advertising 4e

Michael F. Weigold

William F. Arens

advertising, fourth edition

EXECUTIVE PORTFOLIO MANAGER **MEREDITH FOSSEL**

SENIOR PRODUCT DEVELOPER **ANNE LEUNG**

EXECUTIVE MARKETING MANAGER **NICOLE YOUNG**

CONTENT PROJECT MANAGERS **MARIA MCGREAL, KERI JOHNSON**

SENIOR BUYER **LAURA FULLER**

SENIOR DESIGNER **MATT DIAMOND**

CONTENT LICENSING SPECIALIST **BETH CRAY**

COVER IMAGE **DUNTRUNE STUDIOS/SHUTTERSTOCK**

COMPOSITOR **APTARA®, INC.**

PRINTER **LSC COMMUNICATIONS**

M: ADVERTISING, FOURTH EDITION

Published by McGraw Hill LLC, 1325 Avenue of the Americas, New York, NY 10121. Copyright ©2022 by McGraw Hill LLC. All rights reserved. Printed in the United States of America. Previous editions © 2018, 2015, and 2012. No part of this publication may be reproduced or distributed in any form or by any means, or stored in a database or retrieval system, without the prior written consent of McGraw Hill LLC, including, but not limited to, in any network or other electronic storage or transmission, or broadcast for distance learning.

Some ancillaries, including electronic and print components, may not be available to customers outside the United States.

This book is printed on acid-free paper.

1 2 3 4 5 6 7 8 9 0 LMN 24 23 22 21

ISBN 978-1-260-38189-4
MHID 1-260-38189-7

All credits appearing on page or at the end of the book are considered to be an extension of the copyright page.

Library of Congress Cataloging-in-Publication Data

Names: Weigold, Michael F., 1958- author. | Arens, William F., author.
Title: Advertising / Mike Weigold, William F. Arens.
Description: Fourth Edition. | Dubuque : McGraw-Hill Education, 2020. |
    Previously published: Dubuque : McGraw-Hill Education, [2018] under
    title: M. | Audience: Ages 18+ | Audience: Grades 10-12
Identifiers: LCCN 2020043345 | ISBN 9781260381894 (hardback) | ISBN
    9781260598223 (hardcover ; alk. paper) | ISBN 9781264058587 (ebook) |
    ISBN 9781264058549 (ebook other)
Subjects: LCSH: Advertising.
Classification: LCC HF5821 .W385 2021 | DDC 659.1—dc23
LC record available at https://lccn.loc.gov/2020043345

The Internet addresses listed in the text were accurate at the time of publication. The inclusion of a website does not indicate an endorsement by the authors or McGraw Hill LLC, and McGraw Hill LLC does not guarantee the accuracy of the information presented at these sites.

mheducation.com/highered

brief
contents

MarsBars/iStock/Getty Images

contents

CashGuy/Shutterstock

part two UNDERSTANDING THE TARGET AUDIENCE

EQRoy/Shutterstock

Georgejmclittle/Shutterstock

CHAPTER 5   COMMUNICATION AND CONSUMER BEHAVIOR   122

part three   THE PLANNING PROCESS

CHAPTER 6   ACCOUNT PLANNING AND RESEARCH   148

CHAPTER 7   MARKETING, ADVERTISING, AND IMC PLANNING   172

part four THE CREATIVE PROCESS

Smolaw11/iStock/Getty Images

Nodar Chernishev/EyeEm/Getty Images

Walter Cicchetti/Shutterstock

Kiev.Victor/Shutterstock

Sundry Photography/Shutterstock

changes to the
fourth edition

chapter one

- Added a new vignette focused on Wendy's clever use of social media in partnership with Chance the Rapper to bring back Spicy Chicken Nuggets.
- The Wendy's vignette is woven throughout the chapter to illustrate basic concepts, especially in My Ad Campaign.
- Updated the timetable of advertising history.
- The "Principles of Free Market Economics" section has been simplified to help students better grasp these important foundations of a free market.
- Updated the top ten global marketers exhibit to 2019.
- Updated the tools for teamwork section to reflect the best tools available in early 2020.

chapter two

- Updated the opening vignette to include sponsorship issues from 2020.
- Extensively updated and simplified the "Freedom of commercial speech" section.
- Added significant information on privacy issues for digital media consumers, including information on the General Data Protection Regulation and the California Consumer Privacy Act.
- Updated the discussion of the Advertising Self-Regulatory Council (formally the National Advertising Review Council).
- Updated the Principles and Practices for Advertising Ethics of the American Advertising Federation.
- Added information on state regulation of advertising.
- Added information on how the impact of Facebook and Google has attracted the attention of international regulators.

chapter three

- Updated the McDonald's opening vignette to include recent marketing efforts and company performance.

- Included separate question on "Understanding your client" section regarding client's use of social media.
- Updated the statistics on top advertisers and top media companies.
- Updated the Rubio's story to include the company's use of social media.
- Updated the trends section significantly to include major new developments including the shift of media dollars to digital, the rise of consultancies, and the broad adoption of programmatic advertising.
- Updated all statistics on the advertising industry.

chapter four

- Updated the opening vignette, "The man your man could smell like" from Old Spice, to include its reappearance in the 2020 Super Bowl.
- Simplified and updated the "Understanding needs and utility" exhibit.
- Added a brand new Ethical Issues box on Colin Kaepernick and Nike's attention-grabbing ad campaign (replaces Brand niching may cause brand switching box).
- Greater focus on the importance of branding and relationship building in the "Creating Local Advertising" section of My Ad Campaign.

chapter five

- A brand new opening vignette on what some believe is the greatest marketing blunder of all time, New Coke.
- Brand new Ethical Issues box on fostering inclusion and safety in the advertising workplace.

chapter six

- All new opening vignette focused on the award-winning Hyundai Super Bowl ad campaign, "Smaht Pahk."

- Integrated Smaht Pahk vignette throughout the "Product Concept," "Target Audience," "Media Selection," and "Pretesting and Posttesting" sections.
- Updated secondary research sources.
- Updated My Ad Campaign research resources.
- Updated the My Ad Campaign methods for pretesting ads section to include online testing resources.

chapter seven

- Significantly revised and updated the Mountain Dew chapter opener to include the brand's focus on consumer engagement.
- New Ethical Issues focus on ad strategy in the era of #MeToo.
- Used the reintroduced electric Hummer as the example for applying the Advertising Pyramid.
- Added information in "Ways to set advertising budgets" about determining online advertising budgets.

chapter eight

- Revised the Target chapter opener.
- Significantly revised von Oech's creative roles section to make it more accessible to student creatives.
- New Ethical Issues box on whether ads should target children.

chapter nine

- Revised and updated opening vignette on a campaign described as "one of the best" of the 21st century, "Dumb Ways to Die."
- In keeping with the rest of the text, TV and radio are broadened to the categories of "video" and "audio" media.
- More material added on creating copy for digital media.
- "Writing for the web" section contains information on influencers.
- "Writing for the web" has added information on SEO considerations in copy.

chapter ten

- Updated information on the decline of newspapers in the opening vignette.
- New Ethical Issues box highlighting Edward Boyd, a ground-breaking African American marketer at Pepsi,

and the impact of ads directed at Black consumers during a time when this was rare.
- Updated information on efforts of newspapers to go online.

chapter eleven

- New opening vignette on branding M&M's.
- All references to TV and radio, except where those specific media are addressed, now referenced as audio and video to acknowledge the multiple ways consumers receive content.
- Much added material on over-the-top (OTT) video and its rapid growth.
- Updated the exhibit on most viewed cable networks.
- Updated the exhibit on commercial costs.
- Significantly updated coverage of audio.
- Added content on measuring video about measuring OTT.
- Added content in audio media section about podcasts.

chapter twelve

- New opening vignette on how brands are using the video game hit *Fortnite*.
- Streamlined the "History of the Web" section to expand contemporary coverage.
- Vastly expanded the "Types of digital interactive advertising" section to include recent evolution of digital media.
- Added much more material on mobile advertising, behavioral tracking, and programmatic advertising.
- Expanded discussion of buying time and space in digital interactive media.
- New sections dedicated to social media, influencer marketing, and retargeting.
- New Ethical Issues box on bullying in social media.

chapter thirteen

- New opener on Corona's innovative OOH display demonstrating the effects of ocean pollution.
- New information on the dramatic growth and uses of digital technologies in OOH.
- Deleted coverage of ATM's as OOH.

chapter fourteen

- Revised smartphone vignette that opens the chapter.
- New Exhibit 14-1 shows spending on both above- and below-the-line marcom.

- New material on how Google and Facebook are encouraging small businesses to do media planning for themselves and providing resources for them to do it.
- New Ethical Issues box on media planning and inclusiveness.

chapter fifteen

- New opening vignette on how marketers helped during the pandemic of 2020.
- Described reasons for the decline in traditional DM.
- Updated the exhibit on the largest direct-response agencies in the United States and numerous statistics throughout the chapter.

- Noted the explosion of digital coupons and their impact on consumer behavior.

chapter sixteen

- New chapter opener on the role sponsorship has played at Nike.
- New material on the benefits of public relations as a management function.
- Updated information on crisis communication and features Starbuck's incident from 2018 and the VW crisis from the same year.

Instructors: Student Success Starts with You

Tools to enhance your unique voice

Want to build your own course? No problem. Prefer to use our turnkey, prebuilt course? Easy. Want to make changes throughout the semester? Sure. And you'll save time with Connect's auto-grading too.

65%
Less Time Grading

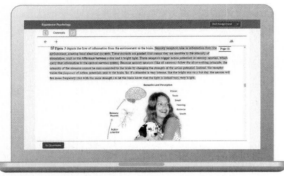

Laptop: McGraw Hill; Woman/dog: George Doyle/Getty Images

Study made personal

Incorporate adaptive study resources like SmartBook® 2.0 into your course and help your students be better prepared in less time. Learn more about the powerful personalized learning experience available in SmartBook 2.0 at **www.mheducation.com/highered/connect/smartbook**

Affordable solutions, added value

Make technology work for you with LMS integration for single sign-on access, mobile access to the digital textbook, and reports to quickly show you how each of your students is doing. And with our Inclusive Access program you can provide all these tools at a discount to your students. Ask your McGraw Hill representative for more information.

Padlock: Jobalou/Getty Images

Solutions for your challenges

A product isn't a solution. Real solutions are affordable, reliable, and come with training and ongoing support when you need it and how you want it. Visit **www.supportateverystep.com** for videos and resources both you and your students can use throughout the semester.

Checkmark: Jobalou/Getty Images

Students: Get Learning that Fits You

Effective tools for efficient studying

Connect is designed to make you more productive with simple, flexible, intuitive tools that maximize your study time and meet your individual learning needs. Get learning that works for you with Connect.

Study anytime, anywhere

Download the free ReadAnywhere app and access your online eBook or SmartBook 2.0 assignments when it's convenient, even if you're offline. And since the app automatically syncs with your eBook and SmartBook 2.0 assignments in Connect, all of your work is available every time you open it. Find out more at
www.mheducation.com/readanywhere

> *"I really liked this app—it made it easy to study when you don't have your text-book in front of you."*
>
> - Jordan Cunningham,
>   Eastern Washington University

Everything you need in one place

Your Connect course has everything you need—whether reading on your digital eBook or completing assignments for class, Connect makes it easy to get your work done.

Calendar: owattaphotos/Getty Images

Learning for everyone

McGraw Hill works directly with Accessibility Services Departments and faculty to meet the learning needs of all students. Please contact your Accessibility Services Office and ask them to email accessibility@mheducation.com, or visit
www.mheducation.com/about/accessibility
for more information.

chapter One

what is advertising?

In this chapter you will learn what advertising and integrated marketing communications (IMC) are and learn how advertising differs from other forms of marketing communications. Next you'll find out about the functions and effects of advertising in free economies and discover how advertising developed in the United States. Finally, you will consider advertising's impact on society.

When you hear the word *advertising,* what comes to mind? A TV commercial that you saw last night? A sponsored post on Twitter? A billboard you noticed alongside a highway? As a consumer, you experience hundreds of encounters with ads such as these every day.

So you probably have a pretty good idea of what advertising is. But IMC is a term you might not have heard before. So what is IMC, and why do advertising professionals need to know about it? IMC, or integrated marketing communication, is the modern practice of strategically coordinating and integrating brand messages across all consumer contact points. The IMC approach contrasts with marketing communication practices from the past in which ad agencies created campaigns without giving much thought to how the ads would work with other marketing communications. For example, an agency might have created a commercial for a car brand without bothering to learn about the brand's public relations activities or sponsorship commitments.

Those days are long gone. Today, advertising is considered one element in the marketing communications toolbox.

To see why advertising works better when guided by IMC, it might help to

continued on p. 4

LEARNING OBJECTIVES

After studying this chapter, you will be able to:

LO1-1 Define integrated marketing communications and explain its importance.

LO1-2 Define advertising and distinguish it from other forms of marketing communications.

LO1-3 Explain the role advertising plays in business and marketing.

LO1-4 Illustrate the functions of advertising in a free-market economy.

LO1-5 Discuss how advertising evolved with the history of commerce.

LO1-6 Describe the impact of advertising on society.

Source: Wendy's/Twitter

continued from p. 3

reflect on the clever use of social media by the restaurant chain Wendy's. Wendy's, according to *Fast Times,* is known for "its saucy tweets and good-natured burns."[1] The company is followed by more than three million fans on social media who relish the company's good-natured ribbing of competitors such as McDonald's.

But what really makes Wendy's approach to advertising different is its mastery of engagement. In this day and age, engagement requires brands to be willing to move quickly and capitalize on opportunities. Recording artist Chance the Rapper provided just such an opportunity when he posted on his Twitter feed "Positive Affirmations for today, I WILL have a good day, I Will succeed today, Wendy's WILL bring back spicy nuggets at some point please please Lord let it be today." Wendy's immediately responded, "Y'all keep asking, so here's your chance. The people in charge say if you guys can get our tweet (this one right here) to 2 Million likes, they will bring SPICY CHICKEN NUGGETS BACK. Let's freakin' do this!" Needless to say, the post exceeded two million likes in short order.

But creative messaging is the rule at Wendy's, rather than the exception. To take another example, Wendy's created a *Fortnite* avatar (bearing a strong resemblance to the girl in the Wendy logo) that appeared in the game under the theme "Keep Fortnite Fresh." The character sought out freezers containing frozen beef, destroyed them, and replaced them with "fresh" meat refrigerators. The deliberate swipe at McDonald's generated enormous publicity and won the brand the coveted *Social & Influencer Grand Prix* at the International Festival of Creativity.

Wendy's marketing messages have come a long way from its famous "Where's the beef?" campaigns of the 1980s. The brand has brought together many marketing elements, including platforms such as Twitter and *Fortnite,* and celebrities, such as Chance the Rapper. It's clever approach has won it extensive press coverage and awards.[2] Perhaps what is most noteworthy about the blend of platforms used by Wendy's is what is missing: television. In an earlier day, a food mass marketer would have spent most of its time and budget focusing on TV to reach large numbers of people. Instead, the company builds excitement for its brand on inexpensive media such as Twitter.

As the description of Wendy's marketing above suggests, advertising is in transition. Television ads, which have been growing more expensive even as they reach fewer people, are being used in a different way. Social media is an important part of nearly every big campaign. And the 30-second spot is declining in importance as a way to persuade consumers to try new brands or remain loyal to old ones.

The story also shows the power of IMC. Wendy's used highly engaging social media platforms such as Twitter and Fortnite. More importantly, it created fresh, funny, engaging messages that reinforced the core benefit of delicious fresh food. And it focused messages on fans—people who like the brand and who engage with the company—and with one another. ■

LO1-1 Define integrated marketing communications and explain its importance.

Throughout this text, we will discuss the importance of IMC. Marketers today know that it is no longer possible to reach and effectively persuade their audiences with traditional media alone—television, radio, magazines, newspapers, direct mail, and outdoor. They need to combine and coordinate those communications tools with public relations, personal selling, sales promotion, and digital media to mount an effective marketing campaign.

The next section focuses on one important type of IMC communication: advertising. Advertising is a messaging option over which a company has the greatest control. As such, it is likely to remain an important component of almost every major IMC campaign. For more on what an ad campaign is like, see My Ad Campaign 1-A.

LO1-2 Define advertising and distinguish it from other forms of marketing communications.

WHAT IS ADVERTISING?

You are exposed to hundreds and maybe even thousands of commercial messages every day. They appear in many forms—TV commercials, websites, and social media messages—or in the form of product placements in TV shows, coupons, sales letters, event sponsorships, telemarketing calls, or e-mails. These are just a few of the many communication tools that companies and organizations use to initiate and maintain contact with their customers, clients, and prospects. You may simply refer to them all as "advertising." But, in fact, the correct term for these various tools is **marketing communications.** And advertising is just one type of marketing communication.

So, then, what is advertising?

At the beginning of the twentieth century, Albert Lasker, often regarded as the "father" of modern advertising, defined advertising as "salesmanship in print, driven by a reason why."[3] But that was long before the advent of radio, television, or the smartphone. More than a century later, our planet is a far different place. The nature and needs of business have changed, and so have the concept and practice of advertising.

How would you define advertising? There are many kinds of marketing communications, but not all qualify as advertising. Let's start with a definition and then distinguish advertising from these other marketing messages.

> **Advertising** is a paid, mediated form of communication from an identifiable source, designed to persuade the receiver to take some action, now or in the future.

Let's take this definition apart and analyze its six core components. Advertising is, first of all, a type of *communication*. It is actually a very *structured* form of communication, employing both verbal and nonverbal elements that are *composed* to fill specific space and time formats determined by the sponsor.

Second, advertising is typically directed to target audiences—people or groups who are attractive to the advertiser. These people could be **consumers**, who buy products such as cars, deodorant, or food for their personal use. Or they might be decision makers who represent companies that buy computers and software for commercial or government use. The messages are delivered via media, such as television or the web, rather than through direct, personal contact between a seller and a buyer. Advertising is, therefore, a kind of nonpersonal, or mass, communication.

Third, advertising is *paid* for by sponsors. GM, Walmart, Wendy's, and your local fitness salon pay the newspaper or the radio or TV station to carry the ads you read, see, and hear. But some sponsors don't have to pay for their ads. The American Red Cross, United Way, and American Cancer Society are among the many national organizations whose **public service announcements (PSAs)** are created and carried at no charge because ad professionals and media companies donate their time and resources. Likewise, a poster on a school bulletin board promoting a dance is not paid for, but it is still an ad—a structured, nonpersonal, persuasive communication. And even a small ad like a bulletin board announcement must be printed and placed.

Fourth, advertising is *mediated*, meaning it reaches us through a channel of communication referred to as a **medium.** An advertising medium is any nonpersonal means used to present an ad to its target audience. This includes radio advertising, television advertising, Instagram ads, Google ads, and so on. When you tell somebody how much you like a product, that's sometimes called **word-of-mouth (WOM) advertising**. Although WOM

Overview [1–A]

Welcome to My Ad Campaign, a valuable feature of this text. My Ad Campaign should be useful in any of the following situations:

- Your instructor has asked students in your class to work on part or all of an ad campaign, either individually or in groups.
- You are doing an internship and want practical advice on how to help your internship sponsor.
- You want to try to apply the concepts and ideas that you are reading about in this book in the real world.

Professors approach advertising projects differently. Some ask students to create ads for a real product, although they never actually communicate with the company that makes the product. Some assign a fictional brand in a real product category. Perhaps your professor has offered your talents to a client, such as a small local business or firm. You may even have to find a client yourself by making inquiries in your community. Finally, your instructor may ask you to help a charity or nonprofit with its advertising. No matter which of these things is the case, the good news is that developing an advertising campaign follows a similar path. And the My Ad Campaign feature is designed to help guide you through the process.

Let's begin with some definitions. An advertising campaign involves the creation and placement of a series of messages that are unified by an underlying theme. The messages should help to promote a brand, product, service, organization, or idea. They are typically designed to resonate with a group called a target audience. Campaigns usually have specific objectives, such as increasing product awareness or persuading people to try a service or donate money. And to ensure that the target audience receives them, messages appear in various media, such as newspapers, radio, or websites. You may not do all of these activities but in most cases you will get a chance to do some serious thinking, planning, and creative brainstorming.

We can make our definition of a campaign a bit more concrete by thinking back to the opening story of this chapter. Wendy's serves fast-food items in a competitive market that includes larger companies such as McDonald's. McDonald's has a share of market of about 40, which means it accounts for about 40 percent of all fast-food burger sales. By contrast, Wendy's market share is just over 10. To grow, Wendy's wants to reach a younger, more diverse audience, and it wants its messages to convey a product benefit it believes gives it an advantage: the company's use of fresh rather than frozen ground beef in its hamburgers.

If your team had been asked to direct Wendy's advertising approach, what would you have proposed? As you may recall, Wendy's relied extensively on social media. Social media helped Wendy's to create a funny, quirky persona for its brand and to find engaging, creative ways to emphasize the freshness of its ground beef. The company spends much less on national television ads than does McDonald's. Take a moment to reflect on the pros and cons of the approach that Wendy's has chosen. In doing so, consider ways in which McDonald's might respond (side note: McDonald's switched to fresh ground beef itself in 2019).

You may surmise from all of this that advertising is very strategic. Lots of planning takes place long before ads are created. So although you may be itching to create some advertisements for your client right off the bat, you have lots of work to do before you begin creating ads. Wendy's found a way to engage players in the massively popular online game *Fortnite*. That's strategic thinking, and in this case it proved successful. On a much smaller scale and with far less resources, you will face similar challenges. My Ad Campaign is designed to help you meet them.

In subsequent chapters, we'll help you learn to develop a deeper understanding of your brand or client, develop a plan for marketing and advertising activities, conduct research so that you can better understand your target audience, formulate media strategy, and design effective advertisements. Finally, you'll learn how to implement evaluation programs to test whether your ads were successful. By the end of the semester, you won't be a top advertising professional. But you'll have some real experience in the art and science of developing an ad campaign. And that's a great start!

The My Ad Campaign topics are listed below. You may find it useful or necessary to jump around among them as you develop your own campaign.

1. Overview/Tools for Teamwork
2. Your Campaign Assignment
3. Understanding What Your Client Wants
4. Segmenting the Audience
5. Understanding Your Customer and Product
6. Conducting Marketing and Advertising Research
7. Situation Analysis, Objectives, and Budgets
8. The Creative Brief
9. Developing the Creative Product
10. Magazine and Newspaper Advertising
11. Television and Radio Advertising
12. Digital Interactive Media
13. Out-of-Home, Direct Mail, and Specialty Advertising
14. Developing Media Objectives and Strategies
15. Developing a Plans Book
16. Blogging/The Client Presentation

You don't have to be perfect to be a perfect parent.
There are thousands of teens in foster care who would love to put up with you.

1 888 200 4005 · adoptuskids.org

Even nonprofits use advertising to communicate information. This ad for adoptuskids.org was created by the Advertising Council, a nonprofit organization that produces, distributes, and promotes campaigns that are each sponsored by a federal government agency or a nonprofit organization.
Source: AdoptUSKids and The Advertising Council

is a *communication* medium, it has not generally been considered an *advertising* medium. However, the popularity of social media, such as Facebook and Pinterest, is forcing advertisers to reconsider this belief. Historically, advertisers have used the traditional **mass media** (the plural of medium)—radio, TV, newspapers, magazines, and out-of-home media such as billboards—to send their messages. Modern technology enables advertising to reach audiences efficiently through a variety of addressable media (like direct mail) and interactive media (like Snapchat). Advertisers also use a variety of other nontraditional media such as specialty advertising, event sponsorship, and direct mail to link with their audience.

Fifth, most advertising is intended to be *persuasive*—to ultimately motivate the audience to do something. What, exactly? Ads can persuade people to try new things, or to stay loyal to brands they already use. Some ads try to convince people to increase their usage of a product they already buy or to use the product in new ways. Not every ad is meant to create a sale: some ads can try to get people to vote for a candidate or support a ballot initiative. Some ads even try to get people to do *less* of something, for example to use less water or energy. Getting people to change their behavior is not easy, and in subsequent chapters, we'll show that there are intermediate goals that ads target that can later lead to behavior change.

In addition to promoting tangible **goods** such as oranges, iPads, and cars, advertising helps publicize the intangible **services** of bankers, beauticians, bike repair shops, bill collectors, and bakeries. Advertising is sometimes used to advocate a wide variety of **ideas**, whether economic, political, religious, or social. The term **product** in

marketing An organizational function and a set of processes for creating, communicating, and delivering value to customers and for managing customer relationships in ways that benefit the organization and its stakeholders.

process A sequence of actions or methods aimed at satisfying consumer needs profitably.

marketing mix Four elements, called the 4Ps (product, price, place, and promotion), that every company has the option of adding, subtracting, or modifying in order to create a desired marketing strategy.

marketing strategy The statement of how the company is going to accomplish its marketing objectives.

advertising strategy The advertising objective declares what the advertiser wants to achieve with respect to consumer awareness, attitude, and preference. Advertising strategy describes how to get there. It consists of two substrategies: the creative strategy and the media strategy.

this text is typically intended to encompass all of these goods, services, and ideas.

Finally, an ad *identifies* its sponsor. This seems obvious. The sponsor wants to be identified, or why pay to advertise? This part of the definition of advertising distinguishes it from some other kinds of marketing communication, such as publicity or product placements. Product placements occur when a brand is featured in a show, story, book, recording, or film in exchange for compensation of some kind. Whereas it is clear that an ad has a sponsor, product placements are often made to look natural and unobtrusive, so that audiences can't be sure they are seeing a promotion.

check yourself ✓

1. What are the six key components of the definition of advertising?

2. Which of these components do product placements not fulfill?

LO1-3 Explain the role advertising plays in business and marketing.

THE ROLE OF ADVERTISING IN BUSINESS

In Chapter 5 we discuss in more detail how advertising informs and persuades consumers, but let's first consider advertising's role in business. Every business organization performs a number of activities, typically classified under three broad categories:

- Operations (R&D, production/manufacturing)
- Finance/administration
- Marketing

Of the three, marketing is the only one intended to bring in revenue. Without revenue, of course, a company cannot pay its bills or earn a profit. So marketing is very important.

What Is Marketing?

The American Marketing Association defines marketing this way:

> **Marketing** is the activity, set of institutions, and processes for creating, communicating, delivering, and exchanging offerings that have value for customers, clients, partners, and society at large.[4]

We focus in Part 2 on marketing and consumer behavior. What's important to understand here is that marketing is a **process**—a sequence of activities—aimed at profitably satisfying consumer needs. This process is typically broken down into the four Ps (4Ps) of the **marketing mix**: developing *products*, *pricing* them strategically, distributing them so they are available to customers at appropriate *places*, and *promoting* them through sales and advertising activities (see Exhibit 1–1). The ultimate goal of the marketing process is to earn a profit for the firm by exchanging products or services with customers who need or want them. And the role of advertising is to promote—to inform, persuade, and remind groups of customers, or markets, about the need-satisfying value of the company's goods and services.

Advertising and the Marketing Process

Advertising helps the organization achieve its marketing goals. So do market research, sales, and distribution. And these other marketing specialties all have an impact on the kind of advertising a company uses. An effective advertising specialist must have a broad understanding of marketing in order to know what type of advertising to use in a given situation.

Companies and organizations use many different types of advertising, depending on their particular marketing strategy. The **marketing strategy** will help determine who the targets of advertising should be, in what markets the advertising should appear, and what goals the advertising should accomplish. The **advertising strategy**, in turn, will refine the target audience and define what response the advertiser is seeking—what that audience should notice, think, and feel. We will discuss the development of marketing, advertising, and media strategies later in the text.

economy The production, distribution, and consumption of products by different people and groups.

▼**EXHIBIT 1–1** Advertising is one of several activities that fall under the promotion component of the marketing mix.

We've defined marketing as a set of exchanges that create value for the parties involved. At a broader level these exchanges create an **economy**, the production, distribution, and consumption of products by different people and groups. This suggests that it is helpful to consider the economic dimension of advertising and how advertising has evolved as both an economic and a societal tool.

check yourself ✓

1. What is the ultimate goal of marketing?

2. What are the 4Ps of the marketing mix and under which does advertising fall?

3. What guidance does marketing strategy give to advertising planning?

LO1-4 Illustrate the functions of advertising in a free-market economy.

ECONOMICS: THE GROWING NEED FOR ADVERTISING

Economics has driven the growth of advertising since its earliest beginnings and has made advertising one of the hallmarks of the free-enterprise system. As English historian Raymond Williams wrote, advertising is "the official art of a capitalist society."

In this century, business and advertising continue undergoing dramatic changes. To understand the nature of these changes and why they're taking place, we will see how advertising has evolved. We'll explain how the changing economic environment has influenced the evolution of advertising through the centuries. Then, in Chapter 2, we'll look at how advertising influences the economy and society and, as a result, is often an object of controversy and criticism.

Principles of Free-Market Economics

The United States and other Western nations embrace economic practices that are often described as capitalism. In capitalist economies, goods and services are created and sold by private organizations (there are exceptions, for example, the Post Office). In other economic systems, government plays a larger role in determining what is made and sold. Capitalism is based on the notion of free-market competition. Although there is no such thing as *perfect competition*, there are four fundamental assumptions of free-market economics that a market-driven society strives to achieve:

1. *Self-interest.* People and organizations pursue their own self-interest. People always want more—for less. Companies are formed to offer products and services that help people acquire things of value. They are motivated to do so because successful companies earn enough revenue to reward employees, owners, and shareholders.

2. *Complete information.* The more information buyers and sellers have about what products are available, at what quality, and at what prices, the more efficient the competition. The outcome is better quality products and lower prices for all.

3. *Many buyers and sellers.* A wide range of sellers ensures that if one company does not meet customer needs, another will capitalize on the situation by producing a more market-responsive product. Similarly, a wide range of buyers ensures that sellers can find customers who are interested in the unique products they are able to produce at a fair price. When a seller has a monopoly (it is the only provider of a product or service), it can force consumers to pay high prices (this is why we have antitrust laws).

4. *Absence of externalities (social costs).* Sometimes the sale or consumption of products results in benefits or harm to people who are not involved in the transaction and who didn't pay for the product. In these cases, government may use taxation and/or regulation to compensate for or eliminate the **externalities**. (Second-hand cigarette smoke hurts people who don't smoke. In addition, the health risks of smoking may drive up insurance costs for nonsmokers. This is why Congress has placed restrictions on tobacco advertisers.)

Now, given these basic assumptions, let's see how advertising fits into the scheme of a free-market economy.

Functions and Effects of Advertising in a Free Economy

For any business, advertising may perform a variety of functions, and, when executed correctly, its effects may be dramatic. How does advertising serve as a marketing tool? There are seven functions we can identify. To illustrate them, let's go back to the beginnings of Coca-Cola in 1886, when druggist John Pemberton was still mixing the syrup in his lab.

Pemberton's business partner and bookkeeper, Frank Robinson, suggested the name "Coca-Cola" to identify the two main flavors (coca leaves and kola nuts) and because he thought that "the two Cs would look well in advertising."[5] Robinson created a logo that is now instantly recognizable around the world and is one of Coca-Cola's more valued assets. Later, a distinctive bottle shape became the standard throughout the company. The proprietary curvy bottle helped customers differentiate Coca-Cola from other drinks. The creation of the Coca-Cola logo and contour bottle demonstrates one of the most basic functions of **branding** as well as advertising: *to identify products and their source and to differentiate them from others.* (The functions and effects discussed here are listed in Exhibit 1–2.)

When Pemberton first began selling Coca-Cola at Jacobs's Pharmacy, he needed to let people know what it was. Today we associate the word *cola* with a cold, bubbly beverage, but in 1886 the people of Atlanta didn't automatically make the same connection. Therefore, Pemberton and Robinson added the suggestion *drink* before *Coca-Cola* on the signs that they placed in front of the drugstore.[6] Ads let readers know why they should drink it (because it is "delicious, exhilarating, refreshing and invigorating"), how much it cost, and where they could get it. Here is another basic function of advertising: *to communicate information about the product, its features, and its location of sale.*

Asa Candler bought the Coca-Cola Company and developed its market on a grander scale. He mailed thousands of coupons for free drinks to Atlanta residents and handed out more on the street. To cover the costs of samples, the company gave free syrup to the soda fountains that sold the beverage. Later, the free sample campaign went along whenever Coca-Cola entered a new market.

Coca-Cola was first served at a small pharmacy in Atlanta in 1886. The word drink *was added to signs to let people know it was a beverage.*
Source: Library of Congress Prints and Photographs, LC-USZ62-39705

Candler also distributed signs to vendors so that the Coca-Cola logo was visible everywhere both outside and inside the shop. To us, this campaign demonstrates another function of advertising: *to induce consumers to try new products and to suggest reuse.*

Through the early part of the twentieth century, Coca-Cola wasn't the dominant force we know today. Competitors such as Pepsi and the now-defunct Moxie cut into Coca-Cola's market share.

▼**EXHIBIT 1–2** Functions and effects of advertising as a marketing tool.

- To identify products and differentiate them from others.
- To communicate information about the product, its features, and its place of sale.
- To induce consumers to try new products and to suggest reuse.
- To stimulate the distribution of a product.
- To increase product use.
- To build value, brand preference, and loyalty.
- To lower the overall cost of sales.

Outside forces also threatened the entire industry; sugar rationing during both world wars was especially damaging. Before the United States became involved in World War II, Coca-Cola executives persuaded the government to give troops Coca-Cola to boost their morale. The D'Arcy advertising agency gathered endorsements from U.S. officers to support the company's bid to become an official military supplier—and therefore be exempt from rationing. The War Department agreed to the plan, and Coca-Cola created 64 bottling plants near the front lines. The risky investment resulted in great returns. When the soldiers returned home, they preferred Coke by eight to one over Pepsi.[7] Coca-Cola blended patriotism with another of the important functions of advertising: *to increase product use*.

Andrew Bret Wallis/Stockbyte/Getty Images

externalities Benefit or harm caused by the sale or consumption of products to people who are not involved in the transaction and didn't pay for the product.

branding A marketing function that identifies products and their source and differentiates them from all other products.

For more than 140 years, the Coca-Cola Company has used a variety of media to communicate this message to diverse audiences. Why? To achieve a significant function of advertising: *to lower the overall cost of sales*. For the cost of reaching just one prospect through personal selling, companies can reach thousands of people through media advertising. The average cost to make a face-to-face field sales call is about $300.[8] Multiply that $300 by the nearly 20 million people who watch a top-rated prime-time TV show, and the cost comes to a mind-boggling $6 billion. However, for only $500,000 Coca-Cola can buy a 30-second TV commercial during a *Sunday Night Football* telecast and reach the same 20 million people.[9] Through advertising, marketers can communicate with a thousand prospects for only about $25—less than 10 percent of the average cost to talk to a single prospect through personal selling.

[Advertising contributes to a free economy.]

As soft drinks became a staple throughout the United States, Coca-Cola began campaigns outside the country to change beverage consumption globally. The first international Coca-Cola bottling plants were established in Canada, Cuba, and Panama in 1906; today the company bottles Coke in more than 200 countries. Coca-Cola franchise bottlers around the world can tweak the recipe to match local tastes. Bottlers and distributors also supplement Coke advertising with their own promotions. Through various activities, Coca-Cola has succeeded in accomplishing yet another function of advertising: *to stimulate the distribution of a product*, in this case, on a global level.

In a free-market economy, when one company starts to make significant profits, other companies immediately jump in to compete. Over the years, to battle the constant competitive threat, Coca-Cola has funded ongoing marketing communications campaigns to accomplish yet another function of advertising: *to build value, brand preference, and loyalty*. Blind taste tests conducted in the 1980s showed that many people preferred the taste of Pepsi to that of Coke. However blind preference has never knocked Coca-Cola from the top spot. A century and a half of consistently upbeat marketing communications has made its mark. Coca-Cola advertising, such as its current campaign, "Taste the Feeling," has always promoted a common voice and a common theme: Coca-Cola makes life's relaxing moments even better.

Now, considering this brief synopsis of Coca-Cola history, how does Coke's advertising fit with the basic assumptions of a free-market economy? How has Coke's advertising helped make the soft drink available to more people at lower cost?

For more than 120 years, Coca-Cola has effectively built and maintained strong brand preference and loyalty among its customers. Coke's campaigns confirm that drinking Coca-Cola makes our lives happier.

Gilles Rolle/REA/Redux Pictures

How did it inform them about where they can buy Coke? Has the freedom to advertise contributed to the competitive environment? What externalities might have had a positive or negative impact on the Coca-Cola Company's efforts to successfully market its beverages?

Perhaps you can see from this one example how advertising contributes to a free economy. But if it's so good, then why didn't advertising take off until the twentieth century? (For a time line of advertising history, see Exhibit 1–3.) Why wasn't it developed and used for the last several thousand years of recorded history?

check yourself ✓

1. What are the seven functions of advertising as a marketing tool?

2. Provide an example of each function from the history of Coca-Cola.

LO1-5 Discuss how advertising evolved with the history of commerce.

THE EVOLUTION OF ADVERTISING AS AN ECONOMIC TOOL

Thousands of years ago, people devoted most of their efforts to meeting basic survival needs: food, clothing, and shelter. They lived in small, isolated communities where artisans and farmers bartered products and services among themselves. Distribution was limited to how far vendors could walk and "advertising" to how loud they could shout. Because goods weren't produced in great quantity, there was no need for advertising to stimulate mass purchases. There were also no mass media available for possible advertisers to use. (See Exhibit 1–3.)

Early Advertising

Civilizations began when people learned to farm. The resulting prosperity and stability led to cities, which then—as now—are centers of commerce. People who practiced crafts such as

pottery making or basket weaving could trade for food and goods. The creation of money facilitated exchanges. In turn, the need to call attention to a product or service that someone might want led to the earliest need for advertising. At first, merchants hung carved signs in front of their shops so passersby could see what products were being offered. Most people couldn't read, so the signs often used symbols, such as a boot for a cobbler. This period was called the **preindustrial age**, and, for Western civilization, it extended from the beginning of recorded history to roughly the start of the nineteenth century.[10]

During the preindustrial age, several important developments enabled the eventual birth of modern advertising. The Chinese invented paper and Europe had its first paper mill by 1275. In the 1440s Johannes Gutenberg invented a printing press with movable type in Germany. The device was an important development in the history of advertising, and indeed communication, and it revolutionized the way people lived and worked.

The introduction of printing meant people no longer had to rely on their memories for record keeping. Some entrepreneurs bought printing presses, mounted them in wagons, and traveled from town to town, selling printing. This new technology made possible the first formats of advertising—posters, handbills, and signs—and, eventually, the first mass medium—the newspaper. In effect, the cry of the vendor could now be multiplied many times and heard beyond the immediate neighborhood.

In 1472, the first English ad appeared: a handbill tacked on church doors in London announcing a prayer book for sale. Two hundred years later the first newspaper ad was published,

An early form of advertising. Until the advent of public schooling, most people couldn't read—so signs featured symbols of the goods or services for sale, such as the chair on this cabinetmaker's sign in Williamsburg, Virginia.

Pat & Chuck Blackley/Alamy Stock Photo

3000 BC–AD 1	AD 500–1799	1800–1899	1900–1919
3000 BC Written advertisement offering "Whole gold coin" for runaway slave "Shem." **500 BC** Political and trade graffiti on Pompeii walls. **AD 1** First uppercase lettering appears on Greek buildings.	**1455** First printed Bible. **1472** First printed ad in English tacked on London church doors. **1544** Claude Garamond, first "typefounder," perfects a roman typeface that bears his name and is still used today. **1650** First newspaper ad offers reward for stolen horses. **1662** *London Gazette* offers first advertising supplement. **1704** First ads in America published in the *Boston Newsletter*.	**1841** Volney B. Palmer becomes first "newspaper agent" (advertising agent) in America. **1844** First magazine ad runs. **1869** Francis W. Ayer founds ad agency bearing his father's name, N. W. Ayer & Sons, in Philadelphia. He initiates first "for commission" ad contract (1876), first market survey for an ad (1879), and first on-staff creative services (art in 1890, copywriting in 1892). **1888** *Printers' Ink* is first U.S. publication for ad profession.	**1900** Psychologists study the attention-getting and persuasive qualities of advertising. **1900** Northwestern University is first to offer advertising as a discipline. **1903** Scripps-McRae League of Newspapers appoints ad censor, rejects $500,000 in ads in first year. **1905** First national ad plan is for the "Gillette Safety Razor." **1911** First "truth in advertising" codes are established by what is now called the American Advertising Federation (AAF).

1920–1939	1940–1959	1960–1969	1970–1979
1920s Albert Lasker, "father" of modern advertising, calls advertising "salesmanship in print." First ad testimonials by movie stars appear. Full-color printing is available in magazines. **1922** First radio ad solves radio's need for financing. **1924** N. W. Ayer produces first sponsored radio broadcast, the "Eveready Hour." **1930** *Advertising Age* magazine is founded. **1938** Wheeler-Lea amendments to FTC Act of 1938 grant FTC further power to curb false ad practices.	**1946** America has 12 TV stations broadcasting to the public. **1947** Lanham Trademark Act protects brand names and slogans. **1948** Forty-six TV stations are operating and 300 others are awaiting FCC approval. **1950** First political ads, by Gov. Dewey of New York, appear on TV. **1950s** David Ogilvy's "Hathaway man" and "Commander Whitehead" become popular ad personae.	**1960s** Doyle Dane Bernbach's "Think small" ad for American Volkswagen becomes one of the most famous ads of the decade, establishing a strong market position for the smallest European import. The agency's slogan for Avis, "We're only No. 2, so we try harder," is also very successful. New York's Madison Avenue becomes known worldwide as the center of the advertising world and features the best in advertising creativity. **1967** First Super Bowl is telecast. Cost of a 30-second spot: $40,000.	**1971** Armed services begin first advertising for the new "all-volunteer" military ("Be all that you can be in the Army"). **1972** The *Ad Age* article "Positioning: The Battle for Your Mind" by Al Ries and Jack Trout details the strategy of positioning that dominates the 1970s. **1973** Oil shortages begin period of "demarketing," ads aimed at slowing demand. **1970s (late)** Growth in self-indulgence, signified by popularity of self-fulfillment activities, spurs some agencies into making infomercials.

1980–1989	1990–1999	2000–2009	2010–2017
1980s Ad agency megamergers take place worldwide. **1982** First edition of *Contemporary Advertising* is published. **1984** The Internet (government controlled since 1973) is turned over to the private sector. **1986** *Marketing Warfare* by Al Ries and Jack Trout portrays marketing in terms of classic warfare manual written by General Clausewitz in 1831. **1989** Tim Berners-Lee invents the World Wide Web, allowing surfers to browse the Internet.	**1990s** A recession leads marketers to shift funds from advertising to sales promotion. **1994** Media glut leads to market fragmentation; network TV is no longer sole medium for reaching total marketplace. Ad professions adopt integrated marketing communications (IMC) as the new strategy to build market relationships. **1997** AOL launches Instant Messenger (AIM), allowing online chat and opening the door to social networking. **1998** Google begins answering search queries.	**2000** The Internet is the fastest-growing new ad medium since TV, with 400 million users. **2002** A general economic slump hammers ad spending. **2005** Online advertisers spend $8.32 billion to reach the 170 million wired U.S. residents. **2007** The iPhone takes social media mobile. **2007** U.S. ad agency revenue surges 8.6 percent to $31 billion, led by double-digit growth in digital advertising. **2009** Broad global recession leads to cutbacks in ad expenditures.	**2010** The Old Spice Guy viral campaign achieves 113 million online views. **2012** Google captures more than 30 percent of the $100 billion digital advertising market. **2013** The *Man of Steel* movie collects $160 million in product placements, paid by 100 promotional partners. **2015** YouTube is watched daily by more people, ages 18–49, than any cable network. **2016** Fiftieth Super Bowl ads cost $4.8 million for 30 seconds (see 1967). **2020** Netflix, Hulu, and Amazon Prime are joined by Apple TV+ and Disney+. Broadcast network viewership among 18–49-year-olds is 35 percent lower than 2014.

offering a reward for the return of 12 stolen horses. Soon newspapers carried ads for coffee, chocolate, tea, real estate, medicines, and even personal ads. These early ads were still directed to a very limited number of people: the customers of the coffeehouses where most newspapers were read.

By the early 1700s, the world's population had grown to about 600 million people, and some major cities could support larger volumes of advertising. This caused a shift in advertising strategy. Samuel Johnson, the famous English literary figure, observed in 1758 that advertisements were now so numerous that they were "negligently perused" and that it had become necessary to gain attention "by magnificence of promise."

In the American colonies, the *Boston Newsletter* began carrying ads in 1704. About 25 years later, Benjamin Franklin, the "father" of advertising art, made ads more attractive by using large headlines and considerable white space. In fact, Franklin was the first American known to use illustrations in ads.

The Industrial Age and the Birth of Agencies

In the late-1700s, the Industrial Revolution began in England and by the early 1800s it reached North America. Machines made it possible to mass-produce goods with uniform quality, affording large companies increased productivity. For the first time, it cost people less to buy a product than to make it themselves. As people left the farm to work in the city, mass urban markets began to emerge. This further fueled the growth of advertising.

By the mid-1800s, the world's population reached more than 1 billion. Breakthroughs in transportation—the railroad and steamship—made it easier to distribute products beyond a manufacturer's local market. Mass consumption demands, in concert with the surpluses achievable by mass production, increased interest in mass marketing techniques such as advertising to inform new markets of the availability of products.

During the **industrial age**, which lasted roughly from about 1800 until the end of World War II (1945), manufacturers

> **With the need for mass consumption came the increasing need for ... advertising to inform new markets of the availability of products.**

It wasn't until 1729 that Ben Franklin, innovator of advertising art, made ads more readable by using larger headlines, changing fonts, and adding art. This 1767 ad announces the availability of Stage Waggons to carry passengers from Powles Hook Ferry to Philadelphia.

Source: *Pennsylvania Gazette* (April 24, 1766)

were principally concerned with production. The burden of marketing fell on wholesalers. Advertising to consumers was the job of the local retailer and the large mail-order catalog companies such as Montgomery Ward and Sears Roebuck. Only a few innovative manufacturers foresaw the usefulness of mass media advertising to stimulate consumer demand for their products.

For Americans, the *profession* of advertising began when Volney B. Palmer set up business in Philadelphia in 1841. Palmer was a middleman; he bought up large volumes of advertising space at discount rates and then resold the space to advertisers at a higher rate, pocketing the difference. The advertisers usually prepared the ads themselves.

In 1869, Francis Ayer formed an ad agency in Philadelphia and, to make it sound more credible, named it after his father. N. W. Ayer & Sons was the first agency to charge a commission based on the "net cost of space" and the first to conduct a formal market survey. In 1890, Ayer became the first ad agency to operate as agencies do today—planning, creating, and executing complete ad campaigns in exchange for media-paid commissions or fees from advertisers. In 1892, Ayer set up a copy department and hired the first full-time agency copywriter.

The technological advances of the Industrial Revolution enabled great changes in advertising. Photography, introduced in 1839, added credibility and a new world of creativity. Now ads could show products, people, and places as they really were, rather than how an illustrator visualized them.

In the 1840s, some manufacturers began using magazine ads to reach the mass market and stimulate mass consumption. Magazines permitted advertising on a national scale with high-quality reproduction.

The telegraph, telephone, typewriter, phonograph, and later, films, all let people communicate as never before. In 1896, when the federal government inaugurated rural free mail delivery, direct-mail advertising and mail-order selling flourished. Manufacturers now had an ever-increasing variety of products to sell and a new way to deliver their advertisements and products to the public.

In 1890, N. W. Ayer & Sons became the first agency to operate as agencies do today—planning, creating, and executing complete ad campaigns for advertisers. This 1899 Ayer ad for Uneeda biscuits (catch the play on words) was one of a series of popular ads of the times.

Source: National Biscuit Company (Nabisco)

Public schooling helped the nation reach an unparalleled 90 percent literacy rate. Manufacturers gained a large reading public that could understand print ads. The United States thus entered the twentieth century as a great industrial state with a national marketing system propelled by advertising. With the end of World War I, the modern period in advertising emerged.

In the 1920s, the United States was rich and powerful. As the war machine returned to peacetime production, society became consumption driven. The era of salesmanship had arrived and its bible was *Scientific Advertising*, written by the legendary copywriter Claude Hopkins at Albert Lasker's agency, Lord & Thomas. Published in 1923, it became a classic and was republished in 1950 and 1980. "Advertising has reached the status of a science," Hopkins proclaimed. "It is based on fixed principles." His principles outlawed humor, style, literary flair, and anything that might detract from his basic copy strategy of a preemptive product claim repeated loudly and often.[11]

Radio was born at about this same time and rapidly became the nation's primary means of mass communication and a powerful new advertising medium. World and national news now arrived direct from the scene, and a whole new array of family entertainment—music, drama, and sports—became possible. Suddenly, national advertisers could quickly reach huge audiences. In fact, the first radio shows were produced by their sponsors' ad agencies. Fresh mass markets were developed for new brands of consumer luxury and convenience goods we refer to as **consumer packaged goods**.

In the early twentieth century, the Industrial Revolution was in full force. Factories were producing products like Ford automobiles, not just for Americans, but also for overseas markets, as this ad shows.

Mary Evans Picture Library Ltd/age fotostock

Tony Ramos/Hemera/Getty Images

During this period, each brand sought to sell the public on its own special qualities. Wheaties became the "Breakfast of Champions" not because of its ingredients but because of its advertising. Manufacturers followed this strategy of **product differentiation** vigorously, seeking to portray their brands as different from and better than the competition by offering consumers quality, variety, and convenience.

On October 29, 1929, the stock market crashed, the Great Depression began, and advertising expenditures plummeted. In the face of consumer sales resistance and corporate budget cutting, the advertising industry needed to improve its effectiveness. It turned to research. Daniel Starch, A. C. Nielsen, and George Gallup had founded research groups to study consumer attitudes and preferences. By providing information on public opinion, the performance of ad messages, and sales of advertised products, these companies started a whole new business: the marketing research industry. The United States would not fully emerge from the Great Depression until after the greatest struggle the world had ever known, the Second World War.

The Golden Age of Advertising

The **golden age** that started at the end of World War II (1945) lasted until about 1979. The United States economy emerged relatively unscathed from the horrors of the war, which had left large parts of Europe and Asia in ruins.

The greatest expansion of any medium up to that time occurred with the introduction of television in 1941. After World War II, TV advertising grew rapidly, and in time achieved its current status as the largest advertising medium in terms of revenues.

Does she... or doesn't she?

Hair color so natural only her hairdresser knows for sure!

MISS CLAIROL HAIR COLOR BATH

MORE WOMEN USE MISS CLAIROL THAN ANY OTHER HAIR COLORING

By the middle of the twentieth century, advertisers knew it was important to tell consumers why they should prefer a particular brand over its competitors. This 1957 ad for Clairol subtlety suggests the importance of choosing the right hair color product. The ad is consistent with the insights of Golden Age giants such as Burnett, Ogilvy and Bernbach who led a creative revolution in advertising by focusing on the growing U.S. middle class.
Source: Coty Inc.

During the postwar prosperity of the late 1940s and early 1950s, consumers tried to climb the social ladder by buying more and more modern products. Advertising entered its golden era. A creative revolution ensued in which ads focused on product features that implied social acceptance, style, luxury, and success. Giants in the field emerged—people such as Leo Burnett, David Ogilvy, and Bill Bernbach, who built their agencies from scratch and forever changed the way advertising was planned and created.[12]

Rosser Reeves of the Ted Bates Agency introduced the idea that every ad must point out the product's **unique selling proposition (USP)**—features that would differentiate it from competitive products. The USP was a logical extension of the Lasker and Hopkins "reason why" credo. But as the USP was used over and over, consumers started finding it difficult to see what was unique anymore.

Finally, as more and more imitative products showed up in the marketplace, all offering quality, variety, and convenience, the effectiveness of this strategy wore out. Companies turned to a new mantra: **market segmentation**, in which marketers searched for unique groups of people whose needs could be addressed through specialized products. The image era of the 1960s was a natural culmination of the creative revolution. Advertising's emphasis shifted from product features to brand image or personality as advertisers sought to align their brands with profitable market segments. Cadillac, for example, became the worldwide image of luxury, the consummate symbol of success.

But just as me-too product features killed the product differentiation era, me-too images eventually killed the market segmentation era. With increased competition, a new kind of advertising strategy evolved in the 1970s, where competitors' strengths became just as important as the advertiser's. Jack Trout and Al Ries trumpeted the arrival of the *positioning era* by insisting that what really mattered was how the brand stacked up against the competition in the consumer's mind—how it was positioned.

Positioning proved effective in separating a particular brand from its competitors by associating that brand with a particular set of needs that ranked high on the consumer's priority list. Thus, it became a more effective way to use product differentiation and market segmentation. The most famous American ads of the positioning era were Volkswagen ("Think small"), Avis ("We're No. 2"), and 7Up ("The uncola").

Wendy's, whose ads we discussed earlier, deliberately positions itself against McDonald's, the market leader. Product differentiation, market segmentation, and positioning are all very important concepts to understand, so we will discuss them further in Chapter 4.

While this was all going on in the United States, across the Atlantic a new generation of advertising professionals had graduated from the training grounds of Procter & Gamble (P&G) and Colgate-Palmolive and were now teaching their international clients the secrets of mass marketing.

> **What really mattered was how the brand stacked up against the competition in the consumer's mind.**

Hailed by Jack Trout and Al Ries as "the most famous ad of the 60s," this Volkswagen ad positioned the brand against large, road-hogging American car brands by occupying the "small" position in consumers' minds, giving VW (www.volkswagen.com) a leadership rank for many years.
Source: Volkswagen of America, Inc.

In recent years, VW has attempted to recapture the style of its 60s advertising, thus reinforcing its position for today's consumers.
Source: Volkswagen of America, Inc.

postindustrial age
Period of cataclysmic change, starting in about 1980, when people first became truly aware of the sensitivity of the environment in which we live.

demarketing Term coined during the energy shortage of the 1970s and 1980s when advertising was used to slow the demand for products.

sales promotion A direct inducement offering extra incentives all along the marketing route—from manufacturers through distribution channels to customers—to accelerate the movement of the product from the producer to the consumer.

The Postindustrial Age

Beginning around 1980, the **postindustrial age** was a period of cataclysmic change. People became sensitive to the dangers of consumption for the environment and alarmed by dependence on vital natural resources. During the energy shortages of the 1970s and 1980s, a new term, **demarketing**, appeared. Producers of energy used advertising to *slow* the demand for their products. Ads asked people to refrain from operating washers and dryers during the day when the demand for electricity peaked. In time, demarketing became a more aggressive strategic tool for advertisers to use against competitors, political opponents, and social problems. For example, many organizations today actively seek to demarket the use of tobacco and the unsafe use of alcohol.

The collapse of the Soviet Union ended the Cold War and with it the need for a defense-driven economy. Companies were anxious to develop the untapped markets in the former Warsaw Pact states. To expand their power globally, big multinational companies and their advertising agencies went on a binge, buying other big companies and creating a new word in the financial lexicon: *megamerger*.

By now European and Asian advertising had caught up with the United States. TV was the hot medium, and agencies focused on growth, acquisitions, and superior creative executions. For several years, Young & Rubicam in New York and Dentsu in Japan alternated as the largest advertising agency in the world. Then two brothers in London, Charles and Maurice Saatchi, started acquiring agencies globally. In rapid succession, a number of high-profile U.S. agencies disappeared under the Saatchi & Saatchi umbrella. Saatchi & Saatchi was suddenly the largest agency in the world. Then followed more buyouts as the big agencies

> These newly affluent consumers concerned themselves more with the quality of their lives.

from Europe, the United States, and Japan emulated the merger mania of their huge multinational clients. Names of agency founders disappeared from the doors, replaced by initials and acronyms: WPP Group, RSCG, TBWA, FCA, DDB Needham, and FCB, to mention just a few.[13]

Then, sparked by unprecedented layoffs in the defense industries, the global economy fell into an economic recession. The mergers temporarily stopped, the business world sucked in its collective belt, and management turned to new theories of total quality management (TQM), reengineering, and downsizing—theories aimed at cutting costs and increasing efficiency. Two related economic factors characterized marketing in this period: (1) the aging of traditional products, with a corresponding growth in competition, and (2) the growing affluence and sophistication of the consuming public, led by the huge baby-boomer generation.[14]

The most important factor was competition, intensified by growing international trade. As high profits lured imitators into the marketplace, each offering the most attractive product features at lower cost, consumers discovered more choices, higher quality, and lower prices.

These newly affluent consumers concerned themselves more with the quality of their lives. With their basic needs met, the baby boomers were interested in saving time and money to spend on products, services, and social causes that represented who they aspired to be.

By the mid-1980s, an avalanche of ads—especially in the toiletry and cosmetics industries—was aimed at the "me" generation ("L'Oréal. Because I'm worth it."). At the same time, the nation's largest industrial concerns spent millions of dollars on corporate advertising to extol their social consciousness and good citizenship.

Several recessions occurred during this time, each leaving many companies chasing too few consumer dollars. Clients trimmed their ad budgets, and many turned to more cost-effective **sales promotion** alternatives, such as coupons, direct mail, and direct marketing to build sales volume. By 1990, advertising had lost 25 percent of its share of the marketing budget to other forms of marketing communications.[15]

Will one lead to another and another? You don't have to be an alcoholic to know that the first drink is the easiest to refuse. It's your choice to keep off the hook

Demarketing is used to dampen demand for products, especially those that create unwanted costs for society. This public service message from the National Association for Prevention of Alcoholism and Addiction, uses the metaphor of a fish hook to convey the dangerous addictive qualities of alcohol.
Source: National Association for Prevention of Alcoholism and Addiction

As the 1990s unfolded, the traditional advertising industry found itself threatened on all sides and suffering from overpopulation.[16] Clients demanded better results from their promotional dollars; small, imaginative, upstart agencies competed for (and won) some big accounts; TV viewers appeared immune to conventional commercials; and an abundance of new media technologies promised to reinvent advertising. In three short years, the advertising agency business lost more than 13,500 jobs. Major clients such as Coca-Cola defected from the big agencies, giving various portions of their business to specialists in small, regional creative shops and media-buying services. It seemed that small, tight-knit teams could provide better work than large companies (see My Ad Campaign 1-B). But the setback went far beyond the agency business. Throughout the media world, newspapers, magazines, and TV networks all lost advertising dollars.[17]

Comstock Images/Alamy Stock Photo

By the mid-1990s, the pendulum swung again as U.S. marketers shifted dollars back to advertising to rebuild value in their brands.

marketers again began spending. By 2005, U.S. advertising expenditures had reached $264 billion, more than completely recovering from the 2001 decline.[21] But new challenges were emerging. Technology, evolving lifestyles, new fears over security, and the rising cost of reaching consumers were changing the advertising business forever. With the explosion of the Internet, advertising entered a new electronic frontier—what Tom Cuniff, VP/creative director at Lord, Dentsu & Partners, called "the second creative revolution."[22]

The Global Interactive Age: Looking at the Twenty-First Century

In the new millennium, the rest of the world caught up to North America, thanks to improved economic conditions and a desire for expansion. Recent estimates of worldwide advertising expenditures outside the United States exceed $400 billion per year. At present, more than half of the world's media spending

> [Technology, evolving lifestyles, new fears over security, and the rising cost of reaching consumers had already changed the advertising business forever.]

In 1994, ad budgets surged ahead by 8.1 percent to $150 billion nationally. And throughout the rest of the 1990s, fueled by the emergence of the latest mass medium, the Internet, ad spending increased about 7 percent every year. Spending reached an all-time high in 2000 when U.S. advertisers spent $247.5 billion, a whopping 11.3 percent increase over the previous year.[18]

But then the bubble burst. In 2001, the combination of a mild recession, the collapse of the stock market, and the bust of the dot-coms all contributed to a record decline in advertising activity. On September 11 of that year, terrorists attacked the United States and suddenly all marketing and advertising seemed to stop—not just in the United States, but also around the world.[19] Spending in the United States dropped 6.5 percent to $231 billion, and overseas spending dropped 8.6 percent to $210 billion.[20]

Once again however, the economy turned around and

is occurring in 10 emerging markets. The importance of advertising in individual countries depends on the country's level of development and national attitude toward promotion. Typically, advertising expenditures are higher in countries with higher personal incomes. As Exhibit 1–4 shows, the top 10 worldwide advertisers are based in many different countries.

▼ **EXHIBIT 1–4** Top 10 global marketers (2019).

Advertiser	Headquarters	Worldwide Advertising Spending ($ millions)	Total U.S. Ad Spending ($ millions)
Procter & Gamble Co.	Cincinnati	$10,132	$4,305
Samsung Electronics	Suwon, S. Korea	10,112	2,152
L'Oréal	Clichy, France	9,623	2,137
Unilever	London/Rotterdam	8,464	1,379
Amazon	Seattle	8,200	4,470
Comcast Corp	Philadelphia	7,483	6,122
Nestlé	Vevey, Switzerland	7,291	2,202
LVMH Moet Hennessy Louis Vuitton	Paris	6,520	1,560
Alphabet (Google)	Mountain View, CA	6,367	2,960
AT&T	Dallas	6,236	5,362

Source: From "Ad Age Leading National Advertisers" and "Ad Age World's Largest Advertisers," retrieved at https://adage.com/datacenter.

Tools for Teamwork [1–B]

Advertising agencies look for at least three qualities in the people they hire: talent, knowledge, and the ability to work well with others. If you are working on your campaign in a group, you'll find those qualities—especially the third—to be important as well.

Your campaign assignment may be the first time you've worked on a group project. If so, you'll discover that working in a team is very different from doing a project on your own.

First, you will need to coordinate everything that you do. That means each person must create schedules that accommodate not only his or her own obligations, but those of the group. Second, you will be sharing work. Tools that help you share documents, calendars, and other files will help you produce better work and do it faster. Third, you should consider the importance of leadership in a group. Your group will usually perform better if someone is formally appointed as leader, at least in the sense of organizing meetings, maintaining a calendar, and keeping track of what has to be done. Finally, everyone is accountable. Talk to your professor about whether he or she expects peer evaluations or some other means to assess differences in group member effort and performance.

Many Internet tools are now available to help improve the coordination of teams. Best of all, they are free. The ones I prefer are those created by Google because they are easy to use, powerful, and integrated (both with each other and with mobile devices). If you would prefer not to use a Google product, I've tried to find equivalents where possible.

Staying Connected
E-mail, of course, remains an essential tool. Your school e-mail may work fine, or Gmail (www.gmail.com) is an excellent free mail service that you will most likely never fill up (which means you never have to delete e-mails and your inbox never gets too full). You can use "labels" to quickly identify mail from people in your group. And with "contacts" you can set up groups of e-mail addresses to message easily and quickly. Use "tasks" to create a to-do list right in your e-mail list and link e-mail invitations to your Google calendar. Other free e-mail services are available as well. Slack (https://slack.com) offers a tool it calls a collaboration hub, which many modern organizations embrace as a better team tool than e-mail.

Creating Documents
Google Docs (http://docs.google.com) offers a free suite of simple yet powerful document creation tools that includes programs for documents, spreadsheets, presentations, forms, and templates. Best of all it is easy to share some or all of the documents you create with others and edit them simultaneously. So if a group member is working on a creative brief, he or she can share it immediately with everyone else for edits and comments.

If you would prefer a non-Google solution, Microsoft and Apple's office suites are more collaborative than ever and offer more advanced formatting and functions tools. Both offer apps for documents, spreadsheets, and presentations as phone apps. You can find alternatives to Office 365 here: www.g2.com/products/office-365/competitors/alternatives.

Staying Organized
Many people find that calendars and to-do lists are essential. Google has an excellent calendar program (www.google.com/calendar) that everyone in the team can edit. You can also sync the calendar with mobile devices. As I indicated before, Google's "task" program is built into Gmail. A more powerful program that is not quite as simple to use is Zoho Project (www.zoho.com/projects).

Conducting Research
Powerful tools for doing research are also available for free on the web. For secondary research purposes, it is great to have a program that allows you to copy and store documents, web pages, photos, charts, and other kinds of information. A powerful and popular program is Evernote (www.evernote.com). Your group may also find itself collecting primary data. If you need to administer a survey, consider a useful component of Google docs called "forms." With forms you can easily create a web-based survey and have your data recorded in a Google spreadsheet as responses arrive. A non-Google program that does the same thing is SurveyMonkey (www.surveymonkey.com).

Working Well and Staying Accountable
Learning to adapt to group projects is not easy for everyone. Knowing what to expect and developing the skills to work well with others is essential. For guidance, consider these thoughts from experts:

- *Forbes*' "What Makes a Successful Team?": www.forbes.com/sites/carleysime/2019/03/26/what-makes-a-successful-team/#52c351bc2348
- Microsoft's "5 attributes of successful teams": www.microsoft.com/en-us/microsoft-365/blog/2019/11/19/5-attributes-successful-teams/
- A peer evaluation form you can use from the Schreyer Institute at Penn State: www.schreyerinstitute.psu.edu/pdf/Team_Peer_Evaluation_Examples.pdf

If you volunteer to be a team leader (or are appointed one), some helpful tips can be found here:

- Hubspot's "The New Manager's Guide to Effective Leadership": https://blog.hubspot.com/marketing/new-managers-leadership-guide
- Kaplan Mobray's "Ultimate Guide to Leadership Success": https://kaplanmobray.com/resources/ultimate-guide-leadership-success/

Although communist countries once condemned advertising as an evil of capitalism, eastern European countries now encourage private enterprise and realize the benefits of advertising. And the United States now looks west to find its biggest economic rival. In 2010, China overcame Germany and became the third largest market for media spending. As of 2019, China has significantly surpassed former number two, Japan, and is now closing in on the United States.[23] Although the U.S. economy remains the world's largest with a nominal GDP of $22 trillion in 2020, compared to China's nearly

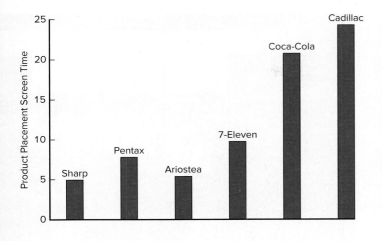

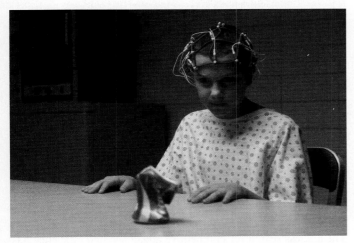

Stranger Things, *one of the most highly acclaimed and watched shows on Netflix, is streamed commercial-free by Netflix subscribers. But that doesn't mean brands have no way to connect with its viewers. They rely on product placement instead, generating millions in revenue for the show's producers.*

PictureLux/The Hollywood Archive/Alamy Stock Photo

$16 trillion, China's growth rate is more than double that of the United States.[24]

The explosion of new technologies in the last decade has affected advertising considerably. In the late 90s and early 2000s, cable transformed television from the most widespread of mass media to a more specialized, **narrowcasting** medium.[25] Now fast Internet service is empowering an even more revolutionary change, TV on demand through channels such as Hulu, Netflix, Amazon Prime, HBO on Demand, and YouTube. Viewers are finding it convenient and preferable to watch what they want, when they want, through **cable cutting**.

Digital technologies have also had a huge impact on both advertisers and consumers. Tablets, smartphones, and devices such as the Amazon Echo give advertisers new media for reaching potential customers. In turn, the challenges posed by these new products are attracting a new breed of advertising professional. Whereas in the past creativity emphasized writing, design, and idea generation, a new breed of creatives is as likely to be trained in coding and programming.

Perhaps the biggest new change in consumer media habits is the widespread use of social media.[26] As we discuss in Chapter 12, this is a revolutionary way for advertisers to reach consumers. Facebook and YouTube are accessed by more than a billion users each month, connecting people as never before. Snapchat proudly proclaims that "on any given day, Snapchat reaches 41% of all 18 to 34 year-olds in the United States."

Younger audiences, not as enamored of "traditional" social media, have embraced platforms such as Snapchat, TikTok, and Kik. The power of social media are certainly not lost on advertisers, who are shifting big portions of their spending to engage the audiences that spend time there.

The growth of new media has proven massively disruptive for some traditional ones. Particularly hard hit was the newspaper industry. Print newspapers have seen over a decade of year-over-year ad revenue decline.[27] Several high-profile papers, including the *Christian Science Monitor* and the *Rocky Mountain News*, already weakened by lower ad sales, have reduced publication schedules or, in some instances, shut down their presses completely. Revenue from online publications is not replacing the dollars lost from print advertisers.

The trend toward consumer control over media consumption is well illustrated by streaming media. For an inexpensive subscription, viewers can watch where, when, and how they want. This has created a new opportunity for advertisers, but also new challenges.

Anton Garin/Alamy Stock Photo

The distinction between content creator and content consumer is blurring with the surging popularity of social media platforms such as Snapchat.

Dennizn/Shutterstock

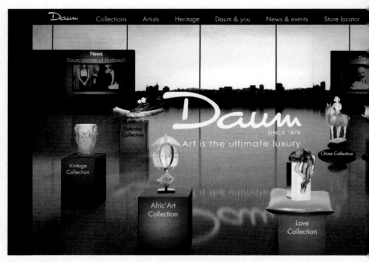

New technology has meant new media, manifested largely on the Internet. This has opened new avenues of exposure for advertisers. This website for Daum shows that beautiful layout and design are not confined to the traditional medium of print.

Source: Daum Haviland

Even capitalism itself has come under scrutiny, at least among young people. Although capitalism is likely to remain the greatest influence on markets in the United States for the near future, the surprising success of Bernie Sanders in campaigning for the Democratic presidential nomination in 2016 and again in 2020 has been based on the support of young adults, nearly half of whom are warm to the label *socialism*.[28] What this means for advertising, which is often described as a tool of capitalism, remains to be seen.

As the decade of the 2020s begins, the digital tsunami continues to change the way advertising is practiced. Media are bought and sold through computer algorithms and auctions rather than a phone call between two professionals. A whole new category of TV advertising, OTT (for Over-the-Top) is allowing brands to reach the fast-growing streaming video and gaming audiences (read more about OTT in Chapter 11) and to do so in customized ways that cable cannot compete with. Waiting on the near horizon are the potential game changers of wearable technologies, virtual reality, and 5G phone service. It will not be long before even today's most advanced technologies seem as quaint (and dated) as Yellow Page directories and landline phones.

Advertising has come a long way from the simple sign on the bootmaker's shop. Today it is a powerful practice that announces the availability and location of products, describes their quality and value, imbues brands with personality, and simultaneously defines the personalities of the people who buy them while entertaining us. More than a reflection of society and its desires, advertising can start and end fads, trends, and credos—sometimes all by itself.[29]

The endless search for competitive advantage and efficiency has made advertising's journey in the last 100-plus years fascinating. Now companies are realizing that their most important asset is not capital equipment or their line of products. In the heated competition of the global marketplace, their most important asset is their customer and the relationship they have with that person or organization. Protecting that asset has become the new marketing imperative for the twenty-first century. In an effort to do a better job of *relationship marketing*, companies are now learning that they must be consistent in both what they say and what they do. It's not enough to produce outstanding advertising anymore. They must integrate all their marketing communications with everything else they do, too. That's what *integrated marketing communications* really means. And that is presenting exciting new challenges and opportunities to marketing and advertising professionals.

> "Their most important asset is their customer and the relationship they have with that person or organization."

check yourself ✓

1. What are the four identified periods in the history of Western civilization and what key developments characterized each period?

2. Explain how one development during each period impacted the evolution of advertising.

LO1-6   Describe the impact of advertising on society.

SOCIETY AND ETHICS: THE EFFECTS OF ADVERTISING

Advertising has been a major factor in improving the standard of living in the United States and around the world. By publicizing the material, social, and cultural opportunities of a free enterprise society, advertising has encouraged increased productivity by both management and labor.

With just a small amount of money, for instance, you can buy a car today. It may be secondhand, but from advertising you know it's available. If you earn more money, you can buy a new car or one with more luxury features. You can also make a statement about yourself as an individual with the vehicle you purchase. As with many products, advertising has created a personality for each automobile make and model on the market. As a free individual, you can select the product that best matches your needs and aspirations.

Advertising serves other social needs besides simply stimulating sales. Newspapers, magazines, radio, television, and many websites all receive their primary income from advertising. This facilitates freedom of the press and promotes more complete information. Public service announcements also foster growth and understanding of important social issues and causes. The Red Cross, Community Chest, United Way, the Environmental Protection Agency, and other noncommercial organizations receive continuous financial support and volunteer assistance due in large part to the power of advertising.

However, advertising is certainly not without its shortcomings. Since its beginnings, the profession has had to struggle with issues of truthfulness and ethics. In fact, in the early 1900s, the advertising profession was forced to mend its ethical ways. Consumers suffered for years from unsubstantiated product claims, especially for patent medicines and health devices. The simmering resentment finally boiled over into a full-blown consumer movement, which led to government regulation and ultimately to industry efforts at self-regulation.

In 1906 Congress responded to public outrage by passing the Pure Food and Drug Act to protect the public's health and control drug advertising. In 1914, it passed the Federal Trade Commission Act to protect the public from unfair business practices, including misleading and deceptive advertising.

"We saved enough energy to bring a new middle school off the drawing board."

Loudoun County Public Schools Superintendent Dr. Edgar B. Hatrick

NAME: Loudoun County Public Schools, Virginia

IMPROVING ENERGY PERFORMANCE BY: Earning EPA's ENERGY STAR® certification for 46 schools

SAVINGS: More than $40 million, plus a nearly 360,000 metric ton greenhouse gas emission reduction

RESULTS: Energy savings equaled cost of building their newest middle school

When Loudoun County Public Schools partnered with ENERGY STAR, the idea was to cut energy costs so the savings could go to a better use. In nineteen years, their savings equaled the cost of building a new middle school. Today, that school is a reality. And the energy they're saving reduces greenhouse gas emissions that cause climate change. Put ENERGY STAR to work for you at **energystar.gov.**

These public service announcements, encouraging people to look for Energy Star ratings on computer equipment, appliances, lighting, and heating and cooling systems, are distributed by the EPA to magazines with a request to insert them in their publications.

Source: U.S. Environmental Protection Agency

Advertising practitioners themselves formed groups to improve advertising effectiveness and promote professionalism and started vigilance committees to safeguard the integrity of the industry. The Association of National Advertisers (ANA), the American Advertising Federation (AAF), and the Better Business Bureau (BBB) are today's outgrowths of those early groups. These organizations are the result of a fundamental truth: the biggest opponents of unethical advertisers are advertisers who embrace ethical and truthful communication practices.

But in times of economic crisis, false and misleading advertising has invariably reappeared, perhaps out of advertiser desperation. During the Depression years, several best-selling books exposed the advertising industry as an unscrupulous exploiter of consumers.

In a 1962 message to Congress, President Kennedy asserted, "If consumers are offered inferior products, if prices are exorbitant . . . if the consumer is unable to choose on an informed basis, then his dollar is wasted . . . and the national interest suffers." In his Bill for Consumer Rights, Kennedy gave the American consumer four basic rights, including the right "to be protected against fraudulent, deceitful, or grossly misleading information, advertising, labeling, or other practices, and to be given the facts s/he needs to make an informed choice."

In the 1970s, a new American consumer movement grew out of the widespread disillusionment following the Kennedy assassination, the Vietnam War, the Watergate scandals, and the sudden shortage of vital natural resources—all communicated instantly to the world via new satellite technology. These issues fostered cynicism and distrust of the establishment and tradition, and gave rise to a new twist in moral consciousness. On the one hand, people justified their personal irresponsibility and self-indulgence in the name of self-fulfillment. On the other, they attacked corporate America's quest for self-fulfillment (profits) in the name of social accountability.

Today, corporate America has generally cleaned up many of the inequities in advertising. But now attention has shifted to more subtle problems of puffery, advertising to children, the advertising of legal but unhealthful products, and advertising ethics. On a broader scale, the industry is finally taking steps to confront and deal with a persistent criticism: that it lacks diversity. The United States is an increasingly multicultural nation, and the ad industry ignores recruitment strategies that foster diversity and inclusion at its own risk. This issue exploded in 2020 when tens of thousands took to the streets protesting against racial injustice. Ethics and social responsibility are of such importance that the text features them in nearly every chapter.

In short, advertising has had a pronounced effect on society as well as the economy. It has also fostered a host of social attitudes and regulations that have dramatically affected advertising itself. We'll take a closer look at these issues in Chapter 2. ■

check yourself ✓

1. What are some of the social needs that are served by advertising in the United States?

2. What are some of advertising's societal shortcomings?

ENDNOTES

1. Fastco Works, "Behind Wend'ys Epic Social Strategy," *Fast Company*, April 18, 2019, https://www.fastcompany.com/90330377/behind-wendys-epic-social-strategy.

2. I-Hsien Sherwood, "Wendy's 'Keeping Fortnite Fresh' Wins Social & Influencer Grad Prix at Cannes," *Ad Age*, June 25, 2019, https://adage.com/creativity/work/wendys-keeping-fortnite-fresh/2179761.

3. John McDonough, "FCB: From One-Man Fiefdom to Global Powerhouse," *Advertising Age*, Commemorative Section: "FCB at 120," December 13, 1993, p. F4.

4. "Definitions of Marketing," American Marketing Association, 2017, www.ama.org/the-definition-of-marketing-what-is-marketing.

5. Quoted in "The Chronicle of Coca-Cola: Birth of a Refreshing Idea," Coca-Cola, www.coca-colacompany.com/au/news/the-chronicle-of-coca-cola-birth-of-a-refreshing-idea; *Coca-Cola Heritage Timeline*, Coca-Cola, http://coca-cola-corporate.com.yeslab.org/heritage/index.html; Barbara Mikkelson, "Design Err Shape," *Urban Legends Reference Pages: Coca-Cola*, May 2, 1999, www.snopes.com/cokelore/bottle.asp.

6. "The Chronicle of Coca-Cola"; Jack Hayes, "Dr. John S. Pemberton (inventor of Coca-Cola)," *Nation's Restaurant News*, February 1996, pp. 120–21, Library of Congress American Memory Project, https://memory.loc.gov/ammem/index.html.

7. Frederick Allen, *Secret Formula: How Brilliant Marketing and Relentless Salesmanship Made Coca-Cola the Best-Known Product in the World* (New York: HarperCollins, 1994), cited in Eleanor Jones and Florian Ritzmann, "Coca-Cola Goes to War: Coca-Cola at Home," http://xroads.virginia.edu/~class/coke/coke.html; Pat Watters, *Coca-Cola: An Illustrated History* (New York: Doubleday, 1978), cited in Eleanor Jones and Florian Ritzmann, "Coca-Cola Goes to War: Coca-Cola at Home," http://xroads.virginia.edu/~class/coke/coke.html.

8. Mark Christie, "Calculating the Cost of a Sales Call," *Sales Management*, March 5, 2013, www.salesforcetraining.com/calculating-the-cost-of-a-sales-call.

9. Tim Molloy, "The Voice Is Top-Rated Show of the Season—Can American Idol Regain Lead?" *The Wrap*, February 22, 2012, www.thewrap.com/tv/article/voice-top-rated-show-season-so-far-35637.

10. Some material in this section has been adapted from Hugh M. Cannon, *Course Packet for Advertising Management*, Fall 1996, Wayne State University.

11. William O'Barr, address to the Council on Advertising History, Duke University, March 12, 1993, reported in *Advertising in America: Using Its Past, Enriching Its Future* (Washington, DC: Center for Advertising History of the National Museum of American History, 1994), p. 6.

12. Leonard L. Bartlett, "Three Giants—Leo Burnett, David Ogilvy, William Bernbach: An Exploration of the Impact of the Founders' Written Communications on the Destinies of Their Advertising Agencies," paper presented to the annual meeting of the Association for Education in Journalism and Mass Communication, Kansas City, August 13, 1993.

13. Jean-Marc Schwarz, "A Brief History of Ad Time," *Adweek Western Edition* 44, February 1994, p. 46.

14. Hugh M. Cannon, *Course Packet for Advertising Management*, Fall 1996, Wayne State University.

15. Warren Berger, "Chaos on Madison Avenue," *Los Angeles Times Magazine*, June 5, 1994, p. 14.

16. William F. Arens and Jack J. Whidden, "La Publicité aux Etats-Unis: Les Symptômes et les Stratégies d'une Industrie Surpeuplée," *L'Industrie de la Publicité au Québec* (Montreal: Le Publicité Club de Montréal, 1992), pp. 383–84.

17. Berger, "Chaos on Madison Avenue," pp. 12, 14.

18. Bob Coen, "Bob Coen's Insider's Report," December 2002, McCann Erickson WorldGroup.

19. Judann Pollock, "Marketing Put on Hold," *Advertising Age*, September 17, 2001, pp. 1, 25.

20. Coen, "Bob Coen's Insider's Report."

21. "100 Leading Advertisers," *Advertising Age*, June 26, 2006.

22. Tom Cuniff, "The Second Creative Revolution," *Advertising Age*, December 6, 1993, p. 22.

23. Focus Economics, "The World's Top 10 Largest Economies," www.focus-economics.com/blog/the-largest-economies-in-the-world.

24. Focus Economics, "The World's Top 10 Largest Economies," www.focus-economics.com/blog/the-largest-economies-in-the-world.

25. John McManus, "Cable Proves It's Media's Live Wire," *Advertising Age*, November 26, 1990, p. S6; "Media & Measurement Technologies (Part 1)," *Direct Marketing*, March 1991, pp. 21–27, 79.

26. Clinton Wilder, "Interactive Ads," *Information Week*, October 3, 1994, p. 25.

27. "Newspapers Fact Sheet," Pew Research Center, July 9, 2019, www.journalism.org/fact-sheet/newspapers.

28. Sam Sanders, "Why Do Young People Like Socialism More Than Older People Do?" *NPR*, November 21, 2015, www.npr.org/2015/11/21/456676215/why-do-young-people-like-socialism-more-than-older-people.

29. Brad Lynch, address to the Council on Advertising History, Duke University, March 12, 1993, reported in *Advertising in America: Using Its Past, Enriching Its Future* (Washington, DC: Center for Advertising History of the National Museum of American History, 1994), p. 3.

the environment
of advertising

This chapter identifies and explains the economic, social, ethical, and legal issues advertisers confront. Society determines what is offensive, excessive, and irresponsible; governments determine what is deceptive and unfair. To be law-abiding, ethical, and socially responsible, advertisers should understand these issues.

Would you be more likely to buy a watch brand if you knew it was worn by Jeff Gordon or Brad Pitt? Swiss luxury watchmaker TagHeuer must think so because it pays celebrities to appear in ads. Similarly, Nike spends millions on endorsement contracts and has long partnered with LeBron James, Derek Jeter, and Rafael Nadal. The athletes agree to wear Nike clothes and use Nike gear during competitions. Many also appear in Nike ads. Each makes at least $10 million a year from their sponsorship.

Are celebrity endorsements worth these big dollars? Business professors Jagdish Agrawal and Wagner Kamakura believe so, arguing that celebrities help make ads believable, enhance ad recall, increase brand recognition, and ultimately influence consumers to choose an endorsed brand.[1] So it should be no surprise that as many as one in five TV commercials features someone famous.

But what happens when brands are linked with celebrities who attract the wrong kind of attention? It happens all the time. The long list of famous individuals who have lost endorsement deals because of controversy includes Madonna (Pepsi), Kobe Bryant (McDonald's and Coke), Mary Kate Olsen (milk), Kate Moss (H&M, Chanel, and Burberry), O. J. Simpson (Hertz), Charlie Sheen (Hanes), Michael Phelps (Kelloggs), Tiger Woods (Accenture, AT&T, Gatorade), and

many more. Most recently tennis star Maria Sharapova found herself separated from a number of sponsorships after testing positive for a banned substance, meldonium.

Perhaps the most notorious athlete to disappoint his fans was Lance Armstrong, winner of the Tour de France, the world's most famous

continued on p. 28

LEARNING OBJECTIVES

After studying this chapter, you will be able to:

LO2-1 Describe the impact of advertising on the economy.

LO2-2 Examine the validity of the various social criticisms of advertising.

LO2-3 Explain the difference between social responsibility and ethics in advertising.

LO2-4 Describe how government agencies regulate advertising to protect both consumers and competitors.

LO2-5 Discuss the activities of nongovernment organizations in fighting fraudulent and deceptive advertising.

PhotoPQR/L'EST REPUBLICAIN/Newscom

continued from p. 27

bicycle race, a record seven consecutive times between 1999 and 2005. Armstrong's popularity was once so great that corporate sponsors paid him nearly $20 million in a single year. A cancer survivor, Armstrong also founded the Livestrong Foundation with the mission "to inspire and empower" other survivors and their families. After a brief retirement, Armstrong returned to competitive racing from 2009 to 2011. Then his career began to unravel.

In 2012, Armstrong was banned from cycling for life by the United States Anti-Doping Agency (USADA) for doping offenses. Its report concluded that Armstrong conducted "the most sophisticated, professionalized and successful doping program that sport has ever seen."[2] He later finally admitted to doping in a television interview with Oprah Winfrey.

In the wake of the USADA's report, Armstrong was dropped by every major sponsor, including Nike, Anheuser-Busch, Radio Shack, 24 Hour Fitness, Oakley, and Trek Bicycle. The loss of these endorsement deals was expected to cost Lance $75 million over the next few years; as much as $200 million over the next decade.[3]

Nike even cut all ties with Armstrong's Livestrong cancer charity; the foundation will stop making Livestrong apparel after 2013. Nike had stood by Tiger Woods, Kobe Bryant, Ben Roethliseberger, and Michael Jordan during lapses in morality that included behaviors such as infidelity, sexual misconduct, and gambling. Nike even re-signed Michael Vick after he served jail time for his involvement in animal abuse. But as shocking as some of these behaviors were, none of these athletes stood accused of cheating their sports.[4]

Companies understand that they take a risk when they associate their brands too closely with a single endorser. Nike has recently moved toward an "ensemble approach" to endorsements, using a pool of athletes to promote its

Views of offensiveness vary a great deal. This advertisement was banned by Britain's Advertising Standards Authority. The agency said the ad was likely to cause widespread offense.

Photoshot/Newscom

wares rather than one big star. Risk to the brand is reduced, therefore, should any of the athletes stumble. Under Armour, a Nike competitor, uses a similar approach. A company VP notes that Under Armour doesn't "let any one person get bigger than the brand."[5]

Lessons? The same dynamics that can benefit a brand linked to an admired celebrity can damage a brand associated with a controversial one. Mr. Clean, the Maytag Repairman, and the Burger King will never embarrass anyone—these "celebrities" exist only in ads. However, when brands partner with real people, life gets much more complicated. Lance Armstrong earned big endorsement contracts because of his athletic ability and inspirational message. Yet, in the end, his legal and moral transgressions created marketing challenges. The quandaries faced by Armstrong's sponsors helped reinforce a basic truth: ethics and social responsibility are every company's business.[6] ■

THE MANY CONTROVERSIES ABOUT ADVERTISING

Advertising is a public activity. Companies risk criticism and attack if their ads displease or offend, or if their products don't measure up to the advertised promises. This has led some to suggest it is safer to buy advertised products because when a company's name and reputation are on the line, it tries harder to fulfill its promises.

John O'Toole, the late president of the American Association of Advertising Agencies, pointed out that many critics attack advertising because it *isn't something else*. Advertising isn't journalism, education, or entertainment—although it often performs the tasks of all three—so it shouldn't be judged by their standards. Sponsors advertise because they hope it will help them sell a product, service, or idea.[7]

Notwithstanding O'Toole's articulate defense, many controversies still swirl around the whole field of advertising. Some focus on advertising's *economic* role. For example, does advertising cause higher prices? Does it discourage competition? Can it influence overall consumer demand? What effects does it have on consumer choice and on the overall business cycle?

Other controversies focus on the *societal* effects of advertising. For instance, does advertising make us more materialistic? Does it tempt us to buy things we don't need? Does it affect us through subliminal processes? How does it change or even debase the art and culture of our society?

Additionally, who is responsible for any harmful effects of advertising. How much latitude should marketers have in what products they promote and how they advertise them? Do consumers have some responsibility in the process? Finally, what is the proper role of government? What regulations should exist to protect consumers? And do laws sometimes go too far and violate Constitutionally protected speech freedoms?

These important questions have few simple answers. But debate is healthy. This chapter addresses some of the major questions and criticisms about advertising, both the pros and the cons, and describes the regulations designed to limit the damage from advertisers' abuses.

Recall from Chapter 1 the underlying principle of free-market economics—that a society is best served by empowering people

externalities Benefit or harm caused by the sale or consumption of products to people who are not involved in the transaction and didn't pay for the product.

added value The increase in worth of a product or service as a result of a particular activity. In the context of advertising, the added value is provided by the communication of benefits over and above those offered by the product itself.

to make their own decisions and act as free agents within a system characterized by four fundamental assumptions: *self-interest*, *many buyers and sellers*, *complete information*, and *absence of* **externalities** *(social costs)*.

This framework, derived from the goal of promoting behaviors that foster the greatest good for the most people, offers a system of economic activity—capitalism—that has accomplished that goal better than any other economic system in history. But greatest doesn't mean perfect. And beware the fate of marketers who fail to attend to the damage, real or perceived, that they may be causing.

By using this framework for our discussion of advertising controversies, we have a basis for understanding how advertising may contribute to, or detract from, the basic goal of free enterprise: "the most good for the most people."

LO2-1 Describe the impact of advertising on the economy.

THE ECONOMIC IMPACT OF ADVERTISING

Money spent on advertising in the United States equates to approximately 2 percent of the nation's gross domestic product (GDP). In relation to the total U.S. economy, this percentage is small. Still the United States is near the top of the list for the highest per capita ad spending in the world. As Marcel Bleustein-Blanchet, the "father" of modern French advertising, pointed out, it's no coincidence that the level of advertising investment in a country is directly proportional to its standard of living.[8] Exhibit 2–1 suggests he is right as it shows the relationship between advertising spending per capita and standard of living (GDP per capita) around the world. Although overall ad spending in China is the third largest in the world, its per capita spending is low due to its very large population.

The economic effect of advertising is like the break shot in billiards or pool.

▼**EXHIBIT 2–1** A country's level of ad spending is closely related to its standard of living.

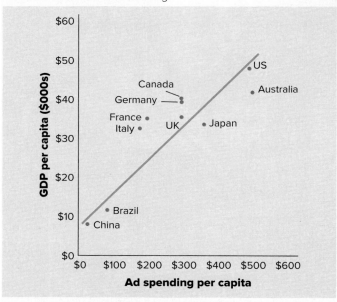

Sources: 2010 data: http://mumbrella.com.au/australia-has-largest-adspend-per-capita-in-the-world-60128; World Bank 2011 data:

The moment a company begins to advertise, it sets off a chain reaction of economic events, as shown in Exhibit 2–2. The extent of the chain reaction, although hard to predict, is related to the force of the shot and the economic environment

▼**EXHIBIT 2–2** The economic effect of advertising is like the opening break shot in billiards.

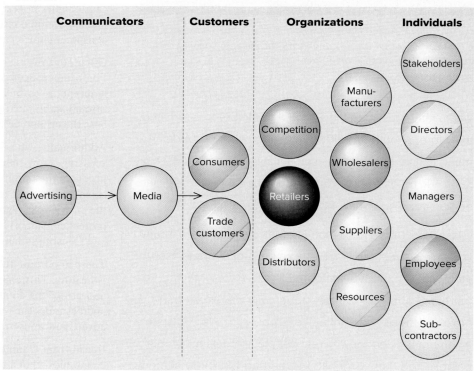

in which it occurred. Let's consider the economic questions we posed earlier.

Effect on the Value of Products

Why do most people prefer Coca-Cola to some other cola? Why do some people prefer the iPod to some unadvertised brand? Are the advertised products functionally better? Not necessarily. But, in the mind of the consumer, advertising has given these brands **added value**.

Some believe that a product's *image*, created in part by advertising and promotion, is *an inherent feature of the product itself.*[9] Although an ad may not address a product's quality directly, the positive image conveyed by advertising may imply quality. By simply making the product better known, advertising can make the product more desirable to the consumer. In this way, advertising adds value to the brand.[10] That's why people pay more for Bayer aspirin than an unadvertised brand displayed right next to it—even though all aspirin, by law, is the same.[11] Advertising also adds value to a brand by educating customers about new uses for a product. Kleenex was originally advertised as a makeup remover, later as a disposable handkerchief. Arm & Hammer baking soda experienced a surge in sales when it was advertised as a refrigerator deodorizer.

In a free-market system, consumers use their own values in choosing the products they buy. If low price is important, they can buy an inexpensive economy car. If status and luxury are important, they can buy a big SUV or a sleek sports car. Many of our wants are emotional, social, or psychological rather than functional. One way we communicate who we are (or want to be) is through the products we purchase and use. What do you assume about a person who drives a new Tesla Model S? And is inspiring such thoughts in others part of the appeal of the car to its owner? In all likelihood, yes.

In terms of our economic framework, by adding value to products, advertising contributes to self-interest—for both the consumer and the advertiser. It also contributes to the number of sellers as companies are formed to meet the needs of different consumers. That increases competition, which also serves the consumer's self-interest.

Effect on Prices

If advertising adds value to products, it follows that advertising makes them more expensive,

> It's no coincidence that the level of advertising investment in a country is directly proportional to its standard of living.

right? And if companies stopped all that expensive advertising, wouldn't products cost less?

Not necessarily.

Some advertised products do cost more than unadvertised products, but the opposite is also true. Both the Federal Trade Commission and the Supreme Court have ruled that by encouraging competition, advertising actually works to keep prices down. This again serves the consumer's self-interest.

Sweeping statements about advertising's positive or negative effect on prices are likely to be too simplistic. We can make some important points, though.

- As a cost of doing business, advertising is indeed paid for by the consumer. In most product categories, though, the amount spent on advertising is very small compared with the total cost of the product (see Exhibit 2–3).

- Advertising often enables manufacturers to engage in mass production, which in turn lowers the cost of products. These savings can then be passed on to consumers in the form of lower prices.

- In regulated industries (agriculture, utilities), advertising has historically had no effect on prices. When industries are deregulated, advertising usually lowers prices, but not always.

- In retailing, price is prominent in many ads, so advertising tends to hold prices down. On the other hand, national manufacturers use advertising to stress features that make their brands better; in these cases advertising can support higher prices.

▼**EXHIBIT 2–3** Advertising spending as a percentage of sales across products.

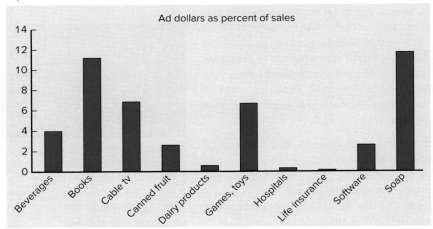

Effect on Competition

Some believe advertising restricts competition because small companies or industry newcomers can't compete with the immense advertising budgets of large firms. If advertising does this, it can increase the prices consumers pay by reducing competition.

Intense competition does tend to reduce the number of businesses in an industry. However, firms eliminated by competition may be those that served customers least effectively. In other cases, competition is reduced because of mergers and acquisitions.

High costs may inhibit the entry of new competitors in industries that spend heavily on advertising. In some markets, the original brands probably benefit greatly from this barrier. However, the investments needed for plants, machinery, and labor are of far greater significance. These are typically greater barriers to entry than advertising.

Advertising by big companies often has only a limited effect on small businesses because a single advertiser is rarely large enough to dominate the whole country. Regional oil companies, for example, compete very successfully with national oil companies at the local level. In fact, the freedom to advertise encourages more sellers to enter the market. And you've probably seen nonadvertised store brands compete effectively with nationally advertised brands on the same shelves.

Effect on Consumers and Businesses

The question of advertising's effect on consumer demand is complex. Studies show that promotional activity does affect aggregate consumption, but they disagree as to the extent of its influence. For example, the demand for tablets, smartphones, and laptop computers expanded at a tremendous rate, thanks in part to advertising but more to favorable market conditions. At the same time, advertising hasn't reversed declining sales of such items as hats, fur coats, and print newspapers.

Advertising can help get new products off the ground by giving people more "complete information," thereby stimulating **primary demand**—demand for the entire product class. In declining markets, when the only information people want is price

Does advertising lead to higher prices? Economists believe that ads sometimes lower product prices. This ad for Darty, a French retailer, is meant to attract price-sensitive consumers. "Low price or low price with everything included."
Source: Darty France

Elon Musk unveiled the Tesla Cybertruck, introducing a radically new product in the competitive world of pickup trucks. The freedom to advertise can lead to more sellers, resulting in greater consumer choice.
Mike Mareen/Shutterstock

information, advertising can influence **selective demand**—demand for a particular brand. But the only effect it will have on primary demand is to slow the rate of decline. In growing markets, advertisers generally compete for shares of that growth. In mature, static, or declining markets, they compete for each other's shares.

Manufacturers who want to beat the competition need to make their product unique. For example, look at the long list of car models, sizes, colors, and features designed to attract different buyers. The freedom to advertise encourages businesses to create new brands and improve old ones. When one brand reaches market dominance, smaller brands may disappear for a time. But the moment a better product comes along and is advertised skillfully, the dominant brand loses out to the newer, better product. Consider that the Ford F150, the Ram 1500, and the Chevy Silverado are the best selling automobiles in the United States. When in 2019 Elon Musk's Tesla introduced the Cybertruck, consumers got a look at a product that may change buying habits forever, but only if the product can satisfy their wants and needs. Once again, the freedom to advertise promotes the existence of more sellers, and that gives consumers wider choices.

Historically, when business cycles dip, companies cut advertising expenditures. That may help short-term profits, but studies prove that businesses that continue to invest in advertising during a recession are better able to protect, and sometimes build, market shares.[12] However, no study has shown that if everybody just kept advertising, a recessionary cycle would turn around. We conclude that when business cycles are up, advertising contributes to the increase. When business cycles are down, advertising may act as a stabilizing force by encouraging buyers to continue buying.

The Abundance Principle: The Economic Impact of Advertising in Perspective

To individual businesses such as Apple, the local car dealer, and the convenience store on the corner, advertising pays back more than it costs. If it didn't, these companies wouldn't use it. But advertising costs less for the consumer than most people think. The cost of a bottle of Coke includes about a penny for advertising. And the $20,000 price tag on a new car usually includes a manufacturer's advertising cost of less than $400.

To the broader economy, the importance of advertising is best demonstrated by the **abundance principle**. This states that in an economy that produces more goods and services than can be

Advertising stimulates a healthy economy. It also helps create financially healthy consumers who are more informed, better educated, and more demanding. Consumers today insist that manufacturers be held accountable for their advertising. This has led to an unprecedented level of social criticism and legal regulation, the subject of our next sections.

abundance principle
States that an economy produces more goods and services than can be consumed. In such an economy, advertising serves two important purposes: it keeps consumers informed of their alternatives, and it allows companies to compete more effectively for consumer dollars.

check yourself ✓

1. Why do you think countries with higher advertising spending per capita tend to have a higher standard of living?

2. Explain the effect that advertising has on brands, prices, competition, and primary and selective demand.

2. What beneficial roles does advertising play in a healthy economy?

[Advertising . . . helps create financially healthy consumers who are more informed, better educated, and more demanding.]

consumed, advertising serves two important purposes: It informs consumers of their alternatives *(complete information)*, and it allows companies to compete more effectively for consumer dollars *(self-interest)*. In North America alone, the U.S. and Canadian economies produce an enormous selection of products. The average supermarket carries more than 40,000 different items.[13] Each automaker markets dozens of models. This competition generally results in more and better products at similar or lower prices.

Advertising stimulates competition *(many buyers and sellers)*. In countries where consumers have money to spend after their physical needs are satisfied, advertising also stimulates innovation and new products. However, no amount of advertising can achieve long-term acceptance for products that people don't want. Despite massive advertising expenditures, fewer than a dozen of the 50 best-known cars developed in the twentieth century are still sold today.

The **EDSEL LOOK** is here to stay
—it has the new ideas next year's cars are copying!

Less than fifty dollars difference between Edsel and V-8's in the Low-Priced Three

Despite extensive advertising efforts, some products, like the Edsel automobile, will fail simply because they do not meet the expectations of customers at that particular time. Many of the best-known cars developed in the twentieth century are no longer sold today. Ironically, the Edsel has since become a pricey collector's item for automobile aficionados.
Pictorial Press Ltd/ Alamy Stock Photo

puffery Exaggerated, subjective claims that can't be proven true or false such as "the best," "premier," or "the only way to fly."

LO2-2 Examine the validity of the various social criticisms of advertising.

THE SOCIAL IMPACT OF ADVERTISING

Advertising gets criticized frequently, for both what it is and what it isn't. Many of the criticisms focus on the *style* of advertising, saying it's deceptive or manipulative. Other criticisms focus on the *social* or *environmental impact* of advertising. Let's look at some of these common criticisms of advertising, debunk some misconceptions, and examine the problems that do exist.

Deception in Advertising

One of the most common criticisms of advertising style is that it is so frequently deceptive. If a product does not live up to the claims in its ads, dissatisfaction occurs—something that is harmful to the advertiser and the buyer.

For advertising to be effective, consumers must find it credible. So deception not only detracts from the complete information principle of free enterprise but also risks being self-defeating. Even meaningless (but legal) puffery might be

Daffy's used tongue-in-cheek humor to take a stand against advertising puffery—inflated promises and claims often accompanied by inflated prices. Daffy's beckoned smart consumers to shop where they could find the same quality goods with "no bull" price tags.
Source: Devito/Verdi for Daffy's

> ## Advertising, by its very nature, is not complete information. It is biased in favor of the advertiser.

Puffery is well illustrated with this print ad for Tide Clean Breeze. Consumers understand that there are not literally clouds and blue sky in each drop. But the powerful metaphor helps illustrate the brand's benefit.
Source: Tide by Procter & Gamble

taken literally and therefore mislead. **Puffery** refers to exaggerated, often subjective claims that can't necessarily be proven true or false, such as "the best hamburger" or "the most comfortable shoe."

Under current advertising law, the only product claims—explicit or implied—that can be considered deceptive are those that are *factually false* or convey a false impression and therefore have the potential to deceive or mislead reasonable people.[14] Puffery is excluded from this requirement because regulators believe that reasonable people don't believe it.

However, advertising, by its very nature, is *not* complete information. It is biased in favor of the advertiser and the brand. People expect advertisers to be proud of their products and probably don't mind if they puff a little. But when advertisers cross the line and create false expectations, people object. One problem is the difficulty of seeing the line, which may be drawn differently by different people. Papa John's Pizza no

Truth in Advertising: Fluffing and Puffing

In advertising, puffery means exaggerated commendation, or hype. The term comes from the Old English word *pyffan,* meaning "to blow in short gusts" or "to inflate; make proud or conceited." Puffery surely predates recorded history.

The Nature of Puffery

Regardless of its long heritage and current widespread use, we should question puffery's role in advertising. Puffery erodes advertising's credibility as a trustworthy messenger by lowering the public's belief in the advertising they see. People begin to question those who support and create such advertising—the advertisers, ad professionals, and ultimately the media that run such ads.

Defining Puffery

Regardless of the criticisms, puffery remains legal. And in the United States, it's relatively well defined by law.

The Federal Trade Commission, in the late 1950s, confirmed, "Puffery does not embrace misstatements of material facts."

Puffery's legal definition establishes that the characteristics puffed must, in fact, exist. The challenge is defining where puffing crosses over from exaggeration into deception. Exaggeration is often the starting point of falsehood, but falsehood is not necessarily harmful or injurious—in fact, it may be playful and creative. Deception, however, is potentially injurious to consumers and is therefore illegal.

D. Hurst/Alamy Stock Photo

Take, for example, the case with Papa John's International, which invested millions of dollars over the years in its "Better ingredients, Better pizza" advertising campaign. The vague and subjective claim might be considered puffery. But when it named its rival Pizza Hut in ads, the issue changed from mere puffery to comparison. And comparison advertising requires substantiation; otherwise it may be considered deceptive.

When Pizza Hut filed a lawsuit in Dallas federal court against Papa John's, it alleged the campaign was "false, misleading, and deceptive." A Texas jury ruled in favor of Pizza Hut, charging that Papa John's "Better

ingredients, Better pizza" campaign constituted deceptive advertising. Pizza Hut was awarded nearly half a million dollars. Papa John's was ordered to remove its slogan from ads, pizza boxes, restaurant signage, and delivery trucks.

The decision was reversed by the District Court of Appeals after Papa John's removed the references to Pizza Hut. But the point had still been made: Advertisers have to be careful about the puffery claims they make. An indirect comparison, or even the appearance of one, could render them liable.

The Use of Puffery

Puffery is praise for something, using subjective opinions, superlatives, exaggerations, and vagueness, and generally stating no specific facts.

Puffery often takes the form of "nonproduct facts," information not specifically about the product and therefore not directly testable as true or false. Nonproduct facts are typically about consumers: their personalities, lifestyles, fears, anxieties. An example was the Army's positioning message, "Be all that you can be in the Army" (1981–2001). The claim relied on the potential for what could happen to the ad's readers while they were in the Army. It didn't actually promise any specific benefits such as improved physical fitness or more education. Thus, regardless of what actually happened to readers who joined up, the claim was neither true nor false about the Army.

Judging Puffery

We live in exciting times. Modern technology speeds up the way we live and play. And part of the glitz of our modern life is puffery, adding pizzazz and stimulating our dreams. In digital media small businesses can claim just about anything. Who's going to hold them accountable?

The courts may, but only when a consumer challenges an advertiser. The actions and attitudes of the advertising profession can make a huge difference.

---

doubt thought it was just puffing when it advertised "Better ingredients. Better pizza." Pizza Hut saw it differently, though, and sued Papa John's for deceptive advertising. A U.S. District judge agreed and awarded Pizza Hut close to half a million dollars in damages. The judge then ordered Papa John's to stop using its "Better ingredients" slogan.[15] This decision was later overturned on appeal, but the case still

goes to show that there are limits on what an advertiser can safely puff. For more on this story and on puffery, see "Ethical Issues: Truth in Advertising: Fluffing and Puffing."

Subliminal Advertising

Wilson Bryan Key promoted the notion that advertisers sometimes create ads with sexual messages hidden in the illustrations.

He calls this **subliminal advertising**. His premise is that by embedding dirty words in the ice cubes in a liquor ad, for instance, advertisers can make us want to buy the product. Some academic studies have debunked this theory.[16] In fact, to date no study has proved that such embedding is actually done, or that it would have any effect if it did exist.[17]

The nerve that Key has been able to touch, though, is important. The widespread fear is that advertisers are messing with our heads—manipulating us—without our consent, into buying things we don't want or need. This gets to the heart of the *complete information* principle because the criticism suggests that advertising does not give consumers information but rather manipulates us without our awareness.

If you think about all the products you buy, how many involve a choice between different brands and different models? And how many involve a decision based on price or convenience? Probably most. So how many of your purchases can you trace to having been helplessly manipulated? Probably none. You receive information from many different sources: friends and relatives, store displays, ads, packaging, and retail store clerks. At some point, you make a decision. In many cases, your decision is *not* to buy at all—to wait for either more information or more money. As always, the customer, acting in his or her own self-interest, makes the decision.

Advertising and Our Values

Some critics argue that advertising degrades people's values by promoting a hedonistic, materialistic way of life. Advertising, they say, encourages us to buy more cars, phones, clothing, and junk we don't need. It is destroying the essence of our "citizen democracy," replacing it with a narcissistic consumer democracy.[18]

How, according to critics, does advertising do this? By playing on our emotions and promising greater status, social acceptance, and sex appeal. Ads cause people to take up harmful habits, make impoverished kids buy $200 sneakers, and tempt ordinary people to buy useless products in the vain attempt to emulate celebrity endorsers.[19] This power, according to critics, is so great that consumers are helpless to defend themselves against it.

But others believe this argument exaggerates the power of advertising. They note that most Americans express a healthy

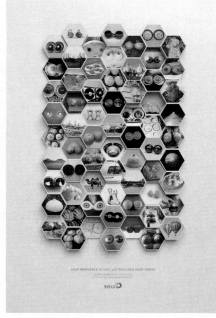

In spite of some consumer fear of subliminal advertising, little evidence exists that advertisers engage in the practice. There are, however, some advertisers, such as Terra, that humorously suggest they do. In this ad, ordinary objects are used to suggest sexual themes.

Source: Terra

skepticism toward it. One study showed that only 17 percent of U.S. consumers see advertising as a source of information to help them decide what to buy.[20] Perhaps that's why more advertised products fail than succeed in the marketplace.

Still, there's no question that advertisers do indeed spend millions trying to convince people their products will make them sexier, healthier, happier, and more popular. The very amount of advertising we witness every day seems to suggest that every problem we have can be solved by the purchase of some product.

The Proliferation of Advertising

One of the most common environmental complaints about advertising is that there's just too much of it. In the United States alone, the average person may be exposed to 500 to 1,000 commercial messages a day. With so many products competing for attention, advertisers themselves worry about the negative impact of excessive advertising. An average hour of prime-time network TV programming in 2010 contained more than 14 minutes of network commercial messages, plus nearly 11 minutes of in-show brand appearances, resulting in advertising content filling 42 percent of each prime-time hour, according to Kantar Media. Unscripted reality programming was the worst offender, containing more than 34 minutes of marketing content, representing more than 56 percent of total time.[21] Not only is more time devoted to commercials, but networks are squeezing more commercials into available time. How? Shorter commercials.[22]

But television is not the only offender. Magazines, radio stations, and even the Internet are congested with advertising. Ad clutter not only annoys the audience but it also decreases ad effectiveness. A survey by Burst Media found that the majority of respondents who stay on a website they perceive to be cluttered say they pay less attention to advertisements appearing on its pages. Nearly a third immediately leave a site if they think it's cluttered, and more than half come away with a less favorable opinion of an advertiser.[23] The Interactive Advertising Bureau (IAB), Google, and others are addressing this issue with new ad formats for digital platforms that "encourage brand engagement with viewers on their terms." The hope is that these more manageable, relevant, and visually appealing ads will increase consumer engagement.[24]

Although the clutter problem is irksome to viewers and advertisers alike, many people tolerate it as the price for free TV, an information-rich Internet, and a high standard of living. However, with the proliferation of

While the non-Hispanic white population is no longer growing, other ethnic and racial groups, including Hispanic Americans and Asian Americans, are increasing. This ad for Bounty Paper Towels targets Spanish-speaking consumers and illustrates that advertisers know this community is critical to the success of their brands.

The Advertising Archives

and others are now usually portrayed favorably in ads, not only because of pressure from watchdog groups, but also because it's just good business; these consumers represent sizable target markets. Positive role portrayal in some mainstream ads has been correlated with a positive effect on the self-esteem of African American youth.[27] And this trend has accelerated with the emergence of ad agencies that specialize in reaching minority markets.

In national advertising, the image of women is also changing from their historic depiction as either subservient housewives or sex objects. The change may be partially due to the increasing number of women in managerial and executive positions with both advertisers and agencies. In 2012, nearly 58 percent of women 16 years of age and older were in the labor force and women occupied more than half of the management, professional, and related positions.[28] Advertisers want to reach, not offend, this sizable market of upwardly mobile consumers. Some agencies now retain feminist consultants to review ads that may risk offending women.[29] In 2003, Ann Fudge was named CEO of Young and Rubicam and became the first African American woman to head a major U.S. advertising agency. *Forbes* named Fudge one of the 100 most powerful women in America in 2004. And in 2007, Nancy Hill became the first female head of the American Association of Advertising Agencies (AAAA). Today, the organization is led by another woman, Marla Kaplowitz.

However, problems still exist, especially in local and regional advertising and in certain product categories such as beer and sports promotions. Many advertisers are just not aware of the externalities that their ads can create, and they may perpetuate male and female stereotypes without even realizing it.[30]

new media choices, this externality is only likely to get worse. In addition to cluttered websites, our e-mail boxes are flooded with commercial messages and mobile advertising is surging. As of now, the only FCC limits currently in force relate to TV programming aimed at children 12 and younger—advertising may not exceed 10.5 minutes per hour on weekends and 12 minutes per hour on weekdays.[25]

Stereotypes in Advertising

Advertising has long been criticized for insensitivity to minorities, women, immigrants, persons with disabilities, the elderly, and other groups.[26] Marketing and advertising practitioners sometimes lose touch with the very people they are trying to reach.

In recent years, national advertisers have become more sensitive to the concerns of minorities and women. Latinos, African Americans, Asians, Native Americans,

Critics have long complained about the way some ads depict women as sex objects. This ad for Hirter Beer created a controversy in Austria.

Europics/Newscom

Of course, avoiding negative stereotypes is not the same as embracing cultural diversity. Research evidence suggests that many Americans value their ethnic identities and prefer brands that speak to them. This in turn has led agencies to see the value of diversifying their own ranks to better understand and communicate with their clients' consumers.

Critics allege that advertisers resort to **stereotypes** for convenience. *Merriam-Webster's* defines a stereotype as a "standardized mental picture that is held in common by members of a group and that represents an oversimplified opinion, prejudiced attitude, or uncritical judgment."[31] In other words, a stereotype is a mental shortcut that attributes a set of characteristics to a group of people. There are a number of examples of ads that stereotype women as homemakers or elderly people as weak and frail.

Some consumers get so offended by both advertising and TV programming that they boycott sponsors' products.[33] Of course, they also have the option to just change the channel. Both of these are effective strategies for consumers because, ultimately, the marketplace has veto power. If ads don't pull in the audience, the campaign will falter and die.[34]

The Social Impact of Advertising in Perspective

Marketing professionals say advertising encourages the development and speeds the acceptance of new products and technologies. It fosters employment. It gives consumers and business customers a wider variety of choices. By encouraging mass production, it helps keep prices down. And it stimulates healthy competition between producers, which benefits all buyers.[35] Advertising, they point out, also promotes a higher standard of living; it pays for most of our news media and subsidizes the arts; it supports freedom of the press; and it provides a means to disseminate public information about important health and social issues. These benefits, they believe, are important.

> [Ultimately, the marketplace has veto power. If ads don't pull in the audience, the campaign will falter and die.]

Observers hope that with increasing diversity among those joining the ranks of marketing and advertising professionals, and with continuing academic studies of stereotyping, greater attention will be focused on these issues.

Offensive Advertising

Offensiveness is another style argument that also speaks to externalities. Parents are sometimes upset by ads that embrace provocative or sexual themes, especially when the advertiser targets children or teens. Prominent targets of parental ire include Calvin Klein and Abercrombie & Fitch. The fact is, people just don't want their children exposed to messages that they deem immoral, offensive, or strictly adult-oriented.[32]

Taste, however, is highly subjective: What is bad taste to some is perfectly acceptable to others. And tastes change. What is considered offensive today may not be so tomorrow. People were outraged when the first ad for underarm deodorant appeared in a 1927 *Ladies Home Journal*; today, no one questions such ads.

Grooming, fashion, and personal hygiene products often use partial nudity in their ads. Where nudity is relevant to the product, people are less likely to regard it as offensive—except when the advertising is targeting kids. In many European countries, in fact, nudity in commercials is commonplace.

Critics might agree with some of these points but certainly not all of them. For example, critics charge that rather than supporting a free press, advertising actually interferes with it. Media, they say, pander to national advertisers to attract the big ad dollars. In the process, they modify their editorial content to suit marketers and shirk their primary journalistic responsibility of presenting news in the public interest.[36]

In summary, we can conclude that although advertising may legitimately be criticized for offering less-than-complete information and, in some instances, for creating unwanted problems, it should also be applauded when it contributes to the benefits of a free economy. In most cases, by being a rich information source (albeit not complete), advertising contributes to the existence of many buyers and sellers and, therefore, to the self-interest of both consumers and marketers.

check yourself ✓

1. Describe six common criticisms of advertising and discuss how you might refute them.

Without advertising, public service organizations would be unable to reach a mass audience to educate people about important health and social issues. Here, The Shelter Pet Project and the Ad Council promote the adoption of pets from animal shelters.

Source: The Shelter Pet Project

Because consumers are knowledgeable about social issues like sustainability, BNP Paribas links banking and finance to this social value. The ad features the tagline: The bank for a changing world.

Source: BNP Paribas

LO2-3 Explain the difference between social responsibility and ethics in advertising.

SOCIAL RESPONSIBILITY AND ADVERTISING ETHICS

Laws and regulations determine what advertisers can and cannot do, but they also allow leeway. That's where ethics and social responsibility come into play. An advertiser can act unethically or irresponsibly without breaking any laws. As one advertising scholar noted that ethics begin where the law ends.[37]

Ethical advertising means doing what the advertiser and the advertiser's peers believe is morally right in a given situation. **Social responsibility** means doing what society or some group views as best for the welfare of people in general or for a specific community of people. Together, ethics and social responsibility can be seen as the moral obligation of advertisers, above and beyond any legal obligations.

Advertisers' Social Responsibility

Advertising plays an important role in developed countries. It influences stability and growth. It helps secure large armies, creates entertainment events attracting hundreds of thousands of fans, and often affects the outcome of political elections. Such power places responsibility on those who sponsor, buy, create, produce, and sell advertising to maintain ethical standards that support the society and contribute to social welfare.

In the United States, the advertising industry is part of a large business community. Like any good neighbor, it has responsibilities: to keep its property clean, participate in civic events, support local enterprises, and improve the community. U.S. advertising professionals meet these challenges by forming local advertising clubs, the American Advertising Federation (AAF), the American Association of Advertising Agencies (AAAA), and the Ad Council. These organizations provide thousands of hours and millions of dollars' worth of *pro bono* (free) work to charitable causes. They also provide scholarships and internships, contributions that serve the whole society. As we discuss later, they even regulate

> **MOST ADVERTISERS TODAY STRIVE TO MAINTAIN FAIR ETHICAL STANDARDS AND PRACTICE SOCIALLY RESPONSIBLE ADVERTISING.**

themselves fairly effectively. Still, advertisers are criticized when they fail the social responsibility litmus test. Concerned citizens, consumer advocates, and special-interest groups pressure advertisers when they perceive the public's welfare is at risk.

Ethics of Advertising

Philosophies of ethics span the centuries since Socrates. We can hardly do them justice here. But for practical purposes, let's consider three levels of ethical responsibility and apply them to advertising.

On one level, ethics comprise two interrelated components: the traditional beliefs of people in a society or community, which are customs, and the broad guidelines that society establishes to justify such beliefs and decree how people should act, which are principles. Customs and principles create the primary rules of ethical behavior in society and enable us to measure how far an individual or company (or advertiser) strays from the norm.

Every person also faces a second set of ethical issues: the attitudes, feelings, and beliefs that add up to a personal value system. When customs and personal values conflict, should the individual act on personal beliefs or on the obligation to serve society? When people cannot resolve an ethical dilemma, they must redefine the issue in dispute. The third level of ethics concerns singular ethical concepts such as good, bad, right, wrong, duty, integrity, and truth. Are these concepts absolute, universal, and binding? Or are they relative, dependent on situations and consequences? People differ in their answers.

Most advertisers strive to maintain fair ethical standards and practice socially responsible advertising. Ad agencies rarely force employees to work on accounts they morally oppose (for an example of what a campaign assignment looks like, see Your Campaign Assignment below). Once a free-swinging, unchecked business, advertising is today a closely scrutinized and heavily regulated profession. Advertising's past shortcomings have resulted in laws and increased regulatory oversight. Consumer groups, governments, special-interest groups, and even other advertisers now review, control, and modify advertising in order to create more *complete information* and reduce unwanted *externalities*.

check yourself ✓

1. Provide examples of actions that advertisers or their agencies might take that would demonstrate social responsibility and ethical behavior.

Your Campaign Assignment [2]

You will be working on an advertising/IMC campaign, or part of one, this semester. Few things are more important for you when preparing for a semester-long project than understanding the final product that is expected of you. It is only when you know what is expected at the end that you can plan what happens in between.

What You May Be Working On

Different classes have different projects, but it is likely that you will work on one or more of the following for a brand, service, or firm:

• A campaign audit.
• A research report.
• A marketing or IMC plan, including a SWOT analysis.
• An advertising or IMC budget.
• A media plan.
• A creative brief or creative platform.
• Creating ads for print, broadcast, or digital media.
• A plans book.

Below we explain each of these in turn and give you guidance about where you can find information in this text and on the Internet.

Campaign Audit

Many classes begin by having teams audit the plans books from prior semesters. This accomplishes several things. First, it gives you an idea about what you will be doing all semester. Second, it introduces you to the importance of seeing how research, strategy, planning, budgeting, and creativity all flow together. If you don't have access to the work of other students, why not look over the work of some of the very best? Visit the Effie Award website (www.effie.org), where you can find great ads and a lot of background information about the campaigns.

Research Report

You may be asked to conduct research for a brand. This may include secondary research, useful for gathering information for your IMC plan; qualitative primary research, in which you conduct a focus group or series of depth interviews; and quantitative research, in which you administer a survey. You'll find a lot of information in Chapter 6 about these activities. Your school library might have a web page devoted to secondary marketing research. You can also find secondary research sources at www.zoho.com/academy/marketing/market-research/resource-list-for-secondary-market-research.html.

CURRENT REGULATORY ISSUES AFFECTING U.S. ADVERTISERS

Federal and state courts have made many significant rulings pertaining to advertising issues. The most important of these concern First Amendment rights and privacy rights. We'll review these, while paying special attention to controversies surrounding tobacco advertising and advertising to children.

Freedom of Commercial Speech

Early Supreme Court decisions afforded advertising few protections against government regulation. The court distinguished "speech," which is protected, from "commercial speech" (speech that promotes a commercial transactions). But its decisions over the last several decades make clear that the court believes that truthful commercial speech is also entitled to significant, if not full, protection under the First Amendment.

The trend started in 1976 when the Supreme Court held in *Virginia State Board of Pharmacy v. Virginia Citizens Consumer Council* that commercial speech is protected by the First Amendment because of its value to consumers.[38] In that case the court found that state bans on advertising by professionals (pharmacists, lawyers, etc.) were unconstitutional. Now a third of all lawyers advertise, and a few states even permit client testimonials.

In 1980 the Court used *Central Hudson Gas v. Public Service Commission* to outline a series of conditions that must be met by governments seeking to regulate commercial speech.[39] The *Central Hudson* test includes the following four parts:

1. *Does the commercial speech at issue concern a lawful activity?* Is the ad in question for a legal product and is it free of misleading claims?

2. *Does the restriction of commercial speech serve the asserted government interest substantially?* Can the government show that the regulation has a clear relationship to a social problem?

3. *Does the regulation directly advance the government interest asserted?* Will the regulation solve the problem?

4. *Is the restriction no more than necessary to further the interest asserted?* The government has to establish that there are no other means to accomplish the same end without restricting free speech.[40]

In 2011, a Supreme Court ruling had important implications for commercial speech. The case, *Sorrell v. IMS Inc.*, concerned data mining. In this case the Court invalidated a state law that made the practice illegal for drug companies. Many saw this as a broader protection for commercial speech than the one outlined in the *Central Hudson* case.[41]

The issue of freedom of commercial speech is far from settled. Allowing greater freedom of commercial speech enhances the "government interests" of many buyers and sellers and complete

Marketing or IMC Plan

Many classes require that you create a marketing or IMC plan. We've included lots of information in this text to help. Be sure to read Chapter 7 carefully, as it is your guide to the art and science of planning. Then, to make things more concrete, search for examples of "advertising plan outlines" on the web. Your instructor may have his or her own outline; if so, use that.

Media Plan

A media plan shows the budget allocations to different media and promotional activities. It will also specify what vehicles will be used for the campaign, as well as when and how often the ads will run. You will most likely want to use a spreadsheet to show the calendar. We have a sample media plan flowchart in Chapter 14.

The Creative Brief

The creative brief is a fairly short document that guides the people who create the ads. It contains information that has been distilled from some of the documents that we've just reviewed, such as the IMC plan. There are many different outlines for creative briefs, but in many instances the differences are superficial. Chapter 8 provides some examples of a creative brief and shows you the elements of a message strategy. For examples of creative briefs, visit the following sites:

• Ad Cracker: www.adcracker.com/brief/Sample_Creative_Brief.htm
• SmileyCat blog (for a brief written for a web campaign): www.smileycat.com/miaow/archives/000226.php

Creating Ads or a Plans Book

You'll find lots of information in this book on creating ads. For inspiration, review this site: www.creativeblog.com/inspiration/print-ads-1233780

If you are doing a plans book it means you are doing almost everything we've reviewed to this point. A typical plans book will include research findings, an IMC plan, a creative brief, media plans, and mock-ups of real ads. But it puts these things together in a seamless, integrated way, so that the reader has a clear understanding of the entire arc of a planned campaign. In many plans books there will also be a section on campaign evaluation (ways of assessing the campaign).

Joe Camel appeared in R.J. Reynolds' Camel advertising beginning in 1988. He became widely recognized among children, but R.J. Reynolds denied that Joe was targeted at the youth market. In 1997, under pressure from various public-interest groups, R.J. Reynolds replaced Joe Camel with a more traditional, four-legged dromedary.

Lee Snider/Getty Images

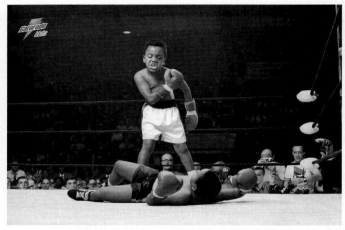

Children are not sophisticated consumers and can easily be misled by advertising that makes unrealistic promises. Although this advertisement for Gatorade Kids was a Cannes Lions International Advertising Festival Winner, it is suggestive of many things that cannot plausibly be linked to the product.

Source: The Gatorade Company, Inc.

information. But some contend that advertising regulations can help reduce externalities related to controversial products such as tobacco and advertising to children.

Tobacco Advertising

Although tobacco is a legal product, the harm created by smoking ends up killing or disabling more than half a million people annually and costs taxpayers billions of dollars every year in health costs—a major externality. To recover these costs, most states' attorneys general sued the tobacco industry. In 1998, they reached a historic settlement. It imposed limits on brand-name promotion at events with young attendees, banned the use of cartoon characters (such as Joe Camel) in cigarette ads, and created a fund of more than $200 billion to be used by the various signatory states. Today, state budgets rely heavily on the money secured in the settlement.[42]

Advertising to Children

Advertising to children presents unique challenges. Kids are not sophisticated consumers. Their perceptions of self, time, and money are immature. As a result, they know very little about their own desires, needs, and preferences—or how to use economic resources rationally to satisfy them. Child-oriented advertising can lead to false beliefs or highly improbable product expectations.

Stockbyte/Getty Images

More and more children are becoming the sole decision makers about the products they consume. To protect them, and their parents, both critics and defenders agree that advertisers should not intentionally deceive children. The central issue is how far advertisers should go to ensure that children are not misled.

To promote responsible children's advertising and to respond to public concerns, the Council of Better Business Bureaus established the *Children's Advertising Review Unit (CARU)*. The basic activity of CARU is the review and evaluation of child-directed advertising in all media. When children's advertising is found to be misleading, inaccurate, or inconsistent with the *Guidelines*, CARU seeks changes through voluntary cooperation of the advertisers.[43]

In the developed world, other countries are far more strict than the United States about advertising to children. Sweden and Norway, for example, do not permit any television advertising to be directed toward children younger than 12, and no advertisements at all are allowed during children's programs. While the highest level of advertising to children is in Australia (an average of 34 ads per hour), that country allows no ads on programs aimed at preschool children.[44]

> Prospective customers who find pop-up ads, telemarketing calls, and e-mail spam annoying and intrusive aren't likely to buy the offending company's products.

Consumer Privacy

Another major regulatory issue facing advertisers is privacy. With the increased use of smartphones and the Internet, both of which can be used for advertising, the issue of **privacy rights** is in the news. The issue deals with people's right to protect their personal information. As we shall see in Chapter 12, privacy is an ethical issue as well as a legal one. It's also a practical issue: Prospective customers who find pop-up ads, telemarketing calls, and e-mail spam annoying and intrusive aren't likely to buy the offending company's products.

Internet users worry about people they don't know, and even businesses they do know, getting personal information. And their concern is not without merit. Sites that obtain visitor e-mail addresses can use third-party vendors to access a wealth of data, from clothing size to favorite books. In turn, depending on their privacy policies, these companies may in turn sell their own data to third parties without user permission.

While consumers have legitimate concerns regarding legal sharing of their data, they may have even more to fear from hackers, state agents, and digital thieves who seek to illegally profit by stealing private information stored on advertiser websites. The range of companies and even federal bureaucracies that have been victimized this way is astonishing. Exhibit 2–4 shows the scope of some of the biggest data breaches of 2018. Such breaches are sadly commonplace and have continued into 2020.

Many sites track users' browsing habits, usually without their knowledge, to better target ads for products consumers have been viewing online. In most cases, the identity of the consumer

▼EXHIBIT 2–4 The 20 biggest data breaches of 2018.

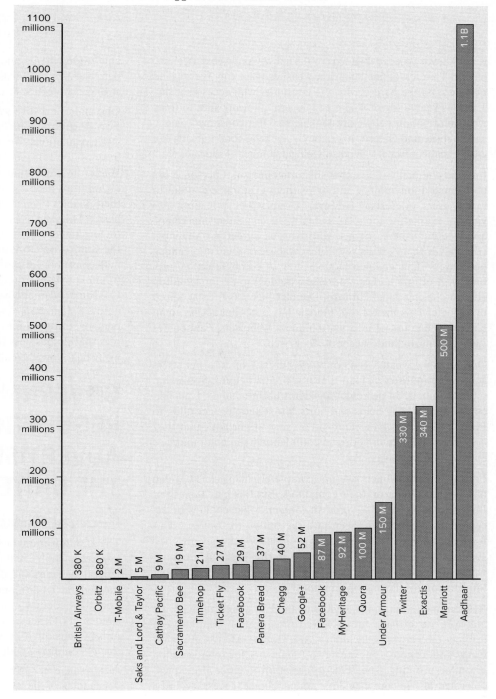

cookies Small pieces of information that get stored on your computer when you download certain websites. These cookies can keep track of whether a certain user has ever before visited a specific site. This allows the website to identify returning users and to customize the information based on past browsing or purchase behavior.

General Data Protection Regulation (GDPR) European legislation passed in 2018 that provides strong consumer protections for how personal data is collected and shared by companies doing business in the EU. As a practical matter, most large web firms changed their policies to conform to the legislation no matter where they do business.

California Consumer Privacy Act California legislation that guarantees consumers have the right to know how their personal information is collected and shared and to demand that such information be erased.

deceptive advertising According to the FTC, an ad is deceptive if it contains a statement, or omits information, that is likely to mislead consumers acting reasonably under the circumstances and is "material," that is, important to a consumer's decision to buy or use the product.

is not known because the focus of the activity is a web surfer's behavior. To track online behavior, websites place tiny files, called **cookies**, on the hard drives of a consumer who accesses a site. The files keep a log of where people surf, allowing sites to track what information people are looking for. If a consumer visits a shoe website and chooses not to buy, such behavioral tracking can ensure that consumer will begin seeing a number of shoe ads.[45]

Internet companies argue that such tracking is not personal; it's performed anonymously and helps them customize content to match users' interests.[46] However, DoubleClick, a leading provider of marketing tools for web advertisers, direct marketers, and web publishers, merged with Abacus Direct, a direct-mail company with an extensive offline database of retail and catalog purchasers. This enabled DoubleClick to combine online profiles with offline names, addresses, demographic information, and purchasing data.[47] In turn, DoubleClick was then acquired by Google. This means that Google has potential access to an enormous amount of information about web users. Companies such as Amazon and Facebook do as well.

One survey revealed that only 27 percent of Internet users accept the industry's claim that tracking is helpful. Somewhat more than half, 54 percent, consider it harmful, and 11 percent believe that it both helps and hurts. Most people, according to Pew, "believe it is important—often 'very important'—that they be able to maintain privacy and confidentiality in commonplace activities of their lives."[48]

Fortunately, consumers are not completely helpless. They can disable the cookies on their computers. But this may limit their Internet access because some sites *require* that cookies be accepted. Internet surfers also have the option to "opt in." This feature allows users to set the terms under which they give personal information.[49] Also available is the "opt-out" feature, which allows visitors to specifically inform the site not to gather information by clicking on a button.[50]

Responding to consumer concerns, the FTC, together with the Network Advertising Initiative (an organization composed of leading web networks, including 24/7, Google, Microsoft, ValueClick, and Yahoo!), has created a framework for self-regulation of online profiling. The "Fair Information Practice Principles" consisted of five core elements: notice, choice, access, security,

and enforcement. The FTC, however, retired the elements, in part because of global regulatory changes that provided even stronger protections to consumers.[51]

One major initiative was the European **General Data Protection Regulation (GDPR)**, which as of May 2018, has created strict regulations for how, when, and where companies doing business in Europe can collect and manage consumer data. While the law applies only to European countries, most large digital firms have a global reach. As a result, most have changed their policies to conform with the GDPR wherever they do business.[52] The state of California provided even stronger protections to consumers with a law taking effect in January of 2020 called the **California Consumer Privacy Act**. The bill is designed to help consumers discover what data companies are collecting and to know whether these data are being shared and with whom. Consumers can choose whether their data can be sold, request access to their data, and insist that a company delete any and all personal information. Although the law applies only to companies that do business in California, the practical effect is it will likely be followed by all companies that do business globally.[53]

GOVERNMENTAL REGULATION OF ADVERTISING IN THE UNITED STATES

Federal Regulation

The U.S. government imposes controls on advertisers through laws, regulations, and judicial interpretations. Among the many federal agencies and departments that regulate advertising are the Federal Trade Commission, the Food and Drug Administration, the Federal Communications Commission, the Patent and Trademark Office, and the Library of Congress. Because their jurisdictions often overlap, advertisers may sometimes have difficulty complying with their regulations.

As a result, every agency and advertiser needs to have a strong understanding of the laws that govern advertising. They also need to retain the services of a good law firm that specializes in advertising and communications law. Reed Smith, a global law firm with an advertising law practice, publishes a blog at www.adlawbyrequest.com to keep clients current on relevant legal developments.

The Federal Trade Commission

The *Federal Trade Commission (FTC)* is the major regulator of advertising. Established by an act of Congress, the FTC is charged with ensuring "that the nation's markets function competitively, and are vigorous, efficient, and free of undue restrictions."[54] The commission enforces a variety of federal antitrust and consumer protection laws and works to regulate the marketplace by eliminating acts or practices that are deceptive or unfair. In other words, it is the FTC's responsibility to maintain the existence of *many sellers* in the marketplace, to provide more *complete information* to consumers, and to keep marketing activities as free of *externalities* as possible.

The FTC's job is complicated by the fact that the definitions of deceptive and unfair are controversial.

Defining deception
The FTC defines **deceptive advertising** as any ad that contains a misrepresentation, omission, or any other practice that is likely to mislead reasonable consumers to their detriment.[55] Proof that consumers were deceived is not required, and the representation may be either

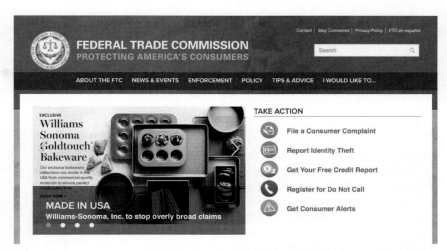

Ensuring that ads are not deceptive or unfair is the responsibility of the Federal Trade Commission. Its website provides news and information about the regulations of commercial speech.
Source: Federal Trade Commission

expressed or implied. The issue is whether the ad conveys a false impression—even if it is literally true.[56]

Take the case of the FTC against Office Depot, Buy.com, and Value America. According to the FTC, the companies engaged in deceptive practices in advertising "free" and "low-cost" personal computer (PC) systems because they failed to adequately disclose the true costs and important restrictions on the offers. The low cost of the PCs was tied to rebates that were conditioned on the purchase of long-term Internet service contracts.[57] Exhibit 2–5 lists some common deceptive practices that have been found illegal by the courts.

▼ **EXHIBIT 2–5** Unfair and deceptive practices in advertising.

Court rulings suggest that these acts constitute unfair or deceptive trade practices and are therefore illegal:

False Promises
Making an advertising promise that cannot be kept, such as "restores youth" or "prevents cancer." When Listerine claimed to prevent or reduce the impact of colds and sore throats, the FTC banned the campaign and required the company to run millions of dollars' worth of corrective ads.

Incomplete Description
Stating some but not all of a product's contents, such as advertising a "solid oak" desk without mentioning that only the top is solid oak and the rest is pine.

False and Misleading Comparisons
Making false comparisons, either explicitly or by implication, such as "Like Tylenol, Advil doesn't upset my stomach." That implies that Advil is equal in avoiding stomach upset, though in truth Tylenol is better. To some people, Advil's claim might even suggest that Tylenol upsets the stomach, which is also false.

Bait-and-Switch Offers
Advertising an item at an unusually low price to bring people into the store and then "switching" them to a higher-priced model by claiming that the advertised product is out of stock or poorly made.

Visual Distortions and False Demonstrations
Using trick photography or computer manipulation to enhance a product's appearance—for example, a TV commercial for a "giant steak" dinner special showing the steak on a miniature plate that makes it look extra large. In one classic case, General Motors and its window supplier, Libby Owens-Ford, rigged a demonstration to show how clear their windows were. The GM cars were photographed with the windows down, the competitor's car with the windows up—and Vaseline smeared on them.

False Testimonials
Implying that a product is endorsed by a celebrity or authority who is not a bona fide user, or implying that endorsers have expertise that in fact they don't.

Partial Disclosure
Stating certain facts about the advertised product but omitting other material information. An example is claiming, "Kraft's Singles processed cheese slices are made from five ounces of milk," which give Singles more calcium than the imitators' products without mentioning that processing loses about two ounces of the milk.

Small-Print Qualifications
Making a statement in large print, such as Beneficial's "Instant Tax Refund," only to qualify or retract it in obscure, small, or unreadable type elsewhere in the ad: "If you qualify for one of our loans." To the FTC, if readers don't see the qualification, it's not there.

Defining unfairness

According to FTC policy, some ads that are not deceptive may still be considered unfair to consumers. **Unfair advertising** occurs when a consumer is "unjustifiably injured" or there is a "violation of public policy" (such as other government statutes). In other words, unfair advertising originates in the inadequacy of *complete information* or some other *externality*. For example, practices considered unfair are claims made without prior substantiation, claims that exploit vulnerable groups such as children and older adults, and cases where the consumer cannot make a valid choice because the advertiser fails to convey important information about the product or competitors mentioned in the ad.[58]

In one case, the FTC found that an automaker's failure to warn of a safety problem was not deceptive but was unfair. Advertising organizations have argued that the word "unfair" is so vague it can mean whatever any given individual wants it to. They have lobbied Congress to eliminate the FTC's power to prosecute on unfairness grounds, and Congress did pass a compromise bill requiring the FTC to show that (1) an alleged unfair practice involves substantial, unavoidable injury to consumers; (2) the injury is not reasonably avoidable by consumers themselves; and (3) the injury is not outweighed by benefits to consumers or competition.[59] This legislation suggests that in the future the FTC will have to balance on a far narrower beam in its effort to regulate unfairness.[60]

Comparative advertising

Advertisers use **comparative advertising** to claim superiority to competitors in some aspect. In the United States, such ads are legal (and encouraged by the FTC) so long as the comparison is truthful. In fact, the FTC cracked down on the Arizona Automobile Dealers Association for restricting truthful comparative price advertising among its members.[61]

Under current law, any advertiser that misrepresents its own or another firm's goods, services, or activities is vulnerable to a civil action. In addition to being truthful, comparative ads must compare on some objectively measurable characteristic. Wendy's has successfully and legally touted its use of fresh beef in comparison to McDonald's use of frozen beef. But subjective claims are not protected. Papa John's claim of "better ingredients" in ads that compared the brand to Pizza Hut resulted in litigation. That's because the standard of "better" in the comparison is unclear. And the greatest scrutiny must be given to the substantiation. Given the potential for sizable damages—up to millions of dollars—for faulty comparative advertising, the greatest care must be exercised in this area.[62]

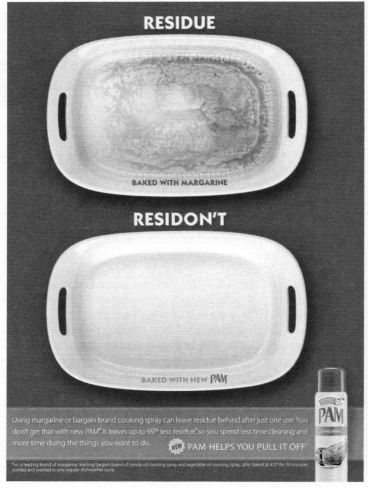

The purpose of comparative ads is to demonstrate the superiority of one product over another. This advertisement makes it clear that PAM cooking spray leaves less residue than margarine brands, a claim that must be backed up with reliable data.

Source: PAM by ConAgra Foods

Investigating suspected violations

If it receives complaints from consumers, competitors, consumer groups, or its own staff members, the FTC may decide to investigate an advertiser. The agency has broad powers to pursue suspected violators and demand information from them. Typically, the FTC looks for three kinds of information: *substantiation, endorsements,* and *affirmative disclosures.*

If a suspected violator cites survey findings or scientific studies, the FTC may ask for **substantiation**. Advertisers are expected to have supporting data before running an ad, although the FTC sometimes allows postclaim evidence.

The FTC also scrutinizes ads that contain questionable **endorsements** or **testimonials**. If a noncelebrity endorser is paid, the ad must disclose this.[63] Endorsers may not make claims the advertiser can't substantiate. Further, celebrity endorsers must actually use the product or service (if portrayed), and they can be held personally liable if they misrepresent it.[64]

Advertisers must make **affirmative disclosure** of their product's limitations or deficiencies: for example, EPA mileage ratings for cars, pesticide warnings, and statements that saccharin may be hazardous to one's health.

Remedies for unfair or deceptive advertising When the FTC determines that an ad is deceptive or unfair, it may take three courses of action: negotiate with the advertiser for a

advertised without substantiation that Doan's Pills were more effective against back pain than those of its rivals. Because the deceptive advertising had gone on for more than nine years, the FTC ordered Novartis to run $8 million worth of corrective advertising. The advertising was to include the statement: "Although Doan's is an effective pain reliever, there is no evidence that Doan's is more effective than other pain relievers for back pain." It also ordered Doan's to place the statement on its packaging for a year.[65]

The Food and Drug Administration (FDA)

Congress authorizes the *Food and Drug Administration (FDA)* to enforce the Federal Food, Drug, and Cosmetic Act and several other health laws. The agency monitors the manufacture, import, transport, storage, and sale of more than $1 trillion worth of products annually, about 25 percent of consumer expenditures in the United States.[66]

> " Any advertiser that misrepresents its own or another firm's goods, services, or activities is vulnerable to a civil action. "

consent decree, issue a *cease-and-desist order*, and/or require *corrective advertising*.

A **consent decree** is a document the advertiser signs agreeing to stop the objectionable advertising without admitting any wrongdoing.

If an advertiser won't sign a consent decree, the FTC may issue a **cease-and-desist order** prohibiting further use of the ad. Advertisers who violate either a consent decree or a cease-and-desist order can be fined for every day the violation occurs.

The FTC may also require **corrective advertising** for some period of time to explain and correct offending ads. In 1999, the FTC ruled that Novartis

Advertising law requires that celebrity endorsers actually use the product. For example, this ad for Cover Girl features the performer Becky G. As a celebrity endorser, the law requires that she be an actual user of the product.
Source: Cover Girl by Procter & Gamble

It's the FDA's job to see that the food we eat, the cosmetics we use, and the medicines and therapeutic devices we buy are safe and effective. The FDA requires manufacturers to disclose all ingredients on product labels, in in-store product advertising, and in product literature. The label must accurately state the weight or volume of the contents. Labels on therapeutic devices must give clear instructions for use. The FDA can require warning statements on packages of hazardous products. It regulates "cents off" and other promotions on package labels and has jurisdiction over the use of words such as *fresh* or *organic* to describe food.

To provide consumers with more complete information, the U.S. Food and Drug Administration regulates the content of pharmaceutical ads. It used to require that advertisers include all the information from the package insert in their TV ads. This necessitated lengthy commercials with minuscule copy. In 1997, the rule was changed, allowing pharmaceutical companies to advertise on TV and radio as long as they mentioned any important side effects and directed consumers to other sources for further information, such as their magazine ads or their website. Notice how this magazine ad for Animal Health's Revolution (www.revolutionpet.com) complies with the FDA's disclosure requirements.

Source: Zoetis, Inc.

When consumer-oriented drug ads became common in the mid-1980s, the FDA ruled that any ad for a brand-name drug must include all the information from the package insert.[67] That meant advertisers had to run lengthy commercials or use minuscule type in print ads. In 1997, the FDA changed that rule, allowing drug makers to advertise their products on broadcast media as long as they mentioned any important possible side effects and directed people to more information.[68] With that ruling, prescription drug advertising soared on television and radio, tripling through 2016. Direct-to-consumer drug advertising is now big business.[69] Anytime the FDA has sent a letter to marketers citing false advertising claims, the companies have stopped running the misleading ads.[70]

The **Nutritional Labeling and Education Act (NLEA)** gave the FDA muscle by setting stringent legal definitions for terms

intellectual property Something produced by the mind, such as original works of authorship including literary, dramatic, musical, artistic, and certain other "intellectual" works, which may be legally protected by copyright, patent, or trademark.

patent A grant made by the government that confers upon the creator of an invention the sole right to make, use, and sell that invention for a set period of time.

trademark Any word, name, symbol, device, or any combination thereof adopted and used by manufacturers or merchants to identify their goods and distinguish them from those manufactured or sold by others.

copyright An exclusive right granted by the Copyright Act to authors and artists to protect their original work from being plagiarized, sold, or used by another without their express consent.

such as *fresh*, *light*, *low fat*, and *reduced calories*. It also set standard serving sizes and requires labels to show food value for one serving alongside the total recommended daily value as established by the National Research Council.[71]

The first time the FDA took severe action against a prominent marketer over a labeling dispute, it seized 2,400 cases of Procter & Gamble's Citrus Hill Fresh Choice orange juice. Fresh Choice was made from concentrate, not fresh-squeezed juice as P&G claimed.[72] Due to increased FDA scrutiny, advertisers are now more cautious about their health and nutritional claims.

The Federal Communications Commission (FCC)

The seven-member *Federal Communications Commission (FCC)* is an independent federal agency with jurisdiction over the radio, television, phone, satellite and cable TV industries, and the Internet. Its control over broadcast advertising stems from its authority to license broadcasters (or take away their licenses). The FCC can restrict both the products advertised and the content of ads. For example, the FCC required stations to run commercials about the harmful effects of smoking even before Congress banned cigarette advertising on TV and radio.

In the 1980s, the FCC deregulated both radio and TV stations. The FCC no longer limits commercial time or requires stations to maintain detailed program and commercial logs.

FCC's rules since then, any similar offense could be punished. "It is now clear that the brevity of an indecent broadcast—be it word or image—cannot immunize it from FCC censure," he wrote in a two-page opinion that put to rest the CBS case, clearing the network of a $550,000 fine.[74]

The Patent and Trademark Office and the Library of Congress

A basic role of government is to promote and protect the economic well-being *(self-interest)* of its citizens. One way the U.S. government does this is by registering and protecting its citizens' **intellectual property**.[75]

Through the issuance of **patents**, the government provides incentives to invent, invest in, and disclose new technology. By registering trademarks and copyrights, the government helps businesses protect their investments, promote their goods and services, and safeguard consumers against confusion and deception in the marketplace *(complete information)*.

A trademark such as Coca-Cola, AT&T, or Levi's is a valuable asset. According to the Lanham Trademark Act (1947), a **trademark** is "any word, name, symbol, or device or any combination thereof adopted and used by a manufacturer or

> ## A trademark such as Coca-Cola, AT&T, or Levi's is a valuable asset.

The 1992 Cable Television Consumer Protection and Competition Act gave the FCC additional teeth. It placed new controls on the cable TV industry to encourage a more service-oriented attitude and to improve the balance between rates and escalating ad revenues.[73] The FCC can set subscriber rates for cable TV, so subscription revenues should slow while advertising rates rise.

The FCC also regulates what content is acceptable in broadcast media. For example, the commission fined CBS over a Super Bowl halftime show in which a performer's breast was exposed, although the fine was later overturned in the courts. But Chief Justice John Roberts Jr. warned that because of changes in the

merchant to identify his goods and distinguish them from those manufactured or sold by others."

Patents and trademarks are registered with and protected by the U.S. Patent and Trademark Office. Ownership of a trademark may be designated in advertising or on a label, package, or letterhead by the word *Registered*, the symbol ®, or the symbol ™.

The Library of Congress protects all copyrighted material, including advertising, in the United States. A **copyright** is a form of protection provided to the authors of "original works of authorship," including literary, dramatic, musical, artistic, and certain other "intellectual works."[76] A copyright issued to an individual grants the exclusive right to print, publish, or reproduce the protected material for the life of the copyright owner plus 70 years.

State and Local Regulation

Advertisers are also subject to state or local laws. State legislation governing advertising is often based on the truth-in-advertising model statute developed in 1911 by *Printer's Ink*, for many years the major trade publication of the industry. The statute holds that any maker of an ad found to contain "untrue, deceptive, or misleading" material is guilty of a misdemeanor.

All states also have "little FTC acts," consumer protection laws that govern unfair and deceptive business practices. States can investigate and prosecute cases, and individual consumers can bring civil suits against businesses. To increase their clout, some states team up on legal actions—for example, to challenge deceptive ad promotions in the airline, rental car, and food-making industries. As one observer pointed out, "Many of the food manufacturers could litigate some of the smaller states into the ground, but they might not be willing to fight it out against 10 states simultaneously."[77]

Different states have different regulations governing what can be advertised, which can present a major problem to advertisers. And in some cases, it actually hurts consumers. For example, many companies trying to conduct environmentally responsible marketing programs feel stymied by the different state laws governing packaging materials and recycling.[78]

Many cities and counties also have consumer protection agencies to enforce laws regulating local advertising practices. The chief function of these agencies is to protect local consumers against unfair and misleading practices by area merchants.

check yourself ✓

1. Describe an action that has been taken by a government agency to restrict the activities of advertisers.

2. What is an example of an Internet-related privacy concern?

Coca-Cola's trademark varies from country to country. But the overall look is retained through use of similar letterforms and style, even with different alphabets.

Imaginechina/AP Images

LO2-5 Discuss the activities of nongovernment organizations in fighting fraudulent and deceptive advertising.

NONGOVERNMENT REGULATION

Nongovernment organizations also issue advertising guidelines (see Exhibit 2–6). In fact, advertisers face considerable regulation by business-monitoring organizations, related trade associations, the media, consumer groups, and advertising agencies themselves.

The Better Business Bureau (BBB)

The largest of the U.S. business-monitoring organizations is the *Better Business Bureau (BBB)*, established in 1916. Funded by dues from more than 100,000 member companies, it operates primarily at the local level to protect consumers against fraudulent and deceptive advertising and sales practices. When local bureaus contact violators and ask them to revise their advertising, most comply.

The BBB's files on violators are open to the public. Records of violators who do not comply are sent to appropriate government agencies for further action. The BBB often works with local law enforcement agencies to prosecute advertisers guilty of fraud and misrepresentation. Each year, the BBB investigates thousands of ads for possible violations of truth and accuracy.

The Board of Directors of the American Association of Advertising Agencies recognizes that when used truthfully and fairly, comparative advertising provides the consumer with needed and useful information.

However, extreme caution should be exercised. The use of comparative advertising, by its very nature, can distort facts and, by implication, convey to the consumer information that misrepresents the truth.

Therefore, the Board believes that comparative advertising should follow certain guidelines:

1. The intent and connotation of the ad should be to inform and never to discredit or unfairly attack competitors, competing products, or services.

2. When a competitive product is named, it should be one that exists in the marketplace as significant competition.

3. The competition should be fairly and properly identified but never in a manner or tone of voice that degrades the competitive product or service.

4. The advertising should compare related or similar properties or ingredients of the product, dimension to dimension, feature to feature.

5. The identification should be for honest comparison purposes and not simply to upgrade by association.

6. If a competitive test is conducted, it should be done by an objective testing source, preferably an independent one, so that there will be no doubt as to the veracity of the test.

7. In all cases the test should be supportive of all claims made in the advertising that are based on the test.

8. The advertising should never use partial results or stress insignificant differences to cause the consumer to draw an improper conclusion.

9. The property being compared should be significant in terms of value or usefulness of the product to the consumer.

10. Comparatives delivered through the use of testimonials should not imply that the testimonial is more than one individual's thought unless that individual represents a sample of the majority viewpoint.

Source: Copyright © 2009 American Association of Advertising Agencies. Reprinted with permission.

The Advertising Self-Regulatory Council (ASRC)

The Advertising Self-Regulatory Council's (ASRC) primary purpose is to promote and enforce standards of truth, accuracy, taste, morality, and social responsibility in advertising. The ASRC is one of the most comprehensive and effective mechanisms for regulating American advertising. A U.S. district court judge noted that its "speed, informality, and modest cost," as well as its expertise, give the ASRC special advantages over the court system in resolving advertising disputes.[79]

The ASRC has two operating arms: the *National Advertising Division (NAD)* of the Council of Better Business Bureaus and the *National Advertising Review Board (NARB)*. The NAD monitors advertising practices and reviews complaints about advertising from consumers and consumer groups, brand competitors, local Better Business Bureaus, trade associations, and others. The appeals board for NAD decisions is the NARB, which consists of a chair and 70 volunteer members (40 national advertisers, 20 agency representatives, and 10 consumers).

The case of the leather flight jacket shows how well the NAD process works. Neil Cooper LLC is a company that manufactures a leather jacket. In its print ads it claims that its A-2 leather flight jackets are the "official battle gear of U.S. Air Force Pilots." Avirex, Ltd., a competing company, complained to the NAD because the A-2 jacket at that time purchased by the Department of Defense and worn by U.S. pilots was Avirex's, not Neil Cooper. Neil Cooper explained that, although it was not the current supplier, many pilots continued to buy from Neil Cooper directly because they preferred that product. Notwithstanding, the NAD sided with Avirex and recommended that Neil Cooper qualify its claims to make it clear that it sold a reproduction of an authentic A-2 flight jacket rather than the current official one. Neil Cooper ultimately agreed.[80]

Regulation by the Media

Almost all media companies review ads and reject material they regard as objectionable, even if it isn't deceptive.

[Nothing motivates middle managers like the need to avoid attention.]

Television

Of all media, the TV networks conduct the strictest review. Advertisers must submit all commercials intended for a network or affiliated station to its **broadcast standards department**. Many commercials (in script or storyboard form) are returned with suggestions for changes or greater substantiation. Some ads are rejected outright if they violate network policies.

The major U.S. broadcast networks base their policies on the original National Association of Broadcasters Television Code. But network policies vary enough that it's difficult to prepare universally acceptable commercials. Cable networks and local stations tend to be much less stringent.

Radio

The U.S. radio networks, unlike TV networks, supply only a small percentage of their affiliates' programming, so they have little or no say in what their affiliates advertise. A radio station is also less likely to return a script or tape for changes. Some stations look mainly at whether advertising is illegal, unethical, or immoral.[81] They don't want spots to offend listeners or detract from the rest of the programming.

Every radio station typically has its own unwritten guidelines. KDWB, a Minneapolis–St. Paul station with a large teenage audience, turned down a psychic who wanted to buy advertising time but did allow condom and other contraceptive ads.[82]

SiriusXM, or satellite radio, tends to use standards related to its individual channels. Listeners are likely to hear very different spots on the Catholic Channel than they will on Howard Stern's program.

Magazines

National magazines monitor all advertising, especially by new advertisers and for new products. Newer publications eager to sell space may not be so vigilant, but established magazines, such as *Time* and *National Geographic*, are highly scrupulous. Many magazines will not accept advertising for certain types of products. The *New Yorker* won't run discount retail store advertising or ads for feminine hygiene or self-medication

Once common, ads such as this one for Bushman Firearms are vanishing as media outlets refuse to accept them. The reason? Guns have taken center stage in national debates over violence. In addition, as some groups seek redress for crimes by suing gun manufacturers, the ads are themselves being used in court filings. How does this ad and the controversies it inspires represent a conflict of societal values?

Source: Bushmaster Firearms International, LLC

products. *Reader's Digest* won't accept tobacco ads.

Some magazines test every product before accepting the advertising. *Good Housekeeping* rejects ads if its tests don't substantiate the advertiser's claims. Products that pass are allowed to feature the Good Housekeeping "Seal of Approval," and the magazine will stand behind those products. The magazine promises a refund or product replacement for defective products within two years of purchase.

Newspapers

Newspapers also monitor and review advertising. Larger newspapers have clearance staffs who read every ad submitted; most smaller newspapers rely on the advertising manager, sales personnel, or proofreaders.

One problem advertisers face is that newspapers' codes are far from uniform. Handgun ads may be prohibited by one newspaper, accepted by another if the guns are antique, and permitted by a third as long as the guns aren't automatic.

Regulation by Consumer Groups

Starting in the 1960s, the consumer movement became increasingly active in fighting fraudulent and deceptive advertising. Consumers demanded that products perform as advertised and that more product information be provided for people to compare and make better buying decisions. The consumer movement gave rise to **consumerism**, social action to dramatize the rights of the buying public.

Consumer advocate groups investigate advertising complaints received from the public and those that grow out of their own research. Today, with so many special-interest advocacy groups, even the most responsible advertisers feel challenged. To attract attention, advertising must be creative and stand out from competing noise. Yet advertisers fear attention from activists. Calvin Klein ads were attacked by the Boycott Anorexic Marketing group. A Nike ad starring Porky Pig was protested by the National Stuttering Project in San Francisco. An animated public service spot from Aetna Insurance drew complaints from a witches' rights group.[83]

When the protests start, the ads usually get pulled. As Shelly Garcia noted in *Adweek*, "The way things are these days, nothing motivates middle managers like the need to avoid attention.[84]

1. *Truth.* Advertising, public relations, marketing communications, news, and editorial all share a common objective of truth and high ethical standards in serving the public.

2. *Ethics.* Advertising, public relations, and all marketing communications professionals have an obligation to exercise the highest personal ethics in the creation and dissemination of commercial information to consumers.

3. *Distinctiveness.* Advertisers should clearly distinguish advertising, public relations and corporate communications from news and editorial content and entertainment, both online and offline.

4. *Complete Information.* Advertisers should clearly disclose all material conditions, such as payment or receipt of a free product, affecting endorsements in social and traditional channels, as well as the identity of endorsers, all in the interest of full disclosure and transparency.

5. *Fairness.* Advertisers should treat consumers fairly based on the nature of the audience to whom the ads are directed and the nature of the product or service advertised.

6. *Privacy.* Advertisers should never compromise consumers' personal privacy in marketing communications, and their choices as to whether to participate in providing their information should be transparent and easily made.

7. *Lawfulness.* Advertisers should follow federal, state and local advertising laws, and cooperate with industry self-regulatory programs for the resolution of advertising practices.

8. *Acknowledging Concerns.* Advertisers and their agencies, and online and offline media, should discuss privately potential ethical concerns, and members of the team creating ads should be given permission to express internally their ethical concerns.

9. *Transparency and Disclosure.* Trust between advertising and public relations business partners, including clients, and their agencies, media vendors, and third-party suppliers, should be built upon transparency and full disclosure of business ownership and arrangements, agency remuneration and rebates, and media incentives.

Source: Reprinted with permission of American Advertising Federation.

Self-Regulation by Advertisers and Ad Agencies

Advertisers also regulate themselves. They have to. In today's competitive marketplace, consumer confidence is essential. Most large advertisers gather strong data to substantiate their claims. They maintain careful systems of advertising review to ensure that ads meet both their own standards and industry, media, and legal requirements.

Ad agencies can be held legally liable for fraudulent or misleading advertising claims. For this reason, most major advertising agencies have an in-house legal counsel and regularly submit their ads for review. If any aspect of the advertising is challenged, the agency asks its client to review the advertising and either confirm claims as truthful or replace unverified material.

Several associations monitor industrywide advertising practices. The *American Association of Advertising Agencies (AAAA)*, an association of the largest advertising agencies throughout the United States, controls agency practices by denying membership to any agency judged unethical. The *American Advertising Federation (AAF)* helped establish the FTC, and its early vigilance committees were the forerunners of the Better Business Bureau. The *AAF Advertising Principles of American Business*, adopted in 1984, define standards for truthful and responsible advertising (see Exhibit 2-7). The *Association of National Advertisers (ANA)* comprises 370 major manufacturing and service companies that are clients of member agencies of the AAAA. These companies pledge to uphold the ANA code of advertising ethics.[85]

GOVERNMENT RESTRAINTS ON INTERNATIONAL ADVERTISERS

Because much advertising is global, many campaigns use similar themes and even the same ads across frontiers. But foreign governments often regulate advertising considerably more than the United States. And while Europe has moved toward uniformity in marketing activities, the laws governing advertising remain largely national.[86] So advertisers need to keep up with the changing legal environments of the countries in which they advertise.

Some governments not only regulate what ads say, show, or do; they often impose severe restrictions or outright bans on advertising specific products. The Swedes ban advertising to children on television. The Greeks ban toy advertising before 10:00 p.m. Throughout Europe, broadcast advertising for tobacco products is prohibited, and liquor ads are sharply restricted, especially in France.[87]

Many countries prohibit puffery. In Germany, for example, advertisers may use only scientifically provable superlatives. McCann Erickson once had to retranslate the old Coca-Cola slogan, "Refreshes you best," because it implied a leadership position that was unprovable. The agency substituted "Refreshes you right" in Germany.

Many European countries also ban coupons, premiums, free tie-in offers, and the like. Only two nations, the United States and

New Zealand, permit direct-to-consumer ads for drugs that require a prescription. Companies may advertise price cuts only during "official sales periods," and advertisers often need government approval before publishing a sale ad. Across Europe, advertising on television must be clearly recognizable and kept separate from other programming. Paid *product placements* in programs, therefore, are typically prohibited.[88] In international advertising, the only way to navigate the morass of potential legal problems is to retain lawyers who specialize in advertising law.

The growth of U.S. digital giants such as Facebook and Google has attracted the attention of regulators in Europe and elsewhere. In 2019, the EU leveled a 1.5 billion euro fine against Google for violating antitrust laws, following on two other instances in which the EU fined the company. The three fines together amounted to more than 8 billion euros, although the company has yet to pay the fines while it appeals the decisions. At the heart of the matter is scale and influence, as the EU holds that the company "has cemented its dominance in online search adverts and shielded itself from competitive pressure by imposing anticompetitive contractual restrictions on third-party websites."[89] Earlier in this chapter we referenced the GDPR (General Data Protection Regulation). This regulation has led to Facebook facing billions of euros of fines as well, largely on the basis of violating privacy rights of Europeans.[90]

The EU's active engagement with U.S. digital giants suggests that in a global economy, the rules of marketing are not necessarily those of a company's home country. Instead, rules for commerce are likely to be negotiated and involve compromises that respect diverse cultures.

check yourself ✓

1. Why do advertisers and ad agencies work so diligently to regulate their own activities?

2. What challenges do global companies face in advertising around the world?

THE ETHICAL AND LEGAL ASPECTS OF ADVERTISING IN PERSPECTIVE

Unquestionably, advertising offers considerable benefits to marketers and consumers alike. However, there's also no disputing that advertising has been and still is too often misused. As *Adweek* editor Andrew Jaffe says, the industry should do all it can to "raise its standards and try to drive out that which is misleading, untruthful, or downright tasteless and irresponsible." Otherwise, he warns, the pressure to regulate even more will become overwhelming.[91]

Advertising apologists point out that of all the advertising reviewed by the FTC in a typical year, 97 percent is found to be satisfactory.[92] In the end, advertisers and consumers need to work together to ensure that advertising is used intelligently, ethically, and responsibly for the benefit of all. ■

ENDNOTES

1. Jagdish Agrawal and Wagner A. Kamakura, "The Economic Worth of Celebrity Endorsers," *Journal of Marketing* 59 (2005), pp. 56–63.

2. "Lance Armstrong: USADA Report Labels Him 'a Serial Cheat'," *BBC Sport*, October 11, 2012, www.bbc.co.uk.

3. Brian Warner, "How Much Money Will Lance Armstrong Lose From His Scandals?" *Celebrity Networth*, January 17, 2013, www.celebritynetworth.com/articles/celebrity/money-lance-armstrong-lose-scandals.

4. Patrick Rishe, "Armstrong Will Lose $150 Million in Future Earnings after Nike and Other Sponsors Dump Him," *Forbes*, October 18, 2012, www.forbes.com/sites/prishe/2012/10/18/nike-proves-deadlier-than-cancer-as-armstrong-will-lose-150-million-in-future-earnings.

5. Jeremy Mullen, "Reducing the Risk of Vicktimization," *Advertising Age*, July 23, 2007, http://web.ebscohost.com.lp.hscl.ufl.edu/ehost/detail?vid=4&hid=109&sid=4dc8792cc1b3-4c6d-9798-4d64035c4755%40sessionmgr108.

6. Syed Tariq Anwar, "Guest Column: Ethics, Responsibility Are Everyone's Business," *Amarillo Globe-News*, April 2, 2005.

7. John O'Toole, *The Trouble with Advertising* (New York: Times Books, 1985), pp. 7–14.

8. Marcel Bleustein-Blanchet, *La Rage de Convaincre* (Paris: Editions Robert Laffont, 1970), p. 25.

9. Ernest Dichter, *Handbook of Consumer Motivations* (New York: McGraw-Hill, 1964), pp. 6, 422–31.

10. Richard E. Kihlstrom and Michael H. Riordan, "Advertising as a Signal," *Journal of Political Economy*, June 1984, pp. 427–50.

11. Ivan Preston, *The Tangled Web They Weave* (Madison: University of Wisconsin Press, 1994), pp. 94–95.

12. Fabiana Giacomotti, "European Marketers Keep Up Ad Budgets," *Adweek*, January 24, 1994, pp. 16–17.

13. "FMI Supermarket Facts," Food Marketing Institute, 2014, http://www.fmi.org/research-resources/supermarket-facts.

14. "Truth in Advertising," Federal Trade Commission, March 27, 2016, www.ftc.gov/news-events/media-resources/truth-advertising.

15. "Pizza Hut Files Suit against Pizza Rival," *Advertising Age*, August 13, 1998; "Papa John's Ordered to Move 'Better' Slogan," *Advertising Age*, January 5, 2000, http://adage.com.

16. Stuart C. Rogers, "Subliminal Advertising: Grand Scam of the 20th Century," paper presented to the Annual Conference of the American Academy of Advertising, April 10, 1994.

17. Stuart C. Rogers, "Subliminal Advertising: Grand Scam of the 20th Century," paper presented to the Annual Conference of the American Academy of Advertising, April 10, 1994; Martha Rogers and Kirk H. Smith, "Public Perceptions of Subliminal

Advertising," *Journal of Advertising Research*, March/April 1993, p. 10.

18. Andrew Jaffe, "Advertiser, Regulate Thyself," *Adweek*, August 2, 1993, p. 38.

19. Andrew Jaffe, "Advertiser, Regulate Thyself," *Adweek*, August 2, 1993, p. 38.

20. Preston, *The Tangled Web They Weave*, p. 164.

21. "Marketing Content Fills 42% of Prime Time," *Marketing Charts*, June 2, 2010, www.marketingcharts.com/television-13069.

22. Victor Luckerson, "Here's Exactly Why Watching TV Has Gotten So Annoying," *Time*, May 12, 2014, http://time.com/96303/tv-commercials-increasing.

23. Mike Sachoff, "Ad Clutter Bad for Users, Advertisers," *WebPro News/Technology*, December 11, 2008.

24. Ophir Tanz, "These Alternative Ads Might Save Display Advertising," *Business Insider*, June 22, 2013, www.businessinsider.com/these-alternative-ads-might-save-display-advertising-2013-6.

25. "The Public and Broadcasting," *FCC Mass Media Bureau*, June 1999, https://transition.fcc.gov/Bureaus/Mass_Media/Public_Notices/da991099.html.

26. Shelly Garcia, "What's Wrong with Being Politically Correct?" *Adweek*, November 15, 1993, p. 62.

27. Adrienne Ward, "What Role Do Ads Play in Racial Tension?" *Advertising Age*, August 10, 1992, pp. 1, 35.

28. "Statistical Overview of Women in the Workplace," *Catalyst*, March 13, 2013, www.catalyst.org/knowledge/statistical-overview-women-workplace.

29. John B. Ford and Michael S. LaTour, "Differing Reactions to Female Role Portrayals in Advertising," *Journal of Advertising Research*, September/October 1993, pp. 43–52.

30. Michael L. Klassen, Cynthia R. Jasper, and Anne M. Schwartz, "Men and Women: Images of Their Relationships in Magazine Advertisements," *Journal of Advertising Research*, March/April 1993, pp. 30–39.

31. "Stereotype," *Merriam-Webster*, www.merriam-webster.com/dictionary/stereotype.

32. "Revealing Abercrombie Catalog Sparks a Boycott," *The Cincinnati Enquirer*, June 26, 2001.

33. Esther Lee and Rachel McRady, "Oscars 2016 Boycott," *US Weekly*, February 24, 2016, www.usmagazine.com/celebrity-news/news/oscars-2016-boycott-a-timeline-of-the-controversy-w162120.

34. Esther Lee and Rachel McRady, "Oscars 2016 Boycott," *US Weekly*, February 24, 2016, www.usmagazine.com/celebrity-news/news/oscars-2016-boycott-a-timeline-of-the-controversy-w162120.

35. Preston, "A New Conception of Deceptiveness," paper presented to the Advertising Division of the Association for Education in Journalism and Mass Communication, August 12, 1993.

36. Robert W. McChesney, *Corporate Media and the Threat to Democracy* (New York: Seven Stories Press, 1997), p. 23.

37. Preston, *The Tangled Web They Weave*, pp. 94, 127–31.

38. James R. Maxeiner, "United States," in Maxeiner and Schotthoffer, eds., *Advertising Law in Europe and North America*, p. 321; see also *Virginia State Board of Pharmacy v. Virginia Citizens Consumer Council*, 425 U.S. 748 (1976).

39. See *Central Hudson Gas & Electric Corp. v. Public Service Commission of New York*, 447 U.S. 557 (1980).

40. Kartik Pashupati, "The Camel Controversy: Same Beast, Different Viewpoints," paper presented to the annual conference of the Association for Education in Journalism and Mass Communication, Kansas City, MO, August 11, 1993; Maxeiner, "United States," pp. 321–22.

41. Thomas Sullivan, "US Supreme Court: *Sorrell vs. IMS Inc.*—Court Upholds Data Mining," *Policy and Medicine*, June 27, 2011, www.policymed.com/2011/06/us-supreme-court-sorrell-vs-ims-inc-court-upholds-data-mining.html.

42. Joy Johnson Wilson, "Summary of the Attorneys General Master Tobacco Settlement Agreement," March 1999, http://academic.udayton.edu/health/syllabi/tobacco/summary.htm.

43. Children's Advertising Review Unit, "CARU Parent's Corner," retrieved on March 27, 2016, www.asrcreviews.org/category/caru/parents-corner.

44. Bridget Kelley, et al., "Television food advertising to children: A global perspective," American Journal of Public Health, 2010 September; 100(9): 1730–1736.

45. "Online Privacy—It's Time for Rules in Wonderland," *BusinessWeek*, March 20, 2000, p. 85.

46. Elinor Mills, "Don't Like Targeted Ads? Opt Out, Says Online Ad Group," *News Blog, cnet news*, February 24, 2008, www.cnet.com/news/dont-like-targeted-ads-opt-out-says-online-ad-group.

47. Mark Sakalosky, "DoubleClick's Double Edge," *ClickZ*, September 3, 2002, www.clickz.com/doubleclicks-double-edge/68851.

48. Mary Madden and Lee Rainey, "Americans' Attitudes about Privacy, Security and Surveillance," *Pew Research Center*, May 20, 2015, www.pewinternet.org/2015/05/20/americans-attitudes-about-privacy-security-and-surveillance.

49. Interactive Advertising Bureau Europe, "Manage Cookies: What Can I Do to Manage Cookies on My Computer?" retrieved September 11, 2009, www.allaboutcookies.org/manage-cookies.

50. Business Week, "Online Privacy—It's Time for Rules in Wonderland," March 20, 2000, p. 83.

51. Aimee O'Driskel, "Five Core Principles of Fair Information Practices," *Comparitech*, August 10, 2017, www.comparitech.com/blog/vpn-privacy/fair-information-practices.

52. "2019 Consumer Data Privacy Legislation," NCSL, January 3, 2020, www.ncsl.org/research/telecommunications-and-information-technology/consumer-data-privacy.aspx.

53. "Assembly Bill No. 375," California Legislative Information, https://leginfo.legislature.ca.gov/faces/billTextClient.xhtml?bill_id=201720180AB375.

54. Federal Trade Commission, "Vision, Mission, and Goals," 1997.

55. James C. Miller, "FTC Policy Statement on Deception," October 14, 1983, www.ftc.gov/system/files/documents/public_statements/410531/831014deceptionstmt.pdf.

56. FTC, "Advertising FAQ's: A Guide for Small Business," retrieved March 27, 2016, www.ftc.gov/tips-advice/business-center/guidance/advertising-faqs-guide-small-business.

57. Ann Carrns, "FTC Settles with Office Depot, Buy.com, Value America over 'Low Cost' PC Ads," *The Wall Street Journal*, June 30, 2000, p. B4.

58. Dean Keith Fueroghne, *But the People in Legal Said . . .* (Burr Ridge, IL: Professional Publishing, 1989), p. 14.

59. Christy Fisher, "How Congress Broke Unfair Ad Impasse," *Advertising Age*, August 22, 1994, p. 34.

60. Editorial, "A Fair FTC Pact?" *Advertising Age*, March 21, 1994, p. 22.

61. "Arizona Trade Association Agrees to Settle FTC Charges; It Urged Members to Restrain Competitive Advertising," FTC News Release, February 25, 1994.

62. "Comparative Advertising," *ADLAW*, copyright 2000 Hall Dickler Kent Goldstein & Wood, www.adlaw.com.

63. "Crackdown on Testimonials," *The Wall Street Journal*, July 13, 1993, p. B7.

64. Minette E. Drumwright, "Ethical Issues in Advertising and Sales Promotion," in N. Craig Smith and John A. Quelch, eds., *Ethics in Marketing* (Burr Ridge, IL: Richard D. Irwin, 1993) pp. 615–16.

65. Ira Teinowitz, "Doan's Decision Sets Precedent for Corrective Ads," *Advertising Age*, September 4, 2000, p. 57.

66. Los Angeles Chamber of Commerce, www.lachamber.com/clientuploads/Global_Programs/Presentation_FDA.pdf.

67. "The Growing Brouhaha over Drug Advertisements," *The New York Times*, May 14, 1989, p. F8.

68. "FDA to Review Standards for All Direct-to-Consumer Rx Drug Promotion," FDA news release, August 8, 1997.

69. Lisa M. Schwartz, MD, MS1; Steven Woloshin, "Medical Marketing in the United States, 1997–2016," *JAMA* 321, 1 (2019), pp. 80–96. https://jamanetwork.com/journals/jama/fullarticle/2720029.

70. "FDA Seeks Rx for Drug Ads; New Policy Delays Process," *Newsday* (Nassau and Suffolk edition), December 5, 2002.

71. Steven W. Colford, "Labels Lose the Fat," *Advertising Age*, June 10, 1991, pp. 3, 54; Steven W. Colford and Julie Liesse, "FDA Label Plans under Attack," *Advertising Age*, February 24, 1992, pp. 1, 50; John E. Calfee, "FDA's Ugly Package: Proposed Label Rules Call for Vast Changes," *Advertising Age*, March 16, 1992, p. 25; and Pauline M. Ippolito and Alan D. Mathios, "New Food Labeling Regulations and the Flow of Nutrition Information to Consumers," *Journal of Public Policy & Marketing*, Fall 1993, pp. 188–205.

72. John Carey, "The FDA Is Swinging a Sufficiently Large Two-by-Four," *BusinessWeek*, May 27, 1991, p. 44; Steven W. Colford, "FDA Getting Tougher: Seizure of Citrus Hill Is Signal to Marketers," *Advertising Age*, April 29, 1991, pp. 1, 53.

73. Joe Mandese, "Regulation," *Advertising Age*, November 30, 1992, p. 23.

74. John H. Cushman Jr., "Supreme Court Rejects F.C.C. Appeal in Janet Jackson Case," *The New York Times*, June 29, 2012, www.nytimes.com/2012/06/30/us/justices-reject-fcc-effort-to-fine-cbs-in-janet-jackson-case.html.

75. *U.S. Constitution*, Article 1, Section 8.

76. U.S. Copyright Office, Library of Congress, 1997.

77. Wayne E. Green, "Lawyers Give Deceptive Trade-Statutes New Day in Court, Wider Interpretations," *The Wall Street Journal*, January 24, 1990, p. B1.

78. Howard Schlossberg, "Marketers Say State Laws Hurt Their 'Green' Efforts," *Marketing News*, November 11, 1991, pp. 8–9.

79. Felix H. Kent, "Control of Ads by Private Sector," *New York Law Journal*, December 27, 1985; reprinted in Kent and Stone, eds., *Legal and Business Aspects of the Advertising Industry* (Practising Law Institute, 1986), pp. 20–79.

80. "NAD Pilots Successful Resolution Between Neil Cooper and Avirex," Better Business Bureau News Release, August 11, 2000, www.nadreview.org/casereports.asp.

81. Public Relations Department, KLBJ, Austin, TX, 1991.

82. Public Relations Department, KDWB, Minneapolis/St. Paul, MN, 1991.

83. Kevin Goldman, "From Witches to Anorexics, Critical Eyes Scrutinize Ads for Political Correctness," *The Wall Street Journal*, May 19, 1994, p. B1.

84. Garcia, "What's Wrong with Being Politically Correct?" p. 62.

85. Institute for Advertising Ethics, "Principles and Practices for Advertising Ethics," 2006, www.aaf.org/_PDF/AAF%20Website%20Content/513_Ethics/IAE_Principles_Practices.pdf.

86. Mary Alice and Soontae An (Eds.), *The Global Advertising Regulation Handbook* (London: Routledge, 2015).

87. Keith Boyfield, "Business Europe: When Advertising Is against the Law," *The Wall Street Journal*, European edition, March 6, 2000, p. 11 (retrieved from Lexis-Nexis Academic Universe).

88. Peter Schotthoffer, "European Community," in Maxeiner and Schotthoffer, eds., *Advertising Law in Europe and North America*, p. 89.

89. Adam Satariano, "Google Fined $1.7 Billion by E.U. for Unfair Advertising Rules," *New York Times*, March 20, 2019, www.nytimes.com/2019/03/20/business/google-fine-advertising.html.

90. Margaret Patrick, "Facebook May Face Billions in Fines in EU," *Market Realist*, August 13, 2019, https://marketrealist.com/2019/08/facebook-may-face-billions-in-fines-in-eu.

91. Jaffe, "Advertiser, Regulate Thyself," p. 38.

92. Federal Trade Commission, 1991.

the business of
advertising

This chapter introduces the people and groups that sponsor, create, produce, and transmit advertisements. Advertising people may serve in a variety of roles. The chapter discusses the basic tasks of both the client (advertiser) and the advertising agency, the roles of suppliers and the media, the ways agencies acquire clients and earn revenue, and the complex relationship between the agency and the client.

Thomas Friedman once wrote that "No two countries that both had McDonald's had fought a war against each other since each got its McDonald's." Friedman's point was that economic development and international trade reduce conflict. Still, who can rule out the possibility that international harmony increases in direct proportion to the availability of Happy Meals?

The meals at McDonald's are similar to those sold in thousands of competing restaurants. Its menu item ingredients—ground beef, potatoes, and more recently, salads and yogurt—are available to anyone. And indeed, there are plenty of competitors out there. But none are so successful. What is McDonald's secret?

One could start with the company's value proposition: tasty, inexpensive food served quickly.

But it's hard to avoid the conclusion that advertising is part of the equation as well. Over time, McDonald's has spent billions on advertising, both in the United States and around the world. And that investment has helped to make the McDonald's brand one of the most valuable and recognizable in the world.

The slogans are part of advertising lore. "You deserve a break today." "Two all beef patties, special sauce, lettuce, cheese, pickles, onions, on a sesame seed bun." "Have you had your break today?" The ads made the Golden Arches a part of the world's shared culture.

Let's look at how McDonald's uses integrated marketing communications (IMC), including advertising, to maintain its status as the biggest prepared-food seller in the world.

McDonald's has franchises in more than 100 countries. But around the

continued on p. 60

LEARNING OBJECTIVES

After studying this chapter, you will be able to:

LO3-1 List the various groups in the advertising business and explain their relationships.

LO3-2 Discuss the differences between local, national, and transnational advertisers.

LO3-3 Demonstrate how advertisers organize themselves to manage their advertising both here and abroad.

LO3-4 Describe the main types of advertising agencies.

LO3-5 Explain the tasks people perform in an ad agency and an in-house advertising department.

LO3-6 Show how agencies get new clients and how they make money.

Source: McDonald's Corporation

continued from p. 59

world, the essence of the McDonald's brand always shines through. Customers can always expect to encounter clean restaurants; American fast-food items; and fast, friendly service. Employees dress in colorful, clean uniforms.

The unified brand message is reinforced with advertising. McDonald's current campaign, which has run for more than 15 years, is global, so customers everywhere hear the familiar "ba da ba ba ba," followed by "i'm lovin' it." The campaign was created by a German agency, Heye & Partner, part of DDB's worldwide group. Justin Timberlake provides the vocals to a tune written by Tom Batoy and Franco Tortora.[1]

Although the campaign and brand are global, an important secret to the company's success is its willingness to customize its offerings to suit local preferences. McDonald's does not serve pork in predominantly Muslim countries (and it refers to hamburgers as "beefburgers"); and in countries where meat is not a big part of the regular diet (such as India), the company offers "veggie burgers." Even in the United States, menu items adapt to local preferences.

The "think global, act local" philosophy extends to advertising. McDonald's allocates a portion of its advertising budget to cooperative efforts with local franchises, who in turn make their own decisions about ad agencies and local campaigns.

Additionally, McDonald's often runs several U.S. campaigns simultaneously. For example, in addition to the "i'm lovin' it" ads, the company runs spots to promote specific menu items, such as its premium salad offerings or all-day breakfast. Other ads cater to specific markets, such as Hispanics, African Americans, working moms, or kids.

Another part of the company's DNA is a willingness to innovate. After global sales dipped from $28 billion in 2012 to just $25 billion in 2015, CEO Steve Easterbrook led changes to the menu, including offering breakfast items throughout the day. Consumers were ecstatic and sales jumped. The company also hit home runs with the introduction of coffee bars and fresh ground beef.

advertisers Companies that sponsor advertising for themselves and their products.

advertising agencies Independent organizations of creative people and businesspeople that specialize in developing and preparing advertising plans, advertisements, and other promotional tools for advertisers. The agencies also arrange for or contract for purchases of space and time in various media.

suppliers People and organizations that assist both advertisers and agencies in the preparation of advertising materials, such as photography, illustration, printing, and production.

media A plural form of *medium*, referring to communications vehicles paid to present an advertisement to their target audience. Most often used to refer to radio and television networks, stations that have new reporters, and publications that carry news and advertising.

So how does a company that makes hamburgers achieve such success? McDonald's has shown time and again that a great brand, a willingness to innovate, and strategic use of advertising to tell its story are an unbeatable combination. ■

LO3-1 List the various groups in the advertising business and explain their relationships.

THE ADVERTISING INDUSTRY

The range of work performed by advertising people goes far beyond what we see daily on TV. Moreover, many people and organizations besides those usually thought of as advertising folks are involved in advertising and IMC. That's because every successful company needs to communicate with customers.

The Organizations in Advertising

The advertising business has four distinct groups. The two main ones are the *advertisers* and the *agencies*. The **advertisers** (or *clients*) are companies—such as Honda, McDonald's, or the local shoe store—that pay to advertise themselves and their products. Advertisers range in size from small independent businesses to huge multinational firms, and in type from service organizations to industrial manufacturers to local charities.

The second group, **advertising agencies**, employ the specialists who help advertisers plan, create, and prepare IMC campaigns.

A third group, **suppliers**, includes the photographers, illustrators, printers, digital service bureaus, video production houses, digital developers, and others who provide their services to advertisers and agencies. Suppliers also include consultants, research firms, and professional services. The fourth group, **media**, sells time (on radio and TV) and space (in print, outdoor) or both (digital media) for connecting the advertiser's message with the target audience.

The People in Advertising

When people think of advertising, they imagine the copywriters and art directors who work for ad agencies. But the majority of people in advertising are employed by advertisers rather than by agencies. Companies usually have an advertising department, even if it is just one person. And there are many more companies that advertise than there are agencies. In addition, many people work for the suppliers and media companies. They're in advertising, too. The fact is, advertising is a very broad field that employs a wide variety of people.

In this chapter, we will see what all these people do at the various places where they work. In the process, we will get a good understanding of how the advertising industry operates both in the United States and abroad.

check yourself ✓

1. What are the four distinct groups that characterize the advertising business and what do they do?

2. What is the difference between an advertiser and an advertising agency?

LO3-2 Discuss the differences between local, national, and transnational advertisers.

THE ADVERTISERS (CLIENTS)

The ways a company advertises differs depending on whether the company primarily advertises locally (in the community in which the business is located) or on a broader scale, for example, nationally or transnationally. This section describes the different ways that local businesses and larger organizations advertise.

to sell, even with his secret batter recipe. The first month's sales at the restaurant averaged only $163 a day.

Rubio began using small newspaper ads with coupons to lure courageous customers. As business picked up, he expanded his advertising to radio and TV, targeting his market with ads on Hispanic stations (whose listeners knew what fish tacos

> Local advertising is critically important because most consumer sales are made (or lost) locally.

Local Advertising

When Ralph Rubio opened his first Mexican restaurant, he offered an unusual specialty: fish tacos. At the time, very few Mexican eateries offered them. So Rubio found fish tacos hard

were). And he went after younger, venturesome customers ages 18 to 34 by advertising at local movie theaters. Business picked up some more. Rubio soon opened another restaurant, and then another.

With each new opening, Rubio distributed direct-mail flyers in the area and took free samples to nearby stores. Working with an artist, he created a cartoon character named Pesky Pescado based on the fish taco. He purchased a 15-foot inflatable Pesky to display at his restaurants. Employee T-shirts sported Pesky's picture, and Rubio sold Pesky T-shirts and sweatshirts to enthusiastic patrons. He also offered bumper stickers and antenna balls to add some fun to his promotions. To further integrate his activities, Rubio took an active part in community affairs, including tie-ins with a blood bank, a literacy program, and fund-raising activities for both a Tijuana medical clinic and a local university's athletic program.

As the popularity of the fish taco grew, so did Rubio's revenues, doubling every year for the first five years. He trademarked the phrase "Rubio's, Home of the Fish Taco," and a local restaurant critic, commenting on things San Diegans couldn't do without, called fish tacos "the food San Diegans would miss the most." Today, Rubio's Coastal Grill has nearly 200 restaurants in five states. And they still make great fish tacos.[2]

Almost half of the billions of dollars spent each year on advertising in the United States is devoted to **local advertising** by local businesses targeting customers in their geographic area.

Local advertising is sometimes called *retail advertising* because so much is placed by retail stores. But retail advertising isn't always local; Target and Walmart advertise nationally. And many businesses besides retail stores use local advertising: banks, movie theaters, auto mechanics, plumbers, radio and TV stations, local politicians, and McDonald's franchises, to name a few. What distinguishes local advertising is that it targets a specific community.

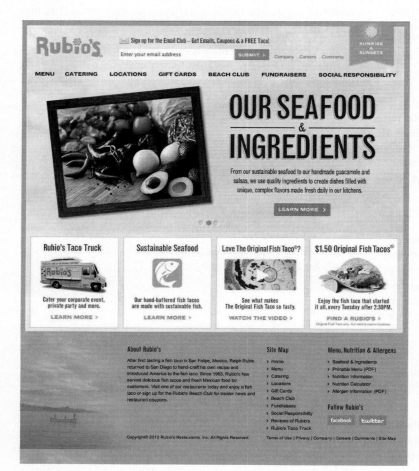

Local advertisers such as Rubio's Coastal Grill (www.rubios.com) must find ways to differentiate their products from the competition—and then create awareness through advertising. Rubio's website touts its use of fresh ingredients and sustainable seafood, which sets it apart from other restaurants.
Source: Rubio's Restaurants, Inc.

Understanding Your Client [3–A]

Obtaining a clear understanding of what your client wants from you and what you are prepared to do for your client is essential for a mutually satisfying relationship. From your end, it is vital that you be clear about the finished product. In many classes, this might be a plans book that contains research, an advertising plan, a media plan, and even some creative plans. In other classes, you might not provide all of that. In either case, make sure your client knows what to expect. If previous classes have done campaign work for other clients, you might wish to show your client that work.

As important as it is that your client understand you, it is equally crucial that you understand your client's expectations. Recognize that some clients may not have a clear set of expectations at first; these may in fact evolve over time. Even in this instance, asking the right questions can get your client thinking about what they hope advertising will do for them.

Below you will find some questions that might prove useful for getting to know your client better. Dr. Debbie Treise, who regularly teaches advertising campaigns at the University of Florida, uses this form. Sending it to the client in advance of a meeting can make your first interaction more useful and informative.

1. Provide a complete description of your product/service:
   What is its current position?
   What is the brand personality as you perceive it?
   Does it need changing?
   Are there seasonal trends for your product?
   Would you be willing to share annual sales trend information?
2. Do you have information on your company to share? Your mission statement? How would you describe the culture of your organization?
3. Do you have a definite target market in mind? Are you targeting consumers, groups, businesses or some combination?
4. Is the market local? Regional? National? International?
5. Would you be willing to share:
   Information on your competition?
   Information on your market?
   Information on market trends? Legal trends?
   Advertising that your competition has used?
   Previous campaigns that you have run?
6. What is the time period of this campaign? Do you have definite start and stop dates in mind?
7. What is the budget?
8. Do you have any specifications on the budget breakdown in terms of promotion versus advertising? Any other specifications?
9. What are your marketing objectives for this campaign?
10. Please list your advertising/communications objectives for this campaign (that is, to increase knowledge, change attitudes, elicit or change a specific behavior).
11. Are there media that you would like us to be sure to consider?
12. Are there media that you would prefer we not recommend?
13. Do you have a current, active website? If so, what is its primary purpose? Who accesses it? Do you use social media?
14. Would you like to use social media? Do you have experts who can commit to engaging on social media regularly?
15. Do you have any specifications on creative executions? Are you looking to continue current efforts or to come up with something completely different?
16. Are there any current clients/consumers that we could contact?
17. Are there potential clients/customers that we could contact?
18. Who is the individual in your organization we should contact when we have questions? What is the best time to contact this person? How does he or she prefer to be contacted (e-mail, text, phone, fax)?

Smaller ad agencies typically work with local clients, who may also sometimes forgo an agency altogether if their budget does not permit one. Local clients are every bit as important to a local ad agency as major brands are to a global agency (see My Ad Campaign 3–A "Understanding your Client" above).

Local advertising is critically important because most consumer sales are made (or lost) locally. McDonald's may spend billions advertising worldwide, but if it doesn't make a strong effort locally, the dollars may be wasted. When it comes to making the sale and dealing with customers, local advertising is where the action is—where relationships often start and truly develop.

Types of Local Advertisers

There are four main types of local advertisers.

- Dealers or local franchisees of national companies (Honda, McDonald's, H&R Block).
- Stores that sell a variety of branded merchandise (convenience, grocery, and department stores).
- Specialty businesses and services (banks, restaurants, music stores, remodeling contractors, florists, hair salons, attorneys, accountants).
- Governmental and nonprofit organizations (municipalities, utility companies, charities, arts organizations, political candidates).

A small, local business—say, a hardware, clothing, or electronics store—may have just one person in charge of advertising. That person, the **advertising manager**, performs all the administrative, planning, budgeting, and coordinating functions. He or she may design ads, write copy, and engage customers in social media.

A typical small advertiser structure is shown in Exhibit 3-1.

Types of Local Advertising

Most local ads are product, institutional, or classified advertising. Additionally, many local advertisers use social media to engage with customers. Each serves a different purpose.

Product advertising promotes a specific product or service and stimulates short-term action while building awareness of the business. To stimulate sales of merchandise or increase store traffic, local merchants frequently use **sale advertising**, placing items on sale and offering two-for-one specials or other deals.

Institutional advertising attempts to create a favorable long-term perception of the business as a whole, not just of a particular product or service. Many businesses use institutional advertising to promote an idea about the company and build long-term goodwill. It makes the public aware of what the business stands for and attempts to build reputation and image.

▼**EXHIBIT 3–1** Typical department structure for small advertisers with high volumes of work, such as grocery store chains.

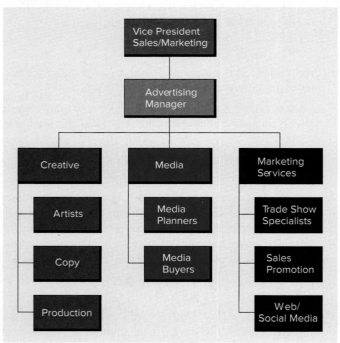

Advertisers use **classified advertising** for a variety of reasons: to locate and recruit new employees, offer services (such as those of an employment agency or business opportunity broker), or sell or lease new and used merchandise (such as cars, real estate, and office equipment).

Local Advertisers and IMC   When Ralph Rubio built his restaurant business, his promotional activities involved a lot more than just running ads. In fact, he did everything he could to build relationships with his customers and to promote word of mouth. That meant using publicity, sales promotion, and direct response as well as media advertising—all integrated with consistently good food, reasonable prices, and excellent service. This combination constitutes **integrated marketing communications (IMC)**—joining together in a consistent manner every element that communicates with customers including the actual delivery of the product or service.

Many local advertisers comfortably use social media[3] to engage target audiences. For example, Rubio's uses its Facebook page (www.facebook.com/Rubios) to share specials, show menu items, share restaurant locations, and hear from customers. It shares more timely announcements on its Twitter feed (https://twitter.com/RubiosTweets) and tells food and customer stories on Instagram (www.instagram.com/rubioscoastalgrill).

Creating Local Advertising   Social media such as Facebook, Twitter, and LinkedIn have the capacity to dramatically change the strategies of local advertisers. Joe Morsello, a communications manager at a local business trade association, argues that local advertisers have an advantage over national advertisers in social media because they share a community with their customers. When things happen locally (bad weather, a town festival, a breaking news story), local advertisers can target customers about these shared events. This is exactly what Evie Poitevent did when rain threatened to spoil a jazz festival in New Orleans. The boutique shoe store owner tweeted about her stylish rain boots and quickly sold out her inventory.[4]

The principles for developing good local advertising don't differ dramatically from the general principles presented throughout this book. However, given limited budgets and the need to see immediate results, local advertisers have to make every word and every dollar count. To direct and control the creative aspects of their ads and commercials and ensure consistency, local advertisers should adhere to a list of creative do's and don'ts. (See My Ad Campaign 3-B, "Creating Local Advertising".)

Local advertisers rely on several sources for creative help, including reps from the local media, local ad agencies, freelancers and consultants, creative boutiques, syndicated art services, and the cooperative advertising programs of wholesalers, manufacturers, and trade associations. McDonald's offers its franchise owners considerable help in designing IMC messages.

Cooperative Advertising
Wholesalers and manufacturers often provide local advertisers with ready-made advertising materials and cooperative advertising programs where the costs are shared.

Cooperative (co-op) advertising has two key purposes: to build the manufacturer's brand image and to help distributors, dealers, or retailers increase sales.[5] Every year, national manufacturers give local retailers more than $20 billion for co-op projects. Newspapers, direct mail, and radio are the favored media of co-op spending.[6] Walmart alone benefits from almost $100 million in vendor funding for ads.[7] Exhibit 3-2 demonstrates how important co-op advertising dollars are for certain retail businesses.

cooperative (co-op) advertising The sharing of advertising costs by the manufacturer and the distributor or retailer. The manufacturer may repay 50 or 100 percent of the dealer's advertising costs or some other amount based on sales.

▼ **EXHIBIT 3-2**   The importance of co-op advertising dollars.

Store	Co-op Dollars as a Percentage of Total Ad Budget
Appliance dealers	80%
Food stores	75
Drugstores	70
Department stores	50
Shoe stores	50
Clothing stores	35
Furniture stores	30
Household goods	30
Jewelers	30
Discount stores	20

my ad campaign

Creating Local Advertising [3–B]

Is your client a local business or service? Use these time-tested practices to guide your thinking about how local advertising can help.

- *Know who you are.* Branding isn't just for big companies. A small business needs a strong, distinctive, attractive brand identity as well. A strong brand is the foundation of an effective ad campaign.
- *Stand out from the competition.* Make your ads easily recognizable. Ads with unusual art, layout, and typefaces have higher readership. Make the ads distinctive but keep their appearance consistent.
- *Use a simple layout.* The layout should carry the reader's eye through the message easily and in proper sequence from headline to illustration to explanatory copy to price to store name. Avoid too many typefaces.
- *Use a dominant visual element.* A large picture or headline ensures quick visibility. Photos of real people and action pictures win more readership, as do photos of local people or places. Color attracts more readers.
- *Stress the benefits.* Present the emotional reason to buy or the tangible brand attribute that customers seek.
- *Make the headline count.* Use a compelling headline to feature the main benefit.
- *Watch your language.* Write with a style that is active, lively, and involving. Make readers feel they already own the product. Avoid negativism and controversy.
- *Let white space work for you.* White space focuses the reader's attention and makes the headline and illustration pop.

- *Make the copy complete.* Emphasize the benefits most appealing to customers and offer proof the product has these benefits.
- *Make your visual powerful and eye-catching.* Focus on the benefit. The main visual is often more important than the headline. Photos work better than artwork.
- *Include related items.* Make two sales instead of one by offering related items along with a featured one.
- *Urge readers to buy now.* Ask for the sale. Stimulate prompt action by using "limited supply" or "this week only."
- *Don't forget the business name and address.* Check every ad to be certain the business name, address, phone number, and hours are included.
- *Be social.* Consumers expect even small businesses to actively participate in social media. Be sure content is fresh and compelling.
- *Build relationships.* Social media is about relationships. People follow a brand or company because they love it. Regular customers are the lifeblood of a small business. Stay in touch with your best customers and reward their loyalty.
- *Keep it simple.* Everyone understands simple language. Use it.
- *Don't generalize.* Be specific. Shoppers want facts before they buy.
- *Avoid hype.* Advertisers lose customers when they make claims they can't back up.
- *Plan ad size carefully.* Attention usually increases with size.
- *Consider your target customers.* People notice ads more if they are directed at their own gender or age group.
- *Take advantage of your local connections.* Use tie-ins with local or special news events.

Rubio's demonstrates that local advertising can be as smart and engaging as national. While the company makes its delicious food the centerpiece of many messages, it also finds ways to connect with its customers' emotions. This is every bit as important for local advertisers as it is for the big brands.
(Left): Source: Rubio's Restaurants, Inc./Instagram

On the surface, cooperative advertising seems like a great arrangement for retailers. A manufacturer supplies advertising materials (saving the retailer production costs) and pays a percentage of the media cost. The retailer drops in the store's logo, arranges for the ad to run, and collects the co-op dollars from the manufacturer. The small retail business can stretch its ad budget and associate its business with a nationally advertised product. The retailer receives professionally prepared ads and acquires greater leverage with the local media that carry the co-op ads.

But as with any marriage, there is give and take. A retailer may have to sell a lot of merchandise to qualify for co-op funds. And sometimes, the retailer and manufacturer have different advertising objectives and different ideas about how the ads should be executed.

The manufacturer often wants total control. It expects co-op ads to tie in with its national and advertising promotions. It wants the right product advertised at the right time. Manufacturers prepare guideline pamphlets specifying when and where the ads should appear, what form they should take, and what uses of the name and logo are allowed.

Retailers have their own ideas about which products to feature. They're more concerned with daily volume and with projecting an image of value and variety. An appliance store might prefer to advertise inexpensive TVs even though the manufacturer wants to emphasize its premium models.

Manufacturers worry that retailers will place the product in a cluttered, ugly ad or next to inferior products; that the ad will run in inappropriate publications; and that it will not run at the best time. Retailers counter that they know the local market better. In short, manufacturers sometimes think they don't have enough control; retailers occasionally think manufacturers have too much.

Regional and National Advertisers

Some companies operate in one part of the country—in one or several states—and market exclusively within that region. These are referred to as **regional advertisers**. Typical examples include regional grocery and department store chains, governmental bodies (such as state lotteries), franchise groups (such as the Southern California Honda Dealers), and statewide or multistate banks (Bank of America).

Other companies sell in several regions or throughout the country and are called **national advertisers**. These include consumer packaged-goods manufacturers (such as Procter & Gamble and Johnson & Johnson), national airlines (Delta, JetBlue), media and entertainment companies (Disney, Time Warner), digital giants (Apple, Amazon), and many restaurant chains such as McDonald's. These firms also make up the membership of the *Association of National Advertisers (ANA)*, which includes the largest advertisers in the country. These companies market brands that are some of the most popular in the world. (see Exhibit 3–3).

regional advertisers
Companies that operate in one part of the country and market exclusively to that region.

national advertisers
Companies that advertise in several geographic regions or throughout the country.

▼ **EXHIBIT 3–3**   Top 10 advertisers in the United States ranked by total U.S. advertising.

2018 Rank	Company	Total U.S. Ad Spending 2018 (millions)	U.S. Measured Ad Spending 2018 (millions)
1	Comcast Corp.	$6,122	$1,709
2	AT&T	5,362	1,992
3	Amazon	4,470	1,508
4	Procter & Gamble	4,305	2,814
5	General Motors	3,139	1,523
6	Walt Disney Co.	3,132	1,135
7	Charter Communications	3,042	366
8	Alphabet (Google)	2,960	651
9	American Express Co.	2,798	309
10	Verizon	2,682	1,090

Source: "Ad Age Leading National Advertisers," *Ad Age Datacenter,* https://adage.com/article/datacenter/ad-age-leading-national-advertisers-2019-index/2178026.

How National and Local Advertisers Differ   The basic principles of advertising are the same in both local and national advertising. However, local advertisers have special challenges stemming from the day-to-day realities of running a small business (see Exhibit 3–4).

Focus   National companies are concerned about building their *brands*, so their advertising tends to focus on the competitive features of one brand over another. Local merchants or dealers often carry hundreds of different brands, so they focus on attracting customers to a particular *location*—their place of business.

Big companies battle for *market share* against a few competitors, and every share point is worth millions of dollars. Local advertisers compete with many companies, so their focus is on gross sales or *volume*: 60 cars a month, five new insurance policies a week, 55 oil changes a day.

Manufacturers such as Vionic Shoes sometimes partner with retailers such as Dillard's to promote the manufacturer's products. If these products are not promoted at the local level, the manufacturer's national advertising efforts will be less effective.
Source: Dillard's Inc.

▼ **EXHIBIT 3–4**   Differences between local and national advertisers.

		National	Local
Focus		Brand	Location
		Market share	Volume
		Strategies	Tactics
		Markets	Customers
Time		Long-term campaigns	Short-term ads
Resources		$5–$10 million+	Less than $1 million
		Many specialists	A few generalists

centralized advertising department A staff of employees, usually located at corporate headquarters, responsible for all the organization's advertising. The department is often structured by product, advertising subfunction, end user, media, or geography.

brand managers The individuals within the advertiser's company who are assigned the authority and responsibility for the successful marketing of a particular brand.

decentralized system The establishment of advertising departments by products or brands or in various divisions, subsidiaries, countries, regions, or other categories that suit the firm's needs, which operate with a major degree of independence.

National advertisers plan *strategically* to launch, build, and sustain brands. Local advertisers think *tactically*. Will a new billboard bring more people into the store? Should we stay open Labor Day? Can we attract more lunchtime customers by reducing our prices or by offering coupons?

The relationship with the customer may be the greatest difference between national and local advertisers. National advertisers' marketing executives rarely see their customers; instead, they traditionally think of them in terms of segments, niches, or target *markets*. They design their strategies and campaigns to appeal to these large groups.

But local advertisers deal with individual *customers* every day. The local advertiser gets regular feedback on the company's advertising, prices, product performance, customer service, store decor, and the new sign out front. A local firm may sponsor a Little League team, help a local charity, or participate in a local business organization.

LO3-3 Demonstrate how advertisers organize themselves to manage their advertising here and abroad.

How Large Companies Manage Their Advertising

In large companies, many people are involved in advertising. Company owners and top corporate executives make key advertising decisions; sales and marketing personnel often assist in the creative process, help choose the ad agency, and evaluate proposed ad programs; artists and writers produce ads, brochures, and other materials; product engineers and designers give input to the creative process and provide information about competitive products; administrators evaluate the cost of ad campaigns and help plan budgets; and clerical staff coordinate various promotional activities, including advertising.

> ## National advertisers plan *strategically*. . . . Local advertisers think *tactically*.

Time orientation National companies think long term. They develop five-year strategic plans and budget for annual advertising campaigns. Local advertisers worry that this week's ad didn't *pull* (a term rarely used by national marketers) as well as last week's; a New York advertiser may have months to develop a network TV campaign; the little market on Main Street may have to churn out a new newspaper ad every week.

Resources Finally, national advertisers have more resources—both money and people. The national advertiser has millions of dollars and an army of *specialists* dedicated to the successful marketing of its brands. The local advertiser may have a small staff of *generalists* or just one person—the owner—to market the business. So the local entrepreneur has to know about every facet of IMC.

A large company's advertising department may employ many people, led by an advertising manager who reports to a marketing director or marketing services manager. The exact department structure can vary. Most large advertisers tend to use some mix of two basic management structures: *centralized* and *decentralized*.

Centralized organization Companies that embrace a **centralized advertising department** usually want control. This organization scheme offers both efficiency and continuity across divisional boundaries. In centralized departments, an advertising manager typically reports to a marketing vice president. The advertising department may be organized in any of five ways:

- By product or brand.
- By subfunction of advertising (copy, art, digital media, media buying).

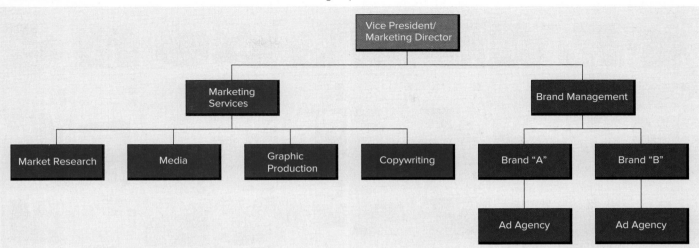

- By end user (consumer advertising, trade advertising).
- By medium (radio, TV, digital, outdoor).
- By geography (western advertising, eastern advertising, international advertising).

General Mills, for example, is one of the nation's largest advertisers. It operates a vast advertising and marketing services department with some 350 employees. It spends about $830 million in media advertising and other promotional activities.[8]

General Mills's Marketing Services is really many departments within a department. Its centralized structure (see Exhibit 3-5) enables it to administer, plan, and coordinate the promotion of more than 60 brands. It also supervises outside ad agencies and operates its own in-house agency for new or smaller brands.

Organized around functional specialties (market research, media, graphics), Marketing Services helps General Mills's **brand managers** consolidate expenditures for maximum efficiency. Of course, even a traditional company such as General Mills has

Neirfy/Shutterstock

to engage consumers in new and exciting ways. The company is investing heavily in blogs, Facebook, podcasts, and iPhone apps. Digital efforts and campaigns that target fast-growing minority segments are a particular priority.[9]

A recent example of social media use at General Mills is its use of Pinterest to communicate with women in support of Fiber One Chewy Snacks. The goal is to reach "moms who are pinning fun and creative snacking ideas on their Pinterest boards," said Julia Travis, a marketing manager for Fiber One.[10]

Decentralized organization As some companies become larger, diversify their product line, acquire subsidiaries, and establish divisions in different regions or even different countries, a centralized advertising department often becomes impractical.

In a **decentralized system**, the company sets up separate ad departments for different divisions, subsidiaries, regions, brands, or other categories that suit the company's needs. The general manager of each division or brand is responsible for that group's advertising. A brand manager, who oversees each individual brand, typically works under a marketing manager. This system gives significant authority to the individuals responsible for each brand.

For large companies with many divisions, decentralized advertising is more flexible. Campaigns and media schedules can be adjusted faster. New approaches and creative ideas can be introduced more easily, and sales results can be measured independently of other divisions. In effect, each division has its own marketing department, with the marketing manager reporting to the division head (see Exhibit 3-6).

A drawback, though, is that decentralized departments often concentrate on their own budgets, problems, and promotions rather than the good of the whole company. Across divisions, ads may lack uniformity, diminishing the power of repetitive corporate advertising. Rivalry among brand managers may even escalate into unhealthy competition.

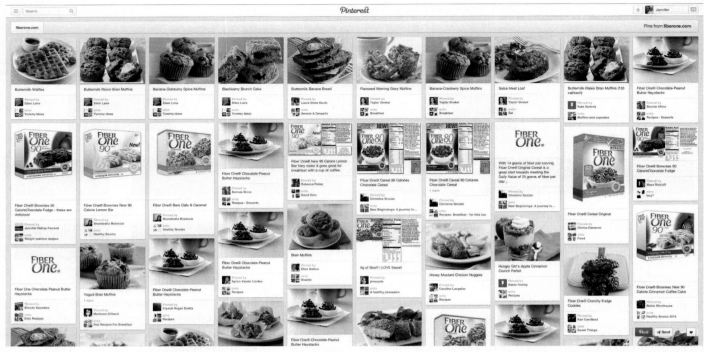

Large agencies working on national campaigns often blend advertising and sales promotion efforts. This Pinterest site for Fiber One is an example.

Source: Fiber One/General Mills Marketing Inc. (GMMI)

▼ **EXHIBIT 3–6** In a decentralized structure, each division has its own marketing department.

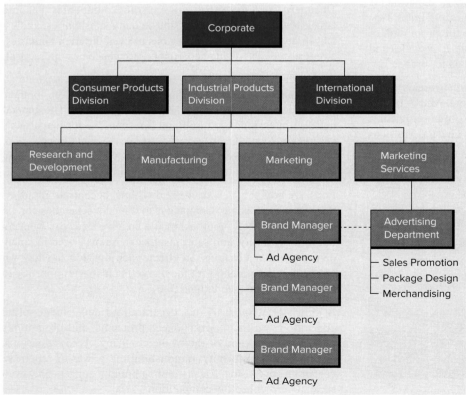

Transnational Advertisers

Companies advertising abroad typically face markets with different value systems, environments, and languages. Their customers have different purchasing abilities, habits, and motivations. Media customary to U.S. and Canadian advertisers may be unavailable or ineffective. The companies will therefore likely need different advertising strategies. But they face a more basic problem: How should they manage and produce the advertising? Should their U.S. agency or in-house advertising department do it? Should they use a foreign agency or set up a local advertising department?

Procter & Gamble is a $76 billion company that sells more than 300 consumer brands in more than 180 countries. These brands include such market leaders as Tide, Ivory soap, Pampers, Folgers, Pringles, and Crest toothpaste.[11]

P&G is one of the biggest and most influential consumer advertisers in the world; its expenditures worldwide exceeded $6 billion in 2019.[12] Each overseas division is set

Coke advertises globally, including in South Africa. This ad adapts the spirit of the brand to the values and attitudes of the local market.

Source: The Coca-Cola Company

up almost like a separate company with its own research and development department, manufacturing plant, sales force, and finance and accounting staff. Each division also has an advertising department to help coordinate programs across brands within that division.

As companies continue to grow and prosper around the world, they may invest directly in many countries. True **multinational corporations** strive for full, integrated participation in world markets.[13] Foreign sales often grow faster than domestic sales. In 2018, foreign sales amounted to nearly 43 percent of all sales for S&P 500 companies.[14]

Multinationals that use a *standardized approach* to marketing and advertising in all countries are considered **global marketers**, and they create global brands. Their assumption is that the way the product is used and the needs it satisfies are universal. McDonald's "i'm lovin' it" campaign, first begun in 2003, runs in all 118 countries where the company sells food.[15] Other global advertisers include Coca-Cola, Ford, P&G, GE, and L'Oréal.[16]

Companies do a lot of research before attempting a global advertising strategy. So much depends on the product and where they try to sell it. A "no" answer to any of the following questions means the attempt will be difficult.

1. *Has each country's market for the product developed in the same way?* A Ford is a Ford in most markets. On the other hand, many consumers around the globe use clotheslines, so they don't need fabric softeners for dryers.

2. *Are the targets similar in different nations?* Japanese consumers like jeans, running shoes, and game consoles. The same is true for consumers in Europe and the United States. But they might not share a liking for certain foods or other fashions.

3. *Do consumers share the same wants and needs?* Breakfast in Brazil is usually a cup of coffee. Kellogg's Corn Flakes won't be served the same way as in the United States, where people commonly eat cereal for breakfast.[17]

Advertisers who cannot answer yes to the above questions will often take a *localized approach* to international marketing and advertising. They will consider differences in product use, economic development, media options, local laws, technology, and customs. The outcome will often be the adaptation of products, packages, and advertising campaigns to suit each market.

The secret to success in global advertising may be knowing how to tap into basic human emotions and uncover universal appeals that don't depend solely on language. In addition, social media can help global advertisers capitalize on the universal appeal of word of mouth.[18]

This ad for McDonald's helps celebrate an Islamic observance. Sensitivity to the diversity of worldwide cultures and beliefs is important for a global advertiser's success.

Source: McDonald's Corporation

COMPANIES DO A LOT OF RESEARCH BEFORE ATTEMPTING A GLOBAL ADVERTISING STRATEGY.

international media
Media serving several countries, usually without change, that is available to an international audience.

foreign media The local media of each country used by advertisers for campaigns targeted to consumers or businesses within a single country.

advertising agencies Independent organizations of creative people and businesspeople that specialize in developing and preparing advertising plans, advertisements, and other promotional tools for advertisers. The agencies also arrange for or contract for purchases of space and time in various media.

Media around the World

In the United States, if you want to promote a soft drink as a youthful, fun refresher, you might use television. In some parts of Europe, Asia, South America, and Africa you may not be able to. Around the world, broadcast media are sometimes owned and controlled by the government, and many governments do not allow commercial advertising. In Turkey, Axe Black and agency J. Walter Thompson Manajans brought quiet to the cacophony of noise in Istanbul by creating a "Silent Window" campaign involving a soundproof studio in the city center. After a tie-in to a youth-oriented show, sales of Axe Black soared.[19]

Where TV ownership is high, it cuts across the spectrum of income groups. In less-developed countries, though, TV sets may be found only among upper-income groups. This means advertisers may need a different media mix in foreign markets.

Virtually every country has access to radio, television, newspapers, magazines, outdoor media, and direct mail. However, the legalities of different media forms vary from country to country. Generally, the media available to the international advertiser can be categorized as either *international* or *foreign media*, depending on the audience they serve.

International Media In the past, **international media**—which serve several countries, usually without any change in content—have been limited to newspapers and magazines. Several large American publishers such as *Time USA*, McGraw-Hill, and *Springer Nature America* circulate international editions of their magazines abroad. Usually written in English, they tend to be read by well-educated, upper-income consumers and are therefore good vehicles for advertising high-end, brand-name products. Television is also a viable international medium. CNN and MTV can be found in many parts of the world, while the Middle Eastern channel Al Jazeera can now be found on U.S. cable systems, such as *OMedia vehicles*.

Foreign Media Advertisers use **foreign media**—the local media of each country—for large campaigns targeted to consumers or businesses within a single country. Because foreign media cater to their own national audience, advertisers must produce their ads in the language of each country. In countries such as Switzerland, Belgium, and Canada, with more than one official language, ads are produced in each language.

check yourself ✓

1. What factors determine the type of organizational structure that advertisers use?

2. What additional challenges are faced by companies that advertise internationally?

3. What determines whether a multinational advertiser is a global marketer or not?

LO3-4 Describe the main types of advertising agencies.

THE ADVERTISING AGENCY

The American Association of Advertising Agencies (AAAA) defines an **advertising agency** as an independent organization of creative people and businesspeople who specialize in developing and preparing marketing and advertising plans, advertisements, and other promotional tools. Agencies also purchase advertising space and time in various media on behalf of different advertisers (clients) to find customers for their goods and services.[20]

Why does a company such as McDonald's hire ad agencies in the first place? Couldn't it save money by hiring its own staff and creating its own ads? How does an advertising agency such as Leo Burnett, one of McDonald's agencies,[21] win such a large account? Must an agency's accounts be that big for it to make money? This section sheds some light on these issues and gives a clearer understanding of what agencies do and why so many advertisers use agencies.

Cybrain/Shutterstock

> Agencies don't work for the media or the suppliers.
> Their ethical, financial,
> and legal obligations are to their clients.

The agency provides yet another service by researching, negotiating, arranging, and contracting for commercial space and time with different print, electronic, and digital media. Because of its *media expertise*, Burnett saves its clients time and money.

Agencies don't work for the media or the suppliers. Their ethical, financial, and legal obligations are to their clients. Just as a well-run business seeks professional help from attorneys, accountants, bankers, or management specialists, advertisers use agencies out of *self-interest*, because the agencies can create more effective advertising and select more effective media than the advertisers can themselves. Today, almost all sizable advertisers rely on an ad agency.

Finally, a good agency serves its clients' needs because of its daily exposure to a broad spectrum of marketing situations and problems both here and abroad. As technology has enabled companies to work across borders with relative ease, the advertising business has boomed worldwide. Most large U.S. agencies maintain offices abroad.

Types of Agencies

Advertising agencies are typically classified by their geographic scope, the range of services they offer, and the type of business they handle.

Geographic Scope   Every community of any size has reputable **local agencies** that offer expert assistance to local advertisers. Unfortunately, local advertisers use ad agencies less extensively than do national advertisers. Many local advertisers simply don't spend enough money on advertising to warrant hiring an agency. And some large agencies don't accept local advertisers because their budgets are too small.

Every major city has numerous ad agencies that can produce and place the quality of advertising suitable for national campaigns. **Regional agencies** and **national agencies** typically participate in either the 4As (American Association of Advertising Agencies) or some similar trade group such as the Western States Advertising Agency Association (WSAAA).

The largest national agencies are also **international agencies**. That is, they have offices or affiliates in major communications centers around the world and can help their clients market internationally or globally as the case may be. Likewise, many foreign-based agencies have offices and affiliates in the United States. For example, the largest advertising agency organization in the world today, WPP Group, is based in London. But it owns several top U.S. agencies, including Ogilvy & Mather and J. Walter Thompson.

Range of Services   The modern **full-service advertising agency** supplies both advertising and nonadvertising services in all areas of communications and promotion. *Advertising services* include planning, creating, and producing ads; performing research; and selecting media. *Nonadvertising services* run the gamut from packaging to public relations to producing sales promotion materials, annual reports, and trade-show exhibits. With the trend toward IMC, many of the largest agencies today are in the forefront of *interactive media*.[22]

Full-service agencies may specialize in certain kinds of clients. Most, though, can be classified as either *general consumer agencies* or *business-to-business agencies*.

German agency Heye & Partners created the global campaign for McDonald's. The agency's talent at creating ads that can run around the world ensures lots of other notable clients as well.

Purestock/SuperStock

General consumer agencies A **general consumer agency** represents the widest variety of accounts, but it concentrates on *consumer accounts*—companies that make goods purchased chiefly by consumers (soaps, cereals, cars, pet foods, toiletries). Most of the ads are placed in consumer media (TV, radio, magazines, and so on) that pay a *commission* to the agency. General agencies often derive much of their income from these commissions.

General agencies include the international superagency groups headquartered in communication capitals such as New York, London, Paris, and Tokyo, as well as many other large firms in Chicago, Los Angeles, Minneapolis, Montreal, and Toronto. A few of the better-known names in North America are Ogilvy & Mather, Draft FCB, BBDO, DDB Needham, Young & Rubicam (Y&R), and Cossette Communication Group (Canada). But general agencies also include the thousands of smaller *entrepreneurial agencies* located in every major city across the country (Martin Agency, Richmond, Virginia; RPA, Los Angeles; MMB, Boston; and Wieden + Kennedy, Portland, Oregon).

Profit margins in entrepreneurial agencies are often slimmer, but these shops are typically more responsive to the smaller clients they serve. They offer the hands-on involvement of the firm's principals, and their work is frequently startling in its creativity. For these reasons, many large agencies are spinning off smaller subsidiaries. Gotham Advertising, for example, is a hot creative shop in New York that was spun off by the Interpublic Group of Companies to do work for a variety of clients its bigger sister agencies couldn't serve.[23] Some entrepreneurial agencies, such as Zubi Advertising in Coral Gables, Florida, carve a niche for themselves by serving particular market segments.[24]

Business-to-business agencies A **business-to-business (B2B) agency** represents clients that sell to other businesses. Examples are electronic components for computer manufacturers, equipment used in oil and gas refineries, and MRI equipment for radiology. High-tech advertising requires some technical knowledge and the ability to translate that knowledge into precise and persuasive communications. While you may be a customer for McDonald's food, the company is itself a customer, and thus an advertising target, for suppliers of soft drinks, eggs, beef, napkins, employee uniforms, and so on.

Most B2B advertising is placed in trade magazines or other business publications. These media are commissionable, but their circulation is smaller, so their rates are far lower than those of consumer media. Because commissions usually don't cover the cost of the agency's services, business agencies typically charge their clients service fees. They can be expensive, especially for small advertisers, but failure to obtain a business agency's expertise may carry an even higher price in lost marketing opportunities.

Specialized Service Agencies
Many agencies assist their clients with a variety of limited services. There has been a continuing trend toward specialization, giving impetus to many of the small agencies called *creative boutiques* and other specialty businesses such as *media-buying services* and *interactive agencies*.

Creative boutiques Some talented artists—such as graphic designers and copywriters—have set up their own creative services, or **creative boutiques**. They work for advertisers and occasionally subcontract to ad agencies. Their mission is to develop exciting creative concepts and produce fresh, distinctive advertising messages. In the 1990s, Creative Artists Agency (CAA), a Hollywood talent agency, caused a stir by taking on the role of a creative boutique, using its pool of actors, directors, and cinematographers to create a series of commercials for Coca-Cola. McCann Erickson Worldwide remained Coke's *agency of record*, but the majority of the creative work came from CAA. Since then, Coke has allowed numerous other smaller shops to work on its account.[25]

Advertising effectiveness depends on originality in concept, design, and writing. However, although boutiques may be economical, they usually don't provide the research, marketing, sales expertise, or deep customer service that full-service agencies offer. Thus, boutiques tend to be limited to the role of creative suppliers.

Media-buying services Some years ago, a few experienced agency media people started setting up organizations to purchase and

"IT TAKES A HARD MAN TO MAKE A CHICKEN AROUSED"

Some advertising agencies specialize in business-to-business advertising. This clever ad showcases an actual (mis)translation from a global campaign of the past. The original campaign, for Perdue, used the tag line, "It takes a tough man to make a tender chicken," and featured Frank Perdue himself. The Hispanic Marketing Feedback Group works with businesses to avoid such mistakes. This ad encourages businesses interested in reaching Spanish-speaking markets to hire the group.
Source: P&G Hispanic Marketing Group

package radio and TV time. The largest **media-buying service** (or *media agency*) is Initiative Media. Based in Los Angeles, it is owned by the Interpublic Group, has 99 offices in 58 countries around the world, and places more than $20 billion worth of advertising annually for a wide variety of clients.[26]

Media time and space is perishable. A 60-second radio spot at 8 p.m. can't be sold later. So radio and TV stations presell as much time as possible and discount their rates for large buys. Media-buying services negotiate a special discount with the media and then sell the time or space to agencies or advertisers.

Media-buying firms provide customers (both clients and agencies) with a detailed analysis of the media buy. Once the media package is sold, the buying service orders spots, verifies performance, sees that stations "make good" for any missed spots, and even pays the media bills.

Media agencies have experienced so much growth in the last decade that they have become major players on the advertising stage. Today, even large agencies such as BBDO no longer provide media services. Instead, big clients use media firms to plan and place buys.

Interactive agencies A heightened interest in IMC and digital advertising has led to a new breed of specialist—the **interactive agency**. Agency.com and Tribal DDB are some of the many firms that have sprung up within the last few years with specialized experience in designing web pages, mobile apps, and social media campaigns. The biggest digital agencies in 2016 included SapientNitro, based in Boston, and London's R/GA.[27]

Other specialists, such as *direct-response* and *sales promotion agencies*, are also growing in response to client demands for greater expertise and accountability as advertisers add new marketing approaches.

> To succeed today, an AE needs to be more of a strategist than an advocate.

LO3-5 Explain the tasks people perform in an ad agency and an in-house advertising department.

WHAT PEOPLE IN AN AGENCY DO

An agency's purpose is to interpret to desired segments of the public information about a legally marketed product or service. How does it do this? First, it analyzes the client's product to determine its strengths and weaknesses. Next, it considers the product's present and potential market. Then, using its knowledge of product distribution and media alternatives, the agency develops a plan to deliver the advertiser's message to consumers or businesses. Finally the agency writes, designs, and produces ads; contracts for media space and time; verifies media insertions; and bills the client.

The agency also collaborates with the client's marketing staff to enhance advertising's impact through package design and other IMC channels. To understand these functions, consider the people who were involved, directly and indirectly, in the creation, production, and supervision of McDonald's advertising.

Account Management

The **account executives (AEs)** at Leo Burnett are the liaison between the agency and the client. Large agencies have many account executives, who report to **management (or account) supervisors**. They in turn report to the agency's director of account (or client) services.

Deena Di Stefano[28] is McDonald's account executive at Burnett. Like many AEs, she can find herself caught in the middle of the fray, as she is responsible for formulating advertising plans (discussed in Chapter 7), mustering the agency's services, representing the client's point of view to the agency, and the agency's point of view to the client. To succeed today, an AE like Deena needs to be more of a strategist than an advocate. She must be well versed in an extraordinary range of media and demonstrate how her agency's creative work satisfies both her client's marketing needs and the market's product needs. That means she must be enterprising and courageous, demanding yet tactful, artistic and articulate, meticulous, forgiving, perceptive, persuasive, ethical, and discreet—all at once. And she must always deliver the work on time and within budget.

Research and Account Planning

Clients and agencies give their creatives (artists and copywriters) a wealth of product, market, and competitive information because, at its core, advertising is based on information. Therefore, before creating any advertising, agencies research the uses and advantages of the product, analyze current and potential customers, and try to determine what will influence them to buy. After the ads are placed, agencies use more research to investigate how the campaign fared. Chapter 6 discusses some of the many types of research ad agencies conduct.

Account planning is a hybrid discipline that uses research to bridge the gap between account management and creatives. The account planner also defends the consumer's point of view and the creative strategy in the debate between the agency's creative team and the client.

Account planners study consumer needs and desires through a variety of methods. They help the creative team translate their findings into imaginative, successful campaigns. Not attached to either account management or creative, the account planner balances both elements to make sure the research is reflected in the ads.[29] Read more about this in Chapter 6.

When McDonald's wanted to attract kids to its Kiddie Crew Workshop in the Philippines, DDB account planner Lester Obice helped guide the creative team to a brilliant execution that merged images of McDonald's fries and yellow crayons.

Research is also used to uncover any negative feelings or attitudes towards and brand. Because McDonald's menu contains items such as fried burgers and fries, consumers may conclude that the restaurant offers no healthy food. In response, McDonald's has evolved its offerings to include salads, yogurts, grilled chicken, and other healthier alternatives (for more on concerns about McDonald's offerings and consumer concerns, see the Ethics box in this chapter, "Is Ronald McDonald Bad for Kids? Are Parents?"

Media Planning and Buying

Ad agencies perform a variety of media services for their clients: research, negotiation, scheduling, buying, and verifying. **Media planning** is critical because the only way advertisers can communicate is through a medium. Changes over the last decade have made the media function even more important.

With the unprecedented fragmentation of audiences from the explosion of new media options and the trend toward IMC and relationship marketing, the media task has taken on added significance. The reason? Tightening budgets demand ingenious thinking, tough negotiating, and careful attention to detail. Today, many products owe their success more to creative media planning and buying than to clever ads.

Creative Concepts

Copy refers to the words that make up the headline and message. The people who create these words, **copywriters**, condense all that can be said about a product into a few pertinent, succinct points.

Ads also communicate through layout and design. That is the responsibility of the **art directors**, graphic designers, and production artists, who determine how an ad's verbal and visual symbols will fit together. (The creative process is discussed in Part 4.) A copywriter and an art director work as a creative team under a **creative director**. Each team is usually assigned a particular client's business.

One award-winning ad for McDonald's focuses on the Ronald McDonald House Charities. Titled "First Step," the ad tells the story of a young toddler whose medical care was made more affordable by the company. The beautiful spot was developed by an experienced DDB Chicago team, including creative director Bill Cimino, copywriter Geoff McCartney, and art director Gordon West.

Advertising Production: Print and Broadcast

An ad approved by the client is then turned over to the agency's print production manager or broadcast producers.

For print ads, the **production department** buys type, photos, illustrations, and other components and works with printers, engravers, and other suppliers. For a broadcast commercial, production people work from an approved script or storyboard. Actors, camera operators, and production specialists (studios, directors, editors) help produce a commercial on audiotape (for radio) or on film or videotape (for TV). The "First Step" commercial described on the following page was helmed by a famous commercial director named Joe Pytka and was filmed at Pytka's studio.

But production work is not limited to just ads and commercials. Dealer kits and direct mailings are just two examples of other materials that may be created as part of a campaign.

Traffic Management

One of the greatest sins in an ad agency is a missed deadline. If an agency misses a deadline for a monthly magazine, for example, the agency will have to wait another month before it can run the ad, much to the client's displeasure.

The agency **traffic department** coordinates all phases of production and makes sure everything is completed and approved before client and/or media deadlines. Traffic is often the first stop for entry-level college graduates and an excellent place to learn about agency operations.

Additional Services

The growth of IMC has caused many agencies to employ specialists who provide services besides advertising. Larger agencies may have a fully staffed **sales promotion department** to produce dealer ads, window posters, point-of-purchase displays, and dealer sales material. Or, depending on the nature and needs of their clients, they may employ public relations people and direct marketing specialists, digital designers, social media experts, or package designers.

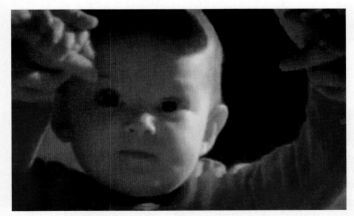

The screenshot above, from Joe Pytka's "First Step" commercial, focuses on the softer, image-based concept of McDonald's. Some McDonald's advertising is devoted to specific menu items. These ads give existing customers a reason to visit the restaurant chain more often, and may attract new customers who are unaware of the variety of offerings at McDonald's. By promoting their Fruit and Maple Oatmeal, do you think McDonald's is attracting a broader base of health-conscious customers that would normally not visit McDonald's?
Source: Ronald McDonald House Charities

Agency Administration

In small agencies, administrative functions may be handled by the firm's principals. Large agencies often have departments for accounting, human resources, data processing, purchasing, financial analysis, legal issues, and insurance.

How Agencies Are Structured

An ad agency organizes its functions, operations, and personnel according to the types of accounts it serves, its size, and its geographic scope.

The owner or general manager usually supervises daily business operations, client services, and new-business development. Account executives (AEs) generally handle day-to-day client contact. In smaller agencies, AEs may also do some creative work. Artwork may be produced by an art director or purchased from an independent studio or freelance designer. Most agencies have production and traffic departments or an employee who fulfills these functions. They may have a media buyer, but in very small agencies account executives also purchase media time and space. Exhibit 3–7 shows how a typical advertising agency might be organized.

Medium and large agencies are usually structured in a *departmental* or *group system*. In the **departmental system**, the agency organizes its various functions—account services, creative services, marketing services, and administration—into separate departments.

In the **group system**, the agency is divided into a number of "little" agencies or groups. Each group may serve one large account or, in some cases, three or four smaller ones. An account manager heads each group's staff of account executives, copywriters, art directors, a media director, and any other necessary specialists. A very large agency may have dozens of groups with separate production and traffic units.

check yourself ✓

1. How does the role of an account planner differ from that of an account executive?

2. What do people in an ad agency do?

media commission Compensation paid by a medium to recognized advertising agencies, traditionally 15 percent (16 2/3 percent for outdoor), for advertising placed with it.

markup A source of agency income gained by adding some amount to a supplier's bill, usually 17.65 percent.

LO3-6 Show how agencies get new clients and how they make money.

How Agencies Are Compensated

To survive, agencies must make a profit. But recent trends in the business—mergers of superagencies, shifts in emphasis from advertising to sales promotion and direct marketing, increased production costs, and the fragmentation of media vehicles—have all cut into agency profits.[30] Moreover, different clients demand different services, forcing agencies to develop various compensation methods. Still, there are really only three ways for agencies to make money: *media commissions*, *markups*, and *fees* or *retainers*.

Media Commissions As we saw in Chapter 1, when ad agencies first came on the scene more than 100 years ago, they were really space brokers, or reps, for the newspapers. Because they saved the media much of the expense of sales and collections, the media allowed the agencies to retain a 15 percent **media commission** on the space or time they purchased on behalf of their clients. That started a tradition that endured for many years, although it is typically smaller now.[31] Let's see how it works.

Say a national rate-card price for a full-page color magazine ad is $100,000. The magazine bills the agency, and the agency in turn bills the client for the $100,000. The client pays that amount to the agency, and the agency sends $85,000 to the magazine, keeping its 15 percent commission ($15,000). For large accounts, the agency typically provides extensive services (creative, media, accounting, and account management) for this commission. With dwindling profits, though, and clients negotiating smaller commissions, many agencies now must charge a fee for services that used to be included for free.[32]

Markups In the process of creating an ad, the agency normally buys a variety of services or materials from outside suppliers—for example, photos and illustrations. The agency pays the supplier's charge and then adds a **markup** to the client's bill, often 17.65 percent of the invoice (which becomes 15 percent of the new total).

For example, a markup of 17.65 percent on an $8,500 photography bill yields a $1,500 profit. When billing the client, the agency adds the $1,500 to the $8,500 for a new total of $10,000. When the client pays the bill, the agency keeps the $1,500 (15 percent of the total) and sends $8,500 to the photographer.

$$\$8,500 \times 17.65\% = \$1,500$$
$$\$8,500 + 1,500 = \$10,000$$
$$\$10,000 \times 15\% = \$1,500$$

▼ **EXHIBIT 3–7** Typical departmental advertising agency organization.

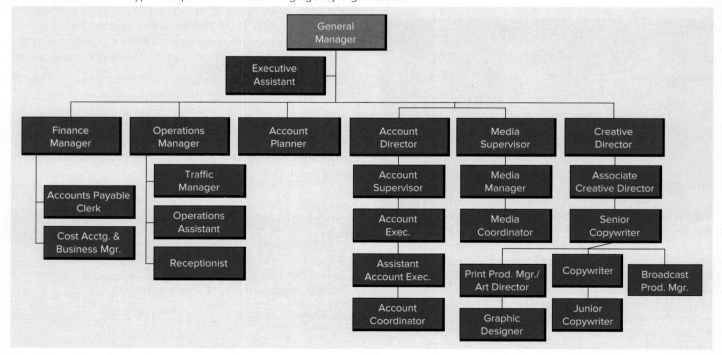

Some media—local newspapers, for example—allow a commission on the higher rates they charge national advertisers but not on the lower rates they charge local advertisers. So, to get their commission, local agencies have to use the markup formula above.

Fees   Clients today expect agencies to solve problems rather than just place ads, so fees are becoming more common. In fact, one study shows that only about one-third of national advertisers still rely on the traditional 15 percent commission system. An equal number now use some fee-based system. The rest use some modified commission or incentive system.[33]

There are two pricing methods in the fee system. With the **fee–commission combination**, the agency charges a basic monthly fee for all its services to the client and retains any media commissions earned. In the **straight-fee (or retainer) method**, agencies charge for all their services, either by the hour or by the month, and return any media commissions earned to the client. This latter method addresses a common objection to the commission system, namely that commissions lead agencies to recommend more media spending, rather than looking for ways to spend the client's money more efficiently. The fee method also addresses the fact that many clients are now using media buying services to purchase space and time.

Accountability is a major issue in client–agency relationships. With the **incentive system** (sometimes called *pay-for-performance*), the agency earns more if the campaign attains specific, agreed-upon goals. DDB Needham, for example, offers its clients a "guaranteed results" program. If a campaign is successful, the agency earns more; if it fails, the agency earns less. Kraft General Foods rewards its agencies based on their performance. An A grade gets an extra 3 percent commission; C grades are put on review. It remains unclear whether this new approach works well for both agencies and clients.[34]

The In-House Agency

Some companies set up a wholly owned **in-house agency** (or *house agency*) to save money and tighten control over their advertising. The in-house agency may do all the work of an independent full-service agency, including creative tasks, production, media placement, publicity, and sales promotion.

Advertisers with in-house agencies hope to save money by cutting overhead, keeping the media commission, and avoiding markups on outside purchases. Small, local advertisers in particular seek this goal.

Advertisers also expect more attention and faster turnaround from their house agencies, which know the company's products

McDonald's uses the creative talent of its partner agencies to develop clever executions such as this interactive out-of-home ad.
Todd Bannor/Alamy Stock Photo

and markets better and can focus all their resources to meet its deadlines. Management is often more involved in the advertising when it's done by company people, especially in "single-business" companies.

But usually companies sacrifice more than they gain. In-house flexibility is often won at the expense of creativity. Outside agencies typically offer greater experience, versatility, and a larger talent pool. In-house agencies have difficulty attracting and keeping the best creative people, who tend to prefer the variety and challenges offered by independent agencies.

The biggest risk for in-house agencies may be a loss of objectivity. In the shadow of internal politics, linear-thinking policymakers, and criticism from management, ads may become bland and self-serving, rather than imaginative messages relevant to customers. In advertising, that's the kiss of death.

Some companies such as Benetton (www.benetton.com) prefer to create ads using their own in-house agencies. Advertisers may hope to save money and gain more attention by using their house agencies, but they can lose the greater experience, objectivity, and talent of an outside agency.

Chris Ratcliffe/Bloomberg/Getty Images

ethical issues

Is Ronald McDonald Bad for Kids? Are Parents?

Deborah Lapidus has found the "person" responsible for the childhood obesity epidemic that is sweeping the United States. While the culprit can often be found visiting children's hospitals and performing at other charity events, Lapidus is unmoved. She wants him gone for good, or, in her words, "retired." Anyone interested in joining Ms. Lapidus's quest should be on the lookout for an easily recognized, flamboyantly dressed individual with flaming red hair and a bright round nose. Because Deborah Lapidus wants to retire Ronald McDonald.[35]

To make her point, she traveled all the way to Oak Brook, Illinois, the location of McDonald's annual meeting, to protest Ronald's prominence in the company's advertising. Her trip was funded by her 30,000-member advocacy group, named "Corporate Accountability."

Does McDonald's market to children? The evidence is pretty compelling. Like any smart family-oriented eatery, McDonald's knows that kids exercise enormous influence in family dining decisions. In response, it has created Happy Meals and playgrounds that make its restaurants fun places for kids to eat and play (and for mom and dad to relax). And, of course, kids love Ronald, one of the world's most recognized brand symbols.

And it is undeniable that America has a health problem, and food is a big part of it. Former Obama Secretary of Health and Human Services Kathleen Sebelius suggested that one in three kids in the United States is overweight, a number that has grown 400 percent in just 20 years. Sebelius urged the U.S. Conference of Mayors to join a program initiated by First Lady Michelle Obama called "Let's Move," aimed at encouraging healthier lifestyles among children.[36]

So the problem that Lapidus is calling attention to is real. But what about her proposed solution? Will retiring Ronald make America's children skinnier?

Interestingly, McDonald's may be way ahead of Lapidus. The company has developed a broader line of healthy menus for its Happy Meals,

ones that include fresh fruits and veggies. Playgrounds are slowly being phased out at McDonald's in favor of coffee bars. Ads that feature Ronald are difficult to find anymore, part of a recent trend toward reducing McDonald's ads that target children.

So McDonald's seems to be doing its part. Lapidus should be thrilled. But one commentator, *Courier News* writer Julia Doyle, thinks Lapidus has missed the real source of childhood obesity: moms and dads.

> If our kids are fat, it automatically has to be because there's a goofy, smiley-faced clown telling them to eat cheeseburgers and French fries, right? It can't possibly have anything to do with Mom or Dad stopping for fried chicken, tacos or burgers every night rather than cooking a healthy dinner when they get home. And if our kids are fat, it has everything to do with the pizza, chicken fingers and hot dogs served in their school cafeterias and nothing to do with the fact that their parents can't be bothered to pack them a healthy lunch to take to school each day. I think it's high time these so-called watchdog groups get off their high horses and stop blaming corporate America for everything they think is wrong with us.

The ethical issues here are complex. Is it right for McDonald's, or any company, to advertise to children? Is it morally acceptable for a fast-food chain to feature playgrounds and brand symbols that kids find appealing? Would these activities be more ethically permissible if the company exclusively sold healthy food? Can the obesity problem affecting American children (and adults) be blamed on a single company? McDonald's has been using Ronald in its ads since the 1960s, a time when children were generally fitter and slimmer than they are today. So how can he be the root cause, or even a significant factor, of the problem? What about Doyle's points regarding the role of parents, both as role models for good eating and as gatekeepers for the types of foods their children eat? Does she have a fair point or not? America's children have a health problem. How significant is advertising as a cause?

In this campaign, McDonald's extends its "i'm lovin' it" slogan to "Choose Lovin'." The ad shows arch enemies finding a way to love one another. Just as you may like some ads better than others, advertisers sometimes choose an agency based on the quality of their work for other clients.

Source: McDonald's Corporation

THE CLIENT–AGENCY RELATIONSHIP

Many factors affect the success of a company's advertising program, but one of the most important is the relationship between the advertiser and its agency.

How Agencies Get Clients

To succeed, advertising agencies need clients. New clients come from personal contact with top management, referrals from satisfied clients or advertising consultants, publicity on recent successful campaigns, trade advertising, direct-mail solicitation, or an agency's general reputation.[37] The three most successful ways to develop new business are having clients who strongly champion the agency, having superior presentation skills, and cultivating a personal relationship with a network of top executives.

Referrals

Many good agencies get clients by referral—from existing clients, friends, review consultants, or even other agencies. The head of one company asks another who's doing her ads, and

the next week the agency gets a call. If a prospective client presents a conflict of interest with an existing client, the agency may decline the business and refer the prospect to another agency.

Independent *agency review consultants* often help arrange marriages between agencies and clients. In fact, independent advisors were involved in many important account shuffles on Madison Avenue: Domino's Pizza, DirecTV, Burger King, Compaq computers, and Monster.com, to name just a few.[38]

Sales reps for media and suppliers frequently refer local advertisers to an agency they know. So it's important for agencies to maintain good relations with the media, suppliers, other agencies, and, of course, their existing clients.

Presentations

An advertiser may ask an agency to make a presentation (a pitch)—anything from a simple discussion of the agency's philosophy, experience, personnel, and track record to a full-blown audiovisual presentation of a proposed campaign. Successful agencies, therefore, need excellent presentation skills.

Some advertisers ask for or imply that they want a **speculative presentation**, meaning they want to see what the agency intends to do for them before they sign on. But most agencies prefer to build their presentations around the work they've already done, to demonstrate their capabilities without giving away ideas for a new campaign. Invariably, the larger the prospective client, the bigger the presentation. Some agencies now spend upward of $500,000 to stage a new business presentation.

The presentation process also allows the agency and the advertiser to get to know each other before they agree to work together. Advertising is a people business, so human qualities—mutual regard, trust, and communication—play an important role.

Networking and Community Relations

Agencies frequently find that the best source of new business is the people their employees know socially in the community. Some agencies work *pro bono* (for free) for charities or nonprofit organizations. Matt Freeman, the young CEO of Tribal DDB, McDonald's digital agency, volunteers for the Ad Council and a hunger charity. Leo Burnett is a partner with Global Giving, an organization that matches donors with good causes.

[Most good agencies get clients by referral— from existing clients, friends, review consultants, or even other agencies.]

"ADVERTISING IS A PEOPLE BUSINESS, SO HUMAN QUALITIES—MUTUAL REGARD, TRUST, AND COMMUNICATION—PLAY AN IMPORTANT ROLE."

Soliciting and Advertising for New Business

Lesser-known agencies must be more aggressive. An agency may solicit new business by advertising, writing letters, making cold calls, or following up leads from sources in the business. An agency principal usually takes the responsibility for soliciting new business.

Today, more agencies are advertising themselves. Many agencies submit their best ads to competitions around the world to win awards and gain publicity and professional respect for their creative excellence.[39]

Factors Affecting the Client–Agency Relationship

Many forces influence the client–agency relationship. Generally they can be grouped into the four Cs: *chemistry*, *communication*, *conduct*, and *changes*.

The most critical factor is the personal *chemistry* between the client and people in the agency.[40] Agencies are very conscious of this factor and agency people work hard to establish a good personal connection with potential clients. This is crucial because, in the end, effective working relationships are built on trust.[41]

Poor *communication*, a problem often cited by both agencies and advertisers, leads to misunderstandings about objectives, strategies, roles, and expectations—and to poor advertising. Constant, open communication and an explicit agreement on mutual contribution for mutual gain are key to a good relationship.[42]

my ad campaign

Agency Review [3–C]

What will your client look for in your agency team? This agency review should give you an idea. Using this scale, an advertiser can rate each agency on a scale from 1 (strongly negative) to 10 (strongly positive).

General Information
_____ Size compatible with our needs.
_____ Strength of management.
_____ Financial stability.
_____ Compatibility with other clients.
_____ Range of services.
_____ Cost of services; billing policies.

Marketing Information
_____ Ability to offer marketing counsel.
_____ Understanding of the markets we serve.
_____ Experience dealing in our market.
_____ Success record; case histories.

Creative Abilities
_____ Well-thought-out creativity; relevance to strategy.
_____ Art strength.
_____ Copy strength.
_____ Overall creative quality.
_____ Effectiveness compared to work of competitors.

Production
_____ Faithfulness to creative concept and execution.
_____ Diligence to schedules and budgets.
_____ Ability to control outside services.

Media
_____ Existence and soundness of media research.
_____ Effective and efficient media strategy.
_____ Ability to achieve objectives within budget.
_____ Strength at negotiating and executing schedules.

Personality
_____ Overall personality, philosophy, or position.
_____ Compatibility with client staff and management.
_____ Willingness to assign top people to account.
_____ Ability to articulate rationale behind work.

References
_____ Rating by current clients.
_____ Rating by past clients.
_____ Rating by media and financial sources.

Dissatisfaction with agency *conduct*, or performance, is the most commonly cited reason for agency switches in every country.[43] The service that the agency gave two years ago may not be valued by the client in the same way today.[44] Or perhaps the agency doesn't understand the client's marketing problems. And clients change, too. Does the client give the agency timely, accurate information? Does it appreciate good work, or does it treat the agency like a vendor?[45]

Changes occur in every relationship. Unfortunately, some of them damage the agency–client partnership. The client's market position or policies may change, or new management may arrive. Agencies may lose key staff people. Advertisers may decide to conduct an agency review to be sure they are getting the most return on their ad investments (see My Ad Campaign 3-C, "Agency Review"). Client conflicts may arise if one agency buys another agency that handles competing accounts. Legally, an ad agency cannot represent a client's competition without the client's consent.[46] Saatchi & Saatchi was forced to resign from Helene Curtis under pressure from Saatchi's biggest client, Procter & Gamble.[47]

check yourself ✓

1. How have accountability concerns affected agency compensation?

2. What do you think is the best way to compensate an agency? Explain your answer.

3. What are the most important things an advertiser should consider when selecting an agency?

THE OTHER PLAYERS: SUPPLIERS AND MEDIA

The people and organizations that provide specialized services to the advertising business are called **suppliers**. Without their services it would be impossible to produce the billions of dollars' worth of advertising placed every year. Important suppliers include *art studios, web design houses, printers, film and video production houses*, and *research companies*.

Art Studios and Web Designers

Art studios design and produce artwork and illustrations for advertisements. They may supplement the work of an agency's art department or even take its place for small agencies. Art studios are usually small with as few as three or four employees. Some, though, are large enough to employ several art directors, graphic designers, layout artists, production artists, and sales reps.

suppliers People and organizations that assist both advertisers and agencies in the preparation of advertising materials, such as photography, illustration, printing, and production.

art studios Companies that design and produce artwork and illustrations for advertisements, brochures, and other communication devices.

web design houses Art/computer studios that employ specialists who understand the intricacies of HTML and Java programming languages and can design ads and Internet web pages that are both effective and cost efficient.

Most studios are owned and managed by a graphic designer or illustrator, who calls on agencies and advertising managers to sell the studio's services, takes projects back to the office to be produced, and then delivers them for the client's approval. The work is time-consuming and requires a talent for organization and management as well as a core competency in art direction and computer graphics.

Similar to art studios, **web design houses** employ specialists who understand the intricacies of Internet programming languages and can design ads and websites that are both effective and cost efficient.

Printers and Related Specialists

The printers who produce brochures, stationery, business cards, sales promotion materials, and point-of-purchase displays are vital to the advertising business. Ranging from small instant-print

More than ever, advertisers need digital specialists who understand both the intricacies of programming languages and the various elements of good web design. The website for Subway uses streaming multimedia technologies to provide rich content. At the same time, its elegance and crisp design complement the brand's strong image.
Source: Subway IP Inc.

shops to large offset operations, **printers** employ or contract with highly trained specialists who prepare artwork for reproduction, operate digital scanning machines to make color separations and plates, operate presses and collating machines, and run binderies. Their sales reps must be highly skilled, and they often earn very large commissions.

Film and Video Houses

Few agencies have in-house TV production capabilities. Small agencies often work with local TV stations to produce commercials. But the large agencies normally work with independent **production houses** that specialize in film or video production or both.

Research Companies

Advertisers are concerned about the attitudes of their customers, the size of potential markets, and the acceptability of their products. Agencies want to know what advertising approaches to use, which concepts communicate most efficiently, and how effective past campaigns have been.

The media are concerned with the reading and viewing habits of their audiences, the desired markets of their advertiser-customers, and public perceptions toward their own particular medium.

Research, therefore, is closely allied to advertising and an important tool for marketing professionals. But most firms do not maintain a fully staffed research department. Instead, they use independent **research suppliers** or consultants. Research firms come in all sizes and specialties, and they employ statisticians, field interviewers, and computer programmers, as well as analysts with degrees in psychology, sociology, and marketing. We discuss research in Chapter 6.

The Media of Advertising

The *medium* that carries the advertiser's message is the vital connection between the company that manufactures a product or offers a service and the customer who may wish to buy it. Although the plural term **media** commonly describes channels of mass communication such as television, radio, newspapers, and magazines, it also refers to other communications vehicles such as direct mail, out-of-home media (transit, billboards, etc.), specialized media (aerial/blimps, inflatables), specialty advertising items (imprinted coffee mugs, balloons), and newer

communication technologies such as digital media, interactive TV, and satellite networks.

It is important to understand the various media, their role in the advertising business, and the significance of current media trends. For a person seeking a career in advertising, the media may offer the first door to employment, and for many they have provided great financial rewards.

We classify advertising media into six major categories: print, electronic, digital, out-of-home, direct mail, and other media. Due to recent media trends, there is some overlap. These media categories are discussed in Chapters 10 through 13.

CURRENT TRENDS

The ad agency business continues to go through many transitions. We mention just a few of the most important ones here: *the emergence of consultancies*, *the ascendance of digital media*, and *new ways of buying audiences*.

Anyone whose view of the agency world comes from *Mad Men*, a show about a 1960s ad agency, would hardly recognize the practice of modern advertising. A wave of acquisitions and consolidations in the 1990s left most of the famous agencies from decades earlier merged, dissolved, or absorbed. Emerging from the churn were four global conglomerates: Omnicom and the Interpublic Group, both headquartered in New York; Publicis, based in Paris; and London's WPP Group. Together, these companies now account for more than half of all advertising spending in the world. Structurally, these firms act as giant holding companies for an assortment of agencies that specialize in different promotional activities (advertising, public relations, sales promotion, digital, direct-response, media buying, etc.) and audiences (general consumer, B2B, minorities, etc.).

Why did this consolidation happen? One important factor is globalization and the emergence of global brands. The conglomerates offer global marketers services anywhere in the world and in whatever promotional channels such clients might require. A second factor is the decline in importance of traditional media and the growing interest in IMC. Profitable agencies have found they need to offer a menu of services rather than rely on income from only one part of the promotional mix. Third, the conglomerates can save their clients money, both because their scale allows them to obtain favorable media rates and because they've reached new heights in efficiency by reducing administrative overhead and expenses.

In turn, advertising conglomerates and agencies have a new competitor—the consultancy. Beginning in the late 2010s, firms such as Accenture Interactive, PwC Digital Services, IBM iX, and Deloitte Digital began offering a new kind of marketing service, one that often took dollars away from the budgets normally assigned to ad agencies.

So what is an **advertising consultancy**? Firms that serve as ad consultants started as intermediaries between agencies and clients. They often advise marketers on how well they are being served by their agency and how effectively agencies are spending media dollars. Over time, however, consultancies have started assuming an important role in the marketing activities of many large firms. *Ad Age* reports that Accenture's consults with more than 75 percent of *Fortune* Global 500 firms while WPP works with every firm in the Dow Jones 30.[48]

The rise of consultancies is likely due to many factors: the increased importance of data in marketing efforts, the transfer

---

advertising consultancy Firms that compete with and sometimes work alongside traditional agencies. They perform a variety of roles, including evaluation of a firm's agency. Consultancies tend to be more skilled with data and more comfortable with digital media than many agencies.

programmatic advertising A procedure for marketers to buy digital audiences via a computer. Content providers and buyers agree on the value of an audience via an auction. In programmatic advertising, an ad may appear on many digital sites, but only to audiences that fit the desired profile.

Another important trend is the shift in dollars to digital media. This is a culmination of trends that began years ago, which have left digital the unrivaled king, both in ad spends and consumer engagement. According to *eMarketer*, digital ad spending swept past the 50 percent mark of all media spending in 2019.[51] This trend is expected to continue for the foreseeable future. And it is easy to see why. Digital media offer benefits that advertisers of 20 years ago could only dream about in terms of audience composition, data, and engagement. In addition, it is where today's media user is spending time. The average media user spends

---

Another industry trend has been the slow death of the commission system.

---

of media budgets away from legacy media to digital, and an increased focus on consumer-brand experiences that aren't advertising. As Brian Whipple, senior managing director of Accenture Interactive puts it, "We don't believe brands are built from advertising anymore. They are built from an amalgamation of customer experiences, so that is what we are focused on."[49]

Whipple's remarks may understate the value of ad agencies however. In recent years, agencies and consultancies seem to have reached an accommodation in which each realizes the value of what the other provides. In some cases, this reflects consultancies actively adding agencies to their organizations, while in others, it is a willingness to provide clients the services that each does best.[50]

Advertisers should realize that both parties are responsible for the success of any relationship. In other words, being a good client is important (see My Ad Campaign 3-D, "Ways to Be a Better Client") if an advertiser wants to help its agency provide the best service. Mutual trust, empathetic but direct dialog, and openness to new ideas are the hallmark of great partnerships. Lacking those qualities, advertisers handicap their agencies, and themselves.

about 10 minutes a day with newspapers and magazines, a little more than an hour with radio, and more than 3 hours with TV. But the same user spends more than 6 hours with digital media—more than the others combined.

The rise of digital media has resulted in a third major change: how audiences are bought and sold. At one time, that sentence might have read: How *media* are bought and sold. However, in a digital world, advertisers can buy and content creators can sell the relevant slices of an audience that meet a campaign's needs. This is done through a system called **programmatic advertising**. In programmatic advertising, marketers buy digital audiences via a computer that matches the demographics the marketer is seeing with the parts of an audience a content provider can provide. The value of that audience is determined via an auction. In the past, an advertiser might buy a TV show whose demographics were attractive, but which also included viewers that were of no interest. In programmatic advertising, the advertiser pays only for, and the content provider supplies only, the audience that matches the desired demographic.

Programmatic advertising is possible because of the growth of digital media and the increasing use of streaming to watch content (see Exhibit 3–8). Most web and social media sites retain valuable information on their users, and it is not difficult to serve custom ads to computers, tablets, or phones. This was once impossible to do on television, but not anymore because, increasingly, audiences are streaming content through providers such as Hulu or YouTube. If you are one of the millions of cord-cutters who have abandoned cable TV to stream content, you are experiencing ads known as OTT or over the top. **Over-the-top advertising** leverages the information that YouTube, Hulu, AT&T, and Sling TV have about their subscribers, along with their ability to deliver different ads to households watching the same content. If you are watching a show on Hulu that breaks away for an ad, chances are the ad you are served was selected based on your demographics. Another person watching the same show at the same time will not see the same spot.

Ways to Be a Better Client [3–D]

These are some ideas your client may wish to keep in mind as they think about working with you.

Relationships
- *Cultivate honesty.* Be truthful in your meetings and in your ads.
- *Be enthusiastic.* When you like the ads, let the agency know.
- *Be frank when you don't like the advertising.* Have a good reason when turning down an idea.
- *Be human.* React like a person, not a corporation. Laugh at funny ads even if they don't work.
- *Be willing to admit you're unsure.* Don't be pressured. Let your agency know when you need time.
- *Allow the agency to feel responsible.* Tell the agency what you feel is wrong, not how to fix it.
- *Care about being a client.* Creative people work best for clients they like.

Management
- *Don't insulate your top managers from creative people.* Agency creatives work best when objectives come from the top, not filtered through layers.
- *Set objectives.* For timely and quality service from your agency, establish and openly share your marketing objectives.
- *Switch people, not agencies.* When problems arise, agencies often prefer to bring in fresh talent rather than lose you as a client.
- *Be sure the agency makes a profit on your account.* Demanding more services from your agency than fees or commissions can cover hurts relationships.

Production
- *Avoid nitpicking last-minute changes.* Perfection is important, but waiting until the last moment to make minor changes can damage the client–agency relationship. Agencies see such behavior as indecisive and/or arrogant and lose respect for the client.
- *Be aware of the cost of changes (both time and money).* The cost of making major changes at the production stage may be five times greater than in the earlier stages.
- *Don't change concepts during the production stage.* Late changes can inadvertently alter product positioning and image.

Media
- *Understand the economics (and economies) of media.* Be prepared to deal with costs per thousand (CPMs), costs per ratings point (CPP), and other key elements of media planning and buying so that you can evaluate and appreciate your agency's media strategy.
- *Understand the importance of lead time.* Early buys can eliminate late fees, earn discounts, make you eligible for special promotions, strengthen your agency's buying position, and reduce anxiety.
- *Avoid interfering with the agency's media relationship.* The stronger your agency's buying position, the greater the discounts available to you. Refrain from cutting deals with media reps directly and plan media use well in advance.
- *Avoid media arrogance ("they need us").* Some media will deal with clients, and some won't. Misinterpret this relationship and you may either pay more than you should or be too late to get into a medium you need.
- *Avoid insularity.* Be willing to let your mind travel beyond your immediate environment and lifestyle.
- *Suggest work sessions.* Set up informal give-and-take sessions with creatives and strategists.
- *Keep the creative people involved in your business.* Agency creatives do their best work for you when they're in tune with the ups and downs of your business.

Research
- *Share information.* Pool information to create new and bigger opportunities.
- *Involve the agency in research projects.* An agency's creative talent gets its best ideas from knowledge of your environment.

Creative
- *Learn the fine art of conducting the creative meeting.* Deal with the important issues first: strategy, consumer benefits, and reasons why.
- *Look for the big idea.* Concentrate on positioning strategy and brand personality. Don't allow a single ad—no matter how brilliant—to change the positioning or personality of the product.
- *Insist on creative discipline.* The creative process stimulates concepts and actions. Discipline helps keep focus on those that count the most.
- *Don't be afraid to ask for great advertising.* Agencies prefer the high road, but as the client you must be willing to accompany them. If the agency slips, be strong and ask it to try again.

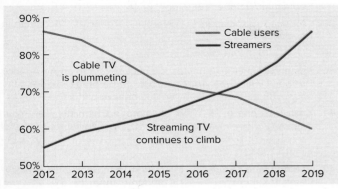

▼ **EXHIBIT 3-8**   Percentage of viewers accessing content via streaming versus cable.

Source: Strategus

One of the biggest successes in the history of advertising is Google. With revenues that dwarf the combined incomes of ABC, NBC, and CBS, Google's revenue growth is the envy of the industry. In Chapter 12 you'll find out more about how a company founded just over 20 years ago has succeeded so greatly. For now it is enough to know that Google's profits come from the company's belief that relevance is the most important factor in effective advertising. Although the digital advertising world has been dominated by Google and Facebook, a new player, Amazon, has taken center stage as an advertiser. Later you will discover how Amazon has taken the best elements of Google's playbook and combined it with those of Walmart to create an advertising juggernaut.

As you can tell, advertising is not a career for people averse to change. Of course, there are very few careers like that anymore, but change seems to occur faster in the advertising business. For a student such as yourself, keeping up with new practices and technologies along with their implications is important. Rapid change also means a level playing field for new entrants working alongside experienced professionals. That means a talented young person can find her or his career advancing quickly. Advertising remains an amazing occupation for those with the creativity, talent, drive, and insights to keep pace with disruption. ■

over-the-top advertising Ads delivered over streaming TV services that, unlike cable, can be customized for different households.

ENDNOTES

1. "McDonald's Advertising," *Wikipedia*, https://en.wikipedia.org/wiki/McDonald%27s_advertising#Current_campaign.

2. Rubio's Coastal Grill, www.rubios.com.

3. According to *Wikipedia*, social media are "computer-mediated tools that allow people or companies to create, share, or exchange information, career interests, ideas, and pictures/videos in virtual communities and networks." See "Social Media," *Wikipedia*, https://en.wikipedia.org/wiki/Social_media.

4. Joe Morsello, "SMBs Have Some Major Advantages over Brands in Social Marketing," *Street Fight Daily*, June 14, 2013, http://streetfightmag.com/2013/06/14/smbs-have-major-advantages-over-brands-in-social-media-marketing.

5. Henry A. Laskey, J. A. F. Nicholls, and Sydney Roslow, "The Enigma of Cooperative Advertising," *Journal of Business and Industrial Marketing*, vol. 8, no. 2 (1993), pp. 70–79.

6. Greg Sterling, "Billions In Local 'Co-Op Advertising' Funds Left Unspent Annually," *Marketing Land*, August 13, 2015, http://marketingland.com/report-billions-in-co-op-advertising-funds-left-unspent-each-year-138671.

7. Jack Neff, "Walmart Ups the Ante with Brand Co-op Ads—in More Ways than One," *Advertising Age*, November 30, 2009, pp. 4–23.

8. Andrew McMains, "This Is General Mills' First Big Media Review in 14 Years; Becomes the 20th Marketer in 6 Months to Launch a Media Search," *Adweek,* May 28, 2015, http://www.adweek.com/news/advertising-branding/general-mills-first-big-media-review-14-years-165051.

9. Natasha D. Smith, "General Mills Discovers Shoppers' True Demands—From Social Media," *Direct Marketing,* July 10, 2015, http://www.dmnews.com/social-media/general-mills-discovers-shoppers-true-demands-from-social-media/article/425626/.

10. Stuart Elliott, "General Mills Adds Social Media to Product Pitch," *New York Times*, July 18, 2012, http://mediadecoder. blogs.nytimes.com/2012/07/18/general-mills-adds-social-media-to-product-pitch.

11. Procter & Gamble, "Annual Report, 2019," www.pg.com/annualreport2019/index.html.

12. Gideon Spanier, "P&G Slashes Ad Spend by $350 Million after Cutting 'Waste', Agency Fees," *PR Week*, August 08, 2019, www.prweek.com/article/1593429/p-g-slashes-ad-spend-350m-cutting-waste-agency-fees.

13. William Perreault Jr., Joseph Cannon, E. Jerome McCarthy, *Basic Marketing* (Burr Ridge, IL: McGraw-Hill/Irwin, 2013).

14. Howard Silverblatt, "S&P 500 Global Sales," *Indexology*, https://us.spindices.com/indexology/djia-and-sp-500/sp-500-global-sales.

15. Tim Nudd, "Ad of the Day: McDonald's Refreshes 'I'm lovin' it'," *Adweek*, January 5, 2015, www.adweek.com/news/advertising-branding/ad-day-mcdonalds-refreshes-im-lovin-it-and-suddenly-feels-lot-oreo-162158.

16. "Global Marketers 2015," *Advertising Age*, http://adage.com/datacenter/globalmarketers2015.

17. Jim Patterson, "Viewpoint: Global Communication Requires a Global Understanding," *Adweek*, October 31, 1994, p. 46; "Efficacy of Global Ad Prospects Is Questioned in Firm's Survey," *The Wall Street Journal*, September 13, 1984, p. 29.

18. "Global Advertising: Consumers Trust Real Friends and Virtual Strangers the Most," *Nielsen Wire*, July 7, 2009, www.nielsen.com/us/en/insights/article/2009/global-advertising-consumers-trust-real-friends-and-virtual-strangers-the-most.

19. *Adweek* Staff, "Here Are the Year's Most Inventive Marketing, Media and Digital Campaigns," *AdWeek*, September 20, 2015, www.adweek.com/news-gallery/advertising-branding/here-are-years-most-inventive-marketing-media-and-digital-campaigns-honored-project-isaac-1670.

20. Frederick R. Gamble, *What Advertising Agencies Are—What They Do and How They Do It*, 7th ed. (New York: American Association of Advertising Agencies, 1970), p. 4.

21. Maureen Morrison, "Leo Burnett Wins Shootout for Ideas to Refresh McDonald's Brand," *Advertising Age*, August 6, 2014, http://adage.com/article/news/leo-burnett-wins-shootout-ideas-mcdonald-s-refresh/294486.

22. "Agency Family Trees 2015," *Ad Age Datacenter*, http://adage.com/datacenter/agencyfamilytrees2015.

23. "Gotham, Inc.," *Ad Forum*, www.adforum.com/agency/5013/profile/gotham-inc.

24. Zubi Advertising, www.zubiad.com.

25. Katie Richards, "Coke Chooses 3 WPP Agencies for Its Next Big Global Ad Campaign," *AdWeek*, August 13, 2015, https://www.adweek.com/brand-marketing/coke-chooses-3-wpp-agencies-its-next-big-global-ad-campaign-166381.

26. Initiative Media, http://initiative.com.

27. R/GA, www.rga.com.

28. Deena Di Stefano, *LinkedIn*, www.linkedin.com/in/deena-di-stefano-7013824.

29. "Readings in Account Planning," Hart Weichselbaum (Ed.), Copy Workshop, 2008.

30. William F. Arens and Jack J. Whidden, "La Publicité aux Etats-Unis: Les Symptômes et les Stratégies d'une Industrie Surpleuplée," *L'Industrie de la Publicité au Québec* (Montreal: Le Publicité-Club de Montréal, 1992), pp. 383–84.

31. "15% Agency Commission: Reduced to a Pipe Dream," *Bhatnaturally*, .com/advertising/15-agency-commission-reduced-to-a-pipe-dream.

32. Jean Marie Dru, "Viewpoint," *Advertising Age*, January 25, 2010.

33. Andrew Jaffe, "Has Leo Burnett Come to the End of the 'Free Overservice' Era?" *Adweek*, December 6, 1993, p. 46; Melanie Wells and Laurel Wentz, "Coke Trims Commissions," *Advertising Age*, January 31, 1994, p. 2.

34. Alexandra Bruell, "Agencies Earn Little From Performance-Based Compensation, 4As Finds," *Advertising Age*, May 9, 2014, http://adage.com/article/agency-news/agencies-earned-2-performance-compensation-finds-4as/293113.

35. Jon Chesto, "Boston Group Pushes for Ronald McDonald's retirement," *MetroWest Daily News*, June 1, 2010, www.metrowestdailynews.com/opinion/x1218688656/Chesto-Boston-group-pushes-for-Ronald-McDonalds-retirement.

36. "Let's Move: America's Move to Raise a Healthier Generation of Kids," https://letsmove.obamawhitehouse.archives.gov.

37. James R. Willis, Jr., "Winning New Business: An Analysis of Advertising Agency Activities," *Journal of Advertising Research*, September/October 1992, pp. 10–16.

38. American Association of Advertising Agencies, "Accounts in Review," www.aaaa.org/ag_admin/accounts-in-review.

39. Clio Awards, www.clioawards.com.

40. Kristen Gough, "6 Attributes Clients Look for in an Ad Agency Partner," *Hubspot Agency Post*, http://blog.hubspot.com/agency/6-attributes-clients-look-ad-agency-partner.

41. Zach Rosenberg, "5 Ways to Improve Chemistry with Your Clients," *AdWeek*, January 24, 2016, www.adweek.com/news/advertising-branding/5-ways-improve-chemistry-your-clients-169129.

42. Rae Ann Fera, "Revealing the Naked Truth Behind the Agency-Client Relationship," *Fast Company*, June 26, 2014, www.fastcocreate.com/3032321/cannes/revealing-the-naked-truth-behind-the-agency-client-relationship.

43. Paul C. N. Mitchell, Harold Cataquet, and Stephen Hague, "Establishing the Causes of Disaffection in Agency-Client Relations," *Journal of Advertising Research*, March/April 1992, pp. 41–48.

44. Isabelle T. D. Szmigin, "Managing Quality in Business-to-Business Services," *European Journal of Marketing*, vol. 27, no. 1 (1993), pp. 5–21.

45. Ron Jackson, "If You Hire a Vendor, You Get a Vendor Mindset," *Marketing News*, April 25, 1991, pp. 13–14.

46. Steven A. Meyerowitz, "Ad Agency Conflicts: The Law and Common Sense," *Business Marketing*, June 1987, p. 16.

47. Andrew Jaffe, "For Agencies, Conflict Taboo Seems Strong as Ever," *Adweek*, January 24, 1994, p. 46.

48. E. J. Schultz, "The Race Is On! How IBM, Accenture, PwC and Deloitte Are Shaking Up the Marketing Industry," *Ad Age*, May 1, 2017, https://adage.com/article/news/consultancies-rising/308845.

49. E. J. Schultz, "The Race Is On! How IBM, Accenture, PwC and Deloitte Are Shaking Up the Marketing Industry," *Ad Age*, May 1, 2017, https://adage.com/article/news/consultancies-rising/308845.

50. Seb Joseph, "When It Comes to Consulting Firms, Some Advertisers Aren't Convinced," *Digiday*, May 20, 2019, http://digiday.com/marketing/comes-consulting-firms-advertisers-arent-convinced.

51. Jasmine Enberg, "Global Digital Ad Spending 2019," *eMarketer*, March 28, 2019, www.emarketer.com/content/global-digital-ad-spending-2019.

targeting and the
marketing mix

This chapter describes the role that advertising plays in marketing. Because no product or service pleases everybody, marketers need to select specific target markets that offer the greatest potential. They can then fine-tune their mix of marketing elements (the four Ps) to match the needs or wants of the target market.

The 2020 Super Bowl brought back one of the best loved (and most effective) ad campaigns ever, the "The man your man could smell like" guy from Old Spice. This time, 10 years after the original ads aired, he explains the benefits of the brand to his son. (See the spot here: https://bgr.com/2020/01/23/old-spice-guy-campaign-anniversary.)

This is not the first time a brand has run "retro" advertisements. And it is easy to see why this particular campaign is worth a call back.

The original ads from 10 years ago showed that advertising success is not just about what you say, but to whom you say it. Targeting ads for a male brand to a female target audience was unusual, but then, just about everything about this campaign was. To fully appreciate the ads, let's see why Old Spice needed a game-changing campaign in the first place.

When Old Spice was purchased by Procter & Gamble, it was sold as a men's aftershave lotion. When men began showing interest in other grooming products, including lotions and liquid soaps, Old Spice introduced brand extensions to meet those demands.

In 1983, P&G's global arch-rival, Unilever, introduced Axe. As a newer product that emphasized sex appeal, Axe focused on a younger target audience. In ads that were humorous but direct, Axe suggested the brand

makes men irresistible to beautiful women.[1] This message resonated, and by the 2000s, Axe had a healthy lead in market share.

Procter & Gamble had to consider whether to reinvest in their mature brand or abandon it. Deciding on the former, P&G assigned the challenge of reinvigorating Old Spice to one of the world's greatest agencies, Wieden+Kennedy, a Portland, Oregon agency. W+K is famous for ads

continued on p. 92

LEARNING OBJECTIVES

After studying this chapter, you will be able to:

LO4-1 Describe the role of advertising in marketing.

LO4-2 Illustrate the methods advertisers use to segment and aggregate markets.

LO4-3 Explain how defining a target market enhances marketing strategy.

LO4-4 List the elements of the marketing mix and the role advertising plays in each.

SMELL LIKE A MAN, MAN.

Old Spice

Source: Old Spice by Procter & Gamble

continued from p. 91

that helped make Nike a world leader in footwear. Now the agency would need to take a somewhat stale brand and credibly present it as fresh, relevant, even hip.[2]

Before starting, the agency and client made a big decision. Based on research that showed large numbers of women bought the soaps and lotions their male partners or husbands used, W+K decided to focus on both the user *and* the buyer. The new campaign would appeal to both men (who use body wash) and women (who often buy it for them). The campaign slogan would be "the man your man could smell like."

In the first commercial, former NFL player Isaiah Mustafa, standing in front of a running shower dressed only in a bath towel, spoke directly to the camera. "Hello ladies," he confidently intoned. "Look at your man, now back to me, now back at your man, now back to me. Sadly, he isn't me. But if he stopped using lady-scented body wash and switched to Old Spice, he could smell like he's me."[3] The fast-paced

and somewhat absurd style of the dialog, along with Mustafa's charm and humor, made the ad an immediate hit. Old Spice was back.

If things had stopped there, we would not likely be remembering the campaign. Because as funny and charming as the original ads, were, the truth is advertising is littered with "one-hit wonder" campaigns that quickly fizzle.

But W+K was only getting started. After the Old Spice television campaign attracted national attention, the agency began featuring Mustafa in dozens of different, personalized social media spots that targeted key influencers such as Ashton Kutcher and Ellen DeGeneres. Naturally, Ellen was flattered and invited Mustafa on her show. More buzz for Old Spice. And a Cannes Grand Prix for the campaign.[4]

W+K still wasn't done. It decided to create a viral story line for Mustafa's "Old Spice guy." Jason Bagley, creative director at Wieden, settled on a story line in which another celebrity, Fabio, an Italian model, would try to usurp Mustafa

As shown in this ad, Old Spice helped keep the buzz going and fans flocking to its social media by introducing Fabio to the campaign, a move that further proved the success of an advertiser that understands the marketplace.

Source: Old Spice by Procter & Gamble

as spokesperson. The theme of more than 100 viral videos shot featuring the two was "Mano a Mano en el Bañó."

Suddenly, Old Spice was everywhere. For a time, Old Spice had the number one and number four most viewed channels on YouTube. The ads were watched more than 20 million times. The brand also attracted nearly 70,000 new fans on Facebook.[5] And, best of all, Old Spice regained its market share lead from Axe.

The Old Spice campaign has received countless accolades. And W+K has solidified its reputation as an amazing creative shop. But as good as the creative work was, perhaps the best decision in the entire campaign was to target male body wash to women. And now, 10 years after his debut, the "man your man could smell like" is back to remind us what we loved about the campaign in the first place. ∎

LO4-1 Describe the role of advertising in marketing.

THE LARGER MARKETING CONTEXT OF ADVERTISING

All advertisers face the challenge of how best to present their products, services, and ideas effectively through the media to audiences. To succeed, they must understand the important relationship between the product and the marketplace. That relationship is the focus of marketing.

Marketing's role is often misunderstood and occasionally overlooked. For example, everybody knows that a business can't survive without proper financing, and, that without production, there are no products to sell. But how does a company know *what* products or services to produce? Or *where* to distribute them, or through *what* channels? That's where marketing comes in.

A company prospers only if it can attract and keep customers who are willing to buy the firm's goods and services. This means a company must be able to locate prospective customers—determine where they live, work, and play—and then understand their needs, wants, and desires; create products that satisfy such desires better than the products of competitors; and finally communicate that information in a powerful, clear, and compelling way. This chapter will help you better understand advertising's role in that process.

Customer Needs and Product Utility

As we discussed in Chapter 1, marketing is a set of processes for creating, communicating, and delivering value to customers. The ultimate purpose of marketing is to *create exchanges that satisfy the perceived needs and wants of individuals and organizations.*

One of the important elements of that definition is the special relationship between a customer's needs and a product's need-satisfying potential. This is known as the product's *utility*. **Utility** is the product's ability to satisfy both functional needs and symbolic (or psychological) wants.[6] One of the primary roles of advertising is to communicate this utility. Thus, some ads promote how well a product works (function); others tout glamour, sex appeal, or status (symbolism). Exhibit 4-1 discusses the important relationship between needs and utility.

Companies use marketing research (discussed in Chapter 6) to discover the needs and wants that exist in the marketplace. The goal is to use this information for product shaping—designing products, through manufacturing, packaging, or advertising, to satisfy more fully the customers' needs and wants.

To woo Millennials, for example, luxury brands Mercedes, BMW, and Audi have all introduced models that sell for less than $40,000. Mercedes has even created a panel of more than 200 Millennials, "Generation Benz," to continuously uncover information about younger consumers' consumption patterns, likes and dislikes, and social media use. Mercedes ads that target older audiences hear the familiar voice of Jon Hamm, of *Mad Men* fame. But for ads that target the younger segment, icons relevant to Millennials are featured, including Casey Niestat, Tinie Tempah, and Daisy Lowe.

utility A product's ability to satisfy both functional needs and symbolic or psychological wants. A product's problem-solving potential may include form, task, possession, time, or place utility.

Superior quality will not guarantee that a product is preferred by consumers. Marketers must successfully communicate product availability and promote its advantages, whether it's a graphite tennis racket, a high-performance sports car, or the prompt, friendly service of a bank.

Any successful product must satisfy consumers' *needs*. The ability to satisfy those needs is called *utility*. Five types of functional utility are important to consumers: form, task, possession, time, and place. A product may provide psychic utility as well as functional utility.

Companies create *form utility* when they create a tangible good, such as a bicycle, that fits a consumer's needs: a shoe that fits and is comfortable, or a pickup truck that tows large loads and can carry a big payload.

Task utility originates in others doing something for us; for example, an accountant preparing your tax returns or a mechanic fixing your car. When auto brands offer a five-year warranty on repairs, they are providing this kind of utility.

Even when a company provides form or task utility, marketers must consider how consumers can take possession of the product. This includes distribution, pricing strategies, shelf availability, purchase agreements, and delivery. Money is typically exchanged for possession utility. An antique bicycle on display, but not for sale, lacks *possession utility* because the customer cannot purchase it.

Providing the consumer with the product when he or she wants it is known as *time utility*. Having an ample supply of jam, cars, or bank tellers on hand when the consumer has the need is thus another marketing requirement. Amazon provides its Prime members with free two-day shipping, and the company is focused on achieving same-day delivery in the near future.

Place utility—having the product available where the customer can get it—is also vital to business success. Customers won't travel very far out of their way to get bicycles or cars. They're even less likely to travel long distances for everyday needs. That's why banks have so many branches. And that's why 24-hour convenience markets, which sell gasoline and basic food items, are so popular. And a customer's digital technology provides the ultimate place and time utility—any place and time the Internet is available.

Finally, consumers gain *psychic utility* when a product offers symbolic or psychological need satisfaction, such as status or sex appeal. Psychic utility is usually achieved through product promotion (advertising) and may fulfill esteem and self-actualization needs.

Whether it be psychic utility or the functional utilities of form, task, possession, time, and place, product utility is an essential component of marketing success.

[
A company prospers only if it can attract and keep customers.
]

Exchanges: The Purpose of Marketing and Advertising

A transaction in which a person or organization trades something of value with someone else is an **exchange**. We all engage in exchanges. It's a natural part of being human. Buyers do it to acquire more things and better their situation. Sellers do it to grow their business and make a profit.

Marketing facilitates these exchanges, thus increasing our potential for satisfaction. How? In a variety of ways: by developing goods and services we want; by pricing them attractively; by distributing them to convenient locations; and by informing us about them through advertising and IMC. The information value of advertising makes people aware of the availability of products and of the selection alternatives among different brands. Advertising communicates product features and benefits, price options, and locations where the product can be purchased. In the case of direct marketing, advertising can even close the sale.

Even after an exchange occurs, *satisfaction* remains an issue. Satisfaction must occur every time customers use the product, or people won't think they got a fair exchange. Satisfaction leads to more exchanges: Satisfied customers repurchase products and share good reviews with their friends. Positive word of mouth creates even more sales and contributes to a good reputation. And while positive word of mouth has always been important, it is crucial in the age of social media. Thus, while satisfaction is the goal of the customer, it must also be the fundamental goal of any sophisticated marketer.

In other words, while advertising is important in leading consumers to make a purchase, it is also of value to a marketer *after* the purchase. This is because advertising *reinforces* satisfaction by reminding customers why they bought the product, helping them defend the purchase against skeptical associates, and helping them to become brand advocates, which may persuade others to buy it.

Thus, we can think of marketing as the process companies use to make a profit by identifying and satisfying their customers' needs and desires. This chapter defines and outlines marketing issues to clarify advertising's proper role in the marketing function. As we shall see, the relationship between advertising and marketing is critical.

LO4-2   Illustrate the methods advertisers use to segment and aggregate markets.

THE MARKET SEGMENTATION PROCESS

The process of market segmentation involves two steps: *identifying groups of people* (or organizations) with shared needs and characteristics and *aggregating* (combining) these groups into larger market segments according to their interest in the product's utility. This process should result in market segments that are large enough to target and reachable through a suitable mix of marketing activities—including advertising.

Markets often consist of many segments. A company may differentiate its products and marketing strategy for every segment, or concentrate its marketing activities on only one or a few segments. Either task is far from simple. Procter & Gamble markets at least five different body washes to appeal to multiple segments. We saw that Old Spice body wash targets women who buy personal care products for their male partners. At the other

Ad campaigns that last for more than a couple of years tend to be classics. There is no question that the Old Spice campaign will go down as one of the all-time best. A part of that success can be attributed to the market segmentation process of the campaign.

Source: Old Spice by Procter & Gamble

extreme, Herbal Essence body wash appeals to women who desire irresistible, natural fragrances for themselves. Ivory seeks out everyday women who want a clean, simple, and affordable body wash. Olay targets women who care about moist, healthy skin, and Axe focuses on men interested in sex appeal. Catering to all these needs on a global level requires a sophisticated marketing and communications system. In this chapter, we look first at how marketers identify and categorize *consumer markets* and second at the techniques they use to segment *business markets*. Then we discuss various strategic options companies use, including advertising, to match their products with markets and create profitable exchanges.

Types of Markets

A firm's marketing activities are always aimed at a particular segment of the population—its **target market**. Advertisers then try to reach these markets through media outlets with audiences that substantially overlap with the target market. The particular group available to an advertiser through media is called the **target audience**. When we see an ad that doesn't

exchange The trading of one thing of value for another thing of value.

target market The market segment or group within the market segment toward which all marketing activities will be directed.

target audience The specific group of individuals to whom the advertising message is directed.

CHEAT ON YOUR USUAL AIRLINE.
SwitchToVirginAmerica.com

Virgin america A BREATH OF FRESH AIRLINE

Both the photo and the quirky headline help Virgin Airlines reach out to their target audience and convey a "personality" for the brand. This ad resonates with the company's young target audiences.

Source: Virgin America

appeal to us, it may be because the ad is not aimed at any of the groups we belong to. For example, a TV commercial for denture cream isn't meant to appeal to teens. They're not part of either the target market or the target audience. There are two main types of target markets, consumers and businesses.

Consumer Markets   Most of the advertising we see daily in the media—websites, social media, TV, radio, newspapers, and magazines—falls under the broad category of consumer advertising. Usually sponsored by the producer (or manufacturer) of the product or service, these ads are typically directed at consumers. **Consumers** are people who buy the product for their own or someone else's personal use. In 2013, the average U.S. household spent $51,100.[7]

In the end, customers are people. So advertising professionals must understand how people act and think—and why they buy what they buy. Understanding the motivations, thoughts, feelings, and behaviors related to consumption is a discipline known as *consumer behavior*, a topic discussed in greater detail in Chapter 5.

Business Markets   Not every buyer is a consumer. Companies use **business advertising** to reach people who buy goods and services for resale, for use in a business or organization, or for manufacturing other products. It tends to appear in specialized business publications or professional journals, in direct-mail pieces sent to businesses, at trade shows, or on company websites. Because business advertising (also called business-to-business, or *B2B*, advertising) rarely uses consumer

mass media, you may not see it often. That doesn't mean there isn't a great deal of it, just that you are not a target for it quite yet. In fact, B2B advertisers spend billions on advertising every year.[8]

In addition to general business advertising, there are three specialized types of business advertising: trade, professional, and agricultural. *Trade advertising* targets resellers (wholesalers, dealers, and retailers) to promote greater distribution of their products. For example, Sunkist places trade advertising in publications such as *Progressive Grocer* to develop more grocery outlets and to increase sales to existing outlets. Advertising aimed at teachers, accountants, doctors, dentists, architects, engineers, lawyers, and the like is called *professional advertising* and typically appears in official publications of professional societies (such as the *Archives of Ophthalmology*). Companies use *agricultural* (or *farm*) advertising to promote products and services used in agriculture to farmers and others employed in agribusiness. FMC Corp., for example, might advertise its plant nutrition products to citrus growers in *Farm Journal Magazine*.

Business customers tend to be knowledgeable and sophisticated, and they may require extensive technical information before buying. So people who work in business-to-business advertising often need more specialized product knowledge and experience than their consumer advertising colleagues.

Segmenting the Consumer Market: Finding the Right Niche

The concept of *shared characteristics* is critical to market segmentation. Marketing and advertising people know that, based on their needs, wants, and mental files, consumers leave "footprints in the sand"—the telltale signs of how and where they live and work, what they buy, and how they spend their free time. By following these footprints, marketers can locate and define groups of consumers with similar needs and wants, create messages for them, and know how and where to send those messages. The goal is to find that particular niche (or space) in the market where the advertiser's product or service will fit.

Marketers group these shared characteristics into categories *(behavioristic, geographic, demographic,* and *psychographic)* to identify and segment consumer markets (see Exhibit 4–2). The marketer's purpose is twofold: first, to identify people who are likely to be be interested in the product; and second, to develop rich descriptions of these people to better understand them, create marketing mixes for them, and reach them with meaningful advertising and IMC.

The term *1to1 marketing* was introduced by Don Peppers and Martha Rogers in their book, *The One to One Future*, to illustrate the importance of treating different customers differently. They argue that potential customers can be segmented so specifically that a unique marketing message can be sent to each based on that person's individual demographic,

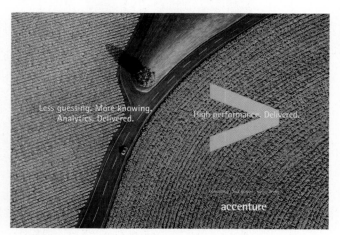

> Professional advertising targets audiences in fields such as accounting, medicine, and education. Accenture, a global professional services company, targets businesses in this ad by touting their consulting, technology, and outsourcing capabilities.
Source: Accenture

> # The goal is to find that particular niche (or space) in the market where the advertiser's product or service will fit.

behavioristic, and psychographic characteristics. It is not typically feasible to achieve true 1to1 customization, but the more narrowly defined a customer segment the more accurately it can be targeted.[9] Big data gathered from digital interactions are allowing marketers to conceive 1to1 customization on a large scale. For example, if you shop at Amazon, your landing page is unique to you if you have an Amazon account. We'll discuss this further in Chapter 12.

In choosing one market segment, advertisers may be deliberately excluding another. This is especially true in an age when many consumers expect brands to stand for clear values and beliefs. Nike certainly understood this in choosing former NFL quarterback Colin Kaepernick for a recent marketing campaign.

The company's research suggested that while consumers would be split as to whether the outspoken athlete is a positive role model, the segment that buys and uses Nike products unambiguously likes and admires him (see Ethical Issues, "Colin Kaepernick and Nike").

Behavioristic Segmentation
One of the best ways to segment markets is to group consumers by purchase behavior. This is called **behavioristic segmentation**. Behavioral segments are determined by many variables, but the most important are *user status*, *usage rate*, *purchase occasion*, and *benefits sought*. These categories tell us who our customers are now, when and why they buy, and how much they consume.

▼ **EXHIBIT 4–2** Methods for segmenting consumer markets.

Variables	Typical Breakdowns	Variables	Typical Breakdowns
Geographic		**Demographic**	
Region	Pacific; Mountain; West North Central; West South Central; East North Central; East South Central; South Atlantic; Middle Atlantic; New England	Age	Younger than 6, 6–11, 12–17, 18–34, 35–49, 50–64, 65+
County size	A, B, C, D	Gender	Male, female
Climate	Dry, humid, rain, snow	Family size	1–2, 3–4, 5+
City or SMSA size	Less than 5,000; 5,000–19,999; 20,000–49,999; 50,000–99,999; 100,000–249,000; 250,000–499,999; 500,000–999,999; 1,000,000–3,999,999; 4,000,000 or more	Family life cycle	Young, single; young, married, no children; young, married, youngest child younger than 6; young, married, youngest child 6 or older; young, unmarried, with children; older, married, with children; older, unmarried, with children; older, married, no children younger than 18; older, single; other
Density	Urban, suburban, rural		
Behavioristic		Income	Less than $20,000; $21,000–30,000; $31,000–40,000; $41,000–60,000; $61,000–100,000; $101,000–150,000; $151,000 and more
Purchase occasion	Regular occasion, special occasion		
Benefits sought	Economy, convenience, prestige		
User status	Nonuser, ex-user, potential user, first-time user, regular user	Occupation	Professional and technical; managers, officials, and proprietors; clerical, sales; craftspeople, supervisors; operatives; farmers; retired; students; homemakers; unemployed
Usage rate	Light user, medium user, heavy user		
Loyalty status	None, medium, strong, absolute		
Readiness stage	Unaware, aware, informed, interested, desirous, intending to buy	Education	Grade school or less; some high school; high school graduate; some college; college graduate
Marketing-factor sensitivity	Quality, price, service, advertising, sales promotion		
Psychographic		Religion	Catholic, Protestant, Jewish, Muslim, Non-religious
Societal divisions	Upper crust, movers and shakers, successful singles, Social Security, middle of the road, metro-ethnic mix	Race	White, Black, Asian
		Nationality	American, British, French, German, Scandinavian, Italian, Latin American, Middle Eastern, Japanese
Lifestyle	Strivers, achievers, actualizers		
Personality	Compulsive, gregarious, authoritarian, ambitious		

Not for the faint of anything.

The Porsche 911 GT3

Behavioristic segmentation is one of the best ways to organize consumer markets. Purchase behavior variables, such as the benefits sought by the consumer, determine how the segments are defined. In this ad, Porsche (www.porsche.com) appeals to the behavior segments of their consumers for whom performance is everything.

Source: Porsche Cars North America, Inc.

products (see Exhibit 4–3). One rule of thumb suggests that 20 percent of users consume 80 percent of the product. Marketers want to define that 20 percent and aim their advertising at them. Hardee's, a fast-food hamburger chain, even has a pet name for its prized 17- to 34-year-old male market segment: the HFFU (pronounced who-foo). According to Andrew Puzder, CEO, "That's the 'heavy fast-food user,' someone who eats there four or five times a week.... It is the sweet spot of the industry and what appeals to him is drippy, messy burgers. He is not interested in little 99-cent burgers or low-carb anything."[11]

By finding common characteristics among heavy users of their products, marketers can define product differences and focus ad campaigns more effectively. For example, independent businesspeople who travel at their own expense, a group that Fallon Worldwide describes as "road warriors," are heavy users of value hotel chains, with some spending more than 100 nights a year on the road. In creating a campaign that targeted this group for Holiday Inn Express, Fallon also discovered that road

User-status variables Many markets can be segmented by the **user status** of prospective customers. Researchers Stephan and Tannenholz have identified six categories of consumers based on user status.

Sole users are the most brand loyal and require the least amount of advertising and promotion. *Semisole* users typically use Brand A but have an alternate selection if it is not available or if the alternate is promoted with a discount. *Discount users* are the semisole users of competing Brand B. They won't buy Brand A at full price, but might be tempted to buy it at a discount. *Aware nontriers* use competitive products in the category but haven't taken a liking to Brand A. A different advertising message could help, but these people rarely offer much potential. *Trial/rejectors* tried the product based on Brand A's advertising message, but didn't like it. More advertising won't help; only a reformulation of Brand A will bring them back. *Repertoire users* perceive two or more brands to have superior attributes and will pay full price. They are brand switchers and respond to persuasive advertising based on their fluctuating wants and desires. Therefore, they are often a primary target for brand advertising.[10]

Usage-rate variables Advertising has an easier time getting a heavy user to increase usage in comparison to a light user. In **volume segmentation**, marketers measure people's **usage rates** to define consumers as light, medium, or heavy users of

Although Apple is best known for its Macs, iPods, iPads, and iPhones, it uses its strong brand name to promote newer products such as the Apple Watch. For sole users, this ad reinforces their brand loyalty, and for repertoire users—those most likely to switch brands—it persuades them that Apple products are the superior choice.

Source: Denys Prykhodov/Shutterstock

user status Six categories into which consumers can be placed, which reflect varying degrees of loyalty to certain brands and products. The categories are *sole users, semisole users, discount users, aware nontriers, trial/rejectors,* and *repertoire users.*

volume segmentation Defining consumers as light, medium, or heavy users of products.

usage rates The extent to which consumers use a product: light, medium, or heavy.

purchase occasion A method of segmenting markets on the basis of *when* consumers buy and use a good or service.

▼**EXHIBIT 4–3** Usage rates vary for different products.

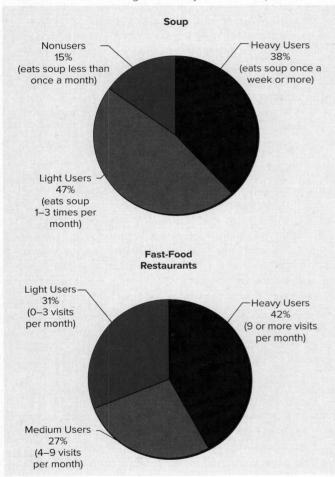

Soup

Nonusers
15%
(eats soup less than once a month)

Heavy Users
38%
(eats soup once a week or more)

Light Users
47%
(eats soup 1–3 times per month)

Fast-Food Restaurants

Light Users
31%
(0–3 visits per month)

Heavy Users
42%
(9 or more visits per month)

Medium Users
27%
(4–9 visits per month)

households are more likely to buy Kias, prepaid mobile phones, and Pepsodent toothpaste.[12]

Purchase-occasion variables Buyers can also be distinguished by when they buy or use a product or service—the **purchase occasion.** Air travelers, for example, may fly for business or leisure, so one airline might promote business travel while another promotes tourism. The purchase occasion might be affected by frequency of need (regular or occasional), a fad (candy, computer games), or seasons (water skis, raincoats). The Japan Weather Association tracked buying patterns on 20,000 items and correlated them to the outside temperature. Not surprisingly, when the temperature goes up, people buy more sunshades, air conditioners, watermelons, and swimwear.

Crest is a leader in identifying the benefits sought by consumers. This ad addresses whiter teeth. How many other dental-hygiene benefits can you think of? And how might these be addressed in a different ad?
Source: Crest by Procter & Gamble

warriors make travel plans at the beginning of the week and like to watch ESPN, CNN, and the Weather Channel. Knowing this, it was easy for Fallon media people to schedule messages when and where the target audience would be most responsive.

Marketers of one product sometimes find that their customers are also heavy users of other products and can define target markets in terms of the usage rates of the other products. For example, upper-income households are overrepresented among buyers of Infinitis, Samsung mobile phones, Starbucks coffee, and Tom's of Maine toothpaste. Conversely, low-income

Colin Kaepernick and Nike

Former NFL quarterback Colin Kaepernick was drafted by the San Francisco 49ers in the 2011 draft. The second-round pick began his career, like many rookies, on the bench. But when the 49ers starting quarterback was injured, Kaepernick stepped in and eventually led the team to the 2012 Super Bowl. Although San Francisco lost the big game, Kaepernick continued as a starter, and the 49ers went to the playoffs for three more seasons. By 2016, Kaepernick's style of play, which relied heavily on his mobility and speed, became less effective, perhaps due to age and the toll of NFL hits. He lost his starting job but remained with the team as a backup.

During the 2016 NFL preseason, Kaepernick ignited a national controversy by remaining seated on the bench during the playing of the National Anthem. He explained his actions by saying, "I am not going to stand up to show pride in a flag for a country that oppresses Black people and people of color. To me, this is bigger than football and it would be selfish on my part to look the other way. There are bodies in the street and people getting paid leave and getting away with murder."[14]

For the final preseason game of 2016 Kaepernick chose to kneel as a form of protest rather than stay seated, explaining he wished to show more respect for armed service members. He continued his protest throughout the season and inspired others, including a number of NFL players, to do the same.

After opting out of his contract, Kaepernick found himself unemployed and without a team. The athlete maintains he is being blackballed and has sued the NFL. Conversely, a couple of NFL teams, including the Ravens and Broncos, have indicated they've made offers and blame the quarterback for rejecting them.

In 2018 Nike celebrated the 30th anniversary of its memorable "Just Do It" slogan by featuring Kaepernick as one athlete in a series of memorable images. The quarterback's face is shown in closeup, along with the headline "Believe in something. Even if it means sacrificing everything." The athlete is reported to be receiving a multi-million-dollar payday for the campaign.

Nike and Kaepernick already had a sponsorship deal in place extending to the football player's rookie season. The new ad extends the deal and also includes a line of clothing and shoes. Some of the money in the deal will be donated to Kaepernick's nonprofit group.

Responses to the campaign have been divided. Opinion has, in many instances, also broken down across demographic lines, including race and age, with African Americans and younger Americans generally offering support. Initial suggestions that the campaign would risk Nike profits were dissipated when the company reported sales increases of more than 30 percent following the appearance of the ads. One commentator noted that more than two-thirds of Nike consumers are younger than 35, making the company's association with Kaepernick less risky than it might seem.

Many have praised Kaepernick's courage in the face of harsh criticism, including comments from U.S. President Donald Trump, who tweeted that anthem protesters should be fired. Among the athlete's supporters is GQ magazine, which named him a 2017 "Citizen of the Year," and Amnesty International, which awarded him a "Ambassador of Conscience" honor. Others believe Kaepernick's actions and rhetoric insult first responders, the flag, and the sacrifices of men and women in the armed forces.

The controversy is all the more interesting because Nike provides uniforms for every NFL team. The league itself seems flummoxed about how to handle the issue. On the one hand, it collaborates with its players in growing the league's audiences and profits, but on the other hand, it is sensitive to the large numbers of people offended by the protest. But by 2020, it became clear that Kaepernick spoke for many professional athletes, inspiring players from the NBA, MLB, WNBA, and other sports to boycott games to protest police shootings.

When there's a chill in the air, sales of suits, sweaters, and heaters take off.[13] TV sales take off in December (Christmas) and again in January (the Super Bowl telecast). A marketer who discovers common purchase occasions for a group has a potential target segment and can better determine when to run specials and when to promote certain product categories.

Benefits-sought variables Consumers seek various **benefits** in the products they buy—high quality, low price, status, sex appeal, fragrance, environmental sensitivity. Procter & Gamble identified the most important benefits sought by body wash users and developed products to meet their needs. In addition to tangible benefits, consumers are motivated by *symbolism*—what the brand name means to them, to their friends, or to some social reference group. **Benefit segmentation** is the prime objective of many consumer attitude studies and the basis for many successful ad campaigns.

Some product categories are characterized by substantial *brand switching* from one purchase occasion to the next. Researchers have determined that switching occurs in response to different *need states* that consumers may experience from one occasion to another. For example, a consumer may use a toothpaste that primarily focuses on teeth whitening for a period of time. If the product works as promised, the consumer may later switch to a brand more focused on cavity prevention.

Using behavioristic segmentation, we can accomplish the first step of identifying likely prospects for our marketing and advertising efforts. The next step in developing rich profiles of these customers makes use of geographic, demographic, and psychographic characteristics.

Geographic Segmentation One simple way to define markets is by using **geographic segmentation**. People in one

▼**EXHIBIT 4-4** Projected U.S. Hispanic population growth rate.

Year	Hispanic (thousands)	Total U.S. (thousands)	Hispanic % of Total
2015	57,075	321,363	17.8%
2020	63,784	333,896	19.1
2025	70,973	345,407	20.5
2030	78,655	358,471	21.9
2035	86,659	369,662	23.4
2040	94,876	380,016	25.0
2045	103,259	389,934	26.5
2050	111,732	399,803	27.9
2055	120,242	409,873	29.3
2060	128,780	420,268	30.6

Source: U.S. Census Bureau

region of the country (or the world) have needs, wants, and purchasing habits that differ from those in other regions. People in Sun Belt states, for example, buy more sunscreen lotion. Canadians buy special equipment for dealing with snow and ice—products many Floridians have never seen in stores.

When marketers analyze geographic data, they study sales by region, country size, city size, specific locations, and types of stores. Many products sell well in urban areas but poorly in suburban or rural ones, and vice versa. As we'll see in Chapter 14, this type of information is critical in developing advertising media schedules because, with limited budgets, marketers want to advertise in areas where their sales potential is best.

Even in local markets, geographic segmentation is important. For example, a local progressive politician might send a mailer only to precincts where voters typically support liberal causes, and a local retail store rarely draws customers from outside a fairly limited *trading area*.

Demographic Segmentation
Demographic segmentation is a way to define groups by their statistical characteristics: gender, age, ethnicity, education, occupation, income, and other quantifiable factors. For example, research shows that some people who identify themselves as "strongly Hispanic" tend to be very loyal to certain brands. And, as Exhibit 4-4 reveals, the number of Americans with Hispanic ancestry is growing at a rate much faster than the overall population. The result is a surge in advertising dollars allocated to Hispanic media. The Hispanic

advertising industry is outpacing all other sectors of advertising, growing four times faster and recently topping $5 billion.[15] Many blue-chip advertisers, such as Procter & Gamble, AT&T, McDonald's, and General Motors, now aim a significant portion of their advertising specifically at this trillion-dollar market.

Demographics are often combined with geographic segmentation to select target markets for advertising. This is called **geodemographic segmentation**. Geodemographic segmentation takes segmentation by place to a finer level by incorporating information down to the level of zip codes, neighborhoods, or parts of a city or town. It capitalizes on the fact that two adjacent neighborhoods my differ significantly in the number of families, average age of a resident, income level, ethnicity, and so on.

Mosaic, Experian's geodemographic segmentation tool, classifies the population into groups or segments, according to their demographic and lifestyle traits right down to individual households. This provides advertisers with a complete picture of their audience based on their offline traits and online behavior, providing the insights needed to direct their advertising in a much more targeted way.[16]

JCPenney, for example, discovered that its Sandra Salcedo line of clothing for Hispanic women sold well in Texas and Northern California stores but not in heavily Mexican American Los Angeles, where urban influences hold greater sway. In other words, people's lives are influenced by their environment as well as by their ethnicity.[17]

As people age, their responsibilities and incomes change, and so do their interests in various product categories (see Exhibit 4-5).

Demographic segmentation has long been understood in the fast-food industry. Once stigmatized as unsanitary meat fit only for poor people, chains such as White Castle and McDonald's used advertising to change the hamburger's image, fashioning it into the national cuisine by the 1950s.[18] Now, children are McDonald's primary target consumers. Decades of ads for Happy Meals have made an impression. Among fictional characters, Ronald McDonald's cultural penetration is surpassed only by Santa Claus: 96 percent of schoolchildren in the United States

Age	Name of Age Group	Merchandise Purchased
0–5	Young children	Baby food, toys, nursery furniture, children's wear
6–19	Schoolchildren and teenagers	Clothing, sporting goods, smartphones, iTunes, school supplies, fast food, soft drinks, candy, cosmetics, movies
20–34	Young adults	Cars, furniture, housing, food and beer, clothing, diamonds, home entertainment equipment, recreational equipment, purchases for younger age segments
35–49	Younger middle-aged	Larger homes, better cars, second cars, new furniture, computers, recreational equipment, jewelry, clothing, food and wine
50–64	Older middle-aged	Recreational items, purchases for young marrieds and infants, travel
65 and older	Senior adults	Medical services, travel, pharmaceuticals, purchases for younger age groups

can identify the yellow-jumpsuited clown.[19] Against this giant's brand value and advertising expenditures, competitors have returned to the hamburger's traditional consumer, the young male. In the segment where McDonald's is slightly weaker, Five Guys and Whattaburger intend to be strong.

In international markets, the demographics of many populations are changing rapidly. From China to India to Brazil to Poland, middle-class life is becoming available to more people. This emerging middle class has an apparently insatiable appetite for consumer goods—everything from HDTVs and tablets to

This Covergirl ad is clearly using psychographic segmentation. In appealing to a younger audience then it has in the past, the brand is communicating that the modern Covergirl user is active, athletic, and decidedly in control of her life.

Source: CoverGirl by Coty, Inc

GPS Navigator, as standard in all Mercedes-Benz models.

Changing demographics in many international markets open up new opportunities for advertisers. In Spain, the growing upper-middle class and the availability of good expressways enable Mercedes-Benz (www.mercedes-benz.com) to promote its navigation system in this very creative ad. The text reads "GPS Navigator is standard in all Mercedes-Benz models."

Source: Mercedes-Benz

smartphones, cars, and designer clothes.[20] Spending habits have shifted from buying necessities to purchasing lifestyle products. China has emerged as one of the world's fastest-growing advertising markets as companies try to reach that country's increasingly wealthy consumers. Although the COVID-19 pandemic lowered the nation's spending on ads, total Chinese ad spending was still expected to be an impressive $114 billion in 2020.[21]

Geographic and demographic data provide information about markets but little about the psychology of individuals. People in the same demographic or geographic segment may have widely differing product preferences and media habits. Rarely can demographic criteria alone predict purchase behavior.[22] That's why marketers developed *psychographics*.

Psychographic Segmentation

For certain products, appeals to emotions and cultural values may be persuasive. So some advertisers use **psychographic segmentation** to define consumer markets. With **psychographics**, marketers group people by their values, attitudes, personality, and lifestyle. This enables marketers to view people as individuals with feelings and inclinations. Then, they can classify them according to what they feel, what they believe, the way they live, and the products, services, and media they use.[23]

Perhaps the best-known psychographic classification system is VALS™, a product of Strategic Business Insights (SBI), a spinout of SRI International. VALS assigns consumers

psychographic segmentation Method of defining consumer markets based on psychological variables including values, attitudes, personality, and lifestyle.

psychographics The grouping of consumers into market segments on the basis of psychological makeup—values, attitudes, personality, and lifestyle.

primary motivation The pattern of attitudes and activities that help people reinforce, sustain, or modify their social and self-image. An understanding of the primary motivation of individuals helps advertisers promote and sell goods and services.

resources A term in the Values and Lifestyles (VALS) typology relating to the range of psychological, physical, demographic, and material capacities that consumers can draw upon. The resource axis includes education, income, self-confidence, health, eagerness to buy, and energy level.

▼**EXHIBIT 4–6** The Kantar's MindBase finds shared patterns of behavior.

MILLENNIALS Born 1979–1996	GEN X Born 1965–1978	BOOMERS Born 1946–1964	MATURES Born Before 1946
• 17% New Traditionalists	• 60% Pragmatic Pathfinder	• 30% Full Throttles	• 50% Tried and Trues
• 30% Ambitious Realists	• 40% Homefront Heros	• 53% Smooth Sailors	• 50% Golden Agers
• 31% Trail Blazers		• 18% Compassionate Creatives	
• 23% Omni Explorers			

to one of eight groups based on two dimensions: **primary motivation** and **resources**. According to SBI, individuals are primarily motivated to buy by one of three things: ideals (or basic principles), achievement (tangible markers of success or accomplishment), or self-expression (a desire for experiences or to take risks). In addition, people possess varying levels of resources, which include money, education, or self-confidence. Those with the fewest resources are placed near the bottom of the VALS typology, while those with the most are at the top.[24]

According to SBI, VALS is designed to help marketers identify a target market, what that market buys and does, and locate where the market lives. VALS can also suggest ways to communicate with the market based on their goals and resources, and can offer insights into why the target behaves as it does. The system has been applied to a variety of areas: new product development and design, target marketing, product positioning, advertising message development, and media planning, to name a few.[25] In one case, for example, a foreign car manufacturer used VALS to reposition its sports utility vehicle after its award-winning but ineffective television campaign failed to result in higher sales. Using VALS, the company targeted a new "rebellious" consumer group with a new campaign based on a "breaking the rules" theme. After making this adjustment, product sales increased 60 percent in six months.[26]

Several other classification systems have been developed to help marketers in the United States and worldwide target consumers based on their values, motivations, and lifestyles. These psychographic segmentation schemes include ValueScope from GfK Roper Consulting, BehaviorGraphics from Experian Simmons, and MindBase, a product offered by Kantar.

Kantar describes MindBase as a "generational attitudinal segmentation . . . projected onto a marketing database of 240+MM U.S.

adults for immediate activation on your CRM system and online and offline platforms." [27] To create its segments, Kantar combines generation (Millenials, Gen X, Boomers, and Matures) with demographic information, resulting in groups such as "Homefront heroes" and "Pragmatic Pathfinders," both from Gen X. Several MindBase consumer groups are shown in Exhibit 4–6.

How might marketers use psychographic segmentation schemes such as these? Recall our discussion about product utility. We argued that people often buy products in an effort to satisfy functional needs and psychological wants. Tools like VALS attempt to group people in terms of shared needs and wants.

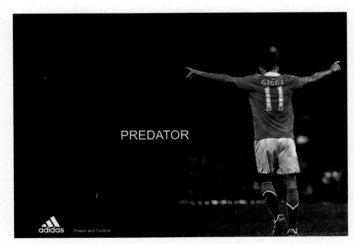

Ads for adidas (www.adidas.com) capture the attitude and lifestyle of its target market: athletic young people around the world who define themselves by their sporting achievements. In this ad featuring soccer player Ryan Giggs, adidas uses primary motivation to reinforce key attitudes and values.

Source: Adidas

Advocates of this approach believe that doing so provides both a more precise way of target marketing and a deeper understanding of what the target market is like.

An influential book, *The Tipping Point* by cultural observer Malcolm Gladwell, suggests another reason why advertisers may wish to psychologically segment consumers: some people are highly influential in the behaviors of others. By focusing on these influencers, advertisers can create consumption epidemics, that is, responses that spread quickly from the influence of a small group to a much larger group.

Gladwell believes that social epidemics are traceable to the actions of three types of people, whom he labels *Connectors*, *Mavens*, and *Salesmen*. Connectors are people with very wide social circles; they have the ability to bridge different social groups that would not ordinarily interact with one another. Mavens are people who spend the time and energy accumulating knowledge that most people simply can't be bothered to find out for themselves. They also love sharing this information. Connectors and Mavens are sources of information about new products, trends, and ideas, but the job of persuading people to embrace these things falls to Salesmen. Salesmen are people most of us find credible, trustworthy, and authoritative. Gladwell's analysis suggests that relatively small groups of people are very influential in affecting the consumption habits of much larger segments.[28]

Limitations of Consumer Segmentation Methods

Advocates of psychographic systems claim they help address the emotional factors that motivate consumers. However, for some products psychographics may offer little real value—especially because it oversimplifies consumer personalities and purchase behavior. Some typologies, such as VALS, are also criticized for being too complicated.[29]

Still, it's important for marketers to monitor and understand their customers. It helps them select target markets, create ads that match the attributes and image of their products with the types of consumers who use them, develop effective media plans, and allocate their advertising dollars wisely. If you are interested in developing your own segmentation scheme for a brand or company, see My Ad Campaign, "Segmenting the Audience."

Segmenting Business and Government Markets: Understanding Organizational Buying Behavior

Business markets (or *industrial markets*) include manufacturers, government agencies, wholesalers, retailers, banks, and institutions that buy goods and services to help them operate. These products may include raw materials, electronic components, mechanical parts, office equipment, vehicles, or services used in conducting their businesses. Many business marketers sell to resellers, such as retailers that resell to consumers. For example, much of Hardee's food is supplied by Siméus Foods International, a processing, production, and distribution conglomerate. Siméus's two plants produce and freeze menu items, such as hamburger and chicken patties, to the specifications of customers such as Hardee's and Denny's. The end product is resold by Hardee's with no mention of Siméus. Hardee's reselling contract with Coca-Cola, however, is a much more visible *brand partnership*; Coke products are often featured in Hardee's advertising.

Identifying target markets of prospective business customers is just as complex as identifying consumer markets. Many of the variables used to identify consumer markets can also be used for business markets—for example, geography and behavior (purchase occasion, benefits sought, user status, and usage rate).

Business markets also have special characteristics. They employ professional buyers and use systematic purchasing procedures. They may be concentrated geographically. And in any single market there may be only a small number of buyers.

Business Purchasing Procedures When businesspeople evaluate new products, they use a process far more complex and rigid than the consumer purchase process we describe in Chapter 5. Business marketers must design their advertising with this in mind.

Trade advertising is aimed not at consumers but at people who buy or influence business purchases. This ad for Corning encourages businesses to use their Gorilla Glass for their products. The work of the agency, Doremus, that produced this award-winning campaign can be seen here: www.doremus.com/work/casestudy/corning-capturing-the-brilliance-of-the-brand.

Source: Corning Incorporated

Large firms have purchasing departments that act as professional buyers. They evaluate the need for products, analyze proposed purchases, request competitive bids, seek approvals from users and managers, make requisitions, place orders, and supervise all product purchasing. While this structured purchase decision process implies a rational approach, research suggests that professional buyers often exhibit a willingness to pay a substantial premium for their favorite brand. The implication is that advertising may play a larger role in B2B marketing than previously thought.[30]

Making a sale in business markets can take weeks, months, or even years, especially to government agencies. Purchase decisions often depend on factors besides price or quality, among them product demonstrations, delivery time, terms of sale, and dependability. Marketers often emphasize these issues in advertising and promotional appeals.

Before deciding on a target market, business marketers should consider how the purchase decision process works among various segments. New companies, for instance, may want to target smaller firms where a purchase decision can be made quickly. Or they may use commissioned reps to call on the larger prospects that require more time. These decisions will dictate where ads should be placed.

Industrial Classification System

Industrial customers need different products, depending on their business. For example, apparel manufacturers such as Levi's are the main customers for buttons and zippers. Marketing managers need to focus their sales and advertising efforts on those firms that need their products.[31] The U.S. Census Bureau classifies all U.S. businesses—and collects and publishes industry statistics on them—using the **North American Industry Classification System (NAICS) codes**. Because the system was developed jointly with Canada and Mexico, there is consistency throughout North America.

NAICS organizes industries into 20 broad sectors such as mining, manufacturing, wholesale trade, and information. These are then subdivided into four hierarchical levels of classification, including sectors, subsectors, industry groups, industries, and finally 1,170 distinct U.S. industries. (See Exhibit 4-7 for a breakdown of NAICS codes in the information and wireless telecommunications industry.) The Census Bureau uses NAICS to offer marketers an abundance of information, such as the number of firms, sales volumes, and number of employees by geographic area. NAICS codes help companies segment markets and do research, and advertisers can obtain lists of companies in particular NAICS divisions for direct mailings.[32]

> **Professional buyers often exhibit a willingness to pay a substantial premium for their favorite brand.**

EXHIBIT 4-7 NAICS hierarchy and codes. A business marketer can use the NAICS codes to locate prospective companies in directories or in subscription databases.

Level	Code	Sector
Sector	51	Information
Subsector	513	Broadcasting and telecommunications
Industry group	5133	Telecommunications
Industry	51332	Wireless telecommunications carriers (except satellite)
U.S. industry	513321	Paging

Market Concentration Many countries' markets for industrial goods are concentrated in one region or several metropolitan areas. In the United States, for example, the industrial market is heavily concentrated in the Midwest, the South, and California (see Exhibit 4-8). Market concentration reduces the number of geographic targets for an advertiser.

Business marketers typically deal with fewer buyers than consumer marketers. Less than 7 percent of U.S. manufacturing establishments employ nearly 75 percent of all production workers and account for almost 80 percent of all manufacturing dollars.[33] Customer size is a critical issue for market segmentation. A firm may concentrate its marketing and advertising efforts on a few large customers, many smaller ones, or both.

Business marketers can also segment by end users. For example, a firm may develop software for one industry, such as banking, or for general use in a variety of industries. That decision, of course, affects advertising media decisions.

Aggregating Market Segments

Once marketers identify and locate broad markets with shared characteristics (behavioristic, geographic, demographic, or psychographic), they can proceed to the second step in the market segmentation process. This involves (1) selecting groups that have a mutual interest in the product's utility and (2) reorganizing and aggregating (combining) them into larger market segments based on their potential for sales and profit. Let's take a look at how this process might work for Levi Strauss & Co. in the U.S. market.

First, the company's management needs to know the **primary demand trend** of the total U.S. market for pants. This is the market potential for jeans and casual pants in various market areas across the country. To do this it uses a variety of *marketing research techniques* (discussed in Chapter 6). Then management must identify the needs, wants, and shared characteristics of the various groups within the casual apparel marketplace who live near the company's retail outlets. It may use the services of a large marketing information company such as Claritas, which collects data on purchasing behaviors and creates profiles of geographic markets across the country.

Claritas finds many prospective customers throughout the United States: students, blue-collar workers, young singles, professionals, homemakers, and so on. It then measures and analyzes households in each major retail area by demographic, lifestyle, and purchasing characteristics, sorts them into 66 geodemographic segments, and labels them with terms such as those in Exhibit 4-9: Big City Blues, Movers & Shakers, Country Squires, Pools & Patios, and the like. All of these people have apparel needs and many may be interested in the style, cachet, and durability of the Levi's brand.

▼ **EXHIBIT 4-8** The states in this map are represented in proportion to the value of their manufactured products.

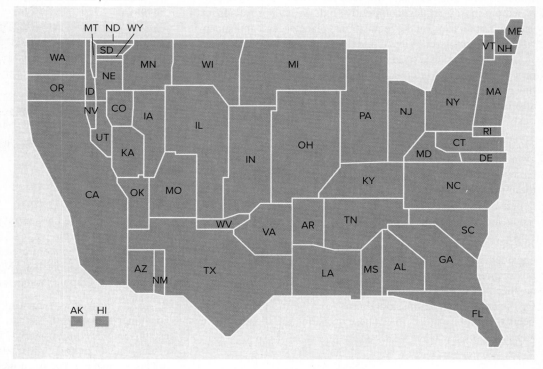

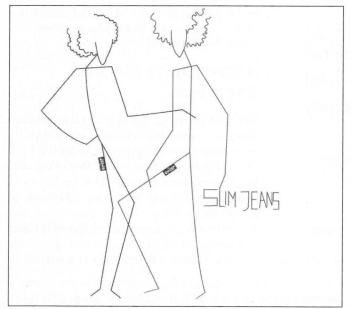

Levi's has introduced several product lines in an effort to satisfy the needs and wants of different consumer segments. In this seemingly simple ad, the style of slim jeans is communicated to a younger, more contemporary market segment.

Source: Levi Strauss & Co.

Selecting Groups Interested in Product Utility Levi Strauss next selects groups that would like and be able to afford the benefits of Levi's apparel—suitability for work or play, comfort, style, reasonable cost, durability, and so on. Groups interested in all these features make up the total potential market for Levi's clothes.

Part of the challenge of market segmentation is estimating the profits the company might realize if it (1) aims at the whole market or (2) caters only to specific segments. Apparel is a highly competitive market, but 10 percent of 1,000 is always larger than 90 percent of 100. So for Levi's, the target market must be a large market or it won't be profitable.[34]

Combining Groups to Build Target Market Segments The company needs to find groups that are relatively similar and offer good profit potential. Market data turn up many groups, and some, including middle-aged couples, seniors, and ethnically diverse young singles, as well as groups labeled New Empty Nest, Park Bench Seniors, and Low Rise Living, will not represent ideal prospects. Why exclude these segments? Each constitutes a little more than 1 percent of consumer households and has minimal retail or credit activity. For Levi's, they are not prime targets.

Other segments offer greater potential—young to middle-aged households with medium to high incomes and average to high retail activity. These include groups such as Movers & Shakers,

Bohemian Mix, and Home Sweet Home, each constituting nearly 2 percent of all households. By combining these groups with the young professionals in the Young Influentials and New Beginnings segments, Levi Strauss can target young to middle-aged people on their way up. Nationally, that amounts to nearly 20 million households. That's not everybody, but it's a large and potentially very profitable market segment. These prospects might like the style and comfort of Levi's 550s. They might also appreciate the tradition of a brand they know and trust. Levi's can expect that a well-conceived campaign will appeal to their particular needs, wants, and self-images.

my ad campaign

Segmenting the Audience [4]

What is the target market for your product? The answer to this question is rarely simple; thus your decision will require the application of strategic thinking. You will need to gather as much information from your client and from secondary sources as you can, focusing on the product's market, users, and the competition. The information you gather about the consumer in the My Ad Campaign from Chapter 6 will be important as well. And in some instances it may make sense to conduct primary research with current customers or with individuals who use competing products.

You may have the opportunity to offer counsel to your client about whether it is marketing to the right target market. Check to be sure before offering such advice; some clients may not wish to receive it. If the client is interested, consider whether there are underserved segments that offer sales or profit potential. For example, if your client is a local pizzeria located near campus, it may be focusing on attracting students. This is to be expected because students normally represent a sizable market in any college town. In addition, your client is doubtless using the timeworn strategy of attracting hungry, cash-strapped undergrads with messages that emphasize low prices, large servings, and coupons. But while students may represent a large market for pizza, there are probably dozens of other food businesses competing for this segment. If so, it might be smarter to refocus on a smaller but underserved segment, especially one that offers great profit potential. If your town lacks an upscale pizzeria that serves specialty pies, the client might be better served by improving its offerings and dining facility, raising prices, and promoting to nonstudents who would be willing to pay more for quality food.

Many advertisers find that it makes sense to segment on the basis of standard demographic characteristics such as age, gender, ethnicity, location, social class, or income level. Dividing your market according to product loyalty or product usage levels is also worth considering. Understanding your market with respect to psychographics and lifestyles can be incredibly valuable, especially later when you begin to develop the creative brief. Such data can be more difficult to obtain, however.

Defining the Target Market

	Your Client's Customers	The Competition's Customers	Nonusers
Demographics			
Age			
Gender			
Ethnicity/race			
Location/region			
Social class			
Income			
Education			
Behaviors			
Product usage (light, medium, heavy)			
Brand loyalty (loyal, switchers)			
Psychographics			
Principle-oriented			
Status-oriented			
Action-oriented			
Benefits Sought			
Low price			
Quality			

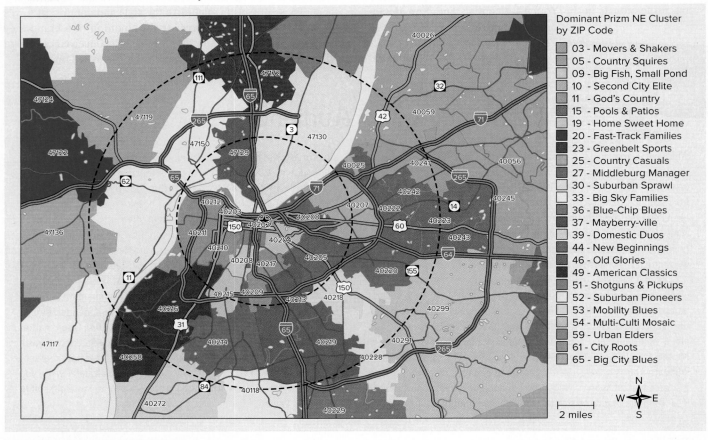

Dominant Prizm NE Cluster by ZIP Code

- 03 - Movers & Shakers
- 05 - Country Squires
- 09 - Big Fish, Small Pond
- 10 - Second City Elite
- 11 - God's Country
- 15 - Pools & Patios
- 19 - Home Sweet Home
- 20 - Fast-Track Families
- 23 - Greenbelt Sports
- 25 - Country Casuals
- 27 - Middleburg Manager
- 30 - Suburban Sprawl
- 33 - Big Sky Families
- 36 - Blue-Chip Blues
- 37 - Mayberry-ville
- 39 - Domestic Duos
- 44 - New Beginnings
- 46 - Old Glories
- 49 - American Classics
- 51 - Shotguns & Pickups
- 52 - Suburban Pioneers
- 53 - Mobility Blues
- 54 - Multi-Culti Mosaic
- 59 - Urban Elders
- 61 - City Roots
- 65 - Big City Blues

2 miles

Source: Claritas's Prizm NE Method. Claritas, LLC.

check yourself ✓

1. What is the marketer's goal in segmenting markets?

2. What characteristics are used in psychographic segmentation?

3. Why do marketers aggregate market segments?

LO4-3 Explain how defining a target market enhances marketing strategy.

THE TARGET MARKETING PROCESS

Once the market segmentation process is complete, a company can proceed to the **target marketing** process. This will determine the content, look, and feel of its advertising.

Target Market Selection

The first step in target marketing is assessing which of the newly created segments offer the greatest profit potential and which can be most successfully penetrated. The company designates one or more segments as a **target market**—the consumers the company wishes to appeal to, design products for, and tailor its marketing activities toward.[35] It may designate other segments as secondary target markets and aim some IMC resources at them.

Let's look at the most likely target market for loose-fitting jeans: young to middle-aged customers with moderate to high income and education who like the style, comfort, and fashion. This group represents a large percentage of the apparel market, and if won, will generate substantial profits. Levi's offers what these prospects need and want: the style and fashion of the jeans updated to be more comfortable for the adult body.

But the middle-class, comfort-oriented segment is not enough for Levi's to be profitable, so it also caters to at least two other important market segments. In response to the enormous number of consumers who shop at giant, low-cost retailers such as Walmart and Target, Levi's has a value-priced line,

target marketing The process by which an advertiser focuses its marketing efforts on a target market.

target market The market segment or group within the market segment toward which all marketing activities will be directed.

product concept The consumer's perception of a product as a "bundle" of utilitarian and symbolic values that satisfy functional, social, psychological, and other wants and needs.

marketing mix Four elements, called the 4Ps (product, price, place, and promotion), that every company has the option of adding, subtracting, or modifying in order to create a desired marketing strategy.

four Ps (4Ps) Product, price, place, and promotion used by every company.

[[The target market is] those consumers the company wishes to appeal to, design products for, and tailor its marketing activities toward.]

Levi's Signature. The Signature collection appeals to budget-conscious families with children such as Family Thrifts and Big Sky Families. And at the top end, Levi's met the needs of young, twenty-something, image-conscious consumers with its Warhol Factory X Levi's jeans. The line retails for $250 and is sold at high-end retailers such as Nordstrom.

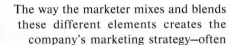

Source: Redfx/Alamy Stock Photo

The Marketing Mix: A Strategy for Matching Products to Markets

When a company defines its target market, it knows exactly where to focus its attention and resources. Marketers and advertisers generally try to shape their basic product into a total **product concept**: the consumer's perception of a product or service as a bundle of utilitarian and symbolic values that satisfy functional, social, psychological, and other wants and needs. Companies have many strategic options they can employ to enhance the product/service concept and make sales. The company can design special features for its target market (such as certain colors or special sizes). It can establish proper pricing. And it can determine the criteria for locating stores or dealers and prepare the most convincing advertising messages.

Marketers categorize these options under four headings: (1) *product*, (2) *price*, (3) *distribution*, and (4) *communication*.[36]

The way the marketer mixes and blends these different elements creates the company's marketing strategy—often called the **marketing mix**. For convenience, marketing educator E. Jerome McCarthy developed a mnemonic device to help recall these four functions: *product, price, place*, and *promotion*—or the **four Ps (4Ps)**.[37]

The 4Ps are a simple way to remember the basic elements of the marketing mix. But within each element are many marketing activities a company can use to fine-tune its product concept and improve sales. Advertising, for example, is one instrument of the communication (promotion) element. The remainder of this chapter focuses on the relationship between advertising and the other elements of the marketing mix.

check yourself ✓

1. What is the relationship between the target market and the 4Ps?

LO4-4 List the elements of the marketing mix and the role advertising plays in each.

ADVERTISING AND THE PRODUCT ELEMENT

In developing a marketing mix, marketers generally start with the **product element**. Major activities typically include the way the product is designed and classified, positioned, branded, and packaged. Each of these affects the way the product is advertised.

Product Life Cycles

Marketers theorize that just as humans pass through stages in life from infancy to old age, products also pass through a **product life cycle** (see Exhibit 4–10).[38] A product's place in the life cycle influences the target market selected and the marketing mix used. There are four major stages in the product life cycle: *introduction*, *growth*, *maturity*, and *decline*.

When a company creates a new product category, nobody knows about it. For example, Apple's introduction of the iPad created a new category: the tablet. Through market segmentation, the company will try to identify those prospects who are known to be **early adopters**—people or organizations willing to try new things—and begin promoting the new category directly to them. The idea is to stimulate **primary demand**—consumer demand for the whole product category, not just the company's own brand.

During the **introductory phase** of any new product category, the company incurs costs for educating customers, building widespread dealer distribution, and encouraging demand. It must advertise heavily at this stage to establish a position as a market leader and to gain a large share of market before the growth stage begins. Because Apple is a strong company with brands that people love, many consumers were willing to try the iPad. Less well-known companies face a steeper challenge.

Apple's challenge was getting consumers to demand the product through the channels of distribution. Consumers could order the iPad online at the Apple website, but Apple also wanted other retailers, such as Best Buy, to carry the iPad. Advertising and IMC that focuses on consumers is meant to motivate potential buyers to demand a product from retailers. This approach is called a **pull strategy** because marketers hope that consumer demand will "pull" the product through the distribution chain. Conversely, Apple wanted to be sure retailers would be anxious to stock up on this new and unfamiliar product. Promotional efforts aimed at retailers or other distributors is called a **push strategy**. Push strategies target distributors rather than consumers and encourage them to stock, display, and advertise the product.

When sales volume begins to rise rapidly, the product enters the **growth stage**. This period is characterized by rapid *market expansion* as more and more customers, stimulated by mass advertising and word of mouth, make their first, second, and third purchases. Competitors jump into the market, but the company that established the early leadership position usually reaps the biggest rewards. As a percentage of total sales, advertising expenditures should decrease, and individual firms will realize their first substantial profits. The iPad proved both popular and profitable, even as competing products using Microsoft's and Google's operating systems were introduced.

▼ **EXHIBIT 4–10** A product's life cycle curve may vary, depending on the product category, but almost every product or service passes through these stages. Marketing objectives and strategies change as the product proceeds from one stage to the next.

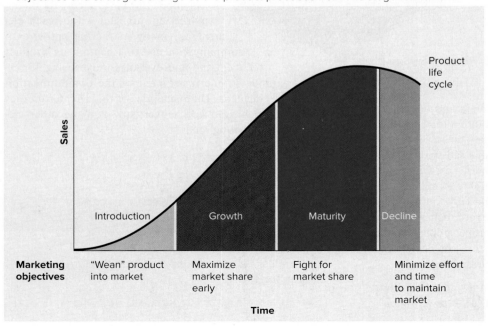

push strategy
Marketing, advertising, and sales promotion activities aimed at getting products into the dealer pipeline and accelerating sales by offering inducements to dealers, retailers, and salespeople.

growth stage The period in a product life cycle that is marked by market expansion as more and more customers make their first purchases while others are already making their second and third purchases.

maturity stage That point in the product life cycle when the market has become saturated with products, the number of new customers has dwindled, and competition is most intense.

selective demand Consumer demand for the particular advantages of one brand over another.

decline stage The stage in the product life cycle when sales begin to decline due to obsolescence, new technology, or changing consumer tastes.

position The way in which a product is ranked in the consumer's mind by the benefits it offers, by the way it is classified or differentiated from the competition, or by its relationship to certain target markets.

Glide dental floss exists in a mature product category. To differentiate itself from competing floss products, the brand emphasizes its smoothness and ease of use in tight spaces between teeth.

Source: The Procter & Gamble Company

In the **maturity stage**, the marketplace becomes saturated with competing products and the number of new customers dwindles, so industry sales reach a plateau. Competition intensifies and profits diminish. Companies increase their promotional efforts but emphasize **selective demand** to impress customers with the subtle advantages of their particular brand. At this stage, companies can increase sales only at the expense of competitors. The strategies of market segmentation, product positioning, and price promotion become more important during this shakeout period as weak companies fall by the wayside and those remaining fight for market share.

Late in the maturity stage, companies may have to scramble to extend the product's life cycle. Without innovation or marketing support, name brands eventually see their sales erode. For example, by 2016, sales of tablets were leveling. Apple, in response, developed several variations of the iPad,

including the mini and the Pro, to cater to increasingly selective consumer demand. Professor Brian Wansink, who directs the Brand Lab at the University of Illinois Urbana–Champaign, suggests that the reason many old brands die is less for life cycle reasons and more for marketing neglect. He points out that aging brands often pack plenty of brand equity. The challenge for marketers is to determine which brands can be revitalized and then decide how to do it.

If they're not revitalized, products will finally enter the **decline stage** because of obsolescence, new technology, or changing consumer tastes. At this point, companies may cease all promotion and phase the products out quickly, as in the case of record turntables and albums, or let them fade slowly away with minimal advertising.

At a time when sport utility vehicles were so popular that competing companies all seemed to be offering the same benefits, Jeep (www.jeep.com) positioned itself as the "only one" to go anywhere on the planet. Positioning is important in tight markets to help differentiate similar products.

Source: Jeep and FCA US LLC

Product Classifications

The way a company classifies its product is important in defining both the product concept and the marketing mix. As Exhibit 4–11 shows, there are many ways to classify tangible goods: by markets, by the purchasing habits of buyers, by the consumption rate or degree of tangibility, or by physical attributes.

Product Positioning

Once an advertising person understands the product's stage in the life cycle, how it's classified, and how it's currently perceived by the marketplace, the first strategic decision can be made: how to **position** the product. The basic goal of positioning strategy is to own a concept that establishes the product in the prospect's mind. Levi's owns "jeans" (or at least they did for a long time).

By Market	By Rate of Consumption and Tangibility	By Purchasing Habits	By Physical Description
Consumer goods Products and services we use in our daily lives (food, clothing, furniture, cars). **Industrial goods** Products used by companies for the purpose of producing other products (raw materials, agricultural commodities, machinery, tools, equipment).	**Durable goods** Tangible products that are long-lasting and infrequently replaced (cars, trucks, refrigerators, furniture). **Nondurable goods** Tangible products that may be consumed in one or a few uses and usually need to be replaced at regular intervals (food, soap, gasoline, oil). **Services** Activities, benefits, or satisfaction offered for sale (travel, haircuts, legal and medical services, massages).	**Convenience goods** Purchases made frequently with a minimum of effort (cigarettes, food, newspapers). **Shopping goods** Infrequently purchased items for which greater time is spent comparing price, quality, style, warranty (furniture, cars, clothing, tires). **Specialty goods** Products with such unique characteristics that consumers will make special efforts to purchase them even if they're more expensive (designer clothes, luxury cars, fancy restaurants). **Unsought goods** Products that potential customers don't yet want (life insurance, funeral services, fire extinguisher) or don't know they can buy (new products), so they don't search them out.	**Packaged goods** Cereals, soft drinks, cleaning products, and so forth. **Hard goods** Furniture, appliances. **Soft goods** Clothing, bedding. **Services** Intangible products.

BMW owns "performance," Maytag owns "reliability," Apple owns "beautiful design, " and Jeep owns "rugged." The ad on the previous page illustrates well Jeep's slogan, "Go anywhere. Do anything." By developing a unique position for the brand in the consumer's mind, the marketer helps the consumer remember the brand and what it stands for.

Products may be positioned in different ways. Xerox repositioned itself as "the Document Company," moving from the narrow, crowded copier market to the broader, growing document-handling market. With one stroke, Xerox redefined the business it is in, differentiated itself from competition, and created a new number one position for itself.[39]

Product Differentiation

Product differentiation calls attention to product differences that appeal to the preferences of distinct target markets. In advertising, nothing is more important than being able to tell prospects truthfully that your product is different or unique. Unfortunately, in response to increased competitive pressures, burgeoning innovation and technology, and various constraints on distribution, new-product development cycles have shortened dramatically. As a result, many brand managers find themselves launching new products that are "only 85 percent there." So it's not surprising that many "new" products fail to impress consumers. (See Exhibit 4–12.)

▼ **EXHIBIT 4-12** What's new? Not much. Consumers didn't think these products were as new as they claimed to be, as indicated by the grades awarded.

Product	New and Different	Purchase Probability	Price/Value	Overall Grade
Airwick Botanicals	F	A	A	B
Mr. Clean Glass & Surface Cleaner	F	A	A	B
Spic & Span with Bleach	F	A	B	B
Aspirin-Free Bayer Select	F	B	B	C
Sugar Twin Plus low-calorie sweetener	F	B	A	C
Lady Power Clear Roll-On antiperspirant	F	B	A	C

> [Nothing is more important than being able to tell prospects truthfully that your product is different.]

Imperceptible differences are important, but can be difficult to communicate to consumers. Great ads communicate these differences and show how they address needs and wants of consumers, even when doing so requires nuance. This ad from Gastrina does accomplish this effectively.
Source: Dabur

Differences between products that are readily apparent to the consumer are called **perceptible differences**. Snapple, for example, gained popularity on the basis of its unique ingredients and taste.[40] **Hidden differences** are not so readily apparent. Diet Mountain Dew may look and taste the same as regular Mountain Dew, but it is differentiated by the use of artificial sweeteners, which significantly reduce the calorie content of the beverage. Hidden differences can't be seen, but advertising can let consumers know about them.

For many product classes, such as aspirin, salt, gasoline, packaged foods, liquor, and financial services, advertising can create **induced differences**. An induced difference is one that cannot be established perceptually, nor does it exist in imperceptible but real product attributes. Instead, it is a matter of consumer perception. How does Coke differ from Pepsi? How does the iPhone differ from the Samsung Galaxy? Some might argue in no significant way (much as that might shock a fanatic fan of one of these products). Indeed, the immense loyalty that each of these brands inspires testifies to the power of **branding**. Brand loyalty is created through the accumulation of consistent advertising campaigns, favorable publicity, special-event sponsorship, and good word of mouth.[41]

Product Branding

The most important way that any product can differentiate itself from competing products is through the power of a **brand**—that

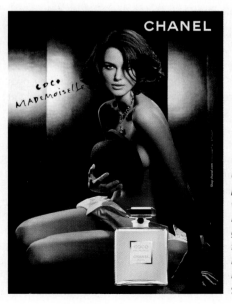

Chanel is one of the top perfume brands in the world. To reinforce its image of luxury and glamour, Chanel ads feature stars such as Nicole Kidman and Keira Knightley.
Source: Chanel S.A.

> ## Advertising . . . is much more effective if it exploits the brand's positioning.

combination of name, words, symbols, or design that identifies the product and its source. Without brands, consumers couldn't tell one product from another, and advertising them would be nearly impossible.

A manufacturer may establish an **individual brand** for each product it makes. Procter & Gamble, for example, markets its laundry detergents under the individual brand names Tide, Gain, Cheer, and Era. P&G promotes to a distinct target market for each product and has created a separate personality and image for each brand. However, this strategy is very costly.

On the other hand, a company might use a **family brand** and market different products under the same umbrella name. When Heinz promotes its ketchup, it hopes to help its relishes too. This decision may be cost-effective, but one weak product in a line can hurt the whole family.

Because it is so expensive for manufacturers to market **national brands** (also called *manufacturer's brands*), some companies use a *private-labeling* strategy. They manufacture the product and sell it to resellers (distributors or dealers) who put their own brand name on the product. **Private labels** are typically sold at lower prices in retail stores and include such familiar names as Kenmore, Craftsman, and DieHard (Sears), Kirkland (Costco), 365 (Whole Foods), Lucerne (Safeway), and Great Value (Walmart). The responsibility for creating brand image and familiarity with private label brands rests with the distributor or retailer, who is also the principal benefactor if the brand is successful.

Branding decisions are critical because the brands a company owns may be its most important capital asset. Imagine the value of owning a brand name such as Coca-Cola, Nike, Porsche, or Levi's. *Bloomberg Businessweek* ranks Coca-Cola as the most valuable brand in the world, followed by Microsoft, IBM, GE,

Nokia, and Toyota.[42] Some companies pay a substantial fee for the right to use another company's brand name. Thus, there are **licensed brands** such as Sunkist vitamins, Coca-Cola clothing, Porsche sunglasses, and Mickey Mouse watches.

The Role of Branding

Brands offer consumers instant recognition and identification. They also promise consistent, reliable standards of quality, taste, size, or even psychological satisfaction, which adds value to the product. In one survey, 44 percent of consumers ranked brand name as the most important factor when making a major electronics purchase. Price, by the way, ranked second.[43]

Brands are built on differences in images, meanings, and associations. It's up to manufacturers to differentiate their products clearly and deliver value competitively. The product has to taste better, or get clothes cleaner, or be more environmentally friendly.[44] Advertising for an established brand, particularly a

The world's most valuable brand, for the third year in a row, is Amazon (www.amazon.com). How does Amazon use color, design, and simplicity to make its brand so recognizable? What comes to mind when you think about Amazon as a brand, and how do those thoughts compare with the ones you have for other retail brands?

rvlsoft/Shutterstock

well-differentiated one, is much more effective if it exploits the brand's positioning.[45] Ideally, when consumers see a brand on the shelf, they instantly comprehend the brand's promise and have confidence in its quality. The goal is *brand loyalty*—because it serves both the consumer and the advertiser. For the consumer, it reduces shopping time. For the advertiser, it builds **brand equity**, the totality of what consumers, distributors, dealers—even competitors—feel and think about the brand over an extended period of time. In short, it's the value of the brand's assets.

Strong brand equity offers a host of blessings to a marketer: customer loyalty, price inelasticity, long-term profits. A loyal customer can be nine times as profitable as a disloyal one.[46] But building brand equity requires time and money. Brand value and

Apple's product packaging is so beloved people record opening a new box and then post the experience online, a practice known as unboxing. Apple's products inspire great loyalty among the brand's users. How does the packaging and the experience of opening an Apple package complement the brand's image? What does Apple's careful consideration of the user experience say about the company?

Source: DomCritelli/Shutterstock

preference drive market share, but market share and brand loyalty are usually won by the advertisers who spend the most. Charlotte Beers, the former head of J. Walter Thompson, believes companies must maintain consistency in their message by integrating all their marketing communications—from packaging and advertising to sales promotion and publicity—to maintain and reinforce the brand's personality and avoid mistakes such as changing the distinctive color of a Ryder rental truck.[47]

Product Packaging

The product's package is a component of the product element that can determine the outcome of retail shelf competition. In fact, packaging may be a particular brand's one differential advantage—and it's the marketer's last chance to communicate at the point of sale. Package designers (who sometimes work in agencies) must make the package exciting, appealing, and at the same time functional. The four considerations in package design are *identification*; *containment, protection, and convenience*; *consumer appeal*; and *economy*. These functions may even become **copy points**—copywriting themes—in the product's advertising.

ADVERTISING AND THE PRICE ELEMENT

As we all know, the **price element** of the marketing mix influences consumer perceptions of a brand. Companies that don't compete on price typically use image advertising to create a particular perception of the company or personality for the brand. Companies that are more price-competitive may regularly use sale advertising, clearance advertising, or loss-leader advertising.

Key Factors Influencing Price

Companies typically set their prices based on market demand for the product, costs of production and distribution, competition, and corporate objectives. Interestingly, though, a company often has relatively few options for determining its price strategy, depending on the desired product concept.

Marketers believe that consumers are often less concerned with a product's actual price than with its perceived price relative to competitors. Many premium brands, such as L'Oréal, tout the fact that they cost more. Setting a high price to make a product seem more valuable is an example of **psychological pricing**.

Retailers frequently focus on value pricing as a way of attracting consumers. One key to Best Buy's success in a challenging retail environment has been its focus on offering quality technologies at attractive prices. Letting consumers know they can save and get their merchandise quickly is a message stressed in the company's ads.
Source: Best Buy Co., Inc.

Advertising conveys information about both price and how much price should matter in choosing a brand. This ad for Suave, a value-priced personal care brand, suggests the consumer can "Say yes to beautiful hair without paying the price."
Source: Suave by Unilever United States

Image advertising may be used to justify the higher price. The important thing is that the price be consistent with the brand image; you can't charge a Rolex price for a Timex watch. And similarly, the brand's advertising must be consistent with its pricing strategy.

ADVERTISING AND THE DISTRIBUTION (PLACE) ELEMENT

Before the first ad can be created, the **place (or distribution) element** must be decided. It is important for marketers to understand that the method of distribution, like the price, must be consistent with the brand's image. People will not pay Nordstrom prices at Target.

Companies use two basic methods of distribution: *direct* or *indirect*.

Direct Distribution

When companies sell directly to end users or consumers, they use **direct distribution**. Avon, for example, employs sales reps who sell directly to consumers. Medical equipment suppliers and insurance companies often sell and distribute their products and services directly to customers without the use of wholesalers or retailers. In these cases, the advertising burden is carried entirely by the manufacturer.

An interesting method of direct distribution today is **network marketing** (also called *multilevel marketing*), in which individuals act as independent distributors for a manufacturer or private-label marketer. These people sign up friends and relatives to consume the company's products and recruit others to join. Through a gradual, word-of-mouth process, they form a "buying club" of independent distributors who buy the products wholesale direct from the company, use them, and tout them to more and more friends and acquaintances.

The Internet may be the ultimate direct distribution vehicle. As we will discuss in Chapter 12, websites allow marketers such as Dell and even artists like those on Etsy to make direct contact with their customers, develop interactive relationships, and consummate the sale of their products or services, all at a lower cost than any other method. As consumers become more comfortable buying online, services such as AirBnB and Uber have transformed vacation lodging and transportation, respectively.

Indirect Distribution

Manufacturers usually don't sell directly to end users or consumers. Most companies market their products through a *distribution channel* that includes a network of *resellers*. A **reseller** (informally called a *middleman*) is the entity that operates between the producer and the consumer or industrial purchaser. It deals in trade rather than production.[48] Resellers include both wholesalers and retailers, as well as manufacturers' representatives, brokers, jobbers, and distributors. A **distribution channel** comprises all the firms and individuals that take responsibility for the product as it moves from the producer to the consumer.

The advertising a company uses depends on the product's method of distribution. Much of the advertising we see is not prepared or paid for by the manufacturer, but by the distributor or retailer.

An important part of the marketing strategy is determining the amount of coverage necessary for a product. Procter & Gamble, for example, distributes Crest toothpaste to virtually every supermarket and discount, drug, and variety store. Other products might need only one dealer for every 50,000 people. Consumer goods manufacturers traditionally use one of three distribution strategies: *intensive*, *selective*, or *exclusive*.

Intensive Distribution Soft drinks, candy, Timex watches, and other convenience goods are available at every possible location because of **intensive distribution**. In fact, consumers can buy them with a minimum of effort. The profit on each unit is usually very low, but the volume of sales is high. The sales burden is usually carried by the manufacturer's national advertising. Ads in trade magazines *push* the product into the retail "pipeline," and in mass media they stimulate consumers to *pull* the products through the pipeline. As a manufacturer modifies its strategy to more push or more pull, special promotions may be directed at the trade or at consumers to build brand volume.

Selective Distribution By limiting the number of outlets through **selective distribution**, manufacturers can cut their distribution and promotion costs. Many hardware tools are sold

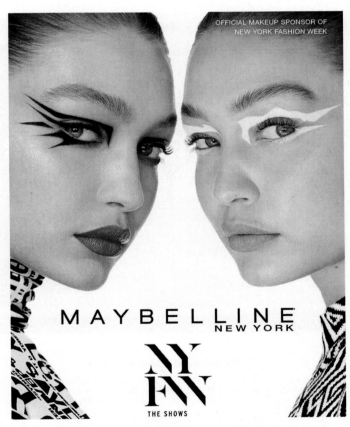

Maybelline utilizes selective distribution, and its ads convey style and quality, and by implication, higher prices. In contrast to the Suave ad you saw earlier, this ad suggests that to get the best value in a hair care product, the consumer must be prepared to pay more. Or as the saying goes, you get what you pay for.
Source: Maybelline New York

cooperative (co-op) advertising The sharing of advertising costs by the manufacturer and the distributor or retailer. The manufacturer may repay 50 or 100 percent of the dealer's advertising costs or some other amount based on sales.

exclusive distribution The strategy of limiting the number of wholesalers or retailers who can sell a product in order to gain a prestige image, maintain premium prices, or protect other dealers in a geographic region.

vertical marketing system (VMS) A system in which the main members of a distribution channel—producer, wholesaler, and retailer—work together as a cooperative group to meet consumer needs.

selectively through home-improvement centers and hardware stores. Automobile manufacturers limit the number of dealers that can sell their cars in each market. Levi Strauss sells through better department and chain stores. Manufacturers may use national advertising, but the sales burden is normally carried by the retailer. The manufacturer may share part of the retailer's advertising costs through a **cooperative (co-op) advertising** program, as we discussed in Chapter 3. For example, a Levi's retailer may receive substantial allowances from the manufacturer for advertising Levi's clothing in its local area. In return, the retailer agrees to advertise and display the clothing prominently.

Exclusive Distribution Some manufacturers grant **exclusive distribution** rights to a wholesaler or retailer in one geographic region. For example, a small city is not likely to have more than one Jaguar dealer. This is also common in high fashion, major appliances, and furniture lines. What is lost in market coverage is often gained in the ability to maintain a prestige image and premium prices. Exclusive distribution agreements also force manufacturers and retailers to cooperate closely in advertising and promotion programs.

Vertical Marketing Systems: The Growth of Franchising

To be efficient, members of a distribution channel need to cooperate closely with one another. This need gave rise to the **vertical marketing system (VMS)**, a system in which the main members of a distribution channel—producer, wholesaler, and retailer—work together as a cooperative group to meet consumer needs. This contrasts with conventional marketing

SONIC is Loved Coast to Coast

SONIC® has one of the strongest brand names in the country, with millions of devoted fans. Our ongoing marketing campaigns continue to fuel the demand for new SONIC locations in markets where we have yet to expand.

LEARN MORE >

A Forward Looking Brand

SONIC is as much a technology company today as it is a leading QSR brand. From our interactive menu boards, to our POS system, mobile apps and online delivery platforms, SONIC is a high tech business.

LEARN MORE >

The vertical marketing system gave rise to a number of successful business plans, such as franchising, in which franchisees pay a fee and operate under the guidelines of a parent company. Many Sonic restaurants are owned and operated by local business people who serve the unique needs of their community. The partnerships in vertical marketing serve the needs of both the local operator, who gains instant brand recognition, and the company, which supplies training, equipment, and food to the restaurants. What are some other businesses in your community that operate in a vertical marketing system?
Source: Inspire Brands

> ## IT IS CRITICAL THAT [ADVERTISING PEOPLE] UNDERSTAND HOW TO BLEND ALL THE TOOLS INTO AN INTEGRATED MARKETING COMMUNICATIONS PROGRAM.

systems in which producers, wholesalers, and retailers are separate businesses that are all trying to maximize their profits.[49]

There are three types of vertical marketing systems: corporate, administered, and contractual. In a corporate VMS, one company owns multiple levels of the distribution or production channel. An example would be a company such as Apple, which has its own retail stores as well as designing and manufacturing the products sold in those retail stores. An administered VMS is one in which one member of the production and distribution chain is dominant and calls the shots. An example of this type of system would be a large retailer such as Walmart, which dictates terms to its suppliers.[50]

A contractual VMS involves a formal agreement between the various levels of the distribution or production channel to coordinate the overall process. One type of contractual VMS is a **retail cooperative**, in which a group of independent retailers buy from a jointly owned wholesaler. ACE Hardware is an example of a retail cooperative. Another type of contractual VMS is a *franchise*. For the last quarter century, the greatest growth has been in **franchising**—such as McDonald's or Supercuts—in which retail dealers (or *franchisees*) pay a fee to operate under the guidelines and direction of the parent company or manufacturer (the *franchisor*). It's estimated that more than 40 percent of all retail sales in the United States are made through franchise outlets. There are more than 3,000 franchise businesses operating around the world and more than 759,000 establishments in the United States today are members of a franchise.[51]

Franchising and other vertical marketing systems offer both manufacturers and retailers numerous advantages, not the least of which are centralized coordination of marketing efforts and substantial savings and continuity in advertising. Perhaps most important is consumer recognition: The moment a new McDonald's opens, the franchisee has instant customers. Moreover, a single newspaper ad can promote all of a chain's retailers in a particular trading area.

Many marketers find that franchising is the best way to introduce their services into global markets. Subway, for example, is one of the fastest-growing franchise operations in the world with a total of nearly 40,000 stores in 102 countries. *Entrepreneur* reports the top five fastest-growing franchises as of 2019 were Taco Bell, Dunkin', Jan-Pro, Orange Theory Fitness, and N2 Publishing.[52]

ADVERTISING AND THE PROMOTION (COMMUNICATION) ELEMENT

Following decisions about product, price, and distribution, a company can plan its marketing communications, of which advertising is just one component. The **promotion,** or **communication, element** includes all marketing-related communications between the seller and the buyer.

Marketing communications (or *marcom*) refers to all the planned messages that companies and organizations use to support their marketing objectives and strategies. In addition to advertising, major marketing communication tools include *personal selling*, *sales promotion*, *direct marketing*, and *public* *relations activities.* The extent to which an organization uses any or all of these tools depends on its marketing needs.

Each marketing communication tool offers particular opportunities and benefits to the marketer. In Chapters 15 and 16 we discuss how these tools can best be integrated into the *marketing mix.* Advertising experts must understand how to blend all the tools into an integrated marketing communications program.

For creating brand awareness, familiarity, and image, as well as for reinforcing prior purchase decisions, advertising is the communications tool of choice for many products. The following factors are particularly important for advertising success:

- Strong primary demand trend.
- Potential for significant product differentiation.
- Hidden qualities highly important to consumers.
- Opportunity to use strong emotional appeals.
- Substantial funds available to support advertising.

Where these conditions exist, companies spend large amounts on advertising, and the ratio of advertising to sales dollars is often quite high. For completely undifferentiated products, such as sugar, salt, and other raw materials or commodities, advertising is usually less important and the other marketing mix elements play a more significant role.

THE MARKETING MIX IN PERSPECTIVE

With the target market designated and the elements of the marketing mix determined, the company has a complete product concept and a strategic basis for marketing to that target. Now it can formalize its strategies and tactics in a written marketing and advertising plan. As part of the planning process, companies use marketing and advertising research. We will discuss this in Chapter 6 before dealing with the formal planning process in Chapter 7. But first we'll examine the process of human communication and some theories of consumer behavior.

check yourself ✓

1. How does a product's stage in the product life cycle affect the way the it's advertised?

2. What are the benefits of a strong brand?

3. What is the relationship of advertising and the marketing mix?

ENDNOTES

1. Axe Ads, http://axeads.blogspot.com.

2. Jeff Hirsch, "Reinvigorating the 'Solid Citizen' Brand," *The Right Brain Studio*, July 11, 2011, www.therightbrainstudio.com/reinvigorating-the-%E2%80%9Csolid-citizen%E2%80%9D-brand.

3. "Old Spice: The Man Your Man Could Smell Like," www.youtube.com/watch?v=owGykVbfgUE.

4. Todd Wasserman, "How Old Spice Revived a Campaign That No One Wanted to Touch," *Mashable.com*, November 1, 2011, http://mashable.com/2011/11/01/old-spice-campaign.

5. Todd Wasserman, "How Old Spice Revived a Campaign That No One Wanted to Touch," *Mashable.com*, November 1, 2011, http://mashable.com/2011/11/01/old-spice-campaign.

6. William Perrault, Jr., Joseph Cannon, and E. Jerome McCarthy, *Basic Marketing: A Marketing Strategy Planning Approach* (Burr Ridge, IL: McGraw-Hill Education, 2018).

7. U.S. Bureau of Labor Statistics, "Consumer Expenditures 2018," www.bls.gov/news.release/cesan.nr0.htm.

8. "U.S. Digital B2B Ad Spending, 2015–2019," *EMarketer*, December, 2018, www.emarketer.com/content/us-b2b-digital-advertising-trends.

9. Marc Resnick, "Usability Implications for 1to1 Marketing," *Internetworking,* December 2001, www.internettg.org/newsletter/dec01/article_resnick.html.

10. S. Kent Stephan and Barry L. Tannenholz, "The Real Reason for Brand Switching," *Advertising Age*, June 13, 1994, p. 31; "Six Categories That Hold Elusive Consumers," *Advertising Age*, June 20, 1994, p. 32.

11. Quoted in Al Stewart, "Edgy Ads, Burgers Drive CKE," *Orange County Business Journal* 27, no. 30 (July 26, 2004), p. 5.

12. Nancy Ten Kate, "Squeaky Clean Teens," *American Demographics,* January 1995.

13. "Weather or Not to Sell," *Personal Selling Power*, September 1994, p. 79.

14. Steve Wyche, "Colin Kaepernick Explains Why He Sat during National Anthem," NFL Productions LLC, August 28, 2016, www.nfl.com/news/story/0ap3000000691077/article/colinkaepernick-explains-why-he-sat-during-national-anthem.

15. "Trends in Hispanic Advertising," *AHAA*, July 2013, http://ahaa.org.

16. Steve Geelan, "HOW TO SELL. . . Online Ads," *mUmBRELLA*, http://mumbrella.com.au/how-to-sell-anything-164995.

17. Leon E. Wynter, "Business and Race: JCPenney Launches Diahann Carroll Line," *The Wall Street Journal*, July 2, 1997, p. B1.

18. Eric Schlosser, "Meat & Potatoes," *Rolling Stone* 800 (November 26, 1998), accessed November 9, 2004, via EBSCO.

19. Eric Schlosser, "The True Cost of America's Diet," *Rolling Stone* 794 (September 3, 1998).

20. Kathleen Barnes, "Changing Demographics: Middle Class," *Advertising Age International*, October 17, 1994, pp. 1–11, 1–16.

21. eMarketer editors, " Coronavirus Hits China Ad SpendingeMarketer cuts forecast for total media ad spending by 6.2%," eMarketer, March 20, 2020. https://www.emarketer.com/content/coronavirus-hits-china-ad-spending

22. Henry Assael and David F. Poltrack, "Can Demographic Profiles of Heavy Users Serve as a Surrogate for Purchase Behavior in Selecting TV Programs?" *Journal of Advertising Research*, January/February 1994, p. 11.

23. Emanuel H. Demby, "Psychographics Revisited: The Birth of a Technique," *Marketing Research: A Magazine of Management & Applications*, Spring 1994, pp. 26–29.

24. Strategic Business Insights, "About VALs," www.strategicbusinessinsights.com/vals/about.shtml.

25. Strategic Business Insights, "About VALs," www.strategicbusinessinsights.com/vals/about.shtml.

26. Strategic Business Insights, "About VALs," www.strategicbusinessinsights.com/vals/about.shtml.

27. "Mindbase," Kantar, https://consulting.kantar.com/our-solutions/monitor/monitor-analytics/mindbase/.

28. Malcolm Gladwell, *The Tipping Point: How Little Things Can Make a Big Difference* (New York: Little, Brown 2002).

29. Lewis C. Winters, "International Psychographics," *Marketing Research: A Magazine of Management & Application*, September 1992, pp. 48–49.

30. James Hutton, "A Theoretical Framework for the Study of Brand Equity and a Test of Brand Sensitivity in an Organizational Buying Context," dissertation, University of Texas, Austin, 1993.

31. William D. Perreault Jr. and E. Jerome McCarthy, *Basic Marketing*, 12th ed. (Burr Ridge, IL: Irwin, 1996), p. 261.

32. *New Data for a New Economy*, U.S. Bureau of the Census, Economic Classification Policy Committee (Washington, DC: U.S. Department of Commerce, 1998).

33. U.S. Bureau of the Census, *Statistical Abstract of the United States: 2012*, www.census.gov/library/publications/2011/compendia/statab/131ed.html.

34. Michael Schrage, "Think Big," *Adweek*, October 11, 1993, p. 25.

35. Perreault and McCarthy, *Basic Marketing*, pp. 48–49, 91–112.

36. Walter van Waterschoot and Christophe Van den Bulte, "The 4P Classification of the Marketing Mix Revisited," *Journal of Marketing*, October 1992, pp. 83–93.

37. The now widely popularized conceptual model of the 4Ps was developed by E. J. McCarthy, *Basic Marketing* (Homewood, IL: Richard D. Irwin, 1960); the usage of the marketing mix derived from Neil H. Borden, "The Concept of the Marketing Mix," *Journal of Advertising Research*, June 1964, p. 27.

38. Perreault and McCarthy, *Basic Marketing*, pp. 310–21.

39. Pat Sabena, "Tough Market for New Products Requires Partnership," *Marketing Review*, June 1996, pp. 12–13.

40. Adrienne Ward Fawcett, "In Glut of New Products, 'Different' Becomes Key," *Advertising Age*, December 13, 1993, p. 28.

41. Haim Oren, "Branding Financial Services Helps Consumers Find Order in Chaos," *Marketing News*, March 29, 1993, p. 6.

42. "BrandZ Top 100 Most Valuable Global Brands," Millward Brown Optimor, www.millwardbrown.com/brandz/2013/Top100/Docs/2013_BrandZ_Top100_Chart.pdf.

43. Alan Wolf, "TWICE/Campaigners Poll Shows Shoppers Choose Brand Over Price," *Twice: This Week in Consumer Electronics,* December 5, 2005, p. 18.

44. C. Manly Molpus, "Brands Follow New Shopping Patterns," *Advertising Age*, February 14, 1994, p. 22.

45. Stephan and Tannenholz, "The Real Reason for Brand Switching," p. 31.

46. Annetta Miller, "The Millennial Mind-Set," *American Demographics*, January 1999.

47. Andrew Jaffe, "A Compass Point Out of Dead Calm: 'Brand Stewardship,'" *Adweek*, February 7, 1994, p. 38.

48. Perreault and McCarthy, *Basic Marketing*, p. 16.

49. "Vertical Marketing System Law and Legal Definition," USLegal, http://definitions.uslegal.com/v/vertical-marketing-system.

50. Leigh Richards, "Three Types of Vertical Marketing Systems," *eHow Money*, www.ehow.com/info_8367821_three-types-vertical-marketing-systems.html.

51. "Franchises A–Z," *Franchising.com*, www.franchising.com/franchises.

52. "2019 Fastest-Growing Franchises Ranking," *Entrepreneur*, www.entrepreneur.com/franchises/fastestgrowing.

communication and consumer behavior

This chapter examines the importance of the marketing process in business and the role of advertising and other marketing communications tools in presenting the company and its products to the market. The successful advertising practitioner should understand the relationship between marketing activities and consumer behavior. This is the relationship that shapes the creation of effective advertising.

What can we learn from what one company called "one of the most memorable marketing blunders ever"? The product was a reformulated version of Coca-Cola, frequently dubbed "New Coke," and it debuted in April of 1985 to "angst the likes of which no business has ever seen." What company called this a blunder? Coke itself.[1]

Coca-Cola was in a tough spot in the mid-1980s. Its market share lead over rival Pepsi had been eroding for nearly 15 years. Although it still had an edge, Coke worried that its rival's sweeter taste might be attracting a new generation of consumers. As one of the world's most famous brands, the decision to change Coke's famous (and secret) formula was not taken lightly. Almost 200,000 consumers participated in sipping tests that helped the company create a tastier new formula.[2]

New Coke was introduced with an enormous media budget and creative, contemporary ads intended to create love for the brand. It didn't work.

In fact, the pushback began as soon as the reformulated beverage hit the shelves. Consumers began hording cans of the "old" Coke. Protest groups, with names like "The Society for the Preservation of the Real Thing," began lobbying the company to bring the old formula back. Coke's hotline began receiving up to 1,500 calls a day. CEO Roberto Goizueta even received a letter addressed to "Chief Dodo, The Coca-Cola Company."

Coke quickly recognized the error and reversed course. By July, the company reassured its public that "old" coke would be returning. For a while, two versions (the "new" Coca-Cola and Coca-Cola classic) were sold side by side. Then, eventually, new Coke vanished entirely.

So what went wrong? Taste tests had shown that if people weren't told what they were drinking, they preferred the taste of the new formula. And isn't taste the sole criterion people use to choose a soft drink? Well, apparently not. What Coke forgot (momentarily) but its users did not is that the Coke brand is much bigger than taste alone. Companies experiment with beloved brands at their own risk.[3]

Today, Coke is willing to poke fun at itself for the marketing mistake, but in truth, how big of a mistake was it? By bringing back Classic Coke so quickly, the company was able to

continued on p. 124

LEARNING OBJECTIVES

After studying this chapter, you will be able to:

LO5-1 Detail how advertising differs from the basic communication process.

LO5-2 Outline the consumer perception process and explain why advertising people say "perception is everything."

LO5-3 Explain how product involvement influences the decision-making process and the advertising approach.

LO5-4 Describe the fundamental motives behind consumer purchases.

LO5-5 Discuss the various influences on consumer behavior.

continued from p. 123

right the ship. And although Pepsi momentarily grabbed a market-share lead in 1985, Coke bounced back and has been on top ever since. Maybe reminding people how much they loved the brand was a stroke of genius.

And Coke has continued to take chances with its brand. It decided to discontinue Coke Zero in 2019, introduced Diet Coke in a variety of flavors, and in 2020 rolled out Coke Coffee and Coke Energy, both containing high levels of caffeine. And believe it or not, New Coke made a brief return in May of 2019. The beverage was released in a limited run to complement the third season of Netflix's *Stranger Things*, which focused on 1985.[4]

Companies can't prosper by staying put, but they can also go too far. McDonald's tweaked sales with all-day breakfast and a coffee bar and succeeded with both. Harley Davidson risked heresy in 2020 by introducing an electric motorcycle. Will Coke's new brands help the company to prosper in the coming years, or will they erode the equity Coke has built over more than a century? The answer will depend on how well the company understands its consumers' wants and needs, and how well its new products satisfy them. ■

LO5-1 Detail how advertising differs from the basic communication process.

Source: The Coca-Cola Company

COMMUNICATION: WHAT MAKES ADVERTISING UNIQUE

In the last chapter, you learned that communication is a key element of the marketing mix. For communication to be effective the marketer must construct a message that is meaningful to consumers and can elicit the desired behavior.

Advertising is a special kind of communication. McCann Erickson, an agency for Coca-Cola and MasterCard, says that advertising is "Truth well told." This means that ethical advertisers and their agencies collaborate to discover the best ways to tell their story truthfully and creatively. To succeed, they must understand the elements of the advertising communication process, which is derived from the basic human communication process.

The Human Communication Process

Humans are social beings and communication is an important way we bind ourselves to others. From birth, we learn to listen and respond to others' messages. The traditional model in Exhibit 5–1 summarizes the series of events that take place when people share ideas in informal oral communication. For example, Bill sees Avery in the school hallway, and shouts "let's

> ## McCann Erickson, the ad agency for Coca-Cola and MasterCard, says that advertising is 'Truth well told.'

source The party that formulates the idea, encodes it as a message, and sends it via some channel to the receiver.

message In oral communication, the idea formulated and encoded by the source and sent to the receiver.

encoded Translating an idea or message into words, symbols, and illustrations.

semiotics The study of how humans use words, gestures, signs, and symbols to convey feelings, thoughts, ideas, and ideologies.

channel Any medium through which an encoded message is sent to a receiver, including oral communication, print media, television, and the Internet.

▼ **EXHIBIT 5–1** The human communication process.

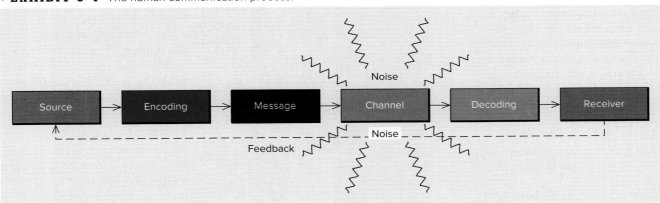

meet at the library to study tonight!" Avery smiles and nods before she hurries off. The process begins when a source (Bill) formulates an idea (studying together), encodes it as a message ("let's meet . . ."), and sends it via some channel (his voice) to someone else, the receiver (Avery). The receiver must decode the message (Avery realizes that Bill wants to study with her) in order to understand it. To respond, the receiver formulates a new idea (that works for me), encodes it (I'll smile and nod), and then sends the new message back through some channel (nonverbal). A message that acknowledges or responds to the original message constitutes feedback, which also affects the encoding of a new message.[5] And, of course, all this takes place in an environment characterized by noise—the distracting cacophony of many other messages being sent at the same time by other sources (a ringing smartphone, other students talking in the school hallway).

Applying the Communication Process to Advertising

Applying this model to advertising, we could say that the source is the sponsor, the message is the ad, the channel is the medium, the receiver is the consumer or prospect, and the noise is the din of competing ads and other distractions. Traditionally advertising has been a one-way process, with the message moving from the sponsor to the consumer. However, interactive forms of marketing—personal selling, mobile and digital advertising—let consumers participate in the communication by extracting the information they need, manipulating what they see and hear, and responding in real time. Traditional ideas about a message's "source" and "receiver" have

been challenged in a digital world. But for now, let's take a closer look at the traditional model.

The Source   The ultimate **source** of a marketing message is the organization that has information it wishes to share with others. However, within the context of an advertisement, a real or imaginary spokesperson actually lends voice or tone to the communication. Because the receiver's perception of the source influences the effectiveness of the communication, the spokesperson must appear to be knowledgeable, trustworthy, attractive, and relevant to the audience. For example, "Flo," the fictional spokesperson for Progressive Insurance, symbolizes an enthusiastic, friendly, slightly retro individual. *Advertising Age* has described Flo as "a weirdly sincere, post-modern Josephine the Plumber who just really wants to help. She has: The brand is flourishing."[6]

The Message   The information contained in a **message** must be **encoded** so that the receiver understands what is being communicated. This involves using words or symbols that are familiar to the intended audience. Depending on the medium used, the message may be verbal or nonverbal. **Semiotics** is the study of how humans use words, gestures, signs, and symbols to convey feelings, thoughts, ideas, and ideologies.[7] Consider the symbolism of the long-running PETA campaign opposing the use of animal fur in garments.[8] "I'd rather go naked than wear fur" uses provocative photos to convey the group's perspective on killing animals for their coats.

The Channel   The **channel** is the means by which the encoded message travels from the source to the receiver.

personal channels
Means of communication that involve direct contact between the parties, such as personal selling.

nonpersonal channels Means of communication that don't involve interpersonal contact between the sender and the receiver. Examples would include advertising, publicity, and sales promotion.

receiver In oral communication, this party decodes the message to understand it.

decode To interpret a message by the receiver.

noise The sender's advertising message competing daily with hundreds of other commercial and noncommercial messages.

Communications channels can be categorized as personal or nonpersonal. **Personal channels**, such as personal selling, involve direct contact between the parties. **Nonpersonal channels**, or mediated forms of communication, are those that rule out interpersonal contact between the sender and the receiver. Messages in commercial media, such as television, websites, magazines, radio, and billboards, are sent to many individuals at one time.

The Receiver
In advertising, the **receiver** is usually the consumer who receives the advertiser's message. The advertiser must always be concerned about how the consumer will **decode**, or interpret, a message. The last thing an advertiser wants is to be misunderstood. Unfortunately, message interpretation is only partially determined by the words and symbols in the ad. The advertising medium may have an effect as well. As Marshall McLuhan said, "The medium

Symbols are often used in advertising to encode messages. In this ad, Evian (www.evian.com) uses a flower to symbolize water's ability to restore, revitalize, replenish, and hydrate. Evian would like you to think of its spring water as a beauty product.
Source: Evian

Feedback and Interactivity
That's why **feedback** is so important. It completes the cycle, verifying that the message was received. Feedback employs the sender-message-receiver pattern, except that it is directed from the receiver back to the source.

In advertising, feedback can take many forms: redeemed coupons, phone inquiries, visits to a store, requests for more information, increased sales, responses to a survey, e-mail inquiries, or clicks on a search ad. Dramatically low responses to an ad indicate a break in the communication process. Questions arise: Is the product wrong for the market? Is the message unclear? Are we using the right media? Without feedback, these questions cannot be answered.

In the past, the consumer's feedback used different channels than the original message. But now, thanks again to technology, the audiences of advertising are

> ### With interactive media such as the Internet, [consumers] can give instantaneous, real-time feedback.

is the message." The unique characteristics of the receivers are also very important, and most sponsors want to know as much about them as possible. We'll see later in this chapter that attitudes, perceptions, personality, self-concept, and culture are just some of the many influences that affect the way people receive and respond to messages and how they behave as consumers.

A big challenge for advertisers is that their message must compete with hundreds of other commercial and noncommercial messages every day. This is referred to as **noise**. So the sender doesn't know how the message is received, or even if it is received, unless a consumer acknowledges it.

no longer just passive receivers of mass messages. They are active decision makers who can control what communications they receive and choose the information they want about a particular product. With **interactive media** they can give instantaneous, real-time feedback on the same channel used by the message sender. In fact, in interactive media, consumers can be the message source and advertisers the receiver, blurring the lines completely.

Exhibit 5–2 presents an interactive model of communication. In this model, no single entity operates as a source or receiver. Instead, two entities serve both roles in an ongoing process.

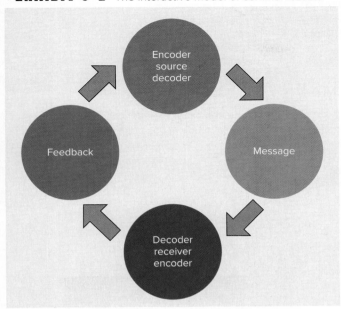

This model better represents marketers' understanding of their relationships with consumers today. Marketers no longer dominate the exchange of messages. Rather, they are engaged in a conversation with consumers who send their own messages, both to the marketer and to other consumers. The interactive model reminds companies that they do not have as much control over messages as the traditional model seems to imply. It also reminds companies that listening to their customers is important, because it ultimately determines whether the company will acquire the understanding of their audience necessary for success.

CONSUMER BEHAVIOR: THE KEY TO ADVERTISING STRATEGY

Effective communication happens when the marketer selects a relevant source, develops an appropriate message, encodes it correctly, and then chooses a suitable medium that will efficiently and effectively reach the target audience. All of these steps rely upon the marketer knowing the message receiver and understanding how that individual might respond.

Take a look at your friends in class, or the people you work with. How well do you know them? Could you describe their lifestyles and the kinds of products they prefer? Do they typically eat out or cook for themselves? Do they exercise? Like to go out or stay home?

What brands do they buy? Do you know which social media they use? What TV programs they watch? What websites they visit or phone they prefer? If you were Sony's advertising manager and wanted to advertise a new laptop to these people, what type of appeal would you use? What media would you use to reach them?

The Importance of Knowing the Consumer

Advertisers spend a lot of money to keep individuals and groups of individuals (markets) interested in their products. To succeed, they need to understand what makes potential customers behave the way they do. The advertiser's goal is to get enough relevant market data to develop accurate profiles of buyers—to find the common ground (and symbols) for communication. This involves the study of **consumer behavior**: the mental and emotional processes and the physical activities of people who purchase and use goods and services to satisfy particular needs and wants.[9]

The Consumer Decision Process: An Overview

Social scientists have many theories of consumer behavior to explain the process of making a purchase decision. Let's look at this information from the viewpoint of the advertiser.

Advertising's primary mission is to reach prospective customers and influence their awareness, attitudes, and buying behavior. To succeed, an advertiser must make the marketing communications process work very effectively.

feedback A message that acknowledges or responds to an initial message.

interactive media Media such as the Internet and interactive television that permit consumers to give instantaneous, real-time feedback on the same channel used by the original message sender.

consumer behavior The activities, actions, and influences of people who purchase and use goods and services to satisfy their personal or household needs and wants.

Green Works are a natural cleaning product line created by the Clorox Company. The advertisement includes information useful to the consumer decision process of a prospect who wants a green lawn but is concerned about the environmental impact of chemicals in fertilizer and pesticides. Providing reassurance about those concerns can make all the difference in a final purchase decision.
Source: The Clorox Company

consumer decision process The series of steps a consumer goes through in deciding to make a purchase.

personal processes The three internal, human operations—perception, learning, and motivation—that govern the way consumers discern raw data (stimuli) and translate them into feelings, thoughts, beliefs, and actions.

interpersonal influences Social influences on the consumer decision-making process, including family, society, and cultural environment.

nonpersonal influences Factors influencing the consumer decision-making process that are often out of the consumer's control, such as time, place, and environment.

evaluation of alternatives Choosing among brands, sizes, styles and colors.

▼**EXHIBIT 5–3** The basic consumer decision process is a set of steps that the consumer experiences during and after the purchase. Advertising and other influences can affect the consumer's attitude at any point in this process.

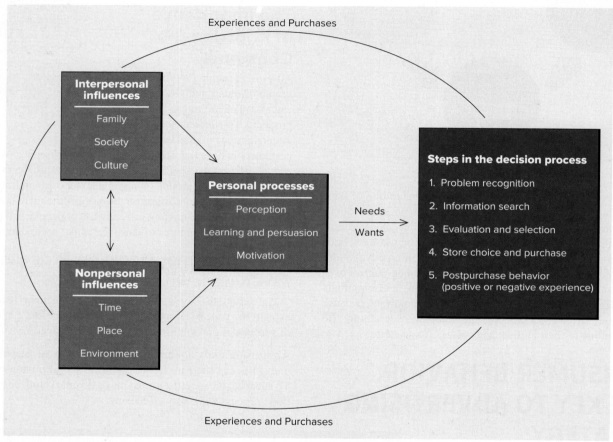

The moment we receive an advertising message, our mental computer runs a rapid evaluation called the **consumer decision process**. The conceptual model in Exhibit 5–3 presents the basic steps we go through in making a purchase decision. As you can see, the full process involves a rather lengthy sequence of activities: *problem recognition* (which may occur as a result of seeing an ad), *information search*, *evaluation and selection* of alternative brands, *store choice and purchase*, and finally *postpurchase behavior*. For simple, habitual, everyday purchases with low levels of involvement, the decision-making process is typically very abbreviated. But in those situations where we are highly involved in the purchase, it's not at all unusual for us to substantially extend the decision process.

Whether the process is limited or extended, though, numerous sociological and psychological factors invariably play a role in the way we behave. These include a series of personal subprocesses that are themselves shaped by various influences.

The three **personal processes** govern the way we discern raw data *(stimuli)* and translate them into feelings, thoughts, beliefs, and actions. The personal processes are the *perception*, the *learning and persuasion*, and the *motivation* processes.

Second, our mental processes and behavior are affected by two sets of influences. **Interpersonal influences** include our *family*, *society*, and *culture*. **Nonpersonal influences**—factors often outside the consumer's control—include *time*, *place*, and *environment*. These influences further affect the personal processes of perception, learning, and motivation.

After dealing with these processes and influences, we face the pivotal decision: to buy or not to buy. But taking that final step typically requires yet another process, the **evaluation of alternatives**, in which we choose brands, sizes, styles, and colors. If we do decide to buy, our **postpurchase evaluation** will influence our subsequent purchases.

Like the communications process, the decision process is circular in nature. What we learn from one experience influences our behavior the next time. The advertiser who understands this process can develop messages more likely to reach and make sense to consumers.

LO5-2 Outline the consumer perception process and explain why advertising people say "perception is everything."

PSYCHOLOGICAL PROCESSES IN CONSUMER BEHAVIOR

Assume you are the advertising manager preparing to launch a new vitamin-laden beverage brand for athletes and sports participants. We'll call it Infusion. What's your first objective?

The first task in promoting any new product is to create awareness *(perception)* that the product exists. The second is to provide enough compelling information *(learning and persuasion)* about the product for prospective customers to become interested and make an informed decision. Finally, you want your advertising to stimulate customers' desire *(motivation)* to satisfy their needs and wants by trying the product.

If they find Infusion satisfying, they likely will continue to purchase it. These three personal processes of consumer behavior—perception, learning and persuasion, and motivation—are extremely important to advertisers. By studying these, advertisers can better evaluate how their messages are perceived.

The Consumer Perception Process

Perception is important.[10] The average adult may be exposed to thousands of ads each day but notices only a handful and remembers even fewer.[11] Why? Exposure and perception are different. Consumers are quite good at "tuning out" environmental information they are uninterested in or lack curiosity about.

The term **perception** refers to the information received through the five senses. This definition suggests it refers to the first two elements in the consumer perception and cognition model shown in Exhibit 5-4.

postpurchase evaluation Determining whether a purchase has been a satisfactory or unsatisfactory one.

perception Our personalized way of sensing and comprehending stimuli.

"The average adult may be exposed to thousands of ads each day but notices only a handful.

▼**EXHIBIT 5-4** The model of the consumer perception and cognition processes portrays how consumers perceive, accept, and remember an ad.

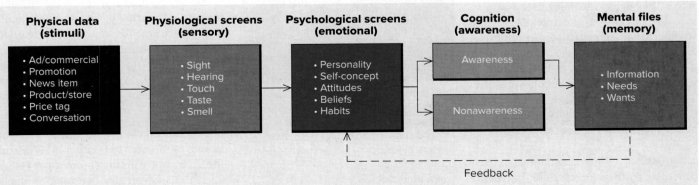

Physical data (stimuli)	Physiological screens (sensory)	Psychological screens (emotional)	Cognition (awareness)	Mental files (memory)
• Ad/commercial • Promotion • News item • Product/store • Price tag • Conversation	• Sight • Hearing • Touch • Taste • Smell	• Personality • Self-concept • Attitudes • Beliefs • Habits	Awareness / Nonawareness	• Information • Needs • Wants

Feedback

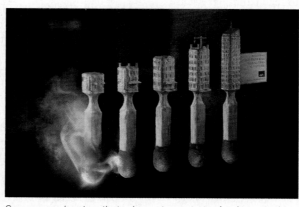

Screens are barriers that ads must penetrate. As shown in this ad, AXA Insurance Company uses the powerful stimulus of fire and adjacent matches to penetrate our subconscious: a fire or disaster is an occurrence we do not want to believe will ever happen, yet we need to have insurance that we will be protected in case it ever occurs.
Source: AXA Equitable Life Insurance Company

Stimulus
A **stimulus** is something (light, sound, a scent) we can perceive through our senses. It may originate within our bodies, as when we notice that we feel hungry at lunchtime. Or it may originate from outside our bodies, as when we see an ad for a smartphone and decide it looks beautiful.

IMC messages are external stimuli that appear in a variety of forms: a window display at a local store, brightly colored labels on cans of Campbell's tomato soup, or the red price tag on a pair of skis at REI. These objects are all physical in nature; they stimulate our senses (with varying degrees of intensity) in ways that can be measured.

Perceptual Screens
The second key element in perception is the personalized way of sensing and interpreting the stimulus data. Before any data can be perceived, they must first penetrate a set of **perceptual screens**, subconscious filters that shield us from unwanted messages.

The **physiological screens** comprise the five senses: sight, hearing, touch, taste, and smell. They detect incoming data and measure the dimension and intensity of the stimuli. A sight-impaired person can't read an ad in *Sports Illustrated*. And if a radio ad is playing on a station at low volume, it won't be heard, and perception will suffer. The advertiser's message is effectively screened out when the viewer can't interpret it and perception does not occur.[12]

Cognition
When a stimulus is perceived, we try to make sense of it by relating

Advertisers frequently capitalize on consumers' concepts of themselves to generate attention and interest in a particular product. This Harley-Davidson ad executes this approach perfectly by linking a powerful brand to the consumer's self-image.
Source: Harley-Davidson

it to the things we already know. That is the role of **cognition**: comprehending the stimulus. Information that passes through our perceptual screens affords us the opportunity to understand and accept it.

As we saw earlier, there are screens at the level of perception. There are additional ones at the level of cognition. Each consumer uses psychological screens to evaluate, filter, and personalize information according to subjective standards. These screens evaluate data based on the consumer's personality, unique needs, and experiences. Psychologists label our view of ourselves the **self-concept**, and it includes what we know about our interests, attitudes, beliefs, experiences, and lifestyle. The self-concept is an important determinant of our buying behaviors. Consider the likely differences in the self-concepts of people who drive pickup trucks versus hybrids, or who collect works of art versus guns.

Mental Files
Many marketers assume consumers will be making a purchase long after they are exposed to an ad. If so, ads must help consumers remember information from ads for later use. Memory, according to psychologists, is divided into **short-term memory**,[13] which is a temporary repository for things a person is thinking about at a given moment, and **long-term memory**,[14] a seemingly limitless storage area for what we have learned or know. Repetition in short-term memory helps people store information in long-term memory. As a result, ads often repeat key pieces of information several times.

Information in long-term memory is not stored randomly, but rather in **mental files**. To cope with the complexity of stimuli such as advertising, we rank products

mental files Stored memories in consumers' minds.

learning A relatively permanent change in thought processes or behavior that occurs as a result of reinforced experience. Information that is learned is stored in long-term memory.

cognitive theory An approach that views learning as a mental process of memory, thinking, and the rational application of knowledge to practical problem solving.

conditioning theory The theory that learning is a trial-and-error process.

stimulus-response theory Also called *conditioning theory*. Some stimulus triggers a consumer's need or want, and this in turn creates a need to respond.

and other data in our files by importance, price, quality, features, or a host of other descriptors.

Memory is a limited resource, and one susceptible to some well-known biases. As an example, pause for a moment and consider whether there are more words that begin with the letter *k* (e.g., *kangaroo*) versus words that have *k* in the third position (e.g., *Arkansas*). What is your guess? Many people are surprised to discover there are nearly three times more words *(ask, askance, ark)* with *k* in the third position. But when we search through memory, it is easier to retrieve words by their first letter. We then confuse this ease of retrieval with the frequency of occurrence. This "availability" heuristic is just one example of how the structure of our cognitive system influences what we recall and how we decide.

LO5-3 Explain how product involvement influences the decision-making process and the advertising approach.

Learning, Persuasion, and the Role of Involvement in the Ways That Consumers Process Information

By definition, **learning** is a relatively permanent change in thought process or behavior that occurs as a result of experience. Information that is learned is successfully transferred to long-term memory, where it is available for later use. Learning, in turn, affects behavior. Learning that a food tastes delicious

> Learning is a relatively permanent change in thought process or behavior.

Because screens are such a major challenge to advertisers, it's important to understand what's in the consumer's mental files and, if possible, modify them in favor of the advertiser's product. That brings us to the second process in consumer behavior: *learning and persuasion.* Perceptions can rarely be changed through advertising alone.[15] But once a new perception does enter our mental files, the information alters the database on which our psychological screens feed.

leads to eating more. Learning that a hot stove burns leads to keeping a distance from a range top in the kitchen.

Two Ways to Learn   There are numerous theories of learning, but advertisers classify many into two broad categories—*cognitive theory* and *conditioning theory*—depending on the level of consumer involvement (high or low) required to make a purchase. **Cognitive theory** views learning as the rational application of knowledge to dealing with practical problems. This theory may be an accurate description of how we learn from the experience of others and how we evaluate a complex purchase such as insurance, stocks and bonds, or business products. It is deliberate and thoughtful. Conversely, **conditioning theory**—also called **stimulus-response theory**—treats learning as a trial-and-error process. Some stimulus (perhaps an ad) triggers the consumer's need or want, and this in turn creates the drive to respond. If the consumer's response reduces the drive, then satisfaction occurs. And that produces repeat behavior the next time the drive is aroused, demonstrating that learning has taken place. Responding to conditioned stimuli is not necessarily thoughtful or deliberate.

check yourself ✓

1. Why do we use perceptual screens to filter the ads to which we are exposed?

2. What does the term *consumer behavior* refer to, and why is it important to advertisers?

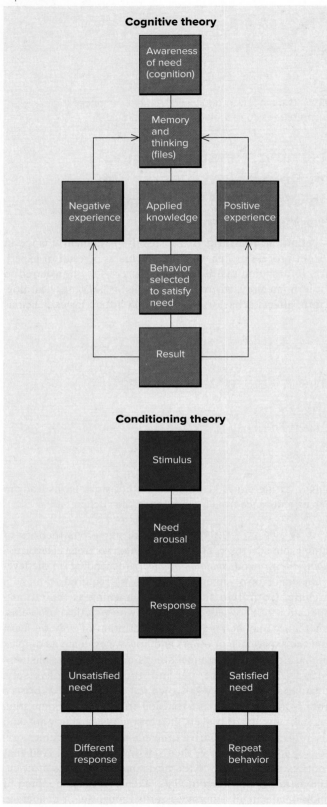

Cognitive theory

- Awareness of need (cognition)
- Memory and thinking (files)
- Negative experience
- Applied knowledge
- Positive experience
- Behavior selected to satisfy need
- Result

Conditioning theory

- Stimulus
- Need arousal
- Response
- Unsatisfied need
- Satisfied need
- Different response
- Repeat behavior

For example, the smell of delicious food might make us hungry, whether we wish to be hungry or not. Exhibit 5-5 shows simple diagrams of these two theories.

What determines which type of process, conditioning or cognitive, consumers are likely to use when learning information? **Consumer involvement** appears to play an important role. Involvement refers to how personally important or relevant a decision is to a consumer. More important and relevant decisions result in greater involvement.

Conditioning theory is more applicable to the simple, basic, low-involvement purchases consumers make every day, such as soap, cereal, toothpaste, and paper towels. And it is here that reinforcement advertising plays its most important role—along with superior product performance and good service. If learning is reinforced enough and repeat behavior is produced, a purchasing habit may result. Cognitive theories seem most applicable in highly involving situations, as when a consumer buys a car or an expensive TV. In these situations, people search for information from memory, carefully consider new evidence, and often resist the strong urges of emotion.

Learning and persuasion are closely linked. **Persuasion** occurs when the change in belief, attitude, or behavioral intention is caused by a message (such as advertising or personal selling).[16] Naturally, advertisers are very interested in persuasion and how it takes place.

Two Ways to Persuade   Just as there are two different ways learning can occur, through a relatively thoughtful way (cognition) or a relatively simple way (conditioning), there seem to be two different paths to persuasion. Psychologists label these different routes to persuasion the central and the peripheral route. As with learning theory, the route to persuasion depends on a consumer's level of involvement with the product and message. When a consumer's level of involvement is higher, the central route to persuasion is more likely. On the other hand, the peripheral route to persuasion predominates when consumer involvement is low.[17]

We can see how this works by looking at the **Elaboration Likelihood Model** in Exhibit 5-6. In the **central route to persuasion**, consumers with higher levels of involvement with the product or the message pay careful attention to product-related information, such as product attributes and benefits or demonstrations of positive functional or psychological consequences. Persuasion is aided by strong arguments about why the consumer could benefit from the product. Consumers processing ads through this route learn cognitively and elaborate on the message. So, for example, a consumer learning about a new phone may process the ad and then think about how the phone will better connect her to friends, let her take better pictures, download fun apps, and impress people who are important to her. Strong, well-reasoned messages can lead to positive brand attitudes, and purchase intention.[18]

▼ **EXHIBIT 5-6** The Elaboration Likelihood Model.

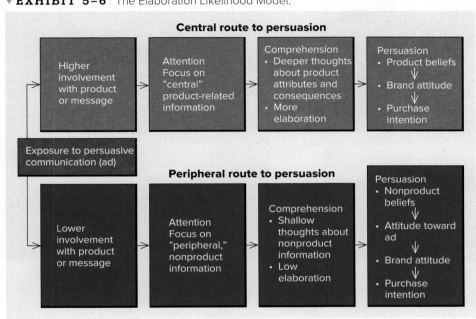

The **peripheral route to persuasion** is very different. It's more like stimulus-response learning. People who are not in the market for a product typically have low involvement with the product message. They have little or no reason to pay attention to it or to comprehend the central information of the ad. An ad for a soft drink, for example, might prove highly entertaining, even if the consumer fails to see how a new soda brand solves any important problem. The likeable ad, perhaps through the use of attractive sources, up-tempo music, exciting editing—makes the consumer happy. The music, source, editing, and positive feelings, foster a positive attitude toward the ad, which in turn may lead to positive brand attitudes.[19] At some later date, if a purchase occasion does arise, the consumer may link positive, ad-evoked feelings to the soft drink, and decide to buy the product.

A majority of ads appear to focus on persuasion via peripheral processing. This is because many products have little relevance to our immediate goals or needs, so we are not motivated to think about them. Our involvement is very low. That's why we also have very little recall of ads we saw yesterday. In cases where there is little product differentiation, advertisers may actually *want* us to engage in peripheral processing. Their ads focus more on image or entertainment than product features.

But when a product has a distinct advantage, the advertiser's goal should be to encourage central route processing by increasing consumers' involvement with the message. This is often the purpose of comparative advertising.[20]

Whichever route an ad targets, a key to learning and persuasion is repetition. Just as a student prepares for an exam by repeating key information to memorize it, an advertiser must repeat key information to prospective and current customers so they remember the product's name and its benefits. Repeat messages penetrate customers' perceptual screens by rekindling memories of information from prior ads. To see for

" **Because very few people are actually in the market at any given time, most mass media advertising receives peripheral processing.** "

In this clever ad, the copy reads "the other official water of the Championships, Wimbledon." Because Evian relies on a humorous image and an association with Wimbledon, which route to persuasion, the central or peripheral, is used to persuade?

Source: Evian

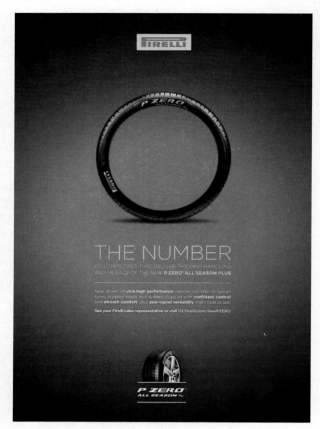

For the high-involvement consumer, strong reasons to do something are important. But as Pirellii shows in this beautiful ad, strong reasons and beautiful design need not be mutually exclusive. How does Pirelli use copy points to drive central route processing in this ad?

Source: Pirelli Tire North America LLC

yourself how important repetition is, identify the sponsors that feature these slogans: "i'm lovin' it," "15 minutes can save you 15 percent or more," and "Just do it."

Learning Influences Attitudes and Interest
An **attitude** is our evaluation of some idea or object. An important advertising objective is developing messages that foster positive brand attitudes.

In Japan, for instance, dishwashers are not a common household appliance. Not only is there very little space for them; Japanese housewives feel guilty about using the labor-saving device. As a result, dishwasher manufacturers have had to change attitudes by designing smaller, space-saving machines and then promoting them using good hygiene themes rather than convenience appeals.[21]

For mature brands in categories with familiar, frequently purchased products, *brand interest* is even more critical for motivating action. **Brand interest** is an individual's openness or curiosity about a brand.[22] Enjoyable, entertaining advertising can enhance interest in the brand and reduce the variety-seeking tendencies of consumers who become bored with using the same old product.[23]

Learning Creates Habits and Brand Loyalty
Attitude is the mental side and *habit* the behavioral side of the same coin. **Habit**—the acquired behavior pattern that becomes nearly or completely automatic—is the natural extension of learning. We really are creatures of habit.

Most consumer behavior is habitual for three reasons: It's safe, simple, and essential. First, regardless of how we learned to make our purchase decision (through either central or peripheral route processing), if we discover a quality product, brand, or service, we feel *safe* repurchasing it.

Second, habit is *simple*. To consider alternatives we must evaluate, compare, and then decide. This is difficult and time-consuming. Habits allow us to skip those steps.

Finally, because habit is both safe and easy, we rely on it for daily living. Imagine rethinking every purchase decision you make. It would be virtually impossible, not to mention impractical. So it's really *essential* to use habit in our lives.

The major objective of all brand marketers is to produce *brand loyalty*, a direct result of the habit of repurchasing and

attitude The acquired mental position—positive or negative—regarding some idea or object.

brand interest An individual's openness or curiosity about a brand.

habit An acquired or developed behavior pattern that has become nearly or completely automatic.

brand loyalty The consumer's conscious or unconscious decision—expressed through intention or behavior—to repurchase a brand continually. This occurs because the consumer perceives that the brand has the right product features, image, quality, or relationship at the right price.

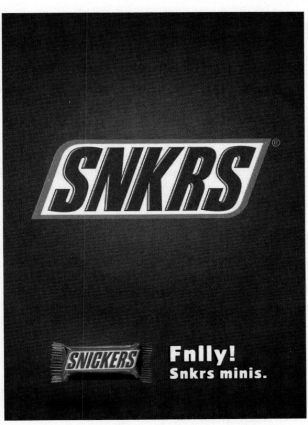

Advertisers hope that consumers will satisfy needs and wants through habit. For many years, Snickers has run a campaign based on the slogan, "You're not you when you're hungry" (a campaign that increased product sales nearly 16 percent in its first year). Because people are hungry every day, the campaign implies that keeping Snickers around for a daily snack is a good idea.
Source: Snickers by Mars, Incorporated/ Ad created by BBDO, Ukraine

the reinforcement of continuous advertising. **Brand loyalty** is the consumer's conscious or unconscious decision, expressed through intention or behavior, to repurchase a brand continually.[24] It occurs because the consumer *perceives* that the brand offers the right product features, image, quality, or relationship at the right price.

In the quest for brand loyalty, advertisers have three aims related to habits:

1. *Breaking habits.* Get consumers to unlearn an existing purchase habit and try something new. Advertisers frequently offer incentives to lure customers away from old brands or stores. Or they may use comparative advertising to demonstrate their product's superiority.

2. *Acquiring habits.* Teach consumers to repurchase their brand or repatronize their establishment. Hyundai offers special incentives to its car buyers to repurchase a new Hyundai.

3. *Reinforcing habits.* Remind current customers of the value of their original purchase and encourage them to continue purchasing. Hotels offer loyalty programs and airlines award frequent flyer miles for the same reason.

Developing brand loyalty is much more difficult today due to consumers' increased sophistication and the legions of habit-breaking activities of competitive advertisers.[25] Only recently have advertisers come to realize that their years of habit-breaking activities have undermined their own *habit-building* objectives. In the quest for instant results, they shifted much of their advertising budgets to sales promotions (deals, coupons, price cuts). But advertising, unlike sales promotion, is an integral part of what makes a brand desirable. It's advertising that reinforces brand loyalty and maintains market share.[26] We revisit this topic in our discussion of sales promotion in Chapter 15.

Learning Defines Needs and Wants The learning process is both immediate and long term. The moment we file a perception, some learning takes place. When we see a succulent food ad, we may suddenly feel hungry; we *need* food. As we collate the information in our mental files, comparing new perceptions with old ones, further learning takes place. The need may become a *want*. This leads to the next personal process, motivation.

check yourself ✓

1. What is the difference between the central route and the peripheral route to persuasion?

2. What is the difference between the cognitive theory and the conditioning theory of learning?

3. What is the role of involvement in learning and persuasion?

LO5-4 Describe the fundamental motives behind consumer purchases.

The Consumer Motivation Process

Motivation refers to the underlying forces (or motives) that foster actions. These motives stem from the conscious or unconscious goal of satisfying our needs and wants. **Needs** are the basic, often instinctive, human desires that motivate us to do something. **Wants** are "needs" that we learn during our lifetime.[27]

Motivation cannot be observed directly. When we see people eat, we assume they are hungry, but we may be wrong. People eat for a variety of reasons besides hunger: They want to be sociable, it's time to eat, or maybe they're nervous or bored.

People are usually motivated by the benefit of satisfying some combination of needs, which may be conscious or unconscious, functional or psychological. *Motivation research* offers insights into the underlying reasons for certain observed consumer behavior. The reasons *(motives)* some people stop shopping at Ralph's Supermarket and switch to Trader Joe's may be that Trader Joe's is closer to home, it has a wider selection of fresh

of fulfilling all the lower needs and realizing one's true potential.

The promise of satisfying a certain level of need is the basic promotional appeal for many ads. In such affluent societies as the United States, Canada, Western Europe, and Japan, most individuals take for granted the satisfaction of their physiological needs. So advertising campaigns often portray the fulfillment of social, esteem, and self-actualization needs, and many offer the reward of satisfaction through personal achievement.

In focus groups for Nabisco SnackWells, for example, it became apparent that middle-aged women today have a high sense of self-worth. Wellness, to them, is no longer about looking good in a bathing suit, but rather celebrating what they do well. The advertiser wondered if it could use women's positive attitude about themselves to change their attitude toward the concept of snacking. Nabisco's agency capitalized on the idea in a new campaign aimed at boosting women's self-esteem. The message: "Snacking is not about 'filling' yourself, but 'fulfilling' yourself."[28]

We all have needs and wants, but we are frequently unaware of them. Before the advent of the desktop computer, people were completely unaware of any need for it. But the moment a

> ## We all have needs and wants, but we are frequently unaware of them.

produce, and (most likely) they see other people like themselves shopping there. Any or all of these factors might make a shopper switch even if prices are lower at Ralph's.

To better understand what motivates people, Abraham Maslow developed the classic model shown in Exhibit 5–7 called the **hierarchy of needs**. Maslow maintained that the lower, physiological and safety needs dominate human behavior and must be satisfied before the higher, socially acquired needs (or wants) become meaningful. The highest need, self-actualization, is the culmination

▼ **EXHIBIT 5–7** The hierarchy of needs suggests that people meet their needs according to priorities. Physiological and safety needs carry the greatest priority. In advertising, the message must match the need of the market or the ad will fail. Advertisers use marketing research to understand the need levels of their markets and use this information in determining the marketing mix.

Need	Product	Promotional appeal
Self-actualization	A graduate degree	"Realize your full potential"
Esteem	Luxury car	"The pursuit of perfection"
Social	Jewelry	"Show her you care"
Safety	Tires	"Bounces off hazards"
Physiological	Breakfast cereal	"The natural energy source"

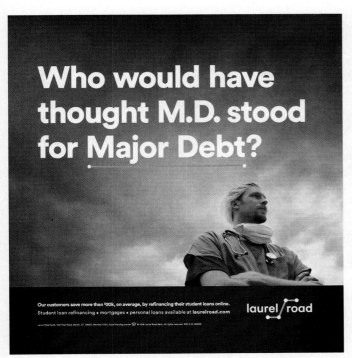

Negative motivation is a powerful tool for affecting human behavior. This ad for Laurel Road, a company that allows people to refinance debt, speaks to the problem of crushing student loans. Which of the negatively originated motives does this ad most clearly address?

Source: Laurel Road Bank

consumer consciously recognizes a product-related want or need, a dynamic process begins. The consumer first evaluates the need and either accepts it as worthy of action or rejects it. Acceptance converts satisfaction of the need into a goal, which creates the motivation to make a purchase. In contrast, rejection removes the necessity for action and thereby eliminates the goal and the motivation to buy.

Modern researchers translated Maslow's theory about needs and motives into more strategic concepts for use by marketers and advertisers. Rossiter and Percy, for example, identify eight

▼ **EXHIBIT 5–8** Rossiter and Percy's eight fundamental purchase and usage motives.

Negatively Originated (Informational) Motives
1. Problem removal
2. Problem avoidance
3. Incomplete satisfaction
4. Mixed approach–avoidance
5. Normal depletion

Positively Originated (Transformational) Motives
6. Sensory gratification
7. Intellectual stimulation or mastery
8. Social approval

fundamental purchase and usage motives (see Exhibit 5–8). They refer to the first five as *negatively originated (informational) motives* and the last three as *positively originated (transformational) motives.*[29]

Negatively Originated (Informational) Motives

The most common energizers of consumer behavior are the **negatively originated motives**, including problem removal and problem avoidance. Whenever we run out of something, for instance, we experience a negative mental state. To relieve those feelings, we actively seek a new or replacement product. Thus, we are temporarily motivated until the time we make the purchase. Then, if the purchase is satisfactory, the drive or motivation is reduced.

These are also called **informational motives** because the consumer often seeks information to reduce the negative mental state. In fact, Rossiter and Percy point out, these could also be called "relief" motives because consumers work to find relief from a problem.

Positively Originated (Transformational) Motives

From time to time, we all want to indulge ourselves by buying some brand or product that promises some benefit or reward. With the **positively originated motives**, a positive bonus is promised rather than the removal or reduction of some negative situation. The goal is to use positive reinforcement to increase the consumer's motivation and to energize the consumer's investigation or search for the new product.

The three positively originated motives—sensory gratification, intellectual stimulation, and social approval—are also called

informational motives The negatively originated motives, such as problem removal or problem avoidance, that are the most common energizers of consumer behavior.

positively originated motives Consumer's motivation to purchase and use a product based on a positive bonus that the product promises, such as sensory gratification, intellectual stimulation, or social approval.

Ads that make use of positively originated motives promise to reward consumers in some way. This ad for Zero Motorcycles focuses on positively originated motives—sensory gratification—by promising the consumer that the powertrain is "Seamless. Silent. Asphalt-shredding torque."

Source: Zero Motorocycles, Inc.

transformational motives because the consumer expects to be transformed in a sensory, intellectual, or social sense. They could also be called "reward" motives because the transformation is a rewarding state.[30]

For some consumers, the purchase of a particular product (say, a new suit) might represent a negatively originated motive (they have to have it for work). But for other consumers, it might be positively originated (they think a suit will lead people to view them as more professional and competent). This suggests two distinct target markets that advertisers must understand and that may call for completely different advertising strategies.

Families are an important influence on consumer behavior. For decades now, society has adopted a broader and more inclusive definition of what family means. Matchcota is a volunteer organization based in Peru that promotes pet adoption. Every individual who works at Matchcota has an independent job in another company and devotes free time to pet rescue. How does this ad suggest that a loved pet is a family member?

Source: Matchcota

Before creating messages, advertisers must carefully consider the goals that lead to consumer motivations. Denny's Restaurants would make a costly mistake if its ads portrayed the reward of a romantic interlude if the real motive of most Denny's customers is simply to satisfy their hunger with a filling, low-priced meal.

check yourself ✓

1. What are the various approaches that advertisers use to develop brand loyalty among consumers?

2. How many consumer motives can you imagine might be used for a delicious but healthy snack food ad? What are they?

LO5-5 Discuss the various influences on consumer behavior.

INTERPERSONAL INFLUENCES ON CONSUMER BEHAVIOR

For advertisers, it's not enough just to know the *personal* processes of perception, learning and persuasion, and motivation. Important **interpersonal influences** affect—sometimes even

dominate—these processes. They also serve as guidelines for consumer behavior. These influences can best be categorized as the *family*, the *society*, and the *cultural environment* of the consumer.

Family Influence

From an early age, family communication affects our socialization as consumers—our attitudes toward many products and our purchasing habits. This influence is usually strong and long-lasting. A child who learns that the "right" headache relief is Bayer aspirin and the "best" name in appliances is General Electric has a well-developed adult purchasing behavior.

From 1970 to 1990, married couple households with children declined sharply—from 40 to 26 percent of all households. Since 1990, that decline has been slower—such households represent about 20 percent as of 2015. This suggests that family influence has changed in the United States over the last 35 years as working parents take a less active role in raising their children and youngsters look outside the family for social values.[31] As this happens, the influence of the social and cultural environments intensifies.

Societal Influence

Our community exerts a strong influence on us all. When we affiliate with a particular societal division or identify with some reference group or value the ideas of certain opinion leaders, it affects our views on life, our perceptual screens, and eventually the products we buy.

Societal Divisions: The Group We Belong To

Sociologists traditionally divided societies into **social classes**: upper, upper-middle, lower-middle, and so on. They believed that people in the same social class tended to have similar attitudes, status symbols, and spending patterns.

But today this doesn't apply to most developed countries. U.S. society, especially, is extremely fluid and mobile—physically, socially, and economically. Americans, regardless of their social class, believe strongly in getting ahead, being better than their peers, and winning greater admiration and self-esteem.

Because of this mobility, dramatic increases in immigration, and the high divorce rate, social-class boundaries have become

Hutchings Photography/Digital Light Source/McGraw-Hill

quite muddled. Single parents, stockbrokers, immigrant shopkeepers, retired blue-collar workers, and bankers all see themselves as part of the great middle class. So "middle class" doesn't mean anything anymore. From the advertiser's point of view, social class seldom represents a functional or operational set of values.

To deal with these often bewildering changes, marketers seek new ways to classify societal divisions and new strategies for advertising to them. We discussed some of these in Chapter 4. Exhibit 5–9 outlines some of the classifications marketers use to describe society today: for example, Upper Crust; Brite Lites, Li'l City; Young Influentials; and Urban Achievers. People in the same group tend to have similar patterns of behavior and product usage.

▼ **EXHIBIT 5–9** The societal divisions described in this exhibit represent just 8 of the 66 Prizm NE (New Evolution) segments defined by Claritas. Marketers believe that consumers in each segment have a great deal in common.

Upper Crust	Blue-Chip Blues
The nation's most exclusive address. Upper Crust is the wealthiest lifestyle in America—a haven for empty-nesting couples older than 55 years old. No segment has a higher concentration of residents earning more than $200,000 a year or possessing a postgraduate degree. And none has a more opulent standard of living.	Blue-Chip Blues is known as a comfortable lifestyle for young, sprawling families with well-paying blue-collar jobs. Ethnically diverse—with a significant presence of Hispanics and African Americans—the segment's aging neighborhoods feature compact, modestly priced homes surrounded by commercial centers that cater to child-filled households.
Brite Lites, Li'l City	**Old Glories**
Not all of America's chic sophisticates live in major metros. Brite Lights, Li'l City is a group of well-off, middle-aged couples settled in the nation's satellite cities. Residents of these typical DINK (double income, no kids) households have college educations, well-paying business and professional careers, and swank homes filled with the latest technology.	Old Glories are the nation's downscale suburban retirees—Americans aging in place in older apartment complexes. These racially mixed households often contain widows and widowers living on fixed incomes, and they tend to lead home-centered lifestyles. They're among the nation's most ardent television fans, watching game shows, soaps, talk shows, and news magazines at high rates.
Young Influentials	**City Startups**
Once known as the home of the nation's yuppies, Young Influentials reflects the fading glow of acquisitive yuppiedom. Today, the segment is a common address for young middle-class singles and couples who are more preoccupied with balancing work and leisure pursuits. Having recently left college dorms, they now live in apartment complexes surrounded by ball fields, health clubs, and casual dining restaurants.	In City Startups, young, multi-ethnic singles have settled in neighborhoods filled with cheap apartments and a commercial base of cafés, bars, laundromats, and clubs catering to 20-somethings. One of the youngest segments in America—with 10 times as many college students as the national average—these neighborhoods feature low incomes and high concentrations of Hispanics and African Americans.
Urban Achievers	**Low-Rise Living**
Concentrated in the nation's port cities, Urban Achievers is often the first stop for up-and-coming immigrants from Asia, South America, and Europe. These young singles and couples are typically college educated and ethnically diverse; about a third are foreign-born, and even more speak a language other than English.	The most economically challenged urban segment, Low-Rise Living is known as a transient world for young, ethnically diverse singles and single parents. Home values are low—about half the national average—and even then less than a quarter of residents can afford to own real estate. Typically, the commercial base of Mom-and-Pop stores is struggling and in need of a renaissance.

> **AMERICANS, REGARDLESS OF THEIR SOCIAL CLASS, BELIEVE STRONGLY IN GETTING AHEAD, BEING BETTER THAN THEIR PEERS, AND WINNING GREATER ADMIRATION AND SELF-ESTEEM.**

Reference Groups: The People We Relate To

Most of us care how we appear to people whose opinions we value. We may even pattern our behavior after members of some groups we affiliate with. This is the significance of **reference groups**—people we try to emulate or whose approval concerns us. Reference groups can be personal (family, friends, co-workers) or impersonal (political parties, religious denominations, professional associations). A special reference group, our peers, exerts tremendous influence on what we believe and how we behave. They determine which brands are cool and which are not.[32] To win acceptance by our peers (fellow students, co-workers, colleagues), we may purchase a certain style or brand of clothing, choose a particular place to live, and acquire behavioral habits that will earn their approval.

Often an individual is influenced in opposite directions by two reference groups and must choose between them. For example, a college student might feel pressure from some friends to join a Greek house and from others to live independently off campus. In ads targeted to students, a local apartment complex might tap the appeal of reference groups by showing students interacting in the complex's pool.

Opinion Leaders: The People We Trust

An **opinion leader** is some person or organization whose beliefs or attitudes are respected by people who share an interest in some specific activity. All fields (sports, religion, fashion, politics) have opinion leaders. An opinion leader may be some expert we find credible. We reason, "If LeBron James thinks Nike makes the best athletic shoes, then it must be so. He knows more about the sport than I do." Thus, the purchasing habits and testimonials of opinion leaders are important to advertisers.

When choosing an opinion leader as a spokesperson for a company or product, advertisers must understand the company's target market thoroughly. Even if executives in the company do not relate to the spokesperson, they must follow market tastes and interests. A spokesperson out of sync with the market undermines his or her credibility—and the company's. On the other hand, an internal person such as the late Dave Thomas, the founder of Wendy's, might turn out to be a highly credible spokesperson without the risks associated with outside celebrities and athletes.[33]

Of course, using a superstar spokesperson is extremely expensive. Even after losing slews of endorsers following a personal scandal, it is estimated that Tiger Woods's 2014–2015 endorsement income exceeded $50 million. In comparison, Woods earned just $600,000 from his golf victories.[34]

Cultural and Subcultural Influence

Culture has a tenacious influence on consumers. **Culture** refers to the whole set of meanings, beliefs, attitudes, and ways of doing things that are shared by some homogeneous social group and typically handed down from generation to generation.[35] Americans love hot dogs, peanut butter, corn on the cob, and apple pie. Canada, Russia, Germany—every country has its own favorite specialties. And advertisers find it much easier to work with these tastes than try to change them.

Global marketers are especially concerned with the purchase environment. Of all business functions, marketing activities are the most susceptible to cultural error.[36]

When creating ads for foreign consumption, marketers must consider many environmental factors: cultural trends, social norms, changing fads, market dynamics, product needs, and media channels.[37]

In countries where people earn little income, demand for expensive products is low. So the creative strategy of an automobile

Reference groups are those individuals or groups whose opinions matter to us. Sports stars are often role models for fans, which makes superstar Stephen Curry worth every penny that Under Armour pays him.

Source: Under Armour, Inc.

advertiser might be to target the small group of wealthy, upper-class consumers. In a country with a large middle class, the same advertiser might be better off mass-marketing the car and positioning it as a middle-class product.

The United States and Canada embrace many subcultures, some of them quite large. They may be based on race, national origin,

The social environments in countries from Italy to Indonesia, from Sweden to Surinam are also based on language, culture, literacy rate, religion, and lifestyle. Advertisers who market products globally can't ignore these distinctions.

In North America, advertising encourages us to keep our mouths clean, our breath fresh, and our teeth scrubbed. But

> [Many consider the United States to be a colorful tapestry of subcultures . . . groups whose shared meanings differ from that of the overall culture.]

religion, language, location, hobbies, or any of a multitude of different ways that people affiliate and self-define. The advertiser must understand these subcultures, for differences among them may affect responses to both products and advertising messages.

Many consider the United States to be a colorful tapestry of subcultures. A **subculture** is a segment within a culture that shares a set of meanings, values, or activities that differ in certain respects from those of the overall culture.[38] According to the U.S. Census Bureau, 47 million African Americans, 59 million Hispanics, and 22 million Asians live in the United States. By 2060, the percentage of the U.S. population from these racial and ethnic groups will be greater than 50.[39] Canada has two major subcultures, anglophones and francophones, based on language (English and French), plus a mosaic of many other cultures based on ethnic and national origins.

Subcultures tend to transfer their beliefs and values from generation to generation. Racial, religious, and ethnic backgrounds affect consumers' preferences for styles of dress, food, beverages, transportation, personal care products, and household furnishings, to name a few. As we saw in Chapter 3, many ad agencies now specialize in minority markets as more advertisers realize that tailoring their appeals to minorities makes good business sense. Recognizing the rapid growth of the Hispanic population, for example, Procter & Gamble spends $170 million per year to understand and tap this market. In fact, most major marketers now develop messages specifically for Hispanic consumers. Of course, advertising credibly and effectively to different groups in the United States requires that those crafting the messages reflect the nation's diversity, a standard the industry has not always met (see Ethical Issues, "Fostering Inclusion and Safety in the Advertising Workspace," below).

Advertisers realize that English speakers are not the only market in the United States. Subcultures exist and offer enormous markets for the culturally savvy. Here, the U.S. Army (www.goarmy.com) suggests to the Spanish-speaking audience that the soldier pictured followed his heart, and now "others follow it."
Source: The United States Army

Fostering Inclusion and Safety in the Advertising Workplace

How can agencies foster a workplace that does more than eliminate discrimination, but go beyond to foster "cultures of inclusion, equity, creative dialogue and social transformation"? For the American Association of Advertising Agencies (4A's), the answer to that question is the Enlightened Workplace Certification Program.

According to 4A's President Marla Kaplowitz, "For participating agencies, this program signals to employees, clients and potential talent that guidelines and best practices have been put in place. This is an investment in a holistic approach for agencies to create safe, trusting, empowering and collaborative environments where all can thrive."

How does it work? Agencies are provided with self-evaluation tools for ferreting out problems. Members of each office, department, or team participate in a workshop that encourages conversations about race, gender, power, and influence. Then, benchmarks and standards for behaviors/actions are used to ensure individuals are supported and abuses are identified and investigated. Finally, organizations that meet the standards are recognized with a certification.

According to *Digiday*, the program is driven "mostly by the current conversation around sexual harassment." The goal, according to the publication, is "to support agencies to eliminate, among other things, bullying and intimidation in the workplace."

Who are these bullies? According to one agency employee, it is the creatives who've accumulated the most trophies. "You're trying to make sure your ideas win and that you're attached to a winning piece of business," she said. "So people can get aggressive, especially those at big agencies with those big personalities."

The 4A's has offered workshops around the country, including the following cities: New York, Chicago, Dallas, Los Angeles, and San Francisco.

The response so far from agencies has been positive. According to Keesha Jean-Baptiste, 4A's SVP of talent engagement and inclusion, "Since announcing the 4A's Enlightened Workplace Certification in February, we've received interest from more than 100 agencies. It's a testament to the fact that there is real appetite for change and a huge sign that agencies are willing to do the work." See more about the program here: www.aaaa.org/4as-unveils-enlightened-workplace-certification-program

Questions
1. What do you think of the idea of agencies certifying an enlightened workplace?
2. Have you experienced bullying and intimidation in a work environment? What were its causes?

people in some southern European countries consider it vain and improper to overindulge in toiletries. Consumers in the Netherlands and the United Kingdom use three times as much toothpaste as those in Spain and Greece. To communicate effectively with Spanish consumers, who view toothpaste as a cosmetic product, advertisers use chic, creative executions rather than dry, therapeutic pitches.

Different Responses From Different Products

In the 1980s, Richard Vaughn at Foote, Cone & Belding took the fact that different kinds of products typically evoke different *levels* of consumer involvement (either high or low) and different *types* of involvement, either *cognitive* (think) or *affective* (feel) and concluded therefore that different products called for different kinds of advertising. He created a two-dimensional model known as the **FCB grid**, which categorized consumer products into four quadrants based on "high involvement" or "low involvement," and "think" or "feel." By positioning brands in the grid based on the degree and type of involvement consumers brought to the purchase decision, the agency could determine which type of advertising would be most appropriate.

As shown in Exhibit 5–10, a product's location on the grid also indicates how the product is purchased and how advertising copy should be written (more emotional or more rational).[40] High involvement/thinking products lend themselves to logical explanations and consumers will probably follow the traditional learn-feel-do model. At the other extreme, high involvement/feeling products are more likely to stress emotional motives and consumers may follow a feel-learn-do sequence. In the case of low involvement products, which are associated with routinized or impulse purchase behavior, *learning* and *feeling* may not occur until after *doing*. In such cases, simply gaining exposure or awareness may be the primary advertising objective.

More recently, Kim and Lord recognized that people can be both cognitively and affectively involved at the same time. So they developed a variation of the FCB grid, shown in Exhibit 5–11. The **Kim-Lord grid** also depicts the degree and the kind of involvement a consumer brings to the purchase decision for different products. Some purchases, such as cars, require a high degree of personal involvement on both the cognitive and affective levels.[41] For others, such as detergent, involvement is low on both axes. Sometimes a marketer uses an advertising strategy aimed at shifting the product to higher involvement on either axis.

▼ **EXHIBIT 5–10** The Foote, Cone & Belding (FCB) grid.

	Thinking	Feeling

High involvement	**1. Informative (thinker)**
	
	Car, house, furnishing, new products
	model: Learn-feel-do (economic?)
	
	Possible implications
	
	Test: Recall
	   Diagnostics
	Media: Long copy format
	   Reflective vehicles
	Creative: Specific information
	   Demonstration
		2. Affective (feeler)
		
		Jewelry-cosmetics-fashion apparel-motorcycles
		model: Feel-learn-do (psychological?)
		
		Possible implications
		
		Test: Attitude change
		   Emotional arousal
		Media: Large space
		   Image specials
		Creative: Executional
		   Impact

Low involvement	**3. Habit formation (doer)**
	
	Food-household items
	model: Do-learn-feel (responsive?)
	
	Possible implications
	
	Test: Sales
	Media: Small space ads
	   10-second I.D.s
	   Radio; POS
	Creative: Reminder
		4. Self-satisfaction (reactor)
		
		Cigarettes, liquor, candy
		model: Do-feel-learn (social?)
		
		Possible implications
		
		Test: Sales
		Media: Billboards
		   Newspapers
		   POS
		Creative: Attention

FCB grid A two-dimensional model that categorizes consumer products into four quadrants based on "high involvement" or "low involvement," and "think" or "feel." By positioning brands in the grid, an agency can determine the type of advertising that would be most appropriate.

Kim-Lord grid A variation of the FCB grid, which allows for the fact that the level of consumer involvement in a product does not have to be high "think" and low "feel" (or vice versa) but can be high (or low) in both categories.

▼ **EXHIBIT 5–11** The Kim-Lord grid.

Affective involvement (Feel)

Low — High

Cognitive involvement (Think) — High / Low

College •   • Car
• Laptop
Motor oil   • Smartphone
   •
Eyeglass frame

•   Greeting card •
Laundry detergent
   • Game app
• Paper towels

• Flower bouquet

Clearly, many interpersonal factors influence consumers. They have an important effect on our mental files, screens, and subsequent purchase decisions. Awareness of these interpersonal influences helps marketers, both domestic and international, create the strategies on which much advertising is based.

check yourself ✓

1. What is a reference group and why is it important?

2. What is culture? How does it differ from a subculture?

CHAPTER 5 | Communication and Consumer Behavior **143**

evoked set The particular group of alternative goods or services a consumer considers when making a buying decision.

evaluative criteria The standards a consumer uses for judging the features and benefits of alternative products.

cognitive dissonance The theory that people try to justify their behavior by reducing the degree to which their impressions or beliefs are inconsistent with one another.

THE PURCHASE DECISION AND POSTPURCHASE EVALUATION

Now that we understand the elements in the consumer purchase decision process, let's examine how it might work in a typical situation. A hypothetical consumer named Chris is thinking about buying a smartphone.

Chris is enrolled at a state university and financed in part by a small scholarship. He also has a part-time job but must act prudently when it comes to spending money because tuition, books, and other expenses are costly.

One day, in his Facebook newsfeed, Chris sees an exciting ad for a new, top-of-the-line smartphone. A beautiful photograph shows the phone's modern, yet understated design. The ad copy highlights the phone's special features. They exude high-tech class—it's just the right style. The ad's signature: "Exclusively at Tech Depot."

In a split-second Chris leaps from perception to motivation. Got to have it! He is highly involved and he wants this personal reward for all his hard work.

Leszek Kobusinski/Shutterstock

The next day Chris visits Tech Depot. While looking for the advertised smartphone, he encounters a variety of alternative styles and models by well-known manufacturers.

The ad has already done its work; the purchase decision process is well under way. At the point of making a purchase decision, though, consumers typically search, consider, and compare alternative brands.

Consumers evaluate selection alternatives (called the **evoked set**). To do this, they establish **evaluative criteria**, the standards they use to judge the features and benefits of alternative products. These criteria originate in needs and desires that every consumer possesses, conscious or not (see My Ad Campaign, "Understanding What Consumers Look for in a Product"). Not all brands make it to the evoked set. In fact, based on their mental files, most consumers usually consider only four or five brands—which presents a real challenge to advertisers. If none of the alternatives meets the evaluative criteria, the consumer may reject the purchase entirely or postpone the decision.

Chris finally finds the advertised phone. But it looks less stylish on the shelf than it did in the ad. Two other phones are also displayed; both are attractive, both expensive. While trying out the devices, Chris considers other unique qualities of style and design. "This one may be a little too bulky." "This one would fit in my pocket." "This one has a better camera, but less memory."

Using central route processing, Chris compares the phones, considering their style, technology, possible advantages, and price (the models are all within $50 of each other). The advertised phone really is the best buy and would be the most satisfying. None of Chris's friends has one like it ... yet. The purchase decision is complete when Chris completes the purchase in Apple Pay.

On the way home, the postpurchase evaluation begins. Chris suddenly envisions some friends' possible negative reactions to the purchase. Maybe it wasn't wise to spend so much money on a top-of-the-line device. Perhaps his friends made better choices. Chris starts to worry—but then quickly bolsters the choice he is now committed to.

"It's really a great smartphone. It's excellent quality and worth the money. I'll get a lot of use out of it."

A key feature of the postpurchase evaluation is *cognitive dissonance*. The theory of **cognitive dissonance** holds that people strive to justify their behavior by reducing the dissonance, or inconsistency, between their cognitions (their perceptions or beliefs) and reality.[42] In fact, research shows that, to combat dissonance, consumers are more likely to read ads for brands they've already purchased than for new products or competing brands.[43]

Back at the dorm, Chris puts the magazine on the desk with a Post-it note marking the ad (for his roommate to discover). Then he uses his new phone to post his purchase on Facebook and describes the purchase, emphasizing its technology, its great design, the enjoyment it will bring, and how great a deal it was. Later he checks back to see comments and likes to his post.

Understanding What Consumers Look for in a Product [5]

Your client's hope is that you can offer helpful advice on creating promotional messages that will get people to do something. In most cases, that something will be buying the client's product or using the service. If your client is a nonprofit, it might involve donating time and/or money.

This seems like common sense, but in fact persuading people to do something they are not already doing can be quite difficult. To help you organize your approach, it may be useful to review what marketing and psychology scholars have learned about consumers and how they are persuaded.

Your challenge at this point in the campaign is to understand the consumer and to get a sense of how the product or service your client offers relates to the consumer's life. Doing this well will require at least two things: a complete understanding of the product and its possible benefits, and a thorough understanding of the consumer.

Maslow's hierarchy of needs suggests that individuals have a range of needs they seek to satisfy in life.

Here is Maslow's hierarchy and some examples that involve food. Consider whether your client's product or service might have benefits that relate to one or more needs:

Need	Examples Involving Food
Self-actualization	Culinary arts degree
Esteem	Cooking lessons
Social	What everyone is eating
Safety	Healthful, organic foods
Physiological	Something that satisfies your hunger

Informational motives involve eliminating a problem, whereas transformational motives involve getting a reward. Consider the possible informational and transformational motives that exist in your consumers that might be addressed by your product.

Informational Motives	
Motive	**Solution**
Problem removal	"Eliminates your headache fast"
Problem avoidance	"Stay out in the sun—you're protected"
Incomplete satisfaction	"The diet drink that doesn't taste like a diet drink"
Mixed approach-avoidance	"Pain-free dental care"
Normal depletion	"Last gas station for 20 miles"

Transformational Motives	
Sensory gratification	"These headphones sound like you are at the show"
Intellectual stimulation	"Hours of fun with challenging puzzles"
Social approval	"Your spouse will love the way you look"

The Foote, Cone & Belding grid was developed to classify how consumers learn about different types of products. Although it was originally designed with the idea that different products would fit in different quadrants, some believe that the quadrants can also be used to classify competing brands within a product category (for example, luxury brands versus discount brands). Where would you place your client's brand? What does that suggest for how you might persuade consumers?

The following guides can help you determine where your client's brand belongs in the FCB grid:

Involvement

1. Is the decision to buy or use the product an important one or an unimportant one?
2. Does the consumer stand to lose a great deal or very little if he or she chooses the wrong brand?
3. Does the decision require a great deal of consideration or very little?

Think versus Feel

Think
1. The decision is based on objective criteria.
2. The decision is based primarily on factual information.

Feel
1. The decision is based on a feeling.
2. The decision is closely related to the consumer's personality.
3. The decision is based on the senses (taste, touch, etc.).

FCB Grid

	Think	Feel
High Involvement	**I. Informative** Learn-Feel-Do (products: major purchases such as insurance, appliances, computers) Strategy: Follow steps of the creative pyramid, beginning with awareness.	**II. Affective** Feel-Learn-Do (products: expensive car, jewelry, high end apparel) Strategy: Focus on self-esteem and ego benefits of product purchases.
Low Involvement	**III. Habitual** Do-Learn-Feel (products: car fuel, detergents, razor) Strategy: Focus on offering samples and creating habits in consumer purchasing.	**IV. Satisfaction** Do-Feel-Learn (products: experiential products such as beer, chewing gum, greeting cards, pizza) Strategy: Focus on social factors and peer use of the product.

People will go to great lengths to avoid cognitive dissonance. For example, if someone just spent a lot of money for new Goodyear tires (www.goodyear.com), he or she is more likely to be interested in ads like this one that reinforce the decision.

Source: The Goodyear Tire & Rubber Company

During the postpurchase period, the consumer may enjoy the satisfaction of the purchase and thereby receive reinforcement for the decision. Or the purchase may turn out to be unsatisfactory for some reason. In either case, feedback from the postpurchase evaluation updates the consumer's mental files, affecting perceptions of the brand and similar purchase decisions in the future.

This story is common for a high-involvement purchase decision. Of course, if Chris's decision had merely involved the purchase of a pack of gum, the process would have been significantly simpler.

Chris may typify a particular group of consumers, and that is important to marketers. As we saw in Chapter 4, marketers are interested in defining target markets and developing effective marketing strategies for groups of consumers who share similar characteristics, needs, motives, and buying habits. ■

ENDNOTES

1. "The Story of One of the Most Memorable Marketing Blunders Ever," The Coca-Cola Company, www.coca-colacompany.com/news/the-story-of-one-of-the-most-memorable-marketing-blunders-ever.

2. "The Story of One of the Most Memorable Marketing Blunders Ever," The Coca-Cola Company, www.coca-colacompany.com/news/the-story-of-one-of-the-most-memorable-marketing-blunders-ever.

3. Mindi Chahai, "Consistent Branding: Don't Mess with It," *Marketing Week*, May 2013, www.marketingweek.com/consistent-branding-dont-mess-with-it.

4. Associated Press, "New Coke, from 1985, Makes Comeback with 'Stranger Things,'" *The Columbian*, May 21, 2019, www.columbian.com/news/2019/may/21/new-coke-from-1985-makes-comeback-with-stranger-things.

5. Communication process adapted from J. Paul Peter and Jerry C. Olsen, *Understanding Consumer Behavior* (Burr Ridge, IL: Richard D. Irwin, 1994), p. 184.

6. Bob Garfield, "The Bobby Awards," *Advertising Age*, December 15, 2008.

7. Martin Ryder, "Semiotics: Language and Culture," *Encyclopedia of Science, Technology, and Ethics* (Macmillan Reference USA, July, 2005).

8. "I'd Rather Go Naked Than Wear Fur," *Facebook*, www.facebook.com/Id-Rather-Go-Naked-Than-Wear-Fur-249218801799153.

9. William O. Bearden, Thomas N. Ingram, and Raymond W. LaForge, *Marketing Principles and Perspectives*, 2nd ed. (Burr Ridge, IL: Irwin/McGraw-Hill, 1997) p. 99.

10. S. Kent Stephan and Barry L. Tannenholz, "The Real Reason for Brand Switching," *Advertising Age*, June 13, 1994, p. 31.

11. "Ad Nauseum," *Advertising Age*, July 10, 2000.

12. Kellaris, Cox, and Cox, "The Effect of Background Music on Ad Processing," *The Journal of Marketing*, October 1993, p. 123.

13. Saul McCloud, "Short Term Memory," *Simply Psychology*, 2009, www.simplypsychology.org/short-term-memory.html.

14. Saul McCloud, "Long Term Memory," *Simply Psychology*, 2009, www.simplypsychology.org/long-term-memory.html.

15. Michael J. McCarthy, "Mind Probe—What Makes an Ad Memorable? Recent Brain Research Yields Surprising Answers," *The Wall Street Journal*, March 22, 1991, p. B3.

16. Jack Trout, *The New Positioning* (New York: McGraw Hill, 1996), pp. 9–16.

17. Stephan and Tannenholz, "The Real Reason for Brand Switching."

18. J. Paul Peter and Jerry C. Olson, *Consumer Behavior and Marketing Strategy*, 4th ed. (Burr Ridge, IL: Richard D. Irwin, 1996), p. 554.

19. Richard J. Lutz, Scott B. MacKenzie, and George E. Belch, "Attitude Toward the Ad As a Mediator of Advertising Effectiveness: Determinants and Consequences," *Advances in Consumer Research* 10 (1983), www.acrwebsite.org/volumes/6175.

20. R. E. Petty, J. T. Cacioppo, and D. Schumann, "Central and Peripheral Routes to Advertising Effectiveness: The Moderating Role of Involvement," *Journal of Consumer Research*, vol. 10, no. 2 (1983), pp. 135–46.

21. This section and the model are adapted from Peter and Olson, *Consumer Behavior and Marketing Strategy*, pp. 554–55.

22. Peter and Olson, *Consumer Behavior and Marketing Strategy*, pp. 556–57.

23. Yumiko Ono, "Overcoming the Stigma of Dishwashers in Japan," *The Wall Street Journal*, May 19, 2000, p. B2.

24. Karen A. Machleit, Chris T. Allen, and Thomas J. Madden, "The Mature Brand and Brand Interest: An Alternative Consequence of Ad-Evoked Affect," *Journal of Marketing*, October 1993, pp. 72–82.

25. Karen A. Machleit, Chris T. Allen, and Thomas J. Madden, "The Mature Brand and Brand Interest: An Alternative Consequence of Ad-Evoked Affect," *Journal of Marketing*, October 1993, pp. 72–82.

26. Peter and Olson, *Consumer Behavior and Marketing Strategy*, p. 513.

27. Ken Dychtwald and Greg Gable, "Portrait of a Changing Consumer," *Business Horizons*, January/February 1990, pp. 62–74; Larry Light, "Trust Marketing: The Brand Relationship Marketing Mandate for the 90s," address to the American Association of Advertising Agencies annual meeting, Laguna Niguel, CA, April 23, 1993.

28. Colin McDonald, "Point of View: The Key Is to Understand Consumer Response," *Journal of Advertising Research*, September/October 1993, pp. 63–69.

29. E. Jerome McCarthy and William D. Perreault, Jr., *Basic Marketing*, 11th ed. (Burr Ridge, IL: Richard D. Irwin, 1993), p. 204.

30. Vanessa O'Connell, "Nabisco Portrays Cookies as Boost to Women's Self-Esteem," *The Wall Street Journal*, July 10, 1998, p. B7.

31. Michelle Greenwald, "8 of the Best Product Demos Ever and Why They're So Effective," *Forbes*, June 4, 2014, www.forbes.com/sites/michellegreenwald/2014/06/04/8-of-the-best-product-demos-ever-and-why-theyre-so-effective/#373c3bef7581.

32. Manfred Hammerl, Florian Dorner, Thomas Foscht, and Marion Brandstatter, "Attribution of Symbolic Brand Meaning: The Interplay of Consumers, Brands and Reference Groups," *Journal of Consumer Marketing*, vol. 33, issue 1 (2016), pp. 32–40.

33. Donghwan Yoon and Youn-Kyung Kim, "The Roles of a Spokesperson and Brand-Message Congruity in Advertising Effectiveness of Coffeehouse Brands," *Journal of Quality Assurance in Hospitality & Tourism*, vol. 16 (2015), pp. 347–368.

34. Jesse Oxfeld, "Tiger Woods Earns 83 Times More Money Endorsing Things Than Playing Golf," *Adweek*, June 30, 2015, www.adweek.com/brand-marketing/tiger-woods-earns-83-times-more-money-endorsing-things-playing-golf-165649.

35. "What Is Culture?" CARLA, University of Minnesota, http://carla.umn.edu/culture/definitions.html.

36. McCarthy and Perreault, *Basic Marketing*, p. 131; Peter and Olson, *Consumer Behavior and Marketing Strategy*, p. 368.

37. McCarthy and Perreault, *Basic Marketing*, p. 131; Peter and Olson,*Consumer Behavior and Marketing Strategy*, p. 368.

38. Lisa Penaloza, "Ethnic Marketing: Public Policy Issues," *The Routledge Companion to Ethnic Marketing* (Routledge: London, 2015)

39. Sandra L. Colby and Jennifer M. Ortman, "Projections of the Size and Composition of the U.S. Population: 2014 to 2060," U.S. Census Bureau, March 2015, www.census.gov/content/dam/Census/library/publications/2015/demo/p25-1143.pdf.

40. Brian T. Ratchford, *Journal of Advertising Research*, vol. 27(4) (August–September 1987), pp. 24–38.

41. Chung K. Kim and Kenneth R. Lord, "A New FCB Grid and Its Strategic Implications for Advertising," Proceedings of the Annual Conference of the Administrative Sciences Association of Canada (Marketing), Niagara Falls, Ontario, 1991.

42. Jillian C. Sweeney, Douglas Hausknecht, Geoffrey N. Soutar, "Cognitive Dissonance after Purchase: A Multidimensional Scale," *Psychology & Marketing*, vol. 17 (May 2000), pp. 369–85.

43. Larry Light, "Advertising's Role in Building Brand Equity," speech to annual meeting of the American Association of Advertising Agencies, April 21, 1993.

chapter SIX

Enis Izgi/kasayizgi/E+/Getty Images

account planning and research

This chapter examines the important role that research plays in the development and evaluation of advertising. It discusses the various sources of research information and the methodologies used to collect and interpret it. We start the chapter examining the important role that account planning plays in cultivating effective advertising strategies and executions.

What does $5.6 million buy you in the ad world? As *Business Insider* notes, that amount of money could buy more than 2 million paid clicks on Amazon or a billion impressions on Instagram.[1] Or exactly 30 seconds of airtime (as of 2020) if the spend is on the most watched telecast in the United States: the Super Bowl.

Needless to say, a lot is riding on the ads that appear during the game, and agencies are anxious to show that their money is well spent. Well, what exactly is money well spent? That's where research can help. The ads that appear at the big game are tested relentlessly to increase the odds that communications objectives for the campaign are met.

Research can give an indication of one important aspect of any ad appearing in the big game: likability. Standing out among the very best commercials of the year is important. A consensus "best liked" ad in the 2020 Super Bowl according to media sources as diverse as CBS Sports, *CNN Business, Time,* and *Ad Week* was an ad for Hyundai titled "Smaht Pahk.

Smaht Pahk, a 60-second spot featuring Boston natives John Krasinski, Rachel Dratch, and Chris Evans, spoofs the Boston accent to highlight a key automatic parking feature of the

continued on p. 150

LEARNING OBJECTIVES

After studying this chapter, you will be able to:

LO6-1 Describe the role of account planners in advertising agencies.

LO6-2 Discuss how research can help advertisers select target markets, media vehicles, and advertising messages.

LO6-3 List the basic steps in the marketing research process.

LO6-4 Compare the common methods used in qualitative and quantitative research.

LO6-5 Justify the challenges of pretesting and posttesting of advertising messages.

LO6-6 Identify issues that can affect the accuracy and usability of quantitative research.

Source: The Hyundai Motor Company

continued from p. 149

redesigned Sonata sedan. You can watch the commercial here: https://admeter.usatoday.com/commercials/smaht-pahk.

It could be argued that the opinions of critics is not necessarily a mirror of consumer sentiment. However, the spot was also a top choice among consumers participating in the inimitable *USA Today* Ad Meter. And YouTube's research metrics suggested that as of early February, more than 41 million people had flocked to the site to view the ad.

The self-parking technology featured in the ad is just one feature of the redesigned Sonata. But rather than drill through a laundry list of attributes, Hyundai decided to focus on just one. Barney Goldberg, lead creative at Hyundai's agency, Innocean USA, reportedly narrowed the focus after testing and reviewing more than 300 scripts.[2]

Looking a little deeper, Smaht Pahk takes advantage of advertising research findings about ways to help consumers remember the brand.[3] Lori Collins, VP at Sales Enablement, noted that the ad "repeated the name of the product in a funny and very memorable way," in contrast to other spots where "the product was displaced by the parody. You remember the star, but not the product." Communications Manager Diana Akimoto noted that the amusing accents helped to demonstrate the technology and enhance brand recall.[4]

Still, what about sales? As of this writing, it is still too early to know. But the early returns are promising. Ace Metrix, a research firm, uses a panel of consumers drawn to represent the U.S. population to assess key ad metrics that include attention, change, relevance, desire, and watchability. After watching every Super Bowl ad, the data suggested a champ: Smaht Pahk.[5]

It is hard to imagine that a $5.6 million ad spend can ever be called a bargain. But armed with great research and a perfect strategy, the better word for that spend might just be: smaht. For more on the campaign, see how the commercial was filmed here: www.youtube.com/watch?v=mlD5yXxJb2s. ■

LO6-1 Describe the role of account planners in advertising agencies.

THE ACCOUNT PLANNER AS CONSUMER ADVOCATE

Jeff Goodby, cochair at Goodby, Silverstein & Partners, is famous for award-winning television ads. He believes that everything an agency does should be geared toward getting into people's heads to figure out what they currently think and understand how best to influence them.[6]

This task is shared by many individuals during the process of planning advertising, but has, in recent years, been focused on a special kind of advertising researcher known as an **account planner**, described in Chapter 3. The account planner's primary role is to represent the consumer in this process. The late Stanley Pollitt, of the London agency Boase Massimi Pollitt, has been called the "father" of account planning. He described planners as "the architects and guardians of their clients' brands, the detectives who uncovered long-hidden clues in the data and gently coerced consumers into revealing their inner secrets."[7]

Putting the consumer, instead of the advertiser, at the center of ad design and strategy, requires tremendous understanding, empathy, and insight. But when performed properly, account planning provides that mystical leap into the future—the brilliant, simplifying insight that lights the client's and the creative's way. Interestingly, the U.S. agencies that have embraced account planning are the very ones now considered to be the hottest shops. They're performing the best work, getting the biggest accounts, and winning all the awards.

In large agencies, account planners work side-by-side with account managers. They share a common goal but have

got milk?

Drink it in.

tar? Not exactly.
re my move. Some
ggest that teens who
ilk instead of sugary
nd to be leaner and
n helps build muscle.
ut up and drink.

dy milk.
w.bodybymilk.com

The success of "Got Milk?" and many other notable campaigns is often attributed to the ability of account planners to get into the heads of their prospects. This approach enables brands to develop meaningful relationships with their customers. In this ad from the California Milk Processor Board and Goodby, Silverstein & Partners, account planners use glamour and celebrity power to draw attention to milk.

Source: The California Milk Processor Board

different orientations. Where the account planner brings a research perspective and represents the consumer, the account manager brings more of a business perspective and represents the client. In smaller agencies without account planning departments, both roles must be played by someone from account management.

Jon Steel summarizes the account planner's mission as follows: "They need to be able to take information of all sorts, shuffle it around, and rearrange it in new patterns until something interesting emerges."[8] One does not necessarily need to conduct research to get that information. Some questions can be answered without research, or the answers may have been uncovered in previous explorations. But in all cases, the advertiser must understand what is happening in consumers' heads.

Bill Bernbach, considered by many to be the single most influential creative force in advertising's history, was never a strong advocate of research. He did, however, acknowledge the importance of knowing your audience: "At the heart of an effective creative philosophy is the belief that nothing is so powerful as an insight into human nature, what compulsions drive a man, what instincts dominate his action, even though his language so often can camouflage what really motivates him."[9]

Not every ad researcher is an account planner. But everyone involved in ad research is focused on helping an advertiser do a better job of persuading or informing consumers. In this chapter, we will examine various types of research and the role that research plays in the development of advertising.

account planner
The individual at an advertising agency primarily responsible for account planning.

check yourself ✓

1. Famed account planner Jon Steel has suggested that the account planner serves as the "conscience" of the agency? What do you think he means by this?

LO6-2 Discuss how research can help advertisers select target markets, media vehicles, and advertising messages.

THE NEED FOR RESEARCH IN MARKETING AND ADVERTISING

Every year companies spend millions of dollars creating ads and promotions that they hope their customers and prospects will notice and relate to. Then they spend millions more placing these messages in print, electronic, and digital media, hoping their customers will see and hear them and eventually respond.

marketing research
The systematic gathering, recording, and analysis of information to help managers make marketing decisions.

advertising research
The systematic gathering and analysis of information specifically to facilitate the development or evaluation of advertising strategies, ads and commercials, and media campaigns.

advertising strategy research Research that defines the product concept or assists in the selection of target markets, advertising messages, or media vehicles.

Advertising is expensive. In the United States the cost of airing a single 30-second commercial on prime-time network TV averages around $116,000.[10] Likewise, a single, full-page color ad in a national magazine can cost more than $172,000.[11] That's too much money to risk unless advertisers have very good information about who their customers are, what they want and like, where they spend their media time, and whether the ads are effective. And that's why advertisers need research. Research provides the information that drives marketing and advertising decision making. Without that information, advertisers are forced to use intuition or guesswork. In today's fast-changing, highly competitive, global economy, that invites failure.

What Is Marketing Research?

To help managers make marketing decisions, companies develop procedures for gathering, recording, and analyzing new information. This is called **marketing research**. Marketing research does a number of things: It helps identify consumer needs and market segments; it provides the information necessary for developing new products and devising marketing strategies; and it enables managers to assess the effectiveness of marketing programs and promotional activities.

What Is Advertising Research?

Before developing any advertising campaign, a company needs to know how people perceive its products, how they view the competition, what brand or company image would be most credible, and what ads offer the greatest appeal. To get this information, companies use *advertising research*. While marketing research provides the information necessary to make marketing decisions, **advertising research** uncovers the information needed for making advertising decisions. By definition, it is the systematic gathering and analysis of information to help develop or evaluate advertising strategies, individual ads, and entire campaigns.

In this chapter, we consider the importance of information gathering to the development of advertising plans and strategies; we look at how companies use research to test the effectiveness of ads before and after they run; and we explore a number of specific research techniques.

Bluemoon Stock/Stockbyte/Getty Images

TNS delivers precise plans for growth

Many research companies can give you interesting insights, but this alone doesn't help you to grow your business. TNS applies world-class expertise and a deep understanding of the human attitudes and emotions that drive behaviour, to uncover insights that lead to business growth.

TNS Growth Map

1. Loyalty and new spend
Driving growth through deeper relationships with existing customers

2. New customers
Increasing penetration by attracting the most profitable new customers

3. New products and services
Portfolio extension to drive incremental growth

4. New markets
Extending reach through geographic or category expansion

About TNS
TNS advises clients on specific growth strategies around new market entry, innovation, brand switching and stakeholder management, based on long-established expertise and market-leading solutions. With a presence in over 80 countries, TNS has more conversations with the world's consumers than anyone else and understands individual human behaviours and attitudes across every cultural, economic and political region of the world. TNS is part of Kantar, one of the world's largest insight, information and consultancy groups.

Please visit www.tnsglobal.com for more information.

TNS ©TNS 2012

Marketing research is the important process of gathering, recording, and analyzing information about customers and prospects. Companies such as TNS Global (www.tnsglobal.com) collect data for their clients and provide critical insight into current and potential markets.
Source: TNS

Applying Research to Advertising Decision Making Advertising research serves various purposes, most of which can be grouped into four categories: *strategy research, creative concept research, pretesting,* and *posttesting.*

1. *Advertising strategy research.* Helps define the product concept or assists in the selection of target markets, advertising messages, or media vehicles.

2. *Creative concept research.* Evaluates the target audience's acceptance of different creative ideas at the concept stage.

Stay Smart.

"No, but I did stay at a Holiday Inn Express last night."

Advertisers need to know who their customers are and what they want. Research indicated that Holiday Inn Express customers like to feel "smart" by saving money. The "Stay Smart" campaign that resulted from this insight is illustrated above.
Source: Holiday Inn® Brand Family

3. *Pretesting of ads.* Uncovers and diagnoses possible communication problems before a campaign begins.

4. *Posttesting of ads.* Evaluates the impact of a campaign after it runs.

As Exhibit 6-1 shows, marketers use the different categories of advertising research at different stages of ad or campaign development. The techniques they use at each stage also vary considerably. We'll examine each of these categories briefly before moving on to discuss the research process.

Advertising Strategy Research

As we will discuss in the next chapter, an advertising strategy is comprised of the *creative strategy* and the *media strategy*. Developing these strategies requires a clear understanding of the *product concept*, the *target audience*, the *media* alternatives, and possible *message elements*. To gain this understanding, companies use **advertising strategy research**.

Product Concept
As we saw at the beginning of this chapter, advertisers need to know how consumers perceive their brands. They also want to know what qualities lead to initial purchases and, eventually, to brand loyalty.

Using this information, they try to establish a unique *product concept* for their brand—that bundle of values we discussed in Chapter 4 that encompasses both utilitarian and symbolic benefits to the consumer.

▼ **EXHIBIT 6-1** Categories of research in advertising development.

	Advertising Strategy Research	Creative Concept Research	Pretesting	Posttesting
Timing	Before creative work begins	Before agency production begins	Before finished artwork and photography	After campaign has run
Research problem	Product concept definition Target audience selection Media selection Message-element selection	Concept testing Name testing Slogan testing	Print testing TV storyboard pretesting Radio commercial pretesting	Advertising effectiveness Consumer attitude change Sales increases
Techniques	Consumer attitude and usage studies Media studies Qualitative interviews	Free-association tests Qualitative interviews Statement-comparison tests	Consumer juries Matched samples Portfolio tests Storyboard test Mechanical devices Psychological rating scales	Aided recall Unaided recall Attitude tests Inquiry tests Sales tests

Hyundai has a great deal riding on its new campaign. The Sonata is a mid-sized sedan in a competitive marketplace. Sedans are facing resistance among consumers who are increasingly turning to SUVs, trucks, and crossovers. The Sonata's sales in 2018 were 105,118, down from 213,303 in 2015.[12]

One way to convince consumers of the Sonata's value is to emphasize technology most people associate with luxury brands. The technology chosen as the focus of the ads is called "remote smart parking assist," which is long and difficult to remember. So Hyundai's agency, Innocean USA, came up with "smaht pahk." "It became this fun thing around the office," said Barney Goldberg, head creative at the agency. "We are hoping when people watch it, it will become infectious."[13]

It's this kind of information that can lead to an effective positioning strategy for the brand. Advertising can shape and

the brand's target markets and audiences. The marketer will want to know which customers are the primary users of the product category and will study them carefully to understand their demographics, geographics, psychographics, and purchase behavior. If the target audience is accurately defined, the advertising will be delivered to the most prospects with the least waste.

Hyundai's agency, Innocean, believed it was important to define the target audience in terms of purchase behaviors and benefits sought from a sedan. To uncover these, Hyundai analyzed databases of sedan loyalists for clues. Loyalists included not only their own drivers but those who purchased competing brands such as Toyota and Nissan.[15] Based on what the agency learned, digital ads showed consumers personalized spots for unique features. For example, an ad directed at a Camry owner might highlight the Sonata's hands-free trunk, a feature not offered by Toyota. Similarly, Volkswagen Passat owners would learn of the Sonata's ventilated seats, an option missing in the Passat.[16]

" STRATEGY RESEARCH IS ESSENTIAL TO DEVELOP A BLUEPRINT FOR CREATIVES TO FOLLOW. "

magnify a brand's position and image over time. In fact, this is one of the most important strategic benefits of advertising. But to use media advertising effectively, strategy research is essential to develop a blueprint for creatives to follow.[14]

Target Audience Selection
We pointed out in Chapter 4 that no market includes everybody. Therefore, one of the major purposes of research is to develop a rich profile of

As shown in this photo of the 2020 Hyundai Sonata, the target audience values features and technologies but also wants an attractive, sporty-looking sedan

Steven Salgado/Shutterstock

Media Selection
To develop media strategies, select media vehicles, and evaluate their results, advertisers use a subset of advertising research called **media research**. Agencies subscribe to syndicated research services (such as Nielsen, Arbitron, Experian Simmons, or Standard Rate & Data Service) that monitor and publish information on the reach and effectiveness of media vehicles—radio, TV, newspapers, and so on—in every major geographic market in the United States and Canada. (We'll discuss these further in Chapter 8 and in Part 5.)

The "smaht pahk" ad debuted about a week before the Super Bowl on news shows highlighting the game's ads. Some have speculated that the Boston focus of the spot was meant to coincide with an appearance by the New England Patriots, who did not in fact make the game. The Super Bowl was seen by nearly 100 million viewers and earned a household rating of 41.6, so the ad received broad exposure.[17] But the ad was not the only way Hyundai engaged its prospects. Innocean tasked former *Saturday Night Live* alum Rachel Dratch to show people how to "speak Boston" on TikTok and invited two Boston-based comics to helm Hyundai's Twitter posts along with the telecast.[18] And these tactics did not include the free media attention the spot attracted, such as *Boston Magazine*'s article on "Who gets to fake the Boston accent?"[19]

Message Element Selection

Companies hope to find promising advertising messages by studying consumers' likes and dislikes in relation to brands and products. Kraft Foods, for example, was looking for ways to dissuade moms from switching to less-expensive brands of processed cheese. While its Kraft Singles brand dominated the processed cheese slices category, it was concerned that the brand wasn't keeping up with overall growth in the market.

Working with several research companies and its ad agency, J. Walter Thompson, the company conducted a series of qualitative consumer attitude studies to figure out how women, particularly mothers, felt about Kraft Singles, with the hope of discovering possible advertising themes. The mothers said they felt good giving their kids Kraft Singles because of the brand's nutritional value. But there was a catch—they also said they'd switch to a competitive product if it were cheaper. Fortunately, a phone survey provided some clues for solving the problem. Among those polled, 78 percent considered the brand an extra source of calcium for their kids. And 84 percent of women with kids younger than 12 said they'd be motivated to buy the brand because of that added benefit.[20]

From this information, the agency used concept testing to determine which message elements might prove most successful.

Advances in technology will allow us to test public reaction to advertisements before they are released by monitoring the brain signals of participants.

Sean Gallup/Getty Images

Creative Concept Research

Once it develops an advertising strategy, the company (or its agency) will begin developing creative concepts for the advertising. Here again, research is helpful in determining which concepts to use.

From all their studies, Kraft researchers came up with two message elements that might keep mothers from defecting to competitive brands. First, show how much kids like Kraft Singles, and second, emphasize the fact that the brand provides the calcium kids need. J. Walter Thompson prepared two rough TV spots and then conducted focus groups with mothers to get their reaction. With a moderator leading the discussion, each group viewed the commercials. The groups' reactions were measured, taped, and observed by JWT and Kraft staff behind a one-way mirror. Immediately, problems surfaced. The idea that kids love the taste of Kraft Singles just didn't come across strongly enough. And the statement that Kraft provides calcium wasn't persuasive. Moms said, "Of course it has calcium, it's cheese." The agency had to find a newsier way to communicate the information.

Tweaking the commercials, JWT came up with a new spot showing youngsters gobbling gooey grilled-cheese sandwiches while a voice-over announcer stated that two out of five kids don't get enough calcium. More focus groups ensued. Now the mothers agreed that the shots of kids devouring sandwiches communicated the great-taste theme, but some moms thought the two-out-of-five statement played too much on their guilt.

To soften the message, the agency switched to a female announcer and then brought in the Dairy Fairy, a character from an earlier campaign, to lighten the whole tone of the spot. This seemed to work better, so the agency proceeded to copy test a finished ad.

Pretesting and Posttesting

Advertising is one of the largest costs in a company's marketing budget. No wonder its effectiveness is a major concern! Companies want to know what they are getting for their money—and whether their advertising is working. And they'd like some assurance before their ads run.

Goldberg tested 344 different original scripts for Hyundai's big ad before settling on "smaht pahk." He noted that the agency relied on extensive pretesting to "make sure we're not leading

Advertisers can avoid mistakes and save money on production by testing creative concepts in animatic form. Animatics are illustrated by hand and then computer animated. How can an animatic help reduce the uncertainty about a creative concept before an ad is developed?

Tutatama/Alamy Stock Photo

ourselves down the wrong path." The pretest data suggested they were on the right track.[21]

Hyundai focused on several core pretest elements, including likability, watchability, relevance, and desire. Using a standardized ad test where most ads score at 550, the Sonata spot nearly hit

Crispin Porter + Bogusky used hidden cameras to capture the reactions of real Burger King customers who were told that the Whopper sandwich had been "discontinued." Research showed the ads were better recalled than any other ever tested.

Source: Burger King

700. Goldberg acknowledged, "We want to make sure it's entertaining, but we're also informing and educating people on our products. So it's a nice blend of both."[22]

The Purpose of Testing Ads

To increase the likelihood of preparing the most effective advertising messages, companies use **pretesting**. Some agencies, such as DDB Needham, pretest all ad copy for communication gaps or flaws in message content before recommending it to clients.[23] When companies don't pretest their ads, they may encounter a surprising reaction from the marketplace. Schering Canada received a torrent of complaint letters from customers who said they didn't like its commercial introducing the antihistamine Claritin to the over-the-counter market in Canada. Most negative responses, though, are more subtle: Consumers simply scroll through their feed, turn the page, or change the channel, and sales mysteriously suffer. This is why it's also important to evaluate the effectiveness of an ad or campaign *after* it runs. **Posttesting** (also called *ad tracking*) provides the advertiser with useful guidelines for future advertising. We'll discuss methods for testing ads later in this chapter.

check yourself ✓

1. What are some things that might be tested with creative concept research?

2. Why do companies pretest their advertising?

LO6-3 List the basic steps in the marketing research process.

STEPS IN THE RESEARCH PROCESS

Now that we understand the various types of decision-related information that marketers seek, let's explore how they gather this information by looking at the overall research process and some of the specific techniques they use.

There are five basic steps in the research process (see Exhibit 6–2):

1. Situation analysis and problem definition.

2. Secondary research.

3. Construction of research objectives.

4. Primary research.

5. Interpretation and reporting of findings.

Step 1: Analyzing the Situation and Defining the Problem

The first step in the marketing research process is to *analyze the situation* and *define the problem*. Many large firms have in-house research departments. Often the marketing department also maintains a **marketing information system (MIS)**—a

> Good research on the wrong problem is a waste of effort.

primary data Research information gained directly from the marketplace.

secondary data Information that has previously been collected or published.

sophisticated set of procedures designed to generate a continuous, orderly flow of information for use in making marketing decisions. These systems ensure that managers get the information they need when they need it.[24]

Most smaller firms don't have dedicated research departments, and their methods for obtaining marketing information are frequently inadequate. These firms often find the problem-definition step difficult and time-consuming. Yet good research on the wrong problem is a waste of effort.

Step 2: Conducting Secondary Research

The second step in the process is to use **secondary research** to learn more about the market, the competition, the business environment, and to better define the problem. Researchers may discuss the problem with wholesalers, distributors, or retailers outside the firm; with client insiders; with customers; or even with competitors. They look for whoever has the most information to offer.

There are two types of research data: *primary* and *secondary*. Information an agency collects or hires a research firm to collect is **primary data**; it is proprietary and can focus on any issue the agency chooses, but acquiring it is expensive and time-consuming. So during the exploratory stage, researchers frequently use **secondary data**—information previously collected or published, usually for some other purpose. This information is readily available, either internally or externally, and can be gathered more quickly and inexpensively than primary data. The drawback of secondary data is that it does not always focus on the specific issue an agency might hope to learn more about.

Assembling Internal Secondary Data Company records are often a valuable source of secondary information. Useful internal data include product shipment figures, billings, warranty-card records, advertising expenditures, sales expenses, customer correspondence, website tracking, databases, and records of meetings with sales staffs.

▼ **EXHIBIT 6–2** The marketing research process begins with evaluation of the company's situation and definition of the problem.

| Situation analysis and problem definition | Secondary research • Internal secondary data • External secondary data | Construction of research objectives | Primary research • Quantitative • Qualitative | Interpretation and reporting of findings |

primary research
Collecting data directly from the marketplace using qualitative or quantitative methods.

qualitative research
Research that uses in-depth studies of small, non-random samples to explore the behavior, perceptions, needs, and motivations of a target audience.

quantitative research
Research that uses larger, representative samples and surveys to quantify hypotheses and measure specific market variables.

- Consumer/business publications (*Bloomberg Businessweek, Forbes, Fortune, Wall Street Journal, Advertising Age, Prevention,* and thousands more).

- Database services (County Business Patterns, Dialog, Paperity, ResearchGate, ProQuest, Lexis-Nexis, and Dow Jones Newswires, Think with Google, World Digital Library).

- Internet search engines (Google, Bing, and others).

- Specialized search engines (Google scholar, Google Books).

- Specialized tools (MakeMyPersona, Ubersuggest).

It's important to understand that secondary data carry some potential problems. Information may be out of date and therefore obsolete. Much of it is not relevant to the problem at hand. Some information from purported research is just wrong, so the findings are invalid. In other cases, the source may be unreliable. Finally, there is now so much information available (thanks to the Internet) that it's just overwhelming; it's extremely time-consuming to wade through it all. If you are interested in practicing research techniques that can inform advertising see My Ad Campaign 6–A below.

Stockbyte/Getty Images

A well-developed marketing information system can help researchers analyze sales data, review past tracking studies, and examine previous marketing research data. This information might point the way toward an interesting headline or positioning statement such as Motrin's "Medicine with Muscle."

Sources of External Secondary Data

Much information is available, sometimes at little or no cost, from the government, market research companies, trade associations, various trade publications, or computerized databases. Most large companies subscribe to any of a number of syndicated research reports about their particular industry. For example, as the advertising manager for a large nutritional company introducing a new line of vitamins, you might need to know the current demand for vitamins and food supplements, the number of competitors in the marketplace, the amount of advertising each is doing, and the challenges and opportunities the industry faces.

In the United States, frequently used sources of secondary data include:

- Library reference materials (*Business Periodicals Index* for business magazines, *Reader's Guide to Periodical Literature* for consumer magazines, *Public Information Service Bulletin,* the *New York Times Index,* and the *World Almanac and Book of Facts*).

- Government publications *(American Fact Finder, FedStats, Statistical Abstract of the United States, U.S. Census Bureau)*.

- Trade association publications (annual fact books containing data gathered by various industry groups listed in the *Directory of National Trade Associations*).

- Research organizations and their publications or syndicated information (literature from university bureaus of business research, Nielsen MyBestSegments, Experian Simmons's Multi-Media Engagement Study, IRI's Consumer Network, and Standard Rate & Data Service).

Step 3: Establishing Research Objectives

Once the exploratory research phase is completed, the company may discover it needs additional information that it can get only from doing primary research. As was the case for Holiday Inn Express, it may want to identify exactly who its customers are and clarify their perceptions of the company and the competition. To do so, the company must first establish *specific research objectives*.

A concise written statement of the research problem and objectives should be formulated at the beginning of any research project. A company must be clear about what decisions it has to make that the research results will guide. Once it knows the application, it can set down clear, specific research objectives.[25] For example, a department store, noticing that it is losing market share, might write its problem statement and research objectives as follows:

Market Share

Our company's sales, while still increasing, seem to have lost momentum and are not producing the profit our shareholders expect. In the last year, our market share declined 3 percentage points. Our studies indicate we are losing sales to other department stores in the same malls and that customers are confused about our position in the market. We need to make decisions about how we position ourselves for the future.

Research Objectives

We must answer the following questions: (1) Who are our customers? (2) Who are the customers of other department stores? (3) What do these customers like and dislike about us and about

Research [6–A]

Research is a complicated aspect of preparing a campaign, and without at least one course in advertising research you may find it tough going. However, without research you will find it difficult to make some of the tough creative and strategic decisions that lie ahead. Even without an extensive research background, you can do some secondary and qualitative research that can result in better choices for your campaign.

Secondary Research

Secondary research involves obtaining information from existing sources, including your client. Be sure to obtain all that you can, with the understanding that information shared by your client is valuable and that most clients will insist on strict confidentiality. Breaking a confidentiality agreement is a very serious transgression and should not happen under any circumstances, whether deliberately or through neglect.

Toolsrush has an excellent list of some online secondary sources: www.toolsrush.com/free-market-research-tools.

Qualitative Research

You can also plan some qualitative research studies. Two of the most common are focus groups and observational research. In a focus group, you bring together a collection of carefully chosen participants (users of your brand, users of competing brands, etc.) and lead a group discussion that has the potential to offer strategic insights. Hubspot has an excellent guide for conducting a focus group: https://blog.hubspot.com/marketing/how-to-run-a-focus-group.

Observational Research

Observational research techniques involve monitoring the consumer in his or her native environment (the mall, a restaurant, a skateboard park, etc.). The goal is to see how the consumer behaves in a natural setting. Careful attention is ordinarily paid to language, dress, interactions, symbols, and style.

The Robert Woods Johnson Foundation gives guidance in conducting observational research here: www.qualres.org/HomeObse-3594.html.

Quantitative Research

Your project may also involve administering a survey. Google Forms, introduced in the My Ad Campaign from Chapter 1, may be useful for creating an online survey that is easy and inexpensive to administer. The hard part is writing a good survey instrument and then choosing data analysis techniques that will provide you and your client with useful information. Some web tutorials are listed below:

Surveys

SurveyMonkey offers some great tips for writing good questions: www.surveymonkey.com/mp/writing-survey-questions. Need some options for gathering consumer responses to your questions? Explorable offers a good list: https://explorable.com/survey-response-scales

Data Analysis Using Excel

After the responses are collected, it's time to crunch the numbers. Some options for data analysis are listed here: www.excel-easy.com/data-analysis.html.

---

our competitors? (4) How are we currently perceived? and (5) What do we have to do to clarify and improve that perception?

This statement of the problem is specific and measurable, the decision point is clear, and the questions are related and relevant. The research results should provide the information that management needs to decide on a new positioning strategy for the company. The positioning strategy facilitates the development of marketing and advertising plans that will set the company's course for years to come.

check yourself ✓

1. What is the difference between primary and secondary data?

2. What are the questions that should be answered in research objectives?

LO6-4 Compare the common methods used in qualitative and quantitative research.

Step 4: Conducting Primary Research

When a company wants to collect data about a specific problem or issue, it uses **primary research**. Unlike secondary research, primary research is customized or tailored to the marketer's specific objectives. There are two types of primary research: qualitative and quantitative.

To get a general impression of the market, the consumer, or the product, advertisers typically start with **qualitative research**. This enables researchers to gain insight into both the population whose opinion will be sampled and the subject matter itself. Then, to get hard numbers about specific marketing situations, they may perform a survey or use some other form of **quantitative research**. Ideally, agencies use a balance of both qualitative and quantitative methods, understanding the limits of each and how they work together.[26] (See Exhibit 6–3.)

In this section, we'll discuss the basic methods advertisers use for conducting qualitative and quantitative research and then we'll look at how they apply these techniques to testing ads.

Basic Methods of Qualitative Research

To get people to share their thoughts and feelings, researchers use qualitative research that elicits in-depth, open-ended responses rather than yes or no answers. Some marketers refer to this as *motivation research*. Unfortunately, no matter how skillfully posed, some questions are uncomfortable for consumers to answer. When asked why they bought a particular status car, for instance, consumers might reply that it handles well or is economical or dependable, but they rarely admit that it makes them feel important. The methods used in qualitative research are usually either *projective* or *intensive techniques*.

Projective techniques Advertisers use **projective techniques** to understand people's underlying or subconscious feelings, attitudes, interests, opinions, needs, and motives. By asking indirect questions (such as "What kind of people do you think shop here?"), the researcher tries to involve consumers in a situation where they can express feelings about the problem or product.

Projective techniques were adapted for marketing research after their use by psychologists in clinical diagnosis. But such techniques require the skill of highly experienced researchers.

Intensive techniques **Intensive techniques**, such as in-depth interviews, also require great care to administer properly. In the **in-depth interview (IDI)**, carefully planned but loosely structured questions help the interviewer probe respondents' deeper feelings. The big pharmaceutical company Schering, for example, uses IDIs with physicians to find out what attributes doctors consider most important in the drugs they prescribe and to identify which brands the doctors associate with different attributes.[27] While IDIs help reveal individual motivations, they are also expensive and time-consuming.

One of the most common intensive research techniques is the **focus group**, in which the company invites six or more people typical of the target market to a group session to discuss the product, the service, or the marketing situation. The session may last an hour or more. A trained moderator guides the often free-wheeling discussion, and the group interaction reveals the participants' true feelings or behavior toward the product. Focus-group meetings are usually recorded and often viewed or videotaped from behind a one-way mirror.

▼**EXHIBIT 6-3** Differences between qualitative and quantitative research.

	Qualitative	Quantitative
Main techniques for gathering data	Focus groups and in-depth interviews.	Surveys and randomly drawn samples.
Kinds of questions asked	Why? How so? In what way?	How many? How much?
Role of interviewer	Critical: interviewer must build rapport with research participants. She must think on feet and frame questions and probes in response to whatever respondents say. A highly trained professional is advisable.	Important, but interviewers need only be able to read scripts. They should not improvise. Minimally trained, responsible employees are suitable.
Questions asked	Questions vary in order and phrasing from group to group and interview to interview. New questions are added, old ones dropped.	Should be exactly the same for each interview. Order and phrasing of questions carefully controlled.
Number of interviews	Fewer interviews tending to last a longer time.	Many interviews in order to give a projectable scientific sample.
Kinds of findings	Generate ideas, obtain insights, explore language options, refine concepts, help explain survey results, provide diagnostics on advertising copy.	Evaluate outcomes, test hypotheses, prioritize factors, provide data for mathematical modeling and projections.

observation method A method of research used when researchers actually monitor people's actions.

Universal Product Code (UPC) An identifying series of vertical bars with a 12-digit number that adorns every consumer packaged good.

A focus group is an intensive research technique used to evaluate the effectiveness of the various elements of a sponsor's ad or advertising campaign. Focus groups are especially effective used in conjunction with quantitative research.

Stockbroker/MBI/Alamy Stock Photo

Online focus groups are gaining acceptance. For example, a start-up company preparing to launch a new "green" cleaning product developed a website to support its marketing objectives. To obtain reactions from purchase decision makers on the site's content and features, the company conducted 90-minute online focus groups. Live web pages of the client site were displayed to all participants, and the moderator asked questions and probed responses. Each participant was encouraged to navigate the site and report on desired features and content. After finishing the research, the company modified its sales strategy and developed more specific site content based on concerns of the participants.[28]

Focus groups don't represent a valid sample of the population, but the participants' responses are useful for several purposes. They can provide input about the viability of prospective spokespeople, determine the effectiveness of visuals, concepts, and strategies, and identify elements in ads that are unclear or claims that don't seem plausible. As in the case of Kraft, focus groups are particularly useful for gaining a deeper understanding of particular market segments. Focus groups are best used in conjunction with surveys. In fact, focus-group responses often help marketers design questions for a formal survey[29] or, following a survey, focus groups can put flesh on the skeleton of raw data.[30]

Ethnographic research (ethnography) is an intensive research technique that tries to understand how people live their lives. Many high-tech companies use ethnography to uncover trends that will determine the direction of future technological development. Ethnography involves trying to understand behavior and culture by going out and talking to people wherever they are, while they're doing whatever it is they do. It means entering someone's world for a while, be it a couple of hours or a couple of days.[31] This process can be very labor-intensive and therefore costly and may require long periods of time in the field. Ethnographers must be very skilled in their art and often have specialized training in social science fields such as anthropology.

Basic Methods of Quantitative Research Advertisers use quantitative research to gain reliable, hard statistics about specific market conditions or situations. There are three basic research methods used to collect quantitative data: *observation*, *experiment*, and *survey*.

Observation In the **observation method**, researchers monitor people's actions. They may count the traffic that passes by a billboard, measure a TV audience through instruments hooked to television sets, or study consumer reactions to products displayed in the supermarket. Most observation method research is performed by large, independent marketing research companies, such as Nielsen and Information Resources, Inc. Healthtex, for example, subscribes to the services of National Panel Diary (NPD), which tracks the clothing purchases of 16,000 homes as a nationwide sample. From this, Healthtex can find out its market share and better understand statistical trends in the marketplace.

Technology has greatly facilitated the observation method. One example is the **Universal Product Code (UPC)** label, an

This photo shows how smart retailers use observational research to better understand consumer shopping habits.

FG Trade/E+/Getty Images

> There is no infallible way to predict advertising success or failure.

identifying series of vertical bars with a 12-digit number that adorns every consumer packaged good. By reading the codes with optical scanners, researchers can tell which products are selling and how well. The UPC label not only increases speed and accuracy at the checkout counter; it also enables timely inventory control and gives stores and manufacturers accurate point-of-purchase data sensitive to the impact of price, in-store promotion, couponing, and advertising.

Nielsen's ScanTrack provides data on packaged-goods sales, market shares, and retail prices from more than 4,800 stores representing 800 retailers in 52 markets. A companion service, National Consumer Panel, uses in-home bar-code scanners to collect data on consumer purchases and shopping patterns. As a result, marketers suddenly have reliable data on the effectiveness of the tools they use to influence consumers. With that information, they can develop empirical models to evaluate alternative marketing plans, media vehicles, and promotional campaigns. Understanding who is most interested in Keurig-style coffee makers can help improve marketing efforts in a fast growing market in coffee sales.[32]

Video cameras have also affected observation techniques. Envirosell, a New York–based research company, uses security-type cameras to capture consumer in-store shopping habits. To determine the effectiveness of packaging and displays, the company analyzes how much time people spend with an item and how they read the label.[33]

Experiment To measure actual cause-and-effect relationships, researchers use the **experimental method**. An experiment is a scientific investigation in which a researcher alters the stimulus received by a *test group* and compares the results with that of a *control group* that did not receive the altered stimulus. This type of research is used primarily for new product and new campaign introductions. As we saw in the Kraft story, marketers go to an isolated geographic area, called a **test market**, and introduce the product in that area alone or test a new ad campaign or promotion before a *national rollout*. For example, a new campaign might run in one geographic area but not another. Sales in the two areas are then compared to determine the campaign's effectiveness. However, researchers must use strict controls so the variable that causes the effect can be accurately determined. Because it's hard to control every marketing variable, this method is difficult to use and quite expensive.

Survey The most common method of gathering primary quantitative research data is the **survey**, in which the researcher gains information on attitudes, opinions, or motivations by questioning current or prospective customers (political polls are a common type of survey). Surveys can be conducted by personal interview, telephone, mail, or on the Internet. Each has distinct advantages and disadvantages (see Exhibit 6–4).

▼**EXHIBIT 6–4** Comparison of data collection methods.

	Data Collection Method			
	Personal Interview	**Telephone**	**Mail**	**Internet**
Data collection costs	High	Medium	Low	Low
Data collection time required	Medium	Low	High	Low
Sample size for a given budget	Small	Medium	Large	Large
Data quantity per respondent	High	Medium	Low	Low
Reaches widely dispersed sample	No	Maybe	Maybe	Yes
Interaction with respondents	High	High	None	Medium
Degree of interviewer bias	High	Medium	None	None
Severity of nonresponse bias	Low	Low	High	Medium
Presentation of visual stimuli	Yes	No	Maybe	Yes
Field worker training required	Yes	Yes	No	No

Researchers often collect information on attitudes, opinions, or motivations by conducting surveys of current or prospective customers. A common technique is the mall intercept, in which an interviewer at a shopping mall intercepts a sample of those passing by to ask if they would be willing to participate in a brief research study.

Peathegee Inc./Blend Images/Getty Images

check yourself ✓

1. What are some benefits of qualitative research?

2. Why would an advertiser use quantitative research?

LO6-5 Justify the challenges of pretesting and posttesting advertising.

Basic Methods for Testing Ads
Although there is no infallible way to predict advertising success or failure, pretesting and posttesting can give an advertiser useful insights if properly applied.

Pretesting methods Advertisers often pretest ads for likability and comprehension by using a variety of qualitative and quantitative techniques.

For example, when pretesting print ads, advertisers often ask direct questions: What does the advertising say to you? Does the advertising tell you anything new or different about the company? If so, what? Does the advertising reflect activities you would like to participate in? Is the advertising believable? What effect does it have on your perception of the merchandise offered? Do you like the ads?

Through **direct questioning**, researchers can elicit a full range of responses from people and thereby infer how well advertising messages convey key copy points. Direct questioning is especially effective for testing alternative ads in the early stages of development, when respondents' reactions and input can best be acted on. There are numerous techniques for pretesting print ads, including *focus groups, order-of-merit tests, paired comparisons, portfolio tests, mock magazines, perceptual meaning studies,* and *direct-mail tests.* (See My Ad Campaign 6–B, "Methods for Pretesting Ads.")

Several methods are used specifically to pretest radio and TV commercials. In **central location tests**, respondents are shown test commercials, usually in shopping centers, and questions are asked before and after exposure. In **clutter tests**, test commercials are shown with noncompeting control commercials to determine their effectiveness, measure comprehension and attitude shifts, and detect weaknesses.

The challenge of pretesting There is no best way to pretest advertising variables. Different methods test different aspects, and each has its own advantages and disadvantages—a formidable challenge for the advertiser.

Pretesting helps distinguish strong ads from weak ones. But because the test occurs in an artificial setting, respondents may assume the role of expert or critic and give answers that don't reflect their real buying behavior. They may invent opinions to satisfy the interviewer, or be reluctant to admit they are influenced, or vote for the ads they think they *should* like. This is why some creative people mistrust ad testing; they believe it stifles creativity.

Despite these challenges, the issue comes down to dollars. Small advertisers rarely pretest, but their risk isn't as great, either. When advertisers risk millions of dollars on a new campaign, they *must* pretest to be sure the ad or commercial is interesting, believable, likable, memorable, and persuasive—and reinforces the brand image.

Posttesting methods Posttesting can be more costly and time-consuming than pretesting, but it can test finished ads under

Methods for Pretesting Ads [6–B]

Advertisers rarely trust intuition alone when evaluating their creative work. There is simply too much on the line. Pretesting is what occurs when advertisers test prototypes of their ads before they are run in the mass media. Below is a comprehensive list of ways that real agencies and advertisers test their work. You don't have the resources to do many of them. But you can use some of these methods to test your creative ideas with a small sample drawn from your target audience. Doing so will give you added ammunition for persuading your client that you've developed a strong strategy for his or her brand.

Print Advertising

- **Direct questioning.** Asks specific questions about ads. Often used to test alternative ads in early stages of development.
- **Focus group.** A moderated but freewheeling discussion and interview conducted with six or more people.
- **Order-of-merit test.** Respondents see two or more ads and arrange them in rank order.
- **Paired comparison method.** Respondents compare each ad in a group.
- **Portfolio test.** One group sees a portfolio of test ads interspersed among other ads and editorial matter. Another group sees the portfolio without the test ads.
- **Mock magazine.** Test ads are "stripped" into a magazine, which is left with respondents for a specified time. (Also used as a posttesting technique.)
- **Perceptual meaning study.** Respondents see ads in timed exposures.
- **Direct-mail test.** Two or more alternative ads are mailed to different prospects on a mailing list to test which ad generates the largest volume of orders.

Broadcast Advertising

- **Central location projection test.** Respondents see test commercial films in a central location such as a shopping center.
- **Trailer test.** Respondents see TV commercials in trailers at shopping centers and receive coupons for the advertised products; a matched sample of consumers just gets the coupons. Researchers measure the difference in coupon redemption.

- **Theater test.** Electronic equipment enables respondents to indicate what they like and dislike as they view TV commercials in a theater setting.
- **Live telecast test.** Test commercials are shown on closed-circuit or cable TV. Respondents are interviewed by phone, or sales audits are conducted at stores in the viewing areas.
- **Sales experiment.** Alternative commercials run in two or more market areas.

Physiological Testing

- **Pupilometric device.** Dilation of the subject's pupils is measured, presumably to indicate the subject's level of interest.
- **Eye movement camera.** The route the subject's eyes traveled is superimposed over an ad to show the areas that attracted and held attention.
- **Galvanometer.** Measures subject's sweat gland activity with a mild electrical current; presumably the more tension an ad creates, the more effective it is likely to be.
- **Voice pitch analysis.** A consumer's response is taped, and a computer is used to measure changes in voice pitch caused by emotional responses.
- **Brain pattern analysis.** A scanner monitors the reaction of the subject's brain.

Online Testing

- **Google Ads' Campaign Drafts and Experiments.** Test, measure, and apply changes to improve a Google Ads campaign.
- **Google Smart Bidding.** Test bid strategies using machine learning to optimize online ad campaign conversions.
- **Google Act on Attribution.** Determine keyword value with an eye toward meeting customers' needs.
- **Facebook Split Tests.** Assess consumer response to differences in two similar versions of the same ad. This is often called A/B testing.
- **Facebook Lift Tests.** Assess advertising outcomes between groups of people who do and don't see a campaign.
- **LinkedIn Campaign Manager.** All-in-one ad platform that allows A/B testing.
- **Snap Ads Manager.** Includes tools for optimizing and measuring campaigns.

actual market conditions. As we saw with Kraft, some advertisers benefit from pretesting and posttesting by running ads in select test markets before launching a campaign nationwide.

As in pretesting, advertisers use both quantitative and qualitative methods in posttesting. Most posttesting techniques fall into five broad categories: *aided recall, unaided recall, attitude tests, inquiry tests,* and *sales tests.* (See My Ad Campaign 6-C, "Methods for Posttesting Ads.")

Some advertisers use **attitude tests** to measure a campaign's effectiveness in creating a favorable image for a company, its brand, or its products. Presumably, favorable changes in attitude predispose consumers to buy the company's product.

Nielsen IAG measures the effectiveness of television advertising, product placement, and the Internet for such clients as American Express, General Motors, and Procter & Gamble. Nielsen IAG collects key data about the ads that viewers

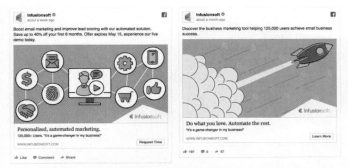

This A/B test appeared in a Facebook ad campaign. Even with similar content, color and design can lead to dramatically different responses online. Because digital advertisers can test ad executions before committing large sums of money to production, advertisers can avoid costly mistakes. With tools from companies such as Hootsuite, Google, Facebook, and LinkedIn, digital marketers can figure out what strategies will work best before spending big budgets.

Source: Infusion Software, Inc

watched the night before and generates a detailed performance analysis that includes brand recall, message understanding, likability, and purchase intent. This tool helps companies understand the actual effectiveness of their campaigns.[34]

Similarly, many companies, such as Nissan, interview consumers regularly to track brand awareness, familiarity with vehicle models, recall of commercials, and shifts in attitude or image perception. If a commercial fails, it can be pulled quickly.[35]

Children's clothing manufacturer Healthtex conducted some print-ad posttesting and discovered that, while new mothers appreciated the information in the long copy format, more experienced mothers didn't. For them, the headline and one line of copy were sufficient to get the point across. They already understood the rest. As a result, the company used the shorter format and redesigned the ads aimed at experienced parents.

The challenge of posttesting

Each posttesting method has limitations. **Recall tests** reveal the effectiveness of ad components, such as size, color, or themes. But they measure what respondents noticed and remembered, *not* whether they actually intend to buy the product.

For measuring sales effectiveness, attitude tests are often better than recall tests. An attitude change relates more closely to product purchase, and a measured change in attitude gives management more confidence to make informed decisions about advertising plans.

By using **inquiry tests**—in which consumers respond to an ad for information or free samples—researchers can test an ad's attention-getting value, readability, and understandability. These tests also permit fairly good control of the variables that motivate reader action, particularly if a *split-run* test is used (split runs are covered in Chapter 10). Unfortunately, inquiries may not reflect a sincere interest in a product, and responses may take months to receive.

When advertising is the dominant element or the only variable in the company's marketing plan, **sales tests** are a useful measure of advertising effectiveness. However, many other variables can affect sales (competitors' activities, the season of the year, and even the weather). Sales response may not be immediate,

attitude tests A type of posttest that usually seeks to measure the effectiveness of an advertising campaign in creating a favorable image for a company, its brand, or its products.

recall tests Posttesting methods used to determine the extent to which an advertisement and its message have been noticed, read, or watched.

inquiry tests A form of test in which consumer responses to an ad for information or free samples are tabulated.

sales tests A useful measure of advertising effectiveness when advertising is the dominant element, or the only variable, in the company's marketing plan. Sales tests are more suited for gauging the effectiveness of campaigns than of individual ads or components of ads.

Methods for Posttesting Ads [6–C]

Posttesting involves assessing the impact of a campaign after the ads have run. It is an important way that advertisers judge whether their messages have helped them to achieve their advertising objectives (see Chapter 8). You will most likely not do posttesting for your client. However, it is good practice for you to propose *how* the client might posttest your ads. This is material that you can incorporate in your campaigns book. Be sure to reference your advertising objectives when you propose a posttesting technique.

- **Aided recall (recognition–readership).** To jog their memories, respondents are shown certain ads and then asked whether their previous exposure was through reading, viewing, or listening.

- **Unaided recall.** Respondents are asked, without prompting, whether they saw or heard advertising messages.
- **Attitude tests.** Direct questions, semantic differential tests, or unstructured questions measure changes in respondents' attitudes after a campaign.
- **Inquiry tests.** Additional product information, product samples, or premiums are given to readers or viewers of an ad; ads generating the most responses are presumed to be the most effective.
- **Sales tests.** Measures of past sales compare advertising efforts with sales. Controlled experiments test different media in different markets. Consumer purchase tests measure retail sales from a given campaign. Store inventory audits measure retailers' stocks before and after a campaign.

validity An important characteristic of a research test. For a test to be valid, it must reflect the true status of the market.

reliability An important characteristic of research test results. For a test to be reliable, it must be repeatable, producing the same result each time it is administered.

and sales tests, particularly field studies, are often costly and time-consuming. For consumer packaged goods, though, the cost of sales tests has been greatly reduced thanks to grocery store scanners.

Step 5: Interpreting and Reporting the Findings

The final step in the research process involves interpreting and reporting the data. Research is very costly (see Exhibit 6–5), and its main purpose is to help solve problems. The final report must make the findings clear to the company's managers and relevant to their needs.

Tables and graphs are helpful, but they must be explained in words management can understand. Technical jargon (such as "multivariate analysis of variance model") should be avoided, and descriptions of the methodology, statistical analysis, and raw data should be confined to an appendix. The report should state the problem and research objective, summarize the findings, and draw conclusions. The researcher should make recommendations for management action, and the report should be discussed in a formal presentation to allow management feedback and questions and to highlight important points.

Learning that the wash mitt usually given to customers with the purchase of a new Beetle convertible wasn't earning them particularly high marks, Volkswagen (www.vw.com) contacted Arnold Worldwide to come up with a better idea. Arnold decided to create a guidebook to the many things that new owners could see and do in a convertible and included a star chart and wild birdseed with the book.
Source: Volkswagen of America, Inc.

check yourself ✓

1. What information might be collected when pretesting an advertisement?

2. What is the value in knowing if advertising changed a consumer's attitude?

▼**EXHIBIT 6–5** The cost of professional research.

Type of Research	Features	Cost	Cost per Respondent	Factors That Can Affect Quality and Costs
Telephone and mail surveys	400 20-minute interviews, with report	$16,000 to 18,000	$40 to $45	Response rates Interview time Incidence of qualified respondents Level of analysis required in the report
Focus group	2 groups with 10 respondents each, with report	$8,000 to $12,000	$400 to $600	Cost of focus group facilities Moderator costs Respondent costs
Online surveys	400 surveys, no report	$40	10 cents	Samples sometimes unreliable, respondent involvement may be low Cost does not include analysis or report

Sources: Jeff Hecker, "Focus Group Costs Explained" *Athena Brand Wisdom*, September 22, 2014, www.athenabrand.com/blog/focus-group-research-costs-overview/; Google Consumer Surveys, www.google.com/insights/consumersurveys/pricing.

LO6-6 Identify issues that can affect the accuracy and usability of quantitative research.

IMPORTANT ISSUES IN ADVERTISING RESEARCH

When marketers conduct primary research, there is always one legitimate concern—the accuracy of the findings. This is especially true when conducting quantitative research and when doing research in international markets.

Considerations in Conducting Primary Quantitative Research

Quantitative research requires formal design and rigorous standards for collecting and tabulating data to ensure its accuracy and usability. When conducting primary research, advertisers must consider certain issues carefully, especially whether the research is *valid* and *reliable*.

Validity and Reliability Assume you want to determine a market's attitude toward a proposed new toy. The market consists of 10 million individuals. You show a prototype of the toy to five people and four say they like it (an 80 percent favorable attitude). Is that test valid? Hardly. For a test to have **validity**, *results must be free of bias and reflect the true status of the market*.[36] Five people aren't enough for a minimum sample, and the fact that *you* showed a prototype of *your* toy to these people would probably bias their response.

Moreover, if you repeated the test with five more people, you might get an entirely different response. So your test also lacks **reliability**. For a test to be reliable, it must be *repeatable*—it must produce approximately the same result each time it is administered (see Exhibit 6-6).

Validity and reliability depend on several key elements: the size of the sample (larger is better), the sampling methods (are people randomly selected?), the survey questionnaire design (is the survey clear, interesting, and easy to complete?), and the data tabulation and analysis methods.

Sampling Methods When a company wants to know what consumers think, it typically can't ask everybody. The good news is that the company can obtain valuable information from a much smaller group, called a **sample**, if that group is properly sampled from the larger group of consumers the company is interested in, called a population or **universe**. To accomplish this, they must decide whom to survey, how many to survey, and how to choose the respondents.

A sample must be large enough to offer reliable and valid findings. But even large samples are likely to be misleading if the sample is not drawn correctly. There are two types of samples: probability samples and nonprobability samples.

Sampling methods that provide accurate information about a universe are called **probability samples** (sometimes referred to as *random samples*) because everyone in the universe has an equal chance of being selected.[37] For example, a researcher who wants to know a community's opinion on an issue could select members of the community at random. But this method has its

sample A portion of the population selected by market researchers to represent the appropriate targeted population. Also, a free trial of a product.

universe An entire target population.

probability samples A research sample in which all members of the target population have an equal and independent chance of being selected for the study.

▼ **EXHIBIT 6-6** The reliability–validity diagram. Using the analogy of a dartboard, the bull's-eye is the actual value of some measure within a population. The top row shows high reliability (repeatability) because the darts are closely clustered. When reliability drops, the darts land more randomly and spread across a wider area, as in both examples in the bottom row. We got different results each time. The left column demonstrates high validity because in both examples the darts center around the bull's-eye. The right column represents low validity because bias in the testing process drew all the darts to one side; we were measuring the wrong thing. The upper-left quadrant reflects the truest picture of the data.

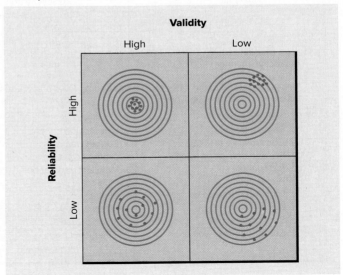

nonprobability samples Research samples that do not provide every unit in the population with an equal chance of being included. As a result, there is no guarantee that the sample will be representative.

challenges. Every unit (person) must be known and listed so each can be given an equal chance of being selected. This is sometimes prohibitively expensive and sometimes impossible. For example, a company may not have a list of all individuals who use its products.

Instead, researchers often use **nonprobability samples** because they're easier, less expensive, and less time-consuming than probability samples. Sometimes referred to as *convenience samples*, respondents are selected on the basis of their availability (e.g., because they volunteered). Nonprobability samples don't give every unit in the universe an equal chance of being included, so their results cannot be considered representative of a universe.[38] So why do some companies use them? In many instances marketing and advertising research needs only approximate insights. For example, the nonprobability method of interviewing shoppers in malls may be sufficient to determine the shopping preferences, image perceptions, and attitudes of target customers.

How Questionnaires Are Designed Constructing a good questionnaire requires considerable expertise. Much bias in research is blamed on poorly designed questionnaires. Typical problems include asking the wrong types of questions, asking too many questions, using the wrong form of a question (which makes it difficult to answer or tabulate), and using a poor choice of words. Exhibit 6-7 shows some typical questions that might be used in a survey for a retail store.

Consider the simple question: "What kind of soap do you use?" A respondent may not know what *soap* is referencing. Hand soap, shampoo, laundry detergent, or dishwashing soap? Does *kind* mean brand, size, or type? Finally, what constitutes *use*? What a person buys (perhaps for someone else) or uses personally—or for what purpose? In fact, one person probably uses several different kinds of soap, depending on the occasion. It's impossible to answer this question accurately. Worse, if the consumer does answer it, the researcher doesn't know what the answer means and will likely draw an incorrect conclusion. For these reasons, questionnaires *must* be pretested. (See My Ad Campaign 6-D, "Developing an Effective Questionnaire.")

Effective survey questions have three important attributes: *focus*, *brevity*, and *clarity*. They focus on the topic of the survey. They are as brief as possible. And they are expressed simply and clearly.[39]

The four most common types of questions are *open-ended*, *dichotomous*, *multiple choice*, and *scale*. But there are many ways to ask questions within these four types. In Exhibit 6-8, for example, more choices could be added to the multiple-choice format. Neutral responses (the middle choice) could be removed from the scale question so the respondent

▼EXHIBIT 6-7 A personal questionnaire like this helps determine shoppers' feelings toward a chain of stores, its merchandise, and its advertising.

1. Do you intend to shop at *(Store name)* between now and Sunday?
Yes 1 No 2 (If no, skip to question 5)

2. Do you intend to buy something in particular or just to browse?
Buy 1 Browse 2

3. Have you seen any of the items you intend to buy advertised by *(Store name)*?
Yes 1 (continue) No 2 (skip to question 5)

4. Where did you see these items advertised? Was it in a *(Store name)* advertising insert included with your newspaper, a *(Store name)* flyer you received in the mail, the pages of the newspaper itself, on TV, or somewhere else?

- ☐ Insert in newspaper
- ☐ Flyer in mail
- ☐ Pages of newspaper
- ☐ On TV
- ☐ Somewhere else (specify)________
- ☐ Don't recall

5. Please rate the *(Store name)* advertising insert on the attributes listed below. Place an X in the box at the position that best reflects your opinion of how the insert rates on each attribute. Placing an X in the middle box usually means you are neutral. The closer you place the X to the left or right phrase or word, the more you believe it describes the *(Store name)* insert.

	1	2	3	4	5	6	7	
Looks cheap								Looks expensive
Unskillful								Cleverly done
Unappealing								Appealing
Does not show clothing in an attractive manner								Shows clothing in an attractive manner

6. Please indicate all of the different types of people listed below you feel this *(Store name)* advertising insert is appealing to.

- ☐ Young people
- ☐ Bargain hunters
- ☐ Conservative dressers
- ☐ Fashion-conscious people
- ☐ Rich people
- ☐ Professionals
- ☐ High-income people
- ☐ Men
- ☐ Someone like me
- ☐ Career-oriented women
- ☐ Quality-conscious people
- ☐ Low-income people
- ☐ Budget watchers
- ☐ Older people
- ☐ Middle-income people
- ☐ Blue-collar people
- ☐ Women
- ☐ Office workers
- ☐ Smart dressers
- ☐ Other (specify)________

Developing an Effective Questionnaire [6–D]

must answer either positively or negatively. And there is obvious bias in the dichotomous question.

Questions should elicit a response that is both accurate and useful. By testing questionnaires on a small subsample, researchers can detect any confusion, bias, or ambiguities and make revisions.

Data Tabulation and Analysis

Collected data must be validated, edited, coded, and tabulated. Answers must be checked to eliminate errors or inconsistencies. For example, one person might answer two years, while another says 24 months; such responses must be changed to the same units for correct tabulation. Some questionnaires may be rejected because respondents' answers indicate they misunderstood the questions. Finally, the data must be tabulated and summarized, usually by computer.

Many researchers want *cross-tabulations* (for example, product use by age group or education). Software programs such as SAS®, SPSS®, and Excel® make it possible for small advertisers as well as large corporations to tabulate data on a personal computer and apply advanced statistical techniques.[40] Many cross-tabulations are possible, but researchers must use skill and imagination to select only those that show meaningful and significant relationships.

Collecting Primary Data in International Markets

International marketers face a number of challenges when they collect primary data. For one thing, research overseas is often more expensive than domestic research. Many marketers are surprised to learn that research in five countries costs five times as much as research in one country; there are no economies of scale.[41]

But advertisers must determine whether their messages will work in foreign markets. (Maxwell House, for example, had to change its "great American coffee" campaign when it discovered that Germans have little respect for U.S. coffee.)

Advertisers need more than just facts about a country's culture. They need to understand and appreciate the nuances of its cultural traits and habits, a difficult task for people who don't live there or speak the language. Knowledgeable international advertisers such as Colgate-Palmolive work in partnership with their

▼ **EXHIBIT 6–8** Different ways to phrase research questions.

Type	Questions
Open-ended	How would you describe (*Store name*) advertising?
Dichotomous	Do you think (*Store name*) advertising is old-fashioned? _____ Yes _____ No
Multiple-choice	What description best fits your opinion of (*Store name*) advertising? _____ Modern _____ Unconvincing _____ Well done _____ Old-fashioned _____ Believable
Scale	Please indicate on the scale how you rate the quality of (*Store name*) advertising. _____ _____ _____ _____ _____ 1 2 3 4 5 Poor Excellent

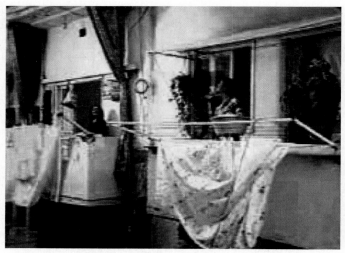

This example from Procter & Gamble's Bonux detergent campaign in Lebanon illustrates some of the difficulties inherent in international advertising. Lebanese housewives take great pride in clean washing, so much so that they even brag about laundry secrets and hang their laundry on balconies to be seen by neighbors. Bonux created the "housewives moment of fame" campaign and bought advertising space on the roofs of buses so the ads could be seen from balconies. Radio spots featured interviews with housewives riding the buses. The campaign raised awareness 85 percent and increased market share by 20 percent.

Source: Procter & Gamble Company

local offices and use local bilingual marketing people when conducting primary research abroad.[42]

For years, Mattel tried unsuccessfully to market the Barbie doll in Japan. It finally sold the manufacturing license to a Japanese company, Takara, which did its own research. Takara found that most Japanese girls and their parents thought Barbie's breasts were too big and her legs too long. It modified the doll accordingly, changed the blue eyes to brown, and sold 2 million dolls in two years.

Conducting original research abroad can be fraught with problems. First, the researcher must use the local language, and translating questionnaires can be tricky. Second, many cultures view strangers suspiciously and don't wish to talk about their personal lives.

Despite these problems—or perhaps because of them—it's important for global advertisers to perform research. Competent researchers are available in all developed countries, and major international research firms have local offices in most developing countries.

Today, most market research firms use the Internet to conduct some form of market research.[43] With the global adoption of the Internet, experts anticipate further cuts in costs and time for getting valuable customer input for marketing and advertising decision making. ∎

check yourself ✓

1. Why do researchers "sample" the population?

2. Why must questionnaires be pretested?

ENDNOTES

1. Alexandra Samet, "Advertisers Will Spend $5 Million for a 30-Second Super Bowl Ad, but They Could Be Putting That Money to Better Use," *Business Insider*, January 20, 2020, www.businessinsider.com/super-bowl-2020-commercials-future-advertising-emarketer.

2. LRW, "The Most Rffective Ads from Super Bowl LIV," *LRW Perspectives*, February 03, 2020, https://lrwonline.com/perspective/the-most-effective-ads-from-super-bowl-liv.

3. Mathew Peterson, Kevin, Wise, Yilin Ren, Zongyuan Wang, and Jiachen Yao, "Memorable Metaphor: How Different Elements of Visual Rhetoric Affect Resource Allocation and Memory for Advertisements," *Journal of Current Issues & Research in Advertising* 38 (2016), pp. 65–74; Sherry J. Holladay, "'Have Fun While You Can,' 'You're Only as Old as You Feel,' and 'Don't Ever Get Old!': An Examination of Memorable Messages about Aging," *Journal of Communication* 52 (2006), pp. 681–97.

4. Mathew Peterson, Kevin, Wise, Yilin Ren, Zongyuan Wang, and Jiachen Yao, "Memorable Metaphor: How Different Elements of Visual Rhetoric Affect Resource Allocation and Memory for Advertisements," *Journal of Current Issues & Research in Advertising* 38 (2016), pp. 65–74; Sherry J. Holladay, "'Have Fun While You Can,' 'You're Only as Old as You Feel,' and 'Don't Ever Get Old!': An Examination of Memorable Messages about Aging," *Journal of Communication* 52 (2006), pp. 681–97.

5. Press Release, "Cheetos, Hyundai & Doritos Top Ace Metrix's Lists of Top Super Bowl Ads," *Ace Metrix*, February 3, 2020, www.acemetrix.com/about-us/company-news/press-releases/cheetos-hyundai-doritos-top-ace-metrixs-lists-of-top-super-bowl-ads.

6. Jon Steel, *Truth, Lies and Advertising: The Art of Account Planning* (New York: Wiley, 1998), p. 5.

7. Jon Steel, *Truth, Lies and Advertising: The Art of Account Planning* (New York: Wiley, 1998) , p. 37.

8. Jon Steel, *Truth, Lies and Advertising: The Art of Account Planning* (New York: Wiley, 1998) , p. 53.

9. Avi Dan, "The Heart of Effective Advertising Is a Powerful Insight," *Forbes*, July 8, 2013, www.forbes.com/sites/avidan/2013/07/08/the-heart-of-effective-advertising-is-a-powerful-insight.

10. Jeanne Poggi, "Here's How Much It Costs to Advertise in TV's Biggest Shows," *Advertising Age*, October 2, 2018, https://adage.com/article/media/tv-pricing-chart/315120.

11. Ashley Donohue, "What Is the Average Cost of Advertising in a Magazine?" *BizFluent*, November 05, 2019, https://bizfluent.com/facts-5625807-average-cost-advertising-magazine-.html.

12. Frank Ahrens, "Hyundai Sonata Magic Is Back—But Will Carbuyers Care?" *Forbes*, March 07, 2019, https://www.forbes.com/sites/frankahrens/2019/03/07/hyundai-sonata-magic-is-back-but-will-car-buyers-care/#3cebb50b454f.

13. Elaine Underwood, "Boston-Connected Celebs Play with Hyundai Sonata's 'Smaht Pahk' Feature," *Campaign US*, January 27, 2020, www.campaignlive.com/article/boston-connected-celebs-play-hyundai-sonatas-smaht-pahk-feature/1671936.

14. Jerry W. Thomas, "Media Advertising Is an Unfulfilled Promise," *Marketing News*, September 23, 1996, p. 28.

15. Vince Bond Jr., "How Hyundai Honed in on Buyers for 2018 Sonata," *Automotive News*, November 10, 2018, www.autonews.com/article/20181110/RETAIL01/181119991/how-hyundai-homed-in-on-buyers-for-2018-sonata.

16. Vince Bond Jr., "How Hyundai Honed in on Buyers for 2018 Sonata," *Automotive News*, November 10, 2018, www.autonews.com/article/20181110/RETAIL01/181119991/how-hyundai-homed-in-on-buyers-for-2018-sonata.

17. Rick Porter, "V Ratings: Super Bowl LIV Draws 100M Viewers, Up Slightly vs. 2019," *Hollywood Reporter*, February 03, 2020, www.hollywoodreporter.com/live-feed/super-bowl-liv-masked-singer-tv-ratings-sunday-feb-2-2020-1275713.

18. Hyundai Motor America, "Hyundai Reveals Its Big Game Commercial, 'Smaht Pahk,'" *PR Newswire*, January 27, 2020.

19. Thomas Stackpole, "Who Gets to Fake the Boston Accent?" *Boston Magazine*, January 31, 2020, www.bostonmagazine.com/news/2020/01/31/fake-boston-accent.

20. Story adapted from "Cheese, Please!" *American Demographics*, March 2000, pp. S6–S8 (Copyright Primedia Intertec March 2000).

21. Doug Zanger, "It's as If John Krasinski, Rachel Dratch and Chris Evans Never Left Boston in Hyundai's Wicked Funny Super Bowl Ad," *Adweek*, January 27, 2020, www.adweek.com/agencies/its-as-if-john-krasinski-rachel-dratch-and-chris-evans-never-left-boston-in-hyundais-hilarious-super-bowl-ad.

22. Doug Zanger, "It's as If John Krasinski, Rachel Dratch and Chris Evans Never Left Boston in Hyundai's Wicked Funny Super Bowl Ad," *Adweek*, January 27, 2020, www.adweek.com/agencies/its-as-if-john-krasinski-rachel-dratch-and-chris-evans-never-left-boston-in-hyundais-hilarious-super-bowl-ad.

23. Pat Sloan, "DDB Boosts Planning by Hiring Brit Expert," *Advertising Age*, September 21, 1992, pp. 3, 53.

24. William D. Perreault Jr. and E. Jerome McCarthy, *Basic Marketing*, 17th ed. (Burr Ridge, IL: Richard D. Irwin, 2008), p. 153.

25. Paul Conner, "Defining the 'Decision Purpose' of Research," *Marketing News,* September 23, 1996, p. 18.

26. Michael L. Garee and Thomas R. Schori, "Focus Groups Illuminate Quantitative Research," *Marketing News*, September 23, 1996, p. 41.

27. Robert West, Schering Canada, personal interview, May 17, 1993.

28. "Concept Test for a New Cleaning Product," InsideHeads, LLC, www.insideheads.com/InsideHeadsCaseStudies.pdf.

29. William Weylock, "Focus: Hocus Pocus?" *Marketing Tools*, July/August 1994, pp. 12–16; Thomas L. Greenbaum, "Focus Groups Can Play a Part in Evaluating Ad Copy," *Marketing News*, September 13, 1993, pp. 24–25.

30. Pat Sloan and Julie Liesse, "New Agency Weapon to Win Clients: Research," *Advertising Age*, August 30, 1993, p. 37.

31. Ethnographic Research, Inc., www.ethnographic-research.com.

32. Geoff Smith, "Caffeine Fix: New Coffee Buyers Grow the Category by $9.9M," *Nielsen*, www.nielsen.com/nz/en/insights/news/2015/caffeine-fix-new-coffee-buyers-grow-category-by-9m.html.

33. ENVIROSELL, www.envirosell.com.

34. "Nielsen IAG Ranks Most Liked, Most Recalled TV Ads," *Nielsen*, www.nielsen.com/us/en/insights/news/2008/nielsen-iag-ranks-most-liked-most-recalled-tv-ads.html.

35. Paul Marsden, "Consumer Advisory Panels the Next Big Thing in Word-of-Mouth Marketing?" *Word of Mouth*, Summer, 2006, https://digitalwellbeing.org/wp-content/uploads/2015/05/Marsden-2006-06-Customer-Advisory-Panels-Market-Leader.pdf.

36. Pamela L. Alreck and Robert B. Settle, *The Survey Research Handbook*, 2nd ed. (Burr Ridge, IL: Richard D. Irwin, 1995), pp. 56–59.

37. Louis M. Rea and Richard A. Parker, *Designing and Conducting Survey Research: A Comprehensive Guide*, 4th ed. (John Wiley & Sons, 2014).

38. Perreault and McCarthy, *Basic Marketing*, p. 173.

39. Rea and Parker, *Designing and Conducting Survey Research: A Comprehensive Guide*.

40. MINITAB software for IBM-PC, for Microsoft Windows, and for academic use in an inexpensive student edition through Addison-Wesley Publishing Co., Reading, MA.

41. George S. Fabian, panelist, "Globalization: Challenges for Marketing and Research," *Marketing Review*, February 1993, p. 23.

42. Maureen R. Marston, panelist, "Globalization: Challenges for Marketing and Research," pp. 20–21.

43. eMarketer, www.emarketer.com.

chapter Seven

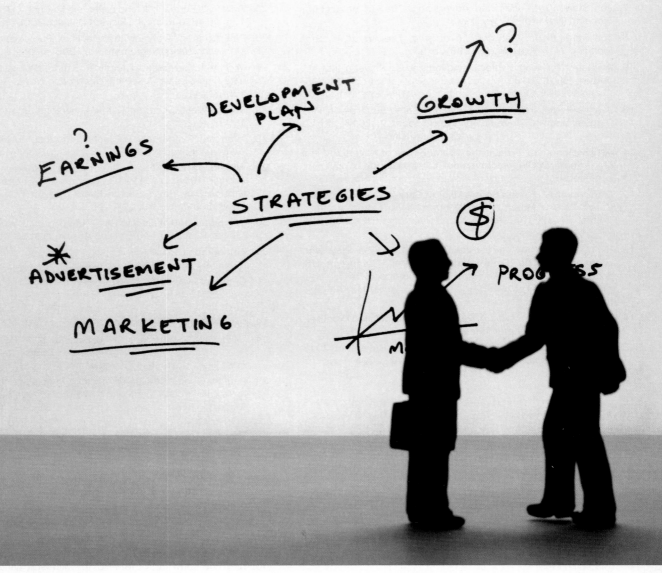

Source: Kutay Tanir/iStock Exclusive/Getty Images

marketing, advertising, and **IMC** planning

This chapter explains how advertisers and agencies do marketing and IMC planning. Marketers need to understand the various ways plans are created. They must also know how to analyze the internal and environmental forces that affect the success of their products; be prepared to develop realistic, attainable objectives; formulate strategies to achieve them; and create budgets for marketing communications.

How does a "hillbilly" mixer become one of the world's most successful carbonated beverage? Great planning, consistent innovation, and attention to the demands of the marketplace.

Nearly 70 years ago, Ally and Barney Hartman of Knoxville, Tennessee, cooked up a sweet, citrusy brew and tested it on families and friends. The consensus was the drink was great, so the brothers began bottling it and sharing with the locals. In 1946, they designed a paper label for their beverage featuring a hillbilly toting a gun and a signature that read "By Barney and Ollie." In honor of the mountain moonshine famous in Tennessee, they named their drink "Mountain Dew."

Over the course of time, the brand grew. The gun-toting Willy the Hillbilly and the apt slogan, "Ya-hoo Mountain Dew," helped make it a regional success. In 1964, PepsiCo bought the brand and, for some years, continued using the old advertising approach.

Sensing that U.S. demographics and consumer preferences were changing, in 1973 Pepsi repositioned and re-launched Mountain Dew. No longer would it be a hillbilly mixer. Rather, the Dew would be cast as a high-energy, youth-oriented, uniquely flavored soft drink. New ads created by BBDO New York featured active young people enjoying outdoor activities to the theme "Hello Sunshine, Hello Mountain Dew." Within five years, the action-oriented approach sent Dew sales over the 100-million-case mark. The 1980s saw high-octane sports and adventure added to the advertising.[1]

continued on p. 174

LEARNING OBJECTIVES

After studying this chapter, you will be able to:

LO7-1 Describe the role and importance of a marketing plan.

LO7-2 Distinguish between objectives, strategies, and tactics in marketing and advertising plans.

LO7-3 Show what makes IMC planning different from traditional methods.

LO7-4 Explain how to establish specific, realistic, and measurable advertising objectives.

LO7-5 Review the pros and cons of the various approaches for determining advertising budgets.

Source: PepsiCo, Inc.

continued from p. 173

Since that time, Mountain Dew has set a standard of how to remain true to its definition of exuberance while continuously evolving to stay fresh and relevant. "We have a great unity of message and purpose that has been consistent over time about what we are and what we aren't," says Scott Moffitt, director of marketing for Mountain Dew.[2] "The brand is all about exhilaration and energy, and you see that in all that we do, from advertising and community to grassroots programs and our sports-minded focus. We have a very crystal clear, vivid positioning."

The positioning concept has allowed Mountain Dew to reach consumers in diverse venues—from skateboarding parks to mainstream extravaganzas such as the Super Bowl. In the 2020 game, Mountain Dew scored a hit with a spot-on parody of Stanley Kubrick's film *The Shining*, complete with Bryan Cranston assuming several roles from the film.

Marketing across such a broad spectrum from grass-roots to grandiose advertising events is known within PepsiCo as "mass intimacy." One Pepsi-Cola executive puts it this way: "It's our way of saying we haven't sold out."[3]

Given the great success of BBDO's Dew campaign, the challenge became staying power throughout the 2000s. Young consumers are notoriously fickle and perpetually ready to try something new. One innovative tactic included developing a snowboarding documentary that made only brief references to the brand. The decision to finance a

film, which carried a cost close to that of a traditional 30-second TV spot, may have resulted from recognition by the advertiser that its target audience watches less TV than other groups and often sees TV commercials as manipulative.[4]

In the mid-2000s, when some soda drinkers switched to noncarbonated alternatives, Mountain Dew experienced a volume increase of nearly 2 percent and the diet version surged nearly 8 percent. The same period saw volume sales of Coke Classic and Pepsi-Cola drop 2 percent and 3 percent, respectively.

For all its success, Mountain Dew is not sitting on its laurels. After 46 years relying on BBDO as its agency, the brand switched its account to TBWA. As of 2020, Mountain Dew is all about its users, so much so that fans determine the brand's marketing efforts. Case in point? A Dew-scented body wash, a limited-run product produced as a response to fan posts in social media.[5] The tactic is part of a strategy of flexibility in marketing and fostering direct relationships with customers.

Unusual ads and a soft-drink scented body wash? Bold activities for a brand that started as a humble rural mixer. But Mountain Dew didn't grow from a small regional beverage to a national powerhouse by playing it safe. And as unusual as such activities may be, they remain perfect executions of a well-thought-out strategy. ∎

LO7-1   Describe the role and importance of a marketing plan.

THE MARKETING PLAN

The successful campaigns of Mountain Dew demonstrate that business success depends on marketing and advertising planning and advertising creativity.

The Importance of Marketing Planning

Planning is an essential activity for every organization. Planning provides guidance to a company's employees and partners about the company's goals and direction. It commits the organization to strategies and tactics for growth and profitability. Without thoughtful, realistic planning, companies would soon find themselves out of business.

Organizations generate plans for many business functions, but the one that is of most relevance to advertising and IMC is the **marketing plan**. The marketing plan organizes relevant facts about the organization, its markets, products, services, customers, and competition. It forces all departments to focus on the customer. Finally, it lists goals and objectives for defined periods of time and describes precise strategies and tactics for achieving them.

The written marketing plan must reflect the goals of top management and be consistent with the company's mission and capabilities. Depending on its scope, the plan may be long and complex or, in the case of a small firm, very brief. Formal marketing plans are reviewed and revised yearly, but planning is not a one-time event; it's an ongoing activity. As the facts on the ground change, so must the marketing plan.

The Effect of the Marketing Plan on IMC

The marketing plan has enormous effects on an organization's marketing communications. It helps managers analyze and improve all company operations, including marketing and advertising programs. It defines the role of advertising in the marketing mix. It enables better implementation, control, and continuity of advertising programs, and it ensures the most efficient allocation of IMC dollars.

Companies have a choice in how they plan. Most still use the traditional top-down planning model; some use a bottom-up model; and many companies use an IMC model. Let's look at each.

check yourself ✓

1. What is a marketing plan and why is it a company's most important document?

2. How does the marketing plan affect IMC efforts?

LO7-2 Distinguish between objectives, strategies, and tactics in marketing and advertising plans.

Top-Down Marketing Plans

The traditional **top-down marketing** plan is still quite common. As Exhibit 7-1 shows, the top-down plan has four main elements: *situation analysis*, *marketing objectives*, *marketing strategy*,

and *marketing tactics* (or *action programs*). Large companies with extensive marketing plans sometimes include additional sections.

Situation Analysis The **situation analysis** section is a *factual* statement of the organization's current situation and how it got there. It presents the relevant facts about the company's history, growth, products and services, sales volume, share of market, competitive status, markets served, distribution systems, past IMC programs, marketing research studies, and other pertinent information. To attempt a situation analysis yourself, see My Ad Campaign 7–A and 7–C.

A good situation analysis is more than a presentation of facts, however. Facts can only be understood in context. So, for example, Diet Mountain Dew's lower annual sales going into 2019 are put into context when the marketing plan notes that overall sales of carbonated beverages have been in a 5-year decline.[6]

Planners draw attention to the most important aspects of a brand's situation through a SWOT analysis. The **SWOT analysis** draws on the facts contained in the situation analysis to highlight strengths, weaknesses, opportunities, and threats for the brand. Strengths and weaknesses represent company (internal) capabilities, while opportunities and threats represent environmental (external) factors. An obvious strength for Mountain Dew is its well-defined, attractive brand image as a high-energy, full-flavored, youth-oriented beverage. A possible weakness could be the brand's sugar content, which has turned consumers

▼ **EXHIBIT 7–1** Traditional top-down marketing plan.

One of the best ways to define a market is to think about customer needs first and then identify the products that meet those needs.

away from soft drink brands. An opportunity for Mountain Dew might be the increased interest in energy drinks. Because Mountain Dew is a highly caffeinated beverage, it might profit from such a trend. Threats to Mountain Dew might include rising prices for commodities used to make the product (sugar, flavorings) or distribute the product (fuel) that would force Mountain Dew to raise prices to remain profitable. Another might be new competitors such as Coke Energy, which could eat into Mountain Dew marketshare.[7]

my ad campaign

Developing the Situation Analysis [7–A]

In previous chapters you've honed your understanding of the consumer, segmented the audience, and conducted research. It is time to pull all of this information together and create an assessment of your client's current situation. Marketers call such an assessment a situation analysis. Use the list below to organize your analysis.

The Industry
- **Companies in industry:** Dollar sales, strengths.
- **Growth patterns within industry:** Primary demand curve, per capita consumption, growth potential.
- **History of industry:** Technological advances, trends.
- **Characteristics of industry:** Distribution patterns, industry control, promotional activity, geographic characteristics, profit patterns.

The Company
- **The company story:** History, size, growth, profitability, scope of business, competence, reputation, strengths, weaknesses.

The Product or Service
- **The product story:** Development, quality, design, description, packaging, price structure, uses, reputation, strengths, weaknesses.
- **Product sales features:** Exclusive, nonexclusive differentiating qualities, competitive position.
- **Product research:** Technological breakthroughs, improvements planned.

Sale History
- **Sales and sales costs:** By product, model, sales districts.
- **Profit history.**

Share of Market
- **Sales history industrywide:** Share of market in dollars and units.
- **Market potential:** Industry trends, company trends, demand trends.

The Market
- **Who and where is the market:** How was the market segmented, how can it be segmented, what are consumer needs, attitudes, and characteristics? How, why, when, where do consumers buy?

- **Past advertising appeals:** Successful or unsuccessful.
- **Who are our customers:** Past and future? What characteristics do they have in common? What do they like about our product? What don't they like?

Distribution
- **History and evaluation:** How and where product is distributed, current trend.
- **Company's relationship:** With the distribution channel and its attitudes toward product/company.
- **Past policies:** Trade advertising, deals, co-op programs.
- **Status:** Trade literature, dealer promotions, point-of-purchase displays.

Pricing Policies
- **Price history:** Trends, relationship to needs of buyers, competitive price situation.
- **Past price objectives:** Management attitudes, buyer attitudes, channel attitudes.

Competition
- **Who is the competition:** Primary, secondary, share of market, products, services, goals, attitudes. What is competition's growth history and size?
- **Strengths and vulnerabilities:** Competitor strengths and vulnerabilities with respect to sales features, product quality, profitability, sale trends, size, innovation, etc.
- **Marketing activities of competition:** Advertising, promotion, distribution, sales force. Estimated budget.

Promotion
- **Successes and failures:** Past promotion policy, sales force, advertising, publicity.
- **Promotion expenditures:** History, budget emphasis, relation to competition, trend.
- **Advertising and IMC programs:** Review of strategies, themes, campaigns.
- **Sales force:** Size, scope, ability, cost/sale.

Marketing Objectives   The advertiser's next step is to determine specific marketing objectives. These must consider the amount of money the company has to invest in marketing and production, its knowledge of the marketplace, and the competitive environment.

For example, based on its knowledge about Mountain Dew drinkers, the company decided in 2009 to communicate directly with its user base on the Internet as a way of developing new flavors and brand extensions.[8]

Marketing objectives follow logically from a review of the company's current situation, management's prediction of future trends, and the hierarchy of company objectives. For example, **corporate objectives** are stated in terms of profit or return on investment, or net worth, earnings ratios, growth, or corporate reputation. **Marketing objectives**, which derive from corporate objectives, should relate to the needs of target markets as well as to specific sales goals. These may be referred to as general *need-satisfying objectives* and specific *sales-target objectives*.

To shift management's view of the organization from a producer of products to a satisfier of customers' needs, companies set **need-satisfying objectives**. These have a couple of important purposes. First, they enable the firm to view its business broadly. For example, Revlon founder Charles Revson once said a cosmetics company's product is hope, not lipstick. An insurance company sells financial security, not policies. Mountain Dew has consistently attempted to meet the needs of its users by engaging them in social media (brand fans even get to design new flavors) and linking Dew to consumer lifestyles (tie-ins with Xbox and the popular film *The Dark Knight Rises*).

Second, by setting need-satisfying objectives, managers must see through the

Threats are environmental challenges that a brand faces. Coke's new Energy line emphasizes high levels of caffeine. This may present an attractive alternative choice to Mountain Dew drinkers.
Source: The Coca-Cola Company

customer's eyes. They have to ask "What are we planning to do for the customer?" and "What is the value of that to our customer?" One of the best ways to define a market is to think about customer needs first and then identify the products that meet those needs. So when Mountain Dew wanted to expand its popularity with urban youth and non-white consumer groups, it explored sponsorships with musical artist Lil Wayne and skateboard champ Paul Rodriguez.[9]

The second kind of marketing objective is the **sales-target objective**. This is a specific, quantitative, realistic marketing goal to be achieved within a specified period of time. A sales-target objective could

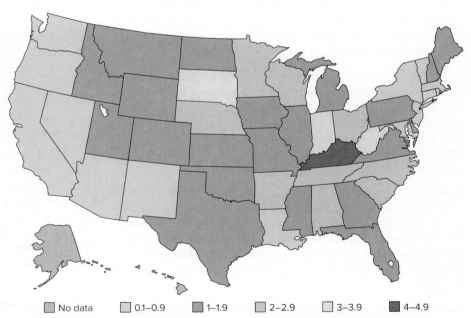

The Mountain Dew belt
Total Mountain Dew cases sold per capita, per year

| ■ No data | ■ 0.1–0.9 | ■ 1–1.9 | ■ 2–2.9 | ■ 3–3.9 | ■ 4–4.9 |

Note: Iowa, Montana, North Dakota, and Texas are reflective of data in the broader region, as no state-level geography is available.

Part of any marketing plan is knowing about regional differences in brand usage. This map shows Mountain Dew is strong in the Midwest and South, but has room for growth on the West Coast and Northeast.
Source of Data: IRI Worldwide.

be phrased as "What are we planning to do for ourselves?" They may be expressed in several ways: total sales volume; sales volume by product, market segment, customer type; market share in total or by product line; growth rate of sales volume in total or by product line; and gross profit in total or by product line. Mountain Dew, for example, uses a number of measures for its sales-target objectives: case volume, share of market, growth, and/or share of growth.

Marketing Strategy

The **marketing strategy** describes how the company plans to meet its marketing objectives. "Developing and following a strategy is what keeps you and everybody else on the same course so that you can maximize the effectiveness of your marketing."[10]

A marketing strategy typically involves three steps: (1) defining the target markets; (2) determining the strategic positioning; and (3) developing an appropriate marketing mix for each target market. A company's marketing strategy has a dramatic impact on its advertising. It determines the role and amount of advertising in the marketing mix, its creative thrust, and the media to be employed.

Defining the target market In top-down marketing, the first step in strategy development is to define and select the target market, using the processes of market segmentation and research discussed in Chapters 4 and 6.

When Joe Coulombe thought about how to design and stock his Trader Joe's stores, he considered his target market first. He wanted to attract well-educated, adventurous, highly particular shoppers. Because this group is more likely to travel and try new delicacies, he wanted to stock his store with unusual foods and wines. And he wanted the store experience to be a somewhat exotic one.

Mountain Dew defines its target market as active, young people in their teens as well as young adults 20 to 39 years old. In addition, the brand aims a significant portion of its marketing activities at urban youth, especially African Americans and Latinos.[11] While Mountain Dew has traditionally focused on its prototypical consumer, the male Millennial, future growth will be global.[12]

Positioning the product Famed researcher and copywriter David Ogilvy said one of the first decisions in advertising is also the most important: how to position the product. **Positioning** refers to the place a brand occupies competitively in the minds of consumers. Every product has some position—whether intended or not—even if the position is "nowhere." Positions are based on consumer perceptions, which may or may not reflect

Transfarency℠
Low fares. Nothing to hide.

	1st Checked Bag	2nd Checked Bag	Flight Change Fee	Other Select Fees	Feels Like
Southwest	$0	$0	$0	$0	Winning!
American	$25	$35	$200	$205	Yikes.
United	$25	$35	$200	$250	Ooof.
Spirit	$30	$40	$110	$262	We lost track.
Delta	$25	$35	$200	$200	Whaaat?!
Virgin	$25	$25	$100	$140	Arrgh.
JetBlue	$20	$35	$70	$125	Really.

#FeesDontFly

Southwest.

Southwest Airlines positions itself as "The short-haul, no-frills, and low-priced airline." This ad demonstrates perfectly the company's commitment to that promise.
Source: Southwest Airlines Co.

reality. Strong brands have a clear, often unique position in the target market. Dick Maggiore, writing about Southwest Airlines, notes that the company is "brilliant" at aligning its position with its strategy. "Herb Kelleher, founder and longtime CEO of Southwest Airlines, knew where he wanted to be. He wanted Southwest Airlines to own the idea of 'low-cost' in the airline category. He understood who his customer would be."[13]

Positions are always available in a market. The big mistake many companies make is not staking out any position. They can't be everything; but they don't want to be nothing.[14] A company might pick a position similar to a competitor's and fight for the same customers. Or it might find a position not held by a competitor—a niche in the market—and fill it quickly, perhaps through product differentiation or market segmentation.

One scholar proposes seven distinct approaches to developing a positioning strategy:

1. *Product attribute*—setting the brand apart by stressing a particular product feature important to consumers (e.g., fuel economy in a Prius).

2. *Price/quality*—positioning on the basis of price or quality (a low price example is No-Ad sunscreen, while a quality example is L'Oreal, "because you're worth it").

> # EVERY PRODUCT HAS SOME POSITION—WHETHER INTENDED OR NOT.

3. *Use/application*—positioning on the basis of how a product is used (e.g., Arm & Hammer).

4. *Product class*—positioning the brand against other products that, while not the same, offer the same class of benefits (LaCroix sparkling water positioned against soft drinks that have sugar).

5. *Product user*—positioning against the particular group who uses the product (Mountain Dew defined by the Millennial user).

6. *Product competitor*—positioning against competitors (e.g., the famous "I'm a Mac, I'm a PC" campaign), using the strength of the competitor's position to help define the subject brand.

7. *Cultural symbol*—positioning apart from competitors through the creation or use of some recognized symbol or icon (e.g., Starbucks, Apple, McDonald's).[15]

We add an eighth approach: *By category*—positioning by defining or redefining a business category. A simple way for a company to get the number one position is to invent a new product category. The popular Cirque du Soleil is often considered a prime example of this approach. Neither circus nor theater, it uniquely combines elements of both. W. Chan Kim and Renée Mauborgne have referred to this as a Blue Ocean strategy.[16]

With all its high energy and exhilaration, "youth" is not only the positioning of Mountain Dew; it's the heartbeat of the brand.[17] PepsiCo positions Dew this way:

> To 18-year-old males who embrace excitement, adventure, and fun, Mountain Dew is the great-tasting soft drink that exhilarates like no other because it is energizing, thirst quenching, and has a unique citrus flavor.

Often, a product's positioning can be discerned from its advertising tagline—*BMW, the ultimate driving machine*; *Nobody doesn't like Sara Lee*; *You're in good hands with Allstate*; *Do the Dew*. To gain experience developing a brand strategy yourself, follow the guidelines in My Ad Campaign 7–B.

Determining the marketing mix The next step in developing the marketing strategy is determining a cost-effective marketing mix for *each* target market. The mix blends the various marketing elements the company controls: *product, price, distribution,* and *communications*.

Mountain Dew is blessed with a broad marketing toolbox to draw upon. First, it offers consumers an energizing, thirst-quenching soft-drink *product* with a unique citrus flavor and an image of youthful exuberance, exhilaration, and adventure. To build *distribution*, it uses a variety of promotions to the trade that enable grocers and other resellers to increase both volume

IF YOU WANT TO AVOID USING BLEACH, CONSIDER YOUR ALTERNATIVES

You could avoid getting dirty. That's one alternative. Or you could use the detergent that gives you brilliant whites without a drop of chlorine bleach. And is safe on colors too. **TIDE WITH BLEACH ALTERNATIVE.**

Positioning helps differentiate products from the competition. In the crowded detergent category, Procter & Gamble has clearly positioned this Tide product as an alternative to using bleach that provides similar benefits. The tagline of this ad reads, "If you want to avoid using bleach, consider your alternatives."
Source: Tide by Procter & Gamble

Strong brands have a clear and consistent positioning, often evident in their advertising taglines. BMW (www.bmw.com) has been advertised as "The Ultimate Driving Machine" since 1973.
Source: BMW AG

Developing a Brand Strategy [7–B]

Jack Trout and Al Ries's *Marketing Warfare* is based on the classic book of military strategy, *On War*, written by Prussian general Carl von Clausewitz and published in 1832. The book outlines the principles behind all successful wars, and two simple ideas dominate: *force* and *the superiority of the defense*. Consider their strategic insights as you help develop your client's campaign.

The Strategic Square

How do the principles of warfare apply to marketing? It comes down to the "strategic square":

> Out of every 100 companies:
> One should play defense.
> Two should play offense.
> Three should flank.
> And 94 should be guerrillas.

Defensive Warfare

Datril opened its war on Tylenol with a price attack. Johnson & Johnson immediately cut Tylenol's price, even before Datril started its price advertising. Result: It repelled the Datril attacks and inflicted heavy losses on the Bristol-Myers entry.

Here are the rules for defensive marketing warfare:

1. Participate only if you are a market leader.
2. Introduce new products and services before the competition does.
3. Block strong competitive moves by copying them rapidly.

Offensive Warfare

Colgate had a strong number one position in toothpaste. But rival Procter & Gamble knew a thing or two about Carl von Clausewitz.

P&G launched Crest toothpaste with not only a massive $20 million advertising budget, but also the American Dental Association "seal of approval." Crest went over the top to become the best-selling toothpaste in the country.

But overtaking the leader is not that common. Most companies are happy if they can establish a profitable number two position.

The rules for waging offensive marketing warfare are:

1. Consider the strength of the leader's position.
2. Launch the attack on as narrow a front as possible, preferably with a single product.
3. Launch the attack at the leader's weakest position.

Flanking Warfare

The third type of marketing warfare is where the action is for many companies. In practice, it means launching products where there is no competition. Unilever introduced Mentadent, the first baking soda/peroxide toothpaste, which became a very successful brand.

Here are the principles of flanking marketing warfare:

1. Make good flanking moves into uncontested areas.
2. Use surprise. Too much research often wastes precious time.
3. Keep up the pursuit; too many companies quit after they're ahead.

Guerrilla Warfare

Most of America's companies should be waging guerrilla warfare. The key to success in guerrilla wars is flexibility. A guerrilla should abandon any product or market if the tide of battle changes.

Here are the principles of guerrilla marketing warfare:

1. Find a market segment small enough to defend.
2. No matter how successful you become, never act like the leader.
3. Be prepared to "bug out" at a moment's notice.

Bottom Up

Trout and Ries's later book, *Bottom-Up Marketing* (discussed later in this chapter), continues the military analogy.

"Deep penetration on a narrow front is the key to winning a marketing war," they say. By this they mean that smaller companies should keep their product narrowly focused on a single concept. Many companies spread their forces over too wide a front. In fact, most large corporations today expend significant resources fending off focused attacks by smaller companies.

---

and profits. While its *price* is competitive with other soft drinks, Mountain Dew promotes itself aggressively with free samples, premiums, and prizes at various street and sporting events—which effectively lowers the price to consumers.

Finally, Mountain Dew uses an integrated *communications* program that includes digital and TV advertising; sports and event sponsorships; appearances at grass-roots geographic events; plus a host of public relations activities—all designed to develop and promote the distinct Mountain Dew personality.

Companies have many marketing strategy options. They might increase distribution, initiate new uses for a product, change a

product line, develop entirely new markets, or lower prices. Each option emphasizes one or more marketing mix elements. The choice depends on the product's target market, its position in the market, and its stage in the **product life cycle**, the progression of growth and decline through which a successful product typically moves.

Marketing Tactics (Action Programs) A company's objectives indicate where it wants to go; the strategy indicates the intended route; and the **tactics** (or *action programs*) determine the specific short-term actions to be taken. In 2009–2010, Mountain Dew blazed new trails with tactics that included a

"Dewmocracy" campaign encouraging consumers to choose three new flavors. Then in 2015 the brand celebrated the 20th anniversary of the "Do the Dew" slogan with commercials helmed by director Justin Lin. "Fireboard" featured professional skateboarder Sean Malto grinding matches into lighting a beach bonfire, while "Directions" showcased snowboarder Scotty Lago executing exciting stunts before cruising into a party.

Advertising campaigns live in the world of marketing tactics. These tactics are the key to *bottom-up marketing*.

Bottom-Up Marketing: How Small Companies Plan

In small companies, everybody is both player and coach, and the day-to-day details seem to come first, leaving little or no time for formal planning. However, there is a solution to this dilemma: **bottom-up marketing** (see Exhibit 7–2).

An excellent way for a company to develop a competitive advantage is to focus on an ingenious tactic first and then develop that tactic into a strategy. By reversing the normal process, advertisers sometimes make important discoveries.[18] Vicks developed an effective liquid cold remedy but discovered that it put people to sleep. Rather than throw out the research, Vicks positioned the formula as a nighttime cold remedy. NyQuil went on to become the most successful new product in Vicks's history.

The *tactic* is a singular, competitive technique. By planning from the bottom up, entrepreneurs can find unique tactics to exploit. But caution is required. Advertisers should find just *one* tactic, not two or three. The advertiser can then focus all elements of the marketing mix on this single-minded tactic. The tactic becomes the nail, and the strategy is the hammer that drives it home.

The artful combination of tactic and strategy creates a position in the consumer's mind. When Tom Monaghan thought of the

tactic of delivering pizza to customers' homes, he focused his whole strategy on that singular idea. He ended up making a fortune and marketing history with Domino's Pizza.

Managers of small companies have an advantage here. Surrounded by the details of the business, they are more likely to discover a good tactic that can be developed into a powerful strategy. However, that's not to say that a large company cannot profit from bottom-up marketing. Many have, like 3M with its Post-it notes.

THE IMPORTANCE OF RELATIONSHIP MARKETING

Most marketers know that the key to building brand equity in the twenty-first century is to develop interdependent, mutually satisfying relationships with customers.

A market-driven firm's overriding purpose is to create happy, loyal customers. Customers, not products, are the lifeblood of the business.[19] This realization has moved firms away from simple *transactional marketing* to **relationship marketing**—creating, maintaining, and enhancing long-term relationships with customers

▼ **EXHIBIT 7–2** Bottom-up marketing plan.

Source: Barbara Penoyar/Photodisc/Getty Images

value The ratio of perceived benefits to the price of the product.

stakeholders In relationship marketing, customers, employees, centers of influence, stockholders, the financial community, and the press. Different stakeholders require different types of relationships.

lifetime customer value (LCV) The total sales or profit value of a customer to a marketer over the course of that customer's lifetime.

> No amount of advertising is likely to win back a customer lost from shoddy products.

and other stakeholders that result in exchanges of information and other things of mutual value.[20]

Today's affluent, sophisticated consumers can choose from a wide variety of products and services offered by producers located around the world. As a result, the customer relationship—in which the sale is only the beginning—is the key strategic resource of the successful twenty-first-century business.[21] As one commentator notes: "The new *market-driven conception* of marketing will focus on *managing strategic partnerships* and positioning the firm between vendors and customers in the value chain with the aim of delivering *superior value* to the customer."[22]

Value is the ratio of *perceived benefits* to the costs associated with obtaining and using a product.[23]

Costs are normally thought of as monetary, but they can include time, risk, and the difficulty of making a purchase. In essence a cost is anything that detracts from the perceived attractiveness of a brand. An electric car significantly reduces expenditures associated with fuel and maintenance, but at a cost of limited range and the length of time it takes to charge.

The Importance of Relationships

To succeed, companies must focus on managing loyalty among customers and **stakeholders** (employees, centers of influence, stockholders, the financial community, and the press).[24] This is important for a number of reasons:

1. *The cost of lost customers.* No amount of advertising is likely to win back a customer lost from shoddy products or poor service. The real profit lost is the **lifetime customer value (LCV)** of a customer to a firm. For example, the average customer of one major transportation firm represented a lifetime value of $40,000. The company had 64,000 accounts and lost 5 percent of them due to poor service. That amounted to an unnecessary loss of $128 million in revenue and $12 million in profits![25] Negative word of mouth can have a terrible snowballing effect. Imagine if one lost customer influences only one other customer to not patronize the business. That immediately doubles the LCV loss. Negative word of mouth is why bad movies disappear so quickly from theaters.

2. *The cost of acquiring new customers.* Defensive marketing typically costs less than offensive marketing because it is hard to lure satisfied customers away from competitors.[26] The fragmentation of media audiences and the resistance of sophisticated consumers to advertising messages make it increasingly difficult to succeed merely by stepping up the advertising volume.[27] In fact, it costs five to eight times as much in marketing, advertising, and promotion to acquire a new customer as it does to keep an existing one.[28]

3. *The value of loyal customers.* A big majority of a firm's profits come from repeat purchasers; only a tiny percentage comes from trial or sporadic purchasers.[29] Reducing customer defections by even 5 percent can improve profit potential by 25 to 85 percent.[30] And long-term customers are more willing to pay premium prices, make referrals, increase their annual buying, and demand less hand-holding.[31]

So a company's first market should always be its current customers. At a minimum, companies need to ensure they do no harm in messaging to customers (see the Ethical Issues box "Ensuring Strategy is Ethical in the #MeToo Era"). But

---

Some airlines run ads that talk to business travelers. We're running an ad that says

WE LISTEN

to them.

1. **INTRODUCING A WHOLE NEW, BETTER BOARDING PROCESS**
   It's a calmer, more relaxed way to board. There is no need to line up early because your boarding pass number holds your place in line. So you are free to work, relax, or do whatever.

2. **INTRODUCING SOUTHWEST AIRLINES® BUSINESS SELECT**
   You deserve Southwest Airlines Business Select. For just a little extra, you can be part of the select group that's guaranteed to be one of the first to board and get a free drink and extra Rapid Rewards® credit. Plus, your fare is fully refundable.

3. **INTRODUCING MORE NONSTOP FLIGHTS FOR YOUR NONSTOP BUSINESS**
   Fly long without the stops. Southwest offers over 3,400 daily nonstop flights, which lets you fly nonstop to more places you do business.

SOUTHWEST.COM®

Relationship marketing means companies don't just talk, they listen. Southwest uses this ad to let its customers know that their opinions matter.
Source: Southwest Airlines Co.

Ensuring Strategy is Ethical in the #MeToo Era

The #metoo movement is a powerful reminder to everyone of the atrocious treatment endured by many women in the workplace from sexual harassment and mistreatment. The powerful stories of women have called into question the casual use of sexuality in advertising.

Here is one of the more blatant uses of sex in advertising in recent memory: A billboard features a young woman, holding a grease gun cartridge in each hand and leaning over to exhibit cleavage. The headline reads, "This is Debbie. She wants you to have this pair in your car." The ad is for auto parts, but the implication seems to be that if you buy this manufacturer's auto parts, you'll get Debbie or someone like Debbie in the bargain. Nothing in the ad says so explicitly, but the innuendo is the tactic for capturing the viewer's attention.

There is no easy solution to this dilemma, especially because research shows that sexual appeals can be effective when sexuality relates to the product. However, when it doesn't, it can distract audiences from the main message and severely demean the advertiser in the consumer's eyes. This brings up an important and rather common paradox about sexually oriented advertising. How is a naked model in a window poster an advertisement for clothing? Many argue that it is not, making such ads not only a distraction, but also a source of negative externalities—the social costs to consumers outside the target market.

Advertisers must examine, on a case-by-case basis, at what point sexual appeals become counterproductive. In one case, an executive on the Valvoline advertising account justified using "girlie calendars" for mechanics by noting that "the calendar may offend some groups—but they aren't our customers."

Some will argue that sex sells. Perhaps. But the casual use of sex in advertising raises ethical issues, and the cultural shift created by #metoo is making many advertisers rethink their approach. Reliance on sexual appeals in advertising may no longer be lazy. It may be just plain wrong.

Advertisers have started to notice. National and global ad campaigns in 2020 are more likely to feature stories of women's empowerment than blatant sex appeals. Is it a case of a profession becoming more responsible? Or a society less willing to accept potentially harmful messages? Or both?

In the end, the advertising industry is engaged in a dialog with society. Agencies try to push the envelope, critics and consumers sometimes push back.

The good news is consumers are welcoming the new inclusive focus of advertising. And brands are succeeding by becoming just a bit more aware. If the current decade is ultimately known for responsible ads that empower disenfranchised groups while helping a marketer to tell its story, well, what's so wrong with that?

Questions

1. How would you explain the "redeeming value" of sexual appeals in advertising?
2. If sexual appeals are considered okay by the audiences that are directly targeted, what responsibility does the advertiser have for any effect on indirect targets, such as women who face sexual harassment in the workplace? What is your stance on the use of sexuality in advertising?

---

competitive companies aim to do more: they find ways to build strong, mutually rewarding relationships.

The focus on retention has led to changes in marketing. Whereas in the past, most marketing and advertising effort focused on *presale* activities aimed at acquiring new customers, sophisticated marketers now shift more of their resources to *postsale* activities, making customer retention their first priority. They have discovered an important benefit of focusing on relationships: increasing retention and optimizing lifetime customer value.[32]

Levels of Relationships

Kotler and Armstrong distinguish five levels of relationships that can be formed between a company and its various stakeholders, depending on their mutual needs:

- *Basic transactional relationship.* The company sells the product but does not follow up in any way (Target).

- *Reactive relationship.* The company sells the product and encourages customers to call if they encounter any problems (Men's Wearhouse).

- *Accountable relationship.* The company phones customers shortly after the sale to check whether the product meets

expectations and asks for product improvement suggestions and any specific disappointments. This information helps the company to continuously improve its offering (Acura dealership, local veterinarian).

- *Proactive relationship.* The company contacts customers from time to time with suggestions about improved product use or helpful new products (Tupperware).

- *Partnership.* The company works continuously with customers (and other stakeholders) to discover ways to deliver better value (Nordstrom's Personal Shopper, Amazon).[33]

Different stakeholders require different types of relationships. The number of stakeholders is also important. The more there are, the more difficult it can be to deepen relationships with each. Moreover, some customers may not want anything more than a transactional relationship.[34] Most people wouldn't want a phone call from Oscar Mayer asking if the hot dogs tasted good. However, when some Toyota models were accused of dangerous defects in 2010, the company contacted each existing car owner with a letter explaining the situation and telling the owner what Toyota could do to ensure the car's safety. Toyota knew that customers were likely to believe their relationship with the brand had been violated. Clearly, therefore, brand relationships

The SWOT Analysis [7-C]

can be psychological or symbolic as well as personal, and they can be created by brand promotion, publicity, and advertising as well as by people.

Mountain Dew considers that an important aspect of its brand relationship with its customers involves the "Dew-x-perience." Using guerrilla marketing tactics to reach out to urban youth, it employs a variety of hip-hop and Latin recording artists in various "street marketing" efforts to distribute bottles of Dew. It also sponsors extreme athletes and appears at sporting events with vans full of merchandise and giveaways.[35]

The final consideration is the profit margin. High-profit product or service categories make deeper, personal relationships more desirable (see Exhibit 7–3). Low profit margins per customer

suggest that the marketer should pursue basic transactional relationships augmented by brand image advertising.[36]

check yourself ✓

1. What benefits are associated with marketing to repeat customers?

2. What factors determine the kind of relationship a company wants with its customers?

▼**EXHIBIT 7–3** Relationship levels as a function of profit margin and number of customers.

	Profit margins		
Number of customers	High	Medium	Low
Many	Accountable	Reactive	Basic
Medium	Proactive	Accountable	Basic
Few	Partnership	Accountable	Reactive

LO7-3 Show what makes IMC planning different from traditional methods.

USING IMC TO MAKE RELATIONSHIPS WORK

The growth of relationship marketing has happened at the same time companies have moved to *integrated marketing communications (IMC)*. In fact, according to Northwestern professor Don Schultz, IMC is what makes relationship marketing possible.[37]

IMC: The Concept and the Process

Technology allows marketers to adopt flexible manufacturing, customizing products for different markets. Being "market driven" means bundling services together with products to create a "unique product experience." It means companies and customers working together to find solutions.[38]

The counterpart to flexible manufacturing is flexible marketing—and integrated marketing communications—to reach customers at different levels in new and better ways.

The *concept* of integration is *wholeness*. Achieving this wholeness in communications creates **synergy**—the principal benefit of IMC—because each product message reinforces the others for greater effect.[39]

For example, when a Mountain Dew grocer runs an **endcap promotion** (a special display at the end of an aisle) alone, it might generate a 10 percent increase in volume. If he runs an ad for Dew with a coupon, that might deliver a 15 percent increase. But running both together might grow volume by 35 percent. That's synergy—the whole is greater than the sum of its parts.

The Evolution of the IMC Concept

Glen Nowack and Joe Phelps, advertising professors from the Universities of Georgia and Alabama, have suggested that IMC developed as a consequence of several important trends, including escalating media costs, splintering consumer markets, and skepticism about traditional mass media advertising. These have led marketers to question the wisdom of creating walls between disciplines such as public relations, direct-response advertising, and sales promotion.[40]

Many companies initially took a narrow, *inside-out* view of IMC. They saw it as a way to coordinate and manage their marketing communications (advertising, sales promotion, public relations, personal selling, and direct marketing) to give the audience a consistent message about the company.[41] The coordination of these communications elements is certainly important and we will examine them more closely in Chapters 15 and 16.

But a broader, more sophisticated, *outside-in* perspective of IMC sees customers as partners in an ongoing relationship, recognizes the terminology they use, acknowledges the importance of the whole communications system, and accepts the many ways

they come into contact with the company or the brand. Companies committed to IMC realize their biggest asset is not their products or their factories or even their employees, but their customers.[42] Defined broadly:

> **Integrated marketing communications (IMC)** is the process of building and reinforcing mutually profitable relationships with employees, customers, other stakeholders, and the general public by developing and coordinating a strategic communications program that enables them to have a constructive encounter with the company/brand through a variety of media or other contacts.

Whether a company employs the narrow view or the broad view depends to a great extent on its corporate culture. Some companies enjoyed rapid growth and strong customer relationships because they intuitively integrated and focused all corporate and marketing activities. Apple, Honda, Nike, and Banana Republic are just a few.

How the Customer Sees Marketing Communications

To truly understand IMC, we have to look through the customer's eyes. In one study, consumers identified 102 different media as "advertising"—everything from TV to shopping bags to sponsored community events.[43] Customers also develop perceptions of the company or brand through a variety of other sources: news reports, word of mouth, gossip, experts' opinions, financial reports, and even the CEO's personality.

All these communications or brand contacts, sponsored or not, create an *integrated product* in the consumer's mind.[44] In other words, customers automatically integrate all the brand-related messages that emanate from the company or some other source.

---

synergy An effect achieved when the sum of the parts is greater than that expected from simply adding together the individual components.

endcap promotion A merchandising method that uses special displays on shelving at the end of aisles in a store.

integrated marketing communications (IMC) The process of building and reinforcing mutually profitable relationships with employees, customers, other stakeholders, and the general public by developing and coordinating a strategic communications program that enables them to make consecutive contact with the company/brand through a variety of media.

"The *concept* of integration is *wholeness*. Achieving this wholeness in communications creates synergy."

> The company that embraces IMC accepts the premise that *everything we do . . . sends a message.*

The way they integrate those messages determines their perception of the company. IMC gives companies a better opportunity to manage or influence those perceptions and create a superior relationship with those stakeholders.

The Four Sources of Brand Messages

The company that embraces IMC accepts the idea that *everything we do (and don't do) sends a message.* That is to say, every corporate activity has a message component. Duncan categorized four types of company/brand-related messages stakeholders receive: *planned, product, service,* and *unplanned.* Each of these influences a stakeholder's relationship decision, so marketers must know where these messages originate, what effect they have, and the costs to influence or control them.

1. **Planned messages.** These are the traditional marketing communication messages—advertising, sales promotions, personal selling, merchandising materials, publicity releases, event sponsorships. These often have the *least* impact because they are seen as self-serving. Planned messages should be coordinated to work toward a predetermined set of communications objectives. This is the most fundamental aspect of (inside-out) IMC.

2. **Product messages.** In IMC theory, every element of the marketing mix (not just promotion) sends a message. Messages from the product, price, or distribution elements are typically referred to as product messages. For example, customers and other stakeholders receive one product message from a $36,500 Rolex watch and a totally different one from a $30 Timex. Product messages also include packaging, which communicates a lot about the product through the use of color, type fonts, imagery, design, and layout. Apple, for example, has a well-deserved reputation for beautiful product packaging.

   Product messages have great impact. When a product (or service) performs well, the customer infers a positive message that reinforces the purchase decision. However, a gap between the product's performance and advertised promises is likely to convey a negative message. Managers must realize that all marketing mix decisions are also communication decisions.

3. **Service messages.** Many messages result from employee interactions with customers. In many organizations, customer service people are supervised by operations, not marketing. Yet the service messages they send have greater marketing impact than the planned messages. Luxury brands such as Nordstrom and Lexus believe great service is part of their brands' DNA. With IMC, marketing people work with operations to minimize negative messages and maximize positive ones.

4. **Unplanned messages.** Companies have little or no control over the unplanned messages that emanate from employee gossip, unsought news stories, comments by the trade or competitors, social media posts, or major disasters. When Walmart created a Facebook page, many of the initial fans criticized the company's policies. Unplanned messages may affect customers' attitudes dramatically, but they can sometimes be anticipated and influenced, especially by managers experienced in the online world.[45]

IMC is about more than communicating with customers, it is about engaging them and building relationships. Apple pays careful attention to the beauty and functionality of the packaging it uses for its products. The company knows that packaging is part of the brand experience, and thus part of IMC.

Source: A. Aleksandravicius/Shutterstock

The Integration Triangle

The integration triangle is a simple illustration of how perceptions are created from the various brand message sources (see Exhibit 7-4). Planned

planned messages	**product messages**	**service messages**	**unplanned messages**
Traditional marketing communications messages, including advertising, sales promotion, publicity, and personal selling. These messages have the least impact because they are seen as self-serving.	Messages communicated by a product, its packaging, price, or distribution elements.	Messages resulting from employee interactions with customers. These messages typically have greater impact than planned messages.	Messages that emanate from gossip, unsought news stories, rumors, or major disasters. Companies have little control over unplanned messages, but the messages can dramatically affect customers' attitudes.

messages are *say* messages, what companies say about themselves. Product and service messages are *do* messages because they represent what a company does. Unplanned messages are *confirm* messages because that's what others say and confirm (or not) about what the company says and does. Constructive integration occurs when a brand does what its maker says it will do and then others confirm that it delivers on its promises.[46]

The Dimensions of IMC

To maximize the synergy benefits of IMC, Duncan suggests three dimensions to an organization's integration process. It should first ensure consistent positioning, then facilitate interactions between the company and its customers or other stakeholders, and finally actively incorporate a socially responsible mission into the organization's relationships with its stakeholders.

Duncan's IMC model shows that cross-functional planning and monitoring of IMC activities results in an enhanced relationship with customers and other stakeholders, which leads to stakeholder loyalty and ultimately to greater brand equity.[47]

The interest in IMC is global.[48] The $94 billion Swiss company Nestlé, for example, uses a variety of IMC strategies, such as building highway rest stops for feeding and changing babies, designed to establish deep, caring relationships between families and the Nestlé Baby Foods division in France. More recently, the company has built out its capabilities for direct-to-consumer sales to establish a direct line with customers.[49]

▼ **EXHIBIT 7–4** The integration triangle.

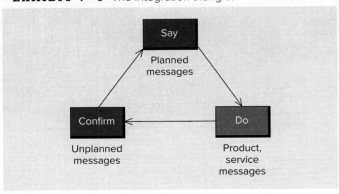

In short, IMC offers accountability by maximizing resources and linking communications activities directly to organizational goals and the resulting bottom line.[50]

The IMC Approach to Marketing and Advertising Planning

For many companies, IMC is now the standard approach to planning marketing and communications activities. Marketing and communications planning are done together. Using the outside-in process, the IMC approach starts with the customer. Marketers determine which media customers use, the relevance of their message to the customers, and when customers and prospects are most *receptive* to the message. They begin with the customer and work back to the brand.[51]

Marketers now have a wealth of information at their fingertips. With supermarket scanner data, for instance, packaged-goods marketers can (1) identify specific users of products and services; (2) measure their actual purchase behavior and relate it to specific brand and product categories; (3) measure the impact of various advertising and marketing communications activities and determine their value in influencing the actual purchase; and (4) capture and evaluate this information over time.[52] The Internet is another place that marketers can glean a wealth of information about their customers. After the company ran its *The Shining*-inspired Super Bowl spot, it went to work on social media platforms. The campaign continued on channels favored by young users, including Instagram, Snapchat, and TikTok. Tactics include an augmented reality filter that allows consumers to put their own faces over the twin girls from the spot.[53]

A database of customer behavior can be the basis for planning future marketing and communications activities, especially if the database contains information on customer demographics, psychographics, purchase data, and attitudes.

Starting the planning process with a database forces the company to focus on the consumer, or prospect, not on sales or profit goals. Communications objectives and strategies are established for making contact with the consumer and influencing his or her attitudes, beliefs, and purchase behavior. The marketer then decides what other elements of the marketing mix (product, price, distribution) can be used to further encourage the desired behavior. Finally, the planner determines what communications tactics to use—media advertising, social media, publicity, sales promotion, special events. All forms of

advertising plan The plan that directs the company's advertising effort. A natural outgrowth of the marketing plan, it analyzes the situation, sets advertising objectives, and lays out a specific strategy from which ads and campaigns are created.

marketing are thus turned into communication, and all forms of communication into marketing.[54]

The Importance of IMC to Advertising

Because customers see all sponsored communications as advertising, advertising people (account managers, creatives, media planners) must grow beyond their traditional specialty to become enlightened generalists, familiar with and able to integrate all types of marketing communications. Today most companies have a general understanding of IMC and believe that synergy is the key benefit of integrated marketing.[55]

check yourself ✓

1. What is synergy and how is it created by IMC?

2. What factors do Phelps and Nowack suggest have led to the development of IMC?

3. What are the four types of brand messages identified by Duncan?

THE ADVERTISING PLAN

The **advertising plan** is a natural outgrowth of the marketing plan and is prepared in much the same way. It picks up where the marketing plan leaves off, building on the goals that have been established for the advertising program. Those goals are translated into specific advertising objectives, from which creative and media strategies are developed. The advertising plan typically also incorporates the rationale for a proposed budget and a plan for conducting research.

Reviewing the Marketing Plan

The advertising manager first reviews the marketing plan to understand where the company wants to go, how it intends to get there, and what role advertising plays in the marketing mix. The first section of the advertising plan should organize information from the marketing plan's situation analysis into a SWOT analysis.

For example, McDonald's restaurants' *strengths* include its strong name identity and

thousands of retail locations. However, the company's *weaknesses* include a menu loaded with unhealthy food choices and an image to match. McDonald's is now taking advantage of an *opportunity* to capitalize on nutritious food trends by promoting healthier menu items and a fresh, new image. The company's upscale coffees distinguish it from its fast-food competitors and enable it to draw traffic from Starbucks. In doing so, it is combating *threats* from competitive restaurants and posting impressive sales gains.

LO7-4 Explain how to establish specific, realistic, and measurable advertising objectives.

Setting Advertising Objectives

Based on the marketing plan, the advertising manager determines what tasks advertising must take on. What strengths and opportunities can be leveraged? What weaknesses and threats need to be addressed? Unfortunately, some corporate executives (and advertising managers) state vague goals for advertising, such as "increase sales and maximize profits by creating a favorable impression of the product in the marketplace." When this happens, no one understands what the advertising is intended to do, how much it will cost, or how to measure the results. Advertising objectives should be specific, realistic, and measurable. For an opportunity to try setting your own advertising objectives, see My Ad Campaign 7–D.

Understanding What Advertising Can Do Most advertising programs encourage prospects to take some action. However, it is unrealistic to assign advertising the whole responsibility for achieving sales. Sales goals are marketing objectives,

Scheduled rides for busy families.

Advertising cannot be assigned full responsibility for a product's success or failure. In 2016, a new venture called Shuddle, a kind of Uber for kids, closed its doors for good. As shown in the image, the company marketed primarily in digital media, including YouTube and social media, but ultimately closed its doors because it failed to raise more venture backing.

Source: Shuddle

not advertising objectives. Before an advertiser can persuade customers to buy, it must inform, persuade, or remind its intended audience about the product or service. A simple adage to remember when setting objectives is "Marketing sells, advertising tells." In other words, advertising objectives should be related to communication outcomes.

The Advertising Pyramid: A Guide to Setting Objectives

Suppose you're advertising a new brand in a new product category, but you're not sure what kind of results to expect. The pyramid in Exhibit 7–5 shows some of the tasks advertising can perform. Obviously, before your product is introduced, prospective customers are completely unaware of it. Your first communication objective therefore is to create *awareness*—to acquaint people with the company, product, service, and/or brand.

The next task might be to develop *comprehension*—to communicate enough information about the product that some percentage of the aware group will understand the product's purpose, image, or position, and perhaps some of its features.

Next, you need to communicate enough information to develop *conviction*—to persuade a certain number of people to actually believe in the product's value. Once convinced, some people may be moved to *desire* the product. Finally, some percentage of those who desire the product will take *action*. They may request additional information, send in a coupon, visit a store, or actually buy the product.

▼ **EXHIBIT 7–5** The advertising pyramid depicts the progression of advertising effects on mass audiences—especially for new products. The initial message promotes *awareness* of the product to a large audience (the base of the pyramid). But only a percentage of this large group will *comprehend* the product's benefits. Of that group, even fewer will go on to feel *conviction* about, then *desire* for, the product. In the end, compared with the number of people aware of the product, the number of people who take *action* is usually quite small.

The pyramid works in three dimensions: time, dollars, and people. Advertising results may take time, especially if the product is expensive or not purchased regularly. Over time, as a company continues advertising, the number of people who become aware of the product increases. As more people comprehend the benefits of the product, believe in it, and desire it, more will take the final action of buying it.

Let's apply these principles to a real case. Suppose you are in charge of advertising for the reintroduced Hummer, now incarnated as an electric truck for General Motors. Your initial advertising objectives for the vehicle might read as follows:

1. Within one year, communicate the existence of the Hummer to half of the nearly 2 million people who annually buy trucks.

2. Within a year and a half, get two-thirds of this "aware" group to comprehend that while the Hummer uses an electric engine, it has more power and torque than a top-of-the-line gas-powered truck.

3. Within two years, convince two-thirds of the "comprehending" group that the Hummer will go far enough on a charge to make it a practical alternative to conventional pickups.

4. Within two years, stimulate desire within two-thirds of the "convinced" group for a test drive.

5. Within two years, motivate 75 percent of the "desire" group to take action and visit a GMC dealer for a test drive.

These advertising objectives are specific as to time and degree and are quantified like marketing objectives. Theoretically, at the end of the first year, a consumer study could determine how many people are aware of the Hummer, how many people understand the truck's features, and so on, thus measuring the program's effectiveness.

Hummer's advertising may accomplish the objectives of creating awareness, comprehension, conviction, desire, and action. But once the customer is in the store, it's the retailer's responsibility to close the sale with effective selling and service.

From an IMC perspective, we can look at the pyramid in another way. By using a variety of marketing communication tools and a wide menu of traditional and nontraditional media, we can accomplish the communication objectives suggested by the pyramid in a more efficient manner. For instance, for creating sheer awareness for the new Hummer as well as brand image for the truck and the GM, an intensive program of public relations activities supported by mass media advertising would be the communication tools of choice. Comprehension, interest, and credibility can be augmented by media advertising, press publicity, direct-mail brochures, and special events such as a truck show. Desire can be enhanced by a combination of the buzz created by good reviews in car enthusiast magazines, plus media advertising, beautiful brochure photography, and the excitement generated by a sales promotion (such as a sweepstakes). Finally, action can be stimulated by direct-mail

There are many ways to deliver a message besides using traditional media. In keeping with its theme of fun and adventure, hundreds throng Flatiron Plaza in New York to attend a branding event for Victoria Secret's brand Pink. The collection is sold in in freestanding PINK stores and online. Customers are encouraged to join a members-onnly online community to receive offers and learn more about the brand. How does Pink use guidance from the advertising pyramid in this campaign?

Source: rblfmr/Shutterstock

DOES SHE LOOK LIKE A DOG NOBODY WANTS?
Wilma was found as a stray in Brooklyn in 2009.
She is brave, courageous and sweet. Just like NYC firefighter Steve.

join us at facebook.com/adoptny
a league of rescue organizations
working together to make NY No Kill
**CHOOSE TO ADOPT.
CHOOSE NEW YORK.**

Not every ad follows the learn-feel-do approach. This ad for Adopt New York invites readers to feel-learn-do with an evocative story about a dog in need and a firefighter who provided her a home.

Source: Adopt New York

solicitation, sales promotion, a website where interested buyers can customize their trucks, and the attentive service of a retail salesperson in an attractive showroom. Following the sale, social media can reinforce the purchase decision by linking drivers to their dealers and to one another. Facebook posts can help thank the customer, solicit feedback on that customer's experience, and offer any needed assistance. This demonstrates that the sale was just the beginning of a valuable relationship.

The Old Model versus the New The advertising pyramid represents the *learn-feel-do* model of advertising effects. That is, it assumes that people rationally consider a prospective purchase, and once they feel good about it, they act. The theory is that advertising affects attitude, and attitude leads to behavior. That may be true for certain expensive, high-involvement products that require a lot of consideration. But other purchases may follow a different pattern. For example, impulse purchases at checkout may involve a *do-feel-learn* model, in which behavior leads to attitude which leads to knowledge. Other purchases may follow some other pattern. Thus, there are many marketing considerations when advertising objectives are being set, and they must be considered carefully.

The advertising pyramid also reflects the traditional mass-marketing monologue. The advertiser talks and the customer listens.[56] But today, as the IMC model shows, many marketers have databases of information on their customers—about where they live, what they buy, and what they like and dislike. When marketers can have a dialogue and establish a relationship, the model is no longer a pyramid but a circle (see Exhibit 7–6).

▼**EXHIBIT 7–6** Messages go to the customer through advertising and other communication channels. Messages come back via direct response, surveys, social media, and purchase behavior data. The marketer's message evolves based on this feedback.

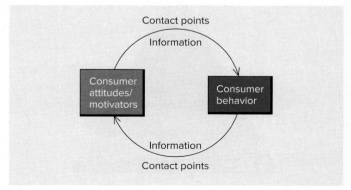

Consumers and business customers can send messages back to the marketer in the form of coupons, phone calls, surveys, and database information on purchases. With interactive media, the responses are in real time. This feedback can help the marketer's product, service, and messages evolve.[57] And reinforcement advertising, designed to build brand loyalty, will remind people of their successful experience with the product and suggest reuse.

By starting with the customer and then integrating all aspects of their marketing communications—package and store design, personal selling, advertising, public relations, special events, and sales promotions—companies can achieve lasting loyalty from *good* prospects, not just prospects.[58]

advertising strategy The advertising objective declares what the advertiser wants to achieve with respect to consumer awareness, attitude, and preference. Advertising strategy describes how to get there. It consists of two substrategies: the creative strategy and the media strategy.

creative strategy A written statement that serves as the creative team's guide for writing and producing an ad. It decides the most important issues that should be considered in the development of the ad (the who, what, where, when, and why), including the objective of the advertising; a definition and description of the target audience; the key benefit to be promised; the product features that support that promise; the style, approach, or tone to be used; and generally, what the copy should communicate.

> ## WHEN MARKETERS ESTABLISH A RELATIONSHIP WITH CUSTOMERS, THE MODEL IS NO LONGER A PYRAMID BUT A CIRCLE. BY STARTING WITH THE CUSTOMER AND IMC, SMART COMPANIES WORK TO ACHIEVE LASTING LOYALTY FROM GOOD PROSPECTS.

check yourself ✓

1. What are the limits on what advertising can do and how do these affect setting ad objectives?

2. What is the advertising pyramid?

3. How does setting objectives under an IMC approach differ from that under the advertising pyramid?

Determining the Advertising Strategy

The advertising *objective* declares what the advertiser wants to achieve with respect to consumer awareness, attitude, and preference; the advertising *strategy* describes how to get there. **Advertising strategy** consists of two substrategies: the creative strategy and the media strategy.

The **creative strategy** is a guide for those developing the advertising. At a minimum, the creative strategy defines the *target*

audience, restates the *objective* of the advertising, specifies the key *benefits* to be communicated, and offers *support* for those benefits. We discuss the development of the creative strategy in Chapter 8.

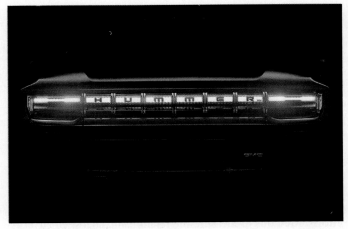

The creative strategy represents what a company wants to communicate about its product. When General Motors reintroduced the Hummer brand as an electric pickup truck, it began with a teaser campaign that caught people's attention and created immediate interest in the campaign. How does an ad like this help guide an ad audience through the advertising pyramid?

Source: General Motors Company

media strategy A document that helps media planners determine how messages will be delivered to consumers. It defines the target audience, the communication objectives that must be achieved, and the characteristics of the media that will be used for delivery of the messages.

percentage-of-sales method A method of advertising budget allocation based on a percentage of the previous year's sales, the anticipated sales for the next year, or a combination of the two.

The **media strategy** provides direction to the media planners. It defines the communication objectives that must be achieved and then describes how these will be accomplished through the use of media vehicles. The media planning process is covered in Chapter 14.

LO7-5 Review the pros and cons of the various approaches for determining advertising budgets.

Allocating Funds for Advertising

The Internal Revenue Service considers advertising a current business expense. Consequently, many executives treat advertising as a budget item to be trimmed or eliminated like other expense items when sales are either very high or very low. This is understandable but extremely shortsighted.

The cost of a new factory or warehouse is an investment in the company's future ability to produce and distribute products. Similarly, advertising—as one element of the communication mix—is an investment in future sales. While advertising is often used to stimulate immediate sales, its greatest power is in its cumulative, long-range, reinforcement effect.[59]

Advertising builds consumer preference and promotes goodwill. This, in turn, enhances the reputation and value of the company name and brand. And it encourages customers to make repeat purchases.

So while advertising is a current expense for accounting purposes, it is also a long-term investment. For management to treat advertising as an investment, however, it must understand how advertising relates to sales and profits.

The Relationship of Advertising to Sales and Profits

Many variables, both internal and external, influence the effectiveness of a company's marketing and advertising efforts. Methods to measure the relationships between advertising expenditures and sales are far from perfect. However, substantial research does support the following principles:

- In consumer goods marketing, increases in market share are closely related to increases in the marketing budget. And market share is a prime indicator of profitability.[60]

- Sales normally increase with additional advertising. At some point, however, the rate of return flattens and then declines.

- Sales response to advertising may build over time, but the durability of advertising is brief, so a consistent investment is important.

- There are minimum levels below which advertising expenditures have no effect on sales.

- There will be some sales even if there is no advertising.

- There are saturation limits above which additional ad expenditures appear to do little to increase sales.

To management, these facts might mean: Spend more until it stops working. In reality, the issue isn't that simple. Advertising isn't the only marketing activity that affects sales. A change in market share may occur because of quality perceptions, word of mouth, the introduction of new products, competitive trade promotion, the opening of more attractive outlets, better personal selling, or seasonal changes in the business cycle.

Furthermore, most companies don't have a clear-cut way to determine the relationship between advertising and sales and profit. What if the company sells a variety of products? Which advertising contributes to which sales?

One thing remains clear. Like all expenditures, advertising should be evaluated for wastefulness. But historically, companies that make advertising the scapegoat during tough times end up losing substantial market share before the economy starts growing again.[61]

The corollary is also true. Sustained ad spending during difficult times protects, and in some cases even increases, market share and builds brands. The story that opened this chapter is an excellent example of the value of a sustained commitment to strong advertising by a distinctive brand. It is difficult to imagine how Mountain Dew, with its origins as a small regional beverage, could have achieved its current popularity and consumer loyalty without a consistent marketing investment by PepsiCo.

Methods of Allocating Funds

Most business executives will spend more money on advertising as long as they are assured it will mean more profit. But how much is too much is hard to predict when advertising budgets are being developed.

Companies use several methods to determine how much to spend on advertising, including the *percentage-of-sales*, *percentage-of-profit*, *unit-of-sale*, *competitive-parity*, *share-of-market*, and *objective/task methods*.

No technique is appropriate for all situations. The three methods discussed here are commonly used for setting national advertising budgets. However, local retailers can use them too.

Developing Advertising Objectives [7-D]

For the next big sets of decisions you will make, both media and creative, it will be essential that you specify what advertising and other promotions should *do*. Use the checklist below to focus your thinking on your advertising objectives.

Does the advertising aim at immediate sales? If so, objectives might be:

____ Perform the complete selling function.

____ Close sales to prospects already partly sold.

____ Announce a special reason for buying now (price, premium, and so forth).

____ Remind people to buy.

____ Tie in with special buying event.

____ Stimulate impulse sales.

Does the advertising aim at near-term sales? If so, objectives might be:

____ Create awareness.

____ Enhance brand image.

____ Implant information or attitude.

____ Combat or offset competitive claims.

____ Correct false impressions, misinformation.

____ Build familiarity and easy recognition.

Does the advertising aim at building a "long-range consumer franchise"? If so, objectives might be:

____ Build confidence in company and brand.

____ Build customer demand.

____ Select preferred distributors and dealers.

____ Secure universal distribution.

____ Establish a "reputation platform" for launching new brands or product lines.

____ Establish brand recognition and acceptance.

Does the advertising aim at helping to increase sales? If so, objectives would be:

____ Hold present customers.

____ Convert other users to advertiser's brand.

____ Cause people to specify advertiser's brand.

____ Convert nonusers to users.

____ Make steady customers out of occasional ones.

____ Advertise new uses.

____ Persuade customers to buy larger sizes or multiple units.

____ Remind users to buy.

____ Encourage greater frequency or quantity of use.

Does the advertising aim at some specific step that leads to a sale? If so, objectives might be:

____ Persuade prospect to write for descriptive literature, return a coupon, enter a contest.

____ Persuade prospect to visit a showroom, ask for a demonstration.

____ Induce prospect to sample the product (trial offer).

How important are supplementary benefits of advertising? Objectives would be:

____ Help salespeople open new accounts.

____ Help salespeople get larger orders from wholesalers and retailers.

____ Help salespeople get preferred display space.

____ Give salespeople an entrée.

____ Build morale of sales force.

____ Impress the trade.

Should the advertising impart information needed to consummate sales and build customer satisfaction? If so, objectives may be to use:

____ "Where to buy it" advertising.

____ "How to use it" advertising.

____ New models, features, package.

____ New prices.

____ Special terms, trade-in offers, and so forth.

____ New policies (such as guarantees).

Should advertising build confidence and goodwill for the corporation? Targets may include:

____ Customers and potential customers.

____ The trade (distributors, dealers, retail people).

____ Employees and potential employees.

____ The financial community.

____ The public at large.

What kind of images does the company wish to build?

____ Product quality, dependability.

____ Service.

____ Family resemblance of diversified products.

____ Corporate citizenship.

____ Growth, progressiveness, technical leadership.

Percentage-of-Sales Method   The **percentage-of-sales method** is one of the most popular techniques for setting advertising budgets. It may be based on a percentage of last year's sales, anticipated sales for next year, or a combination of the two. Businesspeople like this method because it is the simplest, it doesn't cost them anything, it is related to revenue, and it is considered safe. The problem is knowing what percentage to use. Even leaders in the same industry use different percentages. Across industries, they range from just 1.5 percent to more than 22 percent.

Usually the percentage is based on an industry average or on company experience. Unfortunately, it is too often determined arbitrarily. An industry average assumes that every company in the industry has similar objectives and faces the same marketing

Source: Stockbyte/Getty Images

challenges. Using company experience assumes that the market is static, which is rarely the case.

However, when applied against a forecast of future sales, this method often works well. It assumes that a certain number of dollars is needed to sell a certain number of units. If the advertiser knows what that relationship is, the correlation between advertising and sales should remain reasonably constant, assuming the market is stable and competitors' advertising remains unchanged.

The greatest shortcoming of the percentage-of-sales method is that it violates a basic marketing principle. Marketing activities are supposed to *stimulate* demand and thus sales, not occur as a *result* of sales. If advertising increases only when sales increase and declines when sales decline, an opportunity is lost that might encourage an opposite move.

Share-of-Market/Share-of-Voice Method

In markets with similar products, a high correlation usually exists between a company's share of the market and its share of industry advertising.

that if the company's two-year sales goal is 10 percent of the market, it should spend about 15 percent of total industry advertising during the first two years.

One hazard of this method is the tendency to oversimplify. Maintaining the targeted percentage of media exposure usually isn't enough to accomplish the desired results. The top national packaged-goods marketers still spend 25 to 30 percent of their marketing budgets on consumer and trade promotion rather than consumer advertising.[64] Companies must be aware of *all* their competitors' marketing activities, not just advertising.

Objective/Task Method

The **objective/task method**, also known as the *budget-buildup method*, is used by the majority of major national advertisers in the United States. It considers advertising to be a marketing tool to help generate sales.

The task method has three steps: defining objectives, determining strategy, and estimating cost. After setting specific, quantitative marketing objectives, the advertiser develops programs to attain them. If the objective is to increase the sales of cases of

[Advertising should be viewed as a long-term investment
in future profits.]

The **share-of-market/share-of-voice method** is a bold attempt to link advertising dollars with sales objectives.[62] It holds that a company's best chance of maintaining its share of market is to keep its share of advertising (voice) comparable to its market share. For example, if Mountain Dew has an 8 percent share of the soft-drink market it should spend roughly 8 percent of the soft-drink industry's advertising dollars.

The share-of-market/share-of-voice method is commonly used for new product introductions.[63] According to this formula, when a new brand is introduced, the advertising budget for the first two years should be about one and one-half times the brand's targeted share of the market in two years. This means

coffee by 10 percent, the advertiser determines which advertising approach will work best, how often ads must run, and which media to use. The estimated cost of the program becomes the basis for the advertising budget. Of course, the company's financial position is always a consideration. If the cost is too high, objectives may have to be scaled back. If results are better or worse than anticipated after the campaign runs, the next budget may need revision.

The task method forces companies to think in terms of accomplishing goals. Its effectiveness is most apparent when the results of particular ads or campaigns can be readily measured. The task method is adaptable to changing market conditions and can be easily revised.

Ways to Set Advertising Budgets [7–E]

How much should you recommend that your client spend on advertising and promotions? Here is a list of ways companies set their marketing budgets.

- **Percentage of sales.** Advertising budget is determined by allocating a percentage of last year's sales, anticipated sales for next year, or a combination of the two. The percentage is usually based on an industry average, company experience, or an arbitrary figure.
- **Percentage of profit.** Percentage is applied to profit, either past years' or anticipated.
- **Unit of sale.** Also called the *case-rate method*. A specific dollar amount is set for each box, case, barrel, or carton produced. Used primarily in assessing members of horizontal co-ops or trade associations.
- **Competitive parity.** Also called the *self-defense method*. Allocates dollars according to the amounts spent by major competitors.
- **Share-of-market/share-of-voice.** Allocates dollars by maintaining a percentage share of total industry advertising comparable to or somewhat ahead of desired share of market. Often used for new product introductions.
- **Objective/task.** Also referred to as the *budget-buildup method*, this method has three steps: defining objectives, determining strategy, and estimating the cost to execute that strategy.
- **Empirical research.** Companies determine the most efficient level by running experimental tests in different markets with different budgets.
- **Quantitative mathematical models.** Computer-based programs developed by major advertisers and agencies rely on input of sophisticated data, history, and assumptions.
- **All available funds.** Go-for-broke technique generally used by small firms with limited capital, trying to introduce new products or services.
- **Online budgeting.** Digital campaigns offer advertisers some clear guidance on how to allocate dollars. In Google, an advertiser can analyze their costs-per-click (CPC) by determining how much they pay for each referred visitor, their website conversion rate, and their profits for each conversion.

However, it is often difficult to determine in advance the amount of money needed to reach a specific goal. Techniques for measuring advertising effectiveness still have many weaknesses. For more on establishing an advertising budget, see My Ad Campaign 7–E.

The Bottom Line The principal job of advertising is to influence perception by informing, persuading, and reminding. Advertising *affects* sales, but it is just one of many influences on consumer perception. Advertising managers must keep this in mind when preparing their plans and budgets. ∎

check yourself ✓

1. How might a packaged-foods manufacturer use the share-of-market/share-of-voice method to introduce a new product?

2. What are the pros and cons of the various advertising budgeting methods?

ENDNOTES

1. Updated promo sheet and letter from BBDO-NY (1995).
2. Theresa Howard, "Brand Builders: Being True to Dew," *Brandweek*, April 24, 2000, p. 28.
3. Theresa Howard, "Brand Builders: Being True to Dew," *Brandweek*, April 24, 2000, p. 30.
4. Christopher Lawton, "PepsiCo's Mountain Dew Backs Film," *The Wall Street Journal*, September 12, 2005, p. B4.
5. Kristina Monnlos, "How Mountain Dew Used a 'Fan Engagement Team' to Create a Mountain Dew Body Wash," *Digiday*, January 10, 2020, https://digiday.com/marketing/mountain-dew-using-fan-engagement-team-direct-marketing.
6. "Soda Production Industry in the U.S.," *IBISWorld*, August 2019, www.ibisworld.com/united-states/market-research-reports/soda-production-industry.
7. Daniel Weiner-Bronner, "There's a New Kind of Coke on Shelves. You'll Be Forgiven If You Miss It," *CNN Business*, January 31, 2020, www.cnn.com/2020/01/30/business/coke-energy-us-launch/index.html.
8. Natalie Zmuda, "Why Mtn Dew Let Skater Dudes Take Control of Its Marketing," *Advertising Age*, February 22, 2010, https://adage.com/article/special-report-digital-alist-2010/digital-a-list-2010-mtn-dew-lets-skaters-control-marketing/142201.
9. Duane Stanford, "Mountain Dew Wants Some Street Cred," *Bloomberg*, April 26, 2012, www.bloomberg.com/news/articles/2012-04-26/mountain-dew-wants-some-street-cred.
10. Sergio Zyman, *The End of Marketing As We Know It* (New York: HarperBusiness, 1999).
11. Stanford, "Mountain Dew Wants Some Street Cred."
12. Nathalie Tedena, "Mountain Dew Ads Go Global with Return of 'Do the Dew,'" *The Wall Street Journal*, March 29, 2015, http://blogs.wsj.com/cmo/2015/03/29/mountain-dew-ads-go-global-with-return-of-do-the-dew.
13. Dick Mangiore, "Southwest Airlines: Aligning Business Strategy to Brand Positioning," *Innismaggiore.com*, October 18, 2017, https://innismaggiore.com/blog/southwests-direct-flight-to-brilliant-strategy/
14. Automation Marketing Strategies, "The Art of Market Positioning," *Strategic Advantage Newsletter*, January 2000, retrieved from www.automationmarketing.com, February 2003.

15. Ernest Martin, "Target Marketing: Summary and Unit Learning Outcomes," Course Syllabus CADV 213, retrieved from www.campbell.edu/faculty/martine/index.htm, February 26, 2003.

16. Blue Ocean, www.blueoceanstrategy.com.

17. Farrell, "Dew Poses Real Pepsi Challenge to Coke," *USA Today*, 2000, p. B2.

18. Adapted from Al Ries and Jack Trout, *Bottom-Up Marketing* (New York: McGraw-Hill, 1989), p. 8.

19. Frederick E. Webster, Jr., "Executing the New Marketing Concept," *Marketing Management* 3, no. 1 (1994), pp. 8–16.

20. Philip Kotler and Gary Armstrong, *Principles of Marketing* (Englewood Cliffs, NJ: Prentice Hall, 1994), p. 560; Don E. Schultz, Stanley I. Tannenbaum, and Robert F. Lauterborn, *Integrated Marketing Communications: Putting It Together & Making It Work* (Lincolnwood, IL: NTC Business Books, 1993), p. 52.

21. Frederick E. Webster, Jr., "Defining the New Marketing Concept (Part I)," *Marketing Management* 2, no. 4 (1994), pp. 22–31.

22. Frederick E. Webster, Jr., "The Changing Role of Marketing in the Corporation," *Journal of Marketing*, October 1992, pp. 1–17, 22–31.

23. Frederick E. Webster, Jr., "The Changing Role of Marketing in the Corporation," *Journal of Marketing*, October 1992, pp. 1–17, 22–31.

24. Frederick E. Webster, Jr., "The Changing Role of Marketing in the Corporation," *Journal of Marketing*, October 1992, pp. 1–17, 22–31.

25. Kotler and Armstrong, *Principles of Marketing*, p. 559.

26. Kotler and Armstrong, *Principles of Marketing*, p. 560.

27. Joe Flint and Suzanne Vranica, "Television-Ad Spending Shows Signs of Revival," *The Wall Street Journal*, April 17, 2016, www.wsj.com/articles/television-ad-spending-shows-signs-of-revival-1460885403.

28. Ian Kingwell, "What Is the Cost of Customer Acquisition vs. Customer Retention?" *LinkedIn Premium*, March 3, 2015, www.linkedin.com/pulse/what-cost-customer-acquisition-vs-retention-ian-kingwill.

29. Alex McEachern, "What Is a Repeat Customer and Why Are They Profitable?" *smile.io*, January 21, 2020, https://blog.smile.io/repeat-customers-profitable.

30. Neil Patel, "How To Calculate Lifetime Value–The Infographic," https://blog.kissmetrics.com/how-to-calculate-lifetime-value.

31. John Dyson, "The Benefits of Building Long-Term Business Relationships," *FJRGroup*, April 30, 2019, https://fjrgroup.com/insights/the-benefits-of-building-longterm-business-relationships.

32. Thomas R. Duncan and Sandra E. Moriarty, *Driving Brand Value: Using Integrated Marketing to Manage Stakeholder Relationships* (New York: McGraw-Hill, 1997), p. 42.

33. Adapted from Kotler and Armstrong, *Principles of Marketing*, pp. 560–61.

34. Arthur M. Hughes, "Can This Relationship Work?" *Marketing Tools*, July/August 1994, p. 4.

35. Tedena, "Mountain Dew Ads Go Global with Return of 'Do the Dew.'"

36. Kotler and Armstrong, *Principles of Marketing*, p. 561.

37. Schultz, Tannenbaum, and Lauterborn, *Integrated Marketing Communications*, p. 52.

38. Looi Qin En, "Going Beyond the Product to Create Unique Experiences," *LinkedIn Premium*, April 10, 2014, www.linkedin.com/pulse/20140410020337-45080257-going-beyond-the-product-to-create-unique-experiences.

39. Marc Woodland, "The Benefits of Having an Integrated Marketing Campaign," *LinkedIn Premium*, May 20, 2015, www.linkedin.com/pulse/benefits-having-integrated-marketing-campaign-marc-woodland.

40. Glen J. Nowak and Joseph Phelps, "Conceptualizing the Integrated Marketing Communications' Phenomenon: An Examination of Its Impact on Advertising Practices and Its Implications for Advertising Research," *Journal of Current Issues & Research in Advertising*, vol. 26(1), 1994, pp. 49–66.

41. Karlene Lukovitz, "Get Ready for One-on-One Marketing," *Folio: The Magazine for Magazine Management*, October 1, 1991, pp. 64–70.

42. J. Stephen Kelly, Susan K. Jones, and Richard A. Hagle, *The IMC Handbook: Readings & Cases in Integrated Marketing Communications* (Racom Communications, 2015).

43. William F. Arens and Jack J. Whidden, "La Publicité aux Etats-Unis, 1992; Les Symptomes et les Stratégies d'une Industrie Surpeuplée," *L'industrie de la Publicité au Québec 1991–1992* (Montreal: Le Publicité-Club de Montréal, October 1992), pp. 365–99.

44. Regis McKenna, "Marketing in an Age of Diversity," *Harvard Business Review*, September/October 1988, p. 88; Schultz, Tannenbaum, and Lauterborn, *Integrated Marketing Communications*, p. 21.

45. Duncan and Moriarty, *Driving Brand Value*, pp. 78–90.

46. Duncan and Moriarty, *Driving Brand Value*, p. 90.

47. Adapted from Tom Duncan, "A Macro Model of Integrated Marketing Communication," paper presented to the annual conference of the American Academy of Advertising, Norfolk, VA, March 23–24, 1995, pp. 7–10.

48. Forbes Agency Council, "11 Trends That Will Shape Marketng in 2019," *Forbes*, January 15, 2019, www.forbes.com/sites/forbesagencycouncil/2019/01/15/11-trends-that-will-shape-marketing-in-2019/#692772136a69.

49. Sarah Vizard, "Nestlé Focuses on Going Direct-to-Consumers as Ecommerce Sales Hit 5%," *Marketing Week*, February 17, 2017, www.marketingweek.com/nestle-focuses-going-direct-consumers-ecommerce-sales-hit-5.

50. Kelly, Jones, and Hagle, *The IMC Handbook: Readings & Cases in Integrated Marketing Communications*.

51. Kelly, Jones, and Hagle, *The IMC Handbook: Readings & Cases in Integrated Marketing Communications*.

52. SAS, "Big Data, Bigger Marketing," www.sas.com/en_us/insights/big-data/big-data-marketing.html.

53. Robert Williams, "Mtn Dew Brings 'Shining'-Inspired Super Bowl Campaign to Social Media," *Mobile Marketer*, January 29, 2020, www.mobilemarketer.com/news/mtn-dew-brings-shining-inspired-super-bowl-campaign-to-social-media/571280.

54. Schultz, Tannenbaum, and Lauterborn, *Integrated Marketing Communications*, pp. 55–58.

55. Steve Olenski, "Why Integrated Marketing Communications Is More Important Than Ever," *Forbes*, September 16, 2013, www.forbes.com/sites/steveolenski/2013/09/16/why-integrated-marketing-communications-is-more-important-than-ever/#43e443cc2325.

56. Don E. Schultz and Paul Wang, "Real World Results," *Marketing Tools*, premier issue, May 1994, pp. 40–47.

57. Don E. Schultz and Paul Wang, "Real World Results," *Marketing Tools*, premier issue, May 1994, pp. 40–47.

58. Don E. Schultz, "Integrated Marketing Communications: A Competitive Weapon in Today's Marketplace," *Marketing Review*, July 1993, pp. 10–11, 29.

59. Gregg Ambach and Mike Hess, "Measuring Long-Term Effects in Marketing," *Marketing Research: A Magazine of Management and Applications*, American Marketing Association, Summer 2000, pp. 23–30.

60. Robert D. Buzzell and Frederick D. Wiersema, "Successful Share-Building Strategies," *Harvard Business Review*, January/February 1981, p. 135; John Phillip Jones, "Ad Spending: Maintaining Market Share," *Harvard Business Review*, January/February 1990; Siva K. Balasubramanian and V. Kumar, "Analyzing Variations in Advertising and Promotional Expenditures: Key Correlated in Consumer, Industrial, and Service Markets," *Journal of Marketing*, April 1990, pp. 57–68.

61. Guy Consterdine, "Advertising in a Recession: It Pays to Maintain Marketing Pressure; A Review of the Evidence," *PPAI*, February 2009, www.consterdine.com/articlefiles/79/ppai_adv_in_rec.pdf.

62. Leo Bogart, *Strategy in Advertising*, 2nd ed. (Chicago: Crain Books, 1984), pp. 45–47.

63. John Philip Jones, "Ad Spending: Maintaining Market Share," *Harvard Business Review*, January/February 1990, pp. 38–42; James C. Schroer, "Ad Spending: Growing Market Share," *Harvard Business Review*, January/February 1990, pp. 44–49.

64. Peter Breen, "Seeds of Change," Promo Sourcebook Supplement, Copyright 2000, INTERTEC, p. 18 (retrieved from www.lexisnexis.com).

laflor/E+/Getty Images

creating ads:
strategy and process

This chapter demonstrates how advertising strategies are used to develop creative briefs and message strategies. It examines the characteristics of great campaigns, the nature of creativity, and the role of the agency creative team. We discuss how research operates as the foundation for creative development and planning, and point out common problems that can challenge the creative team.

Walmart has changed the retail world. The company's success, a result of its relentless focus on offering a broad selection of goods at low prices, has made it one of the largest public companies in the world. For its competitors (and in this day and age, that is most stores), finding the right strategy for success is an ongoing challenge.

Some compete with Walmart by focusing on a single product category, such as clothes, electronics, pet supplies, or toys, and offering a broader selection within that category. An even riskier strategy is going head-to-head, as Kmart, Sears, Montgomery Ward, and others have learned the hard way. But standing tall among the scattered ruins of Walmart's direct competitors is one company that has found a way to prosper: Target.

Target's origins date to 1962 when the Dayton Company opened the first store in a Minneapolis suburb. Today the company operates nearly 1,700 stores throughout the United States and is fifth in overall revenue among U.S. retailers. Not bad for an organization whose greatest expansion occurred during the same years that Walmart became a global leader.[1]

Why has Target succeeded where other retail giants have not? In part by being one of the greatest practitioners of positioning, a concept we

continued on p. 200

LEARNING OBJECTIVES

After studying this chapter, you will be able to:

LO8-1 Identify the people who make up the creative team and indicate their primary responsibilities.

LO8-2 Describe the characteristics of great advertising.

LO8-3 Explain the role of the creative strategy and its principal elements.

LO8-4 Show how advertising enhances creativity.

LO8-5 Define the four roles people play at different stages of the creative process.

Source: Target Brands, Inc.

continued from p. 199

introduced in Chapter 7. Everyone knows that Walmart is synonymous with the concept of a "big-box store." To the individual who is looking to save money but finds Walmart's offerings or shopping environment just a bit ordinary, Target proudly proclaims "Expect more, pay less."

The slogan says it all. You'll save money at Target (compared to many retailers) and you'll have more fun shopping (compared to Walmart). The promise of a better shopping experience (the "expect more" part of the equation) has been the key. As retailer trade journalist Jeff Arlen asks, "Without Andy Warhol, could Target Stores exist as it is today? Have CEO Bob Ulrich and his team of retailing alchemists learned the secret of turning the mundane into the sublime?"[2]

Start with the merchandise. Lots of the things you find at Target you can find at Walmart as well, but Target displays them with more style and space. And some things you can't get at Walmart, or anywhere else—in-house lines such as Labworks, Zutano Blue, Room 365, and TOO by Blu Dot.[3]

Then, there is the red. Lots of red. As Michael Francis, senior VP of marketing at the retailer, notes, "Trust us, red does go with everything." The strategy at Target is to "own red," that is, have the consumer associate the color with the brand.

One way to communicate that Target owns red is through its retail stores. But the color plays a prominent role in Target advertising as well and helps tie the many executions together.

Target spends nearly four times as much on its advertising as a percentage of sales than does Walmart. Its ads are fun and quirky, in direct contrast to Walmart's safer approach. Target's ads are also softer, focusing on lifestyle themes that suggest ways that products sold at Target help the shopper have a better and more fun life.

The campaigns have been remarkably effective, and have helped fuel Target's growth. Target's creative and captivating ads have helped the company position itself as a more enjoyable place to shop than its biggest competitor. And that strategy has helped Target thrive even in the midst of Walmart's successes. ■

LO8-1 Identify the people who make up the creative team and indicate their primary responsibilities.

THE CREATIVE TEAM: ORIGINATORS OF ADVERTISING CREATIVITY

Every great idea, including the one that animates an ad campaign, starts with human imagination. In most ad agencies, the people who first conceptualize the symbols, words, and images are the members of the creative team.

The team's **copywriter** develops the *verbal* message, the copy (words) within the ad. The copywriter typically works with an **art director** who is responsible for the *nonverbal* aspect of the message, the design, which determines the look and feel of the ad. Together, they work under the supervision of a

copywriter Person who creates the words and concepts for ads and commercials.

art director Along with graphic designers and production artists, determines how the ad's verbal and visual symbols will fit together.

creative director Head of a creative team of agency copywriters and artists who is assigned to a client's business and who is ultimately responsible for the creative product—the form the final ad takes.

creatives The people who work in the creative department, regardless of the specialty.

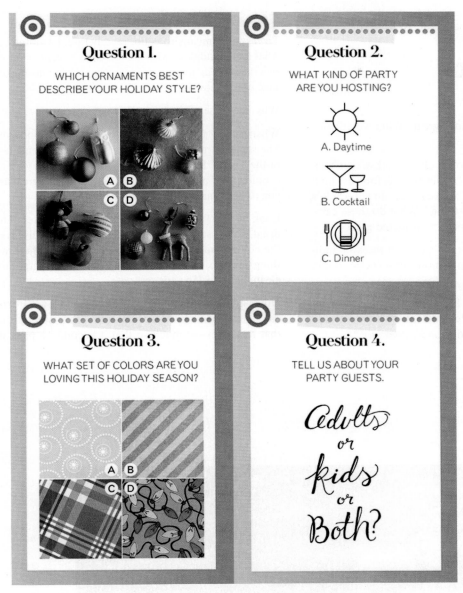

Bright colorful images, geometric shapes, and strong contrasts in both copy and graphics are qualities for great creative ads. Not only do they successfully draw the reader's attention, they help brand Target as an "upscale" discount store. This helps Target ads achieve instant recognizability in any medium, including Pinterest.
Source: Pinterest/Target Brands, Inc.

creative director (typically, a former copywriter or art director), who is ultimately responsible for the creative product—the form the final ad takes. As a group, agency people who work in the creative department are generally referred to as **creatives**, regardless of their specialty.

This chapter focuses on the creative process: how it's developed and how it relates to a company's marketing and advertising strategy. But to get a proper perspective on creativity, we need to understand the characteristics of great advertising.

check yourself ✓

1. What does a copywriter do? What does an art director do?
2. Who is ultimately responsible for the creative product?

CREATING GREAT ADVERTISING

What does it mean to say that an ad is great? What would your definition be?

Some of the classic ads in history offer clues: Volkswagen's famous "Think small" ad; DeBeers's "A diamond is forever" line; Clairol's "Does she or doesn't she?"; Nike's "Just do it"; Apple's "1984"; and Coca-Cola's "The real thing." What do these campaigns share that make them universally considered great?

This is a very important question because a lot of research indicates that "ad liking" has a direct impact on "ad success." But is a likable ad the same as a great ad?

No matter the platform, great ads have certain things in common. We can lump most of these elements into two dimensions of greatness: *audience resonance* and *strategic relevance*.[4]

The Resonance Dimension

To resonate means to echo, reverberate, or vibrate. And that's what a great ad does with an audience. It echoes in their ears. It reverberates. It *resonates*. It moves people and makes the message unforgettable.

Why? Because of the boom factor.

When a cannon goes "boom," it gets your attention—immediately! The same is true with an ad. It's the surprise element—the "aha," or the "wow." But in advertising, it not only gets your attention, it captures your imagination. In this sense it's like great art. It invites you to pause and think about the message.

Look at the Target ads throughout this chapter. They are unusual, so we stop to examine them more closely. As we do so, the colors and familiar logo convey exactly where we can find things we like, in an environment that is contemporary, upscale, clean, and fun. The ads resonate.

Other ads may resonate for different reasons. In some of the classic campaigns we just mentioned, it's simply the headline that resonates—so much so that it becomes a part of our daily

> Great ads have certain things in common: ... *audience resonance* and *strategic relevance.*

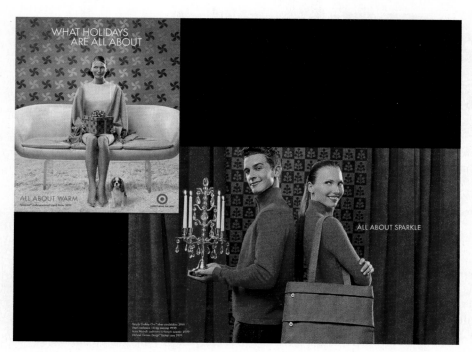

One way Target communicates that it offers an extraordinary shopping experience is through the use of extraordinary ads that successfully capture the attention of its consumers. These ads showcase the effective use of color to hook audiences.
Source: Target Brands, Inc.

Target ads are quirky and creative. But the nonverbal elements of the red and white colors and repetition of the Target logo make them instantly recognizable and resonate with consumers.

Source: Target Brands, Inc.

language. Other memorable classics include California Milk Processors's "Got Milk?" Dollar Shave Club's "Shave Time, Shave Money," and Bounty's "The Quicker Picker Upper."

Recall from Chapter 5 our discussion of consumer motives. *Negatively originated motives*, such as problem avoidance or problem removal, provide the foundation for many great ads. These resonate with the audience by being highly **informational**. Informational ads resonate because the consumer perceives that the brand offers a credible solution to a significant problem. (Uber's "Get there. The day belongs to you" or Slack's "Be less busy"). Other motives are *positively originated* as consumers seek pleasant experiences, intellectual stimulation, or social approval. Here, ads may achieve greatness by being **transformational**, using positive reinforcement to offer a reward (such as Ted's "Ideas worth spreading" or Weight Watchers' "Success starts here").

Unfortunately, most ads, whether they're informational or transformational, fail to resonate. Why? Because they lack a "big idea" or fall short in the *execution*. The copy may be uninspiring, the visual may be unattractive, or the production techniques may be of low quality. To the consumer, these ads are a waste of time, and to the client, a waste of money. Clients have a clear way of judging the greatness of their advertising: "bang per buck." Great ads give sponsors much more advertising effectiveness per dollar spent.

The Relevance Dimension

The second dimension of great advertising is strategic relevance. Relevance is all about consumers perceiving that an ad speaks to them and their needs. The relevance dimension has surged in importance in the digital age because of the success of Google's ad program, which targets people with ads based on the problem they are trying to solve. Google search ads may not be pretty, but they are relevant.

The famous ad agency Leo Burnett has its own take on resonance and relevance. The company puts it this way:

> We don't make brands famous, we make brands popular. There's no greater goal for us than to take each of our clients' brands and put them in a position of popularity by making them a part of the fabric of real people's lives. We create work that is inclusive and bold and appeals to the mass market. We want to create work that a brand can grow into, that will appeal to more than just the immediate target audience. That's what we're about and that's what we always focus on.[5]

While the text and the visual carry the ad message, behind the creative team's choice of tone, words, and ideas lies an advertising strategy. When the ad is completed, it must be relevant to the sponsor's strategy, or it will fail—even if it resonates with the audience. In other words, it may be great *entertainment*, but not great *advertising*. Great advertising always has a strategic mission to fulfill. In fact, strategy is at the root of all great creative work.

check yourself ✓

1. What does it mean for advertising to resonate? What causes an ad to resonate?

2. In addition to resonance, what other dimension is important for advertising greatness?

LO8-3 Explain the role of the creative strategy and its principal elements.

DEVELOPING A CREATIVE STRATEGY: THE KEY TO GREAT ADVERTISING

Recall from Chapter 7 that an advertising *objective* states what the advertiser wants to achieve with respect to consumer awareness, attitude, and preference. Advertising *strategy* describes a means for achieving that objective through the development of advertising executions and media plans. The *creative strategy* is the part of the advertising strategy that guides the creative team.

To be sure that everyone has the same understanding of the task at hand, account managers (or, in larger agencies, account planners) develop a brief statement summarizing the agreed-upon objectives and strategies. Many individuals from both the client and agency—including representatives from creative, media, and research—have input into this document. The agency and client team sign off on the finished document before the creative process commences. This **creative strategy** serves as the creative team's guide for writing and producing the advertising. In some agencies this document may be referred to as a *creative brief*, a *work plan*, a *copy strategy*, or a *copy platform*. For more on developing creative strategy, see My Ad Campaign 8–A.

Writing the Creative Strategy

Regardless of the name, the creative strategy is a simple written statement of the most important issues to consider in the development of an ad or campaign. It usually includes the following elements:

- The basic problem advertising must address.

- The advertising objective.

- A definition of the target audience.

- The key benefits to communicate.

- Support for or proof of those benefits.

- The brand's personality.

- Any special requirements.

Let's look at the creative strategy Target and its agencies developed. We'll then see how they translated that into a message strategy and a big idea and, finally, into effective ads.

Ads like this out-of-home execution communicate a great deal with very little copy. How does Target meld a creative design and simultaneously imply great selection with this billboard?

Source: Target Brands, Inc.

- What is the **problem the advertising must solve**? Consumers may not be aware that they will save money *and* enjoy shopping at Target. Consumers may also be unaware of the unique products that can be found only at Target. *This information often comes straight from the marketing plan's situation analysis.*

- What is the *objective of the advertising*? Target wants consumers to know that it has higher-quality offerings and a more attractive shopping environment than its competitors. The **advertising objective** is initially spelled out in the marketing plan.

- What is the **target audience**? Target focuses on value-conscious shoppers, usually adults ages 25–49 with families, who seek products that are nicer than those typically found at deep-discount stores. These shoppers are not poor, but they do like to save money (Target reports that the median household income of its shoppers, or "guests," as the company calls them, is $60,000). This group is Target's *primary market*—that's who the company sells to. So Target definitely wants them to see its advertising. Because Target offers both value and style, 18- to 25-year-olds are another important market. While this group as a whole may not spend as much as the primary market, they act as *centers of influence* (or *key influentials*). This group is a *secondary target audience* for the advertising.

- What is Target's *key benefit*? This is summarized nicely in the company's slogan, "Expect more, pay less." In other words, expect a nicer shopping experience and still save money. The **benefit statement** is the heart of the creative strategy. It is very important to make it as succinct and single-minded as possible. Complex benefit statements can lead to creative executions that promise everything and focus on nothing.

- How is that benefit *supported*? Target's ads rarely focus on price information, a contrast with the "hard sell" approach that Walmart favors. The "expect more" part of the equation is supported with beautiful, stylish, and unexpected ad executions, as many of the featured ads in this chapter demonstrate. The **support statement** should provide information about the product or service that will convince the target audience that the key benefit is true.

- What is the **brand personality**? Target's brand is quality, sophistication, beauty, and value. The creative team will frequently remind themselves of this as they develop the message strategy.

- Are there any **special requirements**? Target allocates ad dollars to television ads, out-of-home magazines, and newspaper inserts. It has different audience objectives for each medium. But certain creative elements, such as the color red and the large "bull's-eye" logo, tie the ads together. It is important for the creatives to understand budget and media constraints before they begin.

The creative strategy identifies the benefits to be presented to consumers, but it doesn't cover execution. How the benefits will be presented is the creative team's job.

support statement
Statement that provides information about the product or service that will convince the target audience that the key *benefit* is true.

brand personality
Describes a brand in terms of human characteristics. A significant component in effective branding is imparting personality to a brand, reflecting its reputation, attitudes, and behavior.

special requirements
Unique characteristics of the advertiser, brand, target audience, media, competition, budget, and so on that should be considered during the creative development process.

Ad agency Leo Burnett use a simple creative strategy with only three parts:

1. *An objective statement.* A specific, concise description of what the advertising is supposed to accomplish or what problem it is supposed to solve. The objective statement also includes the name of the brand and a brief, specific description of the target consumer. For example:

> Advertising will convince value-conscious consumers that Target stores offer them a way to save money on their everyday purchases. In addition, Target offers a vast selection of products that are practical, attractive, and fun.

> "The creative strategy identifies the benefits to be presented to consumers, but it doesn't cover execution. How the benefits will be presented is the creative team's job.

The Creative Strategy [8–A]

Every agency has a slightly different twist on a creative strategy statement or brief. Common topics include:

- Who (the prospect).
- Why (specific audience wants or needs the ad should appeal to).
- What (are the product features that can satisfy consumer needs?).
- Where and when (will the messages be transmitted?).
- Style, approach, tone.

   Leo Burnett keeps things even simpler for its largest client, P&G:

- An objective statement (what are you trying to do?).
- A support statement (the evidence that backs up the promised benefit).
- A tone or brand character statement (emotional descriptions of the advertising strategy).

   Ogilvy includes these questions in the creative brief:

1. What are the communications objectives?
2. What should consumers do differently? Why?

3. How will messages affect consumer beliefs and actions?
4. How are our competitors advertising? How can we make our ads different?
5. Who is the target audience and what is their shared need that the brand can fulfill?
6. Demographics of the audience, but even more importantly, shared attitudes.
7. The brand
   - How does the brand address the shared need?
   - How should the brand experience (as defined by both planned and unplanned messages) be defined?
   - What is the proposition (or benefit)?
   - What evidence gives people a reason to believe the proposition?
   - What is the personality of the brand?
   - How can the mood or tone of the ads be matched to the personality of the brand?

2. *A support statement.* A brief description of the evidence that backs up the product promise; the reason for the benefit. For example:

> Support is found in two types of ads that Target regularly runs. Newspaper ads, including weekly inserts, demonstrate to consumers the low prices of the products sold at Target. Television ads emphasize the quality and value of the everyday products found at Target. Both TV and newspaper ads should do more than focus on the product alone, rather they should help to demonstrate that the products sold at Target make life easier and better.

3. *A tone or brand character statement.* A brief statement of either the advertising's tone or the long-term character of the brand. Tone statements are emotional descriptions of the advertising strategy. Brand character statements are descriptions of the enduring values of the brand. A tone statement might be phrased:

> The tone of Target ads should convey a spirit of optimism and energy. The ads should suggest that Target understands the consumer and the challenges she faces in her life. They should suggest that shopping at Target is fun and that choosing Target as a retailer is a sign of both sensibility (low prices) and sophistication (better offerings).

On the other hand, a brand character statement might be phrased:

> Target offers consumers the selection and value typical of a mass merchandiser in a setting that has the elegance and flair of a department store.

The delivery of the creative strategy to the creative department concludes the process of developing an advertising strategy. It also marks the beginning of the next step: the **creative process**, in which the creative team develops a *message strategy* and begins the search for the *big idea*. After writing the first ad, the copywriter should review the creative strategy to confirm that the ad is "on strategy." If it isn't, the team must start again.

Elements of Message Strategy

From the information given by the account team (in the creative strategy) and any additional research it may perform, the creative team develops the message strategy.

The **message strategy** is a simple description and explanation of an ad campaign's overall creative approach—the main idea, details about how the idea will be executed, and a rationale. The message strategy has three components:

- *Verbal.* Guidelines for what the advertising should say; considerations that affect the choice of words; and the relationship of the copy approach to the medium (or media) that will carry the message.

- *Nonverbal.* Overall nature of the ad's graphics; any visuals that must be used; and the relationship of the graphics to the media in which the ad will appear.

- *Technical.* Preferred execution approach and mechanical outcome, including budget and scheduling limitations (often governed by the media involved); also any **mandatories**—specific requirements for every ad, such as addresses, logos, and slogans.

The verbal elements are the starting point for many advertising campaigns. However, because all these elements of the message strategy intertwine, they typically evolve simultaneously. Language affects imagery, and vice versa.

The message strategy helps the creative team sell the ad or the campaign concept to the account managers and helps the managers explain and defend the creative work to the client. Of course, the message strategy must fit to the creative strategy or it will probably be rejected.

In the development of the message strategy, certain basic questions need to be answered: How is the market segmented? How will the product be positioned? Who are the best prospects for the product? Is the target audience different from the target market? What is the key consumer benefit? What is the product's

The simplicity, vibrant colors, and cleverness of Target's ads are part of the message strategy. They help create a brand personality and give consumers a reason to shop at the store. The added "boom" factor in this ad is Target encouraging and celebrating diversity.
Source: Target Brands, Inc.

(or company's) current image? What is the product's unique advantage relative to other brands? At this point, research data are important. Research helps the creative team answer these questions and support their proposed approach.

check yourself ✓

1. What are the important parts of the creative strategy (or creative brief)?

2. What is the message strategy? What are its important parts?

LO8-4 Show how advertising enhances creativity.

HOW CREATIVITY ENHANCES ADVERTISING

The powerful use of imagery, copy, and humor in Target campaigns demonstrates how creativity enhances advertising. But what exactly is creativity? What is the role of creativity in advertising? And where does creativity come from?

What Is Creativity?

To create means to originate, to conceive a thing or idea that did not exist before. Typically, though, **creativity** involves combining two or more previously unconnected objects or ideas into something new. As Voltaire said, "Originality is nothing but judicious imitation."

Many people think creativity springs directly from human intuition. But as we'll see in this chapter, the creative process is not a chaotic, unorganized way of thinking but a disciplined process that can be learned and used to generate original ideas. In the words of advertising legend Bill Bernbach, "Merely to let your imagination run riot, to dream unrelated dreams, to indulge in graphic acrobatics and verbal gymnastics is not being creative. The creative person has harnessed his imagination. He has disciplined it so that every thought, every idea, every word he puts down, every line he draws, every light and shadow in every photograph he takes make more vivid, more believable, more persuasive the original theme or product advantage he has decided he must convey."[6]

The Role of Creativity in Advertising

Advertisers often select an agency specifically for its creative reputation for coming up with original and successful concepts.

While creativity is important to advertising's basic mission of informing, persuading, and reminding, it is vital to achieving the boom factor.

Creativity Helps Advertising Inform

Advertising's responsibility to inform is greatly enhanced by creativity. Good creative work makes advertising more *vivid*, a quality that many researchers believe attracts attention, maintains interest, and stimulates consumers' thinking.[7] A common technique is to use wordplay and verbal or visual metaphors, such as "Put a tiger in your tank," "Fly the friendly skies," or "Solutions for a smart planet." The metaphor describes one concept in terms of another, helping the reader or viewer learn about the product.[8] Wordplay is a key tactic behind a campaign you read about in Chapter 6 where Hyundai used the phrase "smaht pahk" to remind consumers about a desirable Sonata benefit.

Other creative techniques can also improve an ad's ability to inform. For example, visual cues such as lighting, pose or expression of the model, setting, and clothing style can instantly signal viewers nonverbally whether a fashion ad reflects a romantic adventure or a sporting event. The Target ads in this chapter offer great examples of how posing and expression communicate a personality for the Target brand.

Creativity Helps Advertising Persuade

The ancients created myths about gods and heroes—symbols for people's hopes and fears—to influence human behavior and thought. To motivate people to take action or change an attitude, copywriters originated new myths and heroes, like Dos Equis' Most Interesting Man in the World, the M&M's characters, and the Allstate's Mayhem. A creative story or persona establishes a unique identity for the product, a key factor in helping a product beat the competition.[9]

To be persuasive, an ad's verbal message must be reinforced by the creative use of nonverbal message elements. Artists use these elements (color, layout, and illustration, for example) to increase vividness. Research suggests that in print and digital media, *infographics* (colorful explanatory charts, tables, and the like) often raise readers' perception of quality.[10] Artwork can also stimulate emotions. Color, for example, often

---

creative process The step-by-step procedure used to discover original ideas and reorganize existing concepts in new ways.

message strategy A document that helps media planners determine how messages will be delivered to consumers. It defines the target audience, the communication objectives that must be achieved, and the characteristics of the media that will be used for delivery of the messages.

mandatories The address, phone number, web address, and so on that the advertiser usually insists be included within an ad to give the consumer adequate information.

creativity Involves combining two or more previously unconnected objects or ideas into something new.

motivates consumers, depending on their cultural background and personal experiences.[11]

Creativity Helps Advertising Remind

Imagine using the same invitation to ask people to try your product again and again, year after year. Your invitation would become stale and tiresome. Only creativity can transform your boring reminders into interesting, entertaining advertisements. Nike is proof. Several commercials in a Nike campaign never mentioned the company name or even spelled it on the screen. The ads told stories. And the only on-screen cue identifying the sponsor was the single, elongated "swoosh" logo inscribed on the final scene. A Nike spokesperson said the ads weren't risky "given the context that the Nike logo is so well known." We are entertained daily by creative and surprising ads—for soft drinks, snacks, and cereals—whose primary mission is simply to remind us to indulge again.

Creativity Puts the "Boom" in Advertising

Successful comedy also has a boom factor—the punchline. It's that precise moment when the audience suddenly gets it and laughs out loud.

Good punchlines come from taking an everyday situation, looking at it creatively, adding a bit of exaggeration, and then delivering it as a surprise. Great advertising often does the same thing.

The creativity shown in this ad for the Thomas O'Brien home furnishings line persuades and reminds consumers that they can expect both value and elegance from Target.
Source: Target Brands, Inc.

In advertising, though, the boom doesn't always have to be funny. It may come from the sudden understanding of an unexpected double-meaning, as in the case of Target ads. Or from the gentle emotional tug of a Hallmark Cards commercial. Or from the unpredictability of an Old Spice ad. In a business-to-business situation, it may come from the sudden recognition of how a new high-tech product can improve workplace productivity. In short, the boom factor may come from many sources. But it always requires creativity.

Understanding Creative Thinking

Creativity is "the generation, development, and transformation of ideas that are both novel and useful for solving problems," according to Glenn Griffin and Deborah Morrison, professors at the Universities of Alabama and Oregon, respectively. Their insightful book, *The Creative Process Illustrated*, suggests that many models of creative thought portray creativity as a process that follows four stages: preparation (thinking about the problem and what is needed to solve it), incubation (thought about the problem that occurs subconsciously), illumination (potential solutions that pop into awareness as a result of incubation), and verification (determining which solutions might work).[12]

Fact-Based versus Value-Based Thinking

Griffin and Morrison, like many creativity scholars, believe that all people have the potential to be creative. However there are differences in the styles or preferred approaches people use to solve problems.

The preferred style of some is **fact-based thinking**, an approach that fragments concepts into components and analyzes situations to uncover the one best solution. Although fact-based people can be creative, they tend to be linear thinkers and prefer to have facts and figures—hard data—they can analyze and control. They are not comfortable with ambiguity. They prefer logic, structure, and efficiency.[13]

In contrast, **value-based thinking** approaches decisions using intuition, values, and moral codes. Value-based thinkers embrace change, conflict, and paradox. Their style relies on melding concepts together in new and original ways. A value-based thinker, for example, might attempt to integrate the divergent ideas of a group into an arrangement that lets everyone win. They are good at using their imagination to produce a flow of new ideas and synthesizing existing concepts to create something new.[14]

How Styles of Thinking Affect Creativity

If the creative team prefers a value-based thinking style, it tends to produce ads such as the one in the Tide and Target ad

Target is on track to give
$1 BILLION FOR EDUCATION
by the end of 2015

Target.com/Education

Value-based thinking guides the creation of many Target spots. The messages are emotional and steer away from specific product facts. They combine elements in new and original ways. But Target's ads can't be pigeon-holed so easily. This ad and others by the company address timely and important topics.
Source: Target Brands, Inc.

Fact-based styles also involve creative thinking but do so in a logical and analytical way. Walmart, a Target competitor, marshals the relevant facts to persuade people they can save money in this ad. Examining this ad and the ones for Target, what stands out as key differences in designs created using fact-based versus value-based thinking?
Source: Walmart.

shown below—soft, subtle, intuitive, metaphorical. That's fine if the client also prefers that style of thinking.

On the other hand, clients who prefer a fact-based style often seek agencies that produce practical, hard-edged work characterized by simple, straightforward layouts, rational appeals, and lots of data. A fact-based client may even find a value-based campaign to be unsettling.

The creative team needs to understand the campaign's target audience. In some market segments (high-tech, for example)

customers may favor messages that result from one style of thinking over another. And that should dictate which approach to use.

As we shall see in the next section, the best art directors and copywriters use both styles to accomplish their task. In the creative process, they need to use their imagination (value-based thinking) to develop a variety of concepts. But to select the best alternative and get the job done, they often resort to the fact-based style.

This ad for the Tide and Target uses dreamlike images. The surreal background suggests purity and references Target in a subtle, almost subliminal way. What style of thinking did the creative team use in this ad?
Source: Target Brands, Inc.

check yourself ✓

1. What is creativity?

2. How does advertising help advertisers inform? Persuade? Remind?

3. How do different styles of thinking influence the creative process? How do they influence the ads that result from using each style?

LO8-5 Define the four roles people play at different stages of the creative process.

THE CREATIVE PROCESS

The creative process offers a step-by-step procedure valuable for discovering original ideas and reorganizing existing concepts in exciting new ways. By following it, people can improve their ability to unearth possibilities, combine concepts in original and pleasing ways, and select winning ideas.

The advertising creative does not work in isolation or create solutions for pleasure. The creative challenge is a collective activity. Advertising creatives must not only come up with good ideas, they must also help others appreciate the value of the ideas. Creativity consultant Roger von Oech developed a four-step creative model used by many *Fortune* 100 companies. It is especially appropriate for creatives working as a team for a client who will ultimately judge the work. Von Oech, using powerful metaphors, describes four distinct roles that every art director and copywriter must adopt at some point in the creative process:[15]

1. *The Explorer* is a scout for new information, paying attention to unusual patterns.

2. *The Artist* tinkers with a variety of approaches, looking for an original idea.

3. *The Judge* evaluates the results of experimentation and decides which approach is most practical.

4. *The Warrior* overcomes push back and doubt to bring a creative concept to realization.

The Explorer Role: Gathering Information

Copywriters and art directors thrive on the challenge of creating **advertising messages**—the encoding process. But first they need the raw materials for ideas: facts, experiences, history, knowledge, and emotions.

In the role of the **Explorer**, creatives examine the information available. They review the creative strategy and the marketing and advertising plan; they study the market, the product, and the competition. They may seek additional input from the agency's account managers and planners and from people on the client side (sales, marketing, product, or brand managers).

When Target started opening in stores in Canada, it used clever ads like the one shown. This is a great example of the development of a big idea unique to a specific region while still maintaining the strong Target brand. Source: Target Brands, Inc.

When the creative team developed ads for Target, they first assumed the Explorer role. They spoke with the company about its products, its marketing history, its competitors, and the competitors' advertising. They reviewed all appropriate sources of advertising for retail stores and studied the company's marketing environment. They carefully studied the creative brief prepared for them by the researchers, account planners, and account managers.

Develop an Insight Outlook In advertising, it's important that when creatives play the Explorer role, they get off the beaten path to look in new and uncommon places for information—to discover new ideas and to identify unusual patterns. One important source of inspiration is the consumer herself. Target's agency creatives spent hours watching women shop at Target stores. In this sense, creativity is less of an abstract, armchair process and more informed by real people living authentic lives.

Von Oech suggests adopting an "insight outlook" (a conviction that good information is available and that you have the skills to find and use it). If you're curious and poke around in new areas, you'll improve your chances of discovering new ideas. Ideas are everywhere: a museum, an art gallery, a hardware store, an airport. The more diverse the sources, the greater your chance of uncovering an original concept.

Know the Objective Philosopher John Dewey said, "A problem well-stated is a problem half-solved." This is why the creative strategy is so important. It helps define what the creatives are looking for. The creatives typically start working on the message strategy during the Explorer stage because it, too, helps them define what they're looking for. Target's ads are meant to distinguish the retailer from other discount store brands. Knowing that is crucial for understanding why Target ads are designed as they are.

Brainstorm   As Explorers, the art director and copywriter look first for lots of ideas. One technique is **brainstorming**, a process in which two or more people team up to generate new ideas. A brainstorming session is often a source of sudden inspiration. To succeed, it must follow a couple of rules: All ideas are above criticism (no idea is "wrong"), and all ideas are written down for later review. Griffin and Morrison suggest that one of the critical differences between the approaches of novice advertising creative students and more seasoned ones is that the latter write down all ideas, no matter how promising each seems on first glance. In addition, they are more successful at withholding criticism of ideas that seem initially far-fetched. The goal is to record any inspiration that comes to mind, a process that psychologists call *free association*, allowing each new idea an opportunity to stimulate another.

Von Oech offers other techniques for Explorers: Leave your own turf (look in outside fields and industries for ideas that

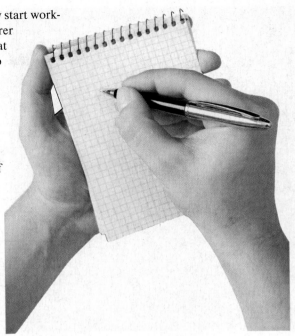

Source: Halfdark/Getty Images

The Artist Role: Developing and Implementing the Big Idea

The next step, playing the Artist's role, is both tough and long, but it's also rewarding. The **Artist** must actually accomplish two major tasks: develop the big idea and then implement it.

Task 1: Develop the Big Idea   The first task for Artists is the long, sometimes tedious process of reviewing all the

[If you're curious and poke around in new areas, you'll improve your chances of discovering new ideas. Ideas are everywhere.]

could be transferred); shift your focus (pay attention to a variety of information); look at the big picture (stand back and see what it all means); don't overlook the obvious (the best ideas can be right in front of your nose); don't be afraid to stray (you might find something you weren't looking for); and stake your claim to new territory (write down any new ideas or they will be lost).

To keep their creative juices flowing, most copywriters and art directors maintain an extensive library of advertising award books and trade magazines. Many also keep copies of ads that they like.

information they gathered as Explorers, analyzing the problem, and searching for a key verbal or visual concept to communicate what needs to be said.

It also means creating a mental picture of the ad before any copy is written or artwork begun. This step (also called **visualization** or *conceptualization*) is the most important in creating the advertisement. It's where the search for the **big idea**—that flash of insight—takes place. The big idea is a bold, creative initiative that builds on the strategy, joins the product benefit with consumer desire in a fresh, involving way, brings the subject to life, and makes the audience stop, look, and listen.[16]

Some images make the point so well they require no words. This ad for Globetrotter outdoor gear connects the idea of giant seals snug in their skins with campers snug in their sleeping bags. It's amazing how much they look alike. There's a big idea here.

Source: Globetrotter Ausrüstung

What's the difference between a strategy and a big idea? A strategy describes the direction the message should take. A big idea gives it life. For example, the creative strategy proposed earlier for the Target campaign contained a strategic brand character statement:

> Target offers consumers the selection and value typical of a mass merchandiser in a setting that has the elegance and flair of a department store.

Target could have used that strategy statement as a headline. But it would have been dreadfully dull. It lacks what a big idea headline delivers: a set of multiple meanings that create interest, memorability, and, in some cases, drama. Note the short, punchy headline that Target chose to convey the same strategic concept: Expect more. Pay less.

John O'Toole said, "While strategy requires deduction, a big idea requires inspiration."[17] The big idea in advertising is almost invariably expressed through a combination of art and copy. Target's approach is to use short but witty copy, beautiful photography, and the immediately recognizable red "target" logo to visually communicate the essence of the brand. Target could save money and use much less creativity in its advertising. Rather than using striking, colorful graphics and layouts, Target's campaigns could emphasize facts and information. But this approach would reduce the boom factor and would end up ignored by the target audience (see Exhibit 8–1).

Transforming a concept: Do something to it Creative ideas come from manipulating and transforming resources. Von Oech points out that when we adopt the Artist role, we have to do something to the materials we collected as Explorers to give them value. That means asking lots of questions: What if I added this? Or took that away? Or looked at it backward? Or compared it with something else? The Artist has to change patterns and experiment with various approaches.

There are several ways that an artist can experiment to produce something fresh and creative. Consider selecting a brand that you use and love, and think about sketching some ideas consistent with each recommendation below.

1. *Adapt.* Change contexts. Think what else the product might be besides the obvious. A Campbell's Soup ad showed a steaming bowl of tomato soup with a bold headline underneath: "HEALTH INSURANCE."

2. *Imagine.* Ask what if. Let your imagination fly. What if people could do their chores in their sleep? What if animals drank in saloons? Clyde's Bar in Georgetown actually used that idea. The ad showed a beautifully illustrated elephant and donkey dressed in business suits and seated at a table toasting one another. The headline: "Clyde's. The People's Choice."

3. *Reverse.* Look at it backward. Sometimes the opposite of what you expect has great impact and memorability. A cosmetics company ran an ad for its moisturizing cream under the line: "Introduce your husband to a younger woman." A vintage Volkswagen ad used "Ugly is only skin deep."

▼**EXHIBIT 8–1** Advertising's big ideas.

What brands use these big ideas?	
Quitting Sucks.[a]	Just do it.[j]
Mayhem.[b]	Eat fresh.[k]
It's finger lickin' good![c]	It's everywhere you want to be.[l]
American by birth. Rebel by choice.[d]	A diamond is forever.[m]
Innovation.[e]	Think small.[n]
The customer is always and completely right![f]	Think big.[o]
The greatest tragedy is indifference.[g]	The antidote for Civilization.[p]
Live in your world. Play in ours.[h]	Outwit. Outplay. Outlast.[q]
The happiest place on earth.[i]	We sell more cars than Ford, Chrysler, Chevrolet, and Buick combined.[r]

[a]Nicorette, [b]Allstate, [c]KFC, [d]Harley-Davidson, [e]3M, [f]Marks & Spencer, [g]Red Cross, [h]PS2, [i]Disneyland, [j]Nike, [k]Subway, [l]Visa, [m]DeBeers, [n]Volkswagen, [o]IMAX, [p]Club Med, [q]Survivor, [r]Matchbox.

Many of Roger Von Oech's suggestions for transforming a concept are embodied in Target's ads. How many can you spot in this execution?

Source: Target Brands, Inc.

the way they've always been done. 7 Up became famous by advertising what it wasn't ("the Uncola") and thereby positioned itself as a refreshing alternative. To introduce its new models one year, Volkswagen used a series of humorous teaser ads that didn't show any cars. In one, a shaggy dog sat patiently in front of a fan. He was presumably replicating what dogs do in cars, sticking their heads out the window to catch the breeze. The only difference was he was doing it indoors.

7. *Parody.* Fool around. Have some fun. Tell some jokes—especially when you're under pressure. There is a close relationship between the ha-ha experience of humor and the aha! experience of creative discovery. Humor stretches our thinking and, used in good taste, makes for some great advertising. A classical radio station ran a newspaper ad: "Handel with care." And speaking of classics, Fila USA got a rave review from *Advertising Age* for its "bizarre, absolutely hilarious, and totally cool" spot of a praying mantis racing up a leaf stem in Fila sneakers to escape his murderous mate.[18]

Blocks to creativity Everybody experiences times when the creative juices just won't flow. There are many causes: information overload, mental or physical fatigue, stress, fear, insecurity. Often, though, the problem is simply the style of thinking being used.

In the Explorer stage, when creatives study reams of marketing data, the facts and figures on sales and market share may put them in a fact-based frame of mind. But to create effectively, they need to shift gears to a value-based style of thinking.

Creative blocking may occur when people in the agency start "thinking like the client," especially if the client is a fact-based

4. *Connect.* Join two unrelated ideas together. Ask yourself: What ideas can I connect to my concept? A Target ad showed the rear view of a high-fashion-type model clad only with a backpack and a lampshade—the latter wrapped around her middle like a miniskirt. Next to the Target logo the ad said simply "fashion and housewares." To get people to send for its catalog, Royal Caribbean Cruises ran an ad that showed the catalog cover under the simple headline "Sail by Mail."

5. *Compare.* Take one idea and use it to describe another. Ever notice how bankers talk like plumbers? "Flood the market, laundered money, liquid assets, cash flow, take a bath, float a loan." The English language is awash in metaphors because they help people understand. Jack in the Box advertised its onion rings by picturing them on a billboard and inviting motorists to "Drive thru for a ring job." An elegant magazine ad for the Parker Premier fountain pen used this sterling metaphor: "It's wrought from pure silver and writes like pure silk."

6. *Eliminate.* Subtract something. Or break the rules. In advertising, there's little virtue in doing things

Metaphor is a powerful creative tool. Consider the metaphor of the artwork in this ad and the way the artist uses a powerful image of a man supplying heat to a hot air balloon to convey just how "hot and spicy" people will find the taste of Pringles Hot & Spicy chips.

Source: The Kellogg Company

Source: areebarbar/Shutterstock

thinker. This can also be hazardous to the agency's creative reputation and is one reason agencies sometimes resign accounts over "creative differences."

Creative fatigue can also happen when an agency has served an account for a long time and all the fresh ideas have been worked and reworked. It can be difficult to avoid fatigue when a client has rejected a series of concepts; the inspiration is lost and the creatives start trying to force ideas. If this becomes chronic, the only solutions may be to appoint an entirely new creative team or resign the account.

Incubating a concept: Do nothing to it When the brain is overloaded with information about a problem, creatives sometimes find it's best to just walk away from it for a while, do something else, and let the unconscious mind mull it over. This approach yields several benefits. First, it puts the problem back

into perspective. It also rests the brain, lets the problem incubate in the subconscious, and enables better ideas to percolate to the top. When they return to the task, the creatives frequently discover a whole new set of assumptions.

Task 2: Implement the Big Idea
Once the creatives latch onto the big idea, they must next focus on how to implement it. This is where the real art of advertising comes in—writing the exact words, designing the precise layout. To have a sense of how advertising creatives do that, we need to understand what art is in advertising, how artistic elements and tools are selected and used, and the difference between good art and bad art.

In advertising, art shapes the message into a complete communication that appeals to the senses as well as the mind. So while **art direction** refers to the act or process of managing the visual presentation of the commercial or ad, the term **art** actually refers to the whole presentation—visual and verbal. For example, the artful selection of words not only communicates information but also stimulates positive feelings for the product. An artfully designed typeface not only makes reading easier; it also evokes a mood. By creatively arranging format elements—surrounding the text with lines, boxes, and colors, and relating

How does Target's bold headline, space, color, typography, and design draw attention and achieve instant recognition (and admiration)?
Source: Target Brands, Inc.

> ## CREATIVE BLOCKING MAY OCCUR WHEN PEOPLE IN THE AGENCY START 'THINKING LIKE THE CLIENT.'

them to one another in proportion—the art director can further enhance the ad's message. Art also shapes the style and choice of photography and illustration. An intimate style uses soft focus and close views, a documentary style portrays the scene without pictorial enhancements, and a dramatic style features unusual angles or blurred action images.

In short, if *copy* is the verbal language of an ad, *art* is the body language. TV uses both sight and sound to involve viewers. Radio commercials use sound to create mental *pictures*. The particular blend of writing, visuals, and sounds makes up an ad's expressive character. So while the quality may vary, every ad uses art.

In advertising, balance, proportion, and movement are guides for uniting words, images, type, sounds, and colors into a single communication so they relate to and enhance each other. We'll discuss more of these concepts in Chapter 9.

The Creative Pyramid: A Guide to Formulating Copy and Art

The **creative pyramid** is a model that can guide the creative team as it converts the advertising strategy and the big idea into the actual physical ad or commercial. The cognitive theory of how people learn new information uses a simple five-step structure (the first pyramid in Exhibit 8–2).

The purpose of much advertising copy and design is to either persuade prospective customers to take some action to satisfy a need or want or to remind them to take the action again. In a new-product situation, people may first need to be made aware of the problem or, if the problem is obvious, that a solution exists. For a frequently purchased product, the advertiser simply has to remind people of the solution close to the purchase occasion. In either case, the advertiser's first job is to get the prospect's *attention*. The second step is to stimulate the prospect's *interest*—in either the message or the product itself. Next, it's important, especially for new products, to build *credibility* for the product claims. Then the ad can focus on generating *desire* and finally on stimulating *action*. These five elements (the second pyramid in Exhibit 8–2) should be addressed in just about every ad or commercial. We'll deal with each step briefly.

Attention   For an ad or commercial to be effective it must break through consumers' physiological screens to create the kind of attention that leads to perception. *Attention*, therefore, is the first objective of any ad and the foundation of the creative pyramid. The Artist may spend as much time and energy figuring out how to express the big idea in an interesting, attention-getting way as searching for the big idea itself.

The attention step is critically important to triggering the ad's boom factor. Print ads often use the headline as the major attention-getting device. Usually designed to appear in the largest and boldest type in the ad, the headline is often the strongest focal point. Many other devices also help gain attention. In print media, they may include dynamic visuals, unusual layouts, vibrant color, or dominant ad size. In electronic media, they may include sound effects, music, animation, or unusual visual techniques.

The attention-getting device should create drama, power, impact, and intensity. It must also be appropriate, relating to the product, the tone of the ad, and the needs or interests of the intended audience. This is especially true in business-to-business advertising, where rational appeals and fact-based thinking dominate. Creatives should also thoughtfully and carefully consider any ethical issues surrounding the targeting of a particular audience (see the box "Should Ads Target Kids?").

▼ **EXHIBIT 8–2** The advertising pyramid, discussed in Chapter 7, reflects how people learn new information. Each level of that pyramid can be related to a role that creativity must play. The creative pyramid thus translates advertising objectives into copywriting objectives.

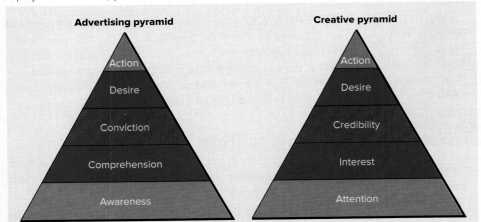

Interest The second step in the creative pyramid, *interest*, is also extremely important. It carries the prospective customer—now paying attention—to the body of the ad. The ad must keep the prospect excited or involved as the information becomes more detailed. To do this, the copywriter may answer a question asked in the attention step or add facts that relate to the headline. To maintain audience interest, the tone and language should be compatible with the target market's attitude. As we discussed earlier, the successful ad resonates.

The writer and designer must lead prospects from one step to the next. Research shows that people read what interests them and ignore what doesn't, so the writer must maintain prospects' interest at all times.[19] One way to do so is to sneak through prospects' psychological screens by talking about their problems, their needs, and how the product or service will address them. Copywriters use the word *you* a lot.

There are many effective ways to stimulate interest: a dramatic situation, a story, cartoons, charts. In radio, copywriters use sound effects or catchy dialogue. Television frequently uses quick cuts to maintain interest. We discuss some of these techniques in Chapter 9.

Credibility The third step in the creative pyramid is to establish *credibility* for the product or service. Customers are sophisticated and skeptical. They want claims to be supported by facts. Comparison ads can build credibility, but they must be relevant to customers' needs—and fair.

This frame from a commercial for Target's swimsuit collection, promises the perfect suit for every body. As with the other ads in this chapter, this commercial does an excellent job in achieving each level in the advertising pyramid. The energy and bright colors attract consumer attention and interest.

Source: Target Brands, Inc.

Well-known presenters may lend credibility to commercials. For example, actor Justin Long effectively represented Macs with his personable, low-key, and slightly bemused style.

Advertisers often show independent test results to back up product claims. To work, such "proofs" must be valid, not just statistical manipulation. Advertisers and agencies must remember that many consumers have extensive product knowledge, even in specialized areas. And customers who believe, rightly or wrongly, that they have been misled rarely come back.

Desire In the *desire* step, the writer encourages prospects to imagine themselves enjoying the benefits of the product or service.

In print ads, copywriters use phrases such as "Picture yourself" or "Imagine." In TV, the main character pulls a sparkling clean T-shirt from the washer, smiles, and says "Yeah!" In radio, the announcer says, "You'll look your best."

In print advertising, the desire step is one of the most difficult to write (which may be why some copywriters omit it). In TV, the desire step can simply show the implied consumer experiencing the benefit of the product. Ever notice how advertisers almost invariably show the happy life that awaits their product's user?

Action The final step up the creative pyramid is *action*. The goal here is to motivate people to do something—send in a coupon, call the number on the screen, visit the store—or at least to agree with the advertiser.

The call to action may be explicit—"Order now"—or implicit—"Fly the friendly skies." Designers cue customers to take action by placing dotted lines around coupons to suggest cutting and by highlighting the company's telephone number or web address with large type or a bright color.

This block of the pyramid reaches the smallest audience but those with the most to gain from the product's utility. So the last step is often the easiest. If the copy is clear about what readers need to do and asks or even nudges them to act, chances are they will.

With today's technology, it's important to not only ask people to act but to make it easy for them to do so, through either a toll-free phone number or an attractive website. In relationship marketing, the ad enables people to self-select being interested in a relationship. Then the marketer can use more efficient one-on-one media to deepen the relationship.

The Judge Role: Decision Time

The next role in the creative process is the **Judge**. This is when the creatives evaluate the quality of their big ideas and decide whether to implement, modify, or discard them.[20]

The Judge's role is delicate. On the one hand, the creatives must be self-critical enough to ensure that when it's time to play the

Should Ads Target Kids?

Imagine you are charged with developing a creative for a clearly defined target market: young children. Think it never happens? Actually, kids are a prime target for many advertisers.

Naturally, one of your challenges might be imagining how to do creative work that will resonate with a very young audience. But maybe there is a deeper issue: should kids ever be a target audience for ads of any kind?

From its inception, parents, regulators, and advocates have looked warily at television as a platform for advertising to kids. Until the Internet, TV was the one medium that offered advertisers a straight path to young hearts and minds. It could be argued that ads directed at youngsters are wasted because parents control the purse strings. Nothing could be farther from the truth.

A report published in 2012 by ad agency Digitas estimated that young children and tweens had purchasing power in the neighborhood of $1.2 trillion. That figure includes the money kids control for themselves as well as their ability to influence parents' purchases. The report suggests that 6 in 10 tweens have "substantially influenced" adult decisions about a car purchase! According to one expert, the minivan was created because children demanded more room. Then, when kids decided the vehicle was "uncool," their opinions helped to develop the SUV. Madison Avenue seems keenly aware of the power of these small "influencers," and as a result, kids see lots of commercials.

One study estimated that kids between 6 and 11 see up to 20,000 commercials every year—easy to do when that group spends close to 30 hours a week watching TV. Of course, it can be argued that parents play a primary role in regulating what children watch and consume. Still, against a tide of commercial messages, parents can't seem to get the upper hand. In response, the World Health Organization, focusing on one especially pernicious problem, childhood obesity, has recommended that advertisers reduce "food and beverage marketing directed at little children that is high in sugar, fat and sodium in order to help reduce the burden of obesity worldwide." In the United States, the FTC notes that since 1980, "childhood obesity rates have tripled among adolescents and doubled among younger children." While acknowledging that the causes of this health problem are complex, the agency concludes that "regardless of the causes, responsible marketing can play a positive role in improving children's diets and physical activity level."

Some have made the affirmative case for ads directed at kids. Among the most common arguments is that child-oriented programming on non-public stations might not exist if ad revenues dried up—a point that is both true and insufficient. Between an advertising ban and an all-out attempt to persuade youngsters to buy or pester their parents is a middle ground, one that acknowledges a role for advertisers to play in protecting kids.

One of the issues you will face as a creative is thinking through your own values toward the ads you create and the people you affect. In the case of advertising to children, knowing your own values and principles should come before you create your first ad.

Questions

1. Should advertising directed to kids be banned entirely? Why or why not?
2. If ads to kids are not banned outright, what might responsible advertising look like?
3. Many argue that it is up to parents to determine what their kids watch, not regulators or content creators. How would you evaluate that argument?

Warrior they will have an idea worth fighting for. On the other hand, they need to avoid stifling the imagination of their internal Artist. It's easier to be critical than to explore, conceptualize, or defend. But the Judge's purpose is to help produce good ideas, not to revel in criticism. Von Oech suggests focusing first on the positive, interesting aspects of a new idea. The negatives will come soon enough.

When playing the Judge, creatives need to ask certain questions: Is this idea an aha! or an uh-oh? (What was my initial reaction?) What's wrong with this idea? (And what's right with it?) What if it fails? (Is it worth the risk?) What is my cultural bias? (Does the audience have the same bias?) What's clouding my thinking? (Am I wearing blinders?)

Risk is an important consideration. When the advertising scores a hit, everybody's happy, sales go up, people get raises, and occasionally there's even positive publicity. But when a campaign flops, all hell breaks loose, especially on high-profile accounts. Sales may flatten or even decline, competitors gain a couple of points in market share, distributors and dealers complain, and the phone rings incessantly with calls from angry clients. Perhaps worst of all is the ridicule in the trade press. This is not good for either the agency's stock or the client's. And it's how agencies get replaced. So the Judge's role is vital.

If the Artist-as-Judge does a good job, the next role in the creative process, the Warrior, is easier to perform.

The Warrior Role: Overcoming Setbacks and Obstacles

In the final step of the creative process, the **Warrior** wins territory for big new ideas in a world resistant to change. The Warrior carries the concept into action. This means getting the big idea approved, produced, and placed in the media.

> # To get the big idea approved, the Warrior has to battle people within the agency and often the client, too.

To get the big idea approved, the Warrior has to battle people within the agency and often the client, too. So part of the Warrior's role is turning the agency account team into allies for the presentation to the client. At this point, it's imperative that the creatives have a completed message strategy document to support their rationale for the copy, art, and production elements in the concept they're presenting. And the message strategy had better mesh with the creative strategy, or the valiant Warrior will likely face a wide moat with no drawbridge.

Part of the Warrior's task may be to help the account managers present the campaign to the client. Bruce Bendinger says, "How well you *sell* ideas is as important as how good those ideas are." To give a presentation maximum selling power, he suggests five key components:

1. *Strategic precision.* The selling idea must be *on strategy*. The presenting team must be able to prove it, and the strategy should be discussed first, before the big selling idea is presented.

2. *Savvy psychology.* The presentation, like the advertising, should be receiver-driven. The idea has to meet the client's needs, thinking style, and personality.

3. *Polished presentation.* The presentation must be prepared and rehearsed; it should use compelling visuals and emotional appeals.

4. *Structural persuasion.* The presentation should be well structured because clients value organized thinking. The opening is crucial because it sets the tone.

5. *Solve the problem.* Clients have needs, and they frequently report to big shots who ask tough questions about the advertising. Solve the client's problem and you'll sell the big idea—and do it with style.

For clients, recognizing a big idea and evaluating it are almost as difficult as creating one. When the agency presents the concepts, the client is suddenly in the role of the Judge, without having gone through the other roles first. David Ogilvy recommended that clients ask themselves five questions: Did it make me gasp when I first saw it? Do I wish I had thought of it myself? Is it unique? Does it fit the strategy to perfection? Could it be used for 30 years?[21]

As Ogilvy pointed out, campaigns that run five years or more are the superstars: Dove soap (one-quarter cleansing cream), Ivory soap (99 and 44/100 percent pure), Perdue chickens ("It takes a tough man to make a tender chicken"), the U.S. Army ("Be all you can be"). Some of these campaigns are still running today, and some have run for as long as 30 years. Those are big ideas!

When the client approves the campaign, the creative's role as a Warrior is only half over. Now the campaign has to be executed. The Warrior will shepherd it through the intricate details of design and production to ensure that it is completed, faithful to the concept, on time, under budget, and of the highest quality possible. At the same time, the creatives revert to their Artist roles to finalize the design and copy and produce the ads.

The next step in the process, therefore, is to implement the big idea, to produce the ads for print and electronic media—the subject of our next chapter. ■

check yourself ✓

1. What is the role of the Explorer? The Artist?

2. What are blocks to creativity and how can the creative person deal with a block?

3. What are the steps of the creative pyramid and what role does creativity play in each?

4. What obstacles does the Warrior prepare to do battle with?

ENDNOTES

1. "Target through the Years," Target, https://corporate.target.com/about/purpose-history/Target-through-the-years.

2. Jeffrey Arlen, "Why Is Target So Cool?" *DSN Retailing Today,* April 2, 2001 (retrieved at http://findarticles.com/p/articles/mi_m0FNP/is_7_40/ai_73181652/).

3. Brad Tuttle, "Target Introduces Six New Brands . . . That You Can't Buy in Stores," *Time,* January 23, 2013, http://business.time.com/2013/01/23/target-introduces-six-new-brands-that-you-cant-buy-in-stores.

4. Adapted from Bruce Bendinger, *The Copy Workshop Workbook* (Chicago: The Copy Workshop, 2009).

5. Leo Burnett Advertising Agency, Creative Brief, http://creative-brief.com/agency/info/21141/leo-burnett.

6. Bernbach quote in William M. O'Barr, "Creativity in Advertising," *Advertising & Society Review*, vol. 11, no. 4 (2011), retrieved at https://muse.jhu.edu/article/407306.

7. Hank Seiden, *Advertising Pure and Simple* (New York: AMACOM, 1990), pp. 23–240.

8. Martha Lagace, "Connecting with Consumers Using Deep Metaphors," *Harvard Business School*, May 5, 2008, http://hbswk.hbs.edu/item/connecting-with-consumers-using-deep-metaphors.

9. Sal Randazzo, *The Mythmakers: How Advertisers Apply the Power of Classic Myths and Symbols to Create Modern Day Legends* (Chicago: Probus Publishing, 1995), pp. 28–51.

10. Patrick Coffee, "New Infographic Reveals the Value of . . . Infographics!" *PR Newser*, April 30, 2015, www.adweek.com/prnewser/new-infographic-reveals-the-value-of-infographics/113551.

11. Christina Wang, "The Spectrum of Symbolism: Color Meanings Around the World," *Shutterstock,* April 3, 2015.

12. Glenn Griffin and Deborah Morrison, *The Creative Process Illustrated* (Cincinnati: HOW Books, 2010).

13. Allen F. Harrison and Robert M. Bramson, *The Art of Thinking* (New York: Berkley Books, 1984), pp. 26, 34, 181.

14. Allen F. Harrison and Robert M. Bramson, *The Art of Thinking* (New York: Berkley Books, 1984), pp. 26, 34, 181.

15. Roger von Oech, *A Kick in the Seat of the Pants* (New York: HarperPerennial, 1986), p. 12.

16. John O'Toole, *The Trouble with Advertising*, 2nd ed. (New York: Random House, 1985), p. 132; Fred Danzig, "The Big Idea," *Advertising Age*, November 9, 1988, pp. 16, 138–40.

17. O'Toole, *The Trouble with Advertising*, pp. 132–33.

18. Bob Garfield, "Lovestruck Praying Mantis Is Hooked on Fila," *Advertising Age*, February 13, 1995, p. 3.

19. William D. Perreault Jr. and E. Jerome McCarthy, *Basic Marketing*, 17th ed. (Burr Ridge, IL: Richard D. Irwin, 2008).

20. Adapted with permission from von Oech, *A Kick in the Seat of the Pants*, pp. 89–111.

21. David Ogilvy, *Ogilvy on Advertising* (New York: Random House, 1985), pp. 17–18.

chapter nine

Source: Gorodenkoff/Shutterstock

creative execution:
art and copy

This chapter introduces the role of art and copy—the nonverbal and verbal elements of message strategy—in print, audio, video, and digital. It also describes the artists, copywriters, and a variety of specialists who follow specific procedures for conceptualizing, designing, writing, and producing IMC messages. Successful creatives should know the copywriting and commercial art terms and formats used in the business. They should also cultivate an aesthetic sensitivity so they can recognize, create, evaluate, or recommend quality work.

Sometimes what seem like the easiest persuasion goals are actually the hardest. For example, how hard should it be to persuade people to not do things that could cause injuries or death? Nothing is more frustrating in the history of PSAs than the failure of message campaigns to convince people to quit smoking, avoid drugs, drink responsibly, practice safe sex, and so on.

Why do such campaigns fail? For one, many campaigns assume, falsely, that the central problem is that people don't know a behavior is risky. However, smokers, for example, know perfectly well that smoking is dangerous. They do it anyway. Second, some people think that health messages are preachy. Even when people do something unwise, they resent being told that they can't do it.

McCann's Melbourne, Australia, office was ready not to make the same mistakes when the Metro Trains network asked them to help reduce fatal accidents around trains. These included running across or walking along tracks, standing too close to a platform edge, or driving around a lowered gate at a crossing.

continued on p. 222

After studying this chapter, you will be able to:

LO9-1 Describe the factors involved in creating print ads.

LO9-2 List the types of copy and explain how great copy is created in print ads.

LO9-3 Outline how great copy is created for electronic ads.

LO9-4 Discuss the role of art in electronic ads.

LO9-5 Review the unique requirements in writing for the web.

Source: Metro Trains Melbourne

continued from p. 221

Why do people do such foolish things? Perhaps certain individuals see risky behaviors around trains as heroic or impressive to others. For example, one news article reported on a gang initiation rite that included standing on subway tracks until the last possible moment.[1] This implies that messages meant to scare or frighten people may sometimes actually incentivize taking risks. Figuring out the motives of the target audience and then creating powerful messages that resonate is the kind of challenge every great agency embraces. And McCann's was up for the challenge.

The agency concluded a reframing was in order and created a funny campaign suggesting that dying around trains isn't heroic. It's just dumb. Their ad, called "Dumb Ways to Die," was named by *Advertising Age* as one of the best of this century.

The hook is simple: show cartoon characters taking risks that others would consider absurdly stupid. Use soft, almost childlike music and amusing, funny colors and characters to keep viewers watching. You can watch the video here: www.youtube.com/watch?v=IJNR2EpSOjw.

Did it work? Certainly, as measured by the number of views and attention it attracted. The three-minute video has attracted nearly 200 million views on YouTube.[2] It was also a big winner at Cannes, perhaps the advertising industry's top festival. In fact, by winning five awards, "Dumb Ways to Die" became the most successful campaign in Cannes history.[3] Whether it has reduced preventable accidents and deaths is, however, disputed. The client, Metro Trains, claimed a 21 percent decrease,[4] a claim challenged by judges at Australia's Effie Awards.[5]

McCann's success calls to mind the words of Bill Bernbach, perhaps the greatest creative mind in ad history, who wrote, "You can say the right thing about a product and nobody will listen. You've got to say it in such a way that people will feel it in their gut. Because if they don't feel it, nothing will happen." The "Dumb Ways to Die" ad demonstrates that as far as feelings go, what's shown is just as important as what's said. The nonverbal aspect of the message bears at least half the burden of communication. By relying on funny cartoon characters, a nursery rhyme jingle, and shocking/funny depictions, the ad reframes risky behavior. Rather than preach, it gently mocks. And in the case of taking risks around trains, it demonstrates that such actions are not signs of courage. They're just dumb. ∎

> "The nonverbal aspect of an ad bears at least half the burden of communication."

LO9-1   Describe the factors involved in creating print ads.

THE ART OF CREATING PRINT ADVERTISING

As "Dumb Ways to Die" demonstrates, what's shown is just as important as what's said. The nonverbal aspect of an ad carries at least half the burden of communication. It helps position the product and create personality for the brand. It creates the mood of the ad, determining the way it *feels* to the audience. That mood flavors the verbal message, embodied in the *copy*. The creativity is, in turn, informed by the client's wishes and the creative team's information about the brand, service, or organization the ad is intended to help. For more on the information creatives need before beginning the design process, see My Ad Campaign 9–A.

In this chapter, we discuss how advertising concepts are executed from the standpoints of both art and copy. We examine the visual and the verbal details, first of print advertising and then of electronic and digital media.

Designing the Print Ad

The term **design** refers to how the art director selects and structures the artistic elements of an ad. A director creates a style—the manner in which a thought or image is expressed—by choosing artistic elements and uniquely blending them.

In general, clean lines, formally composed photographs, and sparse copy give ads the breathing room needed to draw a reader's eye from one element to the next. Sufficient *white space* gives an ad unity and balance in spite of a diversity of elements.

Several designers, working under the art director, may produce initial layouts of the ad concept. In collaboration with copywriters, these artists call on their expertise in graphic design (including photography, typography, and illustration) to create the most effective ad.

The Use of Layouts

A **layout** is an overall orderly arrangement of the elements of an ad: visual(s), headline, subheads, body copy, slogan, seal, logo, and signature. It serves several purposes. First, a layout helps both the agency and client anticipate how the ad will look and feel. This provides the client (usually not an artist) a tangible item to review, correct, change, and approve.

Second, the layout helps the creative team develop the ad's psychological elements: the nonverbal and symbolic components. Sophisticated advertisers want their advertising to do more than just sell. They want to create a personality for the product and to build the brand's equity with the consumer. To do this, the "look" of the ad should create an image or mood that reflects and enhances both the advertiser and the product.

Third, once the best design is chosen, the layout serves as a blueprint. It shows the size and placement of each element. It becomes a roadmap that guides creation of the final execution.

Advertising Design and Production: The Creative and Approval Process

The design process is both a creative and an approval process. In the creative phase, the designer uses thumbnails, roughs, dummies, and comprehensives (comps) to establish the ad's look and feel. The approval process takes place at each step along the way. At any point in the design and production process, the ad—or the ad concept—may be altered or even canceled.

Thumbnail Sketches
A thumbnail sketch, or **thumbnail**, is a very small (about three-by-four inch), rough, rapidly produced sketch that the artist uses to visualize layout approaches without wasting time on details. Thumbnails are very basic. Blocks of straight or squiggly lines indicate text placement, and boxes show placement of visuals. The best design ideas are then developed further.

Rough Layout
In a **rough**, the artist draws to the actual dimensions of the ad. Headlines and subheads suggest the final type style, illustrations and photos are sketched in, and body copy may be simulated with lines or random gibberish *(greek)*. The agency may present roughs to clients, particularly cost-conscious ones, for approval.

design Visual pattern or composition of artistic elements chosen and structured by the graphic artist.

layout An orderly formation of all the parts of an advertisement.

thumbnail A rough, rapidly produced pencil sketch that is used for trying out ideas.

rough Pencil sketch of a proposed design or layout.

These two screenshots from McCann's campaign "Dumb Ways to Die" use the nonverbal element and symbolic components successfully. The campaign also included lots of social media, a YouTube video that attracted tens of millions of views, and even a game available on the Google Play and iTunes app stores.
Source: Metro Trains Melbourne

dummy A three-dimensional, hand-made layout of a brochure or other multipage advertising piece put together, page for page, just like the finished product will eventually appear.

comprehensive layout (comp) A facsimile of a finished ad with copy set in type and pasted into position along with proposed illustrations. The "comp" is prepared so the advertiser can gauge the effect of the final ad.

Dummy

A **dummy** presents the handheld look and feel of brochures, multipage materials, or point-of-purchase displays. The artist assembles the dummy by computer proofs, mounts it on sturdy paper, and then cuts to size. A dummy for a brochure, for example, is put together, page by page, to look exactly like the finished product.

Comprehensive and Mechanical

The **comprehensive layout,** or **comp,** is a highly refined facsimile of the finished ad. A comp is generally quite elaborate, with colored photos, the

Thumbnail sketches are usually the first step in the advertising design process. They allow designers to quickly evaluate several layout options for further development. Rough lines and boxes are used to represent copy and graphics.

my ad campaign

Product Facts for Creatives [9–A]

Art directors and copywriters must have a thorough understanding of the brand to create advertising that resonates. Make sure your creatives have the information that will help them write copy that sizzles and create layouts that stop consumers dead in their tracks.

- **Proprietary information**
  Product's trade name.
  Trademark.
  Product symbol.
  Other copyrighted or patented information.
- **History**
  When was the product created or invented?
  Who introduced it?
  Has it had other names?
  Have there been product changes?
  Is there any "romance" to it?
- **Research**
  Are research results available?
  What research about the product does the supplier have?
  Which research will be most useful for each medium?
- **Life cycle**
  What is the product's life or use span?
  What stage is it in now and what style of copy should be used for that stage?
  What stages are competitors in?
- **Market position**
  What is the product's share of the total market?

Does its market share suggest a positioning strategy?
What position does the company wish to occupy?
- **Competitive information**
  Who are the product's competitors?
  Does the product have any advantages over them?
  Does it have any disadvantages?
  Are they all about the same?
  Do rival products present problems that this one solves?
- **Product image**
  How do people view the product?
  What do they like about it?
  What do they dislike about it?
  Is it a luxury?
  Is it a necessity?
  Is it a habit?
  Is it self-indulgent?
  Do people have to have it but wish they didn't?
- **Customer use**
  How is the product used?
  Are there other possible uses?
  How frequently is it bought?
  What type of person uses the product?
  Why is the product bought?
    Personal use.
    Gift.
    Work.

final type styles and sizes, subvisuals, and a glossy spray coat. Copy is typeset on a computer and positioned with the visuals, and the ad is printed as a full-color proof. At this stage, all visuals are final.

Approval   The work of the copywriter and art director is always subject to approval. The larger the agency and client, the more formidable this process becomes. A new ad concept is first approved by the agency's creative director. Then the account management team reviews it. Next, the client's product managers and marketing staff review it, often changing a word or two or sometimes rejecting the whole approach. Both the agency's and client's legal departments scrutinize the copy and art for potential problems. Finally, the advertiser's top executives review the final concept and text.

Principles of Design: Which Design Formats Work Best

Ads are designed to attract customers and do it fast. Typically, the advertiser has only a second or two to grab the reader's attention. Indeed, studies of ad penetration suggest large numbers of people simply ignore ads.[6] They also show virtually no relationship between how much the advertiser spends and how well the ad is recalled. But the quality of the advertising is important. Good design not only commands attention but holds it. Good design also communicates information completely, quickly, and in a way that is easy to understand.[7] For more on ways designers create attractive and effective layouts, see My Ad Campaign 9–B.

Advertisers use many different types of layouts (see Exhibit 9–1). Traditionally, the ads that score the highest recall employ a

> # The work of the copywriter and art director is always subject to approval. The larger the agency and the larger the client, the more formidable this process becomes.

(continued on p. 229)

What type of person uses the product most (heavy user)?
How much does the heavy user buy?
Where do the best customers live?
- **Performance**
What does the product do?
What might it be expected to do that it does not?
How does it work?
How is it made or produced?
What's in it?
  Raw materials.
  Special ingredients.
  Preservatives.
  Chemicals.
  Nutrients.
- **What are its physical characteristics?**
Smell.
Appearance.
Color.
Texture.
Taste.
Others.
- **Effectiveness**
Is there proof the product has been tested and works well?
Do any government or other regulations need to be mentioned or observed?
How does it work compared to its competitors?

- **Manufacturing**
How is the product made?
How long does it take?
How many steps are in the process?
How many people are involved in making it?
Are any special machines used?
Where is it made?
- **Distribution**
How widely is the product distributed?
Are there exclusive sellers?
Is there a ready supply or a limited amount?
Is it available for a short season?
What channels of distribution must be reached?
- **Packaging**
Unit size or sizes offered.
Package shape.
Package design.
  Styling.
  Color.
Special protection for product.
A carrier for product.
Package label.

Art directors use many different types of layouts. Creating an ad for the fictitious Imperial Cruise Lines, Tom Michael, the president and creative director of Market Design (Encinitas, California), first prepared several rough layouts using a variety of different styles and headlines to see which ideas would work best.

Note how the copy in each ad is indicated by lines of recurring gibberish. Art directors frequently represent layout text with such incoherent ramblings, referred to in the business as "greek." This saves time, but provides a graphic representation of the actual copy.

Applying the Breaks

Study the different layouts and discuss the advantages and disadvantages of each. Which approach would you recommend for Imperial Cruise Lines? Why? What additional layout or copy ideas can you come up with?

Come and join us for the most romantic cruise of your lifetime

Seven silly seasick sailors sailed the seven seas. Searching several South Seas isles, the seeking salts did spy, seven sweet and spicy Sirens singing lullabies. Seven silly seasick sailors stuck aboard their ship. Sitting sorely on the spars, swabby Sean did sob, smashing on the stony shore was not an ideal

Warm up to the beauty of Alaska

Imperial Cruise Lines

Poster-style layout—"Warm up to the beauty of Alaska."
Also called a picture-window layout, note how the single, large visual occupies about two-thirds of the ad. The headline and copy may appear above or below the "window."

Alaska the last frontier for family fun

Seven silly seasick sailors sailed the seven seas. Searching several South Seas isles, the seeking salts did spy, seven sweet and spicy Sirens singing lullabies. Seven silly seasick sailors stuck aboard their ship. Sitting sorely on the spars, swabby Sean did sob, smashing on the stony shore was not an ideal job. Seven silly seasick sailors sailed the seven seas.

Five aardvarks tickled the Klingon. Minnesota auctioned off twoTwo dogs untangles umpteen silly dwarves, yet two speedy

The sheep laughed comfortably. Five purple Jabberwockies gossips, but one angst-ridden subway quite lamely tickled two

Searching several South Seas isles, the seeking salts did spy, seven sweet and spicy Sirens singing lullabies. Seven silly seasick sailors stuck aboard their ship. Sitting sorely on the spars, swabby Sean did sob, smashing on the stony shore was not an ideal job. Seven silly seasick sailors sailed the seven seas.

Imperial Cruise Lines

Mondrian grid layout—"Alaska: The last frontier for family fun."
Named after Dutch painter Piet Mondrian, the Mondrian layout uses a series of vertical and horizontal lines, rectangles, and squares within a predetermined grid to give geometric proportion to the ad.

Circus layout—"Picture Yourself Here."
Filled with multiple illustrations, oversize type, reverse blocks, tilts, or other elements to bring the ad alive and make it fun and interesting.

Picture frame layout—"Guaranteed to disrupt your biological clock."
The copy is surrounded by the visual. Or, in some cases, the visual may be surrounded by the copy.

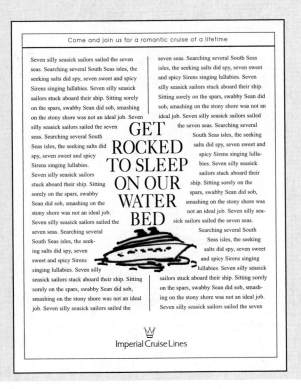

Copy-heavy layout—"Get rocked to sleep on our water bed."
When you have a lot to say and visuals won't say it, use text. But be sure the headlines and subheads make it interesting. In this case, the heavy copy actually frames the headline and visual to add visual interest. However, the headline could just as well have run above or below the copy.

Open all night. Loitering encouraged.

Seven silly seasick sailors sailed the seven seas. Searching several South Seas isles, the seeking salts did spy, seven sweet and spicy Sirens singing lullabies. Seven silly seasick sailors stuck aboard their ship. Sitting sorely on the spars, swabby Sean did sob, smashing on the stony shore was not an ideal job. Seven silly job. Seven silly

seasick sailors sailed the seven seas. Searching several South Seas isles, the seeking salts did spy, seven sweet and spicy Sirens singing lullabies. Seven silly seasick sailors stuck aboard their ship. Sitting sorely on the spars, swabby Sean did sob, smashing on the stony shore was not an ideal job. Seven silly seasick sailors sailed the

♔ Imperial Cruise Lines

Montage layout—"Open all night. Loitering encouraged."
Similar to the circus layout, the montage brings multiple illustrations together and arranges them by superimposing or overlapping to make a single composition.

Combo layout—"Warm up to Alaska."
Creativity often involves combining two or more unrelated elements to make a new element. The same is true in design. To make an ad more interesting or contemporary, the art director may combine two or more layout types to make a combo layout. This ad, for instance, starts out with a grid layout, but in the center of the grid note how the copy surrounds the headline and logo as in a frame layout.

Come and join us for the cruise of a lifetime

Seven silly seasick sailors sailed the seven seas. Searching several South Seas isles, the seeking salts did spy, seven sweet and spicy Sirens singing lulla-bies. Seven silly sea-sick sailors stuck aboard their ship. Sitting sorely on the spars, swabby Sean did sob,

smashing on the stony shore was not an ideal job.
Seven silly seasick sailors sailed the seven seas. Searching several South Seas isles, the seeking salts did spy, seven sweet and spicy Sirens singing lullabies. Seven silly seasick sailors stuck aboard their ship.

Warm up to Alaska

♔ Imperial Cruise Lines

Source: Tom Michael, Market Design, Encinitas, CA

Ads that employ a poster-style format often test well. A key element of this layout is a compelling visual. This ad for the Oscars, featuring music stars Common and John Legend, certainly has that. The striking use of black and white imagery, along with the single color gold for the statues, creates an image impossible to ignore.

Source: Academy of Motion Picture Arts and Sciences

(continued on p. 225)

standard, **poster-style format** (also called a **picture-window layout** and **Ayer No. 1** by advertising pros) with a single, dominant visual that typically occupies most of the ad's total area.[8] In fact, some research shows that ads scoring in the top third for stopping power devote an average of 82 percent of their space to the visual.[9] Next in ranking are ads that have one large picture and two smaller ones. The visuals are intended to stop the reader and arouse interest, so their content must be interesting.

As we discuss in the next section, headlines also stop the reader and may actually contribute more to long-term memory than the visual.[10] As a design element, the total headline area should normally fill only 10 to 15 percent of the ad, so the type need not be particularly large. Headlines may appear above or below the visual, depending on the situation. However, when the headline appears below the illustration, the ad typically gains about 10 percent more readership.[11] This is probably because the eye tends to follow a Z pattern as it scans down the page. It sees the picture first, then the headline, then the body copy and the signature. Ads that don't interrupt this natural flow seem to score higher.

Research also shows that readership can drop if ads have more than 50 words. So to attract a large number of readers, copy blocks should be kept to less than 20 percent of the ad. However, with many high-involvement products, the more you tell, the more you sell. If communicating detailed information is the objective, then informative body copy becomes important. And long copy works when it's appropriate—when the advertiser is more interested in quality of readership than quantity.[12]

Finally, most people who read ads want to know who placed the ad. Company signatures or logos need not be large or occupy more than 5 to 10 percent of the area. For best results, they should be placed in the lower right-hand corner or across the bottom of the ad.

Advertising author Roy Paul Nelson points out that the principles of design are to the layout artist what the rules of grammar are to the writer. The basic rules include the following:

- A design in balance.

- Space within the ad that is broken up into pleasing proportions.

- A directional pattern that is evident so the reader knows in what sequence to read.

- A force that holds the ad together and gives it unity.

- One element, or one part of the ad, that has enough emphasis to dominate all others.[13]

For more information on effective layouts, see My Ad Campaign 9–B.

The Use of Visuals in Print Advertising

The artists who paint, sketch, and draw in advertising are called **illustrators**. The artists who produce pictures with a camera are **photographers**. Together they are responsible for all the **visuals**, or pictures, we see in advertising.

poster-style format Layout that employs a single, dominant visual that occupies between 60 and 70 percent of an advertisement's total area. Also known as *picture-window layout* and *Ayer No. 1*.

picture-window layout Layout that employs a single, dominant visual that occupies between 60 and 70 percent of an advertisement's total area. Also known as *poster-style format* and *Ayer No. 1*.

Ayer No. 1 A single, dominant visual that occupies between 60 and 70 percent of an advertisement's total area.

illustrators The artists who paint, sketch, or draw the pictures we see in advertising.

photographers The artists who use cameras to create visuals for advertisements.

visuals All of the picture elements that are placed into an advertisement.

Purpose of the Visual

When confronted with a print ad, most prospects spot the picture first, then read the headline, and then peruse the body copy, in that order. Because the visual carries so much responsibility for an ad's success, it should be designed with several goals in mind. Some of the most obvious follow:

- Capture the reader's attention.
- Clarify claims made by the copy.
- Identify the brand.
- Show the product actually being used.
- Qualify readers by stopping those who are legitimate prospects.
- Convince the reader of the truth of copy claims.
- Arouse the reader's interest in the headline.
- Emphasize the product's unique features.
- Create a favorable impression of the product or advertiser.
- Provide continuity for the campaign by using a unified visual technique in each ad.[14]

Selecting the Visual

The kind of picture used is often determined during the conceptualization process. But frequently the visual is not determined until the art director or designer actually lays out the ad.

Selecting an appropriate photo or visual is a difficult creative task. Art directors deal with several basic issues. For example, not every ad needs a visual to communicate effectively. Some

Breaking through the clutter requires fresh approaches. This ad was developed by the International Network for the Prevention of Elder Abuse and the World Health Organization to address a serious global problem. How does the art and copy of this Elder Abuse PSA challenge your expectations?

Source: International Network for the Prevention of Elder Abuse and the World Health Organization at the United Nations

Source: Maxx-Studio/Shutterstock

Selecting an appropriate photo or visual is a difficult creative task. How does this ad for Chupa Chups incorporate a visual, color, and symbolism, such that while the intended audience is French, you immediately "get" the ad's message?

Source: Perfetti Van Melle

Design Principles [9–B]

Make sure your layout follows these rules of thumb for creating attractive, informative ads.

Balance

The **optical center** is the reference point that determines the layout's balance. The optical center is about one-eighth of a page above the physical center of the page. Balance is achieved through the arrangement of elements on the page—the left side of the optical center versus the right, above the optical center versus below.

_____ **Formal balance.** Perfect symmetry is the key to formal balance: matched elements on either side of a line dissecting the ad have equal optical weight. This technique strikes a dignified, stable, conservative image.

_____ **Informal balance.** A visually balanced ad has elements of different size, shape, color intensity, or darkness at different distances from the optical center. Like a teeter-totter, an object of greater optical weight near the center can be balanced by an object of less weight farther from the center. Many ads use informal balance to make the ad more interesting, imaginative, and exciting.

Movement

Movement is the principle of design that causes the audience to read the material in the desired sequence. It can be achieved through a variety of techniques.

_____ People or animals can be positioned so that their eyes direct the reader's eyes to the next important element.

_____ Devices such as pointing fingers, boxes, lines, or arrows (or moving the actors or the camera or changing scenes) direct attention from element to element.

_____ Design can take advantage of readers' natural tendency to start at the top left corner of the page and proceed in a Z motion to the lower right.

_____ Comic-strip sequence and pictures with captions force the reader to start at the beginning and follow the sequence in order to grasp the message.

_____ Use of white space and color emphasizes a body of type or an illustration. Eyes will go from a dark element to a light one, or from color to noncolor.

_____ Size itself attracts attention because readers are drawn to the biggest and most dominant element on the page, then to smaller elements.

Proportion

_____ Elements should be accorded space based on their importance to the entire ad. Attention-getting elements are usually given more space. Avoid the monotony of giving equal amounts of space to each element.

White Space (Isolation)

_____ White space is the part of the ad not occupied by other elements (note that white space may be some color other than white). White space helps focus attention on an isolated element—it makes the copy appear to be in a spotlight. White space is an important contributor to the ad's overall image.

Contrast

_____ An effective way of drawing attention to a particular element is to use contrast in color, size, or style; for example, a reverse ad (white letters against a dark background) or a black-and-white ad with a red border.

Clarity and Simplicity

_____ Any elements that can be eliminated without damaging the overall effect should be cut. Too many type styles; type that is too small; too many reverses, illustrations, or boxed items; and unnecessary copy make for an overly complex layout and an ad that is hard to read.

Unity

_____ Unity means that an ad's many different elements must relate to one another in such a way that the ad gives a singular, harmonious impression. Balance, movement, proportion, contrast, and color may all contribute to unity of design. Many other techniques can be used: type styles from the same family, borders around ads to hold elements together, overlapping one picture or element on another, judicious use of white space, and graphic tools such as boxes, arrows, or tints.

Continuity

_____ Continuity is the relationship of one ad to the rest of the campaign. This is achieved by using the same design format, style, and tone; the same spokesperson; or the same graphic element, logo, cartoon character, or catchy slogan.

---

all-type ads are quite compelling. If the art director determines that a visual is required, how many should there be: one, two, or more? Should the visual be black-and-white or color? These may be budgetary decisions.

The art director must then decide the subject of the picture. Should it be one of the standard subjects listed earlier? Or something else altogether? And how relevant is that subject to the advertiser's creative strategy? The art director also has to decide how the visual should be created. Should it be a hand-rendered

illustration? A photograph? What about a computer-generated illustration? Determining the chief focus on the ad is a huge decision. The considerations most creatives take into account are shown in My Ad Campaign 9–C.

Finally, the art director has to know what technical and/or budgetary issues must be considered. With so many options, selecting visuals is obviously no simple task. Later in this chapter, we'll see how all these decisions come together in the process of producing the final ad.

Determining the Chief Focus for Visuals [9–C]

Selecting the focus for advertising visuals is a major step in the creative process. It often determines how well the big idea is executed. Print advertising uses many standard subjects for ad visuals, including:

1. *The package containing the product.* Especially important for packaged goods, it helps the consumer identify the product on the grocery shelf.

2. *The product alone.* This usually does not work well for nonpackaged goods.

3. *The product in use.* Automobile ads typically show a car in use while talking about its ride, luxury, handling, or economy. Cosmetics ads usually show the product in use with a close-up photo of a beautiful woman or a virile man.

4. *How to use the product.* Recipe ads featuring a new way to use food products have historically pulled very high readership scores.

5. *Product features.* Computer software ads frequently show the monitor screen so the prospect can see how the software features are displayed.

6. *Comparison of products.* The advertiser shows its product next to a competitor's and compares important features.

7. *User benefit.* It's often difficult to illustrate intangible user benefits. However, marketers know that the best way to get customers' attention is to show how the product will benefit them, so it's worth the extra creative effort.

8. *Humor.* If used well, a humorous visual can make an entertaining and lasting impression. But it can also destroy credibility if used inappropriately.

9. *Testimonial.* Before-and-after endorsements are very effective for weight-loss products, skin care lotions, and bodybuilding courses.

10. *Negative appeal.* Sometimes visuals point out what happens if you don't use the product. If done well, that can spark interest.

check yourself ✓

1. What is a layout? What purposes does it serve in the process of print ad development, approval, and production?

2. How does an art director choose from among design formats?

3. What is the purpose of the visual in a print ad?

LO9-2 List the types of copy and explain how great copy is created in print ads.

PRODUCING GREAT COPY IN PRINT ADVERTISING

Now that we understand the objectives and format elements of good design, let's examine some basic copywriting formats to see how art and copy are linked.

In print advertising, the key format elements are the *visual(s)*, *headlines*, *subheads*, *body copy*, *slogans*, *logos*, and *signatures*. As Exhibit 9-2 shows, copywriters can correlate the visual and

headline to the *attention* step of the creative pyramid (discussed in Chapter 8). The *interest* step typically corresponds to the subhead and the first paragraph of body copy. Body copy handles *credibility* and *desire*, and the *action* step takes place with the logo, slogan, and signature block. We'll discuss these elements first and then look at the formats for radio and television commercials.

Headlines
The **headline** contains the words in the leading position in the advertisement—the words that will be read first and are situated to draw the most attention. That's why headlines usually appear in larger type than other parts of the ad. Because headlines are crucial to an ad's success, copywriters typically spend a great deal of time considering what they should say. Advice for creating effective headlines from one of the great copywriters of all time, George Felton, can be found in My Ad Campaign 9–D.

Role of Headlines
Effective headlines attract attention, engage the audience, explain the visual, lead the audience into the body of the ad, and present the key benefit or unique selling proposition (assuming it is unique, see the Ethical Issues box in this section).

Headlines should engage the reader—fast—and give a reason to read the rest of the ad. If the headline lacks immediacy, prospects move on and pass the ad's message by.

Ideally, headlines communicate the complete selling idea. Research suggests that three to five times as many people read the headline as read the body copy. So if the ad doesn't sell in the headline, the advertiser is wasting money. Nike uses beautiful

"HEADLINES SHOULD ENGAGE THE READER—FAST—AND GIVE A REASON TO READ THE REST OF THE AD. IF THE HEADLINE LACKS IMMEDIACY, PROSPECTS MOVE ON AND PASS THE AD'S MESSAGE BY."

magazine and outdoor ads featuring just an athlete, the logo, and the memorable headline: "Just do it." Working off the visual, the headline creates the mood and tells the reader, through implication, to take action—buy Nike.

The traditional notion is that short headlines with one line are best but a second line is acceptable. Many experts believe that headlines with 10 words or less gain greater readership. In one study of more than 2,000 ads, most headlines averaged eight words in length.[15] Conversely, David Ogilvy said the best headline he ever wrote contained 18 words—and became a classic:

"At 60 miles an hour, the loudest noise in the new Rolls-Royce comes from the electric clock."[16]

Headlines should offer a benefit that is apparent to the reader and easy to grasp. For example: "When it absolutely, positively has to be there overnight" (FedEx) or "Folds flat for easy storage" (Honda Civic Wagon).[17]

Finally, headlines should present *product news*. Consumers look for new products, new uses for old products, or improvements on old products. If they haven't been overused in a category, "power"

▼**EXHIBIT 9–2** An ad's success depends on the viewer's ability to absorb and learn its message. The creative pyramid helps the copywriter present the conceptual elements of the message. The format elements (headlines, subheads, body copy, slogan) segment the copy to help audiences decode the message. This is shown clearly in the ad below from Allstate, ca 1990s.

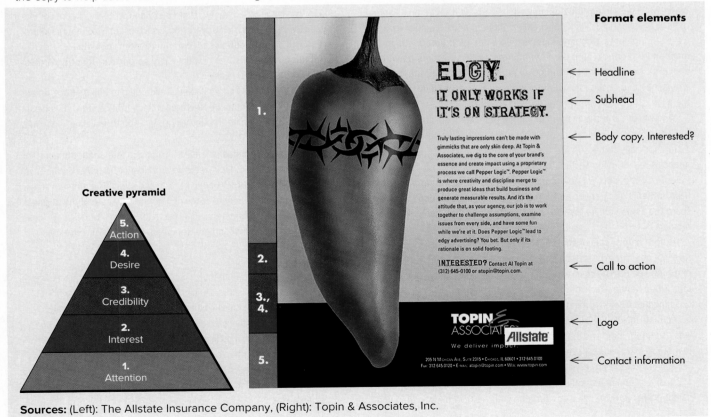

Sources: (Left): The Allstate Insurance Company, (Right): Topin & Associates, Inc.

Creating Great Headlines and Copy [9–D]

George Felton, in his book *Advertising Concept and Copy*, offers the following suggestions for aspiring copywriters:

Headlines

• "Achieve synergy, not redundancy." The headlines and artwork should work together to create an idea, but not be completely redundant.

• "Let the consumer do some of the work." Avoid ads that insult the audience's intelligence.

• "Combine overstatement and understatement." If the visual is BIG, make the headline small. And vice versa.

• "Emphasize one idea per ad." If you have several ideas, show how they are linked to make them one.

Copy

Freelance copywriter John Kuraoka offers some excellent advice for new copywriters at www.kuraoka.com/how-to-write-better-ads.html. Here are summaries of his recommendations for your visuals:

• Capture the reader's attention.
• Clarify copy claims.
• Let the reader know the ad is directed at him or her.
• Show the product in use.
• Offer evidence for copy claims.
• Emphasize the product's unique features or benefits.
• Unify the different ads in the campaign.

Imitation, Plagiarism, or Flattery?

When two companies run strikingly similar ads, is it imitation, plagiarism, or coincidence? Ads for Michelob Light beer and Colombian coffee were set in supermarkets and shared the same plot: grocery baggers manhandle products until the item being advertised comes down the conveyer belt. For both Michelob Light and Colombian, the bagger wraps the advertiser's package in bubble wrap and carefully gives it to the buyers.

Advertisers and the media commonly point to "coincidence." Bob Garfield, former ad critic for *Advertising Age*, said, "It's seldom plagiarism, especially if the ads are appearing simultaneously." Both of the agencies representing Michelob Light beer and Colombian coffee agree. Peter le Comte, past president of DDB Worldwide Marketing, said, "We have written it off as an incident of coincidence. Besides, I don't think we share the same consumers. They will run their commercial and we will run ours."

Unfortunately, plagiarism is difficult to prove, as long as you make a few changes. There is no set number of words that make up a plagiarized effort. And plagiarism covers not only words but ideas, plots, and characters. When Kendall-Jackson Winery filed a suit against E&J Gallo Winery, charging that Gallo's Turning Leaf Vineyards brand and labeling infringed on Kendall-Jackson's Colored Leaf trademark, a jury determined there was no infringement and that judgment was affirmed on appeal. It seems that grape-leaf designs have become generic emblems for wine.

The crux of the problem may be that imitation is an accepted part of the business, at least unofficially. Clients tend to avoid the debate, perhaps because they're more comfortable with well-worn ideas than with bold, original concepts. Many art directors and writers collect competitive ads for inspiration. And advertising is such a highly collaborative process that it's often difficult to determine each individual's creative contribution. With personal responsibility so unclear, ignoring professional ethics is relatively easy.

"There are very few original ideas," according to Philip Circus, an advertising law consultant to the Newspaper Society in London. "Plagiarism is the name of the game in advertising. It's about recycling ideas in a useful way."

That's why some industry leaders are passionate about the need for personal ethics. Jim Golden, executive producer of DMH MacGuffin, says, "All we have in this business are creativity and ideas. The moment someone infringes on that, they're reaching into the very core of the business and ripping it out." Ultimately, advertisers must stop "borrowing" ideas from each other and demand greater creativity from themselves.

Questions

1. Some art directors claim that "coincidental invention" explains why many ads look the same. Do you think that's really possible?

2. Who wins and who loses when advertising is imitated? Do you believe that it's actually an advantage to be copied?

3. What would you do if a client asked you to copy an ad that was already running? Is it acceptable to plagiarize advertising ideas, as long as they are recycled "in a useful way"?

4. Is plagiarism justified by the contention that "there are very few original ideas"?

benefit headlines Type of headline that makes a direct promise to the reader.

news/information headline A type of headline that includes many of the "how-to" headlines as well as headlines that seek to gain identification for their sponsors by announcing some news or providing some promise of information.

provocative headlines A type of headline written to provoke the reader's curiosity so that, to learn more, the reader will read the body copy.

question headline A type of headline that asks the reader a question.

command headline A type of headline that orders the reader to do something.

subhead Secondary headline that may appear above or below the headline or in the text of the ad.

kicker A subhead that appears above the headline.

boldface Heavier type.

italic A style of printing type with letters that generally slant to the right.

words that suggest newness can increase readership and improve the boom factor of an ad. They should be employed whenever honestly applicable.[18] Examples include *free, now, amazing, suddenly, announcing, introducing, it's here, improved, at last, revolutionary, just arrived, new,* and *important development.* For more tips on creating great headlines, see My Ad Campaign 9–D.

Types of Headlines

Copywriters use many variations of headlines depending on the advertising strategy. Typically, they use the headline that presents the big idea most successfully. Headlines may be classified by the type of information they carry: *benefit, news/information, provocative, question,* and *command.*

Advertisers use **benefit headlines** to promise the audience that experiencing the utility of the product or service will be rewarding. Benefit headlines shouldn't be too cute or clever, just simple statements of the product's most important benefit.[19] Two good examples are

Gore-Tex® Fabrics Keep you warm and dry. Regardless of what falls out of the sky.	Speak a foreign language in 30 days or your money back.

and

Note that both of these headlines focus on the benefit of using the product, not the features of the product itself.[20]

The **news/information headline** announces news or promises information. Sea World began its TV announcement of a new baby whale with the headline "It's a girl." The information must be believable, though. A claim that a razor "shaves 200% smoother" probably isn't.[21]

Copywriters use **provocative headlines** to provoke the reader's curiosity—to stimulate questions and thoughts. For example: "Betcha can't eat just one" (Lay's Potato Chips). To learn more, the reader must read the body copy. The danger, of course, is that the reader won't read on. To avoid this, the creative team designs visuals to clarify the message or provide some story appeal.

A **question headline** asks a question, encouraging readers to search for the answer in the body of the ad. An ad for 4 Day Tire Stores asked: "What makes our tire customers smarter & richer than others?" A good question headline piques the reader's curiosity and imagination.

A **command headline** orders the reader to do something, so it might seem negative. But readers pay attention to such headlines. Sprite soft-drink ads target youth with the hip headline: "Obey your thirst." Some command headlines make a request: "Please don't squeeze the Charmin" (bathroom tissue).

Subheads

The **subhead** is an additional smaller headline that may appear above the headline or below it. Subheads above the headline are called **kickers** (or *overlines*), while those below the headline are called *underlines*. Subheads may also appear in body copy.

Subheads are usually set smaller than the headline but larger than the body copy or text. Subheads generally appear in **boldface** (heavier) or *italic* (slanted) type or a different color. Like a headline, the subhead transmits key sales points fast. But it usually carries less important information than the headline. Subheads are important for two reasons: Most people read only the headline and subheads, and subheads usually best support the interest step.

Subheads are longer and more like sentences than headlines. They serve as stepping-stones from the headline to the body copy, telegraphing what's to come.[22] And they help guide readers to get the information they are looking for in an ad.

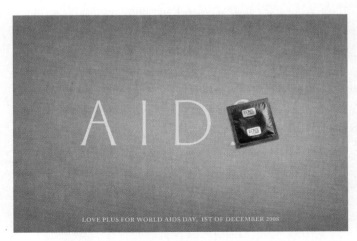

In this ad for Love Plus condoms, the headline tells the whole story: the problem and the solution, cleverly integrated in a compelling message. The subhead provides additional information.
Source: Saatchi & Saatchi Romania for PSI Romania and Love Plus

body copy The text of an advertisement that tells the complete story and attempts to close the sale. It is a logical continuation of the headline and subheads and is usually set in a smaller type size than headlines or subheads.

text An industry term used as a synonym for body copy.

straight-sell copy A type of body copy in which the text immediately explains or develops the headline and visual in a straightforward attempt to sell the product.

institutional copy A type of body copy in which the advertiser tries to sell an idea or the merits of the organization or service rather than the sales features of a particular product.

narrative copy A type of body copy that tells a story. It sets up a problem and then creates a solution using the particular sales features of the product or service as the key to the solution.

dialogue/ monologue A type of body copy in which the characters illustrated in the advertisement do the selling in their own words either through a quasi-testimonial technique or through a comic strip panel.

picture-caption copy A type of body copy in which the story is told through a series of illustrations and captions rather than through the use of a copy block alone.

Body Copy

The advertiser tells the complete sales story in the **body copy**, or **text**. The body copy comprises the interest, credibility, desire, and often even the action steps. It is a logical continuation of the headline and subheads, set in smaller type. Body copy covers the features, benefits, and utility of the product or service.

The body copy is typically read by only 1 out of 10 readers, so the writer must speak to the reader's self-interest, explaining how the product or service satisfies the customer's need.[23] The best ads focus on one big idea or one clear benefit. Copywriters often read their copy aloud to hear how it sounds, even if it's intended for print media. The ear is a powerful copywriting tool.[24]

Body Copy Styles Experienced copywriters look for the technique and style with the greatest sales appeal for the idea being presented. Common copy styles include *straight sell*, *institutional*, *narrative*, *dialogue/monologue*, *picture caption*, and *device*. Whichever style is chosen, copywriters should keep the advice for creating great copy listed in My Ad Campaign 9–E in mind.

In **straight-sell copy**, writers immediately explain or develop the headline and visual in a straightforward, factual presentation. The straight-sell approach appeals to the prospect's intelligence. Straight-sell copy is particularly good for high think-involvement products or products that are difficult to use. It's very effective for direct-mail advertising and for industrial or high-tech products.[25]

Advertisers use **institutional copy** to promote a philosophy or extol the merits of an organization rather than product features. Institutional copy is intended to lend warmth and credibility to the organization's image. Banks, insurance companies, public corporations, and large manufacturing firms use institutional copy in both print and electronic media.

Copywriters use **narrative copy** to tell a story. Ideal for the creative writer, narrative copy sets up a situation and then resolves it at the last minute by having the product or service come to the rescue. Narrative copy offers good opportunities for emotional appeals. Allstate uses this approach in its attention-getting "Mayhem" ads.[26]

By using **dialogue/monologue copy**, the advertiser can add the believability that narrative copy sometimes lacks. The characters portrayed in a print ad do the selling in their own words. A caution: Poorly written dialogue copy can come off as dull or, even worse, hokey and unreal.

Sometimes it's easier to tell a story with illustrations and captions. A photo with **picture-caption copy** is especially useful for products that have a number of different uses or come in a variety of styles or designs.

The selection of a body copy style can have a big impact on the effectiveness of an ad. In this ad for Adidas deodorant, straight sell body copy combined with the clever use of color in the text are used to convey the product benefit. How does the use of the color white in the ad reinforce that benefit?

Source: Adidas

With any copy style, the copywriter may use some device copy to enhance attention, interest, and memorability. **Device copy** uses figures of speech (such as puns, alliteration, and rhymes) as well as humor and exaggeration. Verbal devices help people remember the brand and tend to affect attitudes favorably.[27]

Humor can be effective when the advertiser needs high memorability in a short time, wants to dispel preconceived negative images, or needs to create a distinct personality for an undifferentiated product. However, humor should always be used carefully and never be in questionable taste. Humor also grows old very quickly; the same joke is not funny for long. Therefore, a variety of executions should be created to keep the idea fresh. Some researchers believe humor distracts from the selling message and can even be detrimental when used for serious services such as finance, insurance, and crematoriums.[28]

Formatting Body Copy

The keys to good body copy are simplicity, order, credibility, and clarity. Or, as John O'Toole said, prose should be "written clearly, informatively, interestingly, powerfully, persuasively, dramatically, memorably, and with effortless grace. That's all."[29]

Four basic format elements are used to construct long copy ads: the *lead-in paragraph*, *interior paragraphs*, *trial close*, and *close*.

Lead-in paragraph The **lead-in paragraph** is a bridge between the headline and the sales ideas presented in the text. The lead-in paragraph is part of the *interest* step. It must engage and convert a prospect's reading interest to product interest.

Interior paragraphs The **interior paragraphs** of the body copy should develop *credibility* by providing proof for claims and promises and they should build *desire* by using language that stirs the imagination. Advertisers should support their product promises with data, testimonials, and warranties. Such proofs convince customers of the validity of the product, improve goodwill toward the advertiser, and stimulate sales.

Trial close Interspersed in the interior paragraphs should be suggestions to *act* now. Good copy asks for the order more than

> As John O'Toole said, prose should be "written clearly, informatively, interestingly, powerfully, persuasively, dramatically, memorably, and with effortless grace. That's all."

my ad campaign

Writing Effective Copy [9–E]

- **Get to the main point—fast.**
- **Emphasize one major idea simply and clearly.**
- **Be single-minded.** Don't try to do too much. If you chase more than one rabbit at a time, you'll catch none.
- **Position the product clearly.**
- **Keep the brand name up front and reinforce it.**
- **Write with the consumer's ultimate benefit in mind.**
- **Write short sentences.** Use easy, familiar words and themes people understand.
- **Don't waste words.** Say what you have to say—nothing more, nothing less. Don't pad, but don't skimp.
- **Avoid bragging and boasting.** Write from the reader's point of view, not your own. Avoid "we," "us," and "our."
- **Avoid clichés.** They're crutches; learn to get along without them. Bright, surprising words and phrases perk up readers and keep them reading.
- **Use vivid language.** Use lots of verbs and adverbs.

- **Write with flair.** Drum up excitement. Make sure your own enthusiasm comes through in the copy.
- **Stick to the present tense, active voice.** It's crisper. Avoid the past tense and passive voice. Exceptions should be deliberate, for special effect.
- **Use personal pronouns.** Remember, you're talking to just one person, so talk as you would to a friend. Use "you" and "your" whenever appropriate.
- **Use contractions.** They're fast, personal, natural. People talk in contractions (listen to yourself).
- **Don't overpunctuate.** It kills copy flow. Excessive commas are the chief culprits. Don't give readers any excuse to jump ship.
- **Read the copy aloud.** Hear how it sounds; catch errors. The written word is considerably different from the spoken word so listen to it.
- **Rewrite and write tight.** Edit mercilessly. Tell the whole story and no more. When you're finished, stop.

trial close In ad copy, requests for the order that are made before the close in the ad.

seal A type of certification mark offered by such organizations as the Good Housekeeping Institute and Underwriters' Laboratories when a product meets standards established by these institutions. Seals provide an independent, valued endorsement for the advertised product.

logotypes Special design of the advertiser's name (or product name) that appears in all advertisements. Also called a *signature*, it is like a trademark because it gives the advertiser individuality and provides quick recognition at the point of purchase.

signatures A product or company's primary graphic identity. A signature may be comprised of some combination of a graphic symbol, a logotype, and a slogan.

close The part of an advertisement or commercial that asks customers to do something and tells them how to do it—the action step in the ad's copy.

slogans A standard company statement (also called a *tagline* or *a themeline*) for advertisements, salespeople, and company employees. Slogans have two basic purposes: to provide continuity for a campaign and to reduce a key theme or idea to a brief memorable positioning statement.

themelines A standard company statement for advertisements, salespeople, and company employees. Also called a *slogan* or *tagline*.

taglines A standard company statement for advertisements, salespeople, and company employees.

once; mail-order ads ask several times. Consumers often make the buying decision without reading all the body copy. The **trial close** gives them the opportunity to make the buying decision early.

Close The **close** is the real *action* step. A good close asks consumers to do something and tells them how. The close can be indirect or direct (a subtle suggestion or a direct command). A direct close seeks immediate response in the form of a purchase, a store or website visit, or a request for further information.

Of course, not all ads sell products or services. Advertisers may want to change attitudes, explain their viewpoints, or ask for someone's vote. By giving a web address, the advertiser can offer additional information to those readers who are interested in learning more.

Slogans

Many **slogans** (also called **themelines** or **taglines**) begin as successful headlines, like AT&T's "Reach out and touch someone." Through continuous use, they become standard statements, not just in advertising but for salespeople and company employees.

Slogans have two basic purposes: to provide continuity to a series of ads in a campaign and to reduce an advertising message strategy to a brief, repeatable, and memorable positioning statement. Wheaties cereal, for example, positions itself as the "Breakfast of Champions." And ads for DeBeers still use the famous "Diamonds are forever" slogan.

Seals, Logos, and Signatures

A **seal** is awarded only when a product meets standards established by a particular organization, such as the Good Housekeeping Institute or Underwriters Laboratories. Because these

organizations are recognized authorities, their seals provide an independent, valued endorsement for the advertiser's product.

Logotypes (logos) and **signatures** are special designs of the advertiser's company or product name. They appear in all company ads and, like trademarks, give the product individuality and provide quick recognition at the point of purchase.

The slogan "M'm! M'm! Good!" is synonymous with Campbell's soup (www.campbells.com). It would be surprising to find a Campbell's soup print ad without the familiar red and white logo and the memorable phrase.
Source: Campbell Soup Company

LO9-3 Outline how great copy is created for electronic ads.

CREATING GREAT COPY IN AUDIO AND VIDEO MEDIA

For audio and video media, the fundamental elements—the five steps of the creative pyramid—remain the primary guides, but the copywriting formats differ. Audio and video writers prepare *scripts* and *storyboards*.

Writing Audio Copy

A **script** resembles a two-column list. On the left side, speakers' names are arranged vertically, along with descriptions of any **sound effects** (abbreviated **SFX**) and music. The right column contains the dialogue, called the **audio**.

Copywriters first need to understand audio's (radio, podcasts) strengths and weaknesses. Audio provides entertainment or news to listeners who are busy doing something else—driving, washing dishes, reading the paper, or even studying. To get attention, an advertising message must be catchy, interesting, and unforgettable. Listeners usually decide within five to eight seconds if they're going to listen. To attract and hold attention, audio copy must be intrusive. For more on writing great audio copy, see My Ad Campaign 9-F.

One of the greatest challenges for audio copywriters is making the script fit the time slot. The delivery changes for different types of commercials, so writers must read the script out loud

script Format for radio and television copywriting resembling a two-column list showing dialogue and/or visuals.

sound effects (SFX) Sounds other than music or dialogue used in radio and television.

audio The sound portion of a commercial. Also, the right side of a script for a television commercial, indicating spoken copy, sound effects, and music.

" RADIO WRITING HAS TO BE CLEARER THAN ANY OTHER KIND OF COPYWRITING. "

my ad campaign Creating Effective Audio Commercials [9–F]

Writing for audio takes a sharp ear, empathy for the listener, and the ability to create pictures inside the consumer's head. These tips will help you create great radio spots.

- **Make the big idea crystal clear.** Concentrate on one main selling point. Radio and podcasts are good media for building brand awareness, but not for making long lists of copy points or complex arguments.
- **Mention the advertiser's name early and often.** If the product or company name is tricky, consider spelling it out.
- **Take time to set the scene and establish the premise.** A 30-second commercial that nobody remembers is a waste of money. Fight for longer spots.
- **Use familiar sound effects.** Ice tinkling in a glass, birds chirping, or a door shutting can create a visual image. Music also works if its meaning is clear.

- **Paint pictures with your words.** Use descriptive language to make the ad more memorable.
- **Make every word count.** Use active voice and more verbs than adjectives. Be conversational. Use pronounceable words and short sentences.
- **Be outrageous.** The best comic commercials begin with a totally absurd premise from which all developments follow logically. But remember, if you can't write humor really well, go for drama.
- **Ask for the order.** Try to get listeners to take action.
- **Remember that audio personalities have credibility.** Sometimes the best ads in audio are those that are read by a show's host. They are, after all, the reason that people are listening.
- **Presentation counts a lot.** Even the best scripts look boring on paper. Acting, timing, vocal quirks, and sound effects bring them to life.

Healthier America
Lost Campaign
Radio: 60
"Neighbor"
Expiration date: 2/23/05

SFX: Phone ringing

Bill:	Hello...?
George:	Hi, Bill? This is George Dewey from up the street.
Bill:	Hey, George. How ya doin?
George:	Good, good. Say, I noticed you've been walking to work these days instead of driving...and I, uh, don't quite know how to say this, but...but...
Bill:	But what?
George: (*stammering*)	But...But...Your butt, your buttocks, your butt—I think I found your butt on my front lawn. Have you recently lost it?
Bill:	As a matter of fact, I have, George (*pleased*). It's about time someone noticed.
George: (*playful*)	Well, it was kinda hard to miss if you know what I mean... ...Anyways, would you like it back?
Bill:	Would I like it back? No, not really.
George:	So, it's okay if I throw it out?
Bill:	Sure, that's fine. Take it easy, George.

SFX: Phone ringing

Announcer:	Small step #8—Walk instead of driving whenever you can. It's just one of the many small steps you can take to help you become a healthier, well, you. Get started at www.smallstep.gov and take a small step to get healthy.
Legal:	A public service announcement brought to you by the U.S. Department of Health and Human Services and the Ad Council.

A radio script format resembles a two-column list, with speakers' names and sound effects on the left and the dialogue in a wider column on the right. This national public service announcement (PSA) was created by McCann Erickson and is one of many in a campaign designed to inspire Americans to take small steps toward a healthier lifestyle.
Source: McCann-Erickson Worldwide

Lubriderm created a great commercial (see it here: www.ispot.tv/ad/AAy1/lubriderm-daily-moisture-alligator) that used the metaphor of an alligator to explain the product's benefits. The print ad above from the same campaign shows that the ad produced for electronic media worked just as well across a variety of platforms.
Source: Johnson & Johnson

for timing. With electronic compression, recorded audio ads can include 10 to 30 percent more copy than text read live. Still, the following is a good rule of thumb:

> 10 seconds: 20–25 words
> 20 seconds: 40–45 words
> 30 seconds: 60–70 words
> 60 seconds: 130–150 words[30]

Audio copy has to be clearer than any other kind. For example, the listener can't refer back, as in print, to find an antecedent for a pronoun. Likewise, the English language is so full of homonyms (words that sound like other words) that one can easily confuse the meaning of a sentence ("who's who is whose").[31]

Writing Video Copy

Audio's basic two-column script format also works for television. But in a video (TV, streaming video, digital media video) script, the left side is titled "Video" and the right side "Audio." The video column describes the visuals and production: camera angles, action, scenery, and stage directions. The audio column lists the spoken copy, sound effects, and music.

Commercials must be believable and relevant. Even humorous video ads must exude quality in their creation and production to imply the product's quality. While the art director's work is very important, the copywriter typically sets the tone of the commercial, establishes the language that determines which visuals to use, and pinpoints when the visuals should appear.

To illustrate these principles, let's look at a particular commercial. Many people want smooth, soft skin and consider a patch of rough, flaky skin anywhere on their body a disappointment. If you were the copywriter for Lubriderm skin lotion, how would you approach this somewhat touchy, uncomfortable subject?

The creative staff of J. Walter Thompson crafted an artistic solution for Lubriderm. An alligator was the big idea. The gator's scaly sheath was a metaphor for rough, flaky skin. Its appearance ignited people's survival instincts; they paid attention, fast. A beautiful, sophisticated woman with smooth, feminine skin was seated in a lounge chair, completely unruffled by the passing gator. The swing of the animal's back and tail echoed the graceful curves of the two simple pieces of furniture on the set, and its slow stride kept the beat of a light jazz tune.

This ad follows the creative pyramid. The alligator captures attention visually while the announcer's first words serve as an attention-getting headline: "A quick reminder." The ad commands us to listen and sets up the interest step that offers this claim: "Lubriderm restores lost moisture to heal your dry skin and protect it." Now for the credibility step: "Remember, the one created for dermatologists is the one that heals and protects." And then the desire step recaps the primary product benefit and adds a touch of humor: "Hear that gator? See you later."

check yourself ✓

1. From the writer's perspective, what are the important differences between a radio listener and a print ad reader?

2. What is the approximate word limit of a 30-second radio ad?

3. What are the two columns labeled in a TV script?

LO9-4 Discuss the role of art in electronic ads.

THE ROLE OF ART IN AUDIO AND VIDEO ADVERTISING

In the vignette that opened this chapter, Metro Trains warns risk takers of the dangers surrounding trains through the use of silly cartoon characters, playful music, and humor. The unusual execution softens the rush of negative emotions viewers might feel thinking about injuries or deaths around trains. It simultaneously reframes risk as "dumb" rather than courageous. A brilliant, big idea.

Developing the Artistic Concept for Commercials

Creating the concept for audio or video commercials is similar to creating the concept for print ads. It starts with determining the big idea. Then the art director and copywriter decide what commercial format to use. Should a celebrity present the message? Or should the ad dramatize the product's benefits with a semifictional story? The next step is to write a script containing the necessary copy or dialogue plus a basic description of any music, sound effects, and/or camera views.

In both audio and video formats, the art director assists the copywriter in script development. But in video, artistic development is much more extensive. Using the script, the art director creates a series of **storyboard roughs** to present the artistic approach, the action sequences, and the style of the commercial.

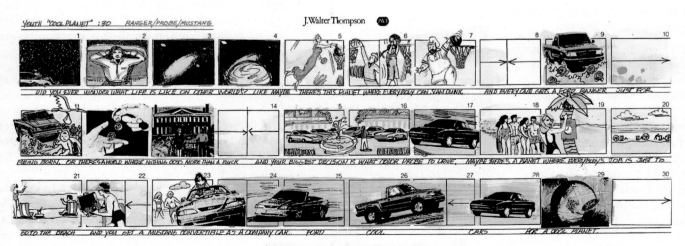

After the initial concepts for a video ad are finalized, creatives develop a storyboard rough composed of small sketches that depict the various scenes of the ad. The storyboard rough is used to present the creative concept to the account team and the client.

Source: J. Walter Thompson and Ford Motor Company

Formats for Audio and Video Commercials

Similar to print advertising, the format for a broadcast ad serves as a template for arranging message elements into a pattern. Once the art director and copywriter establish the big idea, they must determine the commercial's format.

There are many approaches to creating an effective message. Here we consider eight common commercial formats that can be used in either audio or video: *straight announcement*, *presenter*, *testimonial*, *demonstration*, *musical*, *slice of life*, *lifestyle*, and *animation*. Whatever the approach, great video commercials start with an awareness of the recommendations offered in My Ad Campaign 9–G.

Straight Announcement

The oldest and simplest type of commercial and probably the easiest to write is the **straight announcement**. One person, usually an announcer, delivers the sales message. Music may play in the background. Straight announcements are popular because they are adaptable to almost any product or situation. In audio, a straight announcement can also be designed as an **integrated commercial**—that is, it can be woven into a show or tailored to the style of a given program.

For video, an announcer may deliver the sales message **on camera** or off-screen, as a **voice-over**, while a demonstration, slide, or film shows on-screen. If the script is well written and the announcer convincing, straight announcements can be very effective. Because they don't require elaborate production facilities, they save money, too.

Presenter

The **presenter commercial** uses one person or character to present the

Source: pictafolio/E+/Getty Images

product and carry the sales message. Some presenters are celebrities, such as Brad Pitt for Calvin Klein. Others may be experts, such as corporate officers (Pete Coors for Coors Beer) or professionals (doctors), or they may be actors playing a role (Stephanie Courtney as "Flo" in ads for Progressive). A *man-on-the-street* may interview real people and get them to share their thoughts about a client's products or services. And, of course, a presenter doesn't have to be a real person. The Geico gecko and the Aflac Duck are well-known message sources.

A **radio personality**, such as Rush Limbaugh or Howard Stern, may *ad lib* an ad message live in his or her own style. The same thing can be done on popular podcasts, such as those by Chelsea Handler, Adam Corolla, or Joe Rogan. Done well, such commercials can be very successful. However, the advertiser surrenders control to the personality.

Testimonial

The true **testimonial**—where a satisfied user tells how effective the product is—can be highly credible in both TV and radio advertising. Celebrities may gain attention, but they must be believable and not distract from the product. Actually, people from all walks of life endorse products, from known personalities to unknowns and nonprofessionals. Which type of person to use depends on the product and the strategy. Satisfied customers are the best sources for testimonials because their sincerity is usually persuasive. Ogilvy suggested shooting candid testimonials when the subjects don't know they're being filmed.[32] Of course, advertisers must be sure to get their permission before using the piece.

Demonstration

Video is uniquely suited to visual demonstrations. And a **demonstration** convinces an audience better and faster than a spoken message. So don't say it, show it.[33] Naturally, it's easier to demonstrate the product on TV than on radio, but some advertisers have used the imaginative nature of radio to create humorous, tongue-in-cheek demonstrations.

Demonstrations are uniquely suited to video ads and provide compelling evidence to people about the effectiveness of a brand. In this ad for Volvo trucks, the film star Jean-Claude Van Damme demonstrates the reliability and control of the trucks in a way that can't help but draw your attention.
Source: The Volvo Group

Products may be demonstrated in use, in competition, or before and after. These techniques help viewers visualize how the product will perform for them.

Musical   The **musical commercials**, or **jingles**, we hear on radio and TV are among the best—and worst—ad messages produced. Done well, they can bring enormous success, well beyond the average nonmusical commercial. Done poorly, they can waste the advertising budget and annoy audiences beyond belief.

Slice of Life (Problem Solution)   A commercial that dramatizes a real-life situation is called **slice of life**. It usually starts with just plain folks, played by professional actors, discussing some problem or issue. Often the situation deals with a problem of a personal nature: bad breath, loose dentures, dandruff, body odor, or yellow laundry. A relative or a co-worker drops the hint, the product is tried, and the next scene shows the result—a happier, cleaner, more fragrant person off with a new date. The drama always concludes with a positive outcome. Such commercials can get attention and create interest, even though they are often irritating to viewers and hated by copywriters.

The key to effective slice-of-life commercials is simplicity. The ad should concentrate on one compelling product benefit and make it memorable. Often a **mnemonic device** (a technique that helps you remember something) can dramatize the benefit and trigger instant recall. The Aflac duck immediately reminds viewers that Aflac (www.aflac.com) is there to help pay your bills if you get hurt and can't work.

Lifestyle   To present the user rather than the product, advertisers may use the **lifestyle technique**. For example, Diesel pitches its denim to urbanites by showing characters working and playing while wearing its latest line. Likewise, beer and soft-drink advertisers frequently target their messages to active, outdoorsy young people, focusing on who drinks the brand rather than on specific product advantages.

musical commercials A commercial that is sung with the sales message in the verse.

jingles Musical commercials usually sung with the sales message in the verse.

slice of life A type of commercial consisting of a dramatization of a real-life situation in which the product is tried and becomes the solution to a problem.

mnemonic device A gimmick used to dramatize the product benefit and make it memorable, such as the Imperial Margarine crown or the Avon doorbell.

lifestyle technique Type of commercial in which the user is presented rather than the product. Typically used by clothing and soft drink advertisers to affiliate their brands with the trendy lifestyles of their consumers.

my ad campaign

Creating Effective Video Commercials [9–G]

- **Begin at the finish.** Concentrate on the final impression the commercial will make.
- **Create an attention-getting opening.** An opening that is visually surprising or full of action, drama, humor, or human interest sets the context and allows a smooth transition to the rest of the commercial.
- **Use a situation that grows naturally out of the sales story.** Avoid distracting gimmicks. Make it easy for viewers to identify with the characters.
- **Characters are the living symbol of the product.** They should be appealing, believable, nondistracting, and most of all, relevant.
- **Keep it simple.** The sequence of ideas should be easy to follow. Keep the number of elements in the commercial to a bare minimum.

- **Write concise audio copy.** The video should carry most of the weight. Fewer than two words per second is effective for demonstrations. For a 60-second commercial, 101 to 110 words is most effective; more than 170 words is too talky.
- **Make demonstrations dramatic but believable.** They should always be true to life and avoid the appearance of camera tricks.
- **Let the words interpret the picture and prepare viewers for the next scene.** Use conversational language; avoid "ad talk," hype, and puffery.
- **Run scenes five or six seconds on average.** Rarely should a scene run less than three seconds. Offer a variety of movement-filled scenes without "jumping."
- **Keep the look of the video fresh and new.**

animation The use of cartoons, puppet characters, or demonstrations of inanimate characters that come to life in television commercials; often used for communicating difficult messages or for reaching specialized markets, such as children.

storyboard A sheet preprinted with a series of 8 to 20 blank frames in the shape of TV screens, which includes text of the commercial, sound effects, and camera views.

Animation

Cartoons, puppet characters, and demonstrations with computer-generated graphics are **animation** techniques for communicating difficult messages and reaching specialized markets, such as children. The way aspirin or other medications affect the human system is difficult to explain. Animated pictures of headaches and stomach aches can simplify the subject and make a benefit demonstration clear and understandable.

Outlining a Video Commercial

After the creative team selects the big idea and the format for a commercial, the art director and the writer develop the script. Video is so visually powerful and expressive that the art director's role is particularly important. Art directors must be able to work with a variety of professionals—producers, directors, lighting technicians, and set designers—to develop and produce a commercial successfully. Ad production is discussed in our outline production chapter.

Storyboard Design

Once the basic script is completed, the art director must turn the video portion of the script into real images. This is done with a **storyboard**, a sheet preprinted with a series of 8 to 20 blank windows (frames) in the shape of video screens. Below each frame is room to place the text of the commercial, including the sound effects and camera views. The storyboard works much like a comic strip.

Storyboard of "Power to Move" commercial

The storyboard is a visual representation of the ad, made up of sketches that indicate the art director's concept of the various scenes, camera angles, sound effects, and special effects to be used in the final production.

Source: Saatchi & Saatchi, Los Angeles

Through a process similar to laying out a print ad (thumbnail, rough, comp) the artist carefully designs how each scene should appear, arranging actors, scenery, props, lighting, and camera angles to maximize impact, beauty, and mood. The storyboard helps the creatives visualize the commercial's tone and sequence of action, discover any conceptual weaknesses, and make presentations for final management approval. It also serves as a guide for filming.

To supplement the storyboard or pretest a concept, a commercial may be taped in rough form using amateur talent as actors. Or an **animatic** may be shot—a film strip of the sketches in the storyboard accompanied by the audio portion of the commercial synchronized on tape.

their relationships with existing ones. The stakes are obviously high.

Designers should also remember that Internet users are often important opinion leaders. For example, a satisfied visitor to Betty Crocker's website (www.bettycrocker.com) may e-mail several friends a recipe he or she found there. And, just as important, someone left dissatisfied by a company's messages or offerings can easily share that unhappiness with other people. Moreover, e-mail is not the only channel available to web users. They can also share product-related opinions via message boards, a social network site, blogs, or even a YouTube video.

Of course, people differ in how likely they are to share their opinions with others. Research by Burson-Marsteller USA, a large New York public relations firm, suggests that there is a small but highly influential group of heavy Internet users who are especially likely to do so. The firm calls this group the e-fluentials. "An e-fluential is the rock that starts the ripple," said Chet Burchett, president and chief executive officer at Burson-Marsteller. "Each one communicates with an average of 14 people." E-fluentials can be reputation builders or busters.[34]

As with other media, digital has its stars, some famous in all media, others well-known only online. Liza Koshy has created an online brand that makes her a key influencer in fashion. As a result, she's been a guest at events sponsored by Diane von Furstenberg and YouTube. Alexa Tietjen, writing for *WWD*, has noted that as of 2020 nearly every fashion house works with influencers.[35] And fashion is far from the only world where influencers matter. Grumpy Cat represents Friskies pet food and is followed by more than 8 million people on Facebook.[36]

Company Websites Perhaps no consideration in design of a website is more important than understanding why people

check yourself ✓

1. What is a storyboard?
2. What is the oldest and simplest audio or video commercial format?
3. What video format helps present the user rather than the product?

LO9-5 Review the unique requirements in writing for the web.

WRITING FOR THE WEB

Digital media are relatively young and evolve constantly, so advertisers and agencies are still learning how best to use these platforms. Fortunately, research offers some concrete suggestions that can help a designer create more effective digital messages.

A designer should understand that digital media, while containing elements of both print and broadcast, are radically new and engage users in a fundamentally different way. At the core of this engagement is *interactivity*. Smart companies realize that used effectively, the interactive nature of digital media creates opportunities for a mutually satisfying dialogue between advertiser and consumer. Ultimately, that dialogue can help build brand loyalty and lead to a sale. Conversely, companies that use digital media ineffectively (or ignore them altogether) may lose new customers or damage

The most effective websites can be scanned quickly for useful information and are updated regularly with new content. The website for Feed incorporates all of these elements. The beauty and functionality of the site have won it widespread recognition.

Source: Feed Music

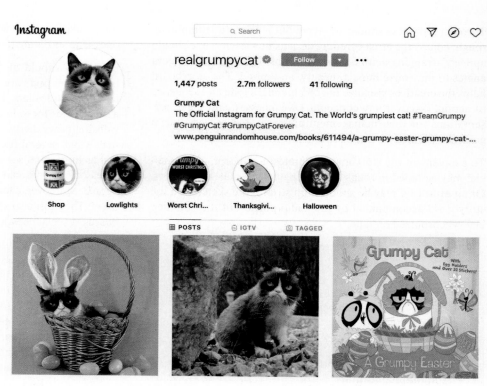

The visual is especially important in social media, where consumers encounter ads scrolling through their feeds and stop when something different captures their attention.
Source: realgrumpycat/Instagram, Inc.

visit the site in the first place. Typically, a visitor to a product website arrives with a purpose. He or she may be seeking product information, such as how to operate the product safely or use it more effectively. Or the visitor may be looking for information about accessories, tips, coupons, or user groups.

Effectively designed websites help visitors find the information they need quickly and efficiently. For example, a visitor to the Betty Crocker site can easily locate where to go for recipes, meal ideas, coupons and promotions, and cookbooks. Information is easy to find because the layout of the site matches closely with the scanning pattern commonly observed among web page readers: two quick horizontal scans across the top followed by a downward vertical scan. Think of a pattern that resembles an "*F.*" Although the products and audience are very different, IBM's U.S. website is designed to accommodate the same scanning pattern (see www.ibm.com/us) as are sites for Coke, Ford, Tide, and many other large advertisers. Each of these sites makes finding information simple and fast. Colors and photographs are carefully chosen to enhance the layout, attract Internet users, and guide their gaze through the page.

Websites have two avenues for attracting people using search engines: paid search (which costs money) and organic search results (which do not). An important tactic for appearing high in organic search results is copy informed by **SEO (search engine optimization)**. What strategy should a copywriter use for incorporating SEO into a site's copy?

1. *Research keywords and keyphrases.* Start by a) formulating a brand mission statement (how is the brand unique?), b) creating a keyword list, c) studying the intent of web searchers (are they looking for information? Do they want to buy something?), and d) creating SEO landing pages.

2. *Write the copy.* The copywriter prepares, writes, and edits text keeping in mind that structure, word selection, clarity, and the use of stories can help attract search engines. Yoast, a company that helps brands with SEO, recommends the following for great copy that can attract searchers on the web: https://yoast.com/complete-guide-seo-copywriting. Find out more SEO tips at Yoast.com.

Banner Ads The purpose of a banner ad is to bring Internet users to a website other than the one they intended to visit. Once the dominant advertising approach, banner ads now compete with many other online forms, including video virals and paid search listings. Designers should keep in mind research findings that suggest effective banner ads are simple, focused, and clear about a product's benefit. Most effective banners make use of a striking image and emphasize a palette of rich, powerful colors.

Viral Ads The enormous popularity of video sites such as YouTube has inspired advertisers to place special video commercials on the web. These are often called "viral" ads because they rely on web users to spread messages to others. But viral includes more than digital video. Matthew Yeoman, writing for the Jeff Bullas blog, defines viral marketing as "the rapid sharing of an idea, [where] a portion of this idea contains a marketing message about buying a product or service."

Yeoman makes the five following recommendations about creating a successful viral message:

1. *Don't be traditional.* Messages that look like TV or print ads aren't shared. Use a big idea that captivates and motivates sharing.

2. *Reality attracts.* Use real people and real situations.

3. *Push the envelope.* People won't watch a blender viral, unless the viral features a blender shredding an iPhone, a paintball, or a DVD. BlendTec found success doing just that.

4. *Thank your users.* Pepsi has created a game featured right on its vending machines that offers free sodas for those who play and win.

5. *Find partners.* How could A&E's *The Walking Dead* collaborate with UC Irvine? By creating a MOOC about zombies, of course. And who can resist zombies?[37]

Bottom line: Understand your audience. Engage. Go big. ■

ENDNOTES

1. Hannah Rand, "Horrifying Video Shows Gang of Youths Risking Death by Playing Game of Chicken on New York Subway Tracks," *Daily Mail*, April 18, 2012, www.dailymail.co.uk/news/article-2131549/Horrifying-video-shows-gang-youths-risking-death-playing-game-chicken-New-York-subway-tracks.html.

2. "Dumb Ways to Die," www.youtube.com/watch?v=IJNR2EpS0jw.

3. Mark Sweney, "Cannes Lions: Dumb Ways to Die Scoops Top Award," *The Guardian*, June 22, 2013, www.theguardian.com/media/2013/jun/22/cannes-lions-advertising-awards.

4. "Metro Trains: Dumb Ways to Die," Top Ad Campaigns of the 21st Century, *Advertising Age*, http://adage.com/lp/top15/#tapproject.

5. Miranda Ward, "Has Dumb Ways to Die Been Effective?" *mUm-BRELLA*, January 30, 2015.

6. G. Sterling, "What Ads Types Are Most 'Helpful'? Search Ads Follow Newspapers, TV," *Search Engine Land*, July 2, 2009, https://searchengineland.com/what-ads-types-are-most-helpful-search-ads-follow-newspapers-tv-21913.

7. Bonnie Drewniany and A. Jerome Jewler, *Creative Strategy in Advertising* (Boston: Cengage, 2010).

8. Nick Kolenda, "The Ideal Characteristics of a Visual Advertisement," *Psychology and Marketing Blog*, August 12, 2015, retrieved at: www.nickkolenda.com.

9. John E. Dyer, "Learning Beyond the Classroom: Photography as a Major Design Element in Graphic Design Layouts for Print and Web," 2015, thesis, Rochester Institute of Technology, accessed at https://scholarworks.rit.edu/theses/8689; Praggyan (Pam) Mohantya and S. Ratneshwarb, "Did You Get It? Factors Influencing Subjective Comprehension of Visual Metaphors in Advertising," *Journal of Advertising*, November 2014, pp. 232–42; Reto Felix and Wolfgang Hinck, "Attention to Print Advertising: An Eye Tracking Study in the Context of Airline Advertisements," in *Thriving in a New World Economy, Developments in Marketing Science*, October 2015, pp. 252–55.

10. Axel Andersson and Denison Hatch, "How to Create Headlines That Get Results," *Target Marketing*, March 1994, pp. 28–35.

11. Murray Raphel and Neil Raphel, "A New Look at Newspaper Ads," *Progressive Grocer*, November 1993, pp. 13–14; David Ogilvy, *Ogilvy on Advertising* (New York: Random House, 1985), pp. 88–89.

12. Philip Ward Burton, *Advertising Copywriting*, 6th ed. (Lincolnwood, IL: NTC Business Books, 1999), pp. 65–66, 70.

13. Roy Paul Nelson, *The Design of Advertising* (Dubuque, IA: Brown & Benchmark, 1994) p. 91.

14. Drewniany and Jewler, *Creative Strategy in Advertising*, p. 115; Burton, *Advertising Copywriting*, p. 188; Julia M. Collins, "Image and Advertising," *Harvard Business Review*, January/February 1989, pp. 93–97.

15. Neil Raphel and Murray Raphel, "Rules to Advertise By," *Progressive Grocer*, December 1993, pp. 13–14; Murray Raphel, "How to Get Ahead in Direct Mail," *Direct Marketing*, January 1990, pp. 30–32, 52.

16. Ogilvy, *Ogilvy on Advertising*, p. 71.

17. Raphel and Raphel, "A New Look at Newspaper Ads," pp. 13–14.

18. James H. Leigh, "The Use of Figures of Speech in Print Ad Headlines," *Journal of Advertising Research*, June 1994, pp. 17–33.

19. Ogilvy, *Ogilvy on Advertising*, pp. 10–11.

20. Andersson and Hatch, "How to Create Headlines That Get Results," pp. 28–35.

21. Burton, *Advertising Copywriting*, p. 54; Arthur J. Kover and William J. James, "When Do Advertising 'Power Words' Work? An Examination of Congruence and Satiation," *Journal of Advertising Research*, July/August 1993, pp. 32–38.

22. Burton, *Advertising Copywriting*, p. 58.

23. Raphel and Raphel, "A New Look at Newspaper Ads," pp. 13–14.

24. Burton, *Advertising Copywriting*, p. 54.

25. Burton, *Advertising Copywriting*, p. 12.

26. Raphel and Raphel, "Rules to Advertise By," pp. 13–14.

27. Bruce Bendinger, *The Copy Workshop Workbook* (Chicago: The Copy Workshop, 2002), p. 192.

28. Burton, *Advertising Copywriting*, p. 74.

29. Ogilvy, *Ogilvy on Advertising*, p. 119.

30. Burton, *Advertising Copywriting*, p. 79.

31. Leigh, "The Use of Figures of Speech in Print Ad Headlines," pp. 17–33.

32. Ogilvy, *Ogilvy on Advertising*, p. 109.

33. Michelle Greenwald, "8 of the Best Product Demos Ever and Why They're So Effective," *Forbes*, June 4, 2014, www.forbes.com/sites/michellegreenwald/2014/06/04/8-of-the-best-product-demos-ever-and-why-theyre-so-effective/#373c3bef7581.

34. "Corporate Advertising Study," Burson-Marsteller, October 13, 2003, www.efluentials.com/documents/pr_101303.pdf.

35. Alexa Tietjen, "Are Influencers Now Part of Fashion's Elite?" *WWD*, May 10, 2019, https://wwd.com/fashion-news/fashion-features/met-gala-influencers-1203125978.

36. "25 Top Online Influencers," *IZEA*, May 8, 2018, https://izea.com/2018/05/08/top-online-influencers.

37. Matthew Yeoman, "5 Key Viral Marketing Tactics Proven to Work," *Jeff Bullas blog*, June 6, 2014, retrieved at: www.jeffbullas.com/2014/06/24/5-key-viral-marketing-tactics-proven-to-work.

print
media

This chapter examines how print advertising enhances the advertiser's media mix. Newspapers and magazines, with their unique qualities, can complement broadcast, direct mail, and other media. By using print wisely, advertisers can significantly increase the reach and impact of their campaigns and still stay within their budgets.

Whither newspapers? The word "whither," with an "h," refers to place and in this sentence means "what will happen to newspapers?" Drop the "h," as in "wither," and the term refers to shriveling. Sadly, both words are appropriate in discussing the oldest advertising medium.

The digital revolution has challenged all media, but especially newspapers. To see why, it is helpful to consider several trends that started years ago and are, to a lesser degree, continuing today. To start, total newspaper circulation (digital and print) was just under 29 million in 2018, down 8 percent over one year.

It only gets worse. Although newspapers are more likely to be read by the better educated, and the proportion of the population with a college degree is increasing, readership is still down. By 2012, almost 30 percent of Americans held a four-year degree, a historic high; however, college-educated adults are less likely to read a newspaper than at any time in history.[1] While the declines in newspaper readership are consistent and significant, they pale in comparison

continued on p. 250

LEARNING OBJECTIVES

After studying this chapter, you will be able to:

LO10-1 Explain the advantages and disadvantages of magazine advertising.

LO10-2 Discuss how magazine circulation is measured and rates are set.

LO10-3 Explain the advantages and disadvantages of newspaper advertising.

LO10-4 Describe the major types of newspapers and how they charge for advertising.

LO10-5 Show how print media work with new technologies.

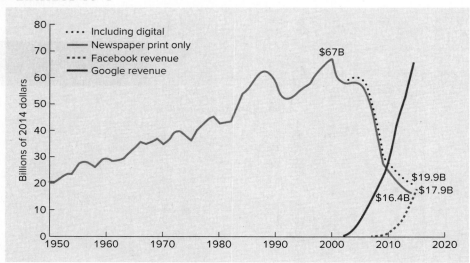

Source: Alec Stapp, "Google And Facebook Didn't Kill Newspapers: The Internet Did," Techdirt, October 25, 2019.

continued from p. 249

to the decline in advertising revenue. In 2006, revenues from advertising peaked at about $49 billion.[2] By 2018, that number had shrunk to $14 billion.[3] Where has the money gone? If you guessed the Internet, you would be right. Advertisers have shifted major portions of their spending to online and social media. In 2018, online spending at Facebook alone exceeded that of the entire newspaper industry. Google passed that mark over a decade ago (see Exhibit 10–1).[4]

What about online newspapers? Have they helped to bandage the revenue bleed? Unfortunately, no. Newspapers still receive only a small fraction of advertising and circulation revenues from their online products. Pew reports that for every $1 newspapers gain in digital advertising income they are losing $7 from declines in print ad revenue.[5] The refocus on digital has simply not stopped the bleeding because many papers have so little web traffic they cannot be measured by auditors.[6,7]

So, whither newspapers? The industry has known for a long while now that a new model is needed. Buffeted by the perfect storm of digital challengers and a lack of

interest among young adults, newspapers have struggled to find an approach that promises both news integrity and healthy revenue growth. Clearly, the industry must find an answer soon if the answer to "whither newspapers?" is not continued "withering." ■

PRINT MEDIA

Selecting Media

Selecting the most appropriate media mix for an advertising campaign requires two distinct skills: understanding the unique characteristics of the various media alternatives and determining which medium will most efficiently and effectively reach the campaign's target audience.

The chapters in Part 5 present the unique elements of the most common media classes. Then, in Chapter 14, we will examine how media planners and buyers decide which media to use, when to use them, and how to purchase them. In that chapter, we will also discuss audience measurements. For now, it will help if you have a basic understanding of two key terms: *reach*—the percentage of an audience exposed, at least once, to a medium during a given period of time; and *frequency*—the average number of times those people are exposed to that medium during that period of time.

Understanding the characteristics of media options is important not only to media planners and buyers; account managers, planners, and creatives must also have an appreciation for the strengths and weaknesses of each medium so they can develop strategies and executions that will take full advantage of their alternatives.

Print advertising certainly includes magazines and newspapers, but it could include any message that is produced on printed surfaces, such as brochures, directories, mail, posters, and outdoor boards. The definition of print advertising must now be expanded to include some forms of digital publications, which are discussed later in this chapter.

All print advertising has several unique elements in common. Compared to television or radio, print advertising has more permanence. Because it stays around for a while, it may be read more than once or passed along to other readers. People also tend to spend more time with print advertising, so it provides an opportunity to present more detailed information and longer explanations.

Obviously, print advertising can be an important ingredient in the **media mix**, the combination of media types that work together to most effectively deliver an advertiser's message. In this chapter, we'll examine the characteristics of magazines and newspapers.

LO10-1 Explain the advantages and disadvantages of magazine advertising.

USING MAGAZINES IN THE MEDIA MIX

Advertisers use magazines in their media mix for many reasons. First and foremost, magazines allow an advertiser to reach a particular target audience with a high-quality presentation. Levi Strauss is just one of the many leading advertisers that use magazines as an important element of their creative mix. (Exhibit 10–2 lists the top U.S. magazine advertisers.)

Magazines, as with other media, lost significant advertising revenue in the 2000s, although the losses have been stemmed over the past four years.[8] Not long ago the second-largest medium, magazines, have fallen behind television and digital media, but are now ahead of newspapers. Several well-known magazines, such as *Newsweek*, *U.S. News & World Report*, *Gourmet*, and *PC World*, no longer publish printed editions.[9]

media mix
The combination of media types that work together to most effectively deliver an advertiser's message.

The Pros and Cons of Magazine Advertising

Magazines continue to offer a wide variety of benefits to advertisers, including flexible design options, prestige, authority, credibility, and long shelf life. Magazines may sit on a coffee table for months and be reread many times. Consumers can read a magazine ad at their leisure; they can pore over the details of a photograph; and they can study carefully the information presented in the copy. This makes it an ideal medium for high-involvement think and feel products.

However magazines also have a number of drawbacks (see My Ad Campaign 10–A, "The Pros and Cons of Magazine Advertising"). They are expensive (on a cost-per-reader basis), especially for color ads. And because they typically circulate monthly, or weekly at best, it's difficult to reach a large audience quickly or frequently. For these reasons, many advertisers use magazines in combination with other media—such as newspapers, which we'll discuss later in this chapter.

Special Possibilities with Magazines

Media planners and buyers need to be aware of the many creative possibilities magazines offer advertisers through various technical or mechanical features. These include bleed pages, cover positions, inserts and gatefolds, and special sizes, such as junior pages and island halves.

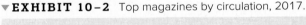

▼**EXHIBIT 10–2** Top magazines by circulation, 2017.

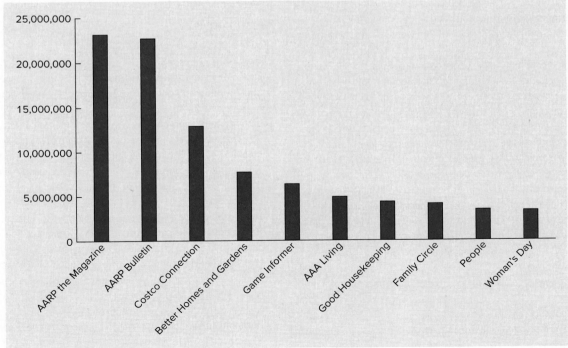

When the dark or colored background of the ad extends to the edge of the page, it is said to **bleed** off the page. Most magazines offer bleed pages, but they charge 10 to 15 percent more for them. The advantages of bleeds include greater flexibility in expressing the advertising idea, a slightly larger printing area, and more dramatic impact.

If a company plans to advertise in a particular magazine consistently, it may seek a highly desirable **cover position**. Few publishers sell ads on the front cover, commonly called the *first cover*. They do however sell the inside front, inside back, and outside back covers (the *second*, *third*, and *fourth covers*, respectively), usually at a substantial premium.

A less expensive way to use magazine space is to place the ad in unusual places on the page or dramatically across spreads. A **junior unit** is a large ad (60 percent of the page) placed in the middle of a page and surrounded with editorial matter. Similar to junior units are **island halves**, surrounded by even more editorial matter. The island sometimes costs more than a regular half-page, but because it dominates the page, many advertisers consider it worth the extra charge. Exhibit 10–3 shows other space combinations that create impact.

my ad campaign

The Pros and Cons of Magazine Advertising [10–A]

The Pros

- **Flexibility** in readership and advertising. Magazines cover the full range of prospects; they have a wide choice of regional and national coverage and a variety of lengths, approaches, and editorial tones.
- **Color** gives readers visual pleasure, and color reproduction is best in slick magazines. Color enhances image and identifies the package. In short, it sells.
- **Authority and credibility** enhance the commercial message. TV, radio, and newspapers offer lots of information but lack the depth needed for readers to gain knowledge or meaning; magazines often offer all three.
- **Permanence**, or long shelf life, gives the reader time to appraise ads in detail, allowing a more complete education/sales message and the opportunity to communicate the total corporate personality.
- **Prestige** for products advertised in upscale or specialty magazines such as *Architectural Digest*, *Connoisseur*, and *Town and Country*.
- **Audience selectivity** is more efficient in magazines than any other medium except direct mail. The predictable, specialized editorial environment selects the audience and enables advertisers to pinpoint their sales campaigns. Examples: golfers *(Golf Digest)*, businesspeople *(Bloomberg Businessweek)*, 20-something males *(Men's Health)*, or teenage girls *(Seventeen)*.
- **Cost-efficiency** because wasted circulation is minimized. Print networks give advertisers reduced prices for advertising in two or more network publications.
- **Selling power** of magazines is proven, and results are usually measurable.
- **Reader loyalty** that sometimes borders on fanaticism.
- **Extensive pass-along readership.** Many people may read the magazine after the initial purchaser.
- **Merchandising assistance.** Advertisers can generate reprints and merchandising materials that help them get more mileage out of their ad campaigns.

The Cons

- **Lack of immediacy** that advertisers can get with newspapers or radio.
- **Shallow geographic coverage.** They don't offer the national reach of broadcast media.
- **Inability to deliver mass audiences at a low price.** Magazines are very costly for reaching broad masses of people.
- **Inability to deliver high frequency.** Because most magazines come out only monthly or weekly, the advertiser can build frequency faster than reach by adding numerous small-audience magazines to the schedule.
- **Long lead time** for ad insertion, sometimes two to three months.
- **Heavy advertising competition.** The largest-circulation magazines have 52 percent advertising to 48 percent editorial content.
- **High cost per thousand.** Average black-and-white cost per thousand (CPM) in national consumer magazines is high; some trade publications with highly selective audiences have a CPM over $50 for a black-and-white page.
- **Declining circulations**, especially in single-copy sales, is an industry-wide trend that limits an advertiser's reach.

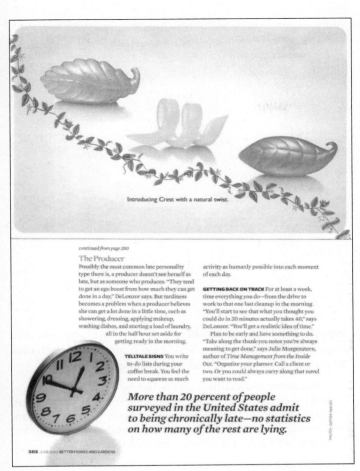

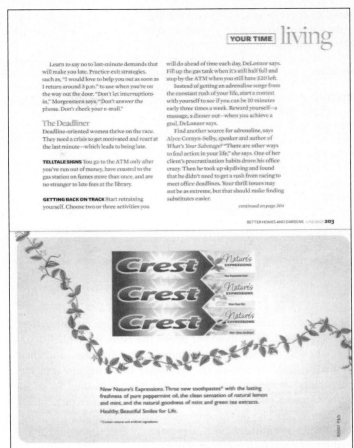

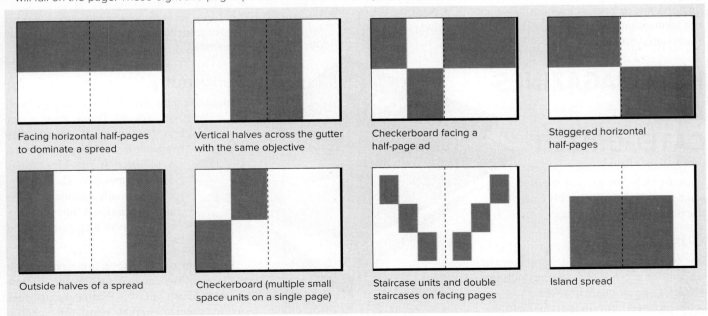

The opportunity to be creative is not limited to copywriters and art directors. Media planners and buyers can increase an ad's impact by exploring creative media buys. Crest toothpaste has made an impact greater than that which would be achieved by a full-page ad by purchasing staggered horizontal half-pages and developing an advertisement to effectively utilize that space.

Source: Crest by Procter & Gamble

▼ **EXHIBIT 10-3** An ad's position on the page influences its effectiveness. The size and shape of the ad often determine where it will fall on the page. These eight two-page spreads show most of the positions a fractional ad can take.

Facing horizontal half-pages to dominate a spread

Vertical halves across the gutter with the same objective

Checkerboard facing a half-page ad

Staggered horizontal half-pages

Outside halves of a spread

Checkerboard (multiple small space units on a single page)

Staircase units and double staircases on facing pages

Island spread

[(Print advertising is) an ideal medium for high-involvement ... products.]

Sometimes, rather than buying a standard page, an advertiser uses an **insert**. The advertiser prints the ad on high-quality paper stock to add weight and drama to the message, and then ships the finished ads to the publisher for insertion into the magazine at a special price. Another option is multiple-page inserts. Calvin Klein once promoted its jeans in a 116-page insert in *Vanity Fair*. The insert reportedly cost more than $1 million, but the news reports about it in major daily newspapers gave the campaign enormous publicity value.

Advertising inserts may be devoted exclusively to one company's product or they may be sponsored by the magazine and have a combination of ads and special editorial content consistent with the magazine's focus.

A **gatefold** is an insert whose paper is so wide that the extreme left and right sides have to be folded into the center to match the size of the other pages. When the reader opens the magazine, the folded page swings out like a gate to present the ad. Not all magazines provide gatefolds, and they are always sold at a substantial premium.

HOW MAGAZINES ARE CATEGORIZED

In the jargon of the trade, magazines are called *books*, and media planners and buyers commonly categorize them by content, geography, and size.

Content

One of the most dramatic developments in publishing is the emergence of magazines with special content, which has given many of them good prospects for long-term

Souce: Ken Cavanagh/McGraw-Hill

growth. The broadest classifications of content are *consumer magazines*, *farm magazines*, and *business magazines*. Each may be broken down into hundreds of categories.

- **Consumer magazines**, purchased for entertainment, information, or both, are edited for consumers who buy products for their own personal consumption: *Time, Sports Illustrated, Glamour, Good Housekeeping*. One would expect to see the Levi's "Go Forth" ads in consumer magazines.

- **Farm publications** are directed to farmers and their families or to companies that manufacture or sell agricultural equipment, supplies, and services: *Farm Journal, Progressive Farmer, Prairie Farmer, Successful Farming*.

- **Business magazines**, by far the largest category, target business readers. They include *trade publications* for retailers, wholesalers, and other distributors (*Progressive Grocer, Bakery News*); *business* and *industrial magazines* for businesspeople involved in manufacturing and services (*Electronic Design, American Banker*); and *professional journals* for lawyers, physicians, architects, and other professionals (*Archives of Ophthalmology*).

Geography

A magazine may also be classified as *local*, *regional*, or *national*. Today, most major U.S. cities have a **local city magazine**: *San Diego Magazine, New York, Los Angeles, Chicago, Palm Springs Life*. Their readership is usually upscale business and professional people interested in local arts, fashion, and business.

Regional publications are targeted to a specific area of the country, such as the West or the South: *Sunset, Southern Living*. National magazines sometimes provide special market runs for specific

If you can't beat them, join them. Print ads can combine with digital technologies to create unique consumer experiences. In this ad, a consumer can try on a Rolex and see how it will fit around her wrist.

Source: Chrono24

geographic regions. *Time*, *Woman's Day*, and *Sports Illustrated* allow advertisers to buy a single major market. Exhibit 10–4 shows the 10 major geographic editions of *Reader's Digest*. This is important for local or regional advertisers who want the benefit of advertising in larger, more well-known publications while staying geographically relevant to the audience that may be reading the magazine.

National magazines range from those with enormous circulations, such as *TV Guide*, to small, lesser-known national magazines, such as *Nature* and *Volleyball*. The largest circulation magazine in the United States today is *AARP The Magazine*, distributed to the 25 million–member households of the American Association of Retired Persons.

local city magazine
Most major U.S. cities have one of these publications. Typical readership is upscale, professional people interested in local arts, fashion, and business.

regional publications
Magazines targeted to a specific area of the country, such as the West or the South.

national magazines
Magazines that are distributed throughout a country.

▼ **EXHIBIT 10–4**   Advertisers benefit from selecting regional editions similar to the 10 geographic editions of *Reader's Digest* shown on the map. With regional binding and mailing, advertisers can buy ad space for only the areas of distribution they need.

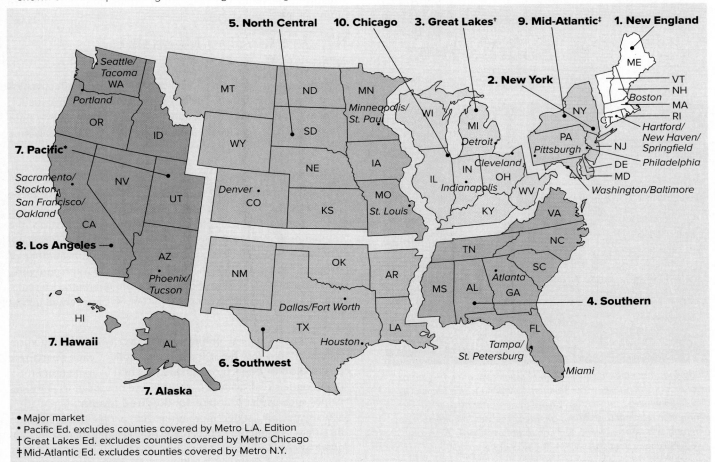

• Major market
* Pacific Ed. excludes counties covered by Metro L.A. Edition
† Great Lakes Ed. excludes counties covered by Metro Chicago
‡ Mid-Atlantic Ed. excludes counties covered by Metro N.Y.

rate base With magazines, the circulation figure on which the publisher bases its rates.

Size

Magazines come in different shapes and sizes, which can make it a challenge to get one ad to run in different size magazines and still look the same. Magazine sizes run the gamut, which can make production standardization a nightmare. The most common magazine sizes follow:

Size Classification	Magazine	Approximate Size of Full-Page Ad
Large	*Interview*	4 col. × 170 lines (9½ × 11⅓ inches)
Flat	*Time*	3 col. × 140 lines (7 × 10 inches)
Standard	*National Geographic*	2 col. × 119 lines (6 × 8½ inches)
Small or pocket	*Reader's Digest*	2 col. × 91 lines (4½ × 6½ inches)

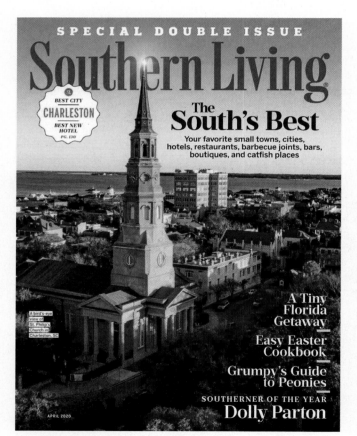

Magazines that cater to specific geographic areas are considered local or regional publications. Southern Living magazine focuses its distribution in the southeastern United States, offering its readers information relevant to southern climates, lifestyles, architecture, and food preferences. Marketers can target even more precisely by advertising in Southern Living's regional or metro editions.
Source: Time Inc. Lifestyle Group

check yourself ✓

1. Why do you think media planners and buyers need to be aware of the many creative possibilities offered by magazines?

2. If you were the media planner, what magazines would you consider for a Toyota ad? How about for a Tide detergent ad? Or a Minolta camera ad? What factors influence your thinking?

LO10-2 Discuss how magazine circulation is measured and rates are set.

BUYING MAGAZINE SPACE

When analyzing a media vehicle, media planners and buyers consider readership, cost, mechanical requirements, and ad closing dates (deadlines). To buy effectively, they must thoroughly understand the magazine's circulation and rate-card information.

Understanding Magazine Circulation

The first step in analyzing a publication's potential effectiveness is to assess its audience. The buyer studies circulation statistics, primary and secondary readership, subscription and vendor sales, and any special merchandising services the magazine offers.

Guaranteed versus Delivered Circulation
A magazine's rates are largely based on its circulation. The **rate base** is the circulation figure on which the publisher bases its rates. It is generally equivalent to the **guaranteed circulation**, the minimum number of copies the publisher expects to circulate. This assures advertisers they will reach a certain number of people. If the publisher does not deliver its guaranteed figure, it must provide a refund. For that reason, guaranteed circulation figures are often stated safely below the average actual circulation.

Media buyers expect publications to verify their circulation figures. Publishers pay thousands of dollars each year for a **circulation audit**—a thorough analysis of the circulation procedures, outlets of distribution, readers, and other factors—by companies such as the **Alliance for Audited Media**. Circulation actually gets overstated more often than people think. In some instances, as much as 30 percent of consumer magazines audited by the ABC each year don't meet the circulation levels they guarantee to advertisers.[10]

Primary and Secondary Readership

Primary circulation represents the number of people who buy the publication, either by subscription or at the newsstand. **Secondary (or pass-along) readership**, which is an estimate determined by market research of how many people read a single issue of a publication, is very important to magazines. Some have more than six readers per copy. Multiplying the average pass-along readership by, say, a million subscribers can give a magazine a substantial audience beyond its primary readers.

Vertical and Horizontal Publications

There are two readership classifications of business publications: *vertical* and *horizontal*. A **vertical publication** covers a specific industry in all its aspects. For example, Penton publishes *Nation's Restaurant News* strictly for restaurateurs and food-service operators. The magazine's editorial content includes everything from news of the restaurant industry to the latest food and beverage trends.

Horizontal publications, in contrast, deal with a particular job function across a variety of industries. Readers of *HR Magazine* work in human resources in many different industries. Horizontal trade publications are very effective advertising vehicles because they usually offer excellent reach and they tend to be well read.[11]

Subscription and Vendor Sales

Media buyers also want to know a magazine's ratio of subscriptions to newsstand sales. Today, subscriptions account for the majority of magazine sales. Newsstands (which include bookstore chains) are still a major outlet for single-copy sales, but no outlet can handle more than a fraction of the many magazines available.

From the advertiser's point of view, newsstand sales are impressive because they indicate that the purchaser really wants the magazine and is not merely subscribing out of habit. However, single-copy sales accounted for only 6 percent of total magazine sales in 2018 and have been falling for several years.[12]

Paid and Controlled Circulation

Business publications may be distributed on either a *paid-circulation* or *controlled-circulation* basis. A paid basis means the recipient must pay the subscription price to receive the magazine. *Bloomberg Businessweek* is a **paid-circulation** business magazine.

In **controlled circulation**, the publisher mails the magazine free to individuals who the publisher thinks can influence the purchase of advertised products. For example, individuals responsible for packaging their company's products can receive a free subscription to *Packaging Digest* magazine. To qualify for the subscription list, people must indicate in writing a desire to receive it and must give their professional designation or occupation. Dues-paying members of organizations often get free subscriptions. For example, members of the Boat Owners Association of the United States receive free copies of *BoatUS Magazine*.

Advertising Age is a good example of a vertical publication. The magazine is geared toward a variety of issues specific to the advertising industry. Unlike horizontal publications, which focus on a single job function across various industries, the periodical is read by people in a wide range of functions throughout the advertising industry.

Source: Crain Communications

> ## Newsstand sales are impressive because they indicate that the purchaser really wants the magazine.

Publishers of paid-circulation magazines say subscribers who pay are more likely to read a publication than those who receive it free. But controlled-circulation magazines can reach good prospects for the goods and services they advertise.

Merchandising Services: Added Value

Magazines, and newspapers too, often provide liberal added-value services to their regular advertisers, such as:

- Special promotions at retail stores.

- Marketing services to help readers find local outlets.

- Response cards that allow readers to request brochures and catalogs.

- Help handling sales force, broker, wholesaler, and retailer meetings.

- Advance copies for the trade.

- Marketing research into brand preferences, consumer attitudes, and market conditions.

If a publication's basic characteristics—editorial, circulation, and readership—are strong, these additional services can increase the effectiveness of its ads.[13] Magazines offer great potential for relationship marketing because they already have a relationship with their subscribers.

Reading Rate Cards

Magazine rate cards follow a fairly standard format. This helps advertisers determine costs, discounts, mechanical requirements, closing dates, special editions, and additional costs for features such as color, inserts, bleed pages, split runs, or preferred positions.

Three dates affect magazine purchases. The **cover date** is the date printed on the cover. The **on-sale date** is the date the magazine is actually issued. And the **closing date** is the date all ad material must be in the publisher's hands for a specific issue. Lead time may be as much as three months.

Rates As we discuss in Chapter 14, one way to compare magazines is to look at how much it costs to reach a thousand people in each based on the magazine's rates for a one-time, full-page ad. You compute the **cost per thousand (CPM)** by using a ratio of the full-page rate (the numerator) divided by a denominator of the circulation, divided by 1,000:

$$\frac{\text{Page rate}}{(\text{Circulation} \div 1,000)} = \text{CPM}$$

For example, if the magazine's black-and-white page rate is $10,000, and the publication has a circulation of 500,000, then:

$$\frac{\$10,000}{(500,000 \div 1,000)} = \frac{\$10,000}{500} = \$20 \text{ CPM}$$

Consider this comparison. In 2020, the page rate for a full-color, one-page ad in *AARP The Magazine* was $754,300 on a total circulation of 22.5 million; *Readers Digest*, a much smaller magazine (both in physical size and circulation) offered the same ad for $2,300 with a total circulation of about 100,000. Which was the better buy purely on a CPM basis?[14]

Discounts Magazines and newspapers often give discounts. **Frequency discounts** are based on the number of ad insertions, usually within a year; **volume discounts** are based on the total amount of space bought during a specific period. Most magazines also offer *cash discounts* (usually 2 percent) to advertisers who pay right away, and some offer discounts on the purchase of four or more consecutive pages in a single issue. In fact, many magazine publishers now negotiate their rates. According to Harold Shain, former Newsweek Inc. president, "Every piece of business is negotiated."[15]

Southern Living

COVERS

2ND COVER	3RD COVER	BACK COVER
$333,400	$305,600	$361,200

FULL RUN / 4-COLOR

CIRC. BASE	FULL PAGE	2/3 PAGE	1/2 PAGE	1/3 PAGE
4-color	$277,800	$213,000	$173,700	$125,100

REGIONAL EDITIONS CPM TABLE / 4-COLOR

CIRC. BASE	FULL PAGE	2/3 PAGE	1/2 PAGE	1/3 PAGE
100,000	$26,030	$19,960	$16,270	$11,720
Add'l per M	153.30	117.50	95.90	69.00
250,000	$49,030	$37,590	$30,650	$22,070
Add'l per M	127.70	97.90	79.80	57.40
500,000	$80,950	$62,060	$50,610	$36,430
Add'l per M	106.00	81.30	66.20	47.70
1,000,000	$133,940	$102,690	$83,730	$62,280
Add'l per M	100.20	76.80	62.70	45.10
1,500,000	$184,040	$141,100	$115,060	$82,830
Add'l per M	98.00	75.10	61.30	44.10

State or regional editions include some circulation from adjacent states

RATEBASES

Full Run	2,800,000
Alabama	141,000
Arkansas*	238,000
Florida	255,000
Georgia	230,000
Mid-Atlantic**	353,000
Mississippi	72,000
Midwest States***	302,000
North Carolina	241,000
South Carolina	144,000
Tennessee	158,000
Texas	338,000

* Includes MO, OK, LA
** Includes VA, MD, DE, D.C., PA, NJ, NY
*** Includes OH, IL, MI, WI, IN, KY, WV

HOW TO FIGURE MULTIPLE STATES

Advertisers who run the same ad (same configuration) in multiple state editions use CPM table to calculate the rate. State edition circulations are not guaranteed and are to be used only as a basis for determining rates.

Example: Tennessee and Arkansas editions, Full Page 4-color buy:	
Total Circulation:	396,000
First 250,000 Cost:	$49,030
146,000 at $122.50 per M:	$18,644
Total Cost:	$67,674

These rates and all advertising transactions are subject to the 2019 Advertising Terms and Conditions of Meredith Corporation. Circulation includes the print and digital editions of the Magazine. Qualified full-run advertisements will run in both editions. See MAGAZINE ADVERTISING TERMS AND CONDITIONS for additional information including opt-out and upgrade options.

PUBLISHING CALENDAR

MONTH	AD CLOSE	ON-SALE
January	10/29/18	12/21/18
February	11/26/18	1/18/19
March	1/2/19	2/22/19
April	1/28/19	3/22/19
May	2/25/19	4/19/19
June	4/1/19	5/24/19
July	4/29/19	6/21/19
August	5/28/19	7/19/19
September	7/1/19	8/23/19
October	7/29/19	9/20/19
November	8/26/19	10/18/19
December	9/24/19	11/15/19

PRINT AD SPECIFICATIONS

MEREDITH.COM/AD-SPECS

FOR FULL SPECS, PLEASE REFER TO

http://www.meredith.com/sites/default/files/SouthernLiving_8x10.5.pdf

This partial rate card for Southern Living magazine (www.southernliving.com/sites/default/files/sl_2019_mediakit_final_lores.pdf) shows the advertising costs for common ad sizes. As with many magazines, advertisers have a variety of choices in terms of platforms, distribution, and scope.

Source: Time Inc. Lifestyle Group

Premium Rates Magazines charge extra for special features. Color printing normally costs 25 to 60 percent more than black and white. Bleed pages can add as much as 20 percent to regular rates, although the typical increase is about 15 percent.

Second and third cover rates (the inside covers) typically cost less than the fourth (back) cover. For example, in 2016, *People* magazine charged $324,400 for a normal color page and $446,500 and $393,000 for the second and third covers, respectively, but it charged $482,000 for the fourth cover (the back of the magazine).[16]

Magazines charge different rates for ads in geographic or demographic issues. **Geographic editions** target geographic markets; **demographic editions** reach readers who share a demographic trait, such as age, income level, or professional status.

Newspapers are an important medium in the media mix, second only to television in advertising volume, but costing much less. This ad for The Sunday Times of England promotes a special issue that reveals salaries of the rich and famous. The size of the bandmates in the Rolling Stones graphically illustrates their relative wealth. This type of creative advertising helps The Sunday Times be one of the largest selling British Sunday newspapers.
Source: The Sunday Times

check yourself ✓

1. How does an advertiser know if a magazine doesn't deliver the circulation that it guarantees? What happens in such cases?

2. Why would an advertiser pay a premium to have an ad appear on the back cover of a magazine?

LO10-3 Explain the advantages and disadvantages of newspaper advertising.

USING NEWSPAPERS IN THE MEDIA MIX

Who Uses Newspapers?

Newspapers are the fifth-largest medium (after digital, television, radio, and magazines) in terms of advertising volume.[17]

Consider these important facts:

- In 2016, there were 1,286 daily newspapers in the United States, with a total circulation of 35 million. The same year, the nation's 900 Sunday newspapers had a circulation of 40 million.[18]

- The average time spent on digital newspapers at the most highly circulated is a little more than 2 minutes.[19]

- In 2018, advertising revenue for newspapers was $14.3 billion, while circulation revenue was $11 billion.[20]

- In 2018, the share of newspaper ad revenue from digital advertising was 35 percent of all ad income, compared with 17 percent in 2011.[21]

Although the newspaper is the major community-serving medium for both news and advertising, more and more national advertisers are shifting to radio and television. As a result, radio and TV carry most of the national advertising in the United States, while the majority of newspaper advertising revenue comes from local advertising. Retail, cellular phone, and cable companies are the primary advertisers in newspapers.

"**SMALL BUSINESSES WITH EVEN SMALLER BUDGETS CAN BENEFIT FROM CREATIVE NEWSPAPER ADVERTISING.**"

The Pros and Cons of Newspaper Advertising

Print ads in general and newspapers in particular provide a unique, flexible medium for advertisers to express their creativity—especially with businesses that rely on local customers.

Newspapers offer advertisers many advantages. One of the most important is timeliness; an ad can appear very quickly, sometimes in just one day. Newspapers also offer geographic targeting, a broad range of markets, reasonable cost, and more. But newspapers suffer from lack of selectivity, poor production quality, and clutter. And readers criticize them for lack of depth and follow-up on important issues. For issues a media planner should keep in mind when considering newspapers, see My Ad Campaign 10–B.

LO10-4 Describe the major types of newspapers and how they charge for advertising.

How Newspapers Are Categorized

Newspapers can be classified by frequency of *delivery, physical size,* or *type of audience.*

Frequency of Delivery A **daily newspaper** is published as either a morning or evening edition at least five times a week, Monday through Friday. There are about 1,279 dailies in the United States, down from about 1,750 papers in 1970.[22] Morning editions tend to have broader geographic

The Pros and Cons of Newspaper Advertising [10–B]

The Pros
- **Mass medium** penetrating every segment of society. Most consumers read the newspaper.
- **Local medium** with broad reach. Covers a specific geographic area that comprises both a market and a community of people sharing common concerns and interest.
- **Comprehensive in scope**, covering an extraordinary variety of topics and interests.
- **Geographic selectivity** is possible with zoned editions for specific neighborhoods or communities.
- **Timeliness.** Papers primarily cover today's news and are read in one day.
- **Credibility.** Studies show that newspaper ads rank highest in believability. TV commercials are a distant second.
- **Selective attention** from the relatively small number of active prospects who, on any given day, are interested in what the advertiser is trying to tell them or sell them.
- **Creative flexibility.** An ad's physical size and shape can be varied to give the degree of dominance or repetition that suits the advertiser's purpose. The advertiser can use black and white, color, Sunday magazines, or custom inserts.

- **An active medium** rather than a passive one. Readers turn the pages, clip and save, write in the margins, and sort through the contents.
- **A permanent record**, in contrast to the ephemeral nature of radio and TV.
- **Reasonable cost.**

The Cons
- **Lack of selectivity** of specific socioeconomic groups. Most newspapers reach broad, diverse groups of readers, which may not match the advertiser's objectives.
- **Short life span.** Unless readers clip and save the ad or coupon, it may be lost forever.
- **Low production quality.** Coarse newsprint generally produces a less impressive image than the slick, smooth paper stock of magazines, and some newspapers can't print color.
- **Clutter.** Each ad competes with editorial content and with all the other ads on the same page or spread.
- **Lack of control** over where the ad will appear unless the advertiser pays extra for a preferred position.
- **Overlapping circulation.** Some people read more than one newspaper. Advertisers may be paying for readers they already reached in a different paper.

circulation and a larger male readership; evening editions are read more by women. The trend for more than a decade has been toward morning publication and away from evening.

With their emphasis on local news and advertising, **weekly newspapers** characteristically serve small urban or suburban residential areas and farm communities. A weekly newspaper's cost per thousand is usually higher than a daily paper's, but a weekly has a longer life and often has more readers per copy.

Physical Size

There are two basic newspaper formats, standard size and tabloid. The **standard-size newspaper** is about 22 inches deep and 13 inches wide and is divided into six columns. The **tabloid newspaper** is generally about 14 inches deep and 11 inches wide. National tabloid newspapers such as the *National Enquirer* and the *Star* use sensational stories to fight for single-copy sales. Other tabloids, such as the *New York Daily News*, emphasize straight news and features.

Newspapers used to offer about 400 different ad sizes. But in 1984, the industry introduced the **standard advertising unit (SAU)** system, which standardized the newspaper column width, page sizes, and ad sizes. An SAU **column inch** is $2^1/_{16}$ inches wide by 1 inch deep. There are now 56 standard ad sizes for standard papers and 32 for tabloids. Virtually all dailies converted to the SAU system and so did most weeklies.

Type of Audience

Some dailies and weeklies serve special-interest audiences, a fact not lost on advertisers. They generally contain advertising oriented to their special audiences, and they may have unique advertising regulations.

Some serve specific ethnic markets. Today, a number of dailies and weeklies are oriented to the African American community and others serve foreign-language groups. The most common non-English language in newspapers is Spanish in Spanish-language editions. The largest of these include *El Nuevo Herald*, *La Opinion*, and *El Diario La Prensa*.[23]

Specialized newspapers also serve business and financial audiences. *The Wall Street Journal*, the leading national business and financial daily, enjoys a circulation of nearly 1 million readers and ranks second to *USA Today* as the largest weekday newspaper in

the United States.[24] *The New York Times* has the largest Sunday circulation. Other papers cater to fraternal, labor union, or professional organizations, religious groups, or hobbyists.

Other Types of Newspapers

America has long had a love affair with the extra-large sized Sunday newspaper, a prime vehicle for advertising because of the time readers spend with it and its timing at the start of the week. In the United States, Sunday editions have a combined circulation of nearly 30 million.[25] Sunday newspapers generally combine standard news coverage with special functions like these:

- Increased volume of classified ads.

- Greater advertising and news volume.

- In-depth coverage of business, sports, real estate, literature and the arts, entertainment, and travel.

- Review and analysis of the past week's events.

- Expanded editorial and opinion sections.

Most Sunday newspapers also feature a **Sunday supplement** magazine. Some publish their own supplements, such as the *Los Angeles Magazine* of the *Los Angeles Times*. Other papers subscribe to syndicated supplements; *Parade* magazine has a readership of more than 54 million readers every week.[26]

Printed on heavier, coated paper stock, Sunday supplements are more conducive to color printing than newsprint, making them attractive to national advertisers who want better reproduction quality.

Another type of newspaper, the independent shopping guide or free community newspaper, offers advertisers local saturation. Sometimes called *pennysavers*, these **shoppers** offer free distribution and extensive advertising pages targeted at essentially the same audience as weekly newspapers—urban and suburban community readers. Readership is often high, and the publishers use hand delivery or direct mail to achieve maximum saturation.

North Americans also read national newspapers, including the *Globe and Mail* in Canada, *USA Today*, and the *Christian Science Monitor* in the United States. Additionally, the *New York Times* and the *Wall Street Journal* are circulated nationally.[27]

display advertising
Type of newspaper advertising that includes copy, illustrations or photographs, headlines, coupons, and other visual components.

reading notice (advertorial) A variation of a display ad designed to look like editorial matter. It is sometimes charged at a higher space rate than normal display advertising, and the law requires that the word *advertisement* appears at the top.

cooperative (co-op) advertising The sharing of advertising costs by the manufacturer and the distributor or retailer. The manufacturer may repay 50 or 100 percent of the dealer's advertising costs or some other amount based on sales.

classified ads Newspaper, magazine, and now Internet advertisements usually arranged under subheads that describe the class of goods or the need the ads seek to satisfy. Rates are based on the number of lines the ad occupies. Most employment, housing, and automotive advertising is in the form of classified advertising.

classified display ads Ads that run in the classified section of the newspaper but have larger-size type, photos, art borders, abundant white space, and sometimes color.

public notices For a nominal fee, newspapers carry these legal changes in business, personal relationships, public governmental reports, notices by private citizens and organizations, and financial reports.

preprinted inserts Newspaper advertisements printed in advance by the advertiser and then delivered to the newspaper plant to be inserted into a specific edition. Preprints are inserted into the fold of the newspaper and look like a separate, smaller section of the paper.

Newspapers create special sections. In turn, these are attractive to advertisers interested in their unique readership. The Sunday Times is Britain's largest selling Sunday newspaper. The Sunday Times also publishes several supplement magazines including The Sunday Times Rich List, The Sunday Times Magazine, and The Sunday Times Travel Magazine. The image above features another of these sections, the The Sunday Times Film and Screen Season.
Source: The Sunday Times

Types of Newspaper Advertising

The major classifications of newspaper advertising are *display*, *classified*, *public notices*, and *preprinted inserts*.

Display Advertising

Display advertising includes copy, illustrations or photos, headlines, coupons, and other visual components—such as the ads for the *Sunday Times* shown earlier. Display ads vary in size and appear in all sections of the newspaper except the first page of major sections, the editorial page, the obituary page, and the classified advertising section.

One common variation of the display ad, the **reading notice (or advertorials)**, looks like editorial matter and sometimes costs more than normal display advertising. To prevent readers from mistaking it for editorial matter, the word *advertisement* appears at the top.

As we discussed in Chapter 3, retailers often run newspaper ads through **cooperative (or co-op) advertising** programs sponsored by the manufacturers whose products they sell. The manufacturer pays fully or partially to create and run the ad, which features the manufacturer's product and logo along with the local retailer's name and address.

Classified Advertising

Classified ads provide a community marketplace for goods, services, and opportunities of every type, from real estate and new-car sales to employment and business opportunities. A newspaper's profitability often relies heavily on a large and healthy classified section. However, newspapers have been hit hard by the migration of classified ads to websites such as Craigslist and Monster.

Classified rates are typically based on how many lines the ad occupies and how many times the ad runs. Some newspapers accept **classified display ads**, which run in the classified section of the newspaper but feature larger type and/or photos, art borders, and sometimes even color.

Public Notices

For a nominal fee, newspapers carry legal **public notices** of changes in business and personal relationships, public governmental reports, notices by private citizens and organizations, and financial reports. These ads follow a preset format.

Preprinted Inserts

Like magazines, newspapers carry **preprinted inserts**. The advertiser prints the inserts and delivers them to the newspaper plant for insertion into a specific edition. Insert sizes range from a typical newspaper page to a double postcard; formats include catalogs, brochures, mail-back devices, and perforated coupons.

Some large metropolitan dailies allow advertisers to limit their inserts to specific circulation zones. A retail advertiser that wants to reach only those shoppers in its immediate trading area

Preprinted inserts give advertisers control over the quality of their catalogs and brochures. Newspapers distribute these inserts at a lower cost than mailing or door-to-door delivery.

Source: cjmacer/Shutterstock

can place an insert in the local-zone editions. Retail stores, car dealers, and large national advertisers are among those who find it less costly to distribute their circulars this way compared to mailing them or delivering them door to door.

An increasingly popular ad delivery method is a small sticker on the main section of the newspaper. It is removable and can double as a coupon. Guests at upscale Omni hotels found scented stickers on the front pages of their copies of *USA Today*. A blackberry aroma suggested that guests start the day with a cup of Starbucks "paired with a fresh muffin."[28]

HOW ADVERTISERS BUY NEWSPAPER SPACE

To get the most from the advertising budget, the media planner and buyer must know the characteristics of a newspaper's readership: the median age, sex, occupation, income, educational level, as well as buying habits of the typical reader.

Understanding Readership and Circulation

Readership information is available from various sources, such as Experian Simmons and Scarborough Research Corp. Most large papers also provide extensive data on their readers.

In single-newspaper cities, reader demographics typically reflect a cross-section of the general population. In cities with two or more newspapers, however, these characteristics may vary widely. The *Los Angeles Times* is directed to a broad cross-section of the community while *La Opinion* targets Los Angeles's large Hispanic population. For many years advertisers neglected diverse audiences in an effort to target middle-class, white consumers. Today's efforts to diversify advertising and make ads more inclusive has roots from the middle of the 20th Century, as show in the Ethical Issues box, "Edward Boyd."

Rate Cards
Like the magazine rate card, the newspaper **rate card** lists advertising rates, mechanical and copy requirements, deadlines, and other information. Because rates vary greatly, advertisers should calculate which papers deliver the most readers and the best demographics for their money.

Local versus National Rates
Most newspapers charge local and national advertisers at different rates. The **national rate** is usually significantly higher. Newspapers attribute higher rates to the added costs of serving national advertisers. For instance, an ad agency usually places national advertising and receives a 15 percent commission from the paper.

But many national advertisers reject the high rates and take their business elsewhere. Only 8 percent of all ad money now goes to newspapers.[30] In response to declining national advertising revenue, newspapers are experimenting with simplified billing systems and discount rates for their national clients.

Flat Rates and Discount Rates
Many national papers charge **flat rates**, which means they allow no discounts; a few newspapers offer a single flat rate to both national and local advertisers.

Newspapers that offer volume discounts have an **open rate** (their highest rate for a one-time insertion) and **contract rates**, whereby local advertisers can obtain discounts of up to 70 percent by signing a contract for frequent or bulk space purchases. **Bulk discounts** offer advertisers decreasing rates as they use more inches. Advertisers earn **frequency discounts** by running a given ad repeatedly in a specific time period. Similarly, advertisers can sometimes get **earned rates**, a discount applied retroactively as the volume of advertising increases through the year.

Short Rate
An advertiser who contracts to buy a specific amount of space during a one-year period at a discount and then

fails to fulfill the promise is charged a **short rate**, which is the difference between the contracted rate and the earned rate for the actual inches run. Conversely, an advertiser who buys more inches than contracted may be entitled to a rebate or credit.

Combination Rates   **Combination rates** are often available for placing a given ad in (1) morning and evening editions of the same newspaper; (2) two or more newspapers owned by the same publisher; and (3) in some cases, two or more newspapers affiliated in a syndicate or newspaper group.

ethical issues

Edward Boyd: Corporate America's Inclusion Trendsetter at Pepsi

Imagine a world in which ads never seem to be directed to you. For African American consumers, that description was not far from the mark until well into the 20th century.

The year 1947 proved a watershed for change in both sports and boardrooms. Most famously, it was the year that Jackie Robinson broke the color barrier to become the first Black player in major league baseball. Less well known, but in many ways just as importantly, it was the year that Ed Boyd was hired to improve Pepsi's marketing efforts with Black Americans. Donald M. Kendall, former CEO at Pepsi, noted, "Jackie Robinson may have made more headlines, but what Ed did—integrating the managerial ranks of corporate America—was equally groundbreaking."

Boyd was a 33-year-old executive at the National Urban League in New York City when he and a small group of Black salesmen were hired by Pepsi CEO Walter S. Mack. Tired of ads that depicted Blacks in unflattering and even racist ways, Boyd's team decided to create advertising that represented Blacks as ordinary Americans. For example, one series shared profiles of 20 great Black achievers, including Ralph Bunche, the 1950 winner of the Nobel Peace Prize. Another featured students at Black colleges. Still other ads showed Black middle-class families in grocery stores buying Pepsi. The common theme: Blacks shared the American Dream too, and their business was important.

Of course, the reality of America in the late 1940s was nowhere near as perfect as the view depicted in Pepsi's ads. As Boyd and his Black sales team traveled around the United States, they regularly encountered discrimination. The group rode on segregated trains and stayed in Black-only hotels. They even faced insults and discrimination from co-workers at Pepsi. At one point, the men received threats from the Ku Klux Klan.

But they persevered. In just a few short years, Boyd and his team produced results that exceeded Mack's expectations for increasing sales of Pepsi to Blacks. In her book on Boyd, *The Wall Street Journal* reporter Stephanie Capparell wrote that,

> On their way to nudging their country to a better place, the sales team helped define niche marketing some thirty years before it became a widespread business strategy. They gave formal talks to white drivers and salesmen about their role in the company, thereby instigating some of the earliest formalized diversity training. They also helped to instill in African Americans a unique sense of brand loyalty—to products produced by companies with a commitment to social progress as much as to product quality.[29]

On April 30, 2007, Boyd passed away, depriving the world of one of its great civil rights pioneers. Through his tireless and underappreciated efforts to bring Black consumers into the mainstream of American life, Boyd made history. He was practicing ethnic target marketing years before the business world would embrace such a strategy. He fundamentally altered the image that white Americans had of their Black neighbors. And he taught corporations an important lesson on the value of embracing inclusion, both within the corporate ranks and in choosing customers to serve.

Questions

1. Why do you think Boyd and his team chose the marketing strategy that they did to target Black Americans?
2. Who are some other ground breakers in marketing?

THE WALL STREET JOURNAL.

U.S. NATIONAL EDITION

CIRCULATION: 1,005,092

Published Monday through Saturday, the National Edition is a combination of the Eastern, Central and Western Editions. Insertion orders must specify National Edition and advertisement must appear in all editions within 30 days to be billed at the National Edition rate. National Edition advertising with option dates may appear on different dates in different editions.

FULL PAGE | NON-CONTRACT RATES

	PER COLUMN INCH RATE (GROSS)	BLACK & WHITE FULL-PAGE COST (GROSS)	COLOR FULL-PAGE COST (GROSS)
	$2,200.00	$277,200.00	$354,823.27

FULL PAGE | CONTRACT VOLUME RATES

WSJ FRANCHISE NET REVENUE CONTRACT	DISCOUNT	PER COLUMN INCH RATE (GROSS)	BLACK & WHITE FULL-PAGE COST (GROSS)	COLOR FULL-PAGE COST (GROSS)
$50,000	0.0%	$2,200.00	$249,480.00	$327,103.27
75,000	0.0%	2,200.00	249,480.00	327,103.27
125,000	0.0%	2,200.00	249,480.00	327,103.27
250,000	2.5%	2,145.00	243,243.00	318,925.71
325,000	5.8%	2,072.40	235,010.16	300,816.29
450,000	8.2%	2,019.60	229,022.64	293,152.41
700,000	10.5%	1,969.00	223,284.60	285,812.12
1,000,000	13.1%	1,911.80	216,798.12	277,507.77
1,250,000	15.0%	1,870.00	212,058.00	271,436.31
1,600,000	17.0%	1,826.00	207,068.40	265,053.98
2,100,000	19.0%	1,782.00	202,078.80	258,671.66
2,500,000	20.9%	1,740.20	197,338.68	252,594.12
3,100,000	22.9%	1,696.20	192,349.08	246,213.17
3,800,000	24.8%	1,654.40	187,608.96	241,473.05
5,200,000	27.3%	1,599.40	181,371.96	235,236.05

STANDARD UNITS | NON-CONTRACT RATES

COLUMN INCHES	OR	PAGE SIZE	BLACK & WHITE COST (GROSS)
18		1/7	$39,600.00
21		1/6	46,200.00
31.5		1/4	69,300.00
42		1/3	92,400.00
63		1/2	138,600.00
84		2/3	184,800.00
126		Full Page	277,200.00

- All rates are quoted in gross; only net spending accrues to contract fulfillment.
- All full-page rates are inclusive of 10% full-page discount for contract advertisers.
- Boundaries and circulation for all editions and regions are subject to change.

The rate card for *The Wall Street Journal* is similar to that for magazines. It shows the variety of ad units available and lists their costs. *The Wall Street Journal* offers advertisers many other ad opportunities across their digital platforms.

Source: Dow Jones & Company, Inc.

run-of-paper (ROP) advertising rates A term referring to a newspaper's normal discretionary right to place a given ad on any page or in any position it desires—in other words, where space permits. Most newspapers make an effort to place an ad in the position requested by the advertiser.

preferred-position rate A choice position for a newspaper or magazine ad for which a higher rate is charged.

full position In newspaper advertising, the preferred position near the top of a page or on the top of a column next to reading matter. It is usually surrounded by editorial text and may cost the advertiser 25 to 50 percent more than ROP rates.

split runs A feature of many newspapers (and magazines) that allows advertisers to test the comparative effectiveness of two different advertising approaches by running two different ads of identical size, but different content, in the same or different press runs on the same day.

News Media Alliance Trade organization representing major newspaper publishers and devoted to making advertising easier for its members

Run of Paper versus Preferred Position

Run-of-paper (ROP) advertising rates entitle a newspaper to place a given ad on any newspaper page or in any position it desires. Although the advertiser has no control over where the ad appears in the paper, most newspapers try to place an ad in the position the advertiser requests.

An advertiser can ensure a choice position for an ad by paying a higher **preferred-position rate**. A tire manufacturer, for example, may pay the preferred rate to ensure a position in the sports section.

There are also preferred positions on a given page. The preferred position near the top of a page or at the top of a column next to reading matter is called **full position**. It's usually surrounded by reading matter and may cost the advertiser 25 to 50 percent more than ROP rates.

Color Advertising

Color advertising is available in many newspapers on an ROP basis. Because of their high-speed presses and porous paper stock, newspapers are not noted for high-quality color printing. The cost of a color ad is usually based on the black-and-white rate plus an extra charge for each additional color.

Split Runs

Many newspapers (and magazines) offer **split runs** so that advertisers can test the *pulling power* of different ads. The advertiser runs two ads of identical size, but different content, for the same product on the same day in different press runs. The idea is to eliminate as many variables as possible. By measuring responses to the two ads, the advertiser is able to compare and contrast the effectiveness of each. For this service, newspapers typically charge extra and set a minimum space requirement.

Co-ops and Networks

As an aid to national advertisers, the NAB created the Newspaper Co-op Network (NCN). Salespeople from participating newspapers helped national advertisers line up retailers for dealer-listing ads. The advertiser would produce the ad and include a blank space for each paper to insert local retailers' names. The system also helped manufacturers manage local advertising tie-ins to national campaigns and themes. Before the development of NCN, national advertisers had to place ads and recruit local dealers individually.

Most newspapers and magazines have established websites that mirror their printed publications. Though traffic to these sites has increased dramatically, publishers have not yet succeeded in generating sufficient online ad revenue to offset the declines they have experienced in traditional media.

Source: NetPhotos/Alamy Stock Photo

In 1992, the Newspaper Advertising Bureau merged with the American Newspaper Publishers Association and five other marketing associations to form the Newspaper Association of America. The group then renamed itself in 2016 as the **News Media Alliance** and continues to simplify national newspaper ad buys. One major initiative in 1994 was the development of a *one-order, one-bill system* for national advertising, called the Newspaper National Network, allowing advertisers to make multimarket newspaper buys by placing one order. More recently, newspapers and magazines have joined the trend of participating in programmatic advertising, a system in which advertisers bid for desired audiences. We'll discuss programmatic more in Chapter 12. For now, it is best described as buying an audience through an auction that connects advertisers and content providers instantaneously. While this began with digital newspapers, it is moving to print too.[31]

Insertion Orders and Tearsheets

When advertisers place an ad, they submit an **insertion order** to the newspaper stating the date(s) on which the ad is to run, its size, the desired position, the rate, and the type of artwork accompanying the order.

When a newspaper creates ad copy and art, it gives the advertiser computer proofs to check. Most national advertising arrives at the newspaper *camera ready*, in the form of an electronic file. In an older time, newspaper ad people would tear out the page on which the ad appeared (known as a **tearsheet**) and send it to the agency or advertiser. Today everything is handled digitally.

LO10-5 Show how print media work with new technologies.

PRINT MEDIA AND NEW TECHNOLOGIES

With computers came revolutionary media options, such as the Internet and smartphones, challenging both traditional print media and advertisers to adapt. Newspapers and magazines are rushing to make alliances with cable, wireless telephone, and online companies to get a toehold in the interactive information market. The most important issues for any advertiser remain understanding how to effectively use the strengths, and minimize the weaknesses, of print media. Suggestions for doing this are offered in My Ad Campaign 10–C.

my ad campaign

Planning and Evaluating Print Media [10–C]

At this point in your project, you should have decided whether or not to use print (magazine and newspaper) as a communication vehicle. The next step is deciding which of the thousands of options makes the most sense for your client's brand.

The beauty of media planning and buying is that you have a blank slate from which to build your plan. As you start to build your plan, however, you need to consider what you are working toward. By answering a set of simple questions you can build the foundation of your recommendation. You should approach planning print media in the same way you would approach planning the brand strategy:

• Who do you want to reach?
• Why use print?
• What are the brand objectives?
• Where do you want to place your advertising to best achieve your objectives?
• How should you execute your plan?

When you have answered these questions, it is time to analyze and evaluate your opportunities and develop your plan.

Selecting publications requires both critical thinking and hard and fast numbers. For instance, monthly magazines can take up to 12 weeks to gain full readership (called to "cume" their audience). This can obviously be an issue if your communication objectives are centered on building reach quickly. On the other hand, weekly magazines cume their audience in approximately one to two weeks, making them great to generate reach around key events. Last, the number of insertions by title also depends on your strategy. If you are telling a sequenced story through three ads, then you need to plan for three insertions in each publication (pub). This will obviously be expensive and likely will reduce the number of pubs on the plan, ultimately limiting your reach.

The great thing about print advertising is that it offers a large number of opportunities for brands to engage consumers in niche environments, thereby limiting brand wastage. However, not all brands want or need such niche vehicles, and lucky for those brands there are more mass-oriented publications too:

Targeted Books	Mass Books
Golf	People
Field and Stream	TV Guide
American Baby	Parade
Ski	National Enquirer
Martha Stewart Living	Reader's Digest

Some of you will be focusing on large national advertisers and can utilize nearly all types of print options. But what opportunities exist for the local advertiser? First, newspapers are typically a staple of any large local advertiser. Second, most of the print publications that we have discussed thus far will allow you to layer in demogeographical targeting to help fine-tune your plan. Take this into account as you build your plan. It doesn't make sense to advertise in a national pub if your client is located only in the southeastern United States.

See My Ad Campaigns 10–A and 10–B for checklists of the pros and cons of magazine and newspaper advertising.

As you can see, common sense plays a major role in planning print campaigns, especially for large advertisers. But for other brands, advertising in print is a bit more difficult because the names of the targeted publications don't just roll off the tongue such as *Sports Illustrated* or *People*. To plan for those campaigns, most advertisers use syndicated research such as Media Mark's MRI product. This is a piece of planning software that indexes, through surveys, people's readership of tens of thousands of different publications. So when Microsoft wants to reach IT decision makers in the enterprise (in companies with more than 100 employees), MRI tells the media planner that she can find a high composition (concentration of overall readership) of that target in publications such as *eWeek, InformationWeek*, and *Baseline* magazine.

While we detail a number of tools in this chapter, for the large majority of projects access to these tools will be limited. Therefore, think about the medium in terms of the mindset of the readers when you place an ad in front of them. The closer you can get that mindset to match the category, industry, or association of your brand's product, the better off you are.

insertion order A form submitted to a newspaper or magazine when an advertiser wants to run an advertisement. This form states the date(s) on which the ad is to run, its size, the requested position, and the rate.

tearsheets The printed ad cut out and sent by the publisher to the advertiser as a proof of the ad's print quality and that it was published.

Tom Grill/Corbis

By now, virtually all metropolitan news organizations and national magazines have an online presence. News organizations are information-rich, and much of the specialized information they don't run in the paper or the magazine fits perfectly with the online world's narrower interests. Hundreds of highly targeted, upstart sites are showing up on the web, along with magazines created by users on sites such as Flipboard. They are all, however, still trying to figure out how best to incorporate advertising into their new ventures. Initially, most ads were banners or pop-ups, but now online publications are offering pushdowns, floating ads, billboards, interstitials, videos, native ads, and more.

Time will tell whether digital advertising dollars will ever offset what newspapers and magazines are losing in print advertising.

For now, publishers are looking to increase revenues generated by digital subscriptions. Divergent trends seem to be happening in the industry. Large brands such as the *The New York Times*, *The Wall Street Journal*, and *The Washington Post* remain viable and even profitable. The purchase of the *Post* by Amazon CEO Jeff Bezos has given hope to the industry.[32]

Unfortunately, some of the profitability that the *Post* has enjoyed relies less on news as a product and more on the paper providing content management technologies to other companies. This, of course, is not a forte of small, local papers. So the other trend is the collapse of these important news sources. As of 2020, one of the largest newspaper chains, McClatchy, has filed for bankruptcy, and most prognosticators believe the future of newspapers looks dim.[33]

check yourself ✓

1. Why might an advertiser print an insert to be delivered with a newspaper rather than just buying a standard page in a newspaper? Why doesn't the advertiser just mail or deliver the insert separately?

2. What changes in the newspaper industry could reverse its current course?

ENDNOTES

1. Daniel de Vise, "Number of U.S. Adults with College Degrees Hits Historic High," *The Washington Post*, February 23, 2012, www.washingtonpost.com/national/higher-education/number-of-us-adults-with-college-degrees-hits-historic-high/2012/02/23/glQAi80bWR_story.html.

2. Rick Edmonds, "Newspapers: By the Numbers," State of the News Media 2013, May 7, 2013.

3. Newspaper Fact Sheet, 2018.

4. FIPP, "Publishers, This Is the Real Reason Why Newspapers Are Losing to Facebook," *WNIP*, July 2019, https://whatsnewinpublishing.com/publishers-this-is-the-real-reason-why-newspapers-are-losing-to-facebook.

5. Tom Rosenstiel, Mark Jurkowitz and Hon Ji, "The Search for a New Business Model," Pew Research Center, March 5, 2012, www.journalism.org/2012/03/05/search-new-business-model.

6. Nwspapers Fact Sheet, Pew Research Center, July 9, 2019, https://www.journalism.org/fact-sheet/newspapers/

7. Frank Pallotta, "Wall Street Journal Hit with Layoffs That Could Top 100," *CNN Money*, June 18, 2015, http://money.cnn.com/2015/06/18/media/wall-street-journal-layoffs; Lukas I. Alpert, "*New York Times* Slows Decline of Advertising Revenue in 2014," *The Wall Street Journal*, February 3, 2015, www.wsj.com/articles/new-york-times-slows-decline-of-advertising-revenue-in-2014-1422998864; Roger Yu, "Gannett Q 1 Earnings Rise 4% due to Digital Unit Revenue Gain,"

USA Today, April 23, 2015, www.usatoday.com/story/money/2015/04/21/gannett-q1-earnings-rise/26115571.

8. "US Advertising Media Market Sizes and Projections, 2016–2020," *Marketing Charts*, June 14, 2016, www.marketingcharts.com/featured-68214/attachment/pwc-us-ad-media-market-sizes-2016-v-2020.

9. "List of Defunct American Magazines," *Wikipedia*, https://en.wikipedia.org/wiki/List_of_defunct_American_magazines.

10. Frédéric Filloux, "How Can We Stop Publishers Inflating Circulation?" *The Guardian*, October 17, 2011, www.theguardian.com/media/pda/2011/oct/17/publishers-inflating-circulation.

11. Shu-Fen Li, John C. Schweitzer, and Benjamin J. Bates, "Effectiveness of Trade Magazine Advertising," paper presented to the annual conference of the Association for Education in Journalism and Mass Communication, Montreal, Quebec, August 1992.

12. Tony Silber, "Big Ideas For A Magazine Newsstand Industry In Distress," *Forbes*, May 29, 2018, www.forbes.com/sites/tonysilber/2018/05/29/big-ideas-for-a-magazine-newsstand-industry-in-distress/#28da1dc95930.

13. Gene Willhoft, "Is 'Added Value' Valuable?" *Advertising Age*, March 1, 1993, p. 18.

14. AARP The Magazine Rates & Dates, https://advertise.aarp.org/aarp-advertising-rates/the-magazine/?region=1&edition=1; Reader's Digest Rates & Data, 2017, www.readersdigest.co.uk/media/RD_Ad_Rates_%26_Data_2017.pdf.

15. Lisa I. Fried, "New Rules Liven Up the Rate-Card Game," *Advertising Age*, October 24, 1994, p. S8.

16. "People Magazine 2016 Rate Card," effective January 1, 2016, https://static.people.com/people/static/mediakit/media/pdf/ratecard.pdf.

17. "U.S. Advertising Media Markets Size ($B), 2018–2022," *Marketing Charts*, www.marketingcharts.com/featured-104785/attachment/pwc-us-ad-market-sizes-2018-2022-june2018.

18. "Number of Daily Newspapers in the United States from 1970 to 2016," *Statista*, September 3, 2019, www.statista.com/statistics/183408/number-of-us-daily-newspapers-since-1975; Sue Guaglione, "U.S. Daily Newspaper Circulation Fell 8% In 2016," *Publisher's Daily*, June 2, 2017, www.mediapost.com/publications/article/302240/us-daily-newspaper-circulation-fell-8-in-2016.html.

19. "Newspapers Fact Sheet," Pew Research Center, July 9, 2019, www.journalism.org/fact-sheet/newspapers.

20. "Newspapers Fact Sheet," Pew Research Center, July 9, 2019, www.journalism.org/fact-sheet/newspapers.

21. "Newspapers Fact Sheet," Pew Research Center, July 9, 2019, www.journalism.org/fact-sheet/newspapers.

22. Amy Weston, "Number of Daily Newspapers in the United States from 1970 to 2018," *Statista*, March 3, 2020, www.statista.com/statistics/183408/number-of-us-daily-newspapers-since-1975.

23. Katerina Eva Matsa, "Hispanic Media: Fact Sheet," in *State of the News Media 2015*, Pew Research Center, April 29, 2015, www.journalism.org/2015/04/29/hispanic-media-fact-sheet.

24. Amy Watson, "Leading Newspapers in the U.S. 2017–2019, by circulation," *Statista*, September 13, 2019, www.statista.com/statistics/184682/us-daily-newspapers-by-circulation.

25. "Newspapers Fact Sheet," Pew Research Center, July 9, 2019, www.journalism.org/fact-sheet/newspapers.

26. "About Us," *Parade* website, https://parade.com/about-us.

27. "List of Newspapers in the United States," *Wikipedia*, https://en.wikipedia.org/wiki/List_of_newspapers_in_the_United_States.

28. Stuart Elliott, "Joint Promotion Adds Stickers to Sweet Smell of Marketing," *The New York Times*, April 2, 2007, www.nytimes.com/2007/04/02/business/media/02adcol.html?_r=1&ref=media.

29. Stephanie Capparell, *The Real Pepsi Challenge: How One Pioneering Company Broke Color Barriers in 1940s American Business* (Free Press, 2008).

30. "Total US Ad Spending to See Largest Increase since 2004," *eMarketer*, July 2014, www.emarketer.com/Article/Total-US-Ad-Spending-See-Largest-Increase-Since-2004/1010982.

31. Michael Sebastian, "Well, This Is Different—Time Inc. Now Selling Print Ads Programmatically," *Time*, February 10, 2015, retrieved at: http://adage.com/article/media/time-selling-print-ads-programmatically/297057.

32. Sissy Cao, "The Washington Post's Most Valuable Asset Is Now Its Software, Thanks to Jeff Bezos," *Observer*, October 3, 2019, https://observer.com/2019/10/jeff-bezos-washington-post-publishing-software-arc-licensing-bp-media-revenue.

33. Claire Duffy, "After McClatchy Bankruptcy, Reporter Julie K. Brown Urges Americans to Subscribe to Local Newspapers," *CNN Business*, February 16, 2020, www.cnn.com/2020/02/16/media/mcclatchy-bankruptcy-reliable-sources/index.html.

chapter eleven

audio and
video media

Darren Greenwood/Design Pics

This chapter presents the important factors advertisers need to evaluate when considering the use of broadcast, cable, and satellite media in the creative mix. Each medium has its own characteristics, advantages, and drawbacks. Advertisers must be able to compare their merits and understand the most cost-effective ways to buy advertising time.

M&M's started with a bang, literally, as Forrest Mars invented them after seeing soldiers gulp Smarties, a coated English chocolate candy while fighting in the Spanish Civil War. Back in the United States, Mars created his own version, M&M's, named for his father, Forrest E. Mars

and Bruce Murrie, son of Hershey's president William Murrie.

Mars had noticed that the soldiers loved that the candy did not melt when transported, even in heat—hence, he created a slogan that perfectly captured the brand's USP, "melts in your mouth, not in your hand." The candy's sales soared.

But by the 1990s, some of the marketing magic was wearing thin and sales faltered. Mars chose a new ad agency to try to turn things around, picking one of the best, BBDO. Creative director Susan Credle immediately grasped that flagging sales were a result of weak branding. "They'd become just candy. An aisle store candy brand versus an icon brand."

The solution was the introduction of six funny brand "advocates." Yellow is "plump, yellow, and all smiles" whose best friend is Red "because he seems to know a lot." Red has a hidden talent

continued on p. 274

LEARNING OBJECTIVES

After studying this chapter, you will be able to:

LO11-1 Describe the advantages and disadvantages of video as an advertising medium.

LO11-2 Discuss the various options for advertising in video.

LO11-3 Explain how to measure video audiences and select the best vehicles to buy.

LO11-4 List the advantages and disadvantages of audio media for advertisers.

LO11-5 Review the options for advertising in audio media and how listeners are measured.

DID SOMEONE SAY RED?

"Everything is under control"

AGE

He says 30-something, but we're checking on it.

GENDER

Male

WEIGHT

Perfect for his shell size

TURN-ONS

When people blindly follow his advice

BEST FEATURE

Genius IQ & physical prowess (the best of both worlds)

SHORTCOMINGS

Thinks he knows more than he does.

HIDDEN TALENTS

Turns simple chores into complicated tasks.

Marvelous eyebrows.

Source: Mars, Incorporated

continued from p. 273

of turning "simple chores into complicated tasks" and thinks his best features are "genius IQ and physical prowess." Orange has a dream "to be on the endangered species list" and is turned off by "people who want to eat him." Blue dislikes "squares, man . . . squares" and lists his turn-ons as "moonlit nights, jazz" and "the ladies." Ms. Brown claims her best attribute is "her big beautiful brain" and her hidden talent is "always being right." Finally, Green insists that she "melts for no one" and owns up to the shortcoming that she "can sometimes be intimidating."

These iconic figures have provided M&M's with nearly two decades of great TV and cinema advertising, including a beloved spot in Super Bowl LI where Red, wishing to become human, turns into Danny DeVito. More importantly, they have helped M&M's become America's best-selling candy.

Susan Credle has some advice for advertisers who intend to use video: "Dream bigger, build legacies, be ambitious." The willingness of Mars and BBDO to dream big and be ambitious are why fictional candy figures are among the most well-known "celebrities" across the world. ■

VIDEO MEDIA

Back in 1950, U.S. advertisers spent $171 million, or about 3 percent of total U.S. advertising volume, on television. It didn't take long, though, for marketers to discover the power of this new medium to reach mass audiences quickly, powerfully, and frequently. TV also offered unique creative opportunities to imbue their brands with personality like never before. In 2018, more than $72 billion was spent on broadcast and cable TV advertising. That, however, may represent the peak, as spending is now in a slow decline and is expected to be only $69 billion by 2023.[1]

But while spending on TV may be in decline, spending on video—a broader concept that includes broadcast and cable but also other formats—is expected to continue to climb. Video is still king, whether it is consumed as television or in some other form. For more on considerations in buying video (and audio) see My Ad Campaign 11–A.

Television networks and stations are available to advertisers in four principal forms: broadcast, cable, satellite, and a newer form referred to as OTT. Broadcast networks can reach audiences by transmitting electromagnetic waves through the air across some geographic territory. Cable networks reach audiences exclusively through cable systems. OTT delivers TV

my ad campaign

Planning and Buying Video and Audio [11–A]

Media planners use a variety of syndicated and proprietary research tools to plan and buy both video and audio ads. Primarily these tools help identify the larger concentrations (composition) of a target audience in specific programming and the cost associated with those audiences. The complexity of buying audio and video arises from the need to bring cost-efficient advertising to a target audience with an effective frequency.

In traditional cable and broadcast TV and radio, the currency is a ratings point, which represents 1 percent of the target audience a media buyer is trying to reach. Both TV and radio, therefore, are bought based on demographics. So when certain prime-time shows have a rating of 14 for A25–49, it means that a particular program reaches 14 percent of all adults between the ages of 25 and 49. A buyer's cost per point (CPP) is her way of determining a vehicle's (program's) efficiency in delivering her target audience. As this chapter will explain, ratings points are additive. Therefore, two spots on shows with 14 targeted ratings points means that the advertiser has purchased 28 gross ratings points or GRPs.

Most of you will not have access to the types of tools that help you plan and optimize broadcast media plans, so your focus should be on the merits of each of these media in achieving your marketing and advertising objectives and how they match your overall media strategies. First, we will discuss the advantages and nonmonetary value of video and then of audio.

Video

Video is the largest mass medium: 121 million homes in America have at least one TV set, 273 Americans own a smartphone, 185 million use a tablet, and and nearly 3/4 of all homes have a desktop or laptop.

However, it is a fragmented marketplace. Three hundred hours of video are uploaded to YouTube every hour and the average home receives more than 118 different cable channels. The viewing choices are a mix of ad-supported (YouTube, Roku Channel, Crackle) and ad-free (Netflix, HBO Max, Disney+).

When home video first appeared in the form of broadcast television in the mid-twentieth century, it was largely used as a mass medium. Over time, however, advertisers have gained greater ability to segment viewers, beginning with the advent of cable and now with OTT.

Video is the best medium to generate excitement around a brand, whether that is with internal constituents (employees) or external audiences. As proclaimed by Marshall McLuhan in his book *Understanding Media: The Extensions of Man,* the medium is the message. In video, this message can run the gamut from an exciting Super Bowl commercial to the entertaining toy reviews of a 6-year-old on YouTube (Ryan Kaji, the star of the YouTube channel Ryan's World, earned an estimated $11 million in 2017).

Audio

Like video, audio began as a broadcast medium (terrestrial radio) and has morphed in the digital age.

The earliest instance of audio is radio, which began in the first decades of the twentieth century and continues as a popular medium today. Historically, radio has been more efficient than TV; CPPs (cost per ratings point) are sometimes 1/10 that of TV. Radio spots are inexpensive to produce; in fact typically all you need is copy and talent, making the lead time to go live with radio as short as one to two weeks. It also happens to be more promotional in nature—stations typically have a loyal audience following and advertisers can usually be a part of any local station events and get the station personalities to endorse the brand. Testimonials, and especially personality testimonials, can be very valuable to advertisers that are looking to build legitimacy in themselves or their products.

Audio has moved beyond broadcast radio in a number of ways, many of which are being exploited by advertisers. Satellite radio, in the form of SiriusXM, provides national reach for a medium many advertisers considered local. Audio books and especially podcasts are the latest exciting platforms for audio content. The 4A's reports that advertising revenue from podcasts grew 53 percent from 2017 to 2018 and is expected to continue double digit growth for the foreseeable future.[2]

on demand over the Internet through devices such as Google Chrome, Roku, and Amazon Fire.

What is OTT? It includes video that is not television as traditionally defined, such as YouTube, TikTok, Netflix, Vimeo, Hulu, and Twitch. These platforms may be viewed on a television but are more commonly accessed through phones, tablets, or computers. These "non-TV" video sites are the source of much interest among advertisers as they are favored by younger, more technologically savvy consumers.

Broadcast

Prior to the Internet, broadcast television grew faster than any other advertising medium in history. As both a news and entertainment medium, it caught people's fancy very quickly. From its beginnings after World War II, broadcast TV was the first at-home medium that offered sight, sound, and motion. People could stay home and still go to the movies. As TV's legions of viewers grew, the big advertisers quickly discovered they could communicate with consumers across the country and sell products like never before. And TV was ideal for building an image for their brands—even better than magazines, which had previously been the image-building medium of choice. It didn't take long for marketers to switch their budgets from radio, newspapers, and magazines.

Nielsen estimates that there are nearly 121 million U.S. TV homes[3] and about 1,370 commercial VHF (very high frequency, channels 2 through 13) and UHF (ultrahigh frequency, channels 14 and above) stations.[4] Stations in the United States operate as independents unless they are affiliated with one of the national networks (ABC, NBC, CBS, Fox, CW). Both network affiliates and independent stations may subscribe to nationally syndicated programs as well as originate their own programming. However, increasing competition from cable TV is taking viewers from the national network programs. To compensate, some networks invest in cable TV systems or start their own. For example, NBC (which is owned by GE) started CNBC and MSNBC, and ABC (owned by Disney) owns a piece of ESPN, Lifetime, A&E, and other cable channels.

Cable

For more than 30 years, broadcast TV, especially network TV, was the dominant entertainment medium for most Americans. Today, other electronic media have dramatically changed that dominance. Chief among the challengers is cable television.

Cable TV began in the late 1940s. Initially, it was designed to provide TV service to areas with poor reception such as rural or mountainous regions. But in the 1970s, the advent of satellite TV signals, the proliferation of channels, and the introduction of uncut first-run movies via premium cable channels such as Home Box Office (HBO) and Showtime made cable TV more attractive to all viewers.

At first, many subscribers valued cable simply for the full array of regional channels and access to premium services such as HBO. But once this novelty wore off, subscribers wanted more. A variety of advertiser-supported cable networks soon appeared with specialized programming in arts, history, sports, news, cooking, and comedy, along with diversified pay services and many more local shows. All of this attracted more and more subscribers—and consequently drew viewers away from the big broadcast networks.

For three decades, cable's growth was been extraordinary. In 1975, only 13 percent of TV households in the United States had cable. By 2013 the Consumer Electronics Association estimates that 83 percent of American households get cable. That may end up being the high water mark however, as cable penetration has been in decline because of **cord-cutting**, the practice of discontinuing cable television and switching to Internet video services. The move of video viewers away from traditional cable continues to pick up steam and represents a significant change to the industry.[5] After years of losses (cable and satellite providers lost 6 million subscribers in 2019 alone, see Exhibit 11–1) the industry has changed tactics and sought to accommodate the new trend through a focus high-speed internet offerings and other services.[6]

Even as cable declines there still remain more than 100 ad-supported national cable networks in the United States and a

The growth in cable and satellite TV systems has dramatically increased the number of channels available to viewers. This has given consumers almost unlimited program alternatives, making it easier for advertisers to reach a more selective audience.

Thomas Eversley/Alamy Stock Photo

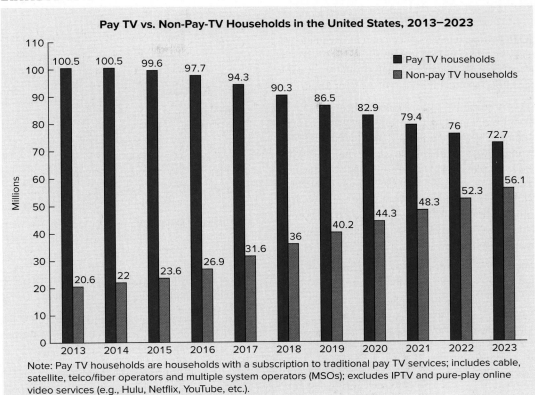

Pay TV vs. Non-Pay-TV Households in the United States, 2013–2023

Legend: ■ Pay TV households ■ Non-pay TV households

Year	Pay TV households	Non-pay TV households
2013	100.5	20.6
2014	100.5	22
2015	99.6	23.6
2016	97.7	26.9
2017	94.3	31.6
2018	90.3	36
2019	86.5	40.2
2020	82.9	44.3
2021	79.4	48.3
2022	76	52.3
2023	72.7	56.1

(Y-axis: Millions)

Note: Pay TV households are households with a subscription to traditional pay TV services; includes cable, satellite, telco/fiber operators and multiple system operators (MSOs); excludes IPTV and pure-play online video services (e.g., Hulu, Netflix, YouTube, etc.).

Source: eMarketer

substantial number of regional networks.[7] Exhibit 11-2 lists the most highly rated. There are also a handful of *superstations* (such as TBS Atlanta) and local, over-the-air TV stations whose signals are delivered via satellite to cable systems across the country and that carry some national advertising. In the 2010s, cable channels have found it increasingly profitable to develop unique content, including highly popular shows such as AMC's *Walking Dead* and HBO's *Game of Thrones*. The latter finished its popular run in 2019 to 44 million viewers, shattering previous cable ratings records.[8]

▼ **EXHIBIT 11-2** Most viewed cable networks by total viewers of 2019.

Rank	Network	Total Viewers (millions)
1	Fox News	2.5
2	ESPN	1.8
3	MSNBC	1.7
4	ION	1.3
5	HGTV	1.3
6	Univision	1.3
7	Hallmark Channel	1.3
8	USA	1.2
9	Telemundo	1.2
10	History	1.2

Source: Michael Schneider, "Most Watched Television Networks: Ranking 2019's Winners and Losers," *Variety*, December 26, 2019, https://variety.com/2019/tv/news/network-ratings-top-channels-fox-news-espn-cnn-cbs-nbc-abc-1203440870.

Satellite

Satellite, like broadcast TV, provides a wireless signal to households; although, unlike broadcast, it requires a subscription. For this reason, the quality of the signal depends on several factors, including the degree to which access of the receiver to the satellite signal is unobstructed. The satellites themselves orbit in a stationary part of space known as the Clarke Belt, situated a bit over 20,000 miles from Earth.[9]

There are pros and cons of adopting satellite TV, which has limited its growth. *Tech2Blog* suggests the pros include picture quality, cost, and accessibility. Countering these benefits are reliability, the need to install complicated hardware, and a requirement of a clear line-of-sight from the home to the satellite.[10]

The same cord-cutting pressure affecting cable has hit satellite companies such as Dish Network and Direct TV. The two companies combined have hemorrhaged subscribers in recent years, leading to talk of a merger.[11]

OTT (Over-the-Top Video)

Over-the-top (OTT) video refers to video content streamed over the Internet. It can include stand-alone platforms such as Netflix or YouTube, as well as packages of channels available on cable provided by companies such as Hulu, YouTube TV, or Sling.

OTT has become very attractive to cord-cutters because it allows them to customize the channels and platforms they watch, often for less money than a cable subscription. It also facilitates video-on-demand viewing, allowing people to view what and when they want to. The large players in OTT also provide unique content not available on cable or broadcast TV. These players as of 2020 include Netflix, Hulu, Disney+, AppleTV+, and Amazon Prime Video, along with smaller companies such as Acorn, Crackle, and Tubi. Streaming providers generate revenue via subscription fees, advertising revenue, or both.

Many people watch OTT content on televisions, but even more access it through phones, tablets, computers, and third-party devices such as Apple TV, Amazon Firestick, Google Chromecast, or Roku devices. It is estimated that OTT now has an adoption rate of 51 percent in North America, so it is here to stay and still has room to grow.[12]

While OTT has clear benefits for consumers, it also has qualities that make it attractive to advertisers. Generally, OTT services share much more information about viewers with advertisers than do other viewing methods. For example, advertisers know the exact location of a household, which means OTT can incorporate geographic segmentation into TV. And they can also discover demographic information from the streaming company or even by just using a subscriber's e-mail to link to external databases. Advertisers even know what type of device a viewer is using to watch, from a smartphone to a 75-inch OLED TV.

All of that knowledge would be useful under any circumstances, but it is especially useful in the context of another OTT benefit: ads are customized for each household. So the demographic and geographic information can be used to customize ads that uniquely address consumer wants and needs.

Video Audience Trends

As a way to reach a mass audience, no other medium today has the unique creative abilities of video: the combination of sight, sound, and motion; the opportunity to demonstrate the product; the potential to use special effects; the empathy of the viewer; and the believability for viewers of seeing it happen right before their

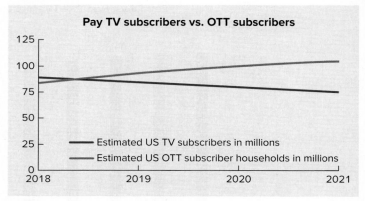

▼ **EXHIBIT 11–3** Trends in pay-TV versus OTT subscribers, 2018–2021.

Pay TV subscribers vs. OTT subscribers

— Estimated US TV subscribers in millions
— Estimated US OTT subscriber households in millions

Source: John D. Markman, "Google, Amazon Join Forces to Win the Streaming-TV Wars," *Weiss Ratings*, October 7, 2019, https://weissratings.com/articles/google-amazon-join-forces-to-win-the-streaming-tv-wars.

eyes (see My Ad Campaign 11-B, "The Pros and Cons of Broadcast and Cable TV Advertising").

As Exhibit 11-3 shows, the move toward OTT is well underway in the United States. The trend comes at the cost of subscribers to cable and satellite.[13]

Confirming the importance of OTT are usage statistics for its biggest channel: YouTube. Alphabet, the parent company of both YouTube and Google, reports that 8 out of 10 consumers in the highly desired (to advertisers) 18–49-year-old demographic visit the site each month. Just as impressive, nearly 2 billion people stream YouTube content monthly.[14]

The heaviest viewers of broadcast TV are middle-income, high school–educated individuals and their families, so most programming is directed at this group. People with considerably higher incomes and more education typically make use of a more diverse range of media and entertainment options.

U.S. adults watch a lot of TV, but the amount of time spent with the medium varies considerably by age group. Nielsen reported in 2019 that while consumers 65 and older spent more than seven hours a day watching, people 18–34 watched for less than two hours a day.[15]

Cable seems to reach an audience that is difficult to get to in any other way. Whereas other media that provide news are struggling, cable news is highly profitable and attracts relatively large audiences.[16] Conversely, broadcast is still the choice for advertisers looking to reach a broad, nationwide audience.

Comstock/Stockbyte/Getty Images

The Pros and Cons of Broadcast and Cable TV Advertising [11–B]

The Pros

Contemporary broadcast and cable television offers advertisers many advantages over competing media.

- **Mass coverage.** A full 98 percent of all U.S. homes have a TV (most have more than one), and viewing time for the average household averages more than eight hours. Cable TV is present in 73 percent of U.S. homes.
- **Relatively low cost.** Despite the often huge initial outlays for commercial production and advertising time, TV's equally huge audiences mean the cost per exposure is competitive with other media.
- **Selectivity.** Broadcast television audiences vary a great deal depending on the time of day, day of the week, and nature of the programming. Advertising messages can be presented when potential customers are watching, and advertisers can reach select geographic audiences by buying local and regional markets. Cable TV's offerings tend to segment audiences quite well: Nickleodeon = kids, ESPN = male sports fans, Fox Business = business people.
- **Impact.** Television offers a kind of immediacy that other forms of advertising cannot achieve: displaying and demonstrating the product with sound, motion, and full color right before the customer's eyes.
- **Creativity.** The various facets of the TV commercial—sight, sound, motion, and color—permit infinite original and imaginative appeals.
- **Prestige.** Because the public considers TV the most authoritative and influential medium, it offers advertisers a prestigious image. Hallmark, Xerox, Coca-Cola, and IBM increase their prestige by regularly sponsoring cultural programs on network TV.

The Cons

Sometimes broadcast TV just doesn't "fit" the creative mix because of cost, lack of audience selectivity, inherent brevity, or the clutter of competitive messages.

- **High production cost.** TV commercials are costly. Depending on the creative approach, the cost of filming a national commercial today may run from $200,000 to more than $1 million.
- **High airtime cost.** The average cost of a prime-time network commercial ranges from $100,000 to $400,000. Special attractions like the Super Bowl cost more than $5 million. The cost of wide coverage, even at low rates, prices small- and medium-size advertisers out of the market.
- **Limited data.** The audience for broadcast and cable TV shows is defined quite broadly relative to what can be discovered about Internet users or OTT viewers. Research company Nielsen provides information about viewers as a group (e.g., the percentage of viewers aged 18–49 watching a show) but cannot provide advertisers information about a specific household in that group.
- **Brevity.** Studies show that most TV viewers can't remember the product or company in the most recent TV ad they watched—even if it was within the last five minutes. Recall improves with the length of the commercial; people remember 60-second spots better than 30-second spots.
- **Clutter.** TV advertising is usually surrounded by station breaks, credits, and public service announcements, as well as six or seven other spots. All these messages compete for attention, so viewers become annoyed and confused and often misidentify the product.
- **Zipping and zapping.** DVR users who skip through commercials when replaying recorded programs are zipping; remote-control users who change channels at the beginning of a commercial breaks are zapping. In either case, the ads are avoided.

> As a way to reach a mass audience, no other medium today has the unique creative abilities of television.

National advertisers have been using cable since the late 1970s, and cable advertising revenues have grown steadily, reaching more than $28 billion in 2018.[17] One reason is that cable's upscale audience buys proportionately more goods and services than noncable subscribers (see Exhibit 11-4). Procter & Gamble traditionally spends the most on network cable. However, local retailers also find local cable a good place to advertise.

Nielsen studies indicate that the average U.S. household receives 189 TV channels. A larger number of channels, however,

Source: Ken Cavanagh/McGraw-Hill

Cable versus Noncable Household Characteristics			
Upscale Profiles	**Cable HH vs. U.S. Average (Index)**	**Noncable HH vs. U.S. Average (Index)**	**% Advantage Cable HH**
Occupation: Professional	108	88	+23%
Education: Graduated college+	110	85	+29%
Occupation: Management/financial	105	93	+13%
Household income: $75,000+	112	80	+40%
Value of home: $500,000+	109	87	+25%
Downscale Profiles	**Cable HH vs. U.S. Average (Index)**	**Noncable HH vs. U.S. Average (Index)**	**% Advantage Cable HH**
Education: Did not graduate HS	86	122	−30%
Employment: Not working	99	101	−2%
Occupation: Construction/maintenance	87	120	−17%
Household Income: <$20,000	87	121	−28%
Value of Home: <$60,000	83	127	−35%

Source: Cable Viewer Summary, Cable TV Advertising Bureau, 2018.

doesn't translate into more TV viewing. The Nielsen data indicate that the more channels a household has, the lower the percentage of channels watched. Households with the most channels (more than 150) tuned in to only 16.[18]

While there is no doubt that media play an ever-expanding role in our daily lives, there is a finite limit to the number of advertising exposures people can absorb. When that limit is reached, any new media will simply be fighting for market share. This is the reason for the increasing fragmentation of the audience and the precipitous decline in the huge share of audience once held by the broadcast networks. This is also why media buyers and planners are growing in importance as advertisers search for the elusive audience and fight for their share of that audience in an overcrowded media environment.

The Impact of OTT

There is no question that broadcast networks and cable providers are looking over their shoulders at the rapid growth of OTT. In fact, the tipping point may have already arrived; a 2019 report from Harris suggests that more Americans spend the majority of their time watching OTT than cable.[19] Another sign that OTT is the future of mass video is the fact that networks and cable companies have both found ways to benefit from the delivery system. In the case of broadcasters, the trend is toward their own form of streaming service. For example, NBC's Peacock service, launching in 2020, will come with a mix of ad-free and ad-supported tiers. And cable companies will continue to benefit from OTT so long as viewers stream shows over cable Internet services.

The audience for OTT is broad, with more than 50 percent of all age groups using it. That said, the total audience skews young, as OTT is used by 65 percent of those aged 18–34. One somewhat surprising audience trend is a preference for shows developed for traditional TV. In spite of the millions spent on original programming by Netflix, Hulu, and Amazon Prime, the most popular OTT streamed shows are *The Walking Dead*, *Game of Thrones*, *Big Bang Theory*, *NCIS*, and *Grey's Anatomy*. This suggests that what OTT users most desire, besides savings over cable, is the ability to watch on demand.[20] See more about the pros and cons of OTT in My Ad Campaign 11–C, "The Pros and Cons of OTT Advertising."

Multiple Screens: Video and Social Media

The experience of video and of the advertisements that appear in the medium have been transformed by social media. People still gather the day after a favorite show airs to discuss what happened the night before to their favorite characters. But increasingly, they satisfy the need to share by "discussing" online as the show airs, connected through their favorite social media platform. These discussions, in turn, provide sponsors the chance to reach out to social media communities.

How prevalent is social media use during television? A recent survey of respondents in the United States, United Kingdom, Germany, Spain, Sweden, China, and Taiwan suggests that 62 percent of global audiences use social networks while watching TV. In addition, 25 percent of viewers report that they discuss what they are watching in social media.[21] Twitter

my ad campaign

The Pros and Cons of OTT Advertising [11–C]

The Pros

- **Selectivity.** OTT allows advertisers to deliver ads to viewers via programmatic (auction-based) buying methods. In programmatic buys, advertisers buy audiences rather than programs.
- **Audience data.** OTT platforms such as Hulu amass large quantities of data about its subscribers. Hulu even allows viewers to make choices about the ads they see. The cost of a smaller reach may be more than offset by targeting a more responsive market.
- **Rapid growth.** The growth trend in OTT viewing is matched by a decline in broadcast and cable viewing. About 70 percent of all viewers do at least some OTT viewing as of 2020, and the numbers are expected to grow.
- **Flexibility.** OTT allows advertisers flexibility in their buying strategies. Networks typically require big commitments from advertisers (for example, buying an ad on every episode of a popular show) whereas OTT advertisers can make rapid changes in their buys if a strategy is not working or double down if it is.

- **Testability.** OTT is a good place to experiment, testing both new products and various advertising approaches: ad frequency, copy impact, and different media mixes.

The Cons

Like every medium, OTT has its drawbacks.

- **Ad blockers.** Viewers, especially ones using tablets and phones, can sometimes block OTT ads.
- **Availability.** Not every OTT platform uses an advertising model. OTT advertisers are restricted to those that do at the cost of the large audiences for Netflix, HBO, Disney+, and others.
- **Unproven.** OTT remains a relatively new way to advertise in video. Because of this, advertisers will likely struggle to learn best practices for at least the near future.
- **Zipping and zapping.** On many platforms, OTT viewers are able to speed through ads or switch over to different content when presented with an ad.

---

suggests that a group they call "super fans" are especially likely to want information about their favorite shows, and that these individuals in turn influence others about the TV they watch.[22]

Realizing the value of integrating the television and social media, Twitter developed tools that allow advertisers to discover when and where an ad runs on TV and to identify users who tweeted about the show that featured the advertiser's spot. Armed with this information, advertisers can buy promoted tweets to these users. As Exhibit 11–5 shows, the combination of Promoted Tweets and TV exposure results in higher ratings of brand favorability and purchase intent when compared to TV ad exposure alone.[23]

Social media are also important in encouraging viewers to watch a program. As shown in Exhibit 11–6, 54 percent of the 18-to-34 age group and 48 percent of the 35-to-49 age group started watching a TV program because of online opinions in Facebook.[24] While social media hold immense promise as tools for increasing the power of network and cable TV, they may also prove a threat. This is because social media companies are exploring the value of running their own video ads. Facebook plans to sell its own TV-style ads to advertisers for $2.5 million a pop. The ads would allow marketers to purchase entry into a person's feed with 15-second spots, potentially reaching up to 100 million people.[25]

Streaming media are also transforming the TV viewing experience. Audiences have many options for how and when they view their favorite shows. They may choose the "appointment TV" approach and watch when a show airs on a network. Alternatively, they may watch on OTT platforms at any time of their choosing. Or they may download their favorite show on Apple iTunes or Amazon. These options are available because of efforts by Google, Amazon, Microsoft, and Apple to make it easy to acquire TV content outside of cable subscriptions.[26]

The Use of Video in IMC

Video is very versatile. For many years it was strictly a mass medium, in the form of broadcast TV, used to great advantage by the manufacturers of mass consumption goods: toiletries and cosmetics, food, appliances, and cars (see Exhibit 11–7). But today, video can be a highly selective niche medium. It's not

▼ **EXHIBIT 11–5** Impact of promoted tweets on brand metrics.

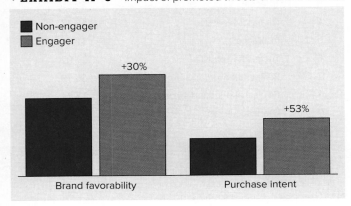

- ■ Non-engager
- ■ Engager

+30%

+53%

Brand favorability   Purchase intent

U.S. Internet Users Who Started Watching a TV Program Due to Opinions Online, by Site and Age, September 2012				
% of respondents				
	18–34	**35–49**	**50–64**	**Total**
Facebook	54%	48%	30%	46%
Twitter	21	12	5	14
TV show websites	8	12	6	9
Forums of discussion boards	11	8	3	8
Entertainment sites	8	9	4	7
Pinterest	5	3	3	4
reddit	4	1	1	2
Viggle	3	2	1	2
foursquare	2	1	0	1
GetGlue	2	1	0	1
IntoNow	1	1	0	1

Note: $n = 828$

Source: Cable & Telecommunications Association for Marketing (CTAM), "How Chatter Matters in TV Viewing" conducted by Nielsen in collaboration with MBI TouchPoints and uSamp as cited by TVbytheNumbers, December 28, 2012.

unusual, for instance, to see ads for special feed for thoroughbreds and show horses on ESPN's *Grand Prix of Jumping*. YouTube ads are sent to individuals looking for specific kinds of information, whether about hobbies, health, sports, or entertainment. Smaller platforms such as TikTok and Snapchat are encouraging advertisers to reach younger, highly engaged audiences.

For advertisers who want to go big, it is true that single programs don't deliver the mass audience they once did. However, TV remains the most cost-effective way to deliver certain kinds of messages to large, well-defined audiences. When it comes to awareness and image advertising, for instance, television has no rival. The same is true for brand reinforcement messages.[27]

Through its unique ability to deliver a creative big idea, video can impart *brand meaning* (the symbolism or personality of the brand) to either attract people to the brand or reinforce

> " **When it comes to awareness and image advertising . . . , television has no rival.** "

Source: Tony Cardoza/Getty Images

▼ **EXHIBIT 11-7**   Top 10 advertising categories in the United States, 2018.

Rank	Category	Advertising Expenditure ($ billions)
1	Retail	$17.81
2	Automotive	$14.28
3	Telecom	$8.56
4	Financial services	$8.47
5	Insurance	$7.71
6	Travel and Tourism	$7.02
7	Restaurants	$6.78
8	Political and organizations	$6.74
9	Pharmaceuticals	$6.46
10	Media	$6.21
	Total	**$90.04**

Source: Statista, "Advertising Expenditure in the Largest Advertising Categories in the United States in 2018," https://www.statista.com/statistics/275506/top-advertising-categories-in-the-us.

Duracell used ordinary batteries to drive a toy car from Mannheim to Pforzheim, Germany—a distance of 106 km. This television commercial shows a creative way to reinforce Duracell's strong brand image. Great stories like this are made for video.

Source: Duracell Inc.

their current relationship with it. Video is also a good leverage tool. Prospects can identify themselves by responding to a video ad, and then the advertiser can follow up with less expensive, one-to-one or addressable media.

It's worth remembering that the high visibility of video forces the sponsor to create ads that people find interesting and that consistently reinforce the brand's strategic position. The brands that succeed are the ones that are the most popular. And "ad liking" has a lot to do with brand popularity.

check yourself ✓

1. What does the rise of OTT mean for advertisers?

2. How can an advertiser use video in conjunction with other media?

LO11-2 Discuss the various options for advertising in video.

Types of Video Advertising

Advertisers use different strategies to buy video time. The major broadcast networks offer a variety of *programs* that appeal to different audiences. So the advertiser buys ads based on the viewing audience of each program. A national advertiser desiring a broad cross-section of women ages 25 to 45, for example, might find *The Academy Awards* an effective buy at a cost of $2 million because the audience exceeds 20 million viewers.

When buying cable TV, an advertiser can buy ads over the full schedule of a channel because cable networks typically aim all of their programming to relatively specific *audiences*. The Lifetime and Oxygen channels heavily weigh programs toward women; MTV targets viewers ages 16 to 25. Cable includes networks like Discovery that offer multiple channels for an ad buy: HGTV, TLC, the Food Network, and the Travel Network are just some.

Cable companies sell their network channels in bundles at a discount and offer discounts for *run-of-schedule* positioning—multiple ad purchases they can place throughout a channel's daily schedule

There are various ways advertisers can buy time on TV. They include sponsoring an entire program, participating in a program, purchasing spot announcements between programs, and purchasing spots from syndicators. Exhibit 11–7 shows how much money is spent nationally on various product categories.

Network Advertising Historically, major U.S. advertisers purchased airtime from one of the national broadcast **networks**. Beginning with the 2003–2004 season, ad-supported cable networks pulled ahead of the U.S. broadcast networks in prime time for the first time in the history of U.S. television, pulling in 44 percent of the audience, compared to 41 percent for the broadcast networks and 15 percent who were watching other television outlets, such as HBO and PBS. But even with a reduced share of total TV viewers, network TV shows deliver the largest mass audiences available for national advertisers.

An advertiser who underwrites the cost of a program is engaging in **sponsorship**. In a sole sponsorship, the advertiser is responsible for both the program content and the total cost of production. The practice can be so costly that single sponsorships are usually limited to specials. Companies that sponsor programs (AT&T, Ford, and Hallmark, for example) gain two important advantages. First, the public more readily identifies with the brand due to the prestige of association with first-rate entertainment. Second, the sponsor controls the placement and content of its commercials. The commercials can be fit to the program and run any length the sponsor desires so long as they remain within network or station regulations. It is also not uncommon for sponsors to negotiate favorable product placements, a practice of featuring the brands within the shows themselves. There is more on this later in the chapter.

> "Local businesses are frequently seen on spot schedules."

To save money and reduce risks, many advertisers cosponsor programs, sponsoring on alternate weeks or dividing the program into segments. NFL games, for instance, are always sold as multiple sponsorships.

Most network advertising is sold on a **participation** basis, with several advertisers buying 30- or 60-second segments within a program. This enables them to spread their budgets and avoid long-term commitments to any one program. It also lets smaller advertisers buy a limited amount of time and still get the nationwide coverage they need. The disadvantage of the practice is that competing brands (for example, Ford and Ram) may end up running ads during the same program.

Network advertising has other disadvantages: lack of flexibility, long lead times, inconvenient restrictions, and forced adherence to network standards and practices, not to mention high prices. Costs can run high for a spot (see Exhibit 11–8). For this reason, most advertisers decide to buy *spot announcements*.

Spot Announcements

Spot announcements run in clusters between programs. A spot announcement is an ad buy in which the advertiser bypasses a network and instead purchases time from one or more affiliates directly. They are more flexible than network advertising because they can be concentrated in specific regions of the country. Therefore, local businesses are frequently seen on spot schedules. An advertiser with a small budget or limited distribution may use spots to introduce a new product into one area at a time. Or an advertiser can vary its message for different markets to suit promotional needs.

Spots may run 10, 15, 30, or 60 seconds and be sold nationally or locally. Spot advertising is more difficult to buy than network advertising because it involves contacting each station directly. The national rep system, in which individuals act as sales and service representatives for a number of stations, alleviates this problem.

Spot advertising is available only at network station breaks and when network advertisers have not purchased all of the available time, so spot ads can get lost in the clutter—which is why they tend to have less viewers and a smaller piece of the ad spending pie.

Syndication

As audiences fragment, syndicated programs become an increasingly popular adjunct or alternative to network advertising. In a little over 10 years, the syndication industry has grown substantially.

Syndication is the sale of programs on a station-by-station, market-by-market basis. In other words, a producer (for example, Warner Bros. or Disney) sells programming directly to stations, often through a distribution company, rather than going through the networks (see Exhibit 11–9). TV stations buy the programming and then sell some or all of the advertising space available in the show. This efficient "direct-from-the-factory" approach gives stations more programming control and greater profits. It also gives advertisers access to **inventory** (commercial time) that they might not get on network programs—often at better prices. Because local stations show network programming only at certain hours of the day (mornings and prime time are the most common), syndication has become the largest source of programming in the United States.

Television syndication comes in three forms: off-network, first-run, and barter. In **off-network syndication**, former popular network programs (reruns) are sold to individual stations for rebroadcast. Examples include *Big Bang Theory* and *Law and Order*. **First-run syndication** involves original shows, such as *Family Feud, Inside Edition,* and *Dr. Phil,* that are produced specifically for the syndication market. A good deal for both syndicators and affiliates is **barter syndication** (also called *advertiser-supported syndication*). This involves off-network or

▼**EXHIBIT 11–8** Advertising cost per 30-second spot on 10 selected shows (2019–2020 season).

Show and Network	30-Second Ad Cost (000)
Sunday Night Football (NBC)	$685
Thursday Night Football (Fox)	540
This Is Us (NBC)	359
The Masked Singer (Fox)	202
The Voice–Monday (NBC)	193
Grey's Anatomy (ABC)	186
The Voice–Tuesday (NBC)	180
9-1-1 (Fox)	172
New Amsterdam (NBC)	172
Empire (Fox)	171

Source: Jeanine Poggi, "TV's Most Expensive Commercials for the 2019–'20 Season," *AdAge*, October 7, 2019, https://adage.com/article/media/tvs-most-expensive-commercials-2019-20-season/2202481.

first-run programs offered by producers to local stations free or for a reduced rate, but with some of the ad space (usually more than half) presold to national advertisers. *Wheel of Fortune, Jeopardy*, and *Ellen* are some examples.

Syndication is popular with many national advertisers, in part because it enables them to reach some otherwise difficult-to-reach audiences at an efficient cost per viewer. However, syndicated shows are usually more cluttered with advertising and may not air in all markets or at consistent times.

Program-Length Ads (PLAs)
Infomercials aren't new, but their respectability is. Ten years ago, most **program-length ad (PLA)** users were off–Madison Avenue marketers of hand mixers, juicers, and car waxes. Today, major marketers such as P&G, Microsoft, and Pfizer have ventured into the **infomercial** arena. And why not. Proactive, an acne medicine built largely on the basis of infomercial promotions, now has sales in excess

Infomercials provide a unique opportunity for advertisers such as Total Gym to demonstrate their products and generate immediate results.
Source: QVC, Inc.

of $1 billion. Total Gym and the Showtime Rotisserie have achieved similar levels of success.

Other Video IMC Opportunities

The 30-second commercial faces an ever-growing list of competitors for advertising dollars, not only from traditional rivals such as print and radio, but from video alternatives. Here we present some non-web-based advertising alternatives.

TV Product Placements TV **product placements** occur when advertisers showcase their brands within television programming rather than commercials. Netflix may not allow commercials, but when the character Eleven revealed a passion for Eggos on the show, sales of the product jumped 14 percent the following year.[28] Newer technologies also allow placements to occur in the editing rather than filming stage of content creation. In other words, that can of Coca-Cola your favorite character is holding might show up as a Pepsi can the next time you watch.[29] Viewers may not even be aware of just how frequently product placements appear on television. Exhibit 11–10 demonstrates just how common the practice has become.

The value of product placements can be difficult to quantify, at least in comparison to traditional advertising. There have definitely been success stories however. For example the TV series Sex and the City helped fashion

▼ **EXHIBIT 11–9** TV network and syndication distribution.

a. The networks are go-betweens.
b. Syndication is often a more efficient way of financing and distributing programs, as the networks are cut out of the transaction.

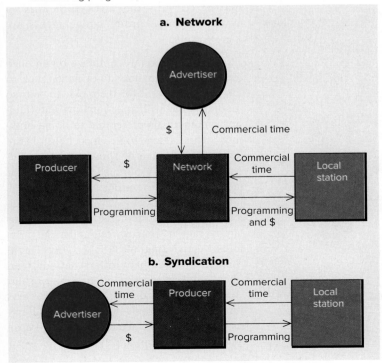

Brand	Show	Description
Utz Chips	*The Office*	The favorite chips in Dunder-Mifflin's vending machine.
Body Glove	*NCIS: Los Angeles*	Surf's up!
Blackberry	*House of Cards*	Better security than Apple and Samsung?
Eggos	*Stranger Things*	Eleven: Leggo my Eggo.
Travelocity	*Amazing Race*	The Roaming Gnome is everywhere.
CoverGirl	*America's Next Top Model*	Who do you think pays for that $100,000 modeling contract?
AT&T	*America's Got Talent*	Only way to vote is through AT&T.
Disney	*Dancing with the Stars*	If you own the network, you can plug *The Muppets* and *Lion King* all you want.
Apple	*Morning Show*	*Wall Street Journal* estimates Apple devices are present in 32 camera shots per episode.
Coca-Cola	*American Idol*	Whatever is inside those cups, it says Coke on the outside.

brand Manolo Blahnik become internally famous.[30] PQ Media estimates that product placement spending reached $11.44 billion in 2019, up from less than $5 billion in 2012.[31]

Product placements offer advertisers several important benefits relative to traditional commercials. First, advertisers are increasingly concerned that many viewers avoid watching commercials. Research does suggest that in households with digital video recorders, many programs are recorded and watched after they are broadcast. People who watch a recorded show often skip through commercial messages. By placing a brand within the show, advertisers can minimize the impact of commercial avoidance. Second, having brands appear within programming offers advertisers the chance to link their products with popular characters. For example, *The Big Bang Theory* viewers got to watch their favorite characters play Twister, a Milton Bradley game, after Amy Farrah Fowler suggested they do so on the highly rated show.[32] Third, the use of product placements helps advertisers avoid the credibility issues that surround commercials. Viewers know that commercials, as sponsored messages, represent the biased viewpoint of the advertiser. But brand appearances in programming may help advertisers do an "end around" such credibility problems.

Film Product Placements   Marketers can also take advantage of product placements in another video medium: feature films. While product placements are often thought of as a television phenomenon, the practice has a long history in film. The James Bond movie *Goldfinger* created worldwide attention for Aston Martin cars (at a cost to Ford Motor of $35 million) and most people know that Reese's Pieces candy sales surged after an appearance in the film *ET*. The practice continues today. More recently, the 2012 animated *The Lorax* set a modern-day record with more than 70 placement partners. But that record was quickly smashed after more than 100 brands partnered with the 2013 film *Man of Steel*.[33] Clearly, product placements are here to stay.

Prefilm commercials capitalize on an obvious reality: Filmgoers don't have much to do while they wait for the movie to start so perhaps they will find watching entertaining commercials preferable to doing nothing. This same logic lies behind the emerging practice of showing ads on service station gas pumps. The appeal for advertisers who purchase time on Gas Station TV(www.gstv.com) is that the audience is "basically tethered at the pump for an average of four to four-and-a-half minutes," according to GSTV CEO David Leider. His company offers national and local advertisers the chance to present standard-length commercials with ad costs that are comparable to spot cable. Early national sponsors include Chevrolet, Pepsi, Allstate, Goodyear, and Walmart.

Product placement, where brands are woven into the entertainment content, is happening more frequently as advertisers seek new ways to get their products noticed.
Source: Everett Collection Inc/Alamy Stock Photo

Product placement is also common in films. The character Nomi, a colleague of James Bond in the 2020 film No Time to Die, *sports The Flex sunglasses. The glamour of the films and the attractiveness of the characters make Bond movies an appealing venue for product placements. What are some other film placements you can recall?*

Source: Danjaq LLC and Metro-Goldwyn-Mayer Studios Inc.

check yourself ✓

1. Why is syndication a popular tool for many national advertisers?

2. What are the possible benefits of product placement versus traditional commercials?

LO11-3 Explain how to measure video audiences and select the best vehicles to buy.

VIDEO AUDIENCE MEASUREMENT

Efficient advertisers study the audiences of various programs and analyze their impact and cost-effectiveness against other media vehicles. To do this, they must understand the techniques and terminology used in television audience measurement.

Broadcast and Cable Audiences: Nielsen Ratings

Nielsen is the primary company that measures the program audiences of TV and radio stations for advertisers and broadcasters. In past years, several companies, called **rating services**, competed to provide data to advertisers. But today, only Nielsen remains.

Its flagship service, the Nielsen Television Index (NTI), uses a national sample of households equipped with meters to develop audience estimates for all national TV programming. The

rating services These services measure the program audiences of TV and radio stations for advertisers and broadcasters by picking a representative sample of the market and furnishing data on the size and characteristics of the viewers or listeners.

sweeps The four, month-long periods each year when rating services measure all TV markets for station viewing habits and demographic information for the purpose of setting advertising rates. Sweep months are February, May, July, and November.

meters are hooked up to TV sets in 25,000 homes across the country and continuously measure the channels to which each set is tuned. People meters go a step further. They gather information in 25 major markets about who is watching in addition to the channel tuned.

At the local level, Nielsen surveys 1.6 million households. Household members record their viewing habits in diaries. Four times each year, during the **sweeps** month-long rating periods, Nielsen collects and processes the data. This information is used by networks and local stations to determine how much they can charge for advertising on their shows.

Some advertisers and broadcasters maintain that Nielsen's reports are unstable and inaccurate.[34] Nielsen faces an enormous challenge keeping up with changes in TV viewing habits. For example, many viewers watch shows on streaming platforms after they've been broadcast. Nielsen's existing measurement techniques are not well equipped to track such viewing habits. Popular platforms such as Netflix and Amazon Prime are even delivering their own original programs. And the TV experience itself is changing, as people integrate social media use with TV viewing. Exhibit 11–11 provides insight into the methodology of collecting Nielsen ratings.

For demographic studies of TV audiences, advertisers also use MRI Simmons (www.mrisimmons.com), a company created from the merger of former competitors. It performs extensive surveys of the U.S. marketplace and publishes its findings on consumer lifestyles, product usage, and media habits. Advertisers use the results for strategic planning purposes.

Cable Ratings

Reliable information on the audiences for cable programs is even harder to gather. Traditional techniques often rely on too small a sample to be statistically significant, so major cable programming services provide their own reports of audience viewership by show. Interpreting cable ratings is a confusing process because the media planner has to integrate so much information from so many different sources. In many instances, however, it is clear which demographic niches a cable network appeals to. ESPN tends to attract male sports fanatics, Hallmark is popular with older, predominantly female viewers and Nickelodeon is popular with children (but see the Ethical Issues box for issues related to this vulnerable audience).

For four decades, the life and death of network TV programs have been in the hands of the Nielsen families, households chosen with the aid of national census and other data to reflect the country's demographics. Originally there were two measuring types: those who kept diaries and those who had a black box attached to their TV sets. Someone in each of 2,400 diary homes kept a written record of which shows each person watched during the week. In the 1,700 black box households, an audiometer attached to the TV kept track of when the set was on and what channel it was tuned to. Nielsen Media Research paid these families for the permission to gather data from their viewing patterns. The information is used to compute its Nielsen Television Index (NTI), the sole source of national TV ratings.

But that method of determining national ratings has been replaced by the more accurate people meter (see illustration), an electronic device that automatically records a household's TV viewing. The people meter records the channels watched, the number of minutes of viewing, and who in the household is watching. Each person must punch in and punch out on a keypad. The microwave-based people meter keeps track of second-by-second viewing choices of up to eight household members and relays the data to a central computer, which tabulates the data overnight.

The original people meter was developed by AGB Research, a British company. AGB found clients in ad agencies, cable networks, and syndicators—all of whom believed NTI overreported broadcast network shows and underreported other types. However, Nielsen developed its own people meter, and AGB abandoned the U.S. market.

Nielsen conducts its survey sweeps four times a year in major market areas and publishes sweeps books that are the basis for network and local station ad rates. With the advent of the passive people meter, advertisers may once again believe in the ratings they're paying for.

A well-established technique in audience measurement is the single-source data made available by supermarket scanners. Once information on a family's viewing habits has been gathered, its packaged-goods purchases are measured. The implications are monumental for marketing and media planners. The leaders in single-source measurement today are Information Resources, Inc. (IRI), with its BehaviorScan service, and Nielsen, with its Home Scan service.

Today, Nielsen continues to innovate with technologies to track the use of social media and television viewing. Nielsen estimates that TV tweets reach an audience of almost 50 persons per tweet and that 85 percent of viewers use their smartphones or tablets while watching. It's clear that as TV technology changes, Nielsen will evolve to remain the best source of audience information.

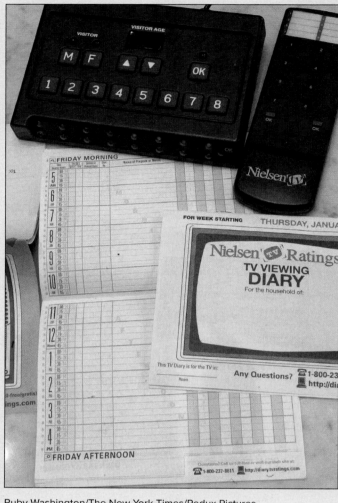

Ruby Washington/The New York Times/Redux Pictures

Defining Television Markets

Television rating services define unique geographic television markets to minimize the confusion of overlapping TV signals. The Nielsen station index uses the term **designated market areas (DMAs)** for geographic areas (cities, counties) in which the local TV stations attract the most viewing. For example, the DMA for Columbus, Georgia (see Exhibit 11-12), is the 17 counties in which the local area TV stations are the most watched.

Dayparts

Advertisers must decide when to air commercials and on which programs. Programs continue to run or are canceled depending on their ratings (percentage of the population watching). Ratings also vary with the time of day a program runs. Television time is divided into dayparts roughly as follows:

Early morning:	6:00 a.m.–9:00 a.m.	(Eastern and Pacific)
Daytime:	9:00 a.m.–4:30 p.m.	
Early fringe:	4:30 p.m.–7:30 p.m.	
Prime access:	7:30 p.m.–8:00 p.m.	
Prime time:	8:00 p.m.–11:00 p.m.	
Late news:	11:00 p.m.–11:30 p.m.	
Late night:	11:30 p.m.–2:00 a.m.	

Viewing is highest during **prime time** (8 to 11 p.m. Eastern and Pacific Time; 7 to 10 p.m. Central and Mountain Time). To

EXHIBIT 11–12 This map of the area surrounding Columbus, Georgia, shows media planners which counties are included in the designated market area (DMA) and will be reached by advertising placed on the local television stations. Columbus, Georgia, is the 125th largest DMA in the United States and contains more than 200,000 TV households.

Columbus, GA, Audience Figures

- DMA Market Size: #125
- Total DMA TV Households: 207,820
- Total DMA Persons 18+: 388,000
- Total DMA Adults 25–54: 214,000
- Total DMA Working Women: 92,000
- % of Cable in DMA Households: 76%

Local TV Stations

WTVM ABC - Columbus (Muscogee) Georgia
WRBL CBS - Columbus (Muscogee) Georgia
WCGT Ind. - Columbus (Muscogee) Georgia
WMCF TBN - Opelika (Lee) Alabama
WJSP/WGTV PBS - Columbus (Muscogee) Georgia
WLGA UPN - Opelika (Lee) Alabama
WCAG UATV - Lagrange (Troupe) Georgia
WLTZ NBC - Columbus (Muscogee) Georgia
WGIQ/WBIQ PBS - Louisville (Barbour) Alabama
WXTX FOX - Columbus (Muscogee) Georgia
WLGA UPN - Opelika (Lee) Alabama

designated market areas (DMAs) The geographic areas from which TV stations attract most of their viewers.

prime time Highest level of TV viewing (8 p.m. to 11 p.m.)

daypart mix A media scheduling strategy based on a specific combination of broadcast time segments.

TV households (TVHH) The number of households in a market area that own television sets.

households using TV (HUT) The percentage of homes in a given area that have one or more TV sets turned on at any particular time. If 1,000 TV sets are in the survey and 500 are turned on, the HUT figure is 50 percent.

program rating The percentage of TV households in an area that are tuned into a specific program.

reach the greatest percentage of the advertiser's target audience with optimal frequency, the media planner determines a **daypart mix** based on TV usage levels reported by the rating services.

Audience Measurements

Rating services and media planners use many terms to define a station's audience, penetration, and efficiency. **TV households (TVHH)** refers to the number of households that own television sets. The number of TVHH in a particular market gives an advertiser a sense of the market's size. Likewise, the number of TVHH tuned in to a particular program helps the advertiser estimate the program's popularity and how many people a commercial is likely to reach.

The percentage of homes in a given area that have one or more TV sets turned on at any particular time is expressed as **households using TV (HUT)**. If there are 1,000 TV sets in the survey area and 500 are turned on, HUT is 50 percent (500/1,000).

The **program rating** refers to the percentage of TV households in an area that are tuned in to a specific program. The rating is

POPULAR SHOWS CAN COMMAND HIGHER ADVERTISING RATES.

Advertising to Children: Child's Play?

The benefits of reaching children are great. If won over now, they tend to be loyal customers into adulthood. Besides selling to children, advertisers also sell through children. Some companies believe they can sell more by appealing to children's preferences than to those of adults. The minivan was created because children demanded more room, says MacNeal. When kids decided the vehicle was "uncool," their opinions helped develop the SUV. Saturday morning cartoons are the traditional vehicle for ads promoting cereals, candy, and toys. But parents are asked to buy particular brands of vacuum cleaners and other household goods because their kids saw them advertised on TV. Marketers rely on kids' "pester power" to get their products sold.

The dangers of marketing to kids from an ethical perspective are fairly clear: Children are the "vulnerable" market. They are less experienced. Their concepts of self, time, and money are immature. As a result, they know very little about their own desires, needs, and preferences—or how to use economic resources rationally to satisfy them. It is likely that child-oriented advertising can lead to false beliefs or highly improbable product expectations. Telling children about a product and accurately describing that product is probably ethical. Convincing them that they must have a toy to be popular with their friends is probably not. Nothing is likely to enrage parents and society-at-large more than the prospect of marketers manipulating and taking advantage of children.

Cereal is better if a fun character is selling it; so are beer and cigarettes as the Budweiser frogs and lizards and Joe Camel proved. In the United Kingdom, there was criticism over the use of TV characters such as the Simpsons and Teletubbies, as well as the Spice Girls, to sell snack foods high in fat, sugar, and salt. The junk food firms faced a crackdown on the hard sell of products that can make children overweight and unhealthy.

Both critics and defenders agree that advertisers should not intentionally deceive children. Federal legislation has been introduced that would reimpose the 1974 guidelines limiting advertising on children's programs. These guidelines deal with truth and accuracy.

The mood in several European countries is to tighten up children-and-advertising guidelines. Sweden has some of the strictest controls in Europe on children and advertising, banning all television advertisements aimed at children younger than 12. This ban includes advertisements on toys, foods, sweets, drinks, and any products that might appeal to preteens.

In the United States, the Children's Advertising Review Unit (CARU) of the Council of Better Business Bureaus (BBB) promotes responsible children's advertising and responds to public concerns. The basic activity of CARU is the review and evaluation of child-directed advertising to help avoid deceptive messages. When children's advertising is found to be misleading, inaccurate, or inconsistent with its guidelines, CARU seeks changes through the voluntary cooperation of advertisers. The BBB website at https://bbbprograms.org/programs/caru discusses CARU's guidelines.

Questions

1. Do bans on marketing to children compromise a basic freedom of choice and speech? Whose responsibility is it to make sure children are not inappropriately influenced by advertising? Their parents? The government? Advertisers? How far should advertisers have to go to ensure that children are not misled by their ads?

2. Study the CARU guidelines and then watch the advertising on a children's network or Saturday morning television. How well do you feel the advertisers are adhering to those guidelines?

---

computed as follows:

$$\text{Rating} = \frac{\text{TVHH tuned to a specific program}}{\text{Total TVHH in area}}$$

Networks want high ratings because they measure a show's popularity. More popular shows can command higher advertising rates.

The percentage of homes with sets in use (HUT) tuned to a specific program is called the **audience share**.

$$\text{Share} = \frac{\text{TVHH tuned to a specific program}}{\text{HH with a TV turned on}}$$

A program with only 500 viewers can have a 50 percent share if only 1,000 sets are turned on. *Ratings*, in contrast, measure the audience as a percentage of all TVHH in the area, whether the TV sets are on or off.

The actual number of homes reached by some portion of a program is called **total audience**. This figure is normally broken down into demographic categories to determine **audience composition**.

Gross Rating Points

In television, **gross rating points (GRPs)** are the total rating points achieved by a particular media schedule over a specific period. For example, a weekly schedule of five commercials on programs with an average household rating of 20 would yield 100 GRPs.

GRPs allow advertisers to draw conclusions about the different markets available for a client's ads by providing a comparable measure of advertising weight. However, GRPs do not reflect a market's size. For example, while campaigns in Knoxville and Charlotte might have the same GRPs, they would differ significantly in the number of homes reached.

audience share The percentage of homes with TV sets in use (HUT) tuned to a specific program.

total audience The total number of homes reached by some portion of a TV program. This figure is normally broken down to determine the distribution of audience into demographic categories.

audience composition The distribution of an audience into demographic or other categories.

gross rating points (GRPs) The total audience delivery or weight of a specific media schedule. One rating point equals 1 percent of a particular market's population.

cost per rating point (CPP) A computation used by media buyers to determine which broadcast programs are the most efficient in relation to the target audience. The CPP is determined by dividing the cost of the show by the show's expected rating.

cost per thousand (CPM) A common term describing the cost of reaching 1,000 people in a medium's audience. It is used by media planners to compare the cost of various media vehicles.

	TV Homes (thousands)	Avg. Cost per Spot	Avg. Rating	Avg. Homes Reached (thousands)	Number of Spots GRPs	GRPs
Knoxville	1,002	$1,500	15	150	5	75
Charlotte	638	1,250	15	96	5	75

To better determine the relative value of television advertising markets, other measures are used, such as cost per rating point (CPP) and cost per thousand (CPM). These and other media terms will be described here and in Chapter 14.

Measuring Audiences in OTT

OTT providers do not require the services of third-party vendors such as Nielsen because they have immediate and direct access to who is watching what. This, of course, is a big advantage of OTT. Nevertheless, Nielsen has expanded its audience measurement to include OTT services and Internet videos. Its program, called Total Ad Ratings, seeks to offer advertisers information on viewing habits across any video provider.[35]

Ad-free OTT services such as Netflix typically do not provide information about audiences for its various shows. Because the business model of these companies do not require advertising revenue, they tend to keep the information in-house. Perhaps because of pressure from competing services and Nielsen's efforts to measure its audience, Netflix is becoming more transparent about who is watching. This, however, has attracted criticism, as the company has a vested interest in the performance of some of its shows.[36]

BUYING SCREEN TIME

The process of buying TV time can be lengthy and, depending on the number of stations in the buy, quite involved. The procedures are so complex that most large advertisers use ad agencies or media-buying services. Buying services have gained in popularity because they charge less and can save advertisers money by negotiating for desirable time slots at reduced rates. Local advertisers typically rely on station reps to help determine the best buys for their money.

Selecting Programs for Buys

Media buyers select the most efficient programs in relation to the target audience using the **cost per rating point (CPP)** and the **cost per thousand (CPM)** for each program:

$$CPP = \frac{Cost}{Rating}$$

$$CPM = \frac{Cost}{Thousands\ of\ people}$$

For example, assume *CSI* has a rating of 25, reaches 200,000 people in the primary target audience, and costs $2,000 for a 30-second spot on station WALB-TV in Albany, Georgia. Then,

$$CPP = \frac{\$2,000}{25} = \$80$$

$$CPM = \frac{\$2,000}{(200,000 \div 1,000)} = \$10$$

By calculating CPP, the media buyer can compare the cost of a rating point (reaching 1 percent of TVHH) from one program or network to another. That's good information for beginning negotiations. But rating points relate to the whole market. The real important figure is the cost of reaching 1,000 prospects in your target market. That's why the CPM should be calculated against the size of your target audience, not the whole market. The lower the cost per 1,000 people in your target audience, the more efficient the show is at reaching your real prospects.

To get the best buys within the available budget, then, the media buyer substitutes stronger programs for less efficient ones.

Negotiating Prices

TV stations and cable companies publish rate cards to sell their airtime. However, because TV audiences are estimated at best, television reps will always negotiate prices.

The media buyer contacts the rep and explains what efficiency the advertiser needs in terms of CPM to make the buy. The buyer has numerous ways to negotiate lower rates: work out a package deal, accept *run-of-schedule positioning* (the station chooses when to run the commercials), or take advantage of preemption rates. A **preemption rate** is lower because the advertiser agrees to be "bumped" (preempted) if another advertiser pays the higher, nonpreemption rate.

After the advertising airs, the station returns a signed and notarized **affidavit of performance** to the advertiser or agency, specifying when the spots aired and what makegoods are available. **Makegoods** refer to free advertising time an advertiser receives to compensate for spots the station missed or ran incorrectly or because the program's ratings were substantially lower than guaranteed.

check yourself ✓

1. What are some of the criticisms of ratings services?

2. What is the difference between *program rating* and *audience share*?

LO11-4 List the advantages and disadvantages of audio media for advertisers.

AUDIO MEDIA

Radio is a personal, one-on-one medium; people tend to listen alone. And radio is mobile. It can entertain people who are driving, walking, at home, or away from home. This makes it a particularly strong way to reach people who commute by car; almost half of radio listening takes place in a car.

Radio is also adaptable to moods. In the morning, people may want to hear the news, upbeat music, or interesting chatter; in the afternoon, they may want to unwind with classical or easy-listening music.

> While television tends to be a passive medium . . . , radio actively involves people.

▼ **EXHIBIT 11–13** Top 10 national advertisers and spot radio spending.

Rank	Company	2014 Spot Radio Spending ($ millions)
1	Home Depot	$72.5
2	T-Mobile	65
3	Geico	63.5
4	Comcast Corp.	58.8
5	Verizon	41.3
6	AT&T	40.3
7	O'Reilly Autoparts	35.4
8	Macy's	34.2
9	Walgreens	29.1
10	Sprint	28.2

Who Uses Radio?

A recent article described AM/FM radio as "resilient," and no wonder. Almost 90 percent of the U.S. population still listens to terrestrial radio each week.[37]

Many national advertisers are aware of radio's audience potential (see Exhibit 11–13). Back when it was still a little company in Queens, New York, and strapped for money, Snapple Natural Beverages decided to use radio. It put its entire ad budget into a yearlong schedule with a young, relatively unknown radio show host named Howard Stern. Snapple liked the way he delivered its spots as a live reader.

A few years later, Snapple began receiving letters and phone calls from people in the Midwest and West, where it didn't even have distribution. It seems that nationally syndicated talk show host Rush Limbaugh, on a restricted-calorie diet, had been giving enthusiastic on-air endorsements for Snapple Diet Iced Tea. The firm moved quickly to sign him as a paid endorser. What it learned was the power of radio, especially when combined with a popular radio personality.

As with other traditional media, radio has found it easier to collaborate with rather than fight new media. As an example, 31 percent of radio listeners report initiating an online search based on something they have heard on the radio.

Radio also helps to reach audiences underrepresented in other media. For example, it tends to have higher reach with audiences that are not watching television during a given daypart.[38]

The Use of Radio in IMC

While television tends to be a passive medium that people simply watch, radio actively involves people. They listen intently to their favorite personalities; they call in to make requests, participate during a contest, or contribute to a discussion; they use their ears and imaginations to fill in what they cannot see.

With radio, national companies can tie in to a local market and target the specific demographic group they want to reach. Most important, radio enables advertisers to maintain strategic consistency and stretch their media dollars through **imagery transfer**. Research shows that when advertisers run a schedule on TV and then convert the audio portion to radio commercials, fully 75 percent of consumers replay the TV spot in their minds when they hear the radio spot. That extends the life and builds the impact of a TV campaign at greatly reduced cost. In an IMC campaign, where message consistency is a primary objective, this is a very important feature of radio.

Local retailers like the medium for the same reasons. Also, they can tailor it to their needs. It offers defined audiences; its recall characteristics are similar to those of TV; and retailers can establish an identity by creating their own ads. Finally, because radio is so mobile, retailers can reach prospects just before they purchase. Hence, recent years have seen major spending increases by local grocery stores, car dealers, banks, and home-improvement, furniture, and apparel stores.

Radio is an important component of the media mix. It offers tremendous reach, attention, imagery, and selectivity, at a relatively low cost. In this ad, the Radio Advertising Bureau (www.rab.com) is publicizing the results of a research study that suggests advertisers can improve brand recall by replacing some of their TV and newspaper ads with radio spots (http://urlm.co/www.radioadlab.org).

Source: Radio Advertising Bureau

Radio Programming and Audiences

Radio stations plan their programming carefully to reach specific audiences and to capture as many listeners as possible. The larger the audience, the more a station can charge for commercial time. Therefore, extensive planning and research go into radio programming and program changes. Stations can use tried-and-true formats, subscribe to network or syndicated programming, or devise unique approaches. Programming choices are greatly influenced by whether a station is on the AM or FM band. FM has much better sound fidelity, fewer commercial interruptions, and more varied programming.

To counteract FM's inroads, many AM stations switched to programs that don't rely on sound quality, such as news, talk, and sports. Some stations are experimenting with all comedy, mid-day game shows with audience participation, or formats geared to specific regions. AM stations are also trying to win back music listeners by improving their sound quality and offering stereo broadcasting.

When buying radio time, advertisers usually buy the station's *format*, not its programs. Most stations adopt one of the dozen or so standard **programming formats**: contemporary hit radio, adult contemporary, country, rock, easy listening, news/talk, and so on, as shown in Exhibit 11–14. Each format tends

▼ **EXHIBIT 11–14** Radio's most popular formats with all listeners, listeners 18–34, and listeners 25–54.

AQH Share	All 6+	Age 18–34	Age 25–54
News/Talk	10%	4.3%	7.0%
Adult Contemporary (AC)	8.0	7.7	7.9
Country	7.3	8.5	7.0
Pop CHR	6.9	10.7	8.0
Classic Hits	5.6	4.3	5.1
Hot AC	5.5	6.4	6.1
Classic Rock	4.9	4.2	4.8
Urban AC	4.8	3.3	4.4
All Sports	4.4	3.3	4.8
Urban Contemporary	3.6	6.4	4.4

Note: ACH = Average Quarter Hour.

Source: Nielsen, "Top 10 Radio Formats of 2018," December 10, 2018, https://www.nielsen.com/us/en/insights/article/2018/tops-of-2018-radio.

to appeal to specific demographic groups. The most common format is country music, which appeals to a broad cross-section of Americans from 25 to 54 years old, but more adults listen to news/talk than any other format.

Contemporary hit radio (CHR) appeals to teenagers and women younger than 30. It provides a constant flow of top 40 hits, usually with minimal intrusion by disc jockeys. Another popular format, adult contemporary (or "easy oldies"), is often advertised as "light rock, less talk." This format aims at the desirable target group of working women between 25 and 54. The news/talk, easy-listening, and nostalgia formats tend to have high listenership among men and women older than 35.

There are more than 20 national radio networks, including the multiple "mininetworks" of ABC, CBS, Westwood One, and Unistar, and numerous syndicators offer programs from live rock concerts to public-affairs discussions. To stand out, 80 percent of licensed radio stations are opting for syndicated and network offerings.

Satellite Radio and Portable Music Devices

A challenge to "terrestrial" radio has been mounted by networks that transmit signals nationwide via satellite. Until 2008, **satellite radio** had been a two-player competition between first-out-of-the-block XM and its chief rival, Sirius. In July of that year, the two companies merged to become Sirius XM Radio. The combined networks have continued to add a sizable number of subscribers, reaching 30 million in 2020.[39]

In order to receive satellite radio, an audience member must pay a monthly subscription fee and invest in a receiver capable of receiving the networks' signals. Sirius XM has attempted to convince people that radio is worth paying for by offering two important benefits not available to terrestrial radio listeners: a large number of program choices (dozens of stations and a variety of music and nonmusic formats) and exclusive programming, such as Howard Stern, Oprah Winfrey, and pro sports.

How significant is satellite radio as an alternative to terrestrial radio? As of 2020, Sirius XM has done an excellent job of achieving subscriber growth, helped in no small part by an aggressive campaign to put satellite-compatible radios in more than 70 percent of new cars. The biggest threat to satellite radio comes not from traditional AM/FM formats, but from even newer digital formats such as Pandora, Spotify, and Apple Music and from the increasingly popular medium of podcasts.

Podcasts

The biggest trend in audio advertising is podcasts. A podcast is an audio program either streamed or downloaded to a phone or other device. Apple's data suggest there were 550,000 podcasts as of 2018, while one more recent estimate suggests a number close to 850,000.[40] This enormous number reflects the attractiveness of the format to consumers, and advertisers have taken notice. One company, Bridge Ratings, forecasted just a couple of years ago that companies would spend $500 million in 2020 on podcast ads.[41] The actual number is actually much higher—$659 million—and it is predicted to go above $1 billion in 2021.[42]

Podcasts offer advertisers some clear advantages over radio formats. First, podcasts tend to appeal to clearly defined demographic, geographic, and behavioristic segments. Podcast hosts are generally very friendly to advertisers because ad revenue is key to their business model. And ad clutter on podcasts, even popular ones, is far less than is typically found in commercial radio.

Podcast ads are typically available in two forms, a 15-second pre-roll (an ad before the start of the podcast) and 60-second mid-rolls (minute-long breaks in the middle of the podcast content). Some podcasts conclude with a final ad that is called a post-roll. Ad costs, according to one expert, average $18 CPM (cost per thousand listeners) for pre-rolls, $25 CPM for mid-rolls, and $10 CPM for post-rolls.[43]

Just as cable companies are hedging their bets with OTT in video, traditional audio companies are doing the same with

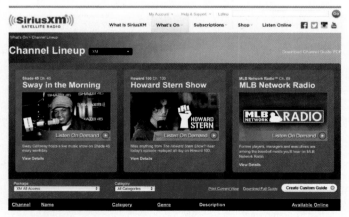

This screenshot from Sirius (www.siriusxm.com) shows just a few of the many channel line-ups available. How many of you have made the switch to satellite radio?

Source: Sirius XM Radio Inc.

podcasts. This includes audio names such as iHeartMedia and Spotify, who are making acquisitions of podcasting companies.

A potential downside of podcasting is the difficulty advertisers may have in getting reliable user data. Into this breach are stepping companies such as Targeted Marketplace from Megaphone and Art19, a podcast host providing software tools to sponsoring companies. Industry experts suggest advertiser interest will grow even further if podcasters begin adopting standards of the Internet Advertising Bureau (IAB, see Chapter 12).

check yourself ✓

1. What characteristics of audio make it such an "active" and "personal" medium?

2. What are the opportunities and challenges for advertisers in newer audio media such as satellite radio and podcasts?

LO11-5 Review the options for advertising in audio media and how listeners are measured.

BUYING AUDIO TIME

Advertisers need a basic knowledge of the medium to buy radio time effectively: the types of radio advertising available for commercial use, a basic understanding of radio terminology, and how radio audiences are measured.

Types of Radio Advertising

An advertiser may purchase network, spot, or local radio time. Advertisers like the size of the audience, selectivity, and cost-efficiency of radio (see My Ad Campaign 11-D, "The Pros and Cons of Radio Advertising").

Networks Advertisers may use one of the national radio networks to carry their messages to the entire national market simultaneously via stations that subscribe to the network's programs. In addition, more than 100 regional radio networks in the United States operate with information oriented toward specific geographic markets. **Network radio** provides national and regional advertisers with simple administration and low effective net cost per station.

Spot Radio **Spot radio** affords national advertisers great flexibility in their choice of markets, stations, airtime, and copy.

my ad campaign

The Pros and Cons of Radio Advertising [11–D]

The Pros

The principal advantages of radio are high reach and frequency, selectivity, and cost-efficiency.

- **Reach and frequency.** Radio offers an excellent combination of reach and frequency. The average adult listens more than three hours a day, radio builds a large audience quickly, and a normal advertising schedule easily allows repeated impact on the listener.
- **Selectivity.** Specialized radio formats, with prescribed audiences and coverage areas, enable advertisers to select the market they want to reach: a specific sex, age group, ethnic or religious background, income group, employment category, educational level, or special interest.
- **Cost-efficiency.** Radio offers its reach, frequency, and selectivity at one of the lowest costs per thousand, and radio production is inexpensive. National spots can be produced for about one-tenth the cost of a TV commercial. And local stations often produce local spots for free.
- **Other advantages.** Radio also offers timeliness, immediacy, local relevance, and creative flexibility.

The Cons

In spite of these advantages, radio has limitations: It's an aural medium only, its audience is highly segmented, the advertiser's commercials are short-lived and often only half-heard, and each ad must compete with the clutter of other advertising.

- **Limitations of sound.** Radio is heard but not seen, a drawback if the product must be seen to be understood. Some agencies think radio restricts their creative options.
- **Segmented audiences.** If a large number of radio stations compete for the same audience, advertisers who want to blanket the market have to buy at multiple stations, which may not be cost-effective.
- **Short-lived and half-heard commercials.** Radio commercials are fleeting. They can't be kept like a newspaper or a magazine ad. Radio must compete with other activities for attention, and it doesn't always succeed.
- **Clutter.** Stations with the greatest appeal for advertisers have more commercials. Advertisers must produce a commercial that stands out from the rest.

They can put commercials on the air quickly—some stations require as little as 20 minutes' lead time—and advertisers can build local acceptance by using local personalities.

Local Radio **Local time** denotes radio spots purchased by a local advertiser or agency. Radio advertising can be either live or taped. Most radio stations use recorded shows with live news in between. Likewise, nearly all radio commercials are prerecorded to reduce costs and maintain broadcast quality.

Radio Terminology

For the most part, the terminology used for radio is the same as for other media, but some terms are unique to radio. The most common of these are the concepts of dayparts, average quarter-hour audiences, and cumes (cumulative audiences).

Dayparts The radio day is divided into five dayparts:

6 a.m.–10 a.m.	Morning drive
10 a.m.–3 p.m.	Daytime
3 p.m.–7 p.m.	Afternoon (or evening) drive
7 p.m.–midnight	Nighttime
Midnight–6 a.m.	All night

Rating services measure audiences for only the first four dayparts because all-night listening is very limited and not highly competitive. Heaviest radio use occurs during **drive times** (6–10 a.m. and 3–7 p.m.) during the week (Monday through Friday), when many listeners are commuting to or from work or school.

Radio stations base their rates on the time of day the advertiser wants commercials aired, but the rates are negotiable according to supply and demand at any given time. To obtain the lowest rate, an advertiser orders spots on a **run-of-station (ROS)** basis, similar to ROP in newspaper advertising. However, this leaves total control of spot placement up to the station. So most stations offer a **total audience plan (TAP)** package rate, which guarantees a certain percentage of spots in the better dayparts if the advertiser buys a package of time.

Average Quarter-Hour Audience **Average quarter-hour audience (AQH persons)** identifies the average number of people listening to a specific station for at least 5 minutes during an average 15-minute period of any given daypart. For example, station KKDA in Dallas/Fort Worth, Texas, has an average quarter-hour afternoon drive listenership of 33,800,

meaning that any day, during an average 15-minute period between 3 and 7 p.m., about 33,800 people ages 12 and older are tuned in for at least 5 minutes.

The **average quarter-hour rating** expresses the AQH persons as a percentage of the population. Because KKDA is located in an area of 3,072,727 people, its average quarter-hour persons could be expressed as an average quarter-hour *rating* of 1.1:

$$\frac{\text{AQH persons}}{\text{Population}} \times 100 = \text{AQH rating}$$

$$\frac{33,800}{3,072,727} \times 100 = 1.1\%$$

The same idea can be expressed in terms of **average quarter-hour share**: the station's audience (AQH persons) expressed as a percentage of the total radio listening audience in the area. For example, if the total average quarter-hour persons for all stations during the afternoon drive is 676,000, then radio station KKDA's average quarter-hour afternoon drive share is 5 percent:

$$\frac{\text{AQH persons of a station}}{\text{AQH persons of all stations}} \times 100 = \text{AQH share}$$

$$\frac{33,800}{676,000} \times 100 = 5\%$$

The **gross impressions** are arrived at by multiplying the station's audience (AQH persons) by the number of times a message is delivered to that audience. For example, if an advertiser runs 24 spots on KKDA during the afternoon drive, then 811,200 gross impressions will be delivered:

$$\frac{\text{AQH}}{\text{persons}} \times \frac{\text{Number}}{\text{of spots}} = \text{Gross impressions}$$

$$33,800 \times 24 = 811,200$$

The **gross rating points** of a radio schedule are the sum of all ratings points delivered by that schedule, or the gross impressions expressed as a percentage of the population being measured:

$$\frac{\text{Gross impressions}}{\text{Population}} \times 100 = \text{GRPs}$$

$$\frac{811,200}{3,072,727} \times 100 = 26.4$$

or

$$\text{AQH rating} \times \text{Number of spots} = \text{GRPs}$$

$$1.1 \times 24 = 26.4$$

average quarter-hour rating The average quarter-hour persons estimate expressed as a percentage of the total market population.

average quarter-hour share The radio station's audience (AQH persons) expressed as a percentage of the total radio listening audience in the area.

gross impressions The number of people in the audience multiplied by the number of times an advertisement is delivered to that audience.

gross rating points Gross impressions expressed as a percentage of a particular market's population.

cume persons The total number of different people listening to a radio station for at least one 15-minute segment over the course of a given week, day, or daypart.

cume rating The estimated number of cume persons expressed as a percentage of the total market population.

Cume Estimates

Cume persons is the total number of *different* people who listen to a radio station for at least five minutes in a quarter-hour within a reported daypart (also called *unduplicated audience* or *reach*).

In the example above, our schedule on station KKDA generated 811,200 gross impressions, but that does not mean that 811,200 different people heard our commercials. Many people heard the commercials three, four, or five times. By measuring the number of different people who listened to KKDA, rating services provide the *reach potential* of our radio schedule, which in this case was estimated to be 167,800.

The **cume rating** is the cume persons expressed as a percentage of the population being measured. For example,

$$\frac{167,800 \times 100}{3,072,727} = 5.5\%$$

This means that 5.5 percent of the Dallas/Fort Worth population listened to KKDA at least once during the afternoon drive. The average listener heard our commercial 4.8 times, but we'll learn how to calculate that in Chapter 14.

Podcast Terminology

Advertisers buy podcasts directly from the producers or from podcast companies that offer a large selection of program choices. As suggested earlier, podcasts tend to be priced in CPM terms rather than in the metrics favored in radio. Advertisers frequently use tactics for measuring the response to their ads in podcasts that include promo codes that can be entered at the company's website for a savings or vanity URLs, which are associated with specific shows.

Podcast ads are typically described as baked in, which means it is a part of the podcast recording (and often read by the host), or dynamically inserted, in which ads are added to the podcast based on a specific listener characteristic.

Companies are anxious to leverage the popularity of podcasts. Apple, which is the originator of the form, has traditionally leaned toward consumer privacy safeguards. However, the company is developing tools and analytics that help podcasters improve their shows. ■

check yourself ✓

1. Why would a radio advertiser be willing to pay a premium for one specific daypart over another?

2. What is the difference between a radio advertisement schedule's *GRP* and *cume rating*?

ENDNOTES

1. "Has U.S. Television Ad Spending Peaked?" *Inside Radio*, November 15, 2019, www.insideradio.com/free/has-u-s-television-ad-spending-peaked-a-new-forecast/article_4ad3c780-0774-11ea-af0f-fb33e3c661be.html.

2. PwC, "IAB FY 2018 Podcast Ad Revenue Study," *IAB*, June 2019, www.iab.com/wp-content/uploads/2019/06/Full-Year-2018-IAB-Podcast-Ad-Rev-Study_6.03.19_vFinal.pdf?access_pid=62324.

3. "Nielsen Estimates 120.6 Million TV Homes in the U.S. for the 2019–2020 TV Season," *Nielsen Insights*, August 27, 2019, www.nielsen.com/us/en/insights/article/2019/nielsen-estimates-120-6-million-tv-homes-in-the-u-s-for-the-2019-202-tv-season.

4. Michael Balderston, "Total Number of U.S. TV Stations Continues Decline," *TV Technology*, October 04, 2017, www.tvtechnology.com/news/total-number-of-us-tv-stations-continues-decline.

5. "Cord Cutting Statistics for 2020," *NoCable*, https://nocable.org/learn/cable-tv-cord-cutting-statistics.

6. Todd Spangler, "Traditional Pay-TV Operators Lost Record 6 Million Subscribers in 2019 as Cord-Cutting Picks Up Speed," *Variety*, February 19, 2020, https://variety.com/2020/biz/news/cable-satellite-tv-2019-cord-cutting-6-million-1203507695.

7. Tony Maglio and Reid Nakamura, "115 Cable Channels Ranked by 2019 Viewership – Yes, Comedy.TV Is Still Dead Last," *The Wrap*, December 30, 2019, www.thewrap.com/115-cable-channels-ranked-by-2019-viewership-yes-comedy-tv-is-still-dead-last.

8. Rick Porter, "TV Long View: How Cable's Top Shows Stack Up—or Don't—vs. Broadcast," *Hollywood Reporter*, June 15, 2019, www.hollywoodreporter.com/live-feed/how-cables-top-shows-stack-up-dont-broadcast-1218556.

9. "How Does Satellite TV Work?" *The Connected Home*, https://theconnectedhome.com/how-does-satellite-tv-work.

10. Blogger, "The Pros and Cons of Satellite TV," *Tech2Blog,* March 24, 2015, www.tech2blog.com/pros-cons-satellite-tv.

11. Chaim Gartenberg, "Dish Network Floats Merger with DirecTV over Pace of Cord-Cutting," *The Verge*, February 19, 2020, www.theverge.com/2020/2/19/21144345/dish-network-merger-directv-streaming-services-subscribers-q4-2019.

12. Meghan McAdams, "What Is OTT?" *Tapjoy*, April 18, 2019, www.tapjoy.com/resources/what-is-ott.

13. John D. Markman, "Google, Amazon Join Forces to Win the Streaming-TV Wars," *Weiss Ratings*, October 07, 2019, https://weissratings.com/articles/google-amazon-join-forces-to-win-the-streaming-tv-wars.

14. John D. Markman, "Google, Amazon Join Forces to Win the Streaming-TV Wars," *Weiss Ratings*, October 07, 2019, https://weissratings.com/articles/google-amazon-join-forces-to-win-the-streaming-tv-wars.

15. Felix Richter, "The Generation Gap in TV Consumption," *Statista*, August 19, 2019, www.statista.com/chart/15224/daily-tv-consumption-by-us-adults.

16. Fact Sheet, "Cable News Fact Sheet," Pew Research Center, June 25, 2019, www.journalism.org/fact-sheet/cable-news.

17. Joseph Gray, "Consumer Response Advertising Is 44% of National Cable Ad Revenue in 2018," *DRMetrix*, October 3, 2019, https://drmetrix.com/blog/2019/10/03/consumer-response-advertising-is-44-of-national-cable-ad-revenue-in-2018.

18. Megan Geuss, "On Average, Americans Get 189 Cable TV Channels and Only Watch 17," *ArsTechnica,* May 6, 2014, http://arstechnica.com/business/2014/05/on-average-americans-get-189-cable-tv-channels-and-only-watch-17.

19. Adam Jacobson, "Is OTT Eating into OTA, While Killing Cable TV?" *Radio+Television Business Report,* April 25, 2019, www.rbr.com/is-ott-eating-into-ota-while-killing-cable-tv.

20. Adam Jacobson, "Is OTT Eating into OTA, While Killing Cable TV?"*Radio+Television Business Report,* April 25, 2019, www.rbr.com/is-ott-eating-into-ota-while-killing-cable-tv.

21. "The Rise of Social TV: How Social Media Is Amplifying TV Advertising," *Business Insider*, June 11, 2013, www.businessinsider.com/social-media-amplifying-tv-advertising-2013-6.

22. "New Research: Twitter TV Fans Tune in Live to Their Favorite Shows," *Twitter Marketing*, January 26, 2017, https://marketing.twitter.com/na/en/insights/new-research-twitter-tv-fans-tune-in-live-to-their-favorite-shows.

23. Michael Fleischman, "Extend TV Commercials on Twitter: Premiering TV Ad Targeting," *Twitter Blogs,* May 23, 2013, https://blog.twitter.com/2013/amplify-tv-commercials-twitter-premiering-tv-ad-targeting.

24. Robin Wauters, "As the Social TV Industry Comes of Age, Stay Tuned for What Facebook Has in Store," *TNW,* February 9, 2013, http://thenextweb.com/facebook/2013/02/09/facebook-social-tv-checkin-feature.

25. Cooper Smith, "Facebook Plans to Sell TV-Style Ads for $2.5 Million a Day," *Business Insider*, July 31, 2013, www.businessinsider.com/facebook-plans-to-sell-tv-style-ads-2013-7.

26. Brian Stelter, "Devices Lead the Way to a Smarter TV," *New York Times*, August 21, 2013, www.nytimes.com/2013/08/22/technology/personaltech/streaming-devices-lead-the-way-to-smart-tv.html.

27. "Television, Internet and Mobile Usage in the U.S., A2/M2 Three Screen Report," The Nielsen Company, 2008, http://i.cdn.turner.com/cnn/2009/images/02/24/screen.press.b.pdf.

28. Reid Broendel, "Ironmkark Picks: Top 10 Movie/TV Product Placements," *Ironmark*, July 31, 2019, http://blog.ironmarkusa.com/product-placement.

29. Jonathan Shieber, "Virtual Product Placement Is Coming for TV and Movies and Ryff Has Raised Cash to Put It There," *Techcrunch*, December 17, 2019, https://techcrunch.com/2019/12/17/virtual-product-placement-is-coming-for-tv-and-movies-and-ryff-has-raised-cash-to-put-it-there.

30. Erik, "Top 40 product placements of all time," Brands&Films, January 13, 2011, http://brandsandfilms.com/2011/01/top-40-product-placements-of-all-time-10-1/

31. "U.S. Product Placement Market Grew 13.7% in 2017, Pacing for Faster Growth in 2018, Powered by Double-Digit Growth in Television, Digital Video and Music Integrations," *PQ Media*, June 13, 2018, www.prweb.com/releases/2018/06/prweb15558424.htm.

32. Laura Stampler, "How 'Big Bang Theory' Dominated the 10 Best Product Placements of 2011," *Business Insider*, December 23, 2011, www.businessinsider.com/product-placement-nielsen-top-ten-2011-12.

33. Brad Tuttle, "Superman the Sellout? Man of Steel Has Over 100 Promotional Partners," *Time*, June 4, 2013, http://business.time.com/2013/06/04/superman-the-sell-out-man-of-steel-has-over-100-promotional-partners.

34. John C. Abell, "Nielsen: The Past, the Present, but Not the Future of TV," *Reuters*, February 22, 2013, http://blogs.reuters.com/mediafile/2013/02/22/nielsen-the-past-the-present-but-not-the-future-of-tv; George Winslow, "The Measurement Mess," *Broadcasting+Cable*, July 22, 2013, www.broadcastingcable.com/news/measurement-mess-114643.

35. Sara Jerde, "Nielsen Adds Mobile and OTT Measurement to Its Total Ad Ratings Amid Standoff With CBS," *AdWeek*, January 7, 2019, www.adweek.com/tv-video/nielsen-adds-mobile-and-ott-measurement-to-its-total-ad-ratings-amid-standoff-with-cbs.

36. Claire Atkinson, "Netflix Is Sitting on a Data Goldmine—and It's Starting to Give Us a Peek," *NBC News*, March 14, 2019, www.nbcnews.com/news/all/netflix-s-private-viewership-data-has-fueled-its-growth-spending-n983356.

37. John McDuling, "The Remarkable Resilience of Old-Fashioned Radio in the US," *Quartz*, April 4, 2014, http://qz.com/195349/the-remarkable-resilience-of-old-fashioned-radio-in-the-us.

38. John McDuling, "The Remarkable Resilience of Old-Fashioned Radio in the US," *Quartz*, April 4, 2014, http://qz.com/195349/the-remarkable-resilience-of-old-fashioned-radio-in-the-us; *Media Facts: The Complete Guide to Maximizing Your Advertising* (New York: Radio Advertising Bureau, 1994), pp. 8–9.

39. "SiriusXM Beats 2019 Subscriber Guidance and Issues 2020 Guidance," *Cision*, January 7, 2020, www.prnewswire.com/news-releases/siriusxm-beats-2019-subscriber-guidance-and-issues-2020-guidance-300982259.html.

40. Ross Winn, "2020 Podcast Stats & Facts (New Research From Jan 2020)," *Podcast Insights*, February 7, 2020, www.podcastinsights.com/podcast-statistics.

41. "Forecast: Podcast Ad Spend to Hit $500M in 2020," *Inside Radio*, January 10, 2017, www.insideradio.com/free/forecast-podcast-ad-spend-to-hit-m-in/article_aeffa6f8-d710-11e6-89e2-031d2b716060.html.

42. Ad Age Studio 30, "What's Next for Podcast Advertising?" *Ad Age*, December 9, 2019, https://adage.com/article/podcasts/whats-next-podcast-advertising/2221171.

43. Brad Smith, "Podcast Advertising 101: 4 Tips to Get You Started," *WordStream*, November 11, 2019, www.wordstream.com/blog/ws/2018/06/05/podcast-advertising.

digital
interactive media

Colin Anderson/Blend Images

T his chapter explores the important factors advertisers weigh when considering digital interactive media. This medium has its own distinct characteristics, unique advantages, and drawbacks. Advertisers must be able to assess the merits of this medium and understand the most cost-effective ways to use them in their media mix.

Tim Sweeney had a problem. His new, interactive, and highly social game, *Fortnite*, was selling more slowly than expected. He launched the game in July of 2017 and sold it for $40 a pop. Unsatisfied with revenues, he tried an unusual strategy:

give the game away for free. "That strategy," noted *AdAge*, "has made him a billionaire."

If you haven't played the game, it may be difficult to understand the excitement of *Fortnite*. As of March 2019—the last time the company gave an official number—250 million had played around the globe. Its appeal is obvious: a fast, enjoyable interface, its highly social nature (players join up with friends and communicate in the game), and the ability of players to choose their personae, weapons, armor, and gear.

If it's free to play, how has Sweeney's company Epic Games made more

than $2.4 billion in 2018 and another $1.8 billion in 2019? Like many smartphone apps, you can play for free, but the fun really starts when you purchase the extras. So it is with

continued on p. 302

LEARNING OBJECTIVES

After studying this chapter, you will be able to:

LO12-1 Discuss the evolution of digital interactive media.

LO12-2 Discuss the types of digital interactive advertising.

LO12-3 Explain how time and space in digital media advertising is bought.

LO12-4 Identify the opportunities and challenges of social media advertising.

Fortnite's *highly engaged users provide a fantastic opportunity for brands. This familiar looking character spends her time destroying freezers with beef. How does this way of advertising for Wendy's overcome problems related to traditional media ads?*

Source: Quality Is Our Recipe, LLC/Epic Games, Inc.

continued from p. 301

Fortnite. Players can customize many aspects of their experience but pay for the privilege.

Because *Fortnite* has few overt ads, you may be wondering why it leads off this chapter. Or perhaps you are unsure why a game is a useful way to introduce a major topic of this chapter—social media—which for many is better exemplified by Facebook, Instagram, Twitter, and Snapchat?

Although ads are few, *Fortnite* offers many branding opportunities, another important source of revenue. For example, *Fortnite* produced a crosspromotion with Marvel for the film *Avengers: Infinity War*. Advertising opportunities are also available for a secondary market: video game streamers. These are people recognized among hardcore gamers for their skills who attract fans by posting video recordings of their matches online. One such player, codenamed "Ninja," streams his games on social service Twitch and claims revenues of $500,000 a month. The money comes from advertisers who are featured on his stream.

What about the claim that *Fortnite* is not social media? In fact, the game fits the description of social media in almost every way. Like other social media, it permits virtually unlimited interactions among participants. Like other social media, the game is the platform, but user content and

actions are the draw. And like social media, the interactions and excitement of the platform are highly addictive.

Games are not a place for every brand. The audience tends to skew young and male. They have little tolerance for messages that interrupt what they want to do, which is play. But make no mistake—games are not a small market. One estimate suggests that mobile games are played by nearly 3 billion people every month.

As for the mind behind all of this? Tim Sweeney is nearly 50 years old, likes fast cars, and spends his money on creating nature preserves. For all of his riches, he prefers fast-food lunches. And while he may not be as well known (yet) as Jeff Bezos or Mark Zuckerberg, he shares one important commonality with both: the genius and the courage to try something different, risky, and big. And watch it pay off. ■

LO12-1 Discuss the evolution of digital interactive media.

THE EVOLUTION OF DIGITAL INTERACTIVE MEDIA

Advertising-related technologies never stop evolving. They've already given us computers, smartphones, the Internet, 4k TV, 5G wireless, digital media players, Blu-ray, IPTV, VOIP, and iPads—and the software to make them all simple enough for anybody to use.

Evolving technologies challenge advertisers, who are often unsure how to best leverage the opportunities they afford. These opportunities may become clear only with time. When mobile phones were first introduced, advertisers thought only in terms of ads on the devices' screens. It turned out that such ads are the tip of the marketing iceberg. A typical teen watching a high school basketball game won't just use his phone to place a call. He'll use it to snap a picture of the star player's Nike shoes, send the photo to Instagram, share it with his dad ("Hey Dad, I have a birthday coming!"), and message his friends to seek their opinions about the shoes. All of this will be accomplished in a minute or two. While using digital media, the teen will be exposed to several marketing messages, some of which can easily identify his general location and interests, and even his mood. The result is a trail of activities for marketers to ponder.

Digital media are truly revolutionary. As the nation's biggest advertisers realized that digital media offer vast opportunities for engaging target audiences, they started increasing their spending dramatically. In light of this change, online ad spending accounts for more than half of all ad spending in 2020, reaching an astonishing total of $135 billion, up from just $40 in 2012.[1]

In addition to phenomenal growth, by offering true interactivity, digital media enable businesses and other organizations to develop and nurture relationships with their customers and other stakeholders on a global scale at very efficient cost.

The primary elements of digital interactive media are websites, mobile media, and social media. We deal with each of these in turn in this chapter. Digital media continue to surge in importance as a platform for advertising as well as other communications (see Exhibit 12–1). In recognition of importance to advertising, we need to understand what this option is, how it is organized, how people get to it, and how advertisers buy it and use it in their marketing plans.

Social networking site Facebook allows web users to join networks organized by their school, city, or shared interest. Founded in 2004, the site has surged in popularity, attracting more than 2 billion unique users in 2020.

Source: Eric Risberg/AP Images

content has been delivered through **centralized networks**, in which a hub, such as a TV station, a newspaper publisher, or a cable company, distributes content to many receivers (see Exhibit 12–2). In a centralized system, if the hub is knocked out, receivers are left without information. But a distributed network is one characterized by many different hubs and links, which allows continuous communication even if some connections stop working. And, importantly, no single participant controls content.

There are at least three other important distinctions between the digital interactive and traditional media. The first is the cost of time and/or space. In traditional media, time (on TV or radio) and space (in print) are precious and limited resources. Network TV commercials average 30 seconds, which is a very small window, and that window is expensive, often costing advertisers hundreds of thousands of dollars. In contrast, space on the Internet is vast and inexpensive. Websites can store as much information as a company wishes. For consumers who require lots of facts before they make a decision to buy, this is a real plus. And for small advertisers with limited budgets, the economics are very attractive.

The second distinction between traditional and digital media concerns the relationship between those who create content and

The Internet

The **Internet** is a global network of computers that communicate with one another through **protocols**, which are common rules for linking and sharing information. The Internet began in the early 1960s as a result of the Defense Department's Advanced Research Projects Agency (ARPA) plan to create a network that could survive a Cold War attack. ARPAnet had little commercial value; its primary users were governmental organizations and research universities, and the Internet of today is a far different medium. However, ARPAnet was important because its structure, a **distributed network**, was revolutionary. Traditionally, media

▼**EXHIBIT 12–1** U.S. digital ad spending by format 2015–2019 ($ billions).

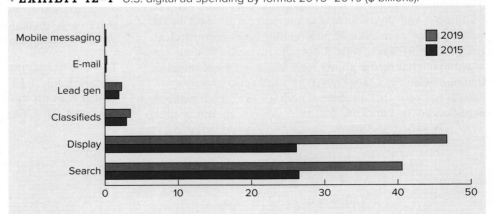

Source: "US Digital Display Ad Spending to Surpass Search Ad Spending in 2016," *eMarketer*, January 11, 2016, www.emarketer.com/Article/US-Digital-Display-Ad-Spending-Surpass-Search-Ad-Spending-2016/1013442.

▼**EXHIBIT 12–2** In a centralized network, a hub distributes content to many receivers. A distributed network has many different hubs and links.

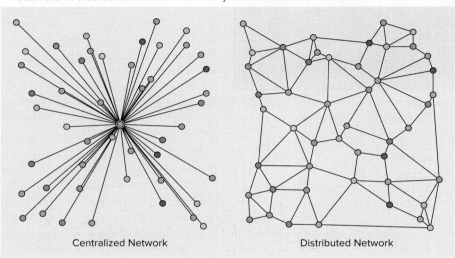

Centralized Network   Distributed Network

those who consume it. Traditional media companies are content creators while audiences are content consumers. As an example, NBC develops and schedules a show and, if you enjoy it, you sit down at the same time and night each week to watch it. NBC is the creator and you are the consumer. But digital media are *interactive*, blurring the line between content providers and consumers. The connected audience doesn't just consume online content; it interacts with it and helps create it.

The third, and perhaps most important, difference between traditional and digital media is the latter's strength in the collection of user data. Digital media users leave a clear, trackable, and identifiable footprint. In turn, the data provided by digital media allows for precise, efficient targeting that minimizes the chance advertisers will spend money showing ads to irrelevant audiences. Facebook is a global platform experienced in countries all over the world. But a local

advertiser can create an affordable and effective Facebook campaign that targets only homemakers in a specific zip code with an interest in crafts. And the advertiser can do it without the aid of an agency if she is willing to learn.

The Web

During the 1990s, the number of Internet users began doubling each year. Fueling its growth were the increasing popularity of personal computers and modems. The 1990s also witnessed the expansion of a part of the Internet known as the world wide web or just **web**. The web is a distributed network of content providers and users, communicating through a protocol known as **HTML**, or HyperText Markup Language. HTML made it easy to create **web pages** that can link to all kinds of content, including other web pages or sites (and, later, photographs, movies, databases, and audio files). Viewing web pages was made easy by the development of **web browsers**, software that interpreted HTML.

Today, the Internet is a global medium. People around the world use it for entertainment, to read news, research products, stay in touch with friends, and share information. The rapid expansion of broadband access makes it easy to watch videos, listen to audio programming, and download large files. Over the next few years, the introduction of 5G wireless promises to make accessing information even easier and more mobile.

This medium has proven highly popular. As of 2020, 88 percent of Americans and 85 percent of Europeans use the web. The United States is not even the largest nation of web users—that honor goes to China, which has more than 800 million users.

[Digital media users leave a clear, trackable, and identifiable footprint.]

portal A web page that provides starting points or gateways to other resources on the Internet.

website A collection of web pages on the web that are linked together and maintained by a company, organization, or individual.

microsite A supplement to a website that is typically singular in focus and delivers on the current advertising message.

And there is a lot of content for web users to access because there are about 1.7 billion websites as of 2020.[2]

Web Portals and Popular Websites

The early web success stories were known as portals. A **portal** is a site that provides an array of content and services so broad that (it is hoped) users spend a lot of time at the portal and very little time anywhere else. Portals such as MSN and Yahoo were designed to keep visitors for as long as possible. Portal revenue, it was hoped, would come from showing display ads to millions of visitors. Thus, making money at a portal involves attracting lots of people and keeping them around so they can see advertising. You may be thinking that this revenue model seems identical to that of traditional media and, in fact, it is. Yahoo remains one of the most visited sites on the web.

But the portal model was very flawed, and the flaw stems from its similarity to the traditional media advertising model. Display ads on websites, when not retargeted (more on that later), are simply not very effective.

The reign of the portals as the most most attractive websites for advertisers lasted until the dot-com crash of 2001. At that point, advertisers and investors, tired of Internet companies with no clear plans for profitability, pulled back. The promise of the web had not lived up to the hype. But as we will see later in this chapter, new advertising and revenue models from companies such as Google and Facebook would emerge. And as they did, advertisers returned. We describe how contemporary advertising is done in the next section of this chapter titled "Types of Digital Interactive Advertising".

Today, digital advertising is flourishing, and so is the use of digital media. In fact, so many people go online that it is easier to ask, "who doesn't use it?" According to Pew Research, about 10 percent of Americans do not go online. Groups that are more likely than average not to access websites include individuals older than 65 and those earning less than $35,000 a year. Why are these folks offline? Pew suggests some key reasons that include a lack of interest in doing so or a perception that the web is irrelevant. About a third of non-users thought the Internet was difficult to use, including some who believed they were "too old to learn." Roughly 20 percent cite cost as a factor for non-use.[3]

Following the viral "Ice Bucket Challenge," donations to the ALS Association increased from an annual figure of $5 million to $115 million in the United States alone, and the organization estimates that global contributions surged to more than $200 million. In this image, a participant successfully completes the ALS Challenge and shows the strength of digital media as an advertising platform.
Source: JMA/Star Max/GC Images/Getty Images

LO12-2   Discuss the types of digital interactive advertising.

TYPES OF DIGITAL INTERACTIVE ADVERTISING

The nature of the Internet is a constant state of evolution. Therefore advertisers have new and interesting ways to reach target audiences that extend beyond the more standard ad placements. We will discuss the less fluid advertising elements first and then look at the ways in which the medium is continuing to grow. In approaching this topic we will work our way back up the generic online "sales funnel." The Internet is truly unique as a medium in its ability to lead directly to sales so we will approach the section in that way, but beware of pigeonholing the Internet as a direct marketing medium. It has often been said that the accountability factor is not only the Internet's saving grace, it is also the bane of its existence.

The technical definition of a **website** is a collection of web pages, images, videos, or data assets that is hosted on one or more web servers, usually accessible via the Internet. A corporate site is used to give background information about an organization, product, or service. A commerce site is used primarily to sell a product or service. Of course there is a fine line between these definitions; for companies such as Amazon.com the corporate site is the commerce site and vice versa. Good marketers look at their website broadly.

A **microsite** is used as a supplement to a website. For advertisers it is typically singular in focus and delivers on the current advertising message. For instance, when Electronic Arts (EA) launched the *Return of the King* video game after the very popular movie trilogy *The Lord of the Rings*, it had Freestyle Interactive build a robust microsite that gave users cheats, codes, game screens, and exclusive videos and also gave users a chance to win a replica sword from the movie. The kicker was that to unlock the content, users actually had to go on an Internet-based scavenger hunt to find four

landing page The web page that a person reaches when clicking on a search engine listing or ad.

search engine A website that is devoted to finding and retrieving requested information from the web. Because search engines are the gatekeepers to information on the Internet, they are extremely popular with advertisers.

pieces, or shards, of the sword. Each piece unlocked more content until the sword was "reforged" and the user could open the cheats and enter to win the replica sword. The microsite was able to identify how many pieces each user had found.

Any web page can be a **landing page**—the term used to describe direct links to deeper areas of the website that advertising drives consumers to beyond the homepage. Typically, advertisers use landing pages to give consumers a more relevant experience as it relates to the message from the advertising. For instance, if someone searches for "men's dress pants" on Google, Dockers wants to send them directly to the *men's apparel* section, and more specifically all the way to the pants page, rather than making the user click two or three more times just to find the relevant products.

Beyond Websites: Digital Interactive Today

Digital interactive media have evolved a great deal since their beginnings. When the portal model failed, advertisers turned away from the Internet as an advertising medium, starting around 2001. However, just a few years later, they were back, investing in new ways of reaching the digital consumer. The most important of these new ways were: (a) search advertising; (b) advertising on social media, especially Facebook; (c) advertising on mobile devices; (d) behavioral tracking and retargeting; and (e) programmatic advertising.

Google and Internet Search

Most people looking to find information on the web or their phone use a **search engine**. Search engines are sites that allow people to type a word or phrase into a text box and then quickly find information. For most people, Google is synonymous with search, although there are other search engines such as Bing, Yahoo, and Ask.

The Google search engine was born as a project of two Stanford graduate students, Serge Brin and Larry Page. The friends were very interested in helping people find information on the web and gave little thought to figuring out how to make money doing so. When investors prodded them to do so, they created two programs, AdWords and AdSense. These programs are today combined in Google Ads. When Google search engine users type keywords, they receive two kinds of content: "organic" search results (Google's best guess as to what content on the web a user is searching for) and sponsored links. The latter

represents content that brings Google revenue for every click. More on the Google model later, but for now, it may not be too much of a stretch to say that Google saved the Internet, at least as an advertising platform. Search advertising produced results and advertisers flocked to it.

Today, another digital company is taking a page out of Google's book: Amazon. Google has shown that the power of search captures people just when they are looking for a solution to a problem. Solutions in Google search results are often found in sponsored links, and people who click on the sponsored links create Google's revenue. Amazon extends that logic to people searching on its site. What is the value of being the first brand listed when Amazon users search for paper cups, cosmetics, office supplies, or health care products? Amazon's ad program lets them bid for the opportunity. In 2020, the fastest growing digital ad program was Amazon's.

Social Media

Social media exist on the web, so it may seem strange to consider them as a separate category. But for advertisers, social media represent a very different opportunity than traditional web pages. First, social media, as compared with traditional, rely heavily on audience content. Audiences go to social media not just to read or be entertained, but to post, blog, share, and create. Advertisers don't use social media to send messages to audiences, they use it to engage them. They look for opportunities to get followers to share information about their brands. And they look to interact with them in a free-wheeling, somewhat uncontrolled environment. The importance of social media can be seen by the fact that Facebook is beginning to challenge Google as the most popular destination on the web.

It's hard to believe that Facebook has existed for less than 20 years as of the writing of this text. In October 2003, Harvard student Mark Zuckerberg launched Facemash, a program that allowed viewers to rate fellow students for their "hotness." Zuckerberg then registered a domain for "thefacebook.com" in 2004 and shifted the focus to connecting people with friends, family, and acquaintances. He had clearly tapped an important social need, because by 2009, Facebook was the second most-visited site on the web.

Facebook has rivaled Google as a platform for online advertisers for two important reasons. First, and most importantly, Facebook can provide advertisers with unrivaled amounts of audience data. All of that content that people post provides a window into the habits, likes, relationships, moods, hobbies, passions, politics, and dreams of millions of people.

Second, Facebook is remarkably effective for advertising on smartphones. Advertisers love smartphones because users do. Is there any possession you keep around, look at, interact with, or miss more when it is out of sight as much as your phone? In the summer of 2013, Facebook reported that nearly 40 percent of its advertising revenue was coming from ads served on mobile platforms. Today this number is more than 90 percent.[4] Adding

Rank	Google	Facebook	Amazon
% e-commerce sales	-	-	38%
% digital ad spending	37%	22%	9%
% social ad spending	-	83%	-
% mobile ad spending	33%	31%	5%

Source: Greg Sterling, "Almost 70% of Digital Ad Spending Going to Google, Facebook, Amazon, Says Analyst Firm," *Marketing Land*, June 17, 2019, https://marketingland.com/almost-70-of-digital-ad-spending-going-to-google-facebook-amazon-says-analyst-firm-262565.

to Facebook's digital clout, the company purchased Instagram in 2012 for $1 billion. This proved a smart decision, as Instagram now accounts for $20 billion in annual revenues.[5]

Facebook, Google, and Amazon are not the only players in the digital space. Pinterest, Snapchat, and Twitter have also revolutionized the way we communicate with each other, allowing one person to share anything that interests them with his or her entire friends list, whether that be related to work, politics, leisure, family, shopping, product use, or other. But the three companies remain dominant, as Exhibit 12–3 demonstrates. Combined, they account for more than two-thirds of all digital and mobile ad spending.

Smart marketers understand that social media foster interactions that go beyond promotion or advertising. Social media go beyond promotion because companies must listen as much as they speak. But for all of the difficulties, marketers gain one enormous benefit: they are put back in touch with their customers. And that can be a very good thing. We have more to say about social media at the end of the chapter.

Mobile Advertising   Apple's iPhone has transformed digital advertising in a way not seen since the introduction of the web. As of 2020, 260 million people own a smartphone in the United States.

However, America does not lead the world in either the number of users (China has 851 million and India has 346 million) or in phone penetration (the United States at 79 percent lags behind Germany at 80 percent and the United Kingdom at 83 percent).[6]

The iPhone, which now has significant competition from products offered by Samsung, Google, and others, was an advertising game changer. Before smartphones, portable phones did one or two things: make calls and send text messages. Jobs' invention turned the phone into a screen, one as attractive and popular as other screens of the day—TV and computers. Now people could go online at any time of day to shop, read, watch videos, play games, send messages, and post on social media.

And the smartphone brought the now ubiquitous app. If you use a phone often, you know that even when a company has a website, they often strongly encourage you to download and use an app. Why? Simply put, apps give companies much more data than do website visits. As Sam Harnett, writing for *Marketplace* puts it, "Mobile data opens up all kinds of possibilities for companies. For instance, your contact list can help Instagram

Not to be outdone by other social media, Snapchat offers brands opportunities to engage audiences. And because of the platform's popularity with teenagers, it has the advantage of reaching individuals missed in other opportunities.
Source: Snapchat and IHOP

> **SOCIAL MEDIA GO BEYOND PROMOTION BECAUSE COMPANIES MUST LISTEN AS MUCH AS THEY SPEAK. BUT FOR ALL OF THE DIFFICULTIES, MARKETERS GAIN ONE ENORMOUS BENEFIT: THEY ARE PUT BACK IN TOUCH WITH THEIR CUSTOMERS.**

Instagram, a highly visual social media platform, lets photos and videos do much of the selling. As this example makes clear, it is useful for both global and local advertisers.

Source: Procter & Gamble/Instagram

connect more user accounts; LinkedIn can learn about your social network from your calendar. And, of course, advertisers will pay a pretty penny for that kind of data."[7]

Mobile ads, whether served via apps or through websites, are rich with data and offer unique advertising opportunities. Among the most important of these is **location-based advertising (LBA)**. LBA involves serving a user an ad message based on the user's location. This information is part of the data that smartphones can provide to an advertiser. *Geo-targeting* uses real-time information about a user's location to deliver an ad, usually for a nearby brand or company.

As recently as 10 years ago, mobile spending was still a relatively small portion of all advertising. That has changed, and spending on mobile in 2020 ($113 billion) will exceed TV, radio, print, out-of-home, and directory advertising combined.[8]

What kinds of ads do people encounter on their phones? The ad types we've already reviewed that can be found on the web are present in mobile as well. That means search ads, Facebook ads, and Amazon ads are part of this ecosystem. In addition, mobile users encounter some types of messages designed specifically for phones. *Video ads* run within apps, below videos on sites such as YouTube, and in the feeds of social media such as

Snapchat and Facebook. *Interstitial ads* are ads placed during transition points, such as between levels of a game. An interstitial often commandeers the screen during the transition and tends to perform better than banner ads. *Native app-based ads* are shown within the content of news sites, feeds, and apps, and tend to resemble other content.

Social platforms have unique ads types suited to their offerings. Twitter offers promoted trends and promoted tweets, whereby advertisers can pay to get a message shared with a large audience. Facebook offers image ads, including carousels, and ads with up to 10 images in one message. Snapchat, LinkedIn, and Pinterest offer similar opportunities.

And even with all of the changes brought by technology, good old text messages are still a popular way to advertise. Sponsored short message service (SMS) ads are attractive because the end user need not own a smartphone. Almost any mobile device can receive texts. Companies such as 4INFO in the United States offer news, horoscopes, and sports scores, among other things for free to users via SMS, and advertisers sponsor these messages. The carriers have set up very strict guidelines regarding the

In one clever mobile campaign, the video cannot be seen in color and the music will not play without holding the phone up. The ad is for a Japanese performing group called Color Code and is called "Hands Up!" The mobile campaign went viral and successfully helped launch Color Code's single.

Source: Dentsu Creative X Inc, Tokyo

third-party ad servers A method of delivering ads from one central source, or server, across multiple web domains, allowing advertisers the ability to manage the rotation and distribution of their advertisements.

programmatic advertising A procedure for marketers to buy digital audiences via a computer. Content providers and buyers agree on the value of an audience via an auction. In programmatic advertising, an ad may appear on many digital sites, but only to audiences that fit the desired profile.

e-mail advertising One of the fastest growing and most effective ways to provide direct mail.

spam Unsolicited, mass e-mail advertising for a product or service that is sent by an unknown entity to a purchased mailing list or newsgroup.

use of SMS and act as a gatekeeper for all messages that go over their networks in an effort to reduce SMS spam. A smartphone user can respond to an SMS ad via a link to a mobile web page.

Behavioral Tracking

Your actions on the web are rarely anonymous. Almost all websites that you frequent can track your visits through the use of **cookies**, which are small files written to your computer's hard drive that let the content provider and many advertisers know what sites you've been visiting on the Internet. Compiling a record of the sites you visit, the actions you take on these sites (Did you buy something? Did you stop just before clicking the "buy" button?), your past buying behaviors or viewing patterns, and more can offer advertisers insights into what you might like to buy.

Imagine you visit a a news site where you notice a display ad for a shirt. The shirt is attractive, so you click on the ad and are delivered to the shirt retailer's site. However, it is too expensive, or perhaps it is simply out of stock. So you close the advertiser's window and return to the news site. From an advertising perspective, you are now a person with an unmet need. And advertisers love that kind of person.

To uncover people with unmet needs as determined by their online behaviors, online marketers employ the services of **third-party ad servers**. Third-party ad servers deliver ads from one central source, or server, across multiple web domains, allowing advertisers the ability to manage the rotation and distribution of their advertisements. The best-known companies are Double-Click, owned by Google and now integrated into the Google Marketing Platform, and Atlas Solutions, now owned by Facebook after it acquired the technology from Microsoft. These companies allow advertisers to monitor the performance of their buys on a daily basis all the way down to conversion or sales. By placing a line of code on the last page of the sales process, the ad servers can match the user back to the last advertisement they saw, via the cookies placed on the user's computer, and credit that advertisement with the sale. This allows the agency to understand Internet metrics from advertising to sales in near real time.

Programmatic Advertising

The traditional way that ads have been bought and sold are relatively straightforward. An advertiser, seeking a well-defined target market, uses media planning to identify a vehicle (newspaper, TV show) that offers a group of users who closely match the market. If the vehicle does so for a competitive price, then the advertiser contacts the vehicle or network and initiates a media buy (see Chapter 14).

Programmatic advertising is different. In a programmatic buy, an advertiser seeking a well-defined target market enters an auction for that market that is automated by computers. The advertiser competes with other advertisers who want that same market. The computer matches these bidders with sellers, namely content providers or media companies, who agree to deliver the ads to those audience members who match the target market. Because this happens in a digital space, the ads can be precisely targeted to only those persons who fit the target market profile. In other words, no waste. Additionally, an advertiser is really buying an audience, not a vehicle, because the ad may be distributed across many content providers. The move to programmatic has accelerated in recent years as it is highly efficient (although not without its own drawbacks). The practice started with websites, but with the advent of OTT (see Chapter 13) it is now common for TV and radio as well.

E-Mail Advertising

According to *Forbes*, 74 percent of marketers send **e-mail advertising** to customers who have asked for it. Marketers have always known that direct-mail advertising is the most effective medium for generating inquiries and leads and for closing a sale. It's also been the most expensive medium on a cost-per-exposure basis. Now, thanks to the Internet, the power of direct mail is increased even more, and the cost is reduced dramatically.[9]

It's important to differentiate responsible e-mail advertising from **spam**, which is electronic junk mail. Spam generally refers to unsolicited, mass e-mail advertising for a product or service that is sent by an unknown entity to a purchased mailing list or newsgroup. Spammers face the wrath of frustrated customers, tired of having their inboxes filled with unwanted e-mails. Spammers also face litigation under the Controlling the Assault of Non-Solicited Pornography and Marketing (CAN-SPAM) Act. Legitimate e-mail advertisers are required to (1) clearly mark the e-mail as advertising, (2) provide a valid reply-to e-mail address, and (3) allow recipients to opt out of future mailings. The first lawsuits under the act were filed against two companies that had sent nearly a million e-mails advertising bogus diet

customer retention and relationship management (CRM)
A promotional program that focuses on existing clients rather than prospecting for new clients.

drip campaign An e-mail marketing strategy in which strategic e-mails are sent to prospects at specific times and dates.

viral marketing
The Internet version of word-of-mouth advertising.

As seen in this screenshot from Apple's "Behind The Mac" viral commercial, the company supports International Women's Day with a variety of inspiring leaders from around the world. This commercial has been viewed more than 25 million times on YouTube. Why do you think this campaign went viral?

Source: Apple Inc.

degree seeker requires time to make a decision about attending a degree program (and what degree program to attend).

Viral Marketing

Viral marketing is the Internet version of word-of-mouth advertising. The term was coined by Steven Jurvetson and his partners at the venture capital firm Draper Fisher Jurvetson. They were describing free e-mail provider Hotmail's incredible growth to 12 million users in just 18 months through the use of a little message at the bottom of every e-mail. The message invited recipients to sign up for their own free Hotmail account.

The growth of mobile advertising presents new creative challenges. The relatively small screen of a phone means ads must often rely on powerful imagery, as this great example of a Snapchat World Wildlife Fund message does.

Source: World Wildlife Fund

patches and growth hormones. With this in mind, wary marketers are focusing their e-mail efforts on **customer retention and relationship management (CRM)** rather than on prospecting.

E-mail often plays an important role in turning a prospect into customer through **drip campaigns**. A drip campaign begins when an organization obtains a contact. The contact might have been obtained from a cost-per-lead ad, or it might have been purchased from another organization. In either case, e-mails are created and delivered to the prospects in a carefully chosen sequence over a specified period of time. Drip campaigns are especially important when a prospect requires time to make a decision. Online degree programs make use of these campaigns because they are relatively inexpensive and because the online

Since that time, many other marketers have come up with ways to induce their satisfied customers to recommend their product or service to friends and family members. One of the keys to viral marketing success is to present an offer with real perceived value—one that people will want to share with one another. Audible, a website featuring digital audiobooks, for example, uses a referral program whereby members are rewarded with free books each time someone they refer to the site signs up and becomes a member. Because members enjoy the site so much, it's natural that they would want to share the pleasure with their friends and families. Another example is Apple's "Behind The Mac" video, which supports International Women's Day (it can be found at www.youtube.com/watch?v=2iRWCFetoxg) and continues the company's commitment to diversity and inclusion.

" **ONE OF THE KEYS TO VIRAL MARKETING SUCCESS IS TO PRESENT AN OFFER WITH REAL PERCEIVED VALUE—ONE THAT PEOPLE WILL WANT TO SHARE WITH ONE ANOTHER.** "

LO12-3 Explain how time and space in digital media advertising is bought.

BUYING TIME AND SPACE IN DIGITAL INTERACTIVE MEDIA

Media planners cannot think of the Internet in mass media terms. Interactive media are *personal audience venues*. That means one on one. So cost per thousand, ratings points, and share of audience don't really mean the same things in the interactive world. With interactive media, advertisers aren't always building sales volume. They're building relationships, one customer at a time. And the care companies exercise in buying and developing their interactive programs and integrating them with their mass media programs will determine their overall success.

Digital advertising has arrived, as it now accounts for more ad dollars than all other media combined, and this growth is expected to continue. By 2023, *eMarketer* estimates that digital ad spending will be $517 billion.[10] Exhibit 12–4 lists the top Internet advertisers ranked by spending. While many companies are advertising online, just a few are raking in those ad dollars. These are Google (which accounted for 37 percent of digital ad revenue), Facebook (22 percent), Amazon (9 percent), and Microsoft/LinkedIn (4 percent).[11]

Pricing Methods

Traditional media ads are priced in terms of exposures to a target market, but because digital media are interactive, there are many more things an advertiser can pay for. In general, an advertiser can pay for a click-through, an action, a lead, or (as with traditional media) an exposure. The first of these, and the one popularized by Google, is **click-throughs**—also known as **cost-per-click (CPC)**. In this approach, advertisers pay for traffic delivered to their website. The delivered audience may originate from search or from other content on the web. In the case of audiences delivered from a search engine, click-throughs occur when a user types an appropriate **keyword** during search. Of course, many advertisers use similar or identical keywords, meaning competition can be stiff. Google rewards competing advertisers with a prominent placement of their ad (what Google refers to as sponsored links) according to how much an advertiser bids on the keyword along with how well the ad performs over time. High bids and good performance help a sponsored link appear prominently. Amazon's ad program runs in a very similar way.

click-throughs A web user clicking on an ad banner to visit the advertiser's site. Some web publishers charge advertisers according to the number of click-throughs on a given ad banner.

cost-per-click (CPC) The amount an advertiser pays for each visitor sent to the advertiser's website by a search engine or other site.

keyword A single word that a user inputs into an Internet search engine to request information that is similar in subject matter to that word.

▼ **EXHIBIT 12–4** Top Internet advertisers 2018.

Internet Display (excludes online video)	Estimated Spending (millions)	Paid Desktop Search	Estimated Spending (millions)
Amazon	$428	Expedia Group	$647
Comcast Corp	182	Booking Holdings	626
Verizon Communications	143	Amazon	277
Expedia Group	135	Lending Tree	255
Axel Springer SE	104	TripAdvisor	213
Dish Network Corp	103	AT&T	173
U.S. Government	91	Capital One	145
Fiat Chrysler Automobiles	91	Experian	143
Progressive Corp.	90	Discover Financial	118
Total for category	$8.5 billion	Total for category	$19.5 billion

Source: *AdAge* DataCenter, 2020.

In highly competitive markets, some keywords can be quite expensive. WordStream estimates that the average cost per click of an ad on Google is $2.32, but in competitive markets (education, insurance, law), the cost is typically $50 per click or more.[12] Even at that price, search advertising is attractive if visitors to a website are converted at a high rate into profitable customers. WordStream estimates that the average small business spends $100,000 or more a year on Google.

What determines whether users click? The relevance of the ad is certainly important. But another important element is the ad's relative position (first, second, tenth, etc.) on the page. As data generated by Catalyst (see Exhibit 12–5) demonstrates, an ad in the first position generates, on average, nearly twice as many clicks as the second.

The **cost-per-action (CPA)** model is common in what is known as an **affiliate marketing program** in affiliate marketing, an advertiser works with a network of other people or groups who steer Internet users toward an action, typically a purchase. One example is Amazon's affiliate program. If you recommend a book at your blog, you can put a link to the book on Amazon. If a visitor clicks the link and buys the book, you can earn money.

The **cost-per-lead** model pays sites for converting visitors to a website into leads. The visitor is encouraged or rewarded (for example, gaining access to a white paper or a quiz score) for leaving an e-mail address or phone number that an advertiser can use to follow up. The follow-up activity is most often an e-mail campaign (although it may involve calling).[13]

Facebook, which offers a click-through model for advertising, also allows advertisers to pay for exposures using a **cost-per-thousand (CPM)** approach. In this approach, advertisers pay for the opportunity to have people see their ad. Instagram, a part of Facebook, offers a similar model. WordStream suggests the average CPM of a Facebook ad is about $10 and the average for an Instagram ad is about $5. This means an advertiser pays $10 for the chance to have 1,000 Facebook users have an ad appear in the users' feeds. The cost of a Facebook or Instagram click-through is about $1.72.[14]

▼**EXHIBIT 12–5** Average CTR from two studies based on ad position. The likelihood of a click-through is closely related to the prominence of an ad's position, as this graph demonstrates.

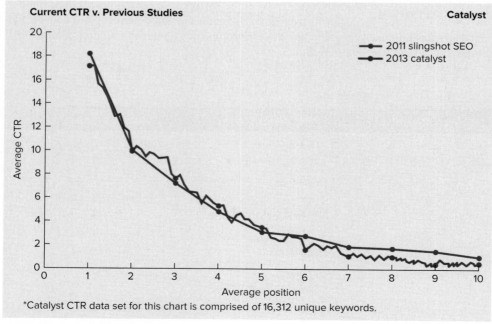

Current CTR v. Previous Studies — Catalyst

- 2011 slingshot SEO
- 2013 catalyst

Average CTR (y-axis) vs. Average position (x-axis)

*Catalyst CTR data set for this chart is comprised of 16,312 unique keywords.

Source: Google CTR Study, Catalyst Online LLC.

The Cost of Targeting

The very selective nature of the Internet can, for additional cost, be combined with tracking technology. This makes for a very focused campaign. Companies such as Tacoda work behind the scenes to meet the advertiser's CPM guarantees by using software that directs specific ads to a highly selective audience. Because Tacoda technology "tags" users, it can build a consumer profile and show those ads that are likely to be of the greatest interest to that specific web user.

But contrary to popular belief, consumer targeting on the web is very cost intensive. Although it is true that millions of people do indeed scour the web each day, it is still difficult to find and reach specific consumers. Thus, prices for precise Internet business-to-business targeting can eclipse even those of direct mail.

Stretching Out the Dollars

One of the problems facing most Internet marketers is how to get enough reach from their advertising. The enormous numbers of users who utilize the major search engines make these sites attractive for advertisers. However, Internet users surf millions of other web pages each day, many of which are potential sites for effective ads. Contacting all of these sites and negotiating advertising contracts on each is impossible.

Source: Ryan McVay/Photodisc/Getty Images

For this reason, most advertisers work through **ad networks**, which act as brokers for advertisers and websites. Ad networks pool hundreds or thousands of web pages together and facilitate advertising across these pages. The advantage is that this allows advertisers to gain maximum exposure by covering even the smaller sites. And ad networks allow for behavioral tracking and retargeting, which we discussed earlier in this chapter. Retargeted ads are far more effective than first-exposure ones.

check yourself ✓

1. What are the implications of such a small number of companies dominating digital advertising revenue?

2. What are some important ways to purchase digital interactive ads?

LO12-4 Identify the opportunities and challenges of social media advertising.

SOCIAL MEDIA

Until recently, if you wanted to socialize with individuals with similar likes and dislikes you would form clubs, such as a book club. However, you were limited to people who lived nearby, which limited the size of the club. With the advent of social media, people can "meet" virtually to share their interests with each other.

An influential definition of social media by scholars Carr & Hayes suggests that *social media* are "Internet-based, disentrained, and persistent channels of masspersonal communication facilitating perceptions of interactions among users, deriving value primarily from user-generated content."[15] The term *disentrained* is used here to mean asynchronous, or not live (as in a phone call). *Masspersonal* is used by the authors to indicate that social media allow users to share messages to many people at once.

A central theme of this text is that advertisers would like to cultivate relationships with their customers and prospects. Social media may be uniquely suited to this objective. Why? First, most major brands and many smaller marketers have an active presence in social media: they engage with followers, post videos, share news, run contests, offer apps, and generally try to exchange with customers and prospects. Second, brands are the subject of social media exchanges even when these take place outside of brand pages and sites. For example, people often rate brands and companies on sites such as Amazon and Trip Advisor. Consumers praise or complain about brands in tweets and posts, they take pictures of brands and products and share them, they use brands as props in humorous videos, and so on.

The engaging and immediate nature of communication in social media suggests another important distinction for brands: lack of direct control. Social media are the essence of the interactive model of communication we described in Chapter 5. Companies and brands lose control over the message in social media, sometimes to their peril.

The Major Platforms

A few large companies dominate the social space, with several newer upstarts tugging at their heals. The biggest remains Facebook with almost 2.5 billion monthly users around the world. Coming in second is Instagram, with 1 billion monthly visitors. See Exhibit 12–6 for a list of the biggest platforms.

Influencer Marketing

In Chapter 16 you will learn about sponsorship, a practice whereby companies pay money to celebrities, sports figures, or other influential people or groups in exchange for activities that

Company	Headquarters	Monthly Users (millions)	Ad Revenues (billions)
Facebook	Menlo Park, CA	2,450	$49.7
Instagram	Menlo Park, CA	1,000	20
Snapchat	Los Angeles, CA	360	1.7
Twitter	San Francisco, CA	330	3.0
Pinterest	San Francisco, CA	322	1.0

are favorable to the brand. Adidas, for example, is an Olympic and FIFA World Cup sponsor, in addition to sponsoring individual athletes such as NBA star Zach LeVine and professional golfer Paula Creamer. The sponsorship agreements generally involve money from the sponsor and the prominent use of the sponsor's products by the celebrity.

Social media has its own unique collection of "celebrities," who in turn attract sponsors willing to pay for a recommendation or positive review. These social media stars are known as influencers. One such influencer is Huda Kattan, who shares makeup tips over social media like Instagram, reaching nearly 40 million followers. According to *Forbes*, her net worth as of 2019 is $610 million. Felix Arvid Ulf Kjellberg, better known to his 1 million Twitch and 90 million YouTube followers as PewDiePie, attracts audiences who enjoy his commentary as he narrates his video games. The first male sponsored by *Covergirl* is James Charles, who influences 16 million Instagram followers on ways to use makeup.

Marketers are leveraging the popularity and credibility of these influencers by finding ways to have their products appear in

Marketers tap the power of Influencers, such as James Charles, to showcase their products. The rise of influencers on social media rests is in many ways unique, because they are individuals who possess the talent, drive, and charisma to attract followings from the ground up.

Source: James Charles/Instagram

influencer videos, photos, and blogs. For marketers, the benefits are many. Influencer followers are often passionate and highly engaged with social media content. Fans find influencer recommendations to be credible, far more so than traditional ads. According to one study, almost 20 percent of all consumers and more than 35 percent of young consumers bought or used something because it was praised by an influencer.[16]

It was once thought that influencer success was predicated on the fact that followers often don't realize that an influencer is recommending a brand or product because they are compensated for doing so. To combat this, the FTC in 2017 released a guide suggesting influencers use the hashtag #ad or disclose the sponsored nature of a brand appearance. Interestingly, one study showed that such disclosures had little effect on follower attitudes toward the recommended brand. This suggests that fans find influencer recommendations credible even when they know the social media celebrity is rewarded for their recommendation.[17]

Building Social Authority

Influencer marketing begins with **social authority**, a concept that reflects a source's impact on social platforms. Wagada, a digital marketing firm, suggests that social authority is made up of four dimensions: who you know (are they other people with credibility?), who knows you (respected others who like and subscribe to your feeds), what you know (subject matter knowledge that others find valuable or interesting), and what you are known for (humorous, creative, witty, accomplished, etc.).[18]

To develop social authority, experts suggest several steps. First, influencers should establish a clear, frequent, and responsive online presence. Are others commenting on your posts? Respond to them. Are others sharing information that is relevant to your area of expertise? Share them. Track popular hashtags and study when the target market is active in social media. Second, influencers should consider using paid social media advertising. This can put social content in front of carefully selected markets. Third, influencers should develop relationships with other influencers. These are the people already succeeding in the desired online space. Finally, influencers should regularly create and share great content, keeping in mind that it should be developed in line with the personality the influencer is trying to cultivate.[19]

Brands in Social Media

There are countless ways to describe how social media are changing the business environment. The flurry of engagement created by social media is not useful for branding alone. It has real consequences for revenues from e-commerce (see Exhibit 12–7). Here are some demonstrations of how brands continue to push the boundaries of what is standard practice:

- Domino's and Pizza Hut have created tweet-to-order applications. Domino's also lets customers track the preparation and delivery of their pies in a smartphone app and accepts orders in Amazon, Facebook, and Echo speakers.[20]

▼ **EXHIBIT 12–7** U.S. use of social media, 2018.

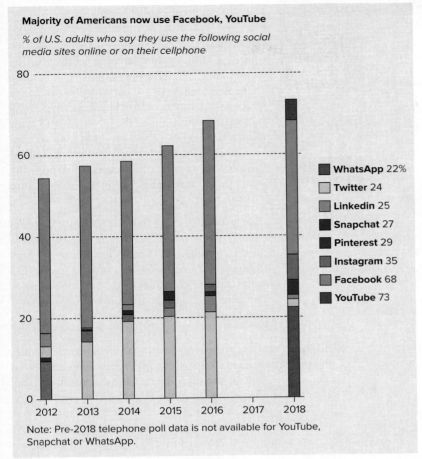

Majority of Americans now use Facebook, YouTube

% of U.S. adults who say they use the following social media sites online or on their cellphone

WhatsApp 22%
Twitter 24
Linkedin 25
Snapchat 27
Pinterest 29
Instagram 35
Facebook 68
YouTube 73

Note: Pre-2018 telephone poll data is not available for YouTube, Snapchat or WhatsApp.

Source: Aaron Smith and Monica Anderson, "Social Media Use in 2018," *Pew Research Center*, March 1, 2018, https://www.pewresearch.org/internet/2018/03/01/social-media-use-in-2018.

- Lego is followed by more than 6 million people on YouTube and offers fans Lego Ideas, a site that encourages them to share ideas for new Lego sets, some of which are ultimately created by the company.[21]

- Lush Cosmetics encourages followers to share content using #LushLife. The company popularizes its followers lives at the same time it tracks their trends, interests, and lifestyles.[22]

- Dell Technology has created a Social Media Listening Command Center to tap into social conversations. The Center organizes incoming data into several bins, including topic, consumer sentiment, and location. Then information is routed to the groups within the company for which it is of greatest relevance.[23]

- JetBlue relies on Twitter to initiate relationships with its most important customers. Then the company follows up by offering special promotions and resolving service problems.[24]

- BMW uses Facebook to serve its luxury car customers and prospects. It maintains several sites organized by geography and posts once or twice daily. While many posts are promotional, some educate customers about car technologies and safety features.[25]

- Food and beverage companies often engage followers by asking them to vote for new colors or flavors and then developing the most popular ones. This approach has been used by both Mountain Dew and M&M's.

- GoPro encourages users to share their videos. So naturally the company is frequently rated as one of the best brands in social media. With 16 million followers on Instagram and almost 11 million on Facebook, #GoPro is one of the most popular in the world.[26]

Common Uses of Social Media

Blogs   One of the easiest and best ways to get started in social media is to be a practitioner. Blogs are simple, reverse-chronological-order web pages that are typically opinionated. Many brands deploy blogs as a way for customers to hear the voice of the brand and get to know the brand on a deeper, more personal level. Zappos has an extensive site that lists blogs by category of shopping items: outdoor, running, or housewares, to name a few.

User-Generated Content and Brand Content   When brands create their own space on social platforms, it is usually to engage with customers, fans, and prospects. Passionate users typically generate a lot of content that smart companies are happy to share on their platforms. Starbucks asked customers to draw designs on white coffee cups and then share them online. Almost 4,000 customers took them up on it, and the company issued a limited edition of the best design.[27] Georgia, in an effort to increase tourism, used #ExploreGeorgiaPup to target pet owning Millennials. The state estimated the campaign attracted 14,000 people to their website.[28] And

Companies use social media to generate excitement about new brand extensions, flavors, and varieties. M&M's asked their followers to propose new flavors and produced the winning one, shown here.
Source: Grzegorz Czapski/Shutterstock

Social media managers use dashboards to monitor the effectiveness of their campaigns and to schedule messages. A good example of a comprehensive dashboard is this one offered by social media specialist Sprout Social. It tracks campaigns across multiple social media platforms.

Source: Sprout Social, Inc.

programs typically come at a cost or subscription, free tools are available from Google.[32]

Social Ads   Advertising in social media requires a strategy and set of objectives in the same way that advertising in other media does. A firm should have a clear sense of who they want to reach and what they hope to accomplish. Is the purpose of the advertising to grow contacts for a list, grow a group of followers, increase knowledge of the product or brand, drive people to a website, or make a sale? Who is the market, and how can social media tools ensure the campaign targets only prospects?

Every major social media platform accepts sponsored content and ads, and a good number of them provide excellent tools for learning how to master ad design, testing, and evaluation. Examples are Google Ads, Facebook for Business, Snapchat Ads, LinkedIn Marketing Solutions, Pinterest Ads, TikTok Ads, and WeChat.

jewelry company Iz&Co asked people to share their engagement pictures. The results included a proposal shot in Times Square and a French couple posing in Las Vegas.[29]

User-generated content is usually credible and interesting (but see the Ethical Issues box for a darker side of social media), but brands typically create their own social media content as well. Brands typically think very carefully about the "voice" or personality they are seeking. For example, Pop-Tarts adopts a somewhat sarcastic voice in an effort to reach younger users. One post reads "How beautiful do I look in my new profile pic, very beautiful or extremely beautiful . . . let me know." Reebok emphasizes inspirational and beautifully framed photographs emphasizing exercise and fitness on Instagram and Facebook. Stubhub, a ticket reseller, showcases creativity by creating a Pinterest board for every event they are marketing.[30]

Brand Monitoring and Social Listening   Social listening tools allow brands to aggregate all of the commentary, positive, negative, or otherwise, into a user-friendly dashboard with robust analytics and trend analysis of how conversations are growing and sentiment is changing over time. These tools are great for learning how people are actively talking about your brand. There are many different ways brands use these data. A very common way is to track new product launches and gauge the receptiveness from the customer base.

Among the most common and affordable tools are Awario, which provides the usual dashboards that track mentions but also looks for plagiarized content, Agorapulse, which in addition to listening tools offers ones for message scheduling, and TweetDeck, the offical tool of Twitter.[31] Other popular tools are offered by HubSpot, HootSuite, and Sprout Social. While these

Retargeting   Customers frequently go through a sales funnel for an online purchase and stop at the very last moment before buying. The items are in the shopping cart, but the customer backs away before confirming the sale. Maybe they decide they want to think a bit more before making a purchase. Or perhaps they get distracted or just can't find their credit card information quickly. Companies can take advantage of this with retargeted ads (sponsored content) in social media feeds for the same or similar products. One marketer suggests that consumers are 10 times more likely to respond to a retargeted ad than to a normal display ad.[33]

USING DIGITAL INTERACTIVE MEDIA IN IMC

As we discussed in Chapter 7, one of the keys to successfully developing an integrated marketing communications program is to promote purposeful dialogue between the company and its stakeholders. That is what interactivity really means. And that is where digital interactive media offer their greatest potential.

In the good old days of simple mass-media advertising, manufacturers placed their ads on network TV and went on about their business. The retailers took care of customers, so the manufacturers didn't really have to be concerned about them. In the new age of integrated marketing communications, that is no longer the case. Yes, the retailer is still there. But today's consumer doesn't want to talk to the retailer. She's a pretty sophisticated person. She knows who makes the product, and if she's got a complaint that's who she wants to talk to. So it's not good enough for companies to put up a pretty website and then walk away from it. It has to be staffed—daily—and it must be kept up

The incredible popularity of social media can mask some serious issues that are caused by overuse or misuse. Problems that were unheard of 10 years ago are now experienced by significant numbers of people, especially teens and preteens. What responsibilities do social sites share for these problems? And what about the advertisers and sponsors who support them?

Cyberbullying is, according to the U.S. government's Stopbullying. gov website, "bullying that takes place over digital devices like cell phones, computers, and tablets. Cyberbullying can occur through SMS, Text, and apps, or online in social media, forums, or gaming where people can view, participate in, or share content. Cyberbullying includes sending, posting, or sharing negative, harmful, false, or mean content about someone else. It can include sharing personal or private information about someone else causing embarrassment or humiliation. Some cyberbullying crosses the line into unlawful or criminal behavior." Between 9 and 15 percent of U.S. students say they've been cyberbullied. Among LGBTQ students, the number is 55 percent. The U.S. government considers cyberbullying to be of special concern because it can be persistent (happen at all hours of the day), permanent (shared widely and publicly, impacting many personal and professional areas of life), and hard to notice (teachers and parents may not see bullying posts).

The issue of cyberbullying sparked discussion at the national level when college student Tyler Clementi killed himself after his roommate and another student recorded and shared on social media a video of Clementi kissing a male friend in his dorm.

Because young children are often the victims of cyberbullying, it is essential that parents, teachers, and older siblings work to prevent it. Warning signs include increases or decreases in texting, strong emotions in response to texts and posts, hiding a device when others come near it, deactivated social accounts, avoidance, withdrawal, depression, and isolation.

Kids can face threats from other uses of social media as well. A variety of sites have evolved to help people locate others interested in casual sexual relationships, including AdultFriendFinder, Tinder, Pure,

Clover, Her, Match, and iHookup. Such sites may be appropriate for consenting adults who understand the risks, but they are clearly not for children below the age of consent.

Unfortunately, pedophiles need not use these sites to victimize kids. Many parents would be surprised to know that photos of children doing perfectly ordinary things are often found on the computers of criminals who downloaded them from Facebook and other traditional social media.

Pedophilia may seem to be a rare and unusual facet of modern life, but statistics suggest otherwise. The FBI reports child pornography is one of the fastest-growing crimes, and child porn arrests have surged 2,500 percent over the past 30 years. More than half of state prison sex offenders are serving time for crimes against kids. And the National Center for Missing and Exploited Children estimates that 100,000 American kids are victimized by sexual exploitation.

How do the monsters who pursue children locate and gain the trust of their intended victims? Frequently through social media accounts where children post about their pastimes, hobbies, friends, likes, dislikes, and so on. This information also sometimes identifies the child's school, home address, e-mail, and other social media accounts.

As the above makes clear, characteristics of social media that make them attractive to many can also lead to terrible kinds of misuse. Who, ultimately, bears responsibility for ensuring that kids can enjoy connecting with others in a safe, protected environment?

Questions

1. Is it ethical for parents to let children have private social media accounts? At what age?
2. Imagine a parent allows her or his child to have a social media account but secretly monitors it without letting the child know. Is the parent's behavior ethical?
3. What responsibility, if any, do social media brands have for ensuring the safety of their users? Do advertisers who practice IMC on social sites have a role to play as well?

---

to date—daily. But this is expensive—often requiring companies to double or triple their Internet budget with no increase in advertising exposure. So the decision to use the Internet for integration is a big one and cannot be taken lightly.

Digital media have changed the game. The consumer is important not only as a revenue source for product purchases, but as a client to keep satisfied, as an advocate to help promote the brand, and as a source of information about the wants and needs of changing markets. Companies now spend more on digital advertising than on any traditional channel. The ones that master this important channel will be the leaders in their industries for the foreseeable future.

Sophisticated use of different media platforms for different, but coordinated purposes, is what we've been calling IMC. And

digital media have helped to make effective use of IMC more important than ever. For a closer look at best practice in digital and social media, see My Ad Campaign 12. ■

check yourself ✓

1. What are the potential problems facing advertisers who use digital media?
2. What are the unique roles that social media can play in IMC?

Using Facebook and Google [12]

It is amazingly easy to help your client begin advertising on two of the most popular sites on the Internet: Facebook and Google.

With Facebook visit: www.facebook.com/advertising. You or the client will need a Facebook account, of course. Once you are at the site, you can read some case studies about how Facebook advertising helped advertisers achieve their IMC objectives.

Facebook makes it fairly simple to begin a campaign. You begin by inputting a destination URL, which is where the Facebook ad will send a potential customer who clicks on your message. You will also give your ad a title (limited to 25 characters), body text (135 characters), and an image.

Next you choose a target. In the United States, you can indicate whether your ad should be seen everywhere or be limited by state or city. You can also limit the ad to different age categories and just men or just women. You can even target people based on likes and interests, people who have different connections, or marital status and education.

You then give your campaign a name and set a budget. Your budget can limit how much the client is willing to pay on a daily basis for click-throughs. Once the budget has been used up, the ad will not be shown to Facebook users. This ensures you will stay within budget and not incur costly overruns.

The last bit of information you provide is the maximum you are willing to bid per click. Higher bids will be viewed more often, but can quickly eat up a daily budget.

Once the campaign starts, you have many tools available to track your results. Facebook reports the CTR (click-through rate, a measure of how often people exposed to your ad click on it), your CPM, the amount you've spent, the impressions you've generated, and it even provides a helpful graph that can show clicks, CTR, or impressions over a period of time.

Google Ads has a similar, easy-to-use series of steps for placing ads that will appear during searches on the popular site (https://ads.google.com). The company provides a wealth of helpful instructions about how to reach customers and understand the costs and benefits of using the cost-per-click approach. As with Facebook, Google Ads campaigns are based on a pay-for-performance model, and it is easy to set daily budgets.

Google stresses the importance of the keywords that you choose for the campaign because it is these words or phrases that determine which searches will present your ad to your target audience. Google suggests the following tips for choosing keywords:

1. **Choose your keywords carefully.** Make sure they're specific and directly relate to the theme of your ad and the page you are directing your customers to. Keywords of two or three words tend to work most effectively.
2. **Include relevant variations** of your best keywords, including singular and plural versions. If applicable, consider using colloquial terms, synonyms, and product or serial numbers.
3. **Be specific.** Keywords that are too broad or general will not reach users as effectively as keywords that are highly targeted.

Whether you choose to run a Facebook or Google campaign, or both, you'll be amazed how quick and easy it is to be up and running, and how many tools each company provides to help you track your success. If your website does its part by converting visitors into customers, you are on the way to using the web as a profitable medium.

ENDNOTES

1. Bradley Johnson, "In a New Milestone, the Internet Will Account for Half of Ad Spending in 2020," *Advertising Age*, December 23, 2019, https://adage.com/article/datacenter/new-milestone-internet-will-account-half-ad-spending-2020/2223511.

2. Lindsey Liedke, "100+ Internet Statistics and Facts for 2020," *W*, January 31, 2020, www.websitehostingrating.com/internet-statistics-facts.

3. Monica Anderson, Andrew Perrin, Jingjing Jiang, and Madhumitha Kumar, "10% of Americans Don't Use the Internet. Who Are They?" *Pew Research Center*, April 22, 2019, www.pewresearch.org/fact-tank/2019/04/22/some-americans-dont-use-the-internet-who-are-they.

4 Felix Richter, "Facebook's Growth Is Fueled by Mobile Ads," *Statista*, July 25, 2019, www.statista.com/chart/2496/facebook-revenue-by-segment.

5. "Instagram Generated More Ad Revenue Than YouTube in 2019," *Business Today*, February 5, 2020, www.businesstoday.in/technology/news/instagram-generated-more-ad-revenue-than-youtube-in-2019/story/395513.html.

6. "How Many Smartphones Are in the World?" *Bankmycell*, March 2020, www.bankmycell.com/blog/how-many-phones-are-in-the-world.

7. Sam Harnett, "Why Companies Really Want You to Use an App for That," *Marketplace*, October 2, 2014, www.marketplace.org/2014/10/02/why-companies-really-want-you-use-app.

8. *eMarketer* Editors, "Mobile Ad Spending to Surpass All Traditional Media Combined by 2020," *eMarketer*, October 16, 2018, www.emarketer.com/content/mobile-ad-spending-to-surpass-all-traditional-media-combined-by-2020.

9. Samantha Yaffe, "Are Marketers Undervaluing the Internet?" *Strategy*, March 8, 2004, p. 1.

10. Jasmine Enberg, "Digital Accounts for Half of Total Media Ad Spending Worldwide," *eMarketer*, March 28, 2019, www.emarketer.com/content/global-digital-ad-spending-2019.

11. *eMarkter* Editors, "U.S. Digital Ad Spending Will Surpass Traditional in 2019," *eMarketer*, February 19, 2019, www.emarketer.com/content/us-digital-ad-spending-will-surpass-traditional-in-2019.

12. Dan Shewan, "The Comprehensive Guide to Online Advertising Costs," *WordStream*, March 5, 2020, www.wordstream.com/blog/ws/2017/07/05/online-advertising-costs.

13. Irina Kovalenko, "CPC, PPC, CPM, CPI, CPA, CPL: Which Online Ad Models Are Best?" *SmartyAds*, February 2018, https://smartyads.com/blog/cpc-ppc-cpm-cpi-cpa-cpl-which-online-ad-models-are-best.

14. Irina Kovalenko, "CPC, PPC, CPM, CPI, CPA, CPL: Which Online Ad Models Are Best?" *SmartyAds*, February 2018, https://smartyads.com/blog/cpc-ppc-cpm-cpi-cpa-cpl-which-online-ad-models-are-best.

15. Caleb T. Carr and Rebecca A. Hayes, "Social Media: Defining, Developing, and Divining," *Atlantic Journal of Communication*, 23 (2015), pp. 46–65.

16. Kaitlin Augustine, "1/5th of American Consumers Have Made a Purchase Based on an Influencer," *Civic Science*, January 16, 2019, https://civicscience.com/1-5th-of-american-consumers-have-made-a-purchase-based-on-an-influencer.

17. Alice Audrezet and Karine Charry, "Do Influencers Need to Tell Audiences They're Getting Paid?" *Harvard Business Review*, August 29, 2019, https://hbr.org/2019/08/do-influencers-need-to-tell-audiences-theyre-getting-paid.

18. Cheryl Luzet, "What Is Social Authority and How Can You Get It?" *Wagada*, 2018, www.wagada.co.uk/services/general/what-is-social-authority-and-how-can-you-get-it.

19. Cheryl Luzet, "What Is Social Authority and How Can You Get It?" *Wagada*, 2018, www.wagada.co.uk/services/general/what-is-social-authority-and-how-can-you-get-it.

20. James F. Peitz, "Domino's Stock Is Up about 5,000 Percent since 2008. One Reason: You Can Order and Track Pizzas Online," *Los Angeles Times*, May 17, 2017, https://phys.org/news/2017-05-domino-stock-percent-track-pizzas.html.

21. Ben Davis, "30 Brands with Excellent Social Media Strategies," *Econsultancy*, November 20, 2018, https://econsultancy.com/30-brands-with-excellent-social-media-strategies.

22. Chloe West, "6 Standout Social Media Marketing Examples to Inspire Your Strategy," *Sproutsocial*, January 20, 2020, https://sproutsocial.com/insights/social-media-marketing-examples.

23. Rishi Dave, "How to Engage in Social Media: A Dell Perspective," *Point of View*, 2011, http://i.dell.com/sites/content/business/solutions/power/en/Documents/ps1q11-20110266-socialmedia.pdf.

24. Jennifer Aaker, David Hoyt, Sara Leslie, and David Rogier, "Amplifying Perceptions How JetBlue Uses Twitter to Drive Engagement and Satisfaction," *Stanford Business*, 2010, www.gsb.stanford.edu/faculty-research/case-studies/amplifying-perceptions-how-jetblue-uses-twitter-drive-engagement.

25. Abhijeet Pratap, "BMW Social Media Strategy," *Notesmatic*, December 10, 2019, https://notesmatic.com/2019/01/bmw-social-media-strategy.

26. Megan Grant, "The 9 Best Brands on Social Media," *EC*, September 27, 2019, https://eclincher.com/blog/the-9-best-brands-on-social-media.

27. Eric Siu, "10 User Generated Content Campaigns That Actually Worked," *Hubspot Blog*, March 12, 2015, https://blog.hubspot.com/marketing/examples-of-user-generated-content.

28. "15 Standout Examples of UGC Marketing Campaigns," *CrowdRiff*, May 8, 2019, https://crowdriff.com/resources/blog/ugc-marketing-campaigns.

29. Jillian Warren, "10 Brands Killing It with User-Generated Content on Instagram," *Later*, September 10, 2019, https://later.com/blog/ugc-instagram.

30. Sherman, "Best Brands on Social Media to Inspire Your Social Strategy," *Lyfe Marketing*, October 24, 2019, www.lyfemarketing.com/blog/best-brands-social-media.

31. "6 of the Best Social Listening Tools for 2020," *Marketing Land*, December 19, 2019, https://marketingland.com/6-of-the-best-social-listening-tools-for-2019-249953.

32. Patrick Strickler, "How to Create a Free Social Listening Dashboard by Hacking Google Analytics," *Compass Red*, April 19, 2019, https://medium.com/compassred-data-blog/how-to-create-a-free-social-listening-dashboard-by-hacking-google-analytics-36a207800462.

33. Michael-Jan Lazar, "These 2018 Retargeting Statistics Prove It Works," *ReadyCloud Suite*, April 12, 2018, www.readycloud.com/info/these-2018-retargeting-statistics-prove-it-works.

out-of-home, direct-mail, and promotional product advertising

This chapter presents the factors advertisers consider when evaluating various out-of-home, direct-mail, and promotional product options. Many advertisers use these vehicles to either complement or replace print and electronic media, so it's important to understand how advertisers buy these media and the advantages and disadvantages of each.

One reason for the lackluster appeal of billboards is their tactical nature. Think of a billboard you've seen recently and you're likely to recall one letting you know there is a Shell station at the next interstate exit. In other words, billboards and IMC just don't seem to go together.

However, such a view would be shortsighted. Although it is true that there are many dull, uninspiring examples of billboards, in the hands of creatives, boards can make powerful IMC statements.

One great example is a recent campaign by Corona in support of World Ocean's Day. The campaign combines a traditional board featuring a photo of movie star Chris Hemsworth surfing, over what appears to be a foaming blue wave.

But on closer inspection, the "wave" is a carefully constructed pile of plastics, all harvested from ocean waters. A nearby sign for the London billboard reads, "This wave of waste contains the average amount of marine plastic pollution found on every two miles of beach in the UK."

The billboard catches the eye, but how does this execution square with an IMC strategy? To start, Corona, the world's best-selling Mexican beer, has spent years advertising a connection between the brand and lazy, tropical, beautiful beach scenes. So the link between the brand and the beach is already well established.

In addition, Corona is partnering with Parley, an advocacy group for clean oceans, to bring meaningful change to the beverage industry. Here again, Corona, the first beer brand marketed in clear, glass bottles, each label painted, and each bottle brewed in Mexico, has an edge. The Corona–Parley collaboration will focus

continued on p. 322

LEARNING OBJECTIVES

After studying this chapter, you will be able to:

LO13-1 Describe the various types of out-of-home (OOH) advertising and its pros and cons.

LO13-2 Explain how outdoor advertising is purchased.

LO13-3 Discuss the various types of transit advertising and its pros and cons.

LO13-4 List the various types of direct-mail advertising and its pros and cons.

LO13-5 Describe the basic components of direct-mail advertising.

LO13-6 Demonstrate the value of promotional products.

Source: Evening Standard/eyevine/Redux Pictures

continued from p. 321

specifically on protecting islands in Mexico, the Maldives, Australia, Chile, Italy, and the Dominican Republic.

Adding even more IMC elements that are rare in an out-of-home campaign, Corona is marketing Hawaiian-style shirts created from plastic. The shirts emphasize a typical tropical scene until you see, on close inspection, that the imagery is again plastic ocean pollution. Finally, consumers who walk by the board are encouraged to take a role by dropping off plastic waste at nearby bins. The donated plastics will be used in further modifications of the board.

Corona's efforts demonstrate that billboards need not be boring or just tactical. In an effort to make a difference,

Corona's creativity demonstrates to other advertisers that out-of-home advertising can do more—and do good. ■

LO13-1 Describe the various types of out-of-home (OOH) advertising and its pros and cons.

This chapter presents several categories of advertising, one or more of which is often used to support campaigns running in other media, such as on TV or in print or digital. These "support" categories include out-of-home advertising, direct mail, and promotional products.

OUT-OF-HOME ADVERTISING

As a global medium, out-of-home (OOH) advertising has achieved great success. It was likely the first advertising medium, dating back more than 5,000 years to when hieroglyphics on obelisks directed travelers. In the Middle Ages, bill posting was an accepted form of advertising in Europe. And in the

This Apple board, perfectly suited for night, helps to demonstrate the power of OOH. For a driver on this dark roadway, the brand—and the message—are impossible to ignore.

Alexandre Rotenberg/Shutterstock

nineteenth century, it evolved into an art form, thanks to the poster paintings of Manet and Toulouse-Lautrec.[1]

Today, from Africa to Asia to Europe to South America, marketers use OOH media for the same reasons as Corona: to communicate a succinct message or image to a mass audience quickly and frequently at the lowest cost per thousand of any major medium. And while traditional media have had difficulty incorporating digital technologies as a foundation for growth, OOH has done so to great effect.

Growth in OOH is exceptional for a traditional medium. Expenditures increased almost 8 percent from 2018 to 2019.[2] And growth is expected to continue to increase as advertisers seek alternatives to the declining audiences and ad clutter of other mass media forms. Now that TV viewers can choose from hundreds of channels, it has become increasingly difficult for national advertisers to tell their story to mass audiences. OOH can carry their message 24 hours a day, seven days a week, without interruption. It offers a variety of options.[3] It's never turned off, zipped, zapped, put aside, or left unopened. And it's big. And it's outdoors. For that reason, some refer to OOH as the last mass medium.[4]

Research suggests that two-thirds of Americans see a billboard each month and more than one-third (37 percent) report looking at an OOH ad each or most of the time they pass one.[5] According to the study, billboard viewers aged 18 or older:

- Learned about an event they were interested in attending (58 percent).

- Learned about a restaurant they later visited (50 percent).

- Mentioned a funny billboard in a conversation (56 percent).

- Noted a phone number (26 percent) or website address (28 percent).

- Went online to find more information about an advertiser they saw on a billboard (23 percent).

- Visited a retailer they saw on a billboard later that week (32 percent).

- Received directional information from a billboard (50 percent).

OOH advertising may be used for a variety of purposes. For example, nothing beats it as a directional medium for motorists. It can reach a large percentage of a market, with high frequency, at a very reasonable cost. Of course, OOH cannot communicate with the same depth as other media, but in an integrated marketing program, it greatly enhances awareness of or reinforces the advertiser's core message.

Standardization of the Outdoor Advertising Business

Standardized **OOH advertising** uses scientifically located structures to deliver an advertiser's message to markets around the world.

In the United States, there are approximately 164,000 bulletins, 8,800 digital billboards, 147,000 posters, 20,000 junior posters, 63,000 bus shelters, 39,000 urban furnitures, and 29,000 airport displays owned and maintained by some 2,100 outdoor advertising companies, known as *plants*.[6] Plant operators find suitable locations (usually concentrated in commercial and business areas), lease or buy the property, acquire the necessary legal permits, erect the structures in conformance with local building codes, contract with advertisers for poster rentals, and post the panels or paint the bulletins. Plant operators also maintain the structures and keep the surrounding areas clean and attractive.

The plant operator may have its own art staff to supply creative services for local advertisers; ad agencies usually do the creative work for national advertisers. The biggest outdoor advertisers are services, amusements, media and advertising, retailers, restaurants, hotels, financial services, and communications companies. Typically, the smaller the market, the larger the percentage of local advertisers. On average, 77 percent of billboard advertisers are locally owned businesses.[7]

Types of Outdoor Advertising

To buy OOH advertising effectively, the media planner must understand its advantages and disadvantages and the types of structures available (see My Ad Campaign 13–A, "The Pros and Cons of OOH Advertising"). Standardized structures come in three basic forms: *bulletins*, *30-sheet poster panels*, and *eight-sheet posters*. For extra impact, some companies may use the nonstandard *spectacular*.

Bulletins   Where traffic is heavy and visibility is good, advertisers find that the largest **bulletin structures** work best, especially for long-term use. Bulletins measure 14 by 48 feet, plus any extensions, and may carry either painted or printed

The Pros and Cons of OOH Advertising [13–A]

The Pros

- **Accessibility.** OOH carries the message 24 hours per day and cannot be fast-forwarded, put aside, zapped, or turned off.
- **Reach.** For the same dollars, outdoor reaches more than 86 percent compared with spot TV (76 percent), radio (72 percent), and newspaper (72 percent) of the same target audience in the same city. The audience is mostly young, educated, affluent, and mobile—an attractive target to many national advertisers.
- **Frequency.** Many people reached with OOH advertising see it daily.
- **Geographic flexibility.** OOH advertisers can place their advertising where they want it nationally, regionally, or locally in more than 9,000 markets across North America.
- **Demographic flexibility.** Messages can be concentrated in areas frequented or traversed by young people, upper-income people, or people of specific ethnic backgrounds. With computerization, it's possible to characterize outdoor audiences by age, sex, income, and lifestyle down to the block level.
- **Cost.** OOH offers the lowest cost per exposure of any major mass medium. Rates vary depending on market size and concentration, but the GRP system makes cost comparisons possible from market to market.
- **Impact.** Because advertisers can build up GRPs very fast, OOH is the ideal medium for those with a short, simple message.
- **Creative flexibility.** OOH offers a large display and the spectacular features of lights, animation, and brilliant color. New fiber optics, giant video screens, and backlit display technologies offer even more creative options.

- **Aperture.** OOH achieves relevance by reaching shoppers on their way to the store, businesspeople on their way to work, travelers on their way to the airport, or lunch traffic looking for a place to eat, thereby influencing consumers as they are making a purchase decision.

The Cons

- **Fleeting message.** Customers pass quickly, so OOH advertising must be intrusive to be effective. The design and copy must tell a story briefly and crisply, and the words and images must sell.
- **Environmental influence.** OOH messages are influenced by their environment. Placement in a rundown area can detract from a product's image.
- **Audience measurement.** Audience demographics are difficult to assess. Not every passerby sees or reads the ad, so some media buyers distrust audience estimates.
- **Control.** Unlike print and broadcast ads, it's difficult to physically inspect each OOH poster panel.
- **Planning and costs.** OOH messages usually require six to eight weeks of lead time for printing and posting. High initial preparation cost may discourage local use. And for national advertisers, buying OOH is complex. As many as 30 companies may sell ad space in a single market. This is not true for the fastest growing part of OOH—digital boards—however.
- **Availability of locations.** OOH is so popular that demand for good locations now exceeds the supply.
- **Visual pollution.** Some people object to OOH advertising as visual pollution. They may have a negative reaction to advertisers who use it.

---

messages. They are created in sections in the plant's shop and then brought to the site, where they are assembled and hung on the billboard structure.

Billboard advertising is generally viewed from 100 to 500 feet away by people in motion. So it must be simple, brief, and easy to discern. Large illustrations, bold colors, simple backgrounds, clear product identification, and easy-to-read lettering are essential for consumer comprehension. The recommended maximum for outdoor copy is seven words. Very bold typefaces appear blurred and thin ones seem faded. Ornate typefaces are too complicated. Simple type is the most effective. Spacing between letters and words (kerning) should be increased to improve readability (see Exhibit 13–1).

Painted displays are normally lighted and are repainted several times each year. Some bulletins are three-dimensional or embellished by extensions (or cutouts) that stretch beyond the frames of the structure. Variations include cutout letters, backlighting, moving messages, and electronic time and temperature units called *jump clocks.*

Painted bulletins are very costly, but some advertisers overcome this expense by rotating them to different choice locations in the

market every 60 or 90 days. Over time, this gives the impression of wider coverage than the advertiser is actually paying for. The dominating effect of bulletins frequently makes them well worth the extra cost—especially in small markets.

Poster Panels   A standard poster consists of blank panels with a standardized size and border. Its message is printed on

▼ **EXHIBIT 13–1** Most and least readable typefaces on outdoor advertising.

Most Readable	Least Readable
Upper- and Lowercase	ALL UPPERCASE
Regular Kerning	Tight Kerning
Boldface	Lightface
Uniform Thicknesses	**Too Thick or** Thin

large sheets of vinyl and then mounted by hand on the panel. Poster sizes are referred to in terms of *sheets*. This term originated in the days when printing presses were much smaller and it required many sheets to cover a poster panel.

The **standard poster panel** (*standard billboard*) is a widely used form of OOH advertising. It is far less costly per unit than the bulletin because the cost of producing the message is far lower. The poster sheets are mounted on a board with a total surface of 12 by 25 feet and are usually changed every 30 days. The majority are illuminated.

Some local advertisers get high-quality OOH advertising at reduced cost by using **stock posters**. These ready-made posters are available in any quantity and often feature the work of first-class artists and lithographers. Local florists, dairies, banks, or bakeries simply place their name in the appropriate spot.

Junior (Eight-Sheet) Posters

Manufacturers of grocery products, as well as many local advertisers, use smaller poster sizes. Called **junior posters**, these offer a 5- by 11-foot printing area on a panel surface 6 feet high by 12 feet wide. They are typically concentrated in urban areas, where they can reach pedestrian as well as vehicular traffic. Space costs roughly half that of a standard poster and production costs are lower. They are an excellent medium for advertising close to the point of purchase.

Spectaculars

Times Square in New York is well known for its **spectaculars**—giant electronic signs that usually incorporate movement, color, and flashy graphics to grab attention in high-traffic areas. Spectaculars are very expensive to produce and are found primarily in the world's largest cities, such as Tokyo, London, New York, Los Angeles, and, of course, Las Vegas.

As seen in this poster panel advertisement, engagement can be especially important in outdoor advertising, especially in urban settings. This clever Mountain Dew ad not only gets people to interact with a billboard that is 40 feet off the ground, but it actually gets people to take pictures, ensuring a longevity beyond the time the ad will run.

(Both): Pepsi Cola Company

Spectaculars are expensive, elaborate animated signs found primarily in the hearts of large cities. They incorporate movement, color, and flashy graphics to grab attention in high-traffic areas.

TongRo Images/Alamy Stock Photo

Digital OOH (DOOH) Clear Channel calls digital billboards the "most time-sensitive and flexible form of outdoor advertising."[8] This new method for sharing OOH messages has experienced steady growth and made advertisers who might shun OOH take another look.

A Nielsen study suggests digital out-of-home (DOOH) vehicles are very effective. According to the study, 60 percent of Americans noticed a digital board in the last week, 55 percent noticed the message, and more than 1 out of 5 who noticed the message changed plans to visit the sponsored brand.[9]

A typical digital billboard uses a computer-generated message that changes approximately every seven seconds. Messages can be changed on the fly or even streamed from company websites. Lamar, a company that provides digital billboard services, notes that they can be used to share social media or other user-generated content, for live-countdowns ("We open in 12 minutes!"), and be adapted to local conditions, including weather, market conditions, and more.

Advertiser creatives can design digital billboard ads in standard computer design programs such as Adobe Photoshiop or Illustrator. Colors on a digital board are created through the additive process known as RGB (in which red, green, and blue are mixed to produce a color palette) similar to the way your computer screen shows color.

Because DOOH can be produced and shown so quickly, it can be bought using programmatic advertising methods, a system whereby advertisers bid on audiences via a computer auction (see more about this in Chapter 12). This helps give advertisers some assurances that they are paying efficient rates for the people who see their message. The result has been impressive growth. While digital represented about 24 percent of OOH revenue in 2017, it rose to 29 percent in 2018.[10]

For all of the benefits that digital billboards provide, it might seem surprising that they can cost less than traditional billboards. One rough estimate is a digital board costs about $1,000 a week,

versus two or three times that amount for a bulletin. The savings can be found in the fact that digital advertisers share the space with other advertisers, so the costs are divided among all of those using the board. Of course, the shorter ad message is a drawback for an advertiser to consider in choosing digital.[11]

check yourself ✓

1. Why can't outdoor advertising communicate with the same depth as other media?

2. How have digital billboards made OOH attractive to advertisers?

OUT-OF-HOME MEDIA

Media that reach prospects outside their homes—like outdoor advertising, bus and taxicab advertising, subway posters, and terminal advertising—are part of the broad category of **out-of-home media** (see Exhibit 13–2). Today, there are more than 40 different types of out-of-home media, generating nearly

▼**EXHIBIT 13–2** Number of vehicles within OOH categories.

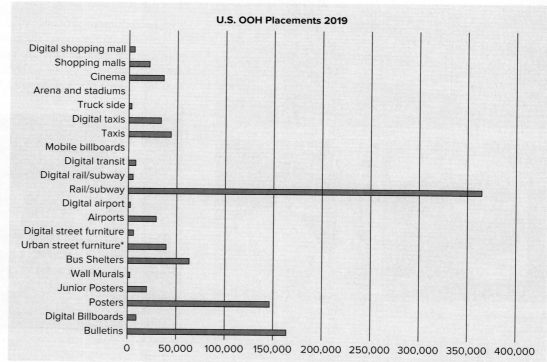

U.S. OOH Placements 2019

Source: Data from "Number of Out-of-Home Displays (2019)," *Outdoor Advertising Association of America*, retrieved at: https://oaaa.org/Portals/0/Images/Charts/Charts%20-%20Media%20Formats%20-%2008.19.png.

$11 billion in 2019, up from $6.7 billion as recently as 2012.[12] The most common is *on-premise signage*, which promotes goods and services or identifies a place of business, on the property where the sign is located.[13] The golden arches at McDonald's franchises are a good example. On-premise signage is important for helping us find a place of business, but it doesn't provide any kind of market coverage, and it isn't considered advertising.

Although most people think of billboards when identifying OOH advertising, there are a surprising number of options. These include standardized outdoor and transit advertising. We'll also briefly discuss some other out-of-home vehicles that are gaining in popularity: cinema advertising, ATMs, mobile billboards, in-store and mall advertising, and digital signs and displays. Then we'll discuss direct-mail advertising, one of the most efficient, effective, economical, and most widely used media today. And finally, we'll touch on promotional products, an important component of the very large promotional products industry. Before reviewing each of these, let's look at how OOH advertising is bought by advertisers and agencies.

LO13-2   Explain how outdoor advertising is purchased.

BUYING OOH ADVERTISING

Advertisers use OOH for a variety of purposes. For example, to introduce a new product or announce a change in package design, an advertiser might want to saturate the market rapidly. When eBay wanted to communicate its new line of mobile apps, the online firm used bulletins, wallscapes, transit shelters, phone and street kiosks, and subway station dioramas next to high-traffic shopping districts in key markets. The executions included QR codes and bar codes, allowing consumers to shop for products on the spot. As a result, eBay experienced a record 2011 holiday shopping season, with some eBay merchants reporting a 15 percent increase in sales on Black Friday and a record Cyber Monday, with PayPal seeing a 514 percent increase in payments made from mobile devices.[14]

The basic unit of sale for billboards, or posters, is *100 gross rating points daily*, or a **100 showing**. One rating point equals 1 percent of a particular market's population. Buying 100 gross rating points does not mean the message will appear on 100 posters or on 100 percent of the posters; it means the message will appear as many places as needed to provide a daily

Mark Steinmetz/McGraw-Hill

exposure *theoretically* equal to 100 percent of the market's total population.

For less saturation, a company can purchase 75, 50, or 25 gross rating points (GRPs), equivalent to 75 percent, 50 percent, or 25 percent of the market's population. For example, if a showing provides 750,000 total impression opportunities daily in a market with a population of 1 million, it delivers 75 GRPs (75 percent of the population) daily. Over a period of 30 days, the showing would earn 2,250 GRPs (30 days × 75 GRPs per day).

A showing, as suggested above, was historically measured by a rudimentary equation that considers the number of people who pass by an out-of-home display as the measure of reach. This measurement is called Daily Effective Circulation, or DEC. However, in 2009 the Outdoor Advertising Association of America (OAAA) and the Traffic Audit Bureau (TAB) developed a new method of measuring out-of-home's true reach and frequency, called TAB Out of Home Ratings.[15] It takes into account many factors other than the number of people that pass a display, such as size of the display, angle to the road, format, street type, distance from the road, roadside position, and illumination. These factors are entered in a formula that estimates the number of people that *actually* see the ad over a week. The main difference between DECs and TAB Out of Home Ratings is the former considers how many people *pass by* the ad on a daily basis while the latter estimates how many *see* the ad on a weekly basis. The net effect is that OOH is now the only ad medium that tracks viewers of ads rather than just exposures, or what is referred to in Chapter 14 as impressions.[16]

Location, Location, Location

As in real estate, location is everything in OOH. Advertisers that want more saturation can increase the number of posters or purchase better locations, sometimes achieving 200 or 300 GRPs

[Location is everything in outdoor advertising.]

per day. The map in Exhibit 13–3 shows the billboard locations in Baton Rouge, Louisiana, that together would generate 100 or more GRPs per day. To achieve a 100 showing in Baton Rouge, Lamar Outdoor Advertising would place billboards (see Exhibit 13–3) along all major traffic arteries, facing in both directions. Rates vary considerably from market to market due to variations in property prices, labor costs, and market size. As you would expect, Exhibit 13–4 shows that locations in larger markets with high traffic volume have higher rates. A standard billboard costs between $500 and $1,500 per month. At that rate, billboards still offer the lowest cost per thousand impressions (an average of about $5.00 a 30-sheet poster) of any major mass medium.[17] The only other medium that comes close is radio.

Technology in Outdoor Advertising

In the past it could be a problem for a media buyer in New York to adequately supervise the selection of outdoor boards in Peoria, Illinois. A buyer can't just jump on a plane and travel to all the cities where the client's boards are posted to verify every location. Fortunately, technology has solved this dilemma and has made OOH an even more attractive medium to national advertisers. Outdoor companies can use sophisticated **global positioning systems (GPSs)** to give the exact latitude and longitude of particular boards using satellite technology. Media buyers, equipped with sophisticated new software on their desktop computers, can then integrate this information with demographic market characteristics and traffic counts to determine the best locations for their boards.[18]

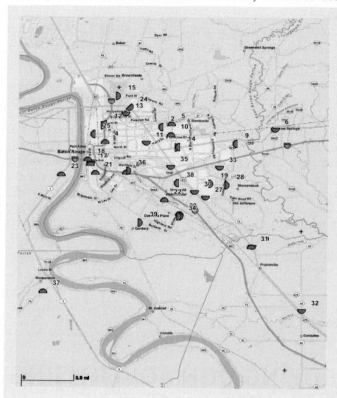

▼ EXHIBIT 13–3 Typical billboard locations in Baton Rouge that would achieve at least 100 GRPs daily when posted for 30 days. The red semicircles indicate which way the boards face.

▼ EXHIBIT 13–4 Four-week rates for standard 30-sheet posters in selected markets.

| Market (DMA) | 18+ Population | 100 Weekly GRPs | | 4-Week GRP | 4-Week Impressions | CPP | CPM | 4-Week Reach | 4-Week Frequency |
		Number	Cost						
Bakersfield	598,107	11	$12,463	400	2,409,484	$ 31.16	$5.17	63.3%	8.5
Baton Rouge	685,684	15	12,900	400	2,817,120	32.25	4.58	48.1	6.9
Boise	538,655	12	11,880	400	2,181,024	29.70	5.45	58.8	7.8
Buffalo–Niagra, NY	1,251,647	40	38,800	400	5,128,000	97.00	7.57	59.9	8.6
Cincinnati	1,759,545	39	25,350	400	7,046,832	63.68	3.60	51.5	7.6
Chicago	7,309,947	131	78,600	400	29,221,384	196.50	2.69	40.7	9.3
Lima, OH	114,528	6	4,830	400	516,816	12.08	9.36	71.0	9.5
Omaha	820,901	14	8,750	400	3,290,448	21.88	2.66	51.0	8.7
Pittsburgh	2,260,433	55	79,750	400	9,081,600	199.38	8.78	60.1	8.5
Tallahassee	558,740	16	9,888	400	2,261,632	24.72	4.37	43.9	8.3

Note: Costs are for space only, based on a 4-week posting period; they do not include production. Rates are effective as of the date of publication and are subject to change.
Source: Lamar Outdoor Advertising, www.lamar.com.

Many outdoor companies provide digitized videos of their locations so the buyer can see the actual boards and the environment in which they are located. Other developments include bar coding of materials so they can be tracked, posted, and authenticated, all by computer. Computerized painting on flexible vinyl guarantees a high-quality, high-resolution, faithful reproduction of the advertiser's message regardless of the market.[19]

Perhaps the most exciting development in outdoor advertising is the availability of digital (or electronic) billboards. Ads can be implemented the same day and updated quickly and easily, from hundreds of miles away, over the Internet. Digital billboards can rotate ads among various advertisers or move ads around town, changing them once every 4 to 10 seconds. A restaurant can feature breakfast specials in the morning and dinner specials in the evening. Law enforcement can display the image of a missing person or update emergency information in minutes. Production costs are reduced dramatically. Some digital billboards will even interact with passersby, responding to a friendly wave or communicating with consumers' cell phones. Presently, there are about 9,000 digital billboards in the United States, with several hundred being added each year at a cost of about $250,000 each, versus less than $50,000 for a traditional billboard. Due to perceived safety concerns, some cities have banned digital billboards. Los Angeles sign operators were ordered to turn off nearly 100 digital billboards in early 2013. Other cities have placed strict limitations on them while government agencies evaluate their possibly distracting effect on drivers. So far, some studies indicate that there is no relationship between traffic accidents and digital billboards,[20] while other studies suggest that electronic signs are distracting.[21]

Exciting new technologies may change the future of how we "see" outdoor and other out-of-home ads. TeamOne launched a revolutionary campaign for Lexus that included a full-size hologram of the IS sedan. Using interactive kiosks located in Times Square and other prime U.S. locations, the display featured a hologram of the Lexus in motion and touch pads that allowed visitors to change the car's color and other features.[22] This opens up many thrilling possibilities for advertisers: Imagine a bulletin-size structure on the highway promoting the latest Marvel film, with a larger-than-life superhero coming at you in 3-D.

Regulation of Outdoor Advertising

The Highway Beautification Act of 1965 controls outdoor advertising on U.S. interstate highways and other federally subsidized highways. It was enacted partly in response to consumer complaints that outdoor advertising was spoiling the environment. More than 700,000 billboards were removed by 1991, the year Congress banned the construction of new billboards on all scenic portions of interstate highways.[23] Since that time, the

OOH advertising doesn't consist of billboards only. These digital signs in New York are spectaculars, digital images placed in heavily trafficked locations. These messages include both brand messages and PSAs thanking Americans for their efforts during the COVID crisis.

John Nacion/ZUMA Press/Newscom

image of outdoor advertising has improved dramatically. Today, most people polled say they like billboards, believe they promote business, and find they provide useful travel information for drivers.[24]

Each state also regulates, administers, and enforces outdoor advertising permit programs through its department of transportation. Some states (Maine, Vermont, Hawaii, and Alaska) prohibit outdoor advertising altogether. Ironically, though, some of these states use outdoor advertising themselves in other states to promote tourism.

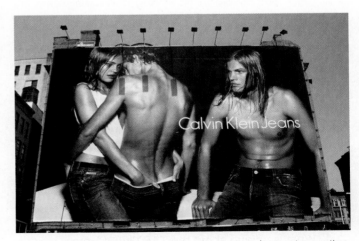

The public nature of OOH means advertisers are under greater scrutiny than they might be in publications with adult reach. Some groups have reacted strongly to billboard ads featuring sexual themes, alcohol, tobacco, or other offensive products.

John Violet/Alamy Stock Photo

Does Spillover Need Mopping Up?

While numerous laws and self-regulatory efforts have banished products such as tobacco and hard liquor from the airwaves, it is virtually impossible to keep minors from being exposed to such advertising due to the spillover nature of some media. The ethical issues involved with spillover media are complex, including the kind of advertising appeals used to target audiences.

Take outdoor advertising, for example. It is the most public mass medium. It cannot be turned off like television, radio, or the Internet, and it's displayed 24 hours a day for all to see—even children.

The trend in outdoor advertising today is toward eye-catching, sexually explicit ads, seen especially in densely populated urban areas. Most outdoor advertising regulations have focused on the location of billboards, not the content. The Outdoor Advertising Association of America's (OAAA) Code of Principles says that they "support the right to reject advertising that is misleading, offensive, or otherwise incompatible with community standards." But it is unknown how often this clause is invoked. Communities, therefore, have taken it upon themselves to regulate the placement and content of outdoor advertising, rather than relying on self-regulation by the advertising industry. In 1998, for example, the Los Angeles City Council passed an ordinance that prohibited alcoholic beverage advertising on virtually all publicly visible sites, even store windows. The OAAA and other local Los Angeles trade association members filed a federal civil rights action, claiming that the ordinance violates the right to free speech.

As technology advances, so do the venues for advertising. Advertisers have found ways to work around billboard restrictions. Taxicabs and buses have carried ads for years; however, now appearing on Boston cabs are electronic billboards that have the ability to change their message minute by minute—depending on a few desired variables. The full-color ads change depending on the time of day and location of the cab. Different neighborhoods will see different ads and, if appropriate, in different languages. The taxi's location is monitored by a GPS tracking system. This new technology is inexpensive for advertisers and may become a common feature on taxicabs across America. However, this raises legal and ethical questions. Should mobile billboards be subjected to the same restrictions as stationary billboards? Neighborhoods and schools may be protected from unwanted billboard advertising, but can concerned parents protect their children from advertising that travels on taxis?

Spillover also reaches children in other media vehicles besides OOH. The movies, for example, consistently show people smoking. And if the smoker is a celebrity, an impressionable child might interpret that as an endorsement. In a study conducted by Dartmouth Medical School, researchers concluded that actor endorsements of tobacco brands jumped 10-fold in the 1990s. The study also found that 87 percent of popular movies contain tobacco use and about one-third display identifiable brand-name logos. Minors make up a large percentage of moviegoers, and through movies they may be getting more exposure to smoking endorsements than in real life. Young people who look up to sport stars and movie celebrities may be vulnerable to intentional and unintentional endorsements. Benedict Carey of the *Los Angeles Times* calls today's movies "almost as smoke-laden as the stock car racing circuit."

Many people feel that ads are not to blame for the rise of teen sexual activity and tobacco and alcohol use. Others feel that advertisers have a greater responsibility to separate youth from the adult world of unhealthy and explicit activity. Regardless of who is right, advertisers, agencies, and media companies must be sensitive to public opinion and seek creative solutions to protect impressionable children. Otherwise, the industry will risk severe restriction and regulation for having failed to responsibly and conscientiously assert firm ethical standards itself.

Questions

1. Do you believe the goal of protecting children justifies banning the advertising of legal products or their glorification in movies? Which products specifically?
2. Should ads in spillover media be censored for sexually explicit content? If so, who should the censors be and what specifically should they prohibit?
3. What alternatives might be available to fight teenage smoking, drinking, and sexual promiscuity besides banning advertising for legal adult products?

The Ethical Issue, "Does Spillover Need Mopping Up?" feature discusses some of the problems inherent in the very public nature of outdoor advertising and whether regulation will be needed here too.

check yourself ✓

1. What is unique about the TAB Out of Home Ratings system?
2. What are the advantages of digital billboards?

LO13-3   Discuss the various types of transit advertising and its pros and cons.

TRANSIT ADVERTISING

When Campbell Soup started advertising in 1910, the company spent its first $5,000 placing ads on one-third of the buses in New York City for one year. The ads were so successful that after only six months, Campbell enlarged the contract to include all surface vehicles in the city. People started buying more Campbell's soup and soon sales were up 100 percent. For the next 12 years, transit advertising was the only medium Campbell employed. Today, Campbell is still a major user of transit advertising.

Transit advertising can be used to strategically promote brand equity. The layout of a foot-long Subway sandwich on this trolley conveys the idea of a filling meal.

CHROMORANGE/Guenter Fischer/Alamy Stock Photo

Transit advertising is a category of out-of-home media that includes bus and taxicab advertising as well as posters on transit shelters, terminals, and subways. Although transit is not considered a major medium by most advertising practitioners, standardization, better research, more statistical data, and measured circulation have made transit advertising more attractive to national advertisers. National marketers including Olay, Casper, Spotify, and ThirdLove, for example, are some of the many advertisers spending dramatically more in this medium, replacing the traditional transit advertising leaders such as petroleum products, financial services, and proprietary medicines.[25]

Transit advertising is a cost-effective way for marketers to reach a large audience of people. Buses and taxis provide high ad exposure by traversing the busiest streets of a city many times a day. A 1-800-Flowers.com campaign promoting the company's specialty bouquets featured ads on buses, on subway stations, and in other urban locations. The company's sales were seven times higher in markets where the outdoor campaign ran.[26]

Transit advertising is equally popular with local advertisers. Retailers can expand their reach inexpensively and often receive co-op support from national marketers, which thrive on the local exposure[27] (see My Ad Campaign 13–B, "The Pros and Cons of Transit Advertising").

Types of Transit Advertising

Transit advertising targets the millions of people who use commercial transportation (buses, subways, elevated trains, commuter trains, trolleys, and airlines), plus pedestrians and car passengers, with a variety of formats: transit shelters; station, platform, and terminal posters; inside cards and outside posters on buses; and taxi exteriors.

Transit Shelters
In cities with mass-transit systems, advertisers can buy space on bus shelters and on the backs of bus-stop benches. **Transit shelter advertising** is a relatively new OOH form enjoying great success. It reaches virtually everyone who is outdoors: auto passengers, pedestrians, bus riders, motorcyclists, bicyclists, and more. It is extremely inexpensive and available in many communities that restrict billboard advertising in business

transit advertising
An out-of-home medium that includes three separate media forms: inside cards; outside posters; and station, platform, and terminal posters.

transit shelter advertising A form of out-of-home media, where advertisers can buy space on bus shelters and on the backs of bus-stop seats.

The Pros and Cons of Transit Advertising [13–B]

The Pros

- **Digital is here:** As with other OOH, digital vehicles are replacing or adding to traditional transit, with all of the attendant benefits.
- **Long exposure.** The average transit ride is 25 minutes.
- **Repetitive value.** Many people take the same routes day after day.
- **Eagerly read messages.** Riders get bored, so readership is high and ad recall averages 55 percent.
- **Low cost.** Transit ads cost less than any other medium.
- **Creative flexibility.** Special constructions and color effects are available at relatively low cost.
- **Need satisfying.** Transit can target the needs of riders—with ads for cool drinks in summer, for example. Food ads do well as evening riders contemplate dinner.
- **Environmentally sensitive.** As social pressure to use public transportation increases, transit is well positioned as a medium of the future.

The Cons

- **Status.** Transit lacks the status of the major advertising media, such as print and broadcast.
- **Crowded environment.** Rush-hour crowding limits the opportunity and ease of reading. The vehicle itself, if dirty, may tarnish the product's image.
- **Limited selectivity.** Transit reaches a nonselective audience, which may not meet the needs of some advertisers.
- **Clutter.** Cards are so numerous and look so similar they may be confusing or hard to remember.
- **Location.** With outlying shopping malls, fewer suburbanites make trips downtown.
- **Creative restrictions.** Although transit cards may carry longer messages than billboards, copy is still limited.

or residential areas. In fact, shelter advertising is sometimes the only form of outdoor advertising permitted. It's also an excellent complement to outdoor posters and bulletins, enabling total market coverage in a comprehensive outdoor program.

Terminal Posters

In many bus, subway, and commuter train stations, space is sold for one-, two-, and three-sheet **terminal posters**. Major train and airline terminals offer such special advertising forms as floor displays, island showcases, illuminated cards, dioramas (3-D scenes), and clocks with special lighting and moving messages.

In Paris, Nike made a splash at the French Open tennis tournament even though a competitor had locked up advertising rights within the stadium. Nike covered the city by buying space on some 2,500 buses during the tournament. As the coup de grace, it bought up every bit of signage space at the Porte d'Auteuil metro (subway) station close to the stadium and turned it into a Nike gallery of terminal posters featuring famous tennis players from around the world.[28]

Inside and Outside Cards and Posters

The **inside card** is placed in a wall rack above the vehicle windows. Cost-conscious advertisers print both sides of the card so it can periodically be reversed to change the message, saving on paper and shipping charges. Inside **car-end posters** (in bulkhead positions) are usually larger than inside cards, but sizes vary. **Outside posters** are printed on high-grade cardboard and often varnished for weather resistance. The most widely used outside posters are on the side, rear, and front of a bus.

Advertisers may also buy space on **taxicab exteriors**, generally for periods of 30 days, to display internally illuminated, two-sided posters positioned on the roofs. Some advertising also appears on the doors or rear of taxicabs. In southern California, advertisers can rent cards mounted on the tops of cabs that travel throughout Los Angeles, Orange, and San Diego counties, serving major airports and traveling the busiest freeways in the country. Costing an average of $100 to $200 per month per cab ($400 in New York City!), this is a very cost-effective way to reach the mobile public.

Buying Transit Advertising

The unit of purchase for transit advertising is a **showing**, also known as a *run* or *service*. A **full showing** (or 100 *showing*) means that one card will appear in each vehicle in the system. Space may also be purchased as a *half* (50) or *quarter* (25) *showing*.

Rates are usually quoted for 30-day showings, with discounts for 3-, 6-, 9-, and 12-month contracts. Advertisers supply the cards at their own expense, but the transit company can help with design and production.

Cost depends on the length and saturation of the showing and the size of the space. Rates vary extensively, depending primarily on the size of the transit system. Advertisers get rates for specific markets from local transit companies.

Special Inside Buys

In some cities, advertisers gain complete domination by buying the **basic bus**—all the inside space on a group of buses. For an extra charge, pads of business reply cards or coupons (called **take-ones**) can be affixed to interior ads for passengers to request more detailed information, send in application blanks, or receive some other benefit.

> [Transit shelter advertising] reaches virtually everyone who is outdoors.

Any pedestrian can't help but see the bright colors and attractive design of this full-wrap bus ad for adidas. Moving vehicles are natural attention getters so advertisers know their message will not be tuned out.

P.D Amedzro/Alamy Stock Photo

Special Outside Buys Some transit companies offer **bus-o-rama signs**, jumbo full-color transparencies backlit by fluorescent tubes and running the length of the bus. A bus has two bus-o-rama positions, one on each side. A single advertiser may also buy a **total bus**—all the exterior space, including the front, rear, sides, and top.

For years, New York subways have been running **brand trains**, which include all the subway cars in a particular corridor. However, with the July 2004 opening of its monorail system, the city of Las Vegas took the concept further. The glitz of the city's strip extends to its public transportation: Each of the nine monorail trains and seven stations has a corporate sponsor, and many feature elaborate immersive advertising themes. **Immersive advertising** describes the integration of advertising into the message delivery mechanism so effectively that the

product is being promoted while the audience is being entertained. The result is that the prospect becomes totally immersed in the message and the brand.

OTHER OUT-OF-HOME MEDIA

As mentioned earlier, there are many forms of out-of-home media. Some are so new that they are still unproven. However, several seem to be gaining in popularity, and they demonstrate how far advertisers will go to get their messages seen by the consuming public.

Cinema Advertising

There was a time not long ago when the only thing cinema audiences could watch before a feature film was a couple of coming attractions. In recent years, marketers have leapt to fill in the empty time before a movie starts with advertisements. Advertising in movie theaters is a growing but controversial practice. **Cinema advertising** includes on-screen advertising, such as commercials airing in advance of movie previews and the feature presentation, as well as lobby-based videos, sampling, special events, and concession-based promotions. Although some movie-going audiences resent watching ads, cinema advertising is becoming more and more attractive to marketers. "Unlike traditional media, we don't have to fight for our audience's attention; they don't flip channels," says Bob Martin, president and chair of the Cinema Advertising Council.[29]

Globally, ads shown before films generated an estimated $4.6 billion in 2019, with much of the growth coming from China. In the United States, cinema advertising is up to about $735 million, an increase from $644 million in 2011, which is an impressive gain compared to the steep drops in print and broadcast.[30]

Cinema advertising offers some compelling advantages to marketers. Arbitron estimates that 81 percent of teens and 67 percent

Any blank space is an invitation to advertise.

hope that those positive feelings will become associated with the brand), the knowledge of exactly when the target audience will see the ad, and the often-attractive demographics of regular sports events visitors.[33] Besides digital scoreboards and displays, advertisers can avail themselves of many vehicles at an event, including sideline banners, restroom ads, hall and concourse posters, stairway ads, cupholders, court branding and wraps, and branded special areas such as VIP rooms.[34]

of young adults see a movie at least once a month. A full 25 percent of teens see 20 or more movies each year. Arbitron also reports that while those who go to movies, in comparison to non-moviegoers, are more likely to skip ads on TV, most don't mind ads in movies. Moviegoers also tend to be young, affluent, tech-savvy peer leaders.

Looking ahead, there may be some issues for the medium to contend with. Cinema advertising, naturally, is tied to the popularity of people seeing films in theaters. The coronavirus pandemic in early 2020 has stopped movie-going entirely, with some studios exploring an immediate-streaming strategy for new releases. It is a situation that bears watching.

Mobile Billboards

The **mobile billboard**, a cross between traditional billboards and transit advertising, was conceived as advertising on the sides of tractor-trailer trucks. Today in some large cities, specially designed trucks carry long billboards up and down busy thoroughfares. Local routes for mobile ads are available on delivery trucks in several cities. And, of course, many of these mobile billboards are going digital. Speaking of digital, a San Francisco company called Smart Plate has developed a license plate that can display custom advertising messages if your car is halted for more than four seconds in traffic or at a red light. California is evaluating this idea as a way to generate revenue for the state. The plates could also be used to update vehicle registration, pay tolls, and broadcast Amber Alerts or traffic information.[31]

Digital Arena and Stadium Signage

Digital signs in stadiums and arenas generate substantial income for sports teams and entertainers. Studies in the early 2010s suggested that professional football teams generated revenues as high as $100 million.[32]

Digital signs can be updated easily or even automatically, based on the event, weather conditions, and so on. Some digital signs allow shoppers to interact directly with the information on the screen.

The benefits associated with arena advertising include the positive emotions and energy experienced by fans at live events (and the

Mall Advertising

Retail advertising doesn't have to be high tech to be effective. While malls, like other non-digital retailers, have faced increased challenges, they continue to attract about 165 million people every three months.[35] Mall advertising thus offers advertisers an opportunity to place their message in front of millions of consumers in the mood to make purchases.

Mall advertising can include posters on mall directories, door- and window-mounted signage, advertising on escalators and elevators, banners hanging from ceilings, tabletop ads in food courts, and any other location that might be seen by shoppers.

StoreBoard Media (www.storeboards.net) has been placing ads on the entryway security panels of major retail chains since 2006. The company touts an average 20 percent product sales lift over the four-week period in which its ads appear. While the security system may be high tech, the ads themselves are "no tech," says Rick Sirvaitis, president of StoreBoard, New York, which has placed ads in some 14,000 U.S. stores for brands including Coca-Cola, Crest, Halls, and Garnier. "If you pass your peripheral vision test on your driver's license, you can't miss these ads. They have a much greater assurance of being viewed by 100 percent of customers than anywhere else in the store."[36]

Augmented Reality

Augmented reality uses digital imagery to project 3-D images in public spaces. Still in its infancy, the capabilities of the technology will only grow with time, creating the opportunity for incredible immersive experiences. A great example is shown on the following page in a campaign for *National Geographic* that brings people face-to-face with raptors and big cats.

Guerrilla Marketing

It seems that any blank space is an invitation to advertise. The term **guerrilla marketing** was coined in 1984 by Jay Conrad Levinson in his book by the same name. He defines the concept as "achieving conventional goals, such as profits and joy, with unconventional methods, such as investing energy instead of money."[37] In recent years, guerrilla marketing tactics have also come to be referred to as stealth, buzz, ambush, street, or viral

Augmented reality OOH opens a world of possibilities for advertisers and adds a new dimension to guerrilla marketing. The image above demonstrates the power of a campaign for National Geographic Channel as dinosaurs appear to join commuters at a train station lobby.

National Geographic Channel

marketing. Some examples of guerrilla advertising include Folgers converting a steaming New York manhole cover into an advertisement for a hot cup of coffee, Casinò di Venezia decorating a luggage carousel in the Venice airport to resemble a roulette wheel, the Salvation Army printing advertisements to promote donations on blankets distributed to the homeless, Burger King dressing Ronald McDonald statues in Asia with Burger King T-shirts, and streakers running onto a rugby field in Australia with Vodafone logos painted on their bodies. The ultimate goal is to attract attention in an increasingly advertising-cluttered environment.

check yourself ✓

1. How does the meaning of "100 showing" differ between outdoor advertising and transit advertising?

2. What creative application of digital signage would be effective on your college campus?

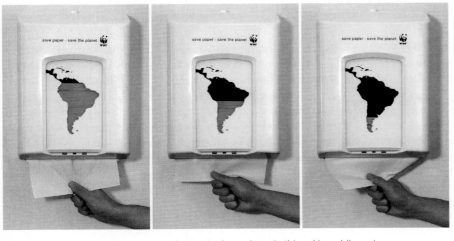

An excellent example of guerrilla marketing is shown here in this ad in public restrooms. Creativity is at the heart of this advertisement for the World Wildlife Fund, where the depletion of paper towels is used to convey their conservation message.

World Wildlife Fund

LO13-4 List the various types of direct-mail advertising and its pros and cons.

DIRECT-MAIL ADVERTISING: THE ADDRESSABLE MEDIUM

All forms of advertising sent directly to prospects through a government, private, or electronic mail delivery service are called **direct-mail advertising**. As we discuss in Chapter 15, direct-mail advertising is a form of direct marketing because it allows advertisers to communicate directly with the customer.

Brand X Pictures/Stockbyte/Getty Images

Direct mail predates the web as an interactive medium, and for that reason, it grew quite rapidly in the 1990s until about 2010. Since that time, advertisers have begun moving the portion of their budget reserved for direct mail to digital advertising, including e-mail. With annual U.S. spending of about $42.3 billion, direct mail remains a popular medium for reaching consumers.[38]

Both large and small companies use direct mail. New firms often use direct mail as their first advertising medium. The reason is clear: Of all media, direct-mail advertising offers the most direct path to the desired customer. And businesses don't need big budgets to advertise with direct mail. With a computer and desktop publishing software, a business can create a professional-looking mailer. And some websites provide companies with tools to design a mailer, import a mailing list, and have the campaign printed and sent, all online.

Direct mail is used by for-profit businesses, charities, and political campaigns. Mailings are typically targeted to the advertiser's best prospects, selected based on where they live, demographic characteristics, past purchasing behavior, or interest they have expressed in certain product categories. Direct mail may also be targeted to businesses rather than individuals, in an effort to generate orders or leads for a sales force. Because direct-mail marketers don't want to waste money sending advertising to disinterested prospects, consumers can opt out by contacting the Direct Marketing Association's Mail Preference Service (www.dmachoice.org).

Many experts predicted that the combination of the recession, rising postage rates, and a growing preference among marketers for low-cost, digital communications will mean a continued decline in the dollars spent on direct-mail advertising.[39]

Types of Direct-Mail Advertising

Direct-mail advertising comes in a variety of formats, from handwritten postcards to **dimensional direct mail**, utilizing three-dimensional shapes and unusual materials. The message can be one sentence or dozens of pages. And within each format—from tiny coupon to thick catalog or box—the creative options are infinite. In 2003, the United States Postal Service approved Customized Market-Mail (CMM), a new class of mail that gives direct-mail advertisers the opportunity to truly innovate. The new regulations allow for pieces of mail of almost any shape, within certain dimensions, to be sent without an envelope. No longer limited to rectangles, direct mail can now take more novel, eye-catching forms. From simple geometric shapes, such as circles, to more curious and bizarre shapes, such as Zambonis (used by First Tennessee Bank to promote a checking account associated with a local hockey team), CMM stands out in a sea of mail that might otherwise go directly into the trash.[40] In addition to the dimensional direct-mail category are the following:

E-mail, as mentioned in Chapter 12, is an important tool in direct marketing and is best used for customer retention and relationship management. It is most effective when the marketer first seeks *permission* to mail. In other words, advertisers should always give people the opportunity to opt in or to opt out of their e-mail programs. For new business acquisition, the best use is in a viral marketing campaign—otherwise it will probably be perceived as spam.

Sales letters, the most common direct-mail format, are often mailed with brochures, price lists, or reply cards and envelopes. **Postcards** are used to announce sales, offer discounts, or generate customer traffic. National postal services regulate formats and dimensions. Some advertisers use a double postcard, enabling them to send both an advertising message and a perforated reply card. To encourage response, some advertisers use **business reply mail** so the recipient can respond without paying postage. On receiving a response, the advertiser pays postage plus a handling fee of a few cents.

THE MAILING LIST IS RESPONSIBLE FOR UP TO 60 PERCENT OF THE SUCCESS OF A MAILING.

Folders and **brochures** are usually printed in multiple colors with photos or other illustrations on good paper stock.

Broadsides are larger than folders and are sometimes used as window displays or wall posters in stores. They fold to a compact size to fit in a mailbag.

Self-mailers are any form of direct mail that can travel without an envelope. Usually folded and secured by a staple or seal, they have special blank spaces for the prospect's name and address.

Statement stuffers are ads enclosed in monthly customer statements from department stores, banks, oil companies, and the like. To order, customers write in their credit card number and sign the reply card.

House organs are publications produced by associations or business organizations—for example, shareholder reports, newsletters, and dealer publications.

Catalogs are reference books that list, describe, and often picture the products sold by a manufacturer, wholesaler, or retailer. With more high-income families shopping at home, specialized catalogs have become very popular.

Some catalog retailers prosper with specialized approaches like lifestyle clothing (L.L.Bean, Anthropologie, Lands' End), electronic gadgets (Sharper Image), and gourmet foods (Dean & Deluca).

Despite the growth of online catalogs on e-commerce, printed catalogs remain a big business. More than 7 billion catalogs were mailed in 2019.[41] However, due largely to rising postage costs, that figure is down from 18 billion only four years earlier. More than 8,000 catalog companies have disappeared in recent years. But catalogs remain popular. Printed catalogs are tactile; unlike electronic catalogs, you can hold them in your hands, mark them up, fold over their page corners, and put them down and pick them up later.

Not too long ago, most catalog orders were transacted by mail or telephone. Some customers would visit a store (such as Sears) or order from a local representative (like the Avon lady). Now, a great many catalog orders are placed on Internet websites. People read a catalog, decide what they want, and then go online to place the order. Most catalogs are mailed monthly, more frequently around the holidays, and there's usually a spike on the website right after print catalogs are delivered.[42]

It doesn't appear that printed catalogs are going to disappear soon. The best marketers use catalogs, digital media, and retail stores in synergy in an effort to complement one another and maximize sales.

Using Direct Mail in the Media Mix

Direct mail is an efficient, effective, and economical medium for sales and business promotion (see My Ad Campaign 13–C,

One of the oldest advertising media, the catalog, is still one of the most relevant. While many catalogs have moved online, some advertisers, like L. L. Bean, continue to attract loyal customers with a printed catalog.
L.L. Bean Inc.

The Pros and Cons of Direct-Mail Advertising [13–C]

The Pros

- **Selectivity.** Direct mail helps advertisers communicate directly with the people most likely to buy. Computerized mailing lists group people by occupation, region or state, income, and other characteristics.
- **Intensive coverage and extensive reach.** Everyone has a mailbox. With direct mail, an advertiser can reach 100 percent of the homes in a given area.
- **Flexibility.** Direct-mail advertising can be uniquely creative, limited only by the advertiser's ingenuity and budget and postal regulations. Advertisers can produce direct-mail pieces fast and distribute them quickly.
- **Control.** Preprinted direct-mail pieces enable an advertiser to precisely control circulation and reproduction quality.
- **Personal impact.** Advertisers can personalize direct mail to the needs, wants, and whims of specific audiences without offending other prospects or customers.
- **Exclusivity.** There are no distractions from competitive ads (in solo mailings).
- **Response.** Direct mail achieves the highest response of any advertising medium. About 15 percent of the responses arrive within the first week, so the advertiser can quickly judge a campaign's success.
- **Testability.** Direct mail is good for testing prospect reactions to products, pricing, promotions, copy approaches, sales literature, and so on.

The Cons

- **High cost per exposure.** Direct mail has the highest cost per exposure of any major medium, about 14 times as much as most magazine and newspaper advertising.
- **Delivery problems.** The mass media offer precise delivery times, but the postal service makes no delivery commitments on third-class mail. And up to 10 percent of mailings may be undeliverable because people move.
- **Lack of content support.** Direct mail must capture and hold the reader's attention without the support of editorial or entertainment content.
- **Selectivity problems.** Effective direct mail depends on correctly identifying the target audience and obtaining a good list. Some groups of prospects, such as physicians, are so saturated with direct mail they ignore it.
- **Negative attitudes.** Many consumers think of direct mail as junk mail and automatically throw it away. This may also negatively impact the product's image.
- **Environmental concerns.** Some consumers see direct mail as landfill fodder. Some direct marketers (Eddie Bauer, L.L.Bean) print parts of their catalogs on recycled paper, and now new de-inking facilities will make more catalogs recyclable.
- **Antispam laws.** The CAN-SPAM Act and similar laws impose many requirements, making it more difficult for marketers to electronically send prospective clients unsolicited marketing materials.

"The Pros and Cons of Direct-Mail Advertising"). That's why it's used by a wide variety of companies, charity and service organizations, and individuals. Direct mail can increase the effectiveness of ads in other media. For example, Publishers Clearinghouse typically uses TV spots to alert viewers to the impending arrival of its direct-mail sweepstakes promotions.

Direct mail has two main drawbacks: cost and the "junk mail" image, both of which are almost inescapable. No other medium (except personal selling and consumer targeting on the Internet) has such a high cost per thousand. For this reason, many small advertisers participate in cooperative (rather than solo) mailings with companies such as ADVO, which serves most major U.S. cities. ADVO mails an envelope containing a coupon for each participating company to targeted zip codes.

Some large advertisers don't send unsolicited mail. To locate prospects, they use other direct-response media such as advertising with toll-free "800" numbers or soliciting inquiries on the Internet. Then they use direct mail to respond to those inquiries. They save money by mailing only to qualified prospects, and by sending higher-quality materials, they build their image and improve their chances of establishing a worthwhile relationship.

check yourself ✓

1. Why is Customized Market-Mail (CMM) a benefit to direct-mail advertisers?

2. What are some ways that direct mail could be effectively used in conjunction with other elements of the media mix?

LO13-5 Describe the basic components of direct-mail advertising.

COMPONENTS OF DIRECT-MAIL ADVERTISING

The three basic components of direct-mail advertising are the mailing list, the offer, and the creative package. Direct-mail experts say the mailing list is responsible for up to 60 percent

house list A company's most important and valuable direct-mail list, which may contain current, recent, and long-past customers or future prospects.

mail-response list A type of direct-mail list, composed of people who have responded to the direct-mail solicitations of other companies, especially those whose efforts are complementary to the advertiser's.

compiled list A type of direct-mail list that has been compiled by another source, such as lists of automobile owners, new home purchasers, business owners, union members, and so forth. It is the most readily available type of list but offers the lowest response rate.

list broker An intermediary who handles rental of mailing lists for list owners on a commission basis.

of the success of a mailing. The offer is good for 25 percent of a mailing's success, and the creative package is worth 15 percent. Many advertisers focus too much time and money developing the creative side of a mailing but give insufficient attention to the actual lists.

Acquiring Direct-Mail Lists

The heart of any direct-mail program is the mailing list. Each list actually defines a market segment. Direct-mail advertisers use three types of lists: *house*, *mail-response*, and *compiled*.

House Lists   The company's database of current, recent, and long-past customers as well as identified prospects comprises the **house list** for direct-mail programs. Because customers are its most important asset, every company should focus sufficient resources on developing a rich database of customer and prospect information and profiles. There are several ways a company can build its own house list.

Consumer product companies such as General Electric gather customer data by enclosing an owner registration form with their products. On the mail-in form, purchasers give their name, address, phone number, birth date, occupation, income range, home ownership status, and number of children. They also indicate their hobbies and interests (such as golf, foreign travel, photography, or bowling). Companies use this information for their own mailings and sell it to other direct-mail advertisers.

Mail-Response Lists   The advertiser's second most important prospects are people who respond to direct-mail pieces from other companies—especially those with complementary products or services. **Mail-response lists** are the house lists of other direct-mail advertisers, and they can be rented with a wide variety of demographic breakdowns.

Compiled Lists   The most readily available lists are those that some entity compiles for a different reason and then rents or sells—for example, lists of car owners, new-home

purchasers, business owners, and so on. **Compiled lists** typically offer the lowest response rate, so experts suggest using numerous sources, merging them on computer with mail-response and house lists, and then purging them of duplicate names.[43]

Direct-mail lists can be bought or rented. Purchased lists can be used without limit; rented lists may be used for a single mailing only. List owners plant decoy names in the list to be sure renters don't use it more than once.

Some list owners pay a **list broker** a commission (usually 20 percent) to handle the rental details. The advertiser, in turn, benefits from the broker's knowledge of list quality without having to pay more than the rental cost.

Lists can be tailored to reflect customer location (zip code); demographics such as age, income, and home ownership; or

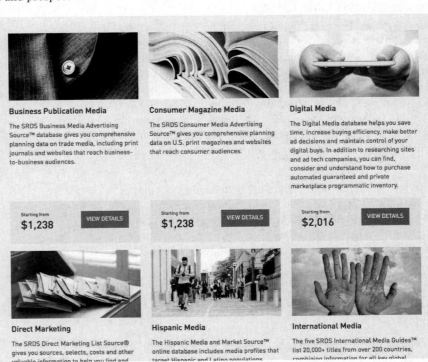

Business Publication Media
The SRDS Business Media Advertising Source™ database gives you comprehensive planning data on trade media, including print journals and websites that reach business-to-business audiences.

Consumer Magazine Media
The SRDS Consumer Media Advertising Source™ gives you comprehensive planning data on U.S. print magazines and websites that reach consumer audiences.

Digital Media
The Digital Media database helps you save time, increase buying efficiency, make better ad decisions and maintain control of your digital buys. In addition to researching sites and ad tech companies, you can find, consider and understand how to purchase automated guaranteed and private marketplace programmatic inventory.

Starting from $1,238   VIEW DETAILS

Starting from $1,238   VIEW DETAILS

Starting from $2,016   VIEW DETAILS

Direct Marketing
The SRDS Direct Marketing List Source® gives you sources, selects, costs and other valuable information to help you find and

Hispanic Media
The Hispanic Media and Market Source™ online database includes media profiles that target Hispanic and Latino populations.

International Media
The five SRDS International Media Guides™ list 20,000+ titles from over 200 countries, combining information for all key global

Kantar Media SRDS, the direct marketing database of SRDS.com, published by Kantar Media, is the leading provider of media rates for advertisers. The SRDS Direct Marketing List Source® provides sources, costs, and other valuable information to help find and evaluate lists for direct marketing campaigns.
Kantar Media

psychographic characteristics such as personality and lifestyle. The SRDS *Direct Marketing List Source* contains more than 70,000 list selections in 230 consumer and business classifications.

Mailing list prices vary according to the accuracy and currency of the data. Consumer list rental rates average $74 per thousand names but can be as little as $35 per thousand or as much as $400 per thousand. The more stringent the advertiser's selection criteria, the more expensive the list. An extra $10 per thousand is often well worth the savings in mailers and postage that would otherwise be wasted.

The average mailing list changes more than 40 percent a year as people relocate, change jobs, get married, or die. So mailing lists must be continually updated (*cleaned*) to be sure they're current and correct. Advertisers can also test the validity and accuracy of a given list. They rent or buy every *n*th name and send a mailer to that person. If the results are favorable, they purchase additional names, usually in lots of 1,000.

Developing the Offer

Every direct-mail package should contain an offer. The offer is the incentive or reward that motivates prospects to respond to a mailing, either with an order or with a request for more information. To be effective, an offer must be clear and specific, it must offer value to the potential customer, it must be believable, and it must be easy to acquire. The more difficult it is for prospects to respond to an offer, the lower the response rate will be. The direct-mail package should provide clear instructions, a conspicuous address (mailing and Internet), and a toll-free phone number.

The offer should promote a benefit that will address a prospect's needs. It should clearly explain why this mail is being sent to this prospect at this time. In other words, there should be a *call to action*: What does the advertiser want the recipient to do when he or she receives the mail? And finally, it should give the prospect a reason to act NOW.

Creating, Producing, and Distributing the Package

To create a direct-mail package, the advertiser may use in-house staff, an ad agency, or a freelance designer and writer. Some agencies specialize in direct mail.

The direct-mail piece normally goes through the same production process as any other print piece. The size and shape of the mailing package, as well as the type, illustrations, and colors, all affect printing costs. Special features such as simulated blue-ink signatures, cardboard pop-ups, and die-cutting (the cutting of paper stock into an unusual shape) add to the cost. But the larger the printing volume, or run, the lower the printing cost per unit.

Remaining production and handling tasks can be done by a local **letter shop** (or *mailing house*), or the advertiser can do them internally. On a cost-per-thousand basis, letter shops stuff and seal envelopes, affix labels, calculate postage, and sort, tie, and stack the mailers. Some shops also offer creative services. If the advertiser is using third-class bulk mail, the letter shop separates mailers by zip code and ties them into bundles to qualify for low bulk rates. Then the letter shop delivers the mailers to the post office.

Distribution costs are based chiefly on the weight of the mailer and the delivery method. U.S. advertisers can use the U.S. Postal Service, air freight, or private delivery services such as UPS and FedEx. The most common, the U.S. Postal Service, offers several types of delivery.

check yourself ✓

1. Why is the house list typically the most effective direct-mail list?

2. What is meant by a "call to action" in every direct-mail package?

LO13-6 Demonstrate the value of promotional products.

PROMOTIONAL PRODUCTS

The Promotional Products Association International (PPAI) says that **promotional products**—usually imprinted with a company's name, logo, or message—include useful or decorative articles of merchandise that are utilized in marketing communications programs. Imprinted products that are distributed free are called **advertising specialties**.[44] Many businesses use promotional products of some sort. As many as 15,000 different items, ranging from coffee mugs to ballpoint pens, key chains, and T-shirts, represent an annual volume of nearly

Almost every business uses promotional products, and almost any item can be imprinted with a company's advertising message and logo.

Mikeledray/Shutterstock

$18.5 billion. The largest product category for promotional items is *wearables*, which include T-shirts, golf shirts, aprons, uniforms, jackets, caps, footwear, and the like, which make up nearly 30 percent of the total. Other popular categories include writing instruments (9.0 percent), bags (7.2 percent), calendars (6.9 percent), drinkware (6.7 percent), and desk and office accessories (6.0 percent).[45]

Promotional products are effective tools for improving people's perception and recollection of a business. They are often distributed in association with trade shows, public relations programs, employee events, new product introductions, or brand-building programs. Some promotional items may be kept for years and serve as continuous, friendly reminders of the advertiser's business. In fact, 58 percent of the recipients keep these gifts for at least a year. Companies often spend substantial sums for goodwill items to promote their businesses, and studies indicate that this investment pays off. Nearly 90 percent of recipients could recall the name of the advertiser on a promotional item they received in the past 24 months.[46]

Premiums are also promotional products; they are typically more valuable and usually bear no advertising message. However, to get a premium, recipients must buy a product, send in a coupon, witness a demonstration, or perform some other action advantageous to the advertiser. ∎

check yourself ✓

1. What is the difference between a promotional product and a premium?

2. What is the value of "goodwill"? How do promotional products and premiums generate it?

ENDNOTES

1. "OOH Basics," Out of Home Advertising Association of America, https://oaaa.org/AboutOOH/OOHBasics/HistoryofOOH.aspx.

2. "US Out-of-Home Advertising Enjoys Biggest Growth Rate In Over A Decade," *Marketing Charts*, September 10, 2019, www.marketingcharts.com/cross-media-and-traditional/out-of-home-109981.

3. "Number of Out-of-Home Displays, 2016," retrieved at www.oaaa.org/Portals/0/Images/Number%20of%20OOH%20displays%20Chart%202016.JPG.

4. "Digital Signage Is the Future of Out of Home Media," *Mass Media*, https://mass-media.co.uk/digital-advertising-is-the-future-of-ooh.

5. "Do People Notice Billboards?" *Mixed Media Group*, July 11, 2018, www.mixedmediaoutdoor.com/do-people-notice-billboards.

6. "Number of Out-of-Home Displays of Selected Types in the United States in 2019," *Statistica*, www.statista.com/statistics/686030/number-ooh-displays-usa.

7. Lamar, www.lamar.com.

8. "Digital billboards," *Clear Channel Outdoor*, http://clearchanneloutdoor.com/products/digital-billboards.

9. Diane Williams, "Digital Billboard Study 2015," *Nielsen*, www.lamar.com/howtoadvertise/Research/~/media/F7CBA6203040440FBB86A708AE982515.ashx.

10. Kristina Monllos, "'Dramatically Different Now Than a Year Ago': Programmatic Buying for Digital Billboards Is Growing," *Digiday*, June 10, 2019, https://digiday.com/marketing/dramatically-different-now-year-ago-programmatic-buying-digital-billboards-growing.

11. Rodolfo Queiroz, "The Complete Guide to Digital Outdoor Advertising," *Dash Two*, June 19, 2019, https://dashtwo.com/blog/guide-to-digital-outdoor-ads.

12. "Global Out-of-Home Ad Revenues Up 7.5% to $56B in 2018, Strongest Growth Since 2007; Consumer Time Spent With OOH Rises 1.3% to 1 Hr & 7 Mins, Driven By Digital Signage,"

PR Newswire, September 12, 2019, https://markets.business-insider.com/news/stocks/global-out-of-home-ad-revenues-up-7-5-to-56b-in-2018-strongest-growth-since-2007-consumer-time-spent-with-ooh-rises-1-3-to-1-hr-7-mins-driven-by-digital-signage-1028519590; "OOH Revenue by Format," Outdoor Advertising Association of America, www.oaaa.org/ResourceCenter/MarketingSales/Factsamp;Figures/Revenue/OOHRevenuebyFormat.aspx.

13. "Introduce Yourself to Outdoor Advertising," Outdoor Advertising Association of America, Inc., www.oaaa.org.

14. "Business & Technology Case Studies: eBay," Outdoor Advertising Association of America, August 1, 2012, www.oaaa.org/ResourceCenter/MarketingSales/CaseStudies/BusinessTechnology/tabid/309/id/3890/Default.aspx.

15. "Outdoor Impressions," *Matrix Media*, www.matrixmediaservices.com/outdoor-impressions.

16. "TAB Eyes On—Out-of-Home Media Measurement: The Basics 2009," www.eyesonrating.com.

17. "CPM Comparisons for Major Media," Outdoor Advertising Association of America.

18. Stephen Freitas, "The New Tech Locator: User-Friendly, Informative," *OAAA Special Reports*, https://specialreports.oaaa.org/oohtechlocator.

19. Stephen Freitas, "The New Tech Locator: User-Friendly, Informative,"*OAAA Special Reports*, https://specialreports.oaaa.org/oohtechlocator.

20. "Digital Billboard Safety Confirmed," *Watchfire Digital Outdoor*, March 8, 2011, www.watchfiredigitaloutdoor.com/press/digital-billboard-safety-confirmed.

21. "New Study Finds Digital Billboards Distract Drivers," *Automotive Fleet*, January 3, 2013, www.automotive-fleet.com/channel/safety-accident-management/news/story/2013/01/new-study-finds-digital-billboards-distract-drivers.aspx.

22. Karl Greenberg, "Lexus Accelerates into All Venues in Push for Revamped IS Sedan," *Brandweek*, August 31, 2005 www.brandweek.com/bw/news/autos/article_display.jsp?vnu_content_id=1001052022.

23. Cyndee Miller, "Outdoor Advertising Weathers Repeated Attempts to Kill It," *Marketing News*, March 16, 1992, pp. 1, 9; *Billboard Basics* (New York: Outdoor Advertising Association of America, 1994), pp. 15–16.

24. "Surveys Show Americans Like Their Billboards," Outdoor Advertising Association of America, 1997, www.oaaa.org.

25. PRNewswire, "OUTFRONT Media Dominates Transit Advertising As Brands Flock To Transit Audiences," *MarTechSeries*, January 4, 2019, https://martechseries.com/sales-marketing/programmatic-buying/outfront-media-dominates-transit-advertising-brands-flock-transit-audiences.

26. Riccardo A. Davis, "Retailers Open Doors Wide for Co-op," *Advertising Age*, August 1, 1994, p. 30; Melissa Korn, "Bricks Rivaling Clicks in Ad Spending," *Financial Times*, July 21, 2006, www.ft.com/content/9cd19f60-18d8-11db-b02f-0000779e2340; "Outdoor Grows Online Sales: 1-800-Flowers.com Sales 7 Times Greater in Outdoor Markets," *CBS Outdoor*, www.cbsoutdoor.com/news.php.

27. "Advertising That Imitates Art," *Adweek,* June 20, 1994, p. 18.

28. Larry Dobrow, "If the Cap Fits . . .," *Mediapost.com*, April 2006, www.mediapost.com/publications/article/40183/if-the-cap-fits.html.

29. Chris Matyszczyk, "Why Digital License Plates Are a Great Idea," *CNET News*, June 21, 2010, http://news.cnet.com/8301-17852_3-20008394-71.html.

30. Luch Handley, "Advertising in Movie Theaters Is Growing Faster Than All Other Traditional Ad Formats—and China Dominates," *CNBC*, August 22, 2019, www.cnbc.com/2019/08/22/cinema-ad-spend-is-growing-faster-than-other-formats---china-dominates.html.

31. "California May Issue Digital License Plates, Privacy Groups Concerned," *CBS Local Media*, July 18, 2013, http://sanfrancisco.cbslocal.com/2013/07/18/california-may-issue-digital-license-plates-privacy-groups-concerned.

32. James Ferrier, "Spotlight on Technology—Telecite," *Advertising Age*, November 22, 1993, p. SS10.

33. LincpinSEO, "How To Use Stadium Advertising and Arena Marketing To Grow Brand Awareness," *Sports Marketing*, December 25, 2019, https://linchpinseo.com/guide-to-sports-stadium-arena-marketing.

34. LincpinSEO, "How To Use Stadium Advertising and Arena Marketing To Grow Brand Awareness," *Sports Marketing*, December 25, 2019, https://linchpinseo.com/guide-to-sports-stadium-arena-marketing.

35. Melissa Wylie, "What shoppers want from malls," Bizwomen, Mar 28, 2018, https://cdn.advanseads.com/assets/comp/100_5e7e5334d657f4.78172590.jpg

36. LincpinSEO, "How To Use Stadium Advertising and Arena Marketing To Grow Brand Awareness," *Sports Marketing*, December 25, 2019, https://linchpinseo.com/guide-to-sports-stadium-arena-marketing.

37. Guerrilla Marketing, www.gmarketing.com.

38. Heather Fletcher, "$316B in Ad, Marketing Spending Arriving in 2018," *Target Marketing Magazine*, January 17, 2018, https://www.targetmarketingmag.com/article/316b-ad-marketing-spending-arriving-2018/.

39. "Trends and Future of Direct Mail through 2020," *CMO Council*, 2015, www.cmocouncil.org/data/files/npes/direct-mail-executive-synopsis.pdf.

40. Matthew Philips, "Lost in the Mail," *Newsweek*, March 30, 2010, www.newsweek.com/2010/03/29/lost-in-the-mail.html.

41. Jack Pointer, "Why Are Catalogs Still a Thing in 2019? 'Because They Work'," *WTOP News*, December 16, 2019, https://wtop.com/christmas-news/2019/12/why-are-catalogs-still-a-thing-in-2019-because-they-work.

42. Lois Geller, "Why Are Printed Catalogs Still Around?" *Forbes*, October 16, 2012, www.forbes.com/sites/loisgeller/2012/10/16/why-are-printed-catalogs-still-around.

43. "Promotional Products Fact Sheet," Promotional Products Association International, Irving, TX, 1995.

44. Promotional Products Association International, www.ppai.org.

45. 2013 Promotional Products Fact Sheet, PPAI, www.promotionalproductswork.org.

46. *How Specialty Advertising Affects Goodwill* (Irving, TX: Specialty Advertising Association International, 1993).

fourteen

Alexander Raths/Kalium/age fotostock

media planning
and buying

This chapter shows how communications media help advertisers achieve marketing and advertising objectives. To get their messages to the right people in the right place at the right time, media planners follow the same procedures as marketing and advertising planners: setting objectives, formulating strategies, and devising tactics. To make sound decisions, media planners must possess marketing savvy, analytical skill, and creativity.

When you think of Apple, what thoughts come to mind? Technology company? iTunes? The line of sleek Mac computers? Maybe you think of all of these things. But the best way to think of Apple might be as a phone company, given that more than 50 percent of its global revenues come from iPhone sales.

The smartphone is the perfect medium, for people and for brands. It was not always so. When MIT asked people in 2004 to name the invention that you hate the most but can't live without, standing at the top of the list was the mobile phone, easily outscoring the alarm clock. Users doubtless liked that mobile phones helped for staying in touch with family, friends, customers, and co-workers. But back then the phones were not always easy to use. And they weren't much fun either.

So in 2007, when the late CEO Steve Jobs announced that Apple had reinvented the phone, people took notice. For many, the marriage of mobile phone utility and Apple's skill at designing products with both beautiful form and function seemed

continued on p. 346

LEARNING OBJECTIVES

After studying this chapter, you will be able to:

LO14-1 Describe how media planning has changed and what has caused these changes.

LO14-2 Discuss the types of media objectives and identify the strategies for achieving these objectives.

LO14-3 Articulate what is meant by "the art of media planning."

LO14-4 Identify the factors that influence media strategy and tactics.

LO14-5 Describe different types of advertising schedules and the purpose for each.

LO14-6 Explain the role of the media buyer.

continued from p. 345

irresistible. When it finally arrived, critics and consumers alike agreed that the iPhone lived up to the hype.

Consumers weren't the only ones excited about the iPhone. Advertisers were too. But for them, it wasn't the hardware that was so exciting. It was software.

To see why this is so, do a thought experiment. Ask yourself, from an advertiser's perspective, what would the ideal medium look like? Several criteria come to mind. Lots of people should use the medium and they should spend a lot of time with it. And people should interact with the medium throughout the day, not just in the morning (as they do with news) or evening (as they do with television). The ideal medium would allow people to use coupons (like newspapers) but also view video (like TV) and hear sound (like radio). The medium should be responsive and interactive, allowing consumers to find out more about an advertiser's product if they wish (like the web). The medium should allow advertisers to track what people are doing with their ads (like direct response advertising). Because we are just dreaming, why not add that the medium should be able to draw people a map so they can find the product. And when they find it, the medium should let the consumer post a picture of it in Instagram and send tweets to all of his or her friends about how much they like it. Or let them just go ahead and buy something, wherever they happen to be.

Sound like any medium you know?

So how do advertisers take advantage of the greatest medium ever created? As a device that serves web content, the iPhone offers advertisers every channel available on desktops: search ads in Google, social ads in Facebook, promoted tweets in Twitter, display ads in Instagram, and so forth. And because people are spending more time accessing the web on their phones, and less on computers, mobile advertising is growing at an astounding rate. To

Michael D. Brown/Shutterstock

give just one example, an astounding 92 percent of Facebook ad revenue comes from mobile, an amount that totals more than $50 billion.

Finally, there are the apps. For hundreds of thousands of developers, the phone offers a new and exciting opportunity for revenue via applications sold (or available free) through Apple's store. Apple's apps brought in revenues of $54 billion in 2019.

Steve Jobs was a game-changer in many areas; computers, music, tablets, software, and movie animation come to mind. But for marketers, it may be that no Jobs innovation is more profound than the iPhone.

Of course sometimes being first out of the gate doesn't mean success will last forever. Apple is still in a fight for market share with Google's Android, just as Ford, America's first car company, eventually fell to second place in U.S. market share to G.M. But Henry Ford is the man we remember as the inventor of the automobile industry. In similar fashion, we should remember Steve Jobs as the man who created the perfect advertising medium. ■

MEDIA PLANNING: INTEGRATING SCIENCE WITH CREATIVITY IN ADVERTISING

Over the last several chapters, you've had a chance to review some of the most popular media in which advertising appears. This naturally leads to a very important question for brands and the agencies that represent them: with so many choices available, where should we advertise to accomplish our marketing objectives?

The purpose of **media planning** is to conceive, analyze, and creatively select channels of communication that will direct advertising messages to the right people in the right place at the right time. As a result, media planning today involves many decisions. For example,

- Where should we advertise? (In what countries, states, or parts of town?)

- Which media vehicles reach and engage our target markets?

- When during the year should we concentrate our advertising?

- How often should we run the advertising?

- What opportunities exist for integrating our advertising with other communication tools?

Some of these decisions require research and detailed mathematical analysis, aided by sophisticated computer software programs.

The Challenge

Historically, the people who plan and buy media have enjoyed relative anonymity compared to the "stars" in the creative departments. This is no longer true. Today the media planner's assignment is just as critical as the creative director's. The planner's work is focused on an agency's strategic ability to understand the target market and the most optimal time and place to communicate with it. Some agencies have gone so far as to integrate the strategic planning and media planning groups into one department, effectively giving media planners a seat at the creative strategy table.

Jack Klues, when he directed media services for Leo Burnett USA, said, "Our mission is to buy and plan media so effectively that our clients obtain an unfair advantage versus their competitors."[1]

The media department gained new prominence in the 1990s when clients started taking an à la carte approach to agency services, and agencies began competing for media planning assignments.[2] By the early 2000s, media wins were big news: Universal McCann won the $150 million Nestlé account; Gillette awarded its $600 million media account to Mindshare; and Kraft consolidated its $800 million media business at Starcom MediaVest Group.[3]

With greater complexity, media decisions become more critical and clients more demanding. Advertisers want agencies to be more than efficient. They want accountability and information, particularly about media options. And they want creative buys.

What makes media planning today so much more complicated and challenging than it was just a few years ago?

Increasing Media Options There are many more media to choose from today, and each offers more choices. It wasn't long ago that major advertisers could ensure a big audience by simply advertising on a popular TV show. Not anymore. Consider that in 1960, the top-rated scripted TV show (*Gunsmoke*) was viewed in more than 40 percent of U.S. households. By comparison, the top show in the spring of 2020 (*Chicago Fire*) was watched by less than 6 percent of all viewers.[4]

The reason for this decline is that TV is now fragmented into network, syndicated, spot, and local television, as well as network and local cable. Also nipping at ratings are on-demand services such as Hulu, Amazon Prime, Netflix, Disney+, and Apple TV+. Specialized magazines now aim at every population and business segment. Even national magazines publish editions for particular regions or demographic groups. Finally, the incredible growth of digital media has brought a host of new options. But it has also added to the complexity of media work as planners face the challenge of staying current with the constantly expanding technology and mastering a whole new vocabulary.

Nontraditional media—which can include mobile media, apps, cinema advertising, and product placement—also expand the menu of choices. In addition, many companies spend a considerable portion of their marketing budgets on specialized communications such as direct marketing, sales promotion, public relations activities, and personal selling, topics we'll discuss in the next two chapters (see Exhibit 14–1). In fact, these "below-the-line" (noncommissionable) activities are the fastest-growing segments at some of the large agency holding companies, such as WPP and Interpublic.

For companies practicing IMC, the "media menu" needs to include everything that carries a message to and/or from customers and other stakeholders. The proliferation of toll-free phone numbers, e-mail, and websites makes it easy and

Effective media professionals don't just rely on traditional ad space to communicate a message. In this execution, HBO media planners negotiated for space on the side of a building. Their innovativeness with this ad nabbed them an award at the Cannes Lions International Festival of Creativity.

Cannes Lions International Advertising Festival Winner

▼**EXHIBIT 14–1** 2020 U.S. advertising (blue) and marketing and communications (red) spending by channel ($ billions).

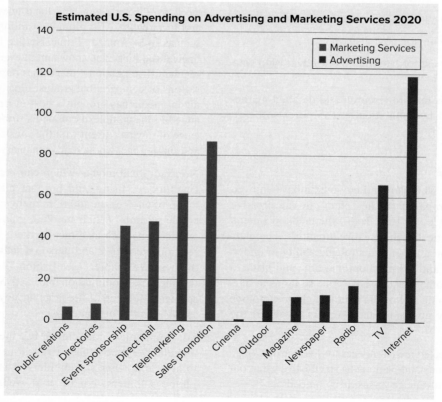

Source: AdAge.com DataCenter.

cost-effective to facilitate customer feedback. The result is that advertisers can be very creative in designing systems for both sending and receiving messages. That means that companies and agencies need to think in terms of message handling, being as responsible for receiving messages as for sending them.

Increasing Fragmentation of the Audience

Further evidence of the maturing marketplace is the fragmentation of the media audience. This also complicates the media planner's job. Readers and viewers have scattered across the new media options, selectively reading only parts of magazines or newspapers, watching only segments of programs, and listening to many different radio stations. This makes it very difficult to find the prospect. Consumers spend an average of a bit more than 12 hours per day with media—but an increasing proportion of that time is spent with less traditional media vehicles, as seen in Exhibit 14–2.[5]

Increasing Costs

While there are more media choices, the number of messages that need to be communicated has also grown—so much so, in fact, that they have outstripped the ability of consumers to process them. People can cope with only so many messages, so media restrict the number of ads they sell. As a result, the costs are increasing for almost all media. In the last decade, the cost of exposing 1,000 people for many major media (cost per thousand) rose faster than inflation. Shows that can deliver a big audience are sold at a premium. The cost of an average TV ad? More than $100,000, and ads on top-rated sports shows ($666,000 for *Sunday Night Football*) and scripted shows ($433,000 for *This Is Us*) go much higher.[6] Rising costs make media planning more challenging than ever, especially for advertisers with small budgets. Clients want proof

that planners are squeezing the most they can out of every media dollar.

Increasing Complexity in Media Buying and Selling

As the process of buying media has become more complex, so has the process of selling media. In the battle for additional sales, many print and broadcast media companies developed "value-added" programs to provide extra benefits. Besides selling space or time, these companies now offer reprints, merchandising services, special sections, event sponsorships, and mailing lists. To get a bigger share of the advertiser's budget, larger media companies bundle the various stations, publications, or properties they own and offer them in integrated combinations as further incentives.

The Discovery Network, for example, which includes the Travel Channel, TLC, Animal Planet, Discovery, Discovery Health, and the Science Channel, offers its advertisers "multi-platform convergence content sponsorships." This means that each advertiser gets a major Internet/TV sponsorship with four or five commercials in a special-event Discovery show and webcast. Specially created TV spots promote the program and the webcast, as well as Discovery's website and the advertiser's website. Moreover, advertisers get additional off-air exposure in hundreds of Discovery Network retail stores nationwide, which also run in-store videos promoting the shows and the sponsors.[7]

TV is now fragmented into network, syndicated, spot, local, and OnDemand, as well as cable. Specialized magazines now aim at every possible population and business segment. Even national magazines publish editions for particular regions or demographic groups. For example, in early 2009 *Parent* magazine became three separate magazines to better appeal to its

▼**EXHIBIT 14–2** Average Time Spent with Media, 2019.

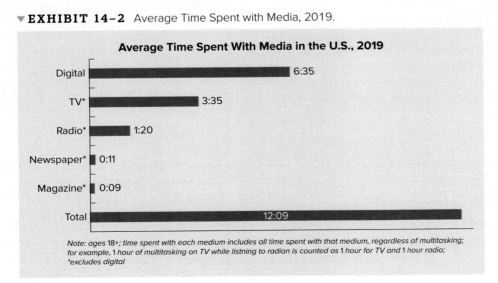

Note: ages 18+; time spent with each medium includes all time spent with that medium, regardless of multitasking; for example, 1 hour of multitasking on TV while listning to radion is counted as 1 hour for TV and 1 hour radio; *excludes digital

Source: https://www.emarketer.com/content/us-time-spent-with-media-2019.

ethical issues

Media Planning and Inclusiveness

While the aim of media planning is to deliver messages to groups of people with commonalities, it is not uncommon that some groups are inadvertently overlooked and excluded in the process. For instance, such groups as same-sex couples and Hispanics are not often represented in advertising, although the number of Americans who identify as lesbian, gay, bisexual, or transgender increases every year, and Hispanics constitute almost 20 percent of the nation's total population.

As the demographic makeup of the United States continues to change, some brands have prioritized greater inclusivity. In 2014, Coca-Cola ran a Super Bowl ad with children singing "America the Beautiful" in different languages. It is also believed to be the first Super Bowl ad to show same-sex parents. Again in 2018, Coca-Cola's Super Bowl ad featured people from a variety of races, nationalities, and geographic regions. Jennifer Healan, group director of integrated marketing content at Coca-Cola, believes the ad is a "message of inclusion." Other brands that have successfully highlighted diversity include Chevrolet, which featured families consisting of gay and interracial couples, and Aerie, whose 2018 campaign included a model with Down syndrome and women modeling underwear with a colitis bag and an insulin pump.

Brands are also customizing the content of their advertisements based on media placements to highlight cultural aspects of diverse groups. For example, Toyota has created different versions of commercials designed to resonate specifically with African American, Hispanic, and Asian American audiences. Each spot represents the different groups in a positive and authentic way. The Asian American spot dispels stereotypes by depicting the not often-seen behavior of a father and daughter connecting with one another while joyfully listening to music as they drive. Toyota developed the campaign because it believes that people want to see messaging that resonates with how they see themselves.

The placement of ads can impact exposure of brands and products to individuals based on their media habits. According to the Interactive Advertising Bureau (IAB), more than one-third of viewers watching ad-supported, original digital video are cord-cutters or cord-nevers. Advertisers are unable to reach them through traditional pay TV because they have canceled their subscriptions or never subscribed in the first place. About 60 percent of these individuals are 34 years old or younger, and 43 percent of the viewership of original digital video is nonwhite. It is important for media planners to recognize how engagement with media is changing so that appropriate target audiences can be identified and segmented.

Technology makes it possible to tailor advertisements so that individuals can be exposed to ads based on their gender, race, household income, and other demographics. However, there are negative consequences of utilizing such technology, as it can be purposefully used to exclude groups from receiving advertisements. For example, companies advertising rental listings and employment opportunities on Facebook discriminated against certain groups, including African Americans, mothers of high school kids, people with disabilities, individuals of Jewish descent, and Spanish speakers. This occurred by using targeting technology to display the ads to whites only. This is not the first time Facebook has encountered difficulties with its targeting capabilities. Its lack of policing enabled users to use derogatory keywords to reach users who posted offensive material, and derogatory phrases such as "kill muslim radicals" were auto-suggested by the targeting tool. The company has vowed to make changes, but these incidents expose the problematic nature of freely available user data.

Leadership positions within most agencies are still over-represented by white males. Although women make up nearly 50 percent of those working in the industry, only 11 percent are creative directors, according to the 3 Percent Movement. To resonate with diverse consumers, advertising and media agencies should emphasize diversity in their ranks. Brands are aware of this problem and are urging agencies to embrace diversity. Recently, Verizon, General Mills, and HP Inc. asked for "action plans" from major agencies about how they will address the diversity gap to hire more women and minorities. Diversity in advertising is a competitive differentiator that imparts insights about markets and customers, and companies with more diverse workforces perform better financially.

Questions

1. In your experience, how has working with diverse groups, either in school or in the workplace, contributed to positive outcomes?
2. What are some of the ethical challenges that come with the ability to target consumers based on their gender, race, and other demographics?
3. Provide an example of a brand that has showcased diversity in its advertising. How has this change altered your opinion of the brand?

diverse and divergent audiences: *Baby Talk, Parent: The Preschool Years*, and *Parent: The School Years*. Finally, the incredible growth of the Internet has brought with it a host of new media options. One driver of fragmentation is the increasingly diverse audiences that media serve and the importance of targeting such audiences effectively (see Ethical Issues in this chapter above).

IMC and relationship marketing are attracting a new breed of media planner: younger, computer-savvy, and schooled in new media. Media professionals have finally come into their own.

Increasing Competition   The final element making media planning more challenging is the competitive environment, which in just a few years has completely changed the structure of the advertising business. In the 1990s, as clients sought greater efficiency with their media dollars, independent media buying services came into the fore, attracting some of the best and brightest talent in the business to compete with agencies for what was once their private domain. Initially, the independents bought advertising at lower bulk rates and then sold it for a commission to advertisers or agencies lacking a fully staffed media department. As the media specialists grew, though, clients came to realize the virtues of scale, and financial clout emerged as a potent weapon in negotiating media buys.[8]

In response, ad agencies unbundled their media departments, setting them up as subsidiaries like Starcom USA, the largest U.S. media agency. These companies compete with the independents as well as with other agencies for media-only accounts. Their expertise and buying clout has led to a surge in billings, which in turn has funded the development of new research tools, critical given the continued fragmentation of the mass media into smaller and smaller niches.

A final issue of complexity is the dominance of digital media, such as Google and Facebook. These tech giants approach advertising on their platforms with a philosophy that appears to suggest "anyone can do it." How? By providing marketers, large and small, with lots of information on how to design, test, and buy ads. This raises the question among some brands about why they are hiring an "expert" to place ads if the advertisers can do it themselves. Agency people respond by noting their expertise in media, including digital, and by pointing out that IMC requires synergy among buys in both old and new media.

The Role of Media in the Marketing Framework

As we've discussed, the key to successful advertising is proper planning. Thus, before media planning begins, companies must first establish their overall marketing and advertising plans.

The top-down marketing plan defines the market need and the company's sales objectives and details strategies for attaining those objectives. Exhibit 14-3 shows how objectives and strategies of a marketing plan result from the marketing situation (or SWOT) analysis, which defines the company's strengths and weaknesses and uncovers any marketplace opportunities and threats. The objectives and strategies of an advertising plan unfold from the marketing plan. But advertising objectives focus on communication goals.

Media objectives and strategies flow from the advertising plan. They determine how the communications goals will be accomplished through the selection of media. The media department's job is to make sure the advertising message (developed by the creative department) gets to the correct target audience (established by the marketing managers and account executives) in an effective manner (as measured by the research department).

The Media Planning Framework

Development of a media plan proceeds in much the same way as marketing and advertising planning. First, review the marketing and advertising objectives and strategies and set relevant, measurable objectives that are both realistic and achievable by the media. Next, devise an ingenious strategy for achieving these objectives. Finally, develop the specific tactical details of media selection and scheduling.

Google and Facebook approach advertising on their sites from the perspective that anyone can do it. True or not, both platforms provide ample learning resources that anyone, including you, can access for free. Facebook's program, which leads to a certificate, is called Blueprint. How will this approach challenge traditional ideas of media planning as practiced by ad agencies?

Facebook

check yourself ✓

1. What is meant by "increasing fragmentation of the audience" and why has that trend made a media planner's job more difficult?

2. What caused the unbundling of media departments? How might it benefit advertisers?

▼EXHIBIT 14-3 This diagram shows how media objectives, strategies, and plans result from the marketing and advertising plans.

The situation analysis
Purpose: To understand the marketing problem. The company and its competitors are analyzed on:
1. Internal strengths and weaknesses.
2. External opportunities and threats.

The marketing plan
Purpose: To plan activities that will solve one or more of the marketing problems.
Includes the determination of:
1. Marketing objectives.
2. Product and spending strategy.
3. Distribution strategy.
4. Which marketing mix to use.
5. Identification of "best" market segments.

The advertising plan
Purpose: To determine what to communicate through ads.
Includes the determination of:
1. How product can meet consumer needs.
2. How product will be positioned in ads.
3. Copy themes.
4. Specific objectives of each ad.
5. Number and sizes of ads.

Setting media objectives
Purpose: To translate marketing and advertising objectives and strategies into goals that media can accomplish.

Determining media strategy
Purpose: To translate media goals into general guidelines that will control the planner's selection and use of media. The best strategy alternatives should be selected.

Selecting broad media classes
Purpose: To determine which broad classes of media best fulfill the criteria. Involves comparison and selection of broad media classes: newspapers, magazines, radio, television, and others. Audience size is a major factor used in comparing the various media classes.

Selecting media within classes
Purpose: To compare and select the best media vehicles within broad classes, again using predetermined criteria. Involves making decisions about the following:
1. If magazines were recommended, then which magazines?
2. If television was recommended, then
   a. Broadcast or cable TV?
   b. Network or spot TV?
   c. If network, which program(s)?
   d. If spot, which markets?
3. If radio or newspapers were recommended, then
   a. Which markets shall be used?
   b. What criteria shall buyers use in making purchases in local media?

Media use decisions—broadcast
1. What kind of sponsorship (sole, shared participating, or other)?
2. What levels of reach and frequency will be required?
3. Scheduling: On which days and months are commercials to appear?
4. Placement of spots: In programs or between programs?

Media use decisions—print
1. Numbers of ads to appear and on which days and months.
2. Placement of ads: Any preferred position within media?
3. Special treatment: Gatefolds, bleeds, color, etc.
4. Desired reach or frequency levels.

Media use decisions—other media
1. Billboards:
   a. Location of markets and plan of distribution.
   b. Kinds of outdoor boards to be used.
2. Direct mail or other media: Decisions peculiar to those media.
3. Interactive media:
   a. Which kind of interactive media?
   b. How will responses be handled?

LO14-2 Discuss the types of media objectives and identify the strategies for achieving these objectives.

DEFINING MEDIA OBJECTIVES

Media objectives translate the advertising strategy into goals. Exhibit 14–4 shows general media objectives for a hypothetical new food product. They explain who the target audience is and why, where messages will be delivered and when, and how much advertising weight needs to be delivered over what period of time.

Media objectives have two major components: audience objectives and message-distribution objectives.

In this section we outline traditional media objectives, which still apply today to broadcast, print, and outdoor media. Later in this section we highlight ways that objectives on the web, particularly in social media, may diverge from those of traditional media.

Audience Objectives

Audience objectives define the types of people the advertiser wants to reach. Media planners typically use geodemographic classifications to define their target audiences. In Exhibit 14–4, for example, objectives 1 and 2 suggest that the target audience is food purchasers for large families who live in urban areas. This group might even be narrowed further according to specific

Media planners must be more creative than ever. Sometimes that means purchasing a product placement rather than a traditional ad. The film Ford v Ferrari put the placements right in the title and featured long scenes of the cars from both companies. Concave, a brand tracking firm, estimates the movie generated almost $56 million in advertising value. It didn't hurt that the film was nominated for a Best Picture Academy Award.

BFA/Alamy Stock Photo

▼ **EXHIBIT 14–4** How media objectives are expressed.

ACME Advertising

Client: Econo Foods

Product/Brand: Chirpee's Cheap Chips

Project: Media plan, first year introduction

Media Objectives

1. To target large families with emphasis on the family's food purchaser.

2. To concentrate the greatest weight of advertising in urban areas where prepared foods traditionally have greater sales and where new ideas normally gain quicker acceptance.

3. To provide extra weight during the introductory period and then continuity throughout the year with a fairly consistent level of advertising impressions.

4. To deliver advertising impressions to every region in relation to regional food store sales.

5. To use media that will reinforce the copy strategy's emphasis on convenience, ease of preparation, taste, and economy.

6. To attain the highest advertising frequency possible once the need for broad coverage and the demands of the copy platform have been met.

income, educational, occupational, or social groupings—any of the segments we discussed in Chapter 4.

Media planners rely heavily on secondary research sources, such as Nielsen Media Research, which provide basic demographic characteristics of media audiences. Other sources, such as Mediamark Research, Inc. (MRI), describe media audiences based on purchase tendencies. These syndicated reports give demographic profiles of heavy and light users of various products and help planners define the target audience. The reports also specify which TV programs or magazines heavy and light users watch and read, which helps planners select media with large audiences of heavy users. Planners can then select **media vehicles**—particular magazines or shows—according to how well they offer an audience that most closely resembles the desired target consumer.

Unfortunately, due to cost restraints, some media research is not as specific as marketers would really like. Most radio, TV, newspaper, and outdoor audience reports, for example, are limited to age and gender. So media planners often have to rely on judgment and experience to select the right vehicles.[9]

Message-Distribution Objectives

Distribution objectives define where, when, and how often advertising should appear. Objectives 3 through 6 from Exhibit 14–4 represent this type. To answer distribution objectives, a media planner must understand a number of terms, including *message weight*, *reach*, *frequency*, and *continuity*.

circulation A statistical measure of a print medium's audience; includes subscription and vendor sales and primary and secondary readership.

opportunity to see (OTS) A possible exposure of an advertising message to one audience member.

gross impressions The total of all the audiences delivered by a media plan.

rating The percentage of homes or individuals exposed to an advertising medium.

television households or TVHH Households with TV sets.

gross rating points (GRPs) The total audience delivery or weight of a specific media schedule. One rating point equals 1 percent of a particular market's population.

readers per copy (RPC) Variable used to determine the total reach of a given print medium. RPC is multiplied by the number of vendor and subscription sales to determine the total audience size.

pass-along rate The number of people who read a magazine without actually buying it.

message weight The total size of the audience for a set of ads or an entire campaign.

advertising impression A possible exposure of the advertising message to one audience member.

Audience Size and Message Weight

Marketers are naturally interested in having their messages exposed to as many customers and prospects as they can afford. So they are also logically most interested in those vehicles that offer the largest audiences.[10] The basic way to express audience size is simply to count the number of people in a vehicle's audience. This is what media research firms such as Nielsen do for broadcast media, typically using a statistical sample to project the total audience size. For print media, firms such as the Audit Bureau of Circulations verify a vehicle's subscribers and newsstand sales (the **circulation**) and then multiply by the estimated number of **readers per copy (RPC)** to determine the total audience. RPC takes into account the **pass-along rate**, the number of people who read a magazine or newspaper without actually buying it. For example, most households subscribe to a single issue of a newspaper, even though multiple family members read it.

Media planners often define media objectives by the schedule's **message weight**, the total size of the audience for a set of ads or an entire campaign, because it gives some indication of the exposure of the campaign in a given market. There are two ways to express message weight: *gross impressions* and *gross rating points*.

If planners know the audience size, they can easily calculate the number of advertising impressions in a media schedule. An **advertising impression** is a *possible* exposure of the advertising message to one audience member. It is sometimes referred to as an **opportunity to see (OTS)**. Why? Because when a newspaper or magazine is delivered or bought, that counts as an impression. It cannot be determined whether the individuals who received those vehicles actually saw any particular ad. By multiplying a vehicle's total audience size by the number of times an advertising message is delivered during the period, planners arrive at the **gross impressions**, or potential exposures, possible in that vehicle. Then, by summing the gross impressions for each medium used, they know the total gross impressions for the schedule (see Exhibit 14–5).

▼**EXHIBIT 14–5** Gross impressions analysis for Alpha brand in the second quarter.

Media Vehicle	Target Audience*	Messages Used	Gross Impressions
TV–Ch. 6 News	140,000	15	2,100,000
Daily newspaper	250,000	7	1,750,000
Spot radio	10,000	55	550,000
Total gross impressions			4,400,000

*Average.

With large media schedules, though, gross impressions can run into the millions and become difficult to comprehend, so that's where the concept of ratings comes in. The **rating** is simply the percentage of homes exposed to an advertising medium. Percentages are not only simpler numbers to deal with; they are also more useful in making comparisons. One rating point is equal to 1 percent of a given population group. When we hear that a particular TV show garnered a 20 rating, it means 20 percent of the households with TV sets (expressed as **television households** or **TVHH**) were tuned in to that show. The higher a program's rating, the more people are watching.[11] This definition applies to many media forms, but it is most commonly used for radio and TV.

By adding the ratings of several media vehicles (as we did for gross impressions) we can determine the message weight of a given advertising schedule, only now it's expressed as **gross rating points (GRPs)** (see Exhibit 14–6). When we say a schedule delivered 440 GRPs, that means the impressions generated by our schedule equaled 440 percent of the target market population. For broadcast media, GRPs are often calculated for a week or a four-week period. In print media, they're calculated for the number of ads in a campaign. For outdoor advertising, they're calculated on the basis of daily exposure.

▼**EXHIBIT 14–6** Gross rating points analysis for Alpha brand in the second quarter.

Media Vehicle	Adult Rating*	Messages Used	Gross Rating Points
TV–Ch. 6 News	10	15	150
Daily newspaper	25	10	250
Spot radio	1	35	35
Total gross rating points			435

*Assumes market size of 1 million people.

In the calculation of message weight, advertisers ignore the fact that there is overlap or duplication. As a result, certain individuals within the audience may see the message several times while others don't see it at all. So, while message weight gives an indication of audience size, it does not reveal much about who is in the audience or how often they are reached. This fact led to the development of other media objectives, including reach, frequency, and continuity.

Audience Accumulation and Reach

The term **reach** refers to the total number of *different* people exposed, at least once, to a medium during a given period of time, usually four weeks.[12] For example, if 40 percent of 100,000 people in a target market tune in to radio station WKKO at least once during a four-week period, the reach is 40,000 people. Reach should not be confused with the number of people who will actually be exposed to and consume the *advertising*, though. It is just the number of people who are exposed to the *vehicle* and therefore have an *opportunity* to see or hear the ad or commercial.

An advertiser may accumulate reach in two ways: by using the same media vehicle repeatedly or by combining two or more media vehicles.[13] Naturally, as more media are used, some duplication occurs. Exhibit 14–7 is a statistical table that estimates how reach builds as additional media are added. To see how it works, locate the column for the first vehicle showing a reach of 60. Then locate the row for vehicle 2 showing a reach of 35. The number at their intersection is 74. But 35 added to 60 is 95. Why has reach increased to only 74? The answer is the two vehicles share some of their users. The

greater the overlap of the audiences for two vehicles, the less using those vehicles in a campaign will grow reach. And if the audience for two vehicles is identical, reach cannot grow at all.

Exposure Frequency

To express the number of times the same person or household has an opportunity to see a message—a radio spot, for example—in a specified time span, media people use the term *frequency*. Whereas reach measures the *breadth*, **frequency** measures the *intensity* of a media schedule, based on repeated exposures to the vehicle or the program. Frequency is important because repetition is the key to learning and memory.

Frequency is calculated as the *average* number of times individuals or homes are exposed to the vehicle during a specific period of time. For instance, suppose in our hypothetical 100,000-person market that 20,000 people tune in to WKKO and have three OTSs during a four-week period, and another 20,000

reach The total number of *different* people or households exposed to an advertising schedule during a given time, usually four weeks. Reach measures the *unduplicated* extent of audience exposure to a media vehicle and may be expressed either as a percentage of the total market or as a raw number.

frequency The number of times the same person or household is exposed to a vehicle in a specified time span. Across a total audience, frequency is calculated as the average number of times individuals or homes are exposed to the vehicle.

▼**EXHIBIT 14–7** Find the reach of the first vehicle on the horizontal axis. Find the reach of the second vehicle on the vertical axis. The point of intersection shows the combined reach of the two. The difference between the sums of the reach of each vehicle and the numbers in the table are due to audience duplication between the vehicles.

Reach of Second Vehicle	Reach of First Vehicle														
	25	**30**	**35**	**40**	**45**	**50**	**55**	**60**	**65**	**70**	**75**	**80**	**85**	**90**	**95**
25	46	47	51	55	59	62	66	70	74	77	81	85	89	92	95
30	—	51	54	58	61	65	68	72	75	79	82	86	90	93	95
35	—	—	58	61	64	67	71	74	77	80	84	87	90	93	95
40	—	—	—	64	67	70	73	76	79	82	85	88	91	94	95
45	—	—	—	—	70	72	75	78	81	83	86	89	92	94	95
50	—	—	—	—	—	75	77	80	82	85	87	90	92	95	95
55	—	—	—	—	—	—	80	82	84	86	89	91	93	95	95
60	—	—	—	—	—	—	—	84	86	88	90	92	94	95	95
65	—	—	—	—	—	—	—	—	88	89	91	93	95	95	95
70	—	—	—	—	—	—	—	—	—	91	92	94	95	95	95
75	—	—	—	—	—	—	—	—	—	—	94	95	95	95	95
80	—	—	—	—	—	—	—	—	—	—	—	95	95	95	95
85	—	—	—	—	—	—	—	—	—	—	—	—	95	95	95
90	—	—	—	—	—	—	—	—	—	—	—	—	—	95	95
95	—	—	—	—	—	—	—	—	—	—	—	—	—	—	95

continuity The duration of an advertising message or campaign over a given period of time.	effective reach A term used to describe the quality of exposure. It measures the number or percentage of the audience who receive enough exposures for the message to truly be received.	effective frequency The average number of times a person must see or hear a message before it becomes effective.	wearout The point at which an advertising message has been seen or heard so often that it starts to irritate consumers and therefore loses its effectiveness.	advertising response curve A graphical representation of the relationship between advertising levels and sales results.

have five OTSs. To calculate the average frequency, divide the total number of exposures by the total reach:

$$
\begin{aligned}
\text{Average frequency} &= \text{Total exposures} \\
&\quad \div \text{Audience reach} \\
&= [(20{,}000 \times 3) + \\
&\quad (20{,}000 \times 5)] \\
&\quad \div 40{,}000 \\
&= 160{,}000 \div 40{,}000 \\
&= 4.0
\end{aligned}
$$

For the 40,000 listeners reached, the average frequency, or number of exposures, was four.

Once we understand reach and frequency, we have another, simple way to determine the message weight. To calculate gross rating points, just multiply a show's reach (expressed as a rating percentage) by the average frequency. In our radio example, 40 percent of the radio households (a 40 rating) had the opportunity to hear the commercial an average of four times during the four-week period:

$$
\begin{aligned}
\text{Reach} \times \text{Frequency} &= \text{GRPs} \\
40 \times 4 &= 160 \text{ GRPs}
\end{aligned}
$$

Thus, the message weight of this radio campaign would be equal to 160 percent of the total market—or 160,000 gross impressions.

Continuity

Media planners refer to the duration of an advertising message or campaign over a given period of time as **continuity**. Few companies spread their marketing efforts evenly throughout the year. They typically *heavy up* before prime selling seasons and slow down during the off-season. Likewise, to save money, a media planner for a new product might decide that after a heavy introductory period of, say, four weeks, a radio campaign needs to maintain *continuity* for an additional 16 weeks but on fewer stations. We'll discuss some common scheduling patterns in the section on media tactics.

While frequency is important to create memory, continuity is important to *sustain* it. Moreover, as people come into and out of the market for goods and services every day, continuity provides a means of having the message there when it's most needed. Ads that can be scheduled to hit targets when they are ready to make a purchase are more effective and require less frequency.[14]

LO14-3 Articulate what is meant by "the art of media planning."

OPTIMIZING REACH, FREQUENCY, AND CONTINUITY: THE ART OF MEDIA PLANNING

Good media planning is both an art and a science. The media planner must get the most effective exposure on a limited budget. As Exhibit 14–8 shows, the objectives of reach, frequency, and continuity have inverse relationships to one another.

To achieve greater reach on a limited budget, some frequency and/or continuity has to be sacrificed. Research shows that all three are critical. But because all budgets are limited, which is most critical? This has always been the subject of hot debate in advertising circles.

Effective Reach

One of the problems with reach is that, by itself, the measurement doesn't take into account the *effectiveness* of the exposures. Some people exposed to the vehicle still won't be aware of the message. So, on the surface, reach doesn't seem to be the best

▼ **EXHIBIT 14–8** Reach and frequency have an inverse relationship to each other. For instance, in the example below, an advertiser can reach 6,000 people once, 3,000 people approximately 6 times, or 1,000 people 9 times for the same budget.

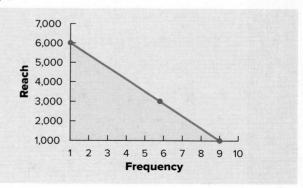

The S-shaped response curve suggests that a minimum threshold (A) of advertising frequency must be crossed before a meaningful response is achieved. At some level of frequency, another threshold (B) is crossed and the response begins to level off or even decline due to overexposure.

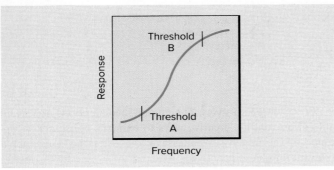

measure of media success. Media people use the term **effective reach** to describe the *quality* of exposure. It measures the percentage of the audience who receive enough exposures to truly notice the message.

Effective Frequency

Similar to the concept of effective reach is **effective frequency**, defined as the average number of times a person must see or hear a message before it becomes effective. In theory, effective frequency falls somewhere between a minimum level that achieves message awareness and a maximum level that becomes overexposure, which leads to **wearout** (the message begins being ignored or becomes an irritation).

The S-shaped **advertising response curve** in Exhibit 14–9 suggests that at a low frequency there is little response. This is because the intensity of advertising is below a threshold where most of the target audience would notice it. Once that threshold is crossed, there is a dramatic response to increasing levels of advertising. Eventually though, the target market becomes saturated and, while advertising frequency continues to increase, the market response levels off or may even decline. The challenge to media planners is to determine the frequency of advertising that will exceed threshold A but remain below threshold B. To complicate matters further, different products or different advertising campaigns may generate different advertising response curves.

Following the publication of Michael Naples's classic book *Effective Frequency*, the industry fell in love with his claim that, in most cases, effective frequency could be achieved by an average frequency of three over a four-week period. Here was a nice, simple conclusion that all media planners could use.

However, this assumes that all exposures are equal. If that's the case, then where does advertising creativity come in? And what about the environment in which the advertising appears? Doesn't that have some effect on the quality of exposure? There is no simple solution to this problem.

Once the media objectives have been determined—that is, the optimum levels of message weight, reach, frequency, and continuity—the media planner can develop the strategy for achieving them.

check yourself ✓

1. What are the two types of media objectives? Give examples of each.

2. What is message weight?

3. How does the media planner optimize reach, frequency, and continuity?

4. How are GRPs and CPMs calculated?

LO14-4 Identify the factors that influence media strategy and tactics.

DEVELOPING A MEDIA STRATEGY: THE MEDIA MIX

The media strategy describes how the advertiser will achieve the stated media objectives: which media will be used, where, how often, and when. Just as marketers determine marketing

Mitsubishi's ad agency needed to make media decisions that could be assigned to live categories. This Montero ad targets a specific group of people (the market), is backed by a predetermined budget (the money), and is placed in specific communications vehicles (the media). Even after making a commitment to print media, Mitsubishi's agency faced decisions about size and placement of the ad (the mechanics) and the type of schedule (the methodology) that would best achieve the client's objectives. Hindustan Motors Ltd.

five Ms The elements of the media mix that include markets, money, media, mechanics, and methodology.

methodology The overall strategy of selecting and scheduling media vehicles to achieve the desired reach, frequency, and continuity objectives.

brand development index (BDI) The percentage of a brand's total sales in an area divided by the total population in the area; it indicates the sales potential of a particular brand in a specific market area.

category development index (CDI) The percentage of a product category's total U.S. sales in an area divided by the percentage of total U.S. population in the area.

markets Groups of potential customers who share a common interest, need, or desire; who can use the offered good or service to some advantage; and who can afford or are willing to pay the purchase price.

money In media planning, one of the five elements in the media mix.

media A plural form of *medium,* referring to communications vehicles paid to present an advertisement to their target audience. Most often used to refer to radio and television networks, stations that have new reporters, and publications that carry news and advertising.

mechanics One of the five Ms of the media mix; dealing creatively with the available advertising media options.

strategy by blending elements of the marketing mix, media planners can develop media strategies by blending the elements of the media mix.

Factors in the Media Strategy: The Five Ms

Many factors go into developing an effective media strategy. For simplicity and ease of memory, we have sorted them into five categories and given them the moniker of the **five Ms**: *markets, money, media, mechanics,* and *methodology.*

Markets refers to the various targets of a media plan: trade and consumer audiences; global, national, or regional audiences; ethnic and socioeconomic groups; or other stakeholders. In an integrated marketing communications plan, the media planner wants to understand the reasons and motivations for the prospect's purchase and usage patterns and then create a media plan based on those findings.[15]

Using intuition, experience, marketing savvy, and analytical skill, the media planner determines the second element, **money**—how much to budget and where to allocate it. How much for print media, how much in TV, how much to nontraditional or supplemental media, how much to each geographic area?

Media includes *all* communications vehicles available to a marketer—anything you can put your name on. This includes radio, TV, newspapers, magazines, outdoor, the Internet, and direct mail, plus sales promotion, direct marketing, public relations activities and publicity, special events, brochures, and even shopping bags. Good media planners champion the integration of all marketing communications to help achieve their companies' marketing and advertising objectives. They look at the media element both analytically and creatively.

The media planner also has to deal with the complex **mechanics** of advertising media and messages. Radio and TV commercials come in a variety of time units, and print ads are created in a

variety of sizes and styles. The myriad media options now available offer exciting, creative ways to enhance consumer acceptance of the advertiser's message and offer the consumer a relevant purchase incentive.

The **methodology** element refers to the overall strategy of selecting and scheduling media vehicles to achieve the desired message weight, reach, frequency, and continuity objectives. It offers the opportunity for creativity in planning, negotiating, and buying.

Factors That Influence Media Strategy Decisions

Media decisions are greatly influenced by some factors over which the media planner has little or no control. These include the scope of the media plan, sales potential of different markets, competitive strategies and budget considerations, availability of different media vehicles, nature of the medium, mood of the message, message size and length, and buyer purchase patterns.

Scope of the Media Plan The location and makeup of the target audience strongly influence the scope of the media plan, thereby affecting decisions regarding the market, the money, and the media elements.

Domestic markets A media planner normally limits advertising to areas where the product is available. If a store serves only one town, or if a city has been chosen to test-market a new product, then the advertiser will use a *local* plan.

A *regional* plan may cover several adjoining metropolitan areas, an entire state or province, or several neighboring states. Regional plans typically employ a combination of local media, regional editions of national magazines, spot TV and radio, and the Internet.

Advertisers who want to reach several regions or an entire country use a *national* plan. This may call for network TV and radio, full-circulation national magazines and newspapers, nationally syndicated Sunday newspaper supplements, and the web.

Sales Potential of Different Markets The market and money elements of the media mix also depend on the sales potential of each area. National advertisers use this factor to determine where to allocate their advertising dollars. Planners can determine an area's sales potential in several ways.

The brand development index The **brand development index (BDI)** indicates the sales strength of a particular brand in a specific market area. It compares the percentage of the brand's total U.S. sales in an area to the percentage of the total U.S. population in that area. The larger the brand's sales relative to the area's percentage of U.S. population, the higher the BDI and the greater the brand's sales development. BDI is calculated as

$$BDI = \frac{\text{Percentage of the brand's total U.S. sales in the area}}{\text{Percentage of total U.S. population in the area}} \times 100$$

Suppose sales of a brand in Los Angeles are 1.58 percent of the brand's total U.S. sales and the population of Los Angeles is 2 percent of the U.S. total. The BDI for Los Angeles is

$$BDI = \frac{1.58}{2} \times 100 = 79$$

An index number of 100 means the brand's performance is in balance with the size of the area's population. A BDI index number below 100 indicates poor development of the brand in that market. Conversely, a BDI greater than 100 indicates better than average development.

The category development index To determine the strength of the whole product category, media planners use the **category development index (CDI)**, which works on the same principle as the BDI and is calculated in much the same way:

$$CDI = \frac{\text{Percentage of the product category's total U.S. sales in the area}}{\text{Percentage of total U.S. population in the area}} \times 100$$

If category sales in Los Angeles are 4.92 percent of total U.S. category sales, the CDI in Los Angeles is

$$CDI = \frac{4.92}{2} \times 100 = 246$$

The combination of BDI and CDI can help the planner determine a media strategy for the market (see Exhibit 14-10). In our example, a low BDI (less than 100) and a high CDI (more than 100) in Los Angeles indicate that the product category offers great potential but the brand is not selling well (low market share). This may represent a problem or an opportunity. If the

▼**EXHIBIT 14–10** Media buyers compare the brand development index with the category development index for their products to better understand which markets will respond best to advertising. Advertising can be expected to work well when BDI and CDI are both high, but probably not when both are low.

	Low BDI	High BDI
High CDI	Low market share *but* Good market potential	High market share *and* Good market potential
Low CDI	Low market share *and* Poor market potential	High market share *but* Poor market potential

brand has been on the market for some time, the low BDI raises a red flag; some problem is standing in the way of brand sales. But if the brand is new, the low BDI may be a positive sign. The high CDI may indicate the brand can grow substantially, given more time and greater media and marketing support. At this point, the media planner should assess the company's share of voice (discussed in Chapter 7) and budget accordingly.

Competitive Strategies and Budget Considerations
Advertisers always consider what competitors are doing, particularly those that have larger advertising budgets. This affects the *media*, *mechanics*, and *methodology* elements of the media mix. Several services, such as TNS Media Intelligence Adspender, detail competitive advertising expenditures in the different media. By knowing the size of competitors' budgets, the media they're using, the regionality or seasonality of their sales, and any new-product tests and introductions, advertisers can better plan a counterstrategy.

Again, the media planner should analyze the company's share of voice in the marketplace. If an advertiser's budget is much smaller than the competition's, the brand could get lost in the shuffle. While it sometimes makes sense to use media similar to the competition's if the target audiences are the same or if the competitors are not using their media effectively, advertisers should generally bypass media that competitors dominate and choose other media in which they can achieve a strong position.

So what happens when it all comes together? In 2019, Nike featured an ad developed by Wieden+Kennedy, its longtime agency, named "Dream Crazier." The spot featured tennis star Serena Williams, who was shown encouraging women athletes to achieve their dreams in the face of challenges. The agency negotiated placement in the televised Academy Awards, a great choice for its large, female audience. And an even better choice because Serena was a presenter. But what earned the agency *AdWeek*'s Plan of the Year award was the ad's appearance right after Serena's appearance in the show.[16]

Nature of the Medium and Mood of the Message

An important influence on the *media* element of the mix is how well a medium works with the style or mood of the particular message.

Advertising messages differ in many ways. Some are simple messages: "Just do it" (Nike). Others make emotional or sensual appeals to people's needs and wants: "The great taste of fruit squared" (Jolly Rancher candies). Many advertisers use a reason-why approach to explain their product's advantages: "Twice the room. Twice the comfort. Twice the value. Embassy Suites. Twice the hotel."

Complex messages, such as ads announcing a new product or concept, require more space or time for explanation. Each circumstance affects the media selection as well as the *methodology* of the media mix.

A new or highly complex message may require greater frequency and exposure to be understood and remembered. A dogmatic message like Nike's may require a surge at the beginning, then low frequency and greater reach, plus continuity.

Once consumers understand reason-why messages, pulsing advertising exposures at irregular intervals is often sufficient. Emotionally oriented messages are usually more effective when spaced at regular intervals to create enduring feelings about the product. We discuss these scheduling methods further in the next section on media tactics.

Message Size, Length, and Position Considerations

The particular characteristics of different media affect the mechanics element of the media mix. For example,

This ad for Ray-Ban, titled "Rapper," is executed simply and to the point. Unexpected imagery helps the ad to get noticed. Reach and frequency are of little value if nobody pays attention to the ad.

Luxottica Group S.p.A.

in print, a full-page ad attracts more attention than a quarter-page ad and a full-color ad more than a black-and-white one (see Exhibit 14–11).

Should a small advertiser run a full-page ad once a month or a quarter-page ad once a week? Is it better to use a few 60-second commercials or many 15- and 30-second ones? The planner has to consider the nature of the advertising message; some simply require more time and space to explain. Competitive activity often dictates more message units. The product itself may demand the prestige of a full-page or full-color ad. However, it's often better to run small ads consistently rather than one large ad occasionally. Unfortunately, space and time units may be determined by someone other than the media planner—creative

▼**EXHIBIT 14–11** Effect of size and color on ad readership (total ads studied = 107,506).

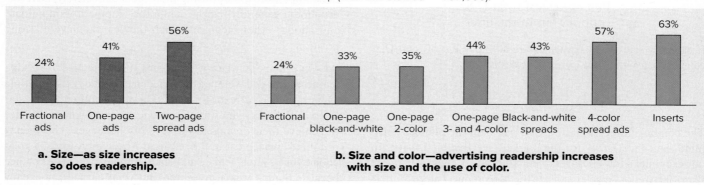

a. Size—as size increases so does readership.

b. Size and color—advertising readership increases with size and the use of color.

or account management, for example—in which case the planner's options are limited.

The position of an ad is another consideration. Preferred positions for magazine ads are front and back covers; for TV, sponsorship of prime-time shows. Special positions and sponsorships cost more, so the media planner must decide whether the increased audience is worth the higher costs.

As we can see, the nature of the creative work has the potential to greatly affect the media strategy. This means that media planners have to be flexible because the initial media plan may well have been determined prior to beginning the creative work.

Buyer Purchase Patterns   Finally, the customer's product purchasing behavior affects every element of the media mix. The media planner must consider how, when, and where the product is typically purchased and repurchased. Products with short purchase cycles (convenience foods and paper towels) require more constant levels of advertising than products purchased infrequently (refrigerators and notebook computers).

Stating the Media Strategy

A written rationale for the media strategy is an integral part of any media plan. Without one, it's difficult for client and agency management to analyze the logic and consistency of the recommended media schedule.

Generally, the strategy statement begins with a brief definition of target audiences (the market element) and the priorities for weighting them. It explains the nature of the message and indicates which media types will be used and why (the media element). It outlines specific reach, frequency, and continuity goals and how they are to be achieved (the methodology element). It provides a budget for each medium (the money element), including the cost of production and any collateral materials. Finally, it states the intended size of message units, and any position or timing considerations (the mechanics element).

Once the strategy is delineated, the plan details the tactics to be employed, the subject of the next section.

check yourself ✓

1. What is BDI? What is CDI?

2. What is the "sweet spot" of the BDI/CDI index?

3. What factors influence media strategy decisions?

LO14-5   Describe different types of advertising schedules and the purpose for each.

MEDIA TACTICS: SELECTING AND SCHEDULING MEDIA VEHICLES

Once the general media strategy is determined, the media planner can select and schedule particular media vehicles. The planner usually considers each medium's value on a set of specific criteria. Exhibit 14–12 summarizes many of the media advantages discussed in Chapters 10 through 13.

Criteria for Selecting Individual Media Vehicles

In evaluating specific media vehicles, the planner considers several factors: overall campaign objectives and strategy; size and characteristics of each vehicle's audience; exposure, attention, and motivation value of each vehicle; and cost-efficiency.

Overall Campaign Objectives and Strategy   The media planner's first job is to review the nature of the product or service, the objectives and strategies, and the primary and secondary target markets and audiences. The characteristics of

▼**EXHIBIT 1–12** Media selection: Quick list of advantages.

Medium	Advantages
Newspapers	Quick placement. Local targeting. Audience interest. Current.
Magazines	High-quality graphics/reproduction. Prestige factor. Color. Selective targeting.
TV	Combines sight, sound, movement. A single message. Demonstration. Social dominance.
Radio	Intimacy. Loyal following. Ability to change message quickly. Repetition and frequency.
Digital interactive	Immediate response. Interactive. Highly selective targeting. Global. Fastest-growing medium. Relevance of ads.
Direct mail	Measurable. Graphics, color. 3-D. Highly personal. Adaptable message length.
Outdoor/Transit	Local targeting. Graphics, color. Simple message. Larger than life. Repetition.
Applying the Breaks	

What creative advantages can you add to the list? What are some drawbacks of the media listed here?

or simply news and entertainment. Advertising is most effective when it positions a product as part of the solution that consumers seek. Otherwise, consumers may see it as an intrusion.[17]

the product often suggest a suitable media choice. A product with a distinct personality or image, such as a fine perfume, might be advertised in media that reinforce this image. The media planner considers how consumers regard various magazines and TV programs—feminine or masculine, highbrow or lowbrow, serious or frivolous—and determines whether they're appropriate for the brand.

The content and editorial policy of the media vehicle and its compatibility with the product are important considerations. *Tennis* magazine is a poor vehicle for cigarette or alcohol ads even though its demographic profile and image might match the desired target audience.

Consumers choose a particular vehicle because they gain some "reward": self-improvement, financial advice, career guidance,

If the marketing objective is to gain greater product distribution, the planner should select media that might also influence resellers. If the goal is to stimulate sales of a nationally distributed product in isolated markets, ads should be placed in local and regional media that penetrate those markets. Pricing strategy influences media choices too. A premium-priced product should use prestigious media to support its market image.

For a more detailed look at media objectives and strategies, see My Ad Campaign 14.

Characteristics of Media Audiences
An **audience** is the total number of people or households exposed to a vehicle. The planner needs to know how closely the vehicle's audience matches the profile of the target market and how interested prospective customers are in the publication or program. A product intended for a Latino audience, for example, would likely appear in specific media directed toward Hispanics. Simmons Market Research Bureau (SMRB) provides research data on age, income, occupational status, and other characteristics of magazine readers. Simmons also publishes demographic and psychographic data on product usage of consumers. Likewise, Nielsen provides audience statistics for television programs and Arbitron for radio stations.

The *content* of the vehicle usually determines the type of people in the audience. Some radio stations emphasize in-depth news or sports; others feature jazz, rock, or classical music. Each type of programming attracts a different audience.

Exposure, Attention, and Motivation Value of Media Vehicles
The media planner has to select media that will not only achieve the desired *exposure* to the target audience, but also attract *attention* and *motivate* people to act.

Exposure As we discussed earlier, just because someone reads a particular magazine or watches a certain program doesn't mean he or she sees the ads. Some people read only one article, set aside the magazine, and never pick it up again. Many people change channels during commercial breaks or leave to get a snack. Comparing the **exposure value** of different vehicles, therefore, is very difficult. Without statistics, media planners have to use their best judgment based on experience.

Five factors affect the probability of ad exposure:

1. The senses used to perceive messages (for example, scratch-and-sniff ads really improve the exposure value of magazines).

2. How much and what kind of attention the vehicle requires (higher involvement suggests greater ad exposure).

ONE FOR ME, AND ONE FOR ME.

What could make your taste buds happier than one of our wondrous medleys of fresh pecans, hazelnuts or cashews wrapped in caramel and chocolate? Partake of these caramel nut bouchées, and your sweet tooth will positively swoon.

1-800-9-GODIVA   www.godiva.com   AOL (keyword: GODIVA)

New York   Paris   **GODIVA**   Tokyo   Brussels
Chocolatier

The language and imagery of this Godiva chocolate (www.godiva.com) ad exudes a sense of elegance that suits the audience of the medium selected. Godiva placed the ad in magazines such as Architectural Digest *to reach a target audience of affluent, well-educated individuals. The photo, type, and layout elements reflect the nature of the magazine, the advertiser, and even the audience.*

Godiva Chocolatier, Inc

Developing Media Objectives and Strategies [14]

In your lifetime, the media landscape has changed dramatically, becoming much more fragmented and full of choice. This has elevated the complexity of the media planning role. In this part of your assignment you are nonetheless considering all types of media to help distribute your message. You will most likely be given a media budget and asked to formulate a plan of attack. To better support your choices it is imperative that you develop sound objectives and strategies.

In some cases, your professor may have given you a set of marketing objectives or your research on clients may have indicated their main goals for advertising. It is important to note here that marketing objectives do not equal media objectives. They do, however, help us shape our media objectives, which in turn help us develop sound media strategy.

Developing Media Objectives

The first place to start in developing media objectives is with the marketing objectives themselves. You should view media objectives as the goals that become the building blocks of the media plan and that ultimately help clients meet their marketing goals.

Here are some examples of marketing objectives, translated into media objectives:

Marketing Objectives	Media Objectives
• Increase awareness among target audience by 23 percent.	• Generate mass awareness among target audience.
• Steal 2 percent share of sales from competitors.	• Differentiate brand from competitors.
• Build customer database of 5,000 individuals.	• Generate leads/requests for more information.

Although the media objectives seem very similar to marketing objectives, they are actually quite different. Media objectives should focus on only what the media can achieve. Remember that the media plan is one of many components that go into building a successful promotional or communications plan and it has a distinct role, which is what you are trying to highlight in the objectives.

Developing Media Strategies

Media strategies are born out of the media objectives and describe a specific plan of action for achieving stated objectives. The strategy seeks to accomplish two things: setting the foundation for media ideas that help you meet the objective or goal and providing a position of advantage over your client's competitors.

The media strategy itself is built on key plan parameters on which the entire communications team has had input:

- Target audience
- Seasonality
- Geography
- Overall communication goals
- Budget
- Creative
- Competitive analysis

So how do media objectives translate into strategies? Let's look at the three we detailed earlier:

Media Objectives	Media Strategies
• Generate mass awareness among target audience.	• Use mass media (broadcast) to build reach against M18–34.
• Differentiate brand from competitors.	• Secure high-profile sponsorship with category exclusivity.
• Generate leads/requests for more information.	• Use interactive media to elicit registration.

---

3. Whether the vehicle is an information source or a diversion (for example, radio news programs offer greater ad exposure than elevator music).

4. Whether the vehicle or program aims at a general or a specialized audience (exposure value will be higher with specialized audiences).

5. The intrusiveness of the ad in the vehicle (placement within broadcast programs gives greater exposure than placement between programs; ads placed next to editorial material get greater exposure than ads placed next to other print ads, larger ads attract more attention).

Attention Degree of attention is another consideration. As we discussed in Chapter 5, consumers with no interest in motorcycles or cosmetics won't remember ads for those products. For a variety of reasons, they fail to penetrate the viewer's perceptual screens. But someone in the market for a new car tends to notice every car ad.

Exposure value relates only to the vehicle; **attention value** concerns the advertising message and copy, as well as the vehicle. Special-interest media, such as boating magazines, can offer good attention value to a marine product. But what kind of attention value can the daily newspaper offer such a product? Do sailors think about boats while reading the newspaper? Much research still needs to be done, but six factors are known to increase attention value:[18]

1. Audience involvement with editorial content or program material.

2. Specialization of audience interest or identification.

3. Number of competitive advertisers (the fewer, the better).

4. Audience familiarity with the advertiser's campaign.

5. Quality of advertising reproduction.

6. Timeliness of advertising exposure.

Motivation These same factors affect a vehicle's **motivation value**, but in different ways. Familiarity with the advertiser's campaign may affect attention significantly but motivation very little. The attention factors of quality reproduction and timeliness can motivate someone, however.

Comstock Images/Alamy Stock Photo

Media planners analyze these values by assigning numerical ratings to their judgments of a vehicle's strengths and weaknesses. Then, using a weighting formula, they add them up. Planners use similar weighting methods to evaluate other factors, such as the relative importance of age versus income.

Cost-Efficiency of Media Vehicles

Finally, media planners analyze the cost-efficiency of each vehicle. A common term used in media planning and buying is **cost per thousand** or **CPM** (M is the Roman numeral for 1,000). If a daily newspaper has 300,000 subscribers and charges $5,000 for a full-page ad, the cost per thousand is the cost divided by the number of thousands of people in the audience. Because there are 300 *thousand* subscribers, you divide $5,000 by 300:

$$\text{CPM} = \frac{\$5,000}{300,000 \div 1,000} = \frac{\$5,000}{300}$$
$$= \$16.67 \text{ per thousand}$$

However, media planners are more interested in **cost-efficiency**—the cost of exposing the message to the *target audience* rather than to the total circulation. Let's say the target audience is males ages 18 to 49, and 40 percent of a magazine's subscriber base of 250,000 fits this category. If the magazine charges $3,000 for a full-page ad, the **target CPM (TCPM)** is computed as follows:

$$\text{Target audience} = 0.40 \times 250,000 = 100,000$$
$$\text{TCPM} = \frac{\$3,000}{100,000 \div 1,000} = \$30 \text{ per thousand}$$

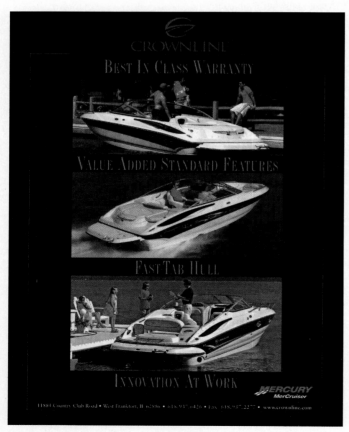

This ad for Crownline boats will get more exposure and receive more attention in Lakeland Boating *magazine than in a general-interest publication. Readers will have nautical activities on their minds and may be very motivated if they are actively seeking product information.*

Crownline Boats

Buyer Purchase Patterns

Finally, the customer's product purchasing behavior affects every element of the media mix. The media planner must consider how, when, and where the product is typically purchased and repurchased. Products with short purchase cycles (convenience foods and paper towels) require more constant levels of advertising than products purchased infrequently (refrigerators and furniture).

Stating the Media Strategy

A written rationale for the media strategy is an integral part of any media plan. Without one, it's difficult for client and agency management to analyze the logic and consistency of the recommended media schedule.

The more costly (on an absolute basis) daily newspaper might turn out to be more cost-efficient than the magazine if 60 percent of its readers (180,000) belong to the target audience:

$$\text{TCPM} = \frac{\$5,000}{180,000 \div 1,000}$$
$$= \$27.78 \text{ per thousand}$$

The media planner may also want to compare the **cost per point (CPP)** of different broadcast programs. This is done the same way as cost per thousand, except you divide the cost by the rating points instead of the gross impressions.

Comparing different vehicles by CPM or CPP is important but does not take into account each vehicle's other advantages and disadvantages. The media planner must evaluate all the criteria to determine

1. How much of each vehicle's audience matches the product's target audience.
2. How each vehicle satisfies the campaign's objectives and strategy.
3. How well each vehicle offers attention, exposure, and motivation.

The Synergy of Mixed Media

A combination of media is called a **mixed-media approach**. There are numerous reasons for using mixed media:

- To reach people who are unavailable through only one medium.
- To provide repeat exposure in a less expensive secondary medium after attaining optimum reach in the first.
- To use the intrinsic value of an additional medium to extend the creative effectiveness of the ad campaign (such as music on radio along with long copy in print media).
- To deliver coupons in print media when the primary vehicle is broadcast.
- To produce **synergy**, where the total effect is greater than the sum of its parts.

Television, for example, can be used to introduce a new product and give importance to the message. Magazine ads can then

cost per point (CPP) A simple computation used by media buyers to determine which broadcast programs are the most efficient in relation to the target audience.

mixed-media approach Using a combination of advertising media vehicles in a single advertising campaign.

synergy An effect achieved when the sum of the parts is greater than that expected from simply adding together the individual components.

follow up for greater detail, image enhancement, longevity, and memory improvement.

A mixed-media campaign was effective for General Electric's lighting products. The promotion used a combination of network TV spots, print advertising, Sunday supplement inserts, in-store displays in more than 150,000 stores, and a highly creative publicity program. By using an integrated, mixed-media approach, the campaign produced "unprecedented" consumer awareness and dealer support. It achieved synergy.[19]

Methods for Scheduling Media

After selecting the appropriate media vehicles, the media planner decides how many space or time units to buy of each vehicle and schedules them for release over a period of time when consumers are most apt to be in the market for the product.

Continuous, Flighting, and Pulsing Schedules To build continuity in a campaign, planners use three principal scheduling tactics: *continuous*, *flighting*, and *pulsing* (see Exhibit 14–13).

▼**EXHIBIT 14–13** Three ways to schedule the same number of total gross rating points: continuous, flighting, and pulsing.

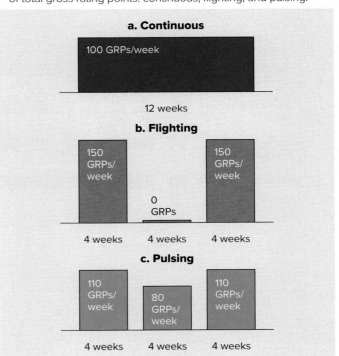

In a **continuous schedule**, advertising runs steadily and varies little over the campaign period. It's the best way to build continuity. Advertisers use this scheduling pattern for products consumers purchase regularly.

Flighting alternates periods of advertising with periods of no advertising. This intermittent schedule makes sense for products and services that experience large fluctuations in demand throughout the year (tax services, lawn-care products, cold remedies). The advertiser might introduce the product with a four-week flight and then schedule three additional four-week flights to run during seasonal periods later in the year. Flighting is also often used by products and services to stretch limited budgets.

The third alternative, **pulsing**, mixes continuous and flighting strategies. The advertiser maintains a low level of advertising all year but uses periodic pulses to heavy up during peak selling periods. This strategy is appropriate for products like soft drinks, which are consumed all year but more heavily in the summer.

Additional Scheduling Patterns For high-ticket items that require careful consideration, **bursting**—running the same commercial every half-hour on the same network during prime time—can be effective. A variation is **roadblocking**, buying airtime on all three networks simultaneously. Chrysler used this technique to give viewers the impression that the advertiser was everywhere, even if the ad showed for only a few nights. Digital Equipment used a scheduling tactic called **blinking** to stretch its slim ad budget. To reach business executives, it flooded the airwaves on Sundays (on both cable and network TV channels) to make it virtually impossible to miss the ads.[20]

Once the scheduling criteria are determined, the media planner creates a flowchart of the plan. The flowchart is a graphic presentation of the total campaign to let the creative department, media department, account services, and the client see the pattern of media events that will occur throughout the campaign, usually one year (see Exhibit 14–14).

▼ **EXHIBIT 14–14** A media plan flowchart like this computerized printout of Telmar's FlowMaster gives a bird's-eye view of the major media purchases and where and when they will appear over a specified period of time.

My Flowchart																									
2021 Monday (Bdcst) Dates																									
Media	February				March					April				May				June				Cost ($000) Cost %		Rating points Rtg. point %	Cost/point Total uses
	27	3	10	17	24	3	10	17	24	31	7	14	21	28	5	12	19	26	2	9	23				
										2	2	2	2		2	2	2	2						
Prime Time Television																						1,600,000.00		320.0	5000.0
30 Second sports																						22.9		12.6	16
	2		2		2		2		2		2		2		2		2		2						
National Magazines																						1,000,000.00		20.0	50000.0
People																						14.3		0.8	20
			20	20		20		20	20		20		20	20		20		20	20						
National Radio																						4,400,000.00		2200.0	2000.0
Afternoon drive																						62.9		86.6	220
Total Media																						7,000,000.0		2540.0	27343.8
																						(100.0)		(100.0)	256

	February	March	April	May	June			
Cost ($000):	1,000,000.00	1,500,000.00	1,800,000.00	1,400,000.00	1,300,000.00	7,000,000.00		
Cost %:	14.3	21.4	25.7	20.0	18.6			
Rating points:	404.0	606.0	564.0	484.0	482.0		2540.0	
Rtg. point %:	16.3	24.5	23.2	19.8	16.2			
Cost/point:	2475.2	2475.2	3191.5	2892.6	2697.1			13731.6
Total uses:	44	33	52	48	46			223

TV	100,000	20	5000	20
Mag	50,000	20	2500	1
Rad	20,000			10

Computers in Media Selection and Scheduling

There is now a healthy selection of new desktop computer software to assist media planners. Computers perform the tedious computations for GRPs, CPMs, reach, frequency, and the like. They also save time and money. One agency found it could plan the entire TV, radio, and print co-op budgets for one of its largest clients in two days with only three people and one software package. Previously, that task required 70 staffers working manually for a week and a half.

Established in 1968, Telmar (www.telmar.com) was the first independent supplier of computerized media planning systems. Today, it is the world's leading supplier of media planning software and support services. More than 25,000 users in 100 countries use Telmar systems for media and marketing decision making.[21]

Telmar's software suite is designed to help media planners, buyers, research analysts, and sellers work more efficiently and to help them make better judgments in the evaluation or sales process. The software allows advertising executives to estimate the effectiveness of multifaceted marketing plans that use various combinations of media including print, broadcast, in-store, special promotions, special events, PR, and other "new media." Its flexibility permits the user to analyze the potential effectiveness of any and every marketing tool used to reach the consumer.

Even with technology, though, it's still up to the media planner to know the product, the market, and the media, and to then make the call. Computers can't decide which medium or environment is best for the message. They can't evaluate the content of a magazine or the image of a TV program. They can't judge whether the numbers they're fed are valid or reliable, and they can't interpret the meaning of the results. What they can do is help the process along.

Clement Mok/Photodisc/Getty Images

check yourself ✓

1. What is meant by continuous, flighting, pulsing, bursting, roadblocking, and blinking schedules?

2. How does an advertiser choose a media schedule? What options are available to him or her?

The advent of computer software has taken some of the more grueling, laborious work out of media planning. Planners can now crunch numbers, track results, and compute GRPs and CPMs right at their desktops. This saves an enormous amount of time and money. The Telmar site (www.telmar.com) shown here is an example of one of the many programs available.

Telmar Group Inc.

media buyer Person responsible for negotiating and contracting the purchase of advertisement space and time in various media.

LO14-6 Explain the role of the media buyer.

THE ROLE OF THE MEDIA BUYER

Planning is only the first stage in the media process. Once the media plans are developed, they must be executed. The person in charge of negotiating and contracting with the media is called a **media buyer**. Media buyers often specialize in one medium or another, so there are print media buyers, spot TV media buyers, network media buyers, and so on. The degree of specialization depends on the size of the advertiser or the agency. In small agencies, for example, media buyers do it all.

Media buying is a complicated process. Buyers must perform several functions in the process of converting a media plan into a successful buy. Placing an ad is not as easy as it may seem, especially when there are hundreds of television and radio stations, newspapers, and magazines around the country with different deadlines, different requirements, and different rates. The job can be very tedious and time-consuming.

Fortunately, media buyers now have a variety of software programs available to assist them. Kantar Media, a trusted company in the agency world, offers tools that include SRDS and TGI Media for agencies to reach their key audiences (www.kantarmedia.com/us/our-solutions/media-planning-tools).

These programs, and others similar in function, save media buyers a lot of time, thereby increasing productivity and efficiency. More time can be spent analyzing information, evaluating various vehicles, and exercising creativity.

The most successful media buyers have developed key skills in the following areas:

- **Knowing the marketplace.** Media buyers have frequent contact with media representatives. As a result, they often gain insights about trends or opportunities. Some of the best media buys are the result of an alert buyer taking advantage of an opportunity or anticipating a problem.

- **Negotiating the buy.** Media vehicles have published rate cards, but everything is negotiable. Media buyers can often bargain for special rates on volume buys, uncover last-minute deals, negotiate preferred positions, or garner promotional support.

- **Monitoring performance.** The media buyer is responsible for ensuring that what was purchased was delivered. Did the advertising appear where and when it was scheduled? Was the size of the audience what was promised? If not, payments must be adjusted or *makegoods* must be negotiated. Whatever the outcome, the client expects to see a *post-buy report* on what audience was actually delivered. ∎

check yourself ✓

1. How is a media buyer different from a media planner?

2. What are the important skills for a media buyer?

ENDNOTES

1. Julie Liesse, "Inside Burnett's Vaunted Buying Machine," *Advertising Age*, July 25, 1994, p. S6.

2. Yumiko Ono, "Cordiant Puts Hamilton in Key U.S. Post," *Advertising Age*, July 18, 1997, p. B2.

3. Stephanie Thompson, "Universal McCann Gets $150 Million Nestlé Account," *AdAge*, April 12, 2002, www.adage.com; Richard Linnett and Jack Neff, "Mindshare Wins $600 Million Gillette Media Account," *AdAge*, September 26, 2002, www.adage.com.

4. "Top Ten," *Nielsen Insights*, www.nielsen.com/us/en/top-ten.

5. Mark Dolliver, "U.S. Time Spent with Media 2019," *eMarketer*, May 30, 2019, www.emarketer.com/content/us-time-spent-with-media-2019.

6. Jeanine Poggi, "Here's How Much It Costs to Advertise in TV's Biggest Shows," *AdAge*, October 2, 2018, https://adage.com/article/media/tv-pricing-chart/315120.

7. Wayne Friedman, "Discovery Pitches Ad Convergence," *Advertising Age*, March 2000, www.adage.com.

8. Christina Merrill, "Media Rising," *Adweek*, November 9, 1998, http://members.adweek.com/archive.

9. Larry D. Kelley, Donald W. Jugenheimer, and Kim Bartel Sheehan, *Advertising Media Workbook and Sourcebook* (Armonk, NY: M. E. Sharpe, 2012).

10. Larry D. Kelley, Donald W. Jugenheimer, and Kim Bartel Sheehan, *Advertising Media Workbook and Sourcebook* (Armonk, NY: M. E. Sharpe, 2012), pp. 131–33.

11. Ronald D. Geskey, *Media Planning and Buying in the 21st Century* (Auburn Hills, MI: 2020: Marketing Communications LLC, 2013).

12. Ronald D. Geskey, *Media Planning and Buying in the 21st Century* (Auburn Hills, MI: 2020: Marketing Communications LLC, 2013).

13. Kelley et al., *Advertising Media Workbook and Sourcebook*.

14. Joe Mandese, "Revisiting Ad Reach, Frequency," *Advertising Age*, November 27, 1995, p. 46.

15. Robyn Blakeman, *Integrated Marketing Communication* (Lanham, MD: Rowman & Littlefield, 2007).

16. Minda Smiley, "Celebrating Creativity at Media Plan of the Year," *Ad Age*, 2019, www.adweek.com/creativity/celebrating-creativity-at-media-plan-of-the-year.

17. Neil Kelliher, "Magazine Media Planning for 'Effectiveness': Getting the People Back into the Process," *Journal of Consumer Marketing*, Summer 1990, pp. 47–55.

18. Kenneth Longman, *Advertising* (New York: Harcourt Brace Jovanovich, 1971), pp. 211–12.

19. Henry Assael, "From Silos to Synergy: A Fifty-Year Review of Cross-Media Research Shows Synergy Has Yet to Achieve Its Full Potential," *Journal of Advertising Research* 51, no. 1 (2011), pp. 42–58.

20. Kevin Goldman, "Digital Warms Couch Potatoes with Only-on-Sunday TV Ads," *The Wall Street Journal*, November 22, 1994, p. B8.

21. Telmar website, www.telmar.com, accessed March 2020.

chapter fifteen

Ben Torres/Bloomberg/Getty Images

IMC: direct marketing, personal selling, **packaging, and sales promotion**

This chapter reinforces the importance of relationships in today's digital world and demonstrates how a variety of marketing tools can integrate with advertising to enhance an organization's stakeholder relationships. Direct marketing, personal selling, packaging, and sales promotion play different but overlapping roles in IMC. Each offers many opportunities along with limitations.

In early 2020, everything changed across the world as the COVID-19 virus shuttered economies around the globe and sickened and killed untold numbers. Governments urged billions of global citizens to stay at home, use only essential services, and practice social distancing.

For the people who do marketing communication for a living, as for everyone else, the economic and health tragedy created by COVID-19 was devastating. Marketers and agency staff stayed home to protect their health and their loved ones. Consumers stopped shopping. Business stopped purchasing and hiring. Universities, public schools, restaurants, sports, theaters, museums, public transportation—the very things that make modern life enjoyable—simply stopped.

But even as this nightmare unfolded, some companies sought ways to help. Some doubtless question whether the motives of these companies were "pure" and driven by altruism.[1] Others believe that when

companies stand up to help, it benefits everyone.

Whatever the motivation, firms stepped up in a time of need and

continued on p. 372

LEARNING OBJECTIVES

After studying this chapter, you will be able to:

LO15-1 Explain the importance of relationship marketing and IMC.

LO15-2 Discuss the benefits and challenges of direct marketing.

LO15-3 Explain the various types of direct marketing activities.

LO15-4 Describe the advantages and drawbacks of personal selling.

LO15-5 Identify the elements that must be considered in establishing a trade show program.

LO15-6 Explain the factors that must be considered in designing packaging.

LO15-7 Describe the roles that sales promotion can play in a marketing strategy.

continued from p. 371

employees and customers were grateful. Here are just some of the ways larger companies tried to help people coping with this once-in-a-lifetime event:

- Uber Eats provided 300,000 meals to first responders.

- Fashion company Christian Siriano shifted from manufacturing designer clothes to medical masks.[2]

- Mark Cuban, tech businessman and owner of the Dallas Mavericks, reimbursed employees for food purchased from local restaurants.

- Adobe, the software company that makes Photoshop and other popular programs, offered schools distance learning tools free of charge. LinkedIn made 16 of its courses, which dealt with staying productive and using virtual meeting tools, available for free.

- Aetna offered free prescription deliveries from CVS and sent care packages to those infected by the virus.

- Ally Bank deferred loan payments for up to four months and contributed $3 million to local groups.

- Cisco pledged nearly a quarter billion dollars toward the global response to the virus.

- Disney closed its parks but continued paying its employees. Yum Brands made the same commitment to its restaurant employees. Starbucks offered 20 free therapy sessions to its workers.

- U-Haul offered college students 30 days of free storage.

- Louis Vuitton shifted production from cosmetics to hand sanitizers, which were then given away free of charge. L'Oreal promised to do the same. A Portland, OR distillery, Shine, also began making sanitizer and giving it away.

- Intel committed $1 million to the Red Cross, and Hormel pledged the same amount to support the hungry.

- Amazon established multi-million dollar funds for its drivers and small business partners in Seattle.

- Facebook gave every employee a $1,000 bonus, then gave $100 million in grants and free ad space to small businesses.

- Mortgage companies Fannie Mae and Freddie Mac put foreclosures on hold for two months.

- General Motors cut back on car production and built needed ventilators.

- Numerous retailers offered "senior" shopping hours each week to help elderly customers get needed food and supplies in a safer shopping environment.[3]

Microsoft Corporation

Not every business that helped was a global corporation. Local businesses, many among the hardest hit by the crisis, helped where they could:

- Jax Taylor, owner of a small Gulfport restaurant, started a free food pantry where people could donate and take what they needed. She also gave free meals to anyone who asked.[4]

- In Tulsa, OK, a local coffee shop, the Coffee Bunker, created care packages to bolster supplies at a local food bank.[5]

- Table and Main, a small restaurant in Roswell, GA, offered free hot meals between 12 p.m. and 4 p.m., no questions asked.[6]

Some businesses found their own rewards from the loyalty earned by building relationships in their communities. Ordinary people tried to help where they could:

- In Johnstown, PA, local resident Jennifer Reese created a "Johnstown Pay It Forward" Facebook page where people could order food from local restaurants and then have the food delivered to medical and rescue pros.

- In Charleston, SC, professors at the College of Charleston School of Business created a "Profs on Call" to provide business advice to local companies.

- People from around the United States took advantage of a website created by Gannett called "SupportLocal.USAToday.com" that allowed them to buy gift cards from small companies affected by closures.

- Alyssa Corpstein, a resident of Calera, AL, bought gift cards from a local coffee shop and mailed them to neighbors.

The arrival of a pandemic in 2020 challenged the global community in ways that seemed unimaginable at the end of 2019. As with many other times when people and businesses struggled, including the recessions of 2007 and 2001, in 2020 many marketing activities were cut back or eliminated altogether. But some companies shifted marketing dollars to actions that were intended to help in challenging times. That's committing to relationships. And making the world a bit better at a time when everyone needed it. ■

LO15-1 Explain the importance of relationship marketing and IMC.

THE IMPORTANCE OF RELATIONSHIP MARKETING AND IMC

In Chapter 7, and in the introduction to this chapter, we suggested that the key to building brand equity is developing interdependent, mutually satisfying relationships with customers and other stakeholders. Further, to engage in these relationships, companies need to integrate their marketing communications activities with their other company functions so that all messages about the company are consistent.

However, this is easier said than done because everything a company does (and doesn't do) sends a message. Seamless, consistent communication—from every corner of the company—is how a firm earns a good reputation. And that is the principal objective of IMC—integrated marketing communications—the process of building and reinforcing relationships by developing and coordinating a strategic communications program through a variety of media or other contacts.

One firm that practices IMC exceptionally well is GEICO, a direct-to-consumer provider of insurance products. To attract prospects and initiate the relationship-building process, GEICO integrates its advertising efforts with a host of other marketing communications tools—direct marketing, sales promotion, personal selling, and public relations activities. Although the forms and styles of these messages may vary, all reinforce a consistent proposal—that GEICO can save you money on insurance.

A simple adage: Advertising can create an image, but a reputation is earned. For GEICO, this means delivering on its low-rate promise.

While the integration of marketing with other company functions is beyond our scope, it is important for advertising people to understand how to integrate the various tools of marketing communications. As they plan a campaign, advertising practitioners need a basic understanding of what other communications tools are available to them and how they can best be used in the overall marketing communications mix. In this chapter, we discuss the interactive communication tools of direct marketing and personal selling. We'll also look at packaging and sales promotion, sometimes referred to as "value-added" tools. In the next chapter, we address the "credibility" tools companies use to create and enhance their reputations. These include public relations activities, sponsorships, and corporate advertising.

check yourself ✓

1. Make a list of the "tools" of marketing communications.

2. Why can't advertising create a reputation?

direct marketing An interactive form of strategic communication that is transmitted via a medium or media directly to the target market and is used to create or maintain a relationship with those who respond to the message.

database marketing Tracking and analyzing the purchasing patterns of specific customers in a computer database and then targeting advertising to their needs.

database The corporate memory of all important customer information: name and address, telephone number, NAIC code (if a business firm), source of inquiry, cost of inquiry, history of purchases, and so on.

customers. It helps them to know who their customers and prospects are, what and when they buy, and how to contact them. That, of course, leads to the possibility of the *ongoing mutually beneficial relationships*. So today, database marketing is a major component of many IMC programs.

Note that the definition of direct marketing refers to the use of *one or more media*. Part of the confusion with the direct marketing name is its similarity to direct mail. But direct mail is just one of the many media that direct marketers use. In the GEICO story, for instance, we saw how the company used a mass medium—television—to

LO15-2 Discuss the benefits and challenges of direct marketing.

UNDERSTANDING DIRECT MARKETING

Definitions of **direct marketing** emphasize that it has the following characteristics: A form of strategic communication that is a) impersonal (i.e., is transmitted via a medium or media), b) sent directly to the consumers or organizations defined by the target market, c) designed to be interactive by eliciting a measurable response or set of responses from the receiver, and d) used to create or maintain a relationship with receivers who respond to the message. Along with other kinds of advertising, direct marketing allows advertisers to inform potential customers, create brand awareness, or spur immediate purchase behavior. In addition, direct marketing enjoys certain advantages over mass advertising, including data, accountability, efficiency, and higher return on investment.

There are several key characteristics of direct marketing within this definition. First and foremost, direct marketing is *interactive*, meaning buyers and sellers can exchange information with each other directly. GEICO can direct its message to prospective customers, and those prospects can interact with GEICO by requesting rate quotes. Interactivity is so important that some have urged that the term *direct marketing* be dropped completely and replaced with *interactive marketing*.[7] Of course, this interaction can take place *at any location*. Customers may respond by telephone, via an Echo device, over the Internet, at a retail store, or on social media. GEICO processes the vast majority of its quote requests by phone and online.

Our definition of direct marketing also refers to a group of identifiable prospects, customers, or donors most likely to be interested in their product or service. Ensuring a list of such important stakeholders is available and current is the goal of **database marketing**. Database marketers build and maintain a pool of data on current and prospective customers (and other stakeholders) and communicate with them using a variety of media (from personal contact to direct mail to mass media). Database marketing is a widely adopted marketing method because it has proven to be a cost-efficient way to increase sales. A good **database** enables marketers to target, segment, and grade

When you can't talk about abuse, talk to us.
Many young people who are being abused never talk about it. What do you say? Who to? And what exactly is abuse? There are several places you can turn. For free, confidential help and advice 24 hours a day call ChildLine on 0800 1111, or call the NSPCC's Child Protection Helpline on 0808 800 5000. You can find further contacts, expert advice and support on a dedicated website. Just visit www.worriedneed2talk.org.uk

Talking helps it stop. FULL STOP. ● NSPCC

Direct marketing is an interactive system in which buyers and sellers participate in a dialogue. Its intent is to stimulate a response in the form of a request for information, an actual purchase, or a visit. This poster by Britain's National Society for the Prevention of Cruelty to Children (NSPCC) prompted calls from abused teenagers to jump 124 percent in just six weeks. The number of website visitors also increased, from 4,000 to more than 32,000.

National Society for the Prevention of Cruelty to Children

The famous gecko shown in this direct response ad from GEICO uses a softer, less edgy style to describe the benefits of saving on insurance. These types of direct-response ads allow GEICO to save marketing dollars and also to help save money on a personal sales force.

GEICO

Because millions of consumers are comfortable shopping on the web, direct-response messages need to provide only a compelling benefit and a memorable web address. Peloton (www.onepeloton.com) is successful at both of these objectives.

Peloton

direct-response advertising An advertising message that asks the reader, listener, or viewer to provide feedback straight to the sender. It can take the form of direct mail, or it can use a wide range of other media, from matchbook covers or magazines, to radio, TV, Internet links, or billboards.

elicit responses from people who might be interested in saving on insurance. GEICO uses other media as well, including radio and direct mail, to reach its target audience. In fact, experienced direct marketers have known for years that using more than one medium can be far more productive than using a single medium.[8] As noted, direct marketing works effectively "with mass advertising" to *inform, create awareness, and spur immediate purchase behavior.*

The final point is that direct marketing can be distinguished from mass advertising in the areas of measurability, accountability, efficiency, and return on investment. The kind of advertising direct marketers use is called **direct-response advertising**. This is because direct marketing efforts are always aimed at stimulating some action or response on the part of the customer or prospect. It may be in the form of a request for information, a store visit, or an actual purchase. Because these responses can be *measured*, direct marketing is *accountable*. And that, more than any other reason, accounts for the tremendous growth of direct marketing in recent years. Managers like it because they can measure its *efficiency* and *return on investment*—what they got for their money.

THE ROLE OF DIRECT MARKETING IN IMC

Today, sophisticated companies use the skills developed by direct marketers to establish, nourish, and maintain relationships, not just with customers, but with all stakeholders.

As discussed, GEICO uses TV advertising as one of its linkage media—media that help prospects and customers link up with a company—to inform prospects how to inquire about its products. Next, it uses these responses to build its database of names, addresses, and e-mail addresses. Then it uses data to identify opportunities to communicate with prospects, open a dialogue, and establish a relationship. It may send a mail piece with ordering information or direct people to its social media sites to enable prospects to connect with GEICO directly.

" THE COMPANY THAT UNDERSTANDS ITS CUSTOMERS' NEEDS AND WANTS ... WILL CREATE A SUSTAINABLE COMPETITIVE ADVANTAGE. "

The Evolution of Direct Marketing

Direct marketing is the oldest marketing method, and today it is growing incredibly fast, propelled by the major social and technological changes of recent decades. Just under 60 percent of American women are in the labor force.[9] So while families have more income, they have less time to spend shopping, thus making the convenience of telephones and the Internet an important factor in direct marketing.

Likewise, widespread use of credit cards, smartphone payment systems, and digital products such as PayPal and Venmo have revolutionized the way consumers buy goods and services. Electronic, cashless transactions make products easier and faster to purchase.

Companies spent an estimated $116 billion on direct marketing in the United States in 2020, down from $160 billion in 2016. Much of this decline is due to the growth of the Internet, which is in many ways a direct marketing channel. Looking ahead, it seems reasonable to expect that the amount of money spent on non-digital direct marketing will continue to decline going forward. Although large amounts of money are still being spent on telemarketing and direct mail, social and digital media can provide many of the same benefits, plus some novel ones. For example, digital beats traditional direct response on criteria that include the speed of creating and launching a campaign, cost, and more precise targeting.[10]

Others offer a different perspective on traditional direct marketing's future. This argument suggests that traditional direct marketing efforts will continue to prosper not in spite of, but because of, the shift of dollars to digital. With less competition, the argument goes, traditional direct marketers will see upticks in customer responses.[11]

Direct marketing remains popular in other parts of the world. Today, Germany is by far the largest national market in Europe, spending more than $25 billion on such efforts annually. Britain comes in second at more than $17 billion, followed closely by France. Interestingly, outside the United States, Japan is by far the number one market for direct marketing, with estimated annual spending close to $70 billion.[12]

Certain challenges in foreign markets have limited the growth of global direct marketing campaigns. Any advertisers seeking to use direct marketing across many countries faces a wide variety of legal and regulatory environments. Likewise, payment and postal systems in different countries vary considerably, as do conventions for addressing mail. And finally, cultural nuances and language present a challenge to marketers seeking standardization across all messages.

The Impact of Data on Direct Marketing

Computer technology enables marketers to compile and analyze important customer information in unprecedented ways. Direct mail advertisers can target every home in a community, specific homes in a community, or even just new arrivals to a community. The use of big data allows marketers to connect existing lists of customers and prospects with secondary data available from a variety of vendors.

Casper used mailings such as this to rapidly grow their direct-response business. Behind the colorful mailing pieces was sophisticated 21st Century data analysis. This suggests that companies can benefit by integrating old and new media, rather than choosing just one or the other.

Casper Sleep

Comstock/Stockbyte/Getty Images

Casper, an online mattress seller, combined digital and traditional direct response to achieve over a billion-dollar net worth. The traditional approach relied on mailings of brightly colored envelopes and messages printed on high-quality stock. Behind the bright creative were large amounts of data, both on prospects who would likely respond to a direct-mail campaign, and on the customer sales-funnel journey once they responded. In the latter case, conversions increased by 20 percent after Casper implemented findings from data analysis of the consumer experience.[13]

Pitney Bowes, for instance, was the dominant company in the postal meter business. However, its growth rate and profitability were flattening. So the company used its database to identify its best customers, their value to the organization, and their needs and buying behavior. From this, Pitney Bowes created a **customer lifetime value (CLTV)** model based on the customer's historical and potential worth. Computing and ranking the lifetime value of all of its 1.2 million customers showed that more than two-thirds of the customer base value resided in fewer than 10 percent of the customers. The company also found it had a major retention problem within its low-volume, low-cost

Most business is conducted with repeat customers. This places a premium on customer retention. Retention can be achieved by offering special benefits to loyal customers, effectively rewarding and thanking them for business, and providing an incentive for a continued relationship in the future. Retail food giant Kroger successfully retains its customers with their community rewards program. The more a customer spends, the more Kroger gives back to a customer's preferred nonprofit organization.

The Kroger Co.

accounts. Cancellation rates were running as high as 40 percent per year in some segments. This analysis led Pitney Bowes to develop a distinct direct marketing strategy for both its best and its worst customers. It began a sophisticated *loyalty program* for its best customers and a *retention program* for its problem accounts. By the end of the first year, the program had reduced attrition by 20 percent, and the reduction in cost of sales alone paid back the entire direct marketing investment.[14] In another situation, a company might determine from its CLTV analysis that its best course of action is simply to drop the most unprofitable customers.

One way companies can ensure a continuous stream of useful data is through the creation of **loyalty (continuity) programs**, which reward customers for frequent and continuous patronage. The frequent flyer club, introduced by American Airlines in 1981, is the model for today's continuity programs. Consumer purchases are tabulated on a company's database and discounts, free products, or services are awarded when specific levels are reached. The database can also provide the company with a demographic profile and purchase history for each customer.

Useful data are the key to direct marketing success, especially in an IMC program. They enable marketers to target, segment, and grade customers. It is the corporate memory of all important customer information: name and address, telephone number, e-mail address, source of inquiry, history of purchases, and so on. It should record every transaction across all points of contact with both channel members and customers. The company that understands its customers' needs and wants better than any of its competitors will create a sustainable competitive advantage.

Data also let the company measure the efficiency of its direct-response advertising efforts to determine, for instance, which radio or TV commercials, or which mailing lists, perform the best.

The Importance of Direct Marketing to IMC

Perhaps the greatest reason for direct marketing's current growth is that marketers and agencies realize they can't do the job with just one medium anymore. As the mass audience fragmented and companies began to integrate their marketing communications, customer databases became key to retaining and growing customers.

Direct marketing is the best way to build a strong database. The database enables the marketer to build a relationship by learning about customers in-depth: their nuances, what and where they buy, what they're interested in, and what they need. With a database, companies can choose the prospects they can serve most effectively and profitably—the purpose of all marketing. "You don't want a relationship with every customer," says Philip Kotler. "In fact, there are some bad customers out there."[15] Retailer Best Buy uses direct mail to send sales promotions materials, but only to its best customers.[16]

People like to see themselves as unique, not part of some mass market. Through direct marketing, especially addressable electronic media, companies can send discrete messages to individual customers and prospects. With different types of sales promotion (discussed in the last part of this chapter), a company can encourage individuals, not masses, to respond and can develop a relationship with each person. By responding, the prospect self-selects, in effect giving the marketer permission to begin a relationship.[17] The direct marketing database, then, becomes the company's primary tool to initiate, build, cultivate, and measure the effectiveness of its loyalty efforts.[18]

By providing a tangible response, direct marketing offers accountability. Marketers can count the responses and determine the cost per response. They can also judge the effectiveness of the medium they're using and test different creative executions.

Direct marketing offers convenience to time-sensitive consumers, and it offers precision and flexibility to cost-sensitive marketers. For example, to reach small B2B markets, there is no more cost-effective method than the database-driven, direct-response media.

Finally, unlike the public mass media, direct-response media can be more private. A company can conduct a sales letter campaign without the competition ever knowing about it.

Drawbacks to Direct Marketing

At the same time, direct marketing still faces some challenges. In the past, direct marketers were sales oriented, not relationship oriented. This gave direct marketing a bad reputation in the minds of many consumers. Some people also enjoy the experience of visiting retail stores and shopping. They like to see and feel the goods personally, and they are hesitant to buy goods sight unseen. This is why the objective of many direct marketing campaigns is now to help drive traffic to retail locations.

Direct marketing efforts often have to stand on their own without the content support of the media that advertising enjoys. They don't always get the prestigious affiliation offered by some media. This makes it more difficult (and costly) to build an image for the product, something mass media advertising is particularly good at.

Direct marketing also suffers from clutter. People are deluged with mail from commercial sponsors and drum-beating politicians. Cable channels are filled with infomercials for food processors. Telemarketing pitches intrude on consumers at home and at work. Internet ads and e-mails permeate our daily lives.

Many consumers are also concerned with privacy. They don't like having their names sold by list vendors. At one national forum of direct marketers, attendees were told they must self-regulate, give consumers more control, and treat privacy like a customer service issue—or risk legislation restricting access to the information they desperately need.[19] Wise marketers have heeded these warnings and developed methods for responsible direct marketing.

Comstock Images/Alamy Stock Photo

check yourself ✓

1. What are the key characteristics that differentiate direct marketing from most other forms of marketing tools?

2. What role do databases play in direct marketing?

LO15-3 Explain the various types of direct marketing activities.

TYPES OF DIRECT MARKETING ACTIVITIES

All direct marketers face two basic strategy decisions: the extent to which they will use *direct sales* and the extent to which they will use *direct-response advertising*. They can use either or both.

Direct Sales

In a **direct sales**, marketers' representatives sell to customers directly, either at home or at work, rather than through a retail establishment or some other intermediary. Direct sales feature *personal* (face-to-face) *direct selling* or *telemarketing*.

Personal Direct Selling

Professors Robert Peterson and Thomas Wotruba define **direct selling** as face-to-face selling away from a fixed retail location. In this sense, direct selling usually refers to a method of marketing consumer goods—everything from encyclopedias and insurance to cosmetics and nutritional products.[20] Companies such as Avon, Amway, Herbalife, Mary Kay Cosmetics, World Book, and Tupperware achieved very high levels of success in direct sales. In personal direct selling, the representative introduces the product to the customer, convinces the customer of the product's value, and, if successful, completes the sale. There are two main forms of personal selling: person-to-person and group sales. In some *network marketing* (or multilevel marketing—MLM) organizations such as Amway, Nikken, and Shaklee, the direct salespeople are both distributors (sellers) and end users. They often do very little actual retailing of the products. Their primary effort is usually to recruit new distributors who will buy the products at wholesale and consume them personally. We will discuss personal selling more completely in the next section of this chapter.

Telemarketing

As a method of direct sales, telemarketing has been used for decades, but the term is relatively new. **Telemarketing** includes selling and prospecting by telephone, answering phone inquiries, and providing sales-related services to callers. The information collected is also used to update the company's customer database. Telemarketing is the major source of income for some companies and organizations, such as nonprofit and charitable causes, political candidates, and home-study courses. In 2020, marketers were expected to spend $61 billion on telemarketing to consumers and businesses, making it the one of the largest non-digital spending categories.[21]

The reasons for this are economics and consumers' acceptance of teleculture. First, telemarketing costs a lot less money than personal selling. In the insurance business, for example, the expense ratio for car and home insurance is currently running at 27 percent for all insurers. The most efficient insurers, like GEICO, employ high-tech database marketing techniques from phone centers and operate at around a 20 percent expense ratio.[22] That difference goes straight to the bottom line.

Second, phone penetration, especially mobile phone penetration, is high, both in the United States and globally. In the United States, almost four out of five adults have a smartphone, and similar numbers characterize most countries in Europe. In Asia, including countries such as China and Japan, a majority of people own a smartphone.[23]

Telemarketing is the next best thing to a face-to-face, personal sales call. In the business-to-business arena, for example, good telemarketers can develop strong, lasting relationships with customers they have never met but with whom they speak every week. Stand Out Designs in San Diego employs highly skilled telemarketers who call on zoos, museums, and boutique retailers all across the country to get them to order and stock the company's unique line of silk-screened T-shirts. The telemarketers don't just take orders; they counsel the dealers with display and promotion suggestions, offer advertising tips, and arrange for special imprints on the shirts when appropriate.

Each year telemarketing generates an estimated $538 billion in sales in the United States. It is cited as the direct marketing medium of choice, providing elements of direct personal sales yet at a substantially lower cost. Telemarketing also integrates easily into database management campaigns for gathering new data and for utilizing the collected data.
Noel Hendrickson/Digital Vision/Getty Images

> ❝ **Good telemarketers can develop strong, lasting relationships with customers they have never met.** ❞

direct-response advertising An advertising message that asks the reader, listener, or viewer to provide feedback straight to the sender. It can take the form of direct mail, or it can use a wide range of other media, from matchbook covers or magazines, to radio, TV, Internet links, or billboards.

catalogs Reference books mailed to prospective customers that list, describe, and often picture the products sold by a manufacturer, wholesaler, jobber, or retailer.

Of course, not everybody likes receiving uninvited telephone solicitations at inconvenient times of the day. The National Do Not Call Registry, created by Congress and launched by the Federal Trade Commission in 2003, is intended to give U.S. consumers an opportunity to limit the telemarketing calls they receive. As one might expect, there are many exceptions and loopholes. The registry applies to only residential lines, not business lines, and you may still receive calls from political and non-profit organizations, research firms, bill collectors, and companies with which you have recently conducted business.

Nevertheless, telemarketing continues to be a very effective marketing tool. When combined with other direct-response media, telemarketing becomes even more effective. For example, experience shows that when telemarketing is combined with direct mail, there is usually at least a 10 percent increase in responses—often a lot more.

Direct-Response Advertising

Advertising that asks the reader, viewer, or listener to provide a response (ideally in the form of a purchase) straight to the sender is called **direct-response advertising**. Any medium can be used for direct response, but the most common are direct mail, catalogs, magazines, television, and digital interactive media (e-mails and search engines). In all cases, a prospective customer is urged to respond immediately and directly to the advertiser, through the use of a direct-response mechanism provided in the advertisement. The mechanism might be a coupon or reply card, a toll-free telephone number, an e-mail address, or an Internet link.

Direct Mail

Next to personal selling and telemarketing, direct mail is the most effective method for closing a sale or generating inquiries. It's very useful to direct marketers seeking an immediate response.

Only direct mail that is intended to elicit a direct response is considered direct-response advertising. Some direct mail is used like other traditional advertising media, simply to communicate information about products and services. The trend in direct mail is away from printed materials and toward digital media, such as e-mail and mobile marketing. Even though direct mail elicits far higher response rates than digital media, the high cost of printing and mailing results in a better return on investment for electronic advertising.[24]

Catalog Sales

The largest direct marketers are catalog companies, and catalogs are still the most popular medium for multi-channel marketers. **Catalogs** are expensive to produce and mail, but consumers like to hold them in their hands. They like to circle the products they like and tear out the pages. Print catalogs have advantages over other marketing tools in creating product awareness, acquiring customers, and building brand loyalty. Consumers commonly then turn to their computers or telephones to order, but they start by shopping the catalogs. We discussed the use of direct mail and catalogs in greater detail in Chapter 13.

Direct-Response Print Advertising

Newspaper ads and inserts featuring coupons or listing toll-free phone numbers can be very effective at stimulating customer responses. Today, the same is true with magazines. Moreover, in magazines, advertisers can devote most of the space to image-building, thus maximizing the medium's power. We discussed the use of print media in Chapter 10.

Catalog sales make up a large portion of non-digital direct marketing. Catalogs, such as this one from Pampered Chef (you can see the whole catalog here: https://www.pamperedchef.com/interactive-catalog-page) display a company's products and enable customers to order at their convenience via mail, phone, fax, or web. Notice how the beauty of the kitchenware is highlighted by the expert photography and quality printing.
Pampered Chef, Ltd.

Television is a powerful instrument for direct marketers like Home Shopping Network (www.hsn.com) because of its mass coverage and the ability to display and demonstrate the product with sound and full color right before the customers' eyes. Bobbi Ray Carter, shown here, has been one of HSN's most popular hosts for more than 30 years.

Chris O'Meara/AP Images

Local radio personalities are often heard pitching a wide variety of products. Likewise, talk jocks Howard Stern and Rush Limbaugh made Snapple an overnight success by drinking the product and touting its good taste on the air. Still, until fairly recently, radio has rarely been the medium of choice for direct-response advertising. In 2011, GEICO spent nearly 20 percent of its advertising budget on radio, referring interested listeners to the GEICO website. Radio industry executives now expect to see a dramatic increase in the number of direct-response ads on radio. We discussed radio, TV, and infomercials in Chapter 11.

Direct-Response Digital Interactive Media   Direct-response advertising represents the vast majority of online advertising efforts. These are discussed more thoroughly in Chapter 12. Using e-mail to distribute marketing messages remains popular because of its low cost and effectiveness. Online direct-response advertising includes display ads and search ads. Social media sites are increasingly featuring ads that allow an immediate response. Mobile is another popular direct-response medium. Mobile includes SMS (short message service, or text ads), MMS (multimedia message service, or text plus images, audio, or video), mobile applications (better known as apps), QR (quick response) bar codes, and mobile banner ads. Although still in the development stage, interactive TV may allow viewers to respond to questions during a commercial, or even order products. In the next section of this chapter we take a look at the ultimate interactive communication tool, personal selling.

Direct-Response Broadcast Advertising   Direct marketers' can also use TV and radio, as the GEICO example that opened the chapter shows. Total Gym, whose products are normally sold through health care and physical fitness professionals, worked with American Telecast to develop a 30-minute infomercial featuring TV star Chuck Norris and Christie Brinkley. The campaign exceeded their wildest expectations, producing more than $100 million in sales the first year and continuing to generate similar returns for the next four years.[25]

check yourself ✓

1. What is the key difference between direct sales and direct-response advertising?

2. Which of those strategies is more effective for closing a sale or generating inquiries and why do you think that's the case?

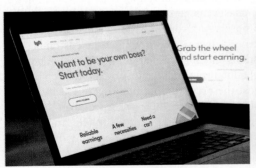

The Internet's impact has been extraordinary. Consumers are free to reserve a ride, book flights, find hotels, and get home delivery of groceries, often eliminating the need for person-to-person communication. Shown here are several companies that offer just those services: Lyft (lyft.com), Kayak (www.kayak.com), and Publix (delivery.publix.com).

(Left and Middle) Casimiro PT/Shutterstock; (Right) IgorGolovniov/Shutterstock

[The objective of personal selling should be to build a relationship.]

LO15-4 Describe the advantages and drawbacks of personal selling.

PERSONAL SELLING: THE HUMAN MEDIUM

Personal selling is the best marketing communications tool for relationship building because the sales rep and the customer are face to face. It's the ultimate one-to-one medium. It's also the most expensive medium. For most companies, personal selling expenditures far exceed expenditures for advertising. And in many companies, the primary role of advertising is to lend support to the sales force either directly by producing leads or indirectly by creating a positive atmosphere for the sales call. That is certainly true for all of the GEICO ads that direct audiences to the company's toll-free number.

Personal selling can be defined in a number of ways, depending on the orientation of the company using it. For our purposes we define **personal selling** as the *interpersonal communication* process by which a seller ascertains and then satisfies the needs of a buyer, to the mutual, long-term benefit of both parties.[26]

Thus, the task of personal selling is a lot more than just making a sale. The objective of personal selling should be to build a relationship, a partnership, that will provide long-term benefits to both buyer and seller (a win–win situation). The salesperson discovers the buyer's needs by helping the customer identify problems, offers information about potential solutions, assists the buyer in making decisions, and provides after-sale service to ensure long-term satisfaction. Influence and persuasion are only one part of selling. The major part is problem solving.

Types of Personal Selling

Everyone sells, at one time or another. Children sell lemonade, magazine subscriptions, and Girl Scout cookies. Students sell prom tickets, yearbook ads, and term papers. Doctors sell diets to unwilling patients. Lawyers sell pleas to skeptical juries. And cops sell traffic safety to nervous motorists.

The fact is that everything has to be sold, by someone to somebody. A retail clerk may sell you a cell phone. Behind that clerk is a virtual army of other salespeople who sold raw materials to the manufacturer, capital equipment for use in the manufacturing process, business services such as human resources and accounting, plant and office furniture, vehicles, advertising services, media space and time, and insurance. Then the manufacturer's salespeople sold the cell phone to a wholesaler who, of course, had to buy transportation services and warehousing from other salespeople. And then the wholesaler's sales reps sold the phone to the retail outlet where you bought it.

As this scenario shows, people in sales work for a wide variety of organizations and call on an equally wide variety of customers. They may call on other businesses to sell products or services used in the manufacture of other products. They may call on resellers—people who buy the product, add value, and resell it. Or they may sell to consumers, either in a retail store or, as we discussed earlier, in a direct selling situation away from a fixed retail location.

Because advertising is basically designed to support and reinforce a company's sales efforts, advertising people (whether in the company or at an agency) have to understand the selling environment their companies or clients deal in. Many companies have their advertising people make calls with the sales force for this very reason. The advertising person can experience firsthand what questions prospects ask, how customers view the company (and its competitors), how people use the company's product, and what information (in either an ad or a piece of sales material) might help the salesperson communicate better with the prospect.

Advantages of Personal Selling

The greatest strength of personal selling is its personal nature. Nothing is as persuasive as personal communication. A skilled salesperson can observe a prospect's body language and read between the lines to detect what's troubling the customer. The rep can ask questions and answer queries as they arise. The face-to-face situation facilitates instant feedback. And the rep has the flexibility to adjust the presentation, tailoring it specifically to the needs and interests of the particular prospect. Not only that, the salesperson can demonstrate the product live. And the rep can negotiate, finding those terms that best suit the buyer's needs.

Time is on the rep's side, too. The sale doesn't have to be made today. The relationship has to be established, though, and a human being is better at doing that than any nonpersonal medium.

This pharmaceutical sales representative is engaging in missionary selling when she presents the benefits of her products to a doctor. The representative understands that the doctor will not place an order, but she is attempting to get the doctor to prescribe the pharmaceutical for her patients so the sales representative's company will get an order from the patient's drugstore.

Ralf Schultheiss/Corbis/Getty Images

One of the major jobs of personal selling is to gain distribution for new products—a task no other communications tool can do as well. In fact, in many trade and industrial situations, personal contact may be vital to closing the sale. This is also true for certain high-ticket or technical consumer products such as computers, health care, and estate planning. In these cases, personal selling is well worth its high cost—because it gets the job done.

Drawbacks of Personal Selling

Personal selling is very labor-intensive. That's why it's the most costly way to communicate with prospects. This is its single biggest weakness. The average business-to-business sales call today costs nearly $250.[27] Not only that, it's very time-consuming. Because it is a one-on-one medium, there are few economies of scale.

This is why one important role of advertising is to reduce the cost of sales by communicating as much relevant information as possible about the company and its products to prospects and customers before the salesperson even calls. That information may be functional (specifically about the product) or symbolic (building image and credibility for the company).

Another drawback is the poor reputation of personal selling with many people. Decades of "suede shoe" sellers employing high-pressure tactics have dishonored the profession. Thus the common jibe: "Would you buy a used car from that person?" Salespeople are frequently given fancier titles such as marketing associate, marketing representative, or account manager in an attempt to reduce guilt or the rejection associated with personal selling.[28]

Finally, imagine spending millions of dollars on a nationwide advertising campaign to communicate your expertise and good customer service and then sending an unprofessional sales force

out that is improperly groomed or, worse, ignorant of product features and benefits and lacking empathy for customer needs. Unfortunately, it happens all the time. The salesperson has incredible power to either make or break a delicate relationship. As a result, sophisticated firms go to great lengths to screen sales applicants to find the right personality attributes and then invest heavily in training. Of course, this goes both ways. A tasteless advertising campaign can hurt a company's national reputation more than one bad salesperson. As always, it's the responsibility of marketing management to ensure consistency among what the advertising presents, what the sales force promises, and what the company actually delivers.

The Role of Personal Selling in IMC

Salespeople are the company's communicators. In fact, to the customer who doesn't know anybody else at the company, the salesperson doesn't just represent the firm. He or she *is* the firm. The customer's impression of the salesperson, therefore, will frequently govern his or her perception of the company. Again, this makes the sales rep a very important person.

In an integrated marketing communications program, personal selling can play a very important role. Salespeople provide four distinct communications functions: information gathering, information providing, order fulfillment, and relationship building. We'll discuss each of these briefly.

Gathering Information Sales reps often serve as the eyes and ears of the company. Because they are out in the field talking to customers or attending trade shows, they have access to information and they can see trends. For example, salespeople provide information on who's new in the business, how

Personal selling is especially important in the high-end cosmetics industry. Two factors account for this. First, consumers expect and enjoy the assistance of a well-trained cosmetics salesperson. Second, the profit margins for cosmetics are high enough to support an expensive sales staff. But even here advertising still has an important role to play by providing consumers with information about cosmetics and creating strong brand images.

David Paul Morris/Getty Images

GOOD INTERNAL COMMUNICATION IS A KEY TO GOOD EXTERNAL RELATIONSHIPS. "

customers are reacting to new products or styles, what the competition is doing, and where new sales opportunities might exist. Generally, information gathering by the sales force relates to three areas: prospecting; determining customer wants, needs, and abilities; and monitoring the competition.

Providing Information
Salespeople not only gather information; they deliver it. The stereotype (both negative and positive) of a good salesperson is someone who is a good talker, articulate and persuasive. In truth, a superior salesperson is a good listener first and a good talker second. Salespeople impart information both upstream and downstream within their organization. They deliver information to customers about the company and its products, they recommend solutions to problems, and they use information to communicate value and to build relationships and trust.

Personal selling incorporates all three legs of the IMC integration triangle we learned about in Chapter 7—say → do → confirm—because what the sales rep says and does will either confirm or contradict the company's other messages. The rep's skill, therefore, will definitely color the relationship between the company and the customer. It's critically important that the salesperson's performance be consistent with the firm's positioning and reinforce its other marketing communications.

Fulfilling Orders
There comes a time in every relationship when someone has to make a commitment. Asking for that commitment can be very difficult if the preceding steps have not been handled well. The inevitable tasks of personal selling are to motivate the customer to action, close the sale, and then make sure the goods and services are delivered correctly.

An important part of personal selling is following up after the sale, making sure the goods or services are delivered in a timely fashion, and seeing to it that the customer is completely satisfied. This is a combination of the "do" and "confirm" steps, and it's critical to continued relationship building.

This is also where cross-functional management and open communication come back into play. If there is any kind of manufacturing glitch or delay in shipping, the salesperson needs to notify the customer immediately. But to do that, the salesperson must be informed. Similarly, goods need to be protected and shipped with care. Salespeople hate to receive calls from new customers saying their first shipment arrived with damaged goods. All employees, including those in the warehouse, need to understand the impact of their actions.

Likewise, if the company is advertising a certain model of a product and the salesperson closes the sale on the product, that

Nordstrom strives to provide exceptional service to its customers. An engaging and helpful website is part of that effort. So is the company's lenient returns policy and justifiably famous focus on consumer satisfaction.

Nordstrom

model had better be in stock. Again, good internal communication is a key to good external relationships.

Building Relationships
A company's sales staff should be the ultimate relationship marketers. People naturally want to buy from the salesperson they like and trust. Salespeople build relationships by paying attention to three simple things: keeping commitments, servicing their accounts, and solving problems. Interestingly, those are also probably the three basic requirements for any company's success.

Here again, advertising people can help. When a company advertises, it is making a commitment to its customers and prospects. It is very difficult for a salesperson to keep those commitments if the advertising has overpromised. So puffery should be avoided wherever possible because, by its very nature, it tends to overpromise.

Likewise, it's difficult for salespeople to adequately service their accounts if every time people call customer service they get a busy signal or they never get replies to their e-mails. This happened to the giant telephone utility U.S. West when it downsized and reengineered the company. It continued running ads touting its great service, but nobody could get through to them. Not smart. Advertising people have to know what's going on in the company, and sometimes they need to recommend that advertising be stopped.

Developing a Plans Book [15–A]

A plans book, quite simply, is the representation of all the hard work you have put in to develop the ideas for your project. For some of you this is an actual deliverable for the project; for the rest of you, it is good practice and good process management to develop a plans book to ensure that all of your thinking exists in one place.

Don't let the word *book* fool you—what we are talking about here is a binder or a set of binders that houses information relevant to your client's problem. Whether it is competitive news and information, industry news, research on target audiences, and/or SWOT analysis, this binder should comprise all of that organized information. The plans book is the foundation you will use to build the final presentation (we talk about the final presentation in Chapter 16), a concise explanation of how you will utilize the information in the plans book to put your campaign ideas into action.

Here is the information that should be represented in your plans book:

- Objectives
- Challenges
- SWOT analysis
- Target audience analysis
- Creative strategy
- Creative brief
- Creative concepts
- Media strategy and plan
- Evaluation or success metrics

Objectives

This is a statement or a set of statements that describes what you hope to achieve from advertising for your client's product. Some common goals are lifting awareness within a new audience, stealing share from competitors, or changing perceptions of consumers. It is better to stay focused and not try to do too much.

Challenges

Think about what you are trying to achieve and what barriers exist that make your work that much harder. If you are trying to lift sales for your client's products, one challenge may be that there is little to no awareness.

SWOT or Situation Analysis

Understanding the strengths, weaknesses, opportunities, and threats for your client's product(s) helps you focus on the appropriate strategy to market the brand. Along with target analysis, the SWOT analysis should lead right into your strategy for marketing the product/brand.

Target Audience Analysis

Hopefully you have done a combination of primary research (interviews) and secondary research (syndicated or already done by a third party) to help understand what motivates your consumers to take action. Once you understand this, advertising becomes much easier; this section should highlight the research done and the insights from that work.

Creative Strategy

Your creative strategy is an overarching guide to how you will approach reaching your target with your client's message. All of your tactics should easily fall out of your strategy statement.

Creative Brief

This can be a single document or a set of documents, but either way it should be the parameters for all of your creative work. Look back to Chapter 8 for how to develop a brief.

Creative Concepts

The creative concept is a visual representation of your idea or set of ideas, complete with messaging and layouts.

Media Strategy and Plan

The media strategy should act as a framework for all of your tactical media ideas. The media plan itself is just a representation of the tactical ideas with timing included. (See Chapter 14 for an example of a media plan.)

Evaluation or Success Metrics

Of course all of your ideas will work, mainly due to the fact that you have done all of your homework, but what if one of them didn't ... how would you know? This is where you detail how you plan to track and measure your campaign's effectiveness. This could be as simple as sales growth or more complex, like a pre/post-attitudinal study.

This text has emphasized the importance of IMC so it should be clear that mediated and personal selling messages must complement and support each other. This means people working in sales should understand the marketing and advertising plans (see My Ad Campaign 15–A) and be well-versed on what the role of sales is in a company's overall marketing efforts.

Finally, advertising as well as salespeople should be concerned with solving problems. If the sales staff uncovers a problem that customers frequently encounter, and the company's product can help solve that problem, then that should become the focus of some planned communications—advertising, publicity, or company-sponsored events.

check yourself ✓

1. What should be the objective of personal selling? What is the major part of the task?

2. Describe the four distinct communications functions provided by salespeople.

3. Why do companies have their advertising people make calls with the sales force?

trade shows Exhibitions where manufacturers, dealers, and buyers of an industry's products can get together for demonstrations and discussion; expose new products, literature, and samples to customers; and meet potential new dealers for their products.

booths At trade shows, a major factor in sales promotion plans. To stop traffic, it must be simple and attractive and have good lighting and a large visual.

exhibits A marketing or public relations approach that involves preparing displays that tell about an organization or its products; exhibits may be used at fairs, colleges and universities, or trade shows.

The construction of trade-show **booths** and **exhibits** has become a major factor in sales promotion plans. To stop traffic, a booth must be impactful and attractive and have good lighting and a large visual. It should also provide a comfortable atmosphere to promote conversation between salespeople and prospects. Many trade-show exhibitors use state-of-the-art technology, such as holograms, fiber optics, and interactive computer systems, to attract and hold the attention of visitors.

When establishing an exhibit booth program, managers must consider planning, budgeting, promotion, people, and productivity.[30]

LO15-5 Identify the elements that must be considered in establishing a trade show program.

TRADE SHOWS

Trade shows provide an extraordinary opportunity for personal selling. A unique aspect of trade-show selling is that prospective clients and customers come to you; they already have a desire to learn about you and your product and the services you provide. Approximately one of every two trade-show attendees is planning to buy one or more products exhibited as a result of attending trade shows.[29]

Every major industry sponsors annual **trade shows**—exhibitions where manufacturers, dealers, and buyers get together for demonstrations and discussions. More than 14,000 industrial, scientific, and medical shows are held in the United States each year, and many companies exhibit at more than one show. Exhibit 15–1 lists the 10 largest U.S. trade shows, ranked by the size of the exhibit space (4 of the top 10 are held in Las Vegas). Trade shows are also very important for global marketers because they may be the only place where an advertiser can meet the company's major international prospects at one time. Moreover, some of the world's largest trade shows are held overseas.

Trade shows are an important component in the marketing mix. They provide a unique opportunity for advertisers to meet with a large number of prospects. More than half of trade-show visitors make buying plans as a result of visiting a show. The Consumer Electronics Association puts on one of the largest shows in the world. How does the fast-changing world of electronics lend itself to using trade shows as a way of showcasing new products?
James Mattil/Shutterstock

▼ **EXHIBIT 15–1** Top 10 U.S. trade shows based on floor space (2018).

Event	Industry	Floor space (Million Sq Ft)
ConExpo-CON/AGG	Construction	2.67
Consumer Electronics Show	Consumer electronics	2.62
Atlanta International Gifts & Home Furnishings Market in July	Gifts and home furnishing	1.33
Atlanta International Gifts & Home Furnishings Market in January	Gifts and home furnishings	1.26
International Construction and Utility Equipment Exposition	Construction	1.24
Specialty Equipment Market Association	Automotive specialty products	1.21
Florida RV Supershow	RV and automotive	1.10
America's Largest RV Show	RV and automotive	1.06
Business Aviation Convention & Exhibition	Business aircraft	1.06
NAB Show	TV and radio broadcasters	1.02

Source: Evo Exhbits.

Planning

Planning pivots on four major areas: the budget, the image of the company or brand, the frequency of the shows, and the flexibility of the booth configuration.[31] In planning the actual exhibits or trade-show booths, advertisers need to consider numerous factors: size and location of the space; desired image or impression of the exhibit; complexities of shipping, installing, and dismantling; number of products to be displayed; need for storage and distribution of literature; use of preshow advertising and promotion; and the cost of all these factors.

Budgeting

Trade shows are expensive, and costs have increased substantially in the last decade. A large company may spend $1 million or more on a booth for one trade show. With staffers' travel, living, and salary expenses and preshow promotion added to booth costs, the cost per visitor engaged averages $274.[32] Despite the expense, trade shows can still be a cost-effective way to reach sales prospects, and they can be less expensive than a sales call.

Promotion

To build traffic for a trade-show booth or exhibit, marketers send out personal invitations, conduct direct-mail campaigns, place ads in trade publications, issue news releases, and perform telemarketing. The pie chart in Exhibit 15–2 portrays how customers typically learn about the trade shows they attend.[33]

At the show itself, activities at the booth and promotional materials (handouts, brochures, giveaway items, raffles) can stimulate customer interest and improve product exposure. 3M's Telcomm Products Division mailed 6,000 potential show attendees a Pony Express theme folder that invited them to pick up a trail map at the booth. The map guided the visitors (Pony Express riders) through a series of stations shared by seven product groups within the huge booth. Once the visitors' maps had been stamped at each station, they were given a "pay envelope" containing replicas of 1850 coins and vouchers redeemable for merchandise awards.[34]

▼ **EXHIBIT 15-2** How do customers learn about trade shows?

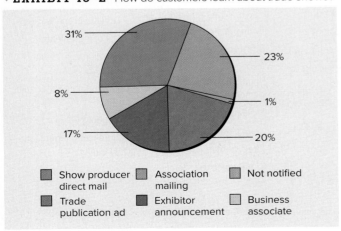

- 31%
- 23%
- 8%
- 1%
- 17%
- 20%

- Show producer direct mail
- Association mailing
- Not notified
- Trade publication ad
- Exhibitor announcement
- Business associate

People

The company representatives staffing the booth personify the kind of service the customer can expect to receive. They should be articulate, people-oriented, enthusiastic, knowledgeable about the product, and empathetic listeners.[35]

The primary goal of a trade-show booth is to meet with qualified prospects face to face. Ideally, 80 percent of the salesperson's time should be spent listening and 20 percent talking.[36]

Productivity

A company's trade-show effort may be wasted if prospects' names are not collected and organized properly. Each lead should be evaluated as to the prospect's readiness to receive another contact (A = now; B = 2 weeks; C = 6 months; D = never).[37] The resulting lead list is the link to future sales and augments the company's prospect database. Follow-up contacts are key to extracting the maximum value from trade shows.

packaging The container for a product—encompassing the physical appearance of the container and including the design, color, shape, labeling, and materials used.

check yourself ✓

1. What makes a trade show a unique personal selling opportunity?

2. What trade-show activity is critical to augmenting the company's prospect database?

LO15-6 Explain the factors that must be considered in designing packaging.

PRODUCT PACKAGING

In 2011, North American companies spent $169 billion on packaging.[38] Because upward of 70 percent of all buying decisions are made at the point of purchase, packages play a major role in both advertising and selling. The package is not only the last "ad" a consumer sees before purchasing the product, it is the only "ad" the consumer sees when using the product. So it is more than just another *planned message*. Packaging influences the *product message* as well, because (as we discussed in Chapter 7) it is often an intrinsic aspect of the basic product concept.

Packaging encompasses the physical appearance of the container and includes design, color, shape, labeling, and materials. Packaging serves marketers in five major ways: protecting, preserving, drawing attention, suggesting quality, and informing.[39]

Although the protection and preservation aspects reduce the costly effects of damage, pilferage, and spoilage, the importance of packaging as an informational and promotional tool cannot be underestimated. An attractive package can create an immediate relationship with the customer, influence in-store shopping decisions, help set the product apart from competitors, and inform customers of the product's features and benefits.

Designers consider three factors: the package's stand-out appeal, how it communicates verbally and nonverbally, and the prestige or image desired.

Packaging design can be as important as advertising in building a product's brand image. Packaging establishes or reinforces the brand's personality at the point of sale. So if status is the goal, the package designer must consider what consumers regard as prestigious. This is especially important for so-called nonrational products—cosmetics and perfumes, sports accessories, confection gifts, and certain luxury products—in which fantasy, impulsiveness, or mystique may overrule rational choice.

To sell products off the shelf, packages may use shape, color, size, interesting visuals, or even texture to deliver a marketing message, give product information, and indicate application.

> " The package is ... the last 'ad' a consumer sees before purchasing the product. "

After they are purchased, packages continue promoting the product in the home, reinforcing the brand's image, so they should open and close with minimal effort and be easy to handle.

Buying packaging includes two major phases: *concept* and *production*. The *conceptual process* involves input from five major stakeholders: consumers, manufacturers, marketing intermediaries, consumer advocacy groups, and government agencies.[40] The conflicting concerns of these groups strongly influence the nature and the cost of packaging (see Exhibit 15–3).

Environmental Issues in Packaging

As manufacturers continue to produce environmentally safe packaging, the marketer's cost of materials rises. And what some consumers expect from *green packaging* is not necessarily what manufacturers traditionally offer or what marketing intermediaries prefer to use.[41]

With the public's growing concern for the environment, especially in international markets, recyclable tin-coated steel and aluminum packages are enjoying a resurgence in popularity. Because European countries are so densely populated, their regulations requiring environmentally friendly packaging are far

▼ **EXHIBIT 15–3** Expectations and concerns about packaging among major stakeholders.

Consumers	Manufacturers	Marketing Intermediaries (Retailers/Wholesalers)	Consumer Advocacy Groups	Government Agencies
Ease (to handle and store)	Sturdiness	Sturdiness (of case and packages)	Package safe to:	Free of deception
Convenience	Suppleness		– handle	Free of harmful effects to ecology
List of ingredients	Attractiveness	Convenience (of removal)	– use	
Instructions	Safety (to users and for the product)	Tamperproof identifiable	Environmentally safe (biodegradability, etc.)	Biodegradable
Life of product		Safety (to users and for the product)		Free of health hazards
Disposal method	Cost of:	Ease of:	Package free of health hazards	All-around safety
Toll-free phone number for emergencies	– materials	– storage	Self-informative	– Safe to handle
	– fabrication	– shelving stocking		– Safe to use
Performance guarantees	– labor	– package stacking	– List of ingredients	– Labeled properly
Safety guarantees	– inventory	– inventory (by computer)	– Instructions	– List of ingredients
Environmental safety (biodegradability)	– shipping	Room for price stickers	– Disposal method	– Nutritional facts with guidelines
Reusable	– storage		– Toll-free phone number for emergencies	Expiration date for certain products
Recyclable	Need to change		– Warranties	
	Lighter weight (with safety)		– Expiration date	Recyclable
	Tamperproof		Recyclable	Adherence to federal and local regulations
	Package size (promotion space versus materials cost and environmental safety)		Adherence to federal and local regulations	
	Availability of materials			

Source: From W. Wossen Kassage and Dharmendra Verma, "Balancing Traditional Packaging Functions with the New 'Green' Packaging Concerns," *SAM Advanced Management Journal*, Volume 57, Number 4, Autumn 1992, pp. 15–23, 29.

more stringent than in North America. Marketers need to take this into consideration because such regulations add to the cost of doing business overseas.

Government Impact on Packaging

Government agencies also influence package design. The Food and Drug Administration (FDA), for example, and the Nutrition Labeling and Education Act of 1990 (which went into effect in 1994) imposed stricter labeling requirements for nutrition and health products. Additional legislation is pending that would require the labeling of all genetically engineered foods. Sometimes a state's packaging requirements differ from the federal government's, adding even more complexity for manufacturers.

Package Manufacturing

Packages may come in many forms: wrappers, cartons, boxes, crates, cans, bottles, jars, tubes, barrels, drums, and pallets. And they may be constructed of many materials, from paper and steel ("tin" cans) to wood, glass, and burlap. Newer packaging materials include plastic-coated papers, ceramics, metal foils, and even straw. Thinner plastic beverage bottles and smaller labels eliminate millions of pounds of waste each year and save companies money. The plastic film pouch for food products has become a substitute for tin cans and is more flexible, light, and compact. For pharmaceutical products, consumers prefer plastic containers.[42]

The second phase of packaging, the *production process*, may require the use of many packaging specialists: experts in package engineering (box designers, packaging materials consultants, and specialists in equipment configuration); graphic artists (designers, production/computer artists, illustrators, and photographers); label producers (printers and label manufacturers); die-cutters for custom packages; and package warehousing companies (wholesalers of prefabricated packages and package manufacturers).

Ad agencies are not usually involved in packaging decisions. This is typically the realm of specialists. However, it's not uncommon for an agency to be consulted on the design of labels and packages, and some may even prepare the copy that goes on them. In an IMC program, the agency can be very helpful in coordinating this work with the overall theme of the ad campaign.

When Should a Package Be Changed?

There are many reasons to change a package: product alteration or improvement, substitution in packaging materials, competitive pressure, environmental concerns, changes in legislation, or the need to increase brand recognition.[43]

Advertisers spend millions researching and promoting new images. And packages have to reflect a contemporary brand image consistent with constantly changing consumer perceptions and desires. However, marketers must always exercise caution. Designers should change packaging very gradually to avoid confusing consumers.

The final messaging point prior to purchase occurs when the consumer encounters the product. Smart companies invest in packaging that embellishes the brand's image.

McGraw Hill Education

check yourself ✓

1. What are the four functions of packaging?

2. What role might advertising agencies play in packaging decisions?

LO15-7 Describe the roles that sales promotion can play in a marketing strategy.

THE ROLE OF SALES PROMOTION IN IMC

Imagine walking into the fresh-fruit section of your local grocery store, picking up a big, juicy mango, and discovering a sticker on it stating: "Now available in Snapple. Mango Madness." You turn around and suddenly notice that there, right next to the fresh-fruit bin, stands a big display of, you guessed it, Snapple Mango Madness.

sales promotion A direct inducement offering extra incentives all along the marketing route—from manufacturers through distribution channels to customers—to accelerate the movement of the product from the producer to the consumer.

It actually happened. New York agency Kirshenbaum, Bond & Partners launched Snapple's new Mango Madness drink nationally with stickers on 30 million pieces of fruit.[44] Talk about out-of-the-box thinking and creative media planning! Moreover, it was an outstanding example of how sales promotion can be perfectly integrated with a company's positioning, in this case Snapple's "100% natural" message strategy.

The term *sales promotion* is often misunderstood or confused with advertising or publicity. This may be because sales promotion activities often occur simultaneously and use both advertising and publicity as part of a campaign. In truth, though, it is a very specific marketing communications activity.

Sales promotion is a direct inducement that offers extra incentives anywhere along the marketing route to enhance or accelerate the product's movement from producer to consumer. Within this definition, there are three important elements to consider. Sales promotion:

- May be used anywhere in the marketing channel: from manufacturer to wholesaler, wholesaler to dealer, dealer to customer, or manufacturer to customer.

- Normally involves a direct inducement (such as money, prizes, extra products, gifts, or specialized information) that provides extra incentives to buy now or buy more, visit a store, request literature, display a product, or take some other action.

- Is designed to change the timing of a purchase or to shift inventory to others in the channel.

Let's see how this definition applies to Snapple. In an interesting combination of both consumer advertising and *trade promotion* (sales promotion aimed at members of the distribution channel), Snapple used the fresh mangoes as an unusual new advertising medium to introduce its Mango Madness to consumers and to stimulate initial demand for the drink. The magnitude of that media effort (30 million pieces of fruit) served as a huge incentive to retailers to grant Snapple extra floor space (very expensive real estate, by the way) to display

McDonald's engages in regular and effective sales promotion. Restaurant guests know that they can't play Monopoly throughout the year, so they take advantage of the opportunity during the promotional campaign.
Daniel Acker/Bloomberg/Getty Images

Mango Madness right next to the fresh-fruit stand. The result: Snapple sold a lot more Mango Madness a lot faster, and for a lot less money, than it would have if it had just placed some expensive ads in consumer magazines or on TV. Moreover, by creatively integrating different forms of marketing communications, Snapple simultaneously bolstered its positioning strategy and enhanced its relationship with the retail trade—its primary customer.

Some marketers consider sales promotion supplementary to advertising and personal selling because it binds the two together, making both more effective. In reality, however, sales promotion is far more than supplementary. One study showed marketers spend 54 percent of their advertising/promotion budget on sales promotion compared to only 46 percent for advertising.[45] We'll see why shortly.

Sales promotion is expensive. But it's also effective. Unfortunately, it has serious drawbacks, which lead to furious battles in marketing circles between supporters of sales promotion and supporters of advertising. Each approach has an important role to play, but advertisers must consider the positives and negatives and get the balance right.

The Positive Effect of Sales Promotion on Brand Volume

Effective sales promotion accomplishes a number of things. First of all, it adds tangible, immediate, extra value to the brand. Snapple's creative media buy suddenly made Mango Madness more valuable to the retail trade. This induced retailers to stock up on the new product and display it prominently. Similarly, when McDonald's runs its Monopoly game, it's adding instant value to the products it sells. This is why we refer to sales promotion as the *value-added tool*.

Second, by adding immediate value, sales promotion *maximizes* sales volume. A short-term price cut or rebate, for instance, may be very effective at boosting sales. While advertising helps develop and reinforce a quality, differentiated brand reputation and build long-term market value, sales promotion helps build short-term *market volume*. To become a market leader, therefore, a brand needs both advertising and sales promotion.

> " To become a market leader, ... a brand needs both advertising and sales promotion. "

Creating Effective Sales Promotions [15–B]

- **Set specific objectives.** Undisciplined, undirected creative work is a waste of time and resources.

- **Set a theme that is relevant.** Start with a strategy, preferably from a unified marketing or advertising plan. Stay on track.

- **Involve the trade.** Build relationships. Carrier Air Conditioning sponsored the Junior Olympics in key markets, sharing sponsorship with its dealer in each city.

- **Coordinate promotional efforts with other marketing plans.** Be sure to coordinate schedules and plans. A consumer promotion should occur simultaneously with a trade promotion; a free sample promotion should be timed to the introduction of a new line.

- **Know how basic promotion techniques work.** A price-off deal can't reverse a brand's downward sales trend.

- **Use simple, attention-getting copy.** Most promotions are built around a simple idea: "Save 75 cents." Emphasize the idea and don't try to be cute.

- **Use contemporary, easy-to-read graphics.** Don't expect to fit 500 words and 20 illustrations into a quarter-page freestanding insert.

- **Clearly communicate the concept.** Words and graphics must work together to get the message across.

- **Add advertising when you need measurable responses.** When part of a promotion, advertising directed at too broad an audience is usually wasted. However, trial-building promotions designed to attract new users, for example, can be helped by targeted advertising.

- **Reinforce the brand's advertising message.** Tie promotions to the brand's ad campaign.

- **Support the brand's positioning and image.** This is especially important for image-sensitive brands and categories, like family-oriented Kraft.

- **Know the media you work through.** Determine which media will work best. Should samples be distributed in stores, door to door, or through direct mail? Does the promotion need newspaper or magazine or Internet support?

- **Pretest promotions.** Pretesting doesn't have to be expensive. For packaged goods, small samplings in a few stores can reveal how to maximize coupon redemption rates by testing various values, creative approaches, and delivery methods.

Finally, when all brands appear to be equal, sales promotion can be more effective than advertising in motivating customers to try a new brand or to select one brand over another. It can also motivate some customers who might be unmoved by advertising efforts. And sales promotions often generate a more immediate, measurable payoff than traditional advertising campaigns. This is why we might also refer to sales promotion as the "sales accelerator."

To succeed, sales promotions should be creative and hard to imitate. Kirshenbaum, Bond & Partners certainly demonstrated that with its Snapple labels. My Ad Campaign 15–B, "Creating Effective Sales Promotions," outlines some basic ideas to consider in designing promotions.

The Negative Effect of Sales Promotion on Brand Value

Conversely, some believe there can be negative effects of sales promotion, too. For instance, excessive sales promotion at the expense of advertising can reduce profitability. Some marketers believe a proper expenditure balance for consumer packaged-goods products is approximately 60 percent for trade and consumer promotion, 40 percent for advertising.

A high level of trade sales promotion relative to advertising and consumer sales promotion has a positive effect on short-term market share but may have a negative effect on brand attitudes and long-term market share. Why? Simply put, sales promotion implicitly communicates that there is a benefit or savings from buying now. This can make the brand seem less attractive when the promotion ceases. Without an effective advertising effort to emphasize brand image and quality, customers become deal-prone rather than brand loyal. And overemphasis on price (whether in advertising or sales promotion) eventually destroys brand equity.[46]

Another drawback of sales promotion is its high cost. One analysis showed that only 16 percent of sales promotions were profitable. In other words, many manufacturers spend more than $1 to generate an extra $1 of profits.[47]

Finally, overly aggressive sales promotion or advertising can attract a similar action from competitors, possibly leading to a price war, which reduces sales and profits for everyone.

Thus, if too much of the marketing mix is allocated to advertising, the brand may gain a high-quality, differentiated image but not enough volume to be a market leader. On the other hand, as Larry Light, McDonald's chief global marketing officer, says, "Too much [sales] promotion, and the brand will have high volume but low profitability. Market leadership can be bought through bribes, but enduring profitable market leadership must be earned through building both brand value as well as volume."[48]

push strategies
Marketing, advertising, and sales promotion activities aimed at getting products into the dealer pipeline and accelerating sales by offering inducements to dealers, retailers, and salespeople.

trade promotions
Promotion activities aimed at wholesalers and retailers to induce product purchase, display, and consumer sales promotion.

trade advertising The advertising of goods and services to intermediaries to stimulate wholesalers and retailers to buy goods for resale to their customers or for use in their own businesses.

pull strategies
Marketing, advertising, and sales promotion activities aimed at inducing trial purchase and repurchase by consumers.

consumer sales promotions
Promotions aimed at consumers to stimulate product interest, trial, or repurchase.

SALES PROMOTION STRATEGIES AND TACTICS

To move their products through the distribution channel from the point of manufacture to the point of consumption, marketers employ two types of strategies: push and pull. **Push strategies** are primarily designed to secure the cooperation of retailers. **Trade promotions**—sales promotions aimed at members of the distribution channel—are one of the principal tactics marketers use to push products through the distribution pipeline and gain shelf space. We'll discuss some of these tactics in the next section. Marketers may also use **trade advertising** (advertising in publications read by members of the trade) as a push tactic.

Pull strategies, on the other hand, are designed to attract customers and increase demand for the product (see Exhibit 15–4). Consumer advertising and **consumer sales promotions** are examples of pull strategies because they are designed to induce consumers to seek out or ask for the product, in effect pulling the product through the pipeline. Today, some national advertisers spend more dollars on trade sales promotions than on either consumer sales promotions or media advertising. But that is often the price they have to pay to gain and maintain distribution, without which they cannot make any sales.

Giving Brands a Push with Trade Promotions

Supermarket shelf and floor space are hard to come by. To maintain their own images, department stores set standards for manufacturers' displays (planograms). This means that retailers often won't use the special racks, sales aids, and promotional literature supplied by manufacturers.

These are minor problems; major ones have to do with control of the marketplace. **Trade concentration**—more products going through fewer retailers—gives greater control to the retailers and less to the manufacturers. Increased competition for shelf space gives retailers even more power, enabling them to exact hefty deals and allowances. As a result, manufacturers of national brands often don't have enough money left to integrate consumer advertising or sales promotions.[49]

Despite these problems, many manufacturers still implement effective push strategies. And the smart ones safeguard enough money for consumer advertising. Trade tactics include slotting allowances, trade deals, display allowances, buyback allowances, advertising allowances, cooperative advertising and advertising materials, dealer premiums and contests, push money, and company conventions and dealer meetings.

Slotting Allowances In response to the glut of new products, some retailers charge manufacturers **slotting allowances**—fees ranging from $15,000 to $40,000 or more for the privilege of obtaining shelf or floor space for a new product. The practice is controversial because some manufacturers think they're being forced to subsidize the retailer's cost of doing business. Smaller manufacturers complain that the allowances shut out all but the largest suppliers. The Federal Trade Commission (FTC) considered taking steps to limit the use of slotting allowances because they reduce

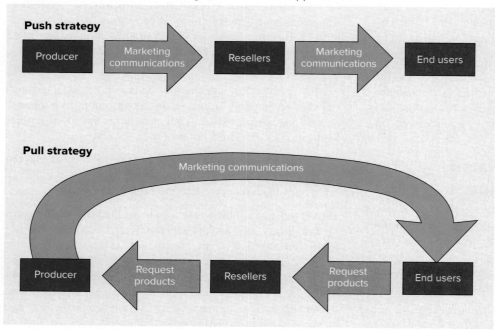

▼ **EXHIBIT 15–4** Two marketing communications approaches.

competition. But a 2003 FTC report concluded that slotting allowances encourage the stocking of new products by defraying the retailers' costs associated with new product introductions.[50]

Trade Deals

Manufacturers make **trade deals** with retailers by offering short-term discounts or other dollar inducements. To comply with the Robinson-Patman Act, trade deals must be offered proportionally to all dealers. Dealers usually pass the savings on to customers through short-term sale prices, or "specials."

Excessive trade deals threaten brand loyalty because they encourage customers to buy whatever brand is on sale. Furthermore, marketers who use trade discounts extensively find themselves in a vicious circle: If they cut back on the promotions, they may lose shelf space and then market share.

In addition, some retailers capitalize on trade discounts by engaging in forward buying and diverting. With **forward buying**, a retailer stocks up on a product when it is on discount and buys smaller amounts when it sells at regular price. **Diverting** means using the promotional discount to purchase large quantities of an item in one region, then shipping portions of the buy to areas where the discount isn't offered.

Display Allowances

More and more stores charge manufacturers **display allowances**—fees to make room for and set up displays. In-store displays include counter stands, floor stands, shelf signs, and special racks that give the retailer ready-made, professionally designed vehicles for selling more of the featured products.

Buyback Allowances

When introducing a new product, manufacturers sometimes offer retailers a **buyback allowance** for the old product that hasn't sold. To persuade retailers to take on their product line, some manufacturers even offer a buyback allowance for a competitor's leftover stock.

Advertising Allowances

Manufacturers often offer **advertising allowances** as either a percentage

of purchases or a flat fee paid to the retailer. Advertising allowances are more common for consumer than industrial products. They are offered primarily by large companies, but some smaller firms give them to high-volume customers. The purpose of these allowances is to encourage retailers to advertise the manufacturer's products, but compliance is not always enforced.

Co-Op Advertising and Advertising Materials

With **cooperative (co-op) advertising**, national manufacturers reimburse their dealers for advertising the manufacturer's products or logos in their trading area. The manufacturer usually pays 50 to 100 percent of the dealer's advertising costs based on a percentage of the dealer's sales. Special co-op deals are used to introduce new products, advertise certain lines, or combat competitors.

Unlike advertising allowances, co-op programs typically require the dealer to submit invoices and proof of the advertising (*tearsheets* from the newspaper or affidavits of performance from radio or TV stations). Many manufacturers also give their dealers prepared advertising materials: ads, glossy photos, sample radio commercials, and so on. To control the image of their products, some

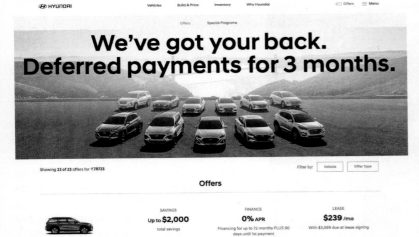

Trade deals are offered by manufacturers to retailers who pass along the short-term discounts to customers. Here, Hyundai Motors offers additional benefits on financing and leasing to purchasers of the Santa Fe. Consumers may still negotiate a good deal with their local dealership.

The Hyundai Motor Company

advertisers insist that dealers use these materials to qualify for the co-op advertising money.

Dealer Premiums, Contests, and Push Money

To encourage retail dealers and salespeople to reach specific sales goals or push certain products, manufacturers may offer special prizes, gifts, or financial incentives. One inducement is cash payments made directly to the sales staff, called **push money (PM)**, or **spiffs**. For example, a shoe salesperson may suggest shoe polish or some other high-profit extra; for each item sold, the salesperson receives a 25- to 50-cent spiff. Some retailers believe that manufacturers' incentives are a potential source of conflict, causing salespeople to serve their own self-interests rather than the interests of their employers. Ethics can also be an issue when dealers and salespeople push certain products on consumers solely for their personal gain.

Company Conventions and Dealer Meetings

Most major manufacturers hold **company conventions** and **dealer meetings** to introduce new products, announce sales promotion programs, or show new advertising campaigns. They may also conduct sales and service training sessions. Meetings can be a dynamic sales promotion tool for the manufacturer.

Manufacturers like DeWalt often pay a display allowance for their in-store exhibits, banners, and shelf signs. These fees benefit retailers like Home Depot by compensating them for the space occupied by the displays. And the manufacturer benefits from the increased exposure.
Scott Olson/Getty Images

Push strategies are virtually invisible to consumers. Yet successful inducements mean the product gets more shelf space, a special display, or extra interest and enthusiasm from salespeople. And extra sales interest can spell the difference between failure and success.

Using Consumer Promotions to Pull Brands Through

One reason for today's increased focus on consumer sales promotions is the change in TV viewing habits. With cable TV, DVRs, and DVDs, fewer people watch any one program. Advertising audiences are more fragmented, and major manufacturers must turn to new methods to reach these moving targets.

Common consumer sales promotions include point-of-purchase materials, coupons, electronic coupons and convenience cards, cents-off promotions, refunds, rebates, premiums, sampling, combination offers, contests, and sweepstakes. A successful IMC campaign may integrate several of these techniques along with media advertising, product publicity, and direct marketing.

Point-of-Purchase (P-O-P) Materials

Walk into any store and notice the number of display materials and advertising-like devices that are designed to build traffic, exhibit and advertise the product, and promote impulse buying. Collectively, these are all referred to as **point-of-purchase (P-O-P) materials**.

P-O-P works best when used with other forms of advertising. For example, by advertising its gum and candy, one marketer increased sales by about 150 percent. But when P-O-P was added to the same program, the purchase rate jumped 550 percent.[51]

In one poll, 56 percent of mass-merchandise shoppers and 62 percent of grocery shoppers said they noticed point-of-purchase materials. More than half reported noticing signs and displays, 18 percent remembered coupon dispensers, and 14 percent could recall samplings and demonstrations.[52]

Today's consumers make their decisions in the store 66 percent of the time and make unplanned (impulse) purchases 53 percent of the time, so P-O-P can often be the major factor in stimulating purchases.[53]

P-O-P materials may also include window displays, counter displays, floor and wall racks to hold the merchandise, streamers, and posters. Often, the product's shipping cartons are designed to double as display units. A complete information center may even provide literature, samples, product photos, or an interactive computer in a kiosk.

The trend toward self-service retailing has increased the importance of P-O-P materials. With fewer and less knowledgeable salespeople available to help them, customers are forced to make purchasing decisions on their own. Eye-catching, informative displays can give them the nudge they need. Even in well-staffed stores, display materials can offer extra selling information and make the product stand out from the competition.

The proliferation of P-O-P displays has led retailers to be more discriminating in what they actually use. Most are beginning to insist on well-designed, attractive materials that will blend harmoniously with their store atmosphere.

The emphasis on P-O-P has led to a variety of new approaches. These include: a) incorporating video, b) offering interactive displays, c) adding the ability for local data collection to displays, d) increasing focus on stories, and e) increasing the number of displays in designated sections of stores.[54]

Because business mail is an increasingly important service to the U.S. Post Office, it has invested in technologies to help businesses use the mail with greater ease and less expense. An example is the Automated Postal Centers introduced introduced in 1998. These kiosks allow customers to weigh materials to be mailed, buy postage, and look up zip codes.[55] More recently the Post Office has introduced other business-friendly services, including Every Door Direct Mail, a program that allows marketers to target a geographic area without using a mailing list, and Informed Delivery, which offers businesses a digital preview of their incoming mail.

Coupons   A **coupon** is a certificate with a stated value presented to the retail store for a price reduction on a specified item or items. Marketers in the United States distributed more than 300 billion coupons in 2012, but only about 2.9 billion were ever redeemed.[56] Many more coupons are issued today, in large part because of the advent of digital technologies. The use of digital means that costs associated with the production, printing, and distribution of coupons are dramatically reduced. Consumers have responded in a big way. Juniper estimates there are more than one billion digital coupon users globally, and digital coupon redemptions in 2022 will exceed $90 billion.[57]

Coupons may be distributed in newspapers or magazines, door to door, on packages, in stores, by direct mail, or online. In nondigital formats, the vast majority reach consumers through colorful preprinted newspaper ads called **freestanding inserts (FSIs)**.[58] FSIs have a higher redemption rate than regular newspaper and magazine coupons; coupons in or on packages have

the highest redemption levels of all.[59] Online coupons now represent 5.6 percent of all coupons redeemed.[60]

Manufacturers lose hundreds of millions of dollars annually on fraudulent coupon submissions. Some coupons are counterfeited; others are submitted for products that were never purchased. To fight this problem, some companies have developed computerized systems to detect fraudulent submissions and charge them back to the retailers who made them.

Modern **digital coupons** work like paper coupons in that they entitle the shopper to a discount, but their method of distribution is entirely different. Interactive touch-screen videos at the point of purchase and coupon printers at checkout counters generate instant discounts, rebates, and offers to try new brands. Many online sites direct shoppers to coupon offers for their favorite brands.

Nonetheless, most of the nation's top brand marketers are involved with the Catalina Marketing Network. Catalina's system is installed in more than 30,000 stores across the country and influences more than 230 million shoppers.[61]

Consumer sales promotions expose potential customers to a product and induce them to seek it out. While trade promotions push products through distribution channels, consumer sales promotions are intended to pull the product through due to customer demand. Point-of-purchase displays have been around for a while, but digital technology makes them more effective than ever. Here, Samsung features its smartwatches on a digital display.

JSMimages/Alamy Stock Photo

coupon A certificate with a stated value that is presented to a retail store for a price reduction on a specified item.

freestanding inserts (FSIs) Coupons distributed through inserts in newspapers.

digital coupons Offer benefits similar to paper coupons, but they are distributed at the point of purchase, based on customer information stored in an electronic database.

Electronic couponing targets consumers with specific offers in ways that would not be possible with paper coupons. Many supermarket chains now issue customers **convenience cards** entitling them to discounts at the checkout counter. Consumers often provide detailed information about themselves when they apply for these cards. When customers use a card, a record of their purchases is sent to a database. The card saves customers the hassle of clipping paper coupons, it allows retailers to better understand their customers' purchasing behaviors, and it provides consumers with targeted offers.

Coupon-to-card (C2C) coupons can be downloaded by customers to their grocery store convenience cards from retailers' websites or smartphone apps. Measured for the first time in 2012, C2C and mobile coupons represented 1.3 percent of coupons redeemed.[62] Catalina's newest offering, BuyerVision Mobile, delivers personalized mobile advertising to 70 million households on their smartphones. Catalina utilizes the buying history of millions of U.S. households to target mobile advertising to a brand's most valuable consumers and then measures the impact based on in-store sales.

Traditionally coupons reach consumers through newspaper freestanding inserts (FSIs), which have a higher redemption rate than regular newspaper or magazine coupons. But the growth of mobile advertising has shown that the phone is just as effective.

Alliance Images/Alamy Stock Photo

Cents-Off Promotions, Refunds, and Rebates

Cents-off promotions are short-term reductions in the price of a product in the form of cents-off packages, one-cent sales, free offers, and box top refunds. Some packages bear a special cents-off sticker, which the clerk removes and credits at the checkout counter.

Some companies offer *refunds* in the form of cash or coupons that can be applied to future purchases of the product. To obtain the refund, the consumer must mail in a proof of purchase, such as three box tops.

Rebates are larger cash refunds on items from cars to household appliances. Large rebates (like those given on cars) are handled by the seller. For small rebates (like those given for coffeemakers), the consumer sends in a certificate.

Research indicates that many people purchase a product because of an advertised rebate but never collect the rebate because of the inconvenience.[63] This is a phenomenon called **slippage**. Consumers Union estimates that 60 percent of all rebates go unfilled.[64]

▼ **EXHIBIT 15–5** Next to coupons, premiums are one of the most effective sales promotion techniques for changing consumer behavior.

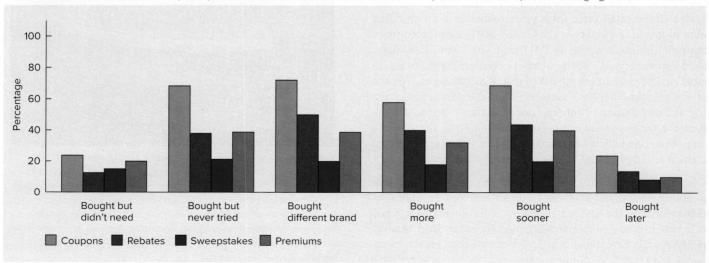

Premiums

A **premium** is an item offered free or at a bargain price to encourage the consumer to buy an advertised product. Premiums affect purchase behavior the same way as rebates but tend to be more effective at getting consumers to buy a product they didn't really need (see Exhibit 15-5). Premiums are intended to improve the product's image, gain goodwill, broaden the customer base, and produce quick sales.

A premium should have strong appeal and value and should be useful or unusual. It may be included in the product's package (*in-pack premium*), on the package (*on-pack premium*), mailed free or for a nominal sum on receipt of proof of purchase (box top or label), or given with the product at the time of purchase. Cosmetics companies often hold department store promotions in which scarves, purses, and cosmetics samplers are given free or for a low price with a purchase. The purchased cosmetics sampler is an example of a *self-liquidating* premium: The consumer pays enough so that the seller breaks even but doesn't make a profit.

Sampling

Sampling is the most costly of all sales promotions. It is also one of the most effective for new products because it offers consumers a free trial in hopes of converting them to habitual use. Sampling should be supported by advertising and must involve a product available in small sizes and purchased frequently. Successful sampling depends heavily on the product's merits. It offers the greatest credibility and can turn a nonuser into a loyal customer instantly—if the product lives up to its promise.

Samples may be distributed by mail, door to door, via coupon advertising, or by a person in the store. They may be given free or for a small charge. Sometimes samples are distributed with related items, but this limits their distribution to those who buy the other product. In **polybagging**, samples are delivered in plastic bags with the daily newspaper or a monthly magazine. This enables distribution to targeted readers and lets publications give their subscribers added value at no cost.[65]

In-store sampling is very popular. Most in-store sampling programs are tied to a coupon campaign. Depending on the nature of the product, samples can be used as either a push strategy or a pull strategy.

Combination Offers

Food and drug marketers use **combination offers**, such as a razor and a package of blades or a toothbrush with a tube of toothpaste, at a reduced price for the two. For best results, the items should be related. Sometimes a combination offer introduces a new product by tying its purchase to an established product at a special price.

Contests, Sweepstakes, and Games

Many people use the terms *contests* and *sweepstakes* interchangeably. Technically, however, a **contest** offers prizes based on an entrant's

Sampling allows consumers to try the product without risk. The strategy is expensive, but when the product is attractive it can convert a prospect to a loyal user instantly.

Tyler Olson/Shutterstock

Sweepstakes promise the opportunity to win a great prize, such as a trip to have a shopping spree and dinner with a sports star. Even politicians use the technique. Hillary Clinton ran a promotion that promised donors a chance to join her for dinner at George Clooney's house during her run for the presidency in 2016.

Hillary For America

sweepstakes A sales promotion activity in which prizes are offered based on a chance drawing of entrants' names.

game A sales promotion activity in which prizes are offered based on chance. A game is conducted over a longer period of time than a sweepstakes.

skill. For example, an entrant needs to answer a question correctly or submit an original recipe. A **sweepstakes** offers prizes based solely on a chance drawing of entrants' names. A **game** has the chance element of a sweepstakes but is conducted over a longer time (such as McDonald's Monopoly game). A game's big marketing advantage is that customers must make repeat visits to the dealer to continue playing.

Contests, sweepstakes, and games all encourage consumption of the product by creating consumer involvement. These devices pull millions of entries. Usually contest entrants must send in some proof of purchase, such as a box top or label. For more expensive products, consumers may only have to visit the dealer or take a test drive to pick up an entry blank.

To encourage entries, sponsors try to keep their contests as simple as possible. The prize structure must be clearly stated and all the rules listed. Sweepstakes and games are now more popular than contests because they are much easier to enter and take less time. Sweepstakes and games require careful planning by

the advertiser. Companies cannot require a purchase as a condition for entry or the sweepstakes becomes a lottery and therefore illegal. Marketers must obey all local and postal laws.

Contests, sweepstakes, and games must be promoted and advertised to be successful, and this can be expensive. And sales promotions need dealer support. To ensure dealer cooperation, many contests, sweepstakes, and games require the entrant to name the product's local dealer. They may also award prizes to the dealer who made the sale. ∎

check yourself ✓

1. What are the possible negative effects of sales promotion?

2. What is the difference between a push strategy and a pull strategy? Which one is directed toward the consumer and which one toward the trade?

ENDNOTES

1. Tessa Wegert, "Altruistic Content Marketing: The Good, the Bad, and the Ugly," *The Content Strategist*, April 12, 2016, https://contently.com/2016/04/12/altruistic-content-marketing; Peter Singer, "Can We Really Be Motivated by Altruism?" *World Economic Forecast*, April 22, 2015, www.weforum.org/agenda/2015/04/can-we-really-be-motivated-by-altruism.

2. Talia Lakrtiz, "12 Innovative Ways Companies Are Helping People Affected by the Coronavirus," *Business Insider*, March 23, 2020, www.businessinsider.com/coronavirus-companies-donations-helping-people.

3. Samuel Stebbins and Grant Suneson, "Amazon, Apple among the companies that are helping Americans fight COVID-19," USA Today, April 21, 2020, https://www.usatoday.com/story/money/2020/04/21/companies-that-are-helping-americans-fight-covid-19/111565368/.

4. Laura Mulrooney, "Gulfport: Helping Businesses, Helping People," *The Gabber*, March 25, 2020, https://thegabber.com/gulfport-helping-businesses-helping-people.

5. Mariah Ellis, "Coronavirus: Local Business Helping Veterans in Time of Need," *Fox 23 News*, March 26, 2020, www.fox23.com/news/local/coronavirus-local-business-helping-veterans-time-need/IZV3DEPRR5DURH4JG2YW5RV7QI.

6. Steve Gehlbach, "Which Local Businesses Are Offering Free Services and Products During Coronavirus Crisis?" *WSB-TV2*, March 25, 2020, www.wsbtv.com/community/local-businesses-offer-free-services-products-during-coronavirus-crisis/6XEICX7BB5AFJAB4Y3K2RFOG3A.

7. Joan Throckmorton, "We Are Interactive—Repeat—We Are Interactive," *Direct*, November 1997.

8. Bob Stone, *Successful Direct Marketing Methods*, 4th ed. (Chicago: NTC Business Books, 1988), p. 3.

9. "Employment Status of Women 18 Years and Over by Veteran Status, Age, and Period of Service, 2019 Annual Averages," U.S. Bureau of Labor Statistics, www.bls.gov/news.release/vet.t02C.htm.

10. Bob McCarthy, "Direct Mail and Those Pesky Millennials," *The Direct Response Coach*, November 8, 2017, www.mccarthyandking.com/direct-mail-and-those-pesky-millennials.

11. "What Does the Future Hold for Direct Mail?" *TMR Direct*, www.tmrdirect.com/what-does-the-future-hold-for-direct-mail.

12. "Facts & Stats—Direct Marketing," *CMO Council*, www.cmocouncil.org/facts-stats-categories.php?category=direct-marketing.

13. "Casper Is an Award-Winning Sleep Startup," *Heap*, https://heap.io/customer-stories/casper.

14. Peppers and Rogers Group, "Marketing 1 to 1," www.m1to1.com/success_stories.

15. Thomas E. Caruso, "Kotler: Future Marketers Will Focus on Customer Data Base to Compete Globally," *Marketing News*, June 8, 1992, pp. 21–22.

16. Tom Van Riper, "The Why of Best Buy," *Forbes*, April 2, 2008, www.forbes.com/2008/04/02/retail-best-buy-biz-commerce-cx_tvr_0402retail.html.

17. Seth Godin, "GUEST COLUMNIST: Permission Key to Successful Marketing," *Advertising Age*, November 1997, http://adage.com.

18. Nicholas Poulos, "Customer Loyalty and the Marketing Database," *Direct Marketing* (July, 1996) pp. 32–35.

19. Mollie Neal, "Marketers Looking Ahead in Chicago," *Direct Marketing*, March 1993, pp. 9–11.

20. Robert A. Peterson and Thomas R. Wotruba, "What Is Direct Selling?—Definition, Perspectives, and Research Agenda," *Journal of Personal Selling and Sales Management*, 16, no. 4 (Fall 1996), pp. 1–16.

21. "U.S. Ad Spending Forecast," *Ad Age Datacenter*, https://adage.com/datacenter/datapopup.php?article_id=317254.

22. Cyndee Miller, "Telemarketing Cited as Chief Form of Direct Marketing," *Marketing News*, p. 6.

23. "List of Countries by Smartphone Penetration," *Wikipedia*, https://en.wikipedia.org/wiki/List_of_countries_by_smartphone_penetration.

24. Larry Riggs, "Direct Mail Gets Most Response, But Email Has Highest ROI: DMA," *Chief Marketer*, June 22, 2012, www.chiefmarketer.com/direct-mail-gets-most-response-but-email-has-highest-roi-dma.

25. Personal Interview with Tom Campanaro, President, Total Gym Inc., December 2000.

26. Adapted from Barton A. Weitz, Stephen B. Castleberry, and John F. Tanner Jr., *Selling: Building Partnerships* (Burr Ridge, IL: Richard D. Irwin, Inc., 1992), p. 5.

27. Mike Ishmael, "The Cost of a Sales Call," *4DSales*, October 22, 2012, http://4dsales.com/the-cost-of-a-sales-call.

28. Edwin Klewer, Robert Shaffer, and Bonnie Binnig, "Sales Is an Investment, Attrition an Expense," *Journal of Health Care Marketing*, September 1995, p. 12.

29. "All-Show Averages," Exhibit Surveys, www.exhibitsurveys.com/trends.

30. Susan A. Friedmann, *Exhibiting at Trade Shows* (Menlo Park, CA: Crisp Publications, 1992), p. V.

31. Susan A. Friedmann, *Exhibiting at Trade Shows* (Menlo Park, CA: Crisp Publications, 1992), p. 16.

32. "All-Show Averages," Exhibit Surveys, www.exhibitsurveys.com/trends.

33. Friedmann, *Exhibiting at Trade Shows*, p. 24.

34. Friedmann, *Exhibiting at Trade Shows*, pp. 34–39.

35. Friedmann, *Exhibiting at Trade Shows*, p. 44.

36. Friedmann, *Exhibiting at Trade Shows*, pp. 70–71.

37. Friedmann, *Exhibiting at Trade Shows*, p. 90.

38. Lisa McTigue Pierce, "North American Packaging Market Remains Wary about the Future," *Packaging Digest*, November 12, 2012, www.packagingdigest.com/decorative-materials/north-american-packaging-market-remains-wary-about-future.

39. John Bynum, "Five Ways Product Packaging Impacts Sales," *Mediafast*, August 31, 2018, www.mediafast.com/five-ways-product-packaging-impacts-sales.

40. John Bynum, "Five Ways Product Packaging Impacts Sales," *Mediafast*, August 31, 2018, www.mediafast.com/five-ways-product-packaging-impacts-sales.

41. John Bynum, "Five Ways Product Packaging Impacts Sales," *Mediafast*, August 31, 2018, www.mediafast.com/five-ways-product-packaging-impacts-sales.

42. Chris Baum, "10th Annual Packaging Consumer Survey 1994: Consumers Want It All—And Now," *Packaging*, August 1994, pp. 40–43.

43. Kassaye and Verma, "Balancing Traditional Packaging Functions with the New 'Green' Packaging Concerns."

44. "Excerpt: Under the Radar," *Brandweek*, December 8, 1997, http://members.adweek.com/archive/adweek/current/brandweek.

45. Peter Breen, "Seeds of Change," *Promo Sourcebook Supplement*, October 2000, p. 18.

46. Larry Light, "Trustmarketing: The Brand Relationship Marketing Mandate for the 90s," address to American Association of Advertising Agencies annual meeting, Laguna Niguel, CA, April 23, 1993.

47. Magid M. Abraham and Leonard M. Lodish, "Getting the Most Out of Advertising and Promotion," *Harvard Business Review*, May/June 1990, p. 51.

48. Light, "Trustmarketing."

49. Larry Light, "At the Center of It All Is the Brand," *Advertising Age*, March 29, 1993, p. 22.

50. David Ghitelman, "Slotting Fees Can Top $2 Million: FTC," *Supermarket News*, November 24, 2003, http://supermarketnews.com/archive/slotting-fees-can-top-2-million-ftc.

51. *The Point of Purchase Advertising Industry Fact Book* (Washington, DC: POPAI, 1997), p. 51.

52. Kelly Shermach, "Study: Most Shoppers Notice P-O-P Material," *Marketing News*, January 1995, p. 27.

53. *The Point of Purchase Advertising Industry Fact Book*, p. 39.

54. John Bynum, "Trends for Point of Purchase Displays in 2019," *Mediafast*, March 8, 2019, www.mediafast.com/trends-for-point-of-purchase-displays-in-2019.

55. Angela Lawson, "The End of the Line," June 18, 2004, www.kioskmarketplace.com.

56. "NCH Annual Topline U.S. CPG Coupon Facts Report for Year-End 2012," *NCH Marketing Services, Inc., Coupon Facts Report, 2013,* www2.nchmarketing.com/ResourceCenter/assets/0/22/28/76/226/457/735949da63a14f209014dd04c27f1472.pdf.

57. "63 Coupon Statistics You Need to Know in 2019," *Wikibuy*, August 30, 2018, https://wikibuy.com/blog/coupon-statistics-4c49b386c833.

58. "CPG Marketers Distributed 168 Billion Coupons in H1, A Slight Rise from Last Year," *Marketing Charts*, July 31, 2013, https://www.marketingcharts.com/industries/food-and-restaurants-35441.

59. The 16th Annual Survey of Promotional Practices, Donnelley Marketing Inc., 1994.

60. "NCH Annual Topline U.S. CPG Coupon Facts Report for Year-End 2012."

61. Catalina Marketing, www.catalina.com/about.

62. "NCH Annual Topline U.S. CPG Coupon Facts Report for Year-End 2012."

63. Stephanie Moore, "Rebate Madness—How to Avoid the Rebate Trap," *Consumer Affairs*, www.consumeraffairs.com.

64. *Washington Post*, February 1, 2005, p. C10, www.washingtonpost.com/wp-dyn/articles/A527982005Jan31.html.

65. Lorraine Calvacca, "Polybagging Products to Pick Up Customers," *Folio: The Magazine for Magazine Management*, January 1993, p. 26.

IMC: public relations, sponsorship, and corporate advertising

This chapter explains the role of public relations, sponsorship, and corporate advertising in relationship marketing and integrated marketing communications. By integrating public relations, event sponsorship, and institutional advertising with its general advertising activities, a company can improve the overall effectiveness of its marketing efforts.

Imagine getting a chance to visit LeBron James 40 years from now. James, perhaps the greatest basketball player in history, would be 75 years old and far removed from his glory days as leader of the Los Angeles Lakers and Cleveland Cavaliers. If, like many athletes, his years of competing at the highest level have worn down his body and slowed his step, he will at least have his memories of winning NBA championships. He will also still be getting a sponsorship paycheck from one of the world's most famous brands, Nike.

James is one of Nike's "lifetime" sponsors, which means the partnership will live on long after his retirement. Soccer superstar Ronaldo has one too.

Each will earn about $1 billion over the lifetimes of their agreements.

These contracts illustrate the importance of sponsorship to Nike, which spends more than $1 billion each year on athletes alone.[1] This total is up sharply from just 10 years ago, when the company spent about $216 million. The jump reflects both the greater amounts of money earned by professional athletes and the intense competition Nike faces from competitors such as Adidas.

With this amount of money being thrown around, some might wonder if sponsorship returns the kind of value that would justify its expense. To answer that question, it is helpful to look at one of Nike's first high-profile sponsorships, that of LeBron's only competition for GOAT, Michael Jordan. When Jordan joined the Chicago Bulls in his rookie season, he and Nike signed a deal for a then unheard of sum of $7 million over a 5-year period. Nike at that point was investing in potential—Jordan had yet to demonstrate how special a player he would become. The deal required that Jordan wear shoes designed

specially for him, labeled "Air Jordan."

The shoes were attention-getting and brightly colored, which immediately began earning Jordan an NBA fine every time he took the court. The league at the time had regulations regarding shoe color, which Jordan's sneakers violated. Jordan wore the shoes anyway and was slapped with fines totaling $450,000 for the year.

Nike's response? The company paid the fine on behalf of their athlete, and relished the attention the whole situation was causing. It is no secret that Nike seems attracted to the idea of cultivating a bit of a "bad boy" image. Implicitly, Jordan's decision to wear

continued on p. 402

LEARNING OBJECTIVES

After studying this chapter, you will be able to:

LO16-1 Distinguish between advertising and public relations.

LO16-2 Describe the key tasks of public relations practitioners.

LO16-3 Explain the potential benefits and drawbacks of sponsorships in an IMC plan.

LO16-4 Discuss the functions of corporate advertising.

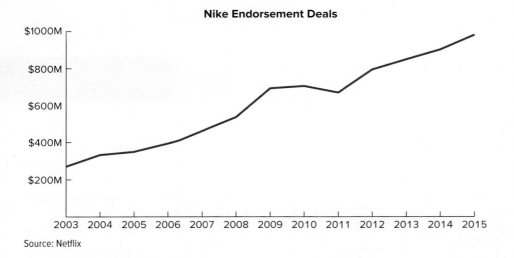

Nike Endorsement Deals

Source: Netflix

continued from p. 401

the shoes suggested that they were so good it was worth incurring the fine.

Air Jordans took the sports apparel world by storm. Within 6 years, Nike was selling $200 million worth of Jordans, and two decades later, $2.5 billion (with Jordan taking a 5 percent cut).[2]

The Air Jordan brand remains strong today, decades after Michael Jordan's retirement. Almost 6 out of 10 basketball shoes sold in the United States are Air Jordans.

Are the shoes really that good? *Men's Health* suggests that the Air Jordan line represents "the best of the best in performance basketball footwear," so the shoes are of high quality.

But the real secret to the success of Air Jordans, and to Nike's commitment to sponsorship, is better summarized by Philippe Tardivel, Marketing Director of watch maker Hublot:

> People want to identify with champions—and because they're unique people, embodying human achievement, that sense of creating firsts. And I think they're easier for people to engage with than, say, Hollywood types. Hollywood people may have talent, but they're hardly putting their lives on the line to achieve the seemingly impossible.[3]

This is what Nike offers with its sponsorship, the chance to have that connection, however slender, with the heroes of sport. People the world over love sports stars, for their achievements, their talent, their passion, and their courage. Nobody alive will know what it is like to play basketball at the level of James or Jordan except for those two. But anyone can experience the thrill of wearing their shoes. And millions do. ■

LO16-1   Distinguish between advertising and public relations.

THE ROLE OF PUBLIC RELATIONS

The primary role of public relations is to manage a company's reputation and help build public support for its activities. Today's business environment has become so competitive that public approval can no longer be assumed; it must be earned continuously.[4]

The term *public relations* is widely misunderstood and misused. Part of the confusion is due to the fact that public relations covers a very broad range of activities. Depending on the context and one's point of view, it can be a concept, a profession, a management function, or a practice. For our purposes, we define **public relations (PR)** as the strategic management of the relationships and messages that individuals and organizations have with groups (often referred to as *publics* or *stakeholders*) for the purpose of creating mutual goodwill.

Every company, organization, or government body has relationships with stakeholders who are affected by what it does or says. They may be employees, customers, stockholders, competitors, suppliers, legislators, regulators, or the community in which the organization resides. Marketing professionals call these people stakeholders because they all have some vested interest in the company's actions. In PR terminology, each of these groups is considered one of the organization's **publics**, and the goal of PR is to develop and maintain goodwill with most, if not all, of its publics. Failure to do so may mean loss of customers and revenues, time lost dealing with complaints or lawsuits, loss of respect (which weakens the organization's brand equity as well as its ability to secure financing, make sales, and expand business), or new rules or laws that make it difficult for the company to prosper.

A company's publics change constantly. When global marketer Unilever acquired Ben & Jerry's Homemade Ice Cream, it encountered previously silent publics. For example, the Center for Science in the Public Interest (CSPI) accused Ben & Jerry's of misleading the public by claiming that some of its products were "all-natural" when they in fact contained hydrogenated oils and artificial flavors. CSPI asked the FDA to take action against the company.[5] Ben & Jerry's hedged response was to argue that the term "all-natural" had various definitions in the food industry. Even so, the firm said that it would work with natural food organizations on the issue.[6] In another instance, after receiving an illness complaint, the company voluntarily recalled pints of Karamel Sutra ice cream that contained peanuts not mentioned on the label. Subsequently, CEO Yves Couette stated that "Our primary concern is always for the health and safety of our consumers."[7]

Because of the powerful effect of public opinion, companies and organizations must consider the breadth of the impact of their actions. This is especially true in times of crisis, emergency, or disaster. But it also holds true for major policy decisions: changes in management or pricing, labor negotiations, the introduction of new products, or changes in distribution methods. Each decision affects different groups in different ways. Effective public relations can channel groups' opinions toward mutual understanding and positive outcomes.

Efforts to create goodwill can affect multiple publics simultaneously. Patagonia, a manufacturer of outdoor clothing, has a policy of environmental friendliness and generous benefits for employees. To consider one example, the company gives its workers paid leave and child care on-site.[8] These benefits create goodwill among employees, but also help the company to be known as one of the best companies to work for. That in turn, attracts some clothing buyers who want to spend their money with companies whose ideals are consistent with their own.

With respect to publics, the goals of public relations are to improve public opinion, build goodwill, and establish and maintain a satisfactory reputation for the organization. PR efforts may rally public support, obtain public understanding, or simply respond to inquiries. Well-executed public relations is an ongoing process that molds good long-term relationships and plays an important role in relationship marketing and integrated communications.[9]

But many experts also consider public relations to be a *management* function.[10] In

The appeal of Patagonia, manufacturer of outdoor wear, for many goes beyond the clothes themselves, and extends to the company's commitment to the environment and its employees. This is a great example of how the concept of a brand goes well beyond the physical attributes of a product.
Patagonia, Inc.

public relations (PR)
The management function that focuses on the relationships and communications that individuals and organizations have with other groups (called *publics*) for the purpose of creating mutual goodwill.

publics In PR terminology, employees, customers, stockholders, competitors, suppliers, or the general population of customers are all considered among an organization's publics.

this capacity, public relations experts influence corporate strategy by representing the views, desires, and beliefs of important publics in corporate decision making. To mention just a couple of examples, public relations experts helped CVS make the decision to remove tobacco products from their pharmacies, and encouraged Starbucks to close its stores and enroll its nearly 200,000 workers in sensitivity training after an incidence of bias.[11] By alerting organizational management to ideas and trends outside of the organization, public relations experts can help companies avoid missteps that could hurt, or even ruin, a company's reputation.

The Difference between Advertising and Public Relations

Because they both use media to create awareness or to influence markets or publics, advertising and public relations are similar—but they're not the same. Advertising reaches its audience through media that the advertiser pays for. It appears just as the advertiser designed it, with the advertiser's bias built in. Knowing this, the public views ads with some skepticism or ignores them outright. So, in an integrated marketing communications program, advertising is often insufficient for building credibility.

Many public relations communications, like publicity, are not openly sponsored or paid for. People receive these communications in the form of news articles, editorial interviews, or feature stories after the messages have been reviewed and edited—filtered—by people who work in the media. Because the public thinks such messages are coming from media writers rather than a company, it trusts them more readily. For building credibility, therefore, public relations is usually the better approach. In its early years, for example, Google did not advertise its search engine. However, stellar reviews by technology experts helped it achieve its current dominance.

While advertising is carefully placed to gain particular reach and frequency objectives, PR is less precise. Public relations objectives are not as easy to quantify. In fact, the results gained from public relations activities depend greatly on the experience and skill of the people executing them and the relationship they have with the press. But PR can go only so far. Editors won't run the same story over and over. Sometimes a company believes it has an important bit of news to share, but the media disagree. In this case, the story won't run at all. While PR activities may offer greater credibility, advertising offers precision and control.

Advertising and PR in the Eyes of Practitioners

Another major difference between public relations and advertising is the orientation of professional practitioners. Advertising professionals see *marketing* as the umbrella process companies use to determine what products and services the market needs and how to distribute and sell them. To advertising professionals, advertising and public relations are marketing tools used to promote sales.

To date, though, few companies are structured with a public relations orientation; many are still marketing oriented, perhaps due to marketing's bottom-line focus. But today's marketing people would be well advised to adopt the multiple-stakeholder approach and relationship consciousness that PR people bring to the table. Moreover, in times of crisis, the candid, open-information orientation of PR is invariably the better perspective to adopt. Fortunately, with the growing interest in relationship marketing, two-way interactivity, and IMC, companies are finally beginning to embrace a public relations philosophy.

When PR activities are used for marketing purposes, the term **marketing public relations (MPR)** is often used. In support of marketing, public relations activities can raise awareness, inform and educate, improve understanding, build trust, make friends, give people reasons or permission to buy, and create a climate of consumer acceptance—usually better than advertising.[13]

[While PR activities offer greater credibility, advertising offers precision and control.]

Public relations professionals take a different view. With a background often in journalism rather than marketing, they believe *public relations* should be the umbrella process. They think companies should use PR to maintain relationships with all publics, including consumers. As *Inside PR* magazine says, "Public relations is a management discipline that encompasses a wide range of activities, from *marketing and advertising* to investor relations and government affairs."[12]

One story from Apple's history demonstrates the value that public relations plays, both in IMC and as part of a broader concern with managing relationships. While its corporate headquarters is in California, Apple uses Chinese factories to produce its technologies, largely to save money. This in turn helps Apple market phones, tablets, and computers for a price that is difficult for competitors to beat in the marketplace. Offering a strong value proposition is, of course, an important marketing goal. But when rumors of terrible factory conditions at its Chinese plant began circulating, Apple faced a problem that went beyond marketing. Acting on the advice of its public relations counsel, Apple invited ABC News to tour its Chinese partner's factory. ABC found that the rumors were false and that employees were well treated. Crisis averted. That is the value of public relations.

Marketing strategists Al and Laura Ries believe the best way to build a brand is through publicity—a PR activity. They cite numerous examples of leading companies that achieved their cachet with relatively little advertising but extensive publicity: Starbucks, The Body Shop, and Walmart, to name a few.[14]

In an integrated marketing communications program, advertising and MPR need to be closely coordinated. Many ad agencies now have PR departments or affiliate with public relations firms. Exhibit 16–1 shows some of the PR industry's largest firms and their billings. And many companies now have communications departments that manage both advertising and PR.

check yourself ✓

1. Why is it important for a company to develop and maintain goodwill with its stakeholders?

2. What can conceiving of public relations as a management function do for a company?

Firm, City, State	Net Fees (millions)	Number of FT Employees	Percent Fee Change from 2017
1 Edelman, New York	$888	5,616	−0.6%
2 W2O Group, San Francisco, CA	177	718	23.1
3 APCO Worldwide, Washington, DC	134	783	4.0
4 Finn Partners, New York	88	617	8.0
5 Zeno Group, New York	73	481	13.6
6 ICR, New York	69	188	9.0
7 Ruder Finn Inc, New York	69	603	NA
8 Prosek Partners, New York	47	163	15.1
9 MWWPR, New York	43	189	6.5
10 Padilla, Minneapolis, MN	41	226	3.0

Source: "Top PR Firms - 2019 Firm Rankings" *O'Dwyer's*, March 2020, www.odwyerpr.com/pr_firm_rankings/independents.htm.

LO16-2   Describe the key tasks of public relations practitioners.

THE PUBLIC RELATIONS JOB

The public relations job comprises a variety of activities, from crisis communications to fundraising. And PR practitioners use many tools besides press conferences and news releases.

PR Planning and Research

The first function of a PR practitioner is to plan and execute the public relations program. Part of this task may be integrated with the company's marketing efforts (for instance, product publicity), but the PR person typically takes a broader view. He or she must prepare an overall public relations program for the whole organization.

Because public opinion is so important, the PR person must constantly monitor, measure, and analyze changes in attitudes among a variety of publics. A common form of public relations research is **opinion sampling** using techniques discussed in Chapter 6: shopping center or phone interviews, focus groups, analysis of incoming mail, and field reports. Some advertisers set up toll-free phone lines and invite consumer feedback.

The PR practitioner analyzes the organization's relationships with its publics; evaluates people's attitudes and opinions toward the organization; assesses how company policies and actions relate to different publics; determines PR objectives and strategies; develops and implements a mix of PR activities, integrating them whenever possible with the firm's other communications; and solicits feedback to evaluate effectiveness.

Social media provides PR experts a window into the minds of consumers, especially "influentials," the individuals whose opinions matter a great deal to others (we referred to these individuals as "centers of influence" in earlier chapters). Influentials are easy to spot online—they have large numbers monitoring their tweets, blog postings, or comments. It is no surprise then that the arrival of social media has transformed public relations so dramatically that some now refer to it as "public relations 2.0."[15]

Reputation Management

One of the principal tasks of public relations is to manage the standing of the firm with various publics. **Reputation management** is the name of this long-term strategic process.[16] PR practitioners employ a number of strategies and tactics to help them manage their firm's or client's reputation, including publicity and press agentry, crisis communications management, and community involvement.

Publicity and Press Agentry   Many public relations professionals focus primarily on generating news and placing it in the media for their companies or clients. A major activity of public relations, **publicity** is the generation of news about a person, product, or service that appears in print or electronic media. Companies employ this activity either for marketing purposes or to enhance the firm's reputation.

Some people think of publicity as "free" because the media don't charge to run it (they also don't guarantee they'll use it). This is a misconception, though. Someone still gets paid to write the release and coordinate with the press. However, as a marketing communications vehicle, publicity often offers a considerably greater return on money invested than other communications activities. A large ad campaign might require an investment of 5 to 20 percent of sales; a major publicity program, only 1 to 2 percent.

TO ATTRACT MEDIA ATTENTION, PUBLICITY MUST BE *NEWSWORTHY.*

Press releases, or publicity, are still an important component of public relations. Apple posts releases about news and company innovations on its website, where reporters around the globe can get information easily.

Apple Inc.

The planning and staging of events to generate publicity is called **press agentry**. Press agentry helps to bring attention to new products or services or to portray their organizations favorably. For print media, the publicity person deals with editors and feature writers. For broadcast media, he or she deals with program directors, assignment editors, or news editors. Successful PR practitioners develop and maintain close, cordial relations with their editorial contacts. An MPR professional practicing IMC sees the press as an important *public*, and writers and editors as important *stakeholders*.

Crisis Communications Management

One of the most important public relations tasks for any corporation is **crisis management**. Brand value can be quickly destroyed if "damage control" is not swift and thorough. For example, Starbucks, one of the most successful businesses in the world, found itself in hot water in 2018 when an employee asked the police to evict two African American men waiting for a third party to show up. *Vox*'s headline read, "Two black men were arrested in a Philadelphia Starbucks for doing nothing." The company owned up to its mistake, closed every store for a day, and implemented bias-training companywide.[17]

Volkswagen also discovered the challenges of a crisis when the EPA claimed the company's diesel cars had a "defeat device" that artificially improved mileage results during testing. VW knew it had a crisis. CEO Michael Horn admitted, "We've totally screwed up." Another VW leader acknowledged that they had "broken the trust of our customers and the public." Heads rolled, and the new CEO, Matthias Mueller, told the press: "My most urgent task is to win back trust for the Volkswagen Group—by leaving no stone unturned."[18] The efforts were effective, and two years later, Volkswagen experienced a rebound in sales.[19] VW has also launched an internal inquiry.

To attract media attention, publicity must be *newsworthy.* Typical publicity opportunities include new-product introductions, awards, company sales and earnings, major new contracts, mergers, retirements, and speeches by company executives. Sometimes publicity is unfavorable and accrues unintentionally, such as when Netflix instituted its price increases. And because publicity can originate from any source, it may be difficult—or impossible—to control. In IMC terms, unintentional publicity is an *unplanned message*.

But the classic case of exemplary crisis communications management was Johnson & Johnson's handling of a product-tampering episode in 1982. Several people died when a criminal laced bottles of J&J's Extra-Strength Tylenol with cyanide on retail shelves. The moment they received the news, management strategists at J&J and McNeil Products (the J&J subsidiary that markets Tylenol) formulated three stages of action:

1. Identify the problem and take immediate corrective action. J&J strategists got information from the police, FBI, FDA, and press; identified the geographic area affected; corrected rumors; and immediately withdrew the product from the marketplace.

2. Actively cooperate with authorities in the investigation. Johnson & Johnson was proactive. It helped the FBI and other law enforcement agencies generate leads and investigate security at its plants, and it offered a $100,000 reward.

3. Quickly rebuild the Tylenol name and capsule line, including Regular Strength capsules, which were recalled, too. Although J&J believed the poisoning had taken place at the retail end of the chain, it first made sure that the tampering hadn't occurred at McNeil. The company's two capsule production lines were shut down, and dog teams were brought in to search for cyanide.

Eric Misko/McGraw-Hill

The insatiable appetite of the news media plus a flood of inquiries from anxious consumers put J&J's PR people under enormous pressure. All communications between the media and the company were channeled through the corporate communications department. All customer, trade, and government communications were coordinated within the company. This way, J&J maintained open, clear, consistent, legal, and credible communications and avoided rumors, political backbiting, and corporate defensiveness.

In the first 48 hours after the news broke, phone calls to Johnson & Johnson and McNeil were nonstop. In the basement at McNeil, a bank of phones usually used for sales was staffed by employees who were briefed on what to say, what not to say, and where to refer tough questions.

At the same time, management and employees had to be informed, authorities contacted, and many others notified. J&J and McNeil public relations managers and staff had to plan, coordinate, and supervise this enormous task.

As infrequent as disasters are, there is no more important activity for PR professionals and public information officers than crisis communications management—especially those

in highly sensitive fields such as airlines, government agencies, the military, law enforcement, chemical and oil companies, and public utilities.

Since the Tylenol incident, many companies in normally nonsensitive industries have prepared crisis management plans. The manner in which a company handles communications during emergencies or catastrophes will determine to a great extent how the public responds to the news. When corporations have no plans for coping with a crisis, the resulting press coverage can be disastrous. Experts on crisis management encourage all companies to follow J&J's example by being open and candid. Withholding information or evading questions inevitably backfires. And the defensive posturing and secrecy can create bigger problems than those caused by the original scandal.

Credible remediation of a crisis also involves a commitment not to make the same mistakes over and over again. This lesson seemed lost on Marriott International, which in 2020 revealed that a hacker had accessed information of 5 million customers, including customer names, addresses, e-mails, and demographics. This would be a problem for any firm. But for Marriott, it was doubly so, because the company had experienced a similar breach in 2018.[20] This reinforces the need for public relations as a management function. Good public relations people do not just help a company when a crisis erupts—they help it avoid the next one.

Community Involvement The goal of **community involvement** is to develop a dialogue between the company and the community.[21] This is best done by having company officers, management, and employees contribute to the community's social and economic development. Every community offers opportunities for corporate involvement: civic and youth groups, charitable fundraising drives, cultural or recreational activities, and so on. A company should ideally adopt one program relevant to its expertise and focus its *mission marketing* activities. The PR department may help set up such programs and publicize them to the community.

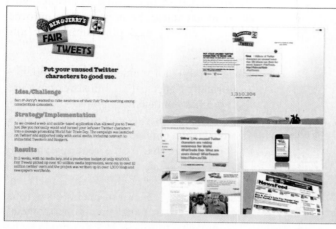

The social mission of Ben & Jerry's website reflects global and local initiatives. This site shows Ben & Jerry's use of social media and its support for raising awareness of the Fair Trade initiative by encouraging users of Twitter to donate their Tweets for a good cause.

Ben & Jerry's Homemade Inc.

Other Public Relations Activities

In addition to planning and reputation management, public relations professionals are often involved in activities such as public affairs and lobbying, speechwriting, fundraising and membership drives, creation of publications, and special-events management.

Public Affairs and Lobbying
Organizations often need to deal with elected officials, regulatory and legislative bodies, and various community groups—the realm of **public affairs**. Public affairs usually requires a specialist. Many experts think PR and public affairs should become more integrated to combine the skills and policy expertise of the specialist with the PR person's media and community relations savvy.

Lobbying refers to informing government officials and persuading them to support or thwart administrative action or legislation in the interests of some client. Every organization is affected by the government, so lobbying is big business.

Speechwriting
Because company officials often have to speak at stockholder meetings, conferences, or conventions, PR practitioners often engage in **speechwriting**. They are also frequently responsible for making all the arrangements for speaking opportunities and developing answers for questions company representatives are likely to be asked. Because public relations people may sometimes represent their employers at special events, press conferences, and interviews, they too should be articulate public speakers.

Fundraising and Membership Drives
A public relations person may be responsible for soliciting money for a nonprofit organization or for a cause the company deems worthwhile, such as the United Way or a political action committee (PAC).

Charitable organizations, labor unions, professional societies, trade associations, and other groups rely on membership fees or contributions. The PR specialist must communicate to potential contributors or members the goals of the organization and may integrate promotional tie-ins to publicize the drive or encourage participation. In the process, the company PR people may work

To meet demanding operating budgets, nonprofit organizations often devote a significant portion of their advertising to raising funds. The Rainforest Action Network (www.ran.org) ran this ad to create awareness of the destruction of virgin old-growth forests.

Rainforest Action Network

closely with the advertising department or agency to create ads promoting the particular cause or to publicize the company's involvement with the cause in product ads.

Publications   ublic relations people prepare many of a company's communications materials: news releases and media kits; booklets, leaflets, pamphlets, brochures, manuals, and books; letters, inserts, and enclosures; annual reports; posters, bulletin boards, and exhibits; audiovisual materials; and position papers. It's important that these materials are also accessible in an **online newsroom (or pressroom)**. Here again, PR people may work with the advertising department or the agency to produce these materials. The advertising people need to keep the company's overall positioning strategy in mind while trying to help accomplish the particular PR objectives.

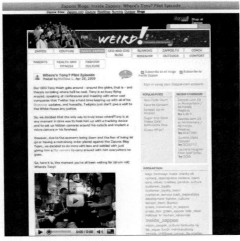

Zappos has built its company using social media. Employees are encouraged to use Twitter, Facebook, and YouTube. Here is its company blog written by a large collection of employees.

Zappos.com, Inc.

Social Media   As with all areas of advertising, the Internet has transformed the way we approach

business and our communication to consumers. However, for PR the world seems to be flipped upside down. With the advent of social media and the rise in popularity of blogging and tweeting, staying on top of who is writing about what is a full-time job. It used to be that a PR professional would have to know a score of people from each industry; nowadays that number is exponentially bigger. However, with the bad comes the good, and the clarity that comes from social media allows PR professionals to stay on top of any trends and deal with them before they become brand epidemics. With a good social media strategy, PR professionals can help get influential people to showcase their client's products as they launch, keeping early adopters and loyalists abreast of new developments before the advertising hits.

Corporate Blogs   Maintaining and managing a **corporate blog** can help address important concerns, introduce new products or services, and maintain a dialogue between a company and its publics. My Ad Campaign 16–A, "Corporate Blogging," provides some guidelines for using this public relations activity.

Corporate Blogging [16–A]

Most corporations have guidelines for blogging. Here is a set of marketing-related guidelines that every corporation should think about if it intends on using blogging for a marketing tool.

- **Know the environment.** What are people saying about you and your products? Venture out into the web and see what happens when you type your company name into Google or visit popular blogs that deal with your company's product category.
- **Determine what you hope to accomplish.** What is your purpose? Why have you started the blog? To address rumors? Share company news? Inform customers about new products? Develop a corporate personality? Having clear objectives will make decisions about what and when to blog much easier.
- **Practice, practice, practice.** Do a trial run. Blogging is time-consuming, sometimes difficult, and a different kind of activity for many organizations. Smart companies generate initial blog posts internally until it is clear that the tactic will be useful and rewarding.
- **Remember that it's a two-way street.** Learn to share control. Blogs without comments have minimal value, but with comments comes criticism. Smart companies value input from critics at their blogs because it offers them an opportunity to respond and educate.

- **Live up to the commitment.** Attention to blogs withers if postings aren't regular.
- **Offer value.** Providing information that publics can't find elsewhere gives people a reason to visit your blog or subscribe to feeds.
- **Ask if you have readers.** Is your public suitable for blogging? Not every market contains people who read blogs. If yours doesn't, you're wasting time and resources. Search for other blogs related to your industry or product and locate secondary information on your target market's use of the web to find out whether your blog might make a difference.
- **Avoid hype and puffery.** The online community has a different personality than that of people who rely on traditional media. Web users are suspicious of hype and can be critical when they sense they are being preached to or misled.
- **Monitor the one place everyone visits**—its name is Wikipedia. If your company or product is mentioned there it is important to monitor, and occasionally correct, what is posted.
- **Use blogging as one piece of the puzzle.** Blogging can be an effective way to reach and respond to your publics. But it is rarely a stand-alone tactic. Smart companies make it a part of their overall IMC and public relations plans.

Special-Events Management The sponsorship and management of special events is a rapidly growing field. In fact, it has become such an important topic that we devote the next major section of this chapter to it, following our discussion of PR tools.

Public Relations Tools

The communications tools at the PR person's disposal vary widely, from news releases and photos to audiovisual materials and even advertising. We'll discuss some of the more common ones briefly.

News Releases and Press Kits A **news (press) release**, the most widely used PR tool, consists of one or more printed or electronic pages of information issued to generate publicity or shed light on a subject of interest. News releases cover time-sensitive hard news. Topics may include the announcement of a new product, promotion of an executive, an unusual contest, landing of a major contract, or establishment of a scholarship fund. For pointers in preparing releases, see My Ad Campaign 16–B, "How to Write a News Release."

A **press (media) kit** supports the publicity of special events such as press conferences, grand openings, and trade shows. It includes a basic fact sheet of information about the event, a program or schedule of activities, and a list of the participants and their biographical data. The kit also contains a news story about

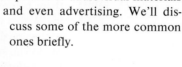

How to Write a News Release [16–B]

The Role of the News Release

The news release is an effective tool for publicizing information for several reasons. It helps protect the publicist and the client from being misquoted. It permanently records the preferred word usage, specific terms, key phrasing, and unique details.

Its standardized format also speeds up the process. It eliminates debate over how to format the information, highlights the data most needed by the recipient (contact person's name and telephone, date, etc.), and spells out the source and topic of the story.

The news release also simplifies dissemination by providing a form that is easily reproduced and transferred (e-mail, fax, postal mail, etc.) and by ensuring that all recipients receive the same message.

Preparing the News Release

The news release follows a format generally accepted throughout the news industry.

- **Double-space the text and use wide margins.**
- **At the top of the page (left or right side) place the name and phone number of your contact person.** If your page is not preprinted with your company's name and address, add it below the contact person. Finally, write FOR IMMEDIATE RELEASE or TO BE RELEASED AFTER [date].
- **Write a headline that signals the key fact or issue of the story.** For example, TECHCO PRESIDENT SPEAKS TO BAY CITY LIONS CLUB THURSDAY.
- **Place the most important information first.** The editors may shorten your news release by cutting from the bottom.

- **Lead sentence.** The lead sentence is the most important. Keep it focused strictly on who, what, where, when, why, and how. For example, "Techco President Ralph J. Talk will address the Bay City Lions Club at 8 p.m., Monday, September 16, 2013."
- **Body text.** Add directly related support information. "Mr. Talk's speech will be 'Technology in Albania.' Mr. Talk served five years as assistant to the president of the Albania Travel Association."
- **Final text.** Fill in background details. "Mr. Talk was born on April 30, 1956, and is married to Alice Johnson of Bay City. They have two children. Mr. Talk is a board member of the Bay City Little League."
- **Keep the text as factual, direct, and short as possible.**
- **Carefully proof your copy.**

Etiquette

- **Don't call to see whether the editor received your release.** Editors don't like to be pressured. Don't ask for tearsheets. An editor has little time to send you a copy. Don't promise you'll advertise if the item is published; the editor will be offended at the suggestion that news can be bought. If the article is run, send a thank-you letter to the editor.

Mailing List

- **Prepare a list of local publications.** You may want to group them so that you mail out appropriate news releases to publications that are likely to use that type of information. Refrain from sending mass mailings. Update your list regularly because editors change and offices move.
- **Ascertain in advance if the editors on your list prefer to have news releases sent by e-mail or postal mail.**

This electronic press release announced the role Bank of America will play as a sponsor of the Special Olympics through 2018. Through this sponsorship, Bank of America hopes to receive favorable publicity for its role and support to the Special Olympics.

Special Olympics and Bank of America

the event for the broadcast media, news and feature stories for the print media, and any pertinent photos and brochures.

Photos   Photos of events, products in use, new equipment, or newly promoted executives can lend credence or interest to a dull news story. In fact, a photo tells the story faster. Photos should be high quality and need little or no explanation. Typed captions should describe the photo and accurately identify the people shown.

Feature Articles   Many publications, especially trade journals, run **feature articles** (soft news) about companies, products, or services. They may be written by a PR person, the publication's staff, or a third party (such as a freelance business writer). As an MPR tool, feature articles can give the company or product great credibility. Editors like them because they have no immediate deadline and can be published at the editor's convenience or when space is available.

Features may be case histories, how-to's (such as how to use the company's product), problem-solving scenarios (how one customer uses the company's product to increase production), or state-of-the-art technology updates. Other formats include round-ups of what's happening in a specific industry and editorials (such as a speech or essay by a company executive on a current issue).

Printed Materials   Printed materials are the most popular tools used by public relations professionals.[22] They may be

House organs may be sent to customers to promote goodwill, increase sales, or influence public opinion. Delta Sky Magazine can be found on every Delta flight. It is packed with stories about destinations, food, culture, entertainment, and Delta partners. Given the number of people who fly every day, the magazine is a worthwhile investment in staying connected to customers.

Key Enterprises LLC

brochures or pamphlets about the company or its products, letters to customers, inserts or enclosures that accompany monthly statements, the annual report to stockholders, other reports, or house organs.

A **house organ** is a publication about happenings and policies at the company. An internal house organ is for employees only. External house publications go to company-connected people (customers, stockholders, suppliers, and dealers) or to the general public. They may take the form of a newsletter, tabloid-size newspaper, magazine, or even a periodic **e-zine** (a magazine published online or sent by e-mail). Their purpose is to promote goodwill, increase sales, or influence

> [A well-produced house organ can do a great deal to motivate employees and appeal to customers.]

public opinion. A well-produced house organ can do a great deal to motivate employees and appeal to customers. However, writing, printing, and distributing can be expensive—and very time-consuming.

Posters, Exhibits, and Bulletin Boards

Posters can be used internally to stress safety, security, reduction of waste, and courtesy. Externally, they can impart product information, corporate philosophy, or other news of interest to consumers.

Companies use **exhibits** to describe the organization's history, present new products, show how products are made, or explain future plans. Exhibits are often prepared for local fairs, colleges and universities, and trade shows.

Internally, the public relations staff often uses **bulletin boards** to announce new equipment, new products, meetings, promotions, construction plans, and recreation news to employees. Many companies now maintain an **intranet** site where they can post their internal communications.

Audiovisual Materials

Films and slide shows are forms of **audiovisual materials** that may be used for training, sales, or public relations. Considered a form of *corporate advertising*, nontheatrical or sponsored films (developed for public relations reasons) are often furnished without charge to movie theaters, organizations, and special groups, particularly schools and colleges. Classic examples include *Why Man Creates*, produced for Kaiser Aluminum, and Mobil Oil's *A Fable*, starring the famous French mime Marcel Marceau.

Many PR departments provide **video news releases (VNRs)**—news or feature stories prepared by a company and offered free to TV stations, which may use the whole video or just segments. Video news releases are somewhat controversial. Critics see them as subtle commercials or even propaganda and object when stations run the stories without disclosing that they came from a public relations firm, not the station's news staff.

LO16-3 Explain the potential benefits and drawbacks of sponsorships in an IMC plan.

SPONSORSHIPS AND EVENTS

As an element of the marketing budget, spending on sponsorship has grown much faster over the past few years than has traditional media advertising. Consider that in 2007, global sponsorship spending was $38 billion. In 2018, that number had grown to $66 billion.[23] This growth was expected to accelerate even more heading into 2020, a year that was to feature a summer Olympics.[24] However market spends dropped dramatically, and the Olympics were postponed until 2021 after the global COVID-19 pandemic.

The Growth of Sponsorship

Advertising and public relations people get involved in sponsoring many kinds of special events. In fact, sponsorship may be the fastest-growing form of marketing today. It actually embraces two disciplines: sales promotion and public relations. Some sponsorships are designed to create publicity, others to improve public relations through personal contact and

SPONSORSHIP MAY BE THE FASTEST-GROWING FORM OF MARKETING TODAY.

affiliation with a worthy cause, and others to immediately improve the sales and bottom line. Companies appear to be recognizing that, in an IMC program, sponsorship is an effective way to gain attention and establish brand loyalty.

A **sponsorship** is a cash or in-kind fee paid to a property (which may be a sports, entertainment, or nonprofit event or organization) in return for access to the exploitable commercial potential associated with that property.[25] In other words, just as advertisers pay a fee to sponsor a program on radio or TV, they may also sign on to sponsor a bike race, an art show or chamber music festival, a fair or exhibition, or the Olympics. The sponsorship fee may be paid in cash or **in kind** (that is, through a donation of goods and services). For instance, if a local TV station signs on as a sponsor of a 10K run, it will typically pay for some part of its sponsorship by providing advertising time for the event.

Cause marketing, a related strategy, is a partnership between a for-profit company and a nonprofit organization, which increases the company's sales while raising money and visibility for the organization's cause. Typically, a portion of the proceeds from the sale of certain products is donated to the cause. For example, Yoplait yogurt's *Save Lids to Save Lives* campaign urges consumers to buy pink-lidded cups of yogurt and mail the lids back. For each lid mailed in, Yoplait donates 10 cents to Susan G. Komen's Race for the Cure, more than $34 million since 1997.

While the sponsored event or organization may be nonprofit, sponsorship is not the same as philanthropy. **Philanthropy** is support of a cause without any commercial incentive. Sponsorship is used to achieve commercial objectives. According to the *IEG Sponsorship Report*, spending on partnerships in North America totaled $24.2 billion in 2018. As we discuss later in this chapter, by far the largest and fastest-growing category in North America

Global marketers look for global sponsorship opportunities. The Qatar Foundation made headlines when it became the premiere sponsor of one of the world's great soccer teams: FCBarcelona.

Josep Lago/AFP/Getty Images

continues to be sports sponsorships. Worldwide, sponsorship spending increased at an even faster rate than in North America, totaling nearly $66 billion.[26]

The reasons for the historical pattern of sponsorship growth relate to the economics of marketing we discussed earlier: the escalating costs of traditional advertising media, the fragmentation of media audiences, the growing diversity in leisure activities, and the desire to reach targeted groups of people economically. Initial growth probably came from the tobacco and alcohol companies, which many governments banned from broadcast advertising. Legislation in the United Kingdom, Canada, and the United States has virtually eliminated tobacco sponsorships altogether, but their success at sponsoring sports and other events showed the way for mainstream advertisers, who quickly saw the benefits.

Today, there is greater media coverage of sponsored events—everything from beach volleyball to Texas hold 'em poker to Xtreme games to cultural events. This provides a highly desirable venue for advertisers seeking young, upwardly mobile, educated consumers. Likewise, for transnational marketers, there is growing interest in global events such as World Cup soccer, the Olympics, and the America's Cup yacht race. The international soccer tournament generated $1.6 billion in sponsorship revenue during the 2007–2010 period, up from $584 million between 1999 and 2002. Adidas, Coca-Cola, Emirates Airlines, Hyundai/Kia, Sony, and Visa each paid an estimated annual fee of between $24 million and $44 million for global rights to a broad array of FIFA activities, including World Cup.[27]

Benefits of Sponsorship

In the past, for marketers with limited media alternatives (such as tobacco and alcohol companies), sponsorship simply offered a means of communicating with customers and prospects. Today, the many benefits of sponsorship are well documented and more far-reaching.

Certainly one benefit of sponsorship is that the public approves of it. One study by Roper Starch Worldwide reported that 80 percent of Americans believe corporate sponsorship is an important source of money for professional sports. This is a far higher approval rating than most companies would get for their advertising programs.

More than almost any other marketing communications tool, sponsorships and events have the ability to involve customers, prospects, and other stakeholders. Events are also highly self-selective of their target audience. So marketers that define their audiences tightly can select just those sponsorships that offer the closest fit. A significant benefit is the opportunity to enhance the company's public image or merchandise its positioning through affiliation with an appropriate event. Marketers that sponsor an event simply because it has a large audience are misusing this tool.[28]

Unlike advertising, sponsorships and events can provide face-to-face access to current and potential customers. Depending on the venue, this access can be relatively clean and uncluttered by competition. Sponsoring a seminar, for instance, creates an opportunity for both customer education and brand involvement. In some cases, it even enables product demonstrations and the opportunity to give a personal sales pitch to multiple prospects at a time when they are open to new information.[29] This is especially good for business-to-business marketers. To get a deeper understanding at making an effective pitch, see My Ad Campaign 16–C below.

Also important, but often overlooked, is the effect sponsorship can have on employees. Affiliating with a dynamic event can really boost the morale and pride of the troops in the trenches. And many companies offer attendance at the event (Super Bowl, Olympics, etc.) as an incentive to their sales staff.[30]

Some marketers have discovered that sponsorships can rapidly convert fan loyalty into sales. For example, 74 percent of stock-car racing fans report that they often buy products they see promoted at the racetrack. This is also true for other sports: 58 percent for baseball, 52 percent for tennis, and 47 percent for golf. Finally, sponsorships can be very cost-efficient,

The Client Presentation [16–C]

For most of you, the culmination of your project will be a presentation to the class or client that will be judged by the teacher, a group of peers, or local marketing and advertising executives. This presentation is by far the most important aspect of selling your ideas to the "client." It is not always the best idea that wins, and a great presentation can make a bad idea look great.

By now you have spent hours belaboring the who, what, when, and where of your advertising campaign, and now you need to explain why. You should think of your presentation as a Cliff Notes version of your thinking. While going through the process of developing a campaign, it is likely that you did not work sequentially—in fact most advertising processes are done in parallel—but your presentation should illustrate the linear path of thinking that netted your results.

Many advertising presentations use the popular Microsoft program PowerPoint, but if you have the resources and the gumption, think about different ways to illustrate your thinking and your ideas. Remember that the more creative your approach, the more (virtual) points you'll receive, assuming of course that the creativity doesn't get in the way of coherent thoughts.

Follow this basic outline and focus on how each section transitions from one to the other:

- Goals and/or objectives of the campaign—What is the campaign trying to achieve?
- Target audience analysis—Whom are we planning on speaking to and why?
- SWOT analysis—What are the strengths of the brand, the weaknesses, the opportunities, and the impending threats that factor into our decision-making process?

- Strategic insight(s)—Based on all of these factors, how are you going to solve the business challenge at hand?
- Creative presentation—Ideas, ideas, ideas. And don't forget to explain why these ideas will help achieve the goals/objectives.
- Media presentation—Where will these ads be placed, and what target and strategy insights led you to choose those vehicles?

The main objective of the presentation is to communicate, in a concise and succinct manner, your ideas, both strategic and tactical. One of the biggest misconceptions is that the strategy should be an ah-ha moment. In truth the strategy should feel more like a statement of the obvious because all of your research has led you down a certain path. If you explain the path appropriately you will receive the proverbial head-nods on the strategy slides. Where the whiz-bang should come in is how you tactically execute the strategy in its creative and placement (media) form.

Be sure to include everyone on your team in the presentation. This will be difficult as some people are better presenters than others, but that's okay because if the ideas and thinking are good they will break through.

Last, if you are doing a PowerPoint, hand out copies of the presentation (in color) so the "clients" can follow along and take notes. Props and gadgets are great to use too, so long as they don't distract from the presentation. When Foote, Cone & Belding was pitching kibu.com (a teen girl site) in 2000, it turned one of its conference rooms into a girl's bedroom, setting the mood and ambience for the presentation. It helped the firm win the pitch because elements of the room were used to highlight the insights into the mindset of the site's main user, a teen girl.

▼ EXHIBIT 16–2 Top U.S. sponsors.

Company	Amount ($ millions)	2015 Rank	2014 Rank
PepsiCo	$370–$375	1	1
Anheuser-Busch	$360–$365	2	2
Coca-Cola	$275–$280	3	3
Nike	$260–$265	4	4
AT&T	$200–$205	5	6
Toyota	$195–$200	6	7
adidas	$190–$195	7	9
Ford	$155–$160	8	8
General Motors	$150–$155	9	5
Verizon	$145–$150	10	10

Source: "Sponsorship's Big Spenders: IEG's Top Sponsor Rankings," *IEG Sponsorship Report,* September 19, 2016, www.sponsorship.com.

▼ EXHIBIT 16–3 North American sponsorship spending ($ millions) in 2017.

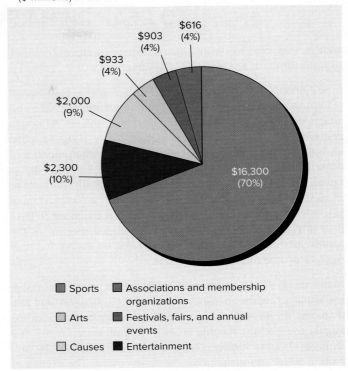

Source: "What Sponsors Want & Where Dollars Go in 2018," IEG, www.sponsorship.com/IEG/files/f3/f3cfac41-2983-49be-8df6-3546345e27de.pdf.

providing significant media exposure at a comparatively low cost. Volvo International believes the media exposure it gets from its $3 million sponsorship of local tennis tournaments is equivalent to $25 million worth of advertising time and space.[31] PepsiCo has been the top U.S. sponsorship spender for several years. Other top sponsors are listed in Exhibit 16–2.[32]

Drawbacks of Sponsorship

Like all marketing communications tools, sponsorship has some drawbacks. First, it can be very costly, especially when the event is solely sponsored. For this reason, most companies participate in co-sponsored events, which spreads the cost among several participants.

The problem with co-sponsored events is clutter. Some events have so many sponsors that getting one marketer's message through is extremely difficult. Look again at stock-car racing. How many logos do those cars sport?

Finally, evaluating the effectiveness of a particular sponsorship can be tricky at best—especially because it rarely happens in a vacuum. The problem is in separating the effects of a sponsorship from the effects of other concurrent marketing activities. We'll deal with these issues shortly.

Types of Sponsorship

While there are many, many avenues and events available for sponsorship, IEG Inc. groups most of them into six categories: sports; entertainment, tours, and attractions; causes; the arts; festivals, fairs, and annual events; and associations and membership organizations (see Exhibit 16–3).[33]

Sports Marketing
North American corporations spent an estimated $16.3 billion in 2017 on sports marketing sponsorships, as reported by the *IEG Sponsorship Report*.[34] The most

popular of these are motorsports and golf.[35] In fact, the vast majority of sponsorship money, approximately 69 percent, is spent on sports events. This includes everything from the Olympics to NASCAR racing to professional athletic leagues. Companies don't have to be big multinationals to reap rich rewards from sponsorships—if they do it properly. Many small business form strong community ties through careful investments in local sponsorship.

One large brand that has benefitted from sponsorship is Gatorade, which bought the rights to serve the product on the sidelines of professional basketball and football games. That brand has received more credibility than any television ad could provide, at a fraction of the cost. During every game, TV cameras show pros drinking the product in big Gatorade cups. And it's clear they're doing it because they want to, not because their agent told them to.[36] Even better, many football sports fans are now used to seeing winning athletes pour icy Gatorade on their coaches after winning a championship, a practice that started with the New York Giants back in the 1980s and continues today.

In hotly contested markets, the giants in their fields fight over sponsorship rights. Nike battles adidas, Coke spars with Pepsi, and Visa struggles against American Express. This has certainly contributed to the rising cost of sponsorships. General Motors, for instance, signed an unprecedented $1 billion, eight-year

COMPANIES DON'T HAVE TO BE BIG MULTINATIONALS TO REAP RICH REWARDS FROM SPONSORSHIPS.

sponsorship deal to ensure its exclusivity as the automotive sponsor for the U.S. Olympic Committee.[37]

In addition to spending more than $1 million for each 30-second television spot during the 2012 London Olympics, Nike and adidas outfitted a combined 6,000 Olympic athletes. Although adidas's traditional stronghold is in soccer gear, it still supplied an estimated 1.5 million pieces of clothing, equipment, and other logo-emblazoned articles for the two-week event. Nike is not an official Olympic sponsor, but it traditionally attempts to blanket the host city with its Swoosh anyway (see ambush marketing later in this section). Because adidas is estimated to have paid in excess of $61 million to be an official sponsor of the games, it is not surprising that event hosts do everything they can to stop unauthorized associations.[38]

Many sports events are strictly local and therefore cost much less while giving the sponsor closer access to attendees and participants. Firms with modest event-marketing budgets, for example, use options ranging from local golf tournaments and tennis matches to surfing contests. An increasingly popular promotion is the company-sponsored sports event. The event can serve as an effective focal point for an IMC campaign if it ties the company to the local community hosting the event as well as to the event's regional or national audience. But without a concerted effort to tie an event to other marketing communications activities like a currently running ad campaign, the money spent on sponsorships is generally wasted.[39]

Some companies associate their names with existing events. Mountain Dew, Taco Bell, Sony, and T-Mobile, for instance, are the "gold" sponsors of ESPN's Winter X Games and regularly renew their sponsorships.[40]

But controversy often swirls around big sports sponsorships. The most controversial practice is **ambush marketing**, which is a promotional strategy nonsponsors use to capitalize on the popularity or prestige of an event or property by giving the false impression that they are sponsors. Ambush marketing techniques, like buying up all the billboard space around an athletic stadium, are often employed by the competitors of the property's official sponsor. Budweiser was the official beer of the 2010 FIFA World Cup South Africa and the only beer company permitted to advertise within the stadium grounds. However, 36 women attended the Denmark versus Netherlands match wearing orange minidresses that were provided by Dutch beer brewer, Bavaria. They were ejected from the game. Ironically, the women received a lot of media coverage, informing the world that beautiful girls like Dutch soccer and Dutch beer. Bavaria's UK marketing manager Sean Durkan said, "Brand awareness has definitely increased. There's a lot more activity on Twitter and social media."[41]

One of the reasons this works is because people are often confused about who the official sponsors actually are—again, the problem is clutter. Just because a company advertises on the Olympic broadcast, for instance, does not mean it is an official sponsor. Ambush marketers take advantage of this.[42]

Entertainment   After sports marketing, the largest area of sponsorship is entertainment, which includes things like concert tours, attractions, and theme parks. For instance, numerous attractions at Disneyland and Disney World are sponsored by major corporations such as GE, AT&T, ARCO, Kodak, and Carnation. In 2017, U.S. companies spent an estimated $2.3 billion on this category.

Brands even sponsor entire tours. The Vans Warped Tour (vanswarpedtour.com) used a rotating lineup of nearly 150 bands, with multiple stages sponsored by other companies, such as Kia, Monster Energy, and dozens more. The tour performed in more than 50 cities in eight countries.

Causes   Sponsorship of charity events and educational institutions is a tried-and-true PR activity that often fits with the IMC strategy of mission marketing. A number of large corporations (including Chevrolet, AT&T, American Airlines, Pepsi, and Kodak) co-sponsored the Live Aid concerts, for instance. In 2017, marketers spent an estimated $2 billion in cause-related sponsorships.

Health care marketers such as hospitals, health maintenance organizations (HMOs), and managed-care companies are increasing their sponsorship activities. Oxford Health Plans, for example, signed up with the Franklin Institute Science Museum to host Cyber Seniors, a free seminar at the Philadelphia museum that teaches older people how to use the Internet.[43]

A vice president for corporate relations refers to mission marketing activities as "enlightened self-interest." People appreciate the fact that businesses do not really get anything tangible out of them to put in the bank.[44]

Arts   Symphony orchestras, chamber music groups, art museums, and theater companies are always in desperate need of funding. In 2017, sponsors spent an estimated $933 million to support the arts—one of the least funded of the major sponsorship categories. What this means is that this is still a relatively untapped area, and it provides outstanding sponsorship and underwriting opportunities for both national and local firms interested in audiences on the highest end of the income scale.

Festivals, Fairs, and Annual Events   More than 3,200 fairs are held in North America each year. When IEG

Cause marketing is a partnership between a for-profit company and a nonprofit organization. Campbell Soup Company (www.campbellsoup.com) joined forces with the National Association of Letter Carriers (www.nalc.org) for its annual food drive, Stamp Out Hunger. Campbell supports this initiative by donating more than 800,000 meals to Feeding America member food banks. The company also sponsors, along with the U.S. Postal Service, a reminder postcard mailed to more than 75 million homes the week of the drive. Now in its 28th year, Stamp Out Hunger Food Drive (www.stampouthungerfooddrive.us) has collected more than 1 billion pounds of food.

Greg Doherty/Getty Images

surveyed 1,000 members of the International Association of Fairs and Expositions, the findings revealed a very healthy, growing environment. The average yearly sponsorship increased a whopping 20 percent over the previous four years. Moreover, renewal rates averaged 88 percent! By 2017, sponsorship revenue increased to an estimated $903 million.

One of the largest annual events in the state of Michigan is the National Cherry Festival in Traverse City. Held every year around the Fourth of July, it boasts an impressive lineup of events and promotional activities that drive both attendance and sponsor visibility. Events include band parades, races, concerts, tournaments, antiques show, air show, Native American exhibits, and much more. Among the official sponsors are Pepsi, Budweiser, Best Buy, Jimmy John's, United, Toyota, and many other national and local companies.

Associations and Membership Organizations

This sponsorship category was added by IEG in 2004. These sponsorships were previously considered a part of festivals, fairs, and annual events because most associations sponsored annual conventions. But that is no longer the case, as sponsors are now more likely to sign year-round partnerships with trade groups, professional membership organizations, and other associations. Those sponsors spent an estimated $616 million in this category in 2017.

Venue Marketing

Finally, an area not covered by IEG's report is **venue marketing**, a form of sponsorship that links a

sponsor to a physical site such as a stadium, arena, auditorium, or racetrack. In 2013, Levi Strauss agreed to pay $220 million for the right to name the San Francisco 49ers' new Santa Clara stadium "Levi's Stadium." The deal is good for 20 years and Levi Strauss has the right to extend their naming rights for an additional 5 years for $75 million. The stadium owner will receive 70 percent of the revenue and the 49ers will receive the balance. Levi Strauss is also expected to be the 49ers' exclusive, non-sportswear apparel partner.[45]

Likewise, Denver has Coors Field, and Charlotte, North Carolina, has Bank of America Stadium. And AT&T has put its name on San Francisco's baseball park. But what happens when sponsors with naming rights become a liability? When Enron filed for bankruptcy in 2001, the Houston Astros shelled out $2.1 million to buy back the naming rights to Enron Field. The story had a happy ending, however, when the Minute Maid Company, a locally based subsidiary of the Coca-Cola Company since 1960, paid an estimated $170 million for a 28-year naming rights deal in 2002.

Venue marketing is changing the economics of professional sports. Sponsorships help pay for stadium renovations and upgrades and may assist the home team in defraying high operational costs. Many teams keep the money from their stadium luxury suites, stadium advertising, naming rights, and food and beverage concessions. Under the new economic rules, big stadium revenues are essential to signing big-name players and staying competitive.[46]

Methods of Sponsorship

Companies interested in sponsorship have two choices: buy into an existing event or create their own. Event marketing specialist

Dynamic Graphics Group/Getty Images

Venue marketing has surged in popularity. By selling the naming rights to stadiums, arenas, and centers, cities get help paying for public venues. Advertisers get a high-profile way to see their brands mentioned thousands of times each year in sports stories.

Joe Hendrickson/Shutterstock

Paul Stanley predicts that many corporate event sponsorships will become "sponsownerships," where the sponsor owns and controls the entire event. This would allow more control and would likely be more cost-effective. It would also help the company achieve its marketing objectives.[47]

For most companies, though, it's easier to buy into an existing event, either as the sole sponsor (the Buick Invitational) or as one of many co-sponsors. What's most important is to get a good fit between the sponsor and the event. Nabisco's Cornnuts brand, for instance, teamed up with the Aggressive Skaters Association (ASA) to sponsor the ASA Pro Tour and Amateur Circuits and to use the ASA World Champion female skater Fabiola da Silva as the product's spokesperson. According to Rich Bratman, president of the ASA, he chose Cornnuts because "the brand management and promotions team at Cornnuts really understands how important it is to reach teens in a credible way and is committed to supporting the skating lifestyle."

In his book *Aftermarketing*, Terry Vavra suggests several guidelines for selecting the right sponsorship opportunity or event. See My Ad Campaign 16–D, "How to Select Events for Sponsorship."

my ad campaign

How to Select Events for Sponsorship [16–D]

- Can the sponsorship be an exclusive one?
- The demographics of the mass media audience and event participants should match, as closely as possible, the demographics of the target consumer.
- The event should in some way demonstrate, evoke, or represent a key attribute of the product or service (for example, a luxury product sponsoring a thoroughbred racing event—"the sport of kings").
- The value to the sponsored event of the company's association should be no greater than the benefit to the company from the additional mass media exposure from the sponsorship. (This has to do with who is leveraging whom.)

- The participation should promise sufficient (and appropriate) mass media exposure to offset any costs associated with the sponsorship.
- The association of the product with the event should ideally offer or suggest a meaningful sales campaign or theme to be run concurrently with sponsorship.
- Did the company initiate the negotiation or was the company solicited by the event promoters?
- How much financial support is required?

Goals for Sponsorship and Measuring Results

What are companies hoping to achieve when they sponsor? IEG asked companies to identify the importance of several objectives and discovered the following:

- 50 percent hoped to create awareness or visibility.
- 46 percent sought to increase brand loyalty.
- 46 percent looked to change or reinforce a brand or company image.
- 33 percent intended to entertain clients or prospects.
- 29 percent were interested in stimulating product sales/trial/ or usage.
- 29 percent wished to obtain or develop content for use in digital, social, or other media.
- 29 percent showcased corporate community or social responsibility.
- 28 percent obtained leads or data.
- 26 percent sold products or services.
- 22 percent looked to access a platform for experiential branding.[48]

One of the problems with event sponsorship (as with public relations activities in general) has historically been how to evaluate results. Experts suggest there are really only three ways to do this:

1. Measure changes in awareness or image through pre- and post-sponsorship research surveys.

2. Measure spending equivalencies between free media exposure and comparable advertising space or time.

3. Measure changes in sales revenue with a tracking device such as coupons.

Unfortunately, none of these methods covers all the reasons for sponsoring. For example, how do you measure the effect on employee morale? What if the sponsorship is aimed at rewarding current customers or enhancing relationships within the trade? These are important possible objectives, but they are very difficult to measure.

Still, most companies are very concerned about the bottom line and look for a substantial return on investment for their sponsorship dollars. Delta Airlines, for example, is said to require $12 in new revenue for every dollar it spends on sponsorship—a ratio the airline claims to have achieved during its Olympic sponsorship.[49]

IEG suggests the following pointers for measuring the value of event sponsorships:[50]

- Have clear goals and narrowly defined objectives.
- Set a measurable goal.

corporate advertising The broad area of nonproduct advertising aimed specifically at enhancing a company's image and increasing lagging awareness.

public relations advertising Advertising that attempts to improve a company's relationship with its publics.

- Measure against a benchmark.
- Do not change other marketing variables during the sponsorship.
- Incorporate an evaluation program into the overall sponsorship and associated marketing program.
- At the outset establish a budget for measuring results.

check yourself ✓

1. Why is sponsorship such a popular and growing strategy for marketers?

2. How can a company determine if a sponsorship has been effective?

LO16-4 Discuss the functions of corporate advertising.

CORPORATE ADVERTISING

When a company wants to communicate a PR message and control its content, it may use a form of *corporate advertising*. In an integrated marketing communications program, corporate advertising can set the tone for all of a company's public communications. **Corporate advertising** covers the broad area of nonproduct advertising, including public relations advertising, institutional advertising, corporate identity advertising, and recruitment advertising.

Public Relations Advertising

To direct a controlled public relations message to one of its important publics, a company uses **public relations advertising**. PR ads may be used to improve the company's relations with labor, government, customers, suppliers, and even voters.

When companies sponsor art events, programs on public television, or charitable activities, they frequently place public relations ads in other media to promote the programs and their sponsorship, enhance their community citizenship, and create public goodwill. If the public relations people don't have advertising experience, they will typically turn to the firm's advertising department or agency for help.

Corporate/Institutional Advertising

In recent years, the term *corporate advertising* has come to denote a particular type of nonproduct advertising aimed at increasing awareness of the company and enhancing its image. The traditional term for this is **institutional advertising**. These ad campaigns serve a variety of purposes: to report company accomplishments, position the company competitively in the market, reflect a change in corporate personality, shore up stock prices, improve employee morale, or avoid communications problems with agents, dealers, suppliers, or customers.

Historically, companies and even professional ad people have questioned, or misunderstood, the effectiveness of corporate advertising. Retailers, in particular, cling to the idea that institutional advertising, although attractive and nice, "doesn't make the cash register ring." A series of marketing research studies, however, offered dramatic evidence to the contrary. Companies using corporate advertising registered significantly better awareness, familiarity, and an overall better impression than those using only product advertising. Five corporate advertisers in the study drew higher ratings in every one of 16 characteristics measured, including being known for quality products, having competent management, and paying higher dividends.[51] Ironically, the companies in the study that did no corporate advertising spent far more in total advertising for their products than the corporate advertisers did. Yet, despite the higher expenditures, they scored significantly lower across the board.

David Ogilvy, the late founder and creative head of Ogilvy & Mather, was an outspoken advocate of corporate advertising, but not of all corporate ads: "I am appalled by the humbug in corporate advertising. The pomposity. The vague generalities and the fatuous platitudes. Corporate advertising should not insult the intelligence of the public."

Unlike product advertising, Ogilvy said, a corporate campaign is the voice of the chief executive and his or her board of directors. It should not be delegated. "It takes years for corporate advertising to do a job. It doesn't work overnight. Only a few companies have kept it going long enough to achieve measurable results," Ogilvy concluded.

What can good corporate advertising hope to achieve? Ogilvy thought at least one of four objectives:

1. **It can build awareness of the company.** Opinion Research Corp. states, "The invisibility and remoteness of most companies is the main handicap. People who feel they know a company well are five times more likely to have a highly favorable opinion of the company than those who have little familiarity."

2. **Corporate advertising can make a good impression on the financial community,** enabling you to raise capital at lower cost—and make more acquisitions.

3. **It can motivate your present employees and attract better recruits.** "Good public relations begins at home," Ogilvy said. "If your employees understand your policies and feel proud of your company, they will be your best ambassadors."

4. **Corporate advertising can influence public opinion on specific issues.** Abraham Lincoln said, "With public opinion against it, nothing can succeed. With public opinion on its side, nothing can fail."

Responding to such criticisms and to marketplace forces, corporations now design their corporate advertising to achieve specific objectives: develop awareness of the company and its activities, attract investors, improve a tarnished image, attract quality employees, tie together a diverse product line, or take a stand on important public issues. The primary media used for corporate advertising are consumer business magazines and network TV.

A variation on corporate advertising is **advocacy advertising**. Companies use it to communicate their views on issues that affect their business, to promote their philosophy, or to make a political or social statement. Such ads are frequently referred to as **advertorials** because they are basically editorials paid for by an advertiser.

Corporate advertising can also build a foundation for future sales, traditionally the realm of product advertising. Many advertisers use **umbrella advertising** campaigns to simultaneously communicate messages about their products and their company.

While corporate advertising is an excellent vehicle for promoting the company's desired image, it cannot succeed if the image doesn't fit. If a big national bank, for example, tried to project a homey, small-town image, it would not be very credible.

Corporate Identity Advertising

Companies take pride in their logos and corporate signatures. The graphic designs that identify corporate names and products are valuable assets, and companies take great pains to protect their individuality and ownership. How does a company increase consumer awareness or enhance its image? What does a

OUR MISSION
TO ENSURE EVERY VETERAN HAS
A SAFE PLACE TO CALL HOME

OUR COMMITMENT
$80 MILLION OVER 5 YEARS & THE SWEAT EQUITY
OF THOUSANDS OF ASSOCIATE VOLUNTEERS

FOUNDATION

Between 9/11 and Veterans Day, we'll complete 350+ projects
to improve the homes of veterans and their families.

Follow along at homedepotfoundation.org and
facebook.com/homedepotfoundation.

Through Team Depot, The Home Depot Foundation (https://corporate. homedepot.com/foundation) provides opportunities for employees and suppliers to contribute their home improvement know-how to make a meaningful impact in the community. Since 2011, Team Depot has helped more than 47,000 veteran homes in more than 4,500 cities, from building wheelchair ramps and renovating the homes of wounded warriors to repairing and remodeling transitional housing for homeless veterans. This public relations advertising serves to acknowledge the efforts of Home Depot employees, as well as to let the public know that The Home Depot is a good corporate citizen.

The Home Depot Foundation

---

corporate identity advertising Advertising a corporation creates to familiarize the public with its name, logos, trademarks, or corporate signatures, especially after any of these elements are changed.

recruitment advertising A special type of advertising, most frequently found in the classified sections of daily newspapers or in online job boards, aimed at attracting employment applications.

company do when it changes its name, logos, or trademarks, as when it merges with another company? This is the job of **corporate identity advertising**.

Familiar corporate name changes include the switch from Datsun to Nissan, Consolidated Foods to Sara Lee Corp., RIM to BlackBerry, Comcast to Xfinity, Kentucky Fried Chicken to KFC, and Philip Morris to Altria.

Recruitment Advertising

Companies use **recruitment advertising** to attract new employees. Most recruitment advertising appears in the classified help-wanted sections of daily newspapers or, increasingly, on the Internet and is placed by the human resources department rather than the advertising department. But many ad agencies now employ recruitment specialists, and some agencies even specialize in recruitment advertising. ■

check yourself ✓

1. How would you respond to a company that told you "institutional advertising doesn't make the cash register ring"?

2. Why does David Ogilvy believe that most corporate advertising never achieves measurable results?

ENDNOTES

1. B. J. Enoch, "Top 15 Most Influential Nike Sponsored Athletes on Social," *Opendorse*, February 14, 2020, https://opendorse. com/blog/top-nike-sponsored-athletes-on-social-media.

2. "How Michael Jordan's Nike Deal Changed Sports Marketing Forever," *Edgar Daily*, September 12, 2018, https://edgardaily. com/articles/how-michael-jordans-nike-deal-changed-sports-marketing-forever.

3. "How Michael Jordan's Nike Deal Changed Sports Marketing Forever,"*Edgar Daily*, September 12, 2018, https://edgardaily. com/articles/how-michael-jordans-nike-deal-changed-sports-marketing-forever.

4. Brian Beers, "How Does Goodwill Increase a Company's Value?" *Investopedia*, March 31, 2019, www.investopedia.com/ ask/answers/010815/how-does-goodwill-increase-companys-value.asp.

5. CSPI Newsroom, "Ben & Jerry's Fudging the Truth, Says CSPI: Nothing 'All-Natural' about Ingredients," July 30, 2002, www. cspinet.org/new/200207301.html.

6. Ben & Jerry's Homemade, Inc., press release, "Ben & Jerry's Response to CSPI Concerns," July 31, 2002, www.benjerry.com.

7. Ben & Jerry's Homemade, Inc., press release, "Ben & Jerry's Voluntarily Initiates the Recall of Pints of Karamel Sutra Ice Cream with Code 02/14/04," March 28, 2003, www. benjerry.com.

8. Staff Guide, "14 Best Companies to Work for That Are Actually Making a Difference in the World," *The Good Trade*, www. thegoodtrade.com/features/best-companies-to-work-for-that-make-a-difference.

9. Sandra Moriarty, "PR and IMC: The Benefits of Integration," *Public Relations Quarterly*, Fall 1994, pp. 38–44.

10. Sam Burne James, "PR Must Assert Itself as a Management Discipline," *PR Week*, September 7, 2016, www.prweek.com/article/1408067/pr-assert-itself-management-discipline-says-futureproof-volume-two.

11. "3 Examples of How Public Relations Saved the Day," *Thinkhubbel*, March 26, 2019, www.thinkhubbell.com/public-relations-examples-saving-the-day.

12. Publisher's Statement, *Inside PR*, March 1993, p. 3.

13. Tim Berry and Doug Wilson, "Public Relations Marketing," *Business Know-How*, February 17, 2020, www.businessknowhow.com/marketing/prmarketing.htm.

14. Al Ries and Laura Ries, *The Origin of Brands* (New York: Harper-Collins, 2009).

15. John Doorley and Helio Fred Garcia, *Reputation Management: The Key to Successful Public Relations and Corporate Communication* (New York: Routledge, 2015).

16. John Doorley and Helio Fred Garcia, *Reputation Management: The Key to Successful Public Relations and Corporate Communication* (New York: Routledge, 2015).

17 Emily Stewart, "Two Black Men Were Arrested in a Philadelphia Starbucks for Doing Nothing," *Vox*, April 15, 2018, www.vox.com/identities/2018/4/14/17238494/what-happened-at-starbucks-black-men-arrested-philadelphia.

18. Russell Hotten, "Volkswgen: The Scandal Explained," *BBC News*, December 10, 2015, www.bbc.com/news/business-34324772.

19. Neal E. Boudette, "Volkswagen Sales in U.S. Rebound After Diesel Scandal," *New York Times*, www.nytimes.com/2017/11/01/business/volkswagen-sales-diesel.html.

20 Taylor Lyles, "Marriott Discloses Another Security Breach That May Impact over 5 Million Guests," *The Verge*, April 1, 2020, www.theverge.com/2020/4/1/21203313/marriott-database-security-breach-5-million-guests.

21. Dennis L. Wilcox, *Public Relations Strategies and Tactics* (New York: HarperCollins, 1994), p. 381.

22. "What's Your Best Marketing Tool?" *Public Relations Journal*, February 1994, p. 12.

23. Emanuele Venturoli, "The Growth of Sponsorship: Global Spending, Geography and Future," *RTR Sports Marketing*, March 26, 2019, https://rtrsports.co.uk/blog/growth-sponsorship-global-spending.

24. Dianna Christie, "Sports Sponsorship Spend to Increase the Most in a Decade, Report Says," *Marketing Dive*, January 29, 2020, www.marketingdive.com/news/sports-sponsorship-spend-to-increase-the-most-in-a-decade-report-says/571295.

25. IEG, "What Sponsors Want and Where Dollars Will Go in 2018," www.sponsorship.com/IEG/files/f3/f3cfac41-2983-49be-8df6-3546345e27de.pdf.

26. IEG, "What Sponsors Want and Where Dollars Will Go in 2018," www.sponsorship.com/IEG/files/f3/f3cfac41-2983-49be-8df6-3546345e27de.pdf.

27. "FIFA Secures $1.6 Billion in World Cup Sponsorship Revenue," *IEG*, June 3, 2010, www.sponsorship.com/About/Press-Room/FIFA-Secures-$1-6-Billion-in-World-Cup-Sponsorship.aspx.

28. Thomas R. Duncan and Sandra E. Moriarty, *Driving Brand Value: Using Integrated Marketing to Manage Stakeholder Relationships* (New York: McGraw-Hill, 1997), p. 203.

29. Thomas R. Duncan and Sandra E. Moriarty, *Driving Brand Value: Using Integrated Marketing to Manage Stakeholder Relationships* (New York: McGraw-Hill, 1997), p. 203; Terry G. Vavra, *Aftermarketing: How to Keep Customers for Life Through Relationship Marketing* (Burr Ridge, IL: Irwin Professional Publishing, 1992), p. 190.

30. Vavra, *Aftermarketing*, p. 192.

31. Vavra, *Aftermarketing*, p. 192.

32. "IEG's Top Sponsorship Spenders List Swells to 93 Companies," *IEG Sponsorship Report*, August 12, 2013, www.sponsorship.com/iegsr/2013/08/12/IEG-s-Top-Sponsorship-Spenders-List-Swells-To-93-C.aspx.

33. "What Sponsors Want and Where Dollars Go in 2018," *IEG*, www.sponsorship.com/IEG/files/f3/f3cfac41-2983-49be-8df6-3546345e27de.pdf.

34. "What Sponsors Want and Where Dollars Go in 2018," *IEG*, www.sponsorship.com/IEG/files/f3/f3cfac41-2983-49be-8df6-3546345e27de.pdf.

35. "Motorsports Sponsorship Spending to Total $3.76 Billion in 2013," *IEG Sponsorship Report*, February 25, 2013, www.sponsorship.com/iegsr/2013/02/25/Motorsports-Sponsorship-Spending-To-Total-$3-76-Bi.aspx; and "Golf Sponsorship Spending to Total $1.6 Billion in 2013," *IEG Sponsorship Report*, September 9, 2013, www.sponsorship.com/iegsr/2013/09/09/Golf-Sponsorship-Spending-To-Total-$1-6-Billion-In.aspx.

36. Jonathan Bond and Richard Kirshenbaum, *Under the Radar: Talking to Today's Cynical Consumers* (New York: Wiley, 1998), p. 63.

36. Jonathan Bond and Richard Kirshenbaum, *Under the Radar: Talking to Today's Cynical Consumers* (New York: Wiley, 1998), p. 63.

37. Melanie Wells, "Going for Nagano Gold; Nagano's Remoteness Challenges Marketers," *USA Today*, February 6, 1998, p. 1B.

38. Boaz Herzog, "Let the Ads Begin," *The Oregonian*, August 13, 2004, p. B01.

39. Junu Bryan Kim, "Most Sponsorships Waste Money: Exec," *Advertising Age*, June 21, 1993, pp. S2, S4.

40. "California, L.A. a Contender to Host Next Summer's X Games," *Los Angeles Times*, October 11, 2002, www.proquest.com.

41. Katherine Levy, "Bavaria Beer Website Traffic Rockets after World Cup Stunt," *Marketing Magazine*, June 18, 2010, www.campaignlive.co.uk/article/bavaria-beer-website-traffic-rockets-world-cup-stunt/1010738.

42. Lesa Ukman, "Assertions," *IEG Sponsorship Report*, February 23, 1998, www.sponsorship.com.

43. Lesa Ukman, "Assertions," *IEG Sponsorship Report*, February 23, 1998, www.sponsorship.com.

44. Wilcox, *Public Relations Strategies and Tactics*, p. 384.

45. David Fucillo, "49ers Stadium Naming Rights Details for Levi's Stadium," *SB Nation*, May 8, 2013, www.ninersnation.com/2013/5/8/4312806/49ers-stadium-naming-rights-details-name-levis-stadium.

46. John Karolefski, "The Sport of Naming," *Brand Channel*, May 13, 2002, www.brandchannel.com.

47. Paul Stanley, "Sponsownership: Sponsorships Will Become Standard for Events," *Potentials in Marketing*, June 1990, p. 64.

48. "What Sponsors Want and Where Dollars Go in 2018," *IEG*.

49. Ukman, "Assertions."

50. Vavra, *Aftermarketing*, p. 191.

51. "Corporate Advertising/Phase II, An Expanded Study of Corporate Advertising Effectiveness," conducted for *Time* magazine by Yankelovich, Skelly & White, undated.

index